A History of Costume in the West

7

A History of Costume in the West

FRANÇOIS BOUCHER

New enlarged edition
with an additional chapter
by Yvonne Deslandres

with 1188 illustrations, 365 in colour

THAMES AND HUDSON

ACKNOWLEDGEMENTS

In the course of the preparation of this book I have been fortunate in receiving much valuable help with research, documentation and illustration material.

For the period up to the Middle Ages I am indebted to Mlle Henriette Vanier for her assistance in research, and for research and the illustrations to Mlle Yvonne Deslandres of the Centre de Documentation du Costume.

I also wish to express my gratitude to my colleagues in Museums and Libraries in France and abroad, and to all those who have allowed me to draw on their private collections, enabling me to assemble this considerable body of documentation.

Finally, I thank my wife for her unfailing understanding during the ten years of preparation and writing of this book.

Translated from the French by John Ross

First published 1966. This new expanded edition published 1987

Published in the USA under the title 20,000 Years of Fashion

Printed in Japan

Contents

Preface

THIS WORK does not claim to be a complete and exhaustive history of costume in all periods and all countries: it sets out to define, within a limited area, the essential characteristics of the forms taken by costume in the Western world, to discover the conditions in which these forms evolved and the causes behind the changes they underwent, and to trace the lines along which innovations spread and interpenetrated. Clearly, such a subject opens a wide field for research: only when it has been studied in depth in each country will it be possible to undertake a comparative study of costume and, perhaps, to establish a complete history of dress throughout the world.

THE PROBLEM OF HISTORICAL SOURCES

The absence of a complete, critical, up-to-date general bibliography of costume makes it difficult to follow the numerous variations in ancient and modern costume. Existing texts and pictorial records leave important gaps to be filled, and when we turn to the basic evidence, the costume itself, we find that the greatest number of surviving garments date from the last two centuries, and even these are scattered round the globe.

Furthermore, although various authorities over the last hundred years have treated the history of costume in general works such as, in France, the dictionary of Viollet-le-Duc or the archaeological works of C. Enlart and Victor Gay, these authors have considered only particular aspects of the question, subordinated to archaeology or the study of ancient texts; they wrote without having studied costume as such and without comparing texts and pictorial evidence. Only A. Harmand, in his detailed study of costume at the time of Joan of Arc, provided a complete survey of iconography, texts and the technical aspects of the subject.

Quicherat's history of costume, which covers a much wider period than the preceding works, is limited by the amount of documentation available to the author, who was in any case not a specialist in costume.

For the present study, more recent and authoritative sources have been consulted, where available, but while excellent work has been published concerning some countries and periods, there are still large gaps, not satisfactorily filled by popular publications.

Where non-French costume is concerned, information has been taken from a wide range of recent works, many of whose authors are specialists of long standing in their fields and took part in the first International Congress for the History of Costume, which I helped to organize in Venice in 1952. Similarly, consideration has been given to the most recent works on prehistoric and archaeological discoveries, which have thrown new light on the subject.

THE GEOGRAPHY AND CHRONOLOGY OF COSTUME

This book has been divided into groupings that are both geographical and chronological. Before the Renaissance, the material distribution of different types of costume was established by outside factors which few historians have taken into account: an unfortunate omission, as these outside factors differed so widely that sometimes they ensured the survival intact of certain types of clothing in a given region while they were disappearing or undergoing modification elsewhere.

The geographical limits of a given element of costume vary according to the period. For instance, in the fifteenth century the *atour* or elongated conical head-dress, erroneously known as a *hennin*, was worn in Burgundy and Flanders, but not in England or Italy: therefore to claim as some writers have done that 'the hennin was fashionable throughout Europe in the Middle Ages' is to show a total ignorance of its geographical spread.

In the present state of knowledge concerning the history of costume, it is still virtually impossible to establish a continuous, precise chronological table of the first appearances of the various elements of costume.

For the protohistoric and ancient periods, and the Middle Ages until the fourteenth century, costume archetypes are few, fairly simple and widely worn; clothes were generally long, swathed and draped or fitted and sewn, worn in a varying number of layers. Their long life-span and limited zones of occurrence make a summary of this type possible, if we allow for a very broad, relative chronology.

But after the sixteenth century, when men's and women's garments became sharply differentiated, with men in short, fitted costumes with clearly separate garments for the upper and lower body, and all styles were interpreted with increasing originality and varied according to the social class of the wearer, it becomes impossible to formulate any accurate summary, for we should have to take into account innumerable essential factors: the multiplication of types of garment, the accelerating pace of fashion changes, which differed from country to country and even between the sexes, and the existence of national characteristics which spread more rapidly and widely beyond their original frontiers. An attempt at summary would yield a shapeless mass overloaded with dates and details, or else remain incomplete and subject to justified criticism. It seems preferable to follow the general lines of the history of costume, with all its overlappings and interpenetrations, rather than compress it into an arbitrary chronological framework.

THE VOCABULARY

The vocabulary of costume further complicates study by its changing applications and, particularly in French, its variety.

The term *costume* itself, in the sense it has today, had only been employed since the middle of the eighteenth century. When originally introduced to France, during the reign of Louis XIII, it retained its Italian pronunciation and meant 'custom' or 'usage'. And so this word, which has been accepted for only the last two centuries, is now paradoxically applied to a history that predates it by several millennia.

The meaning of other terms also varies with the period: *robe* in the Middle Ages, *habit* in seventeenth century France, are applied to costume ensembles and not to separate pieces of clothing.

More often, certain garments change their name from period to period, although their forms undergo little modification: for instance, it is difficult to decide exactly how and when the *doublet*, the *gambeson* and the *gippon* merged into the *pourpoint*. The modern male *waistcoat* was called a *vest* in the eighteenth century. Conversely, the same name can be applied to entirely different garments according to the period: there is no relationship between the *saie*, the short coat worn by the Franks, and the *saye* or *sayon* of the sixteenth century. In France, *collet* was first applied to a standing collar, then to a leather waistcoat, to a linen facing and, in the nineteenth century, to a woman's tippet. In the same century *pardessus* refers to all the short coats worn by women as well as to the male *surtout*, or overcoat. In the case of the *cote*, which in the Middle Ages was an undergown, in the sixteenth century its lower part took the name of *jupe* which until then had been given to a sort of waistcoat or jerkin. Today advertising gives any name it cares to any type of garment, regardless of the original meaning.

Similarly, the meaning of certain adjectives has changed over the centuries: in the Middle Ages, *ajusté* referred to sewn garments, such as the tunic, contrasting with draped garments, but not necessarily moulding the body, as the eighteenth century *juste* did.

The passage from Latin to French during the Merovingian period also contributed to confusions between identical garments which were duly named in different ways.

Many writers on costume in the last century have side-stepped the problem of the concordance of parts of costume and their names, and their approximate terminology has been adopted without criticism or verification by later writers. When we come to examine texts, we see that certain articles of dress have been given names which appeared in the language as much as a century after the date of the garment; two cases in point are the *touret* and the *escoffion*, indicated as having been worn at the beginning of the thirteenth century and the end of the fourteenth respectively. Now, the first is mentioned only after the end of the thirteenth century, and the second, introduced with the Italian *scuffia*, first appears only in the sixteenth century; consequently these terms can bear no contemporary relation to the head-dresses to which they were assigned.

Some etymological dictionaries, despite the erudition of their compilers, still contain erroneous definitions: the course of costume terminology has yet to be traced. It is evident that the life-span of a type of costume does not always coincide with the span of the word designating it, but the appearance and disappearance of a term are nonetheless pointers which must not be neglected.

FRENCH COSTUME, OUR MAIN PREOCCUPATION

Since its aim is to present the essential information, this work has naturally taken as its basis middle- and upper-class French civilian costume, which is used as the central point of reference for costumes of other countries, whose principal traits are defined in terms of it. However, it is impossible to discuss this type of dress without relating it to the ancient costume from which it is descended and which, in its turn, could be established only in relation to the primitive costume that dates from the very origins of man.

ORIGINAL COSTUMES, THE BASIC SOURCE MATERIAL

It is necessary to give the first place here to costume itself, referring, wherever possible, to the various garments that have been preserved from destruction; the majority surviving in private or public collections rarely date from before the late seventeenth century. We have few seventeenth-century specimens, except in England and the Nordic countries, and medieval examples are very rare indeed. Specialized museums are still few and far between; on the other hand, costume sections are to be found in general museums, but few of these collections were founded before 1850 and in many of them costume is considered as a decorative element, if not actually as a secondary accessory.

Unlike certain works, this book does not separate the study of essential types of costume from the examination of accessories or specialized garments for each period.

Folk, military or religious costumes have been mentioned only when it was possible to establish some relationship between them and the characteristic types of civilian costume of the same period. The study of folk costume, in particular, which is more advanced in the Northern and Central European countries, has not yet been the subject of a complete synthesis in France, and it is scarcely possible to disentangle the various inheritances from the many types of clothing which, from the sixteenth century on, contributed to its very diverse elements.

6

ICONOGRAPHICAL SOURCES

The almost complete disappearance of garments before the eighteenth century obliges us to search for evidence elsewhere, in works of art: paintings, sculptures, frescos, miniatures, stained glass, coins, seals, tapestries and engravings; for just over a century these sources have been supplemented by photography. But each of these sources has interpreted costume in accordance with a particular technique: the postures of Egyptian sculpture or the colours of medieval miniatures do not correspond exactly to the reality of the costume represented.

Similarly, it is as well to attach only a very relative degree of importance to the garments represented in sacred art; they are often conventionalized. We must also eliminate all the retrospective elements in works of art: they are more often than not interpreted imaginatively, and are far removed from an authentic record, as, for instance, in the costumes for biblical figures in medieval miniatures.

On the other hand, it is necessary to stress the documentary value of an exactly dated costume for the dating of certain works of art or even archaeological periods. Glotz has shown the help costume can give, in the case of Middle Minoan I.

ILLUSTRATIONS, CAPTIONS AND BIBLIOGRAPHIES

Illustrations must form an essential part of any history of costume; drawings based on original documents are subject to incomplete, inaccurate interpretation and have therefore been ruled out. All the reproductions collected here, representing a considerable and extremely varied body of documentation, have been chosen to form an integrated extension of the text.

Beside the individual picture captions, the reader will find fuller general notes on groups of pictures, indicated by ruled lines above and below.

In addition to the list of general reference works, there is a bibliography at the end of each chapter; items are arranged as far as possible in the order of reference to the text.

2 *The Lovers.* German embroidery on white linen. Fifteenth century (Photo Ciba)

Introduction

1 F. BOUCHER: *The Haberdasher,* 1746.
Stockholm, Nationalmuseum. (Museum photo)

THE ORIGINS OF COSTUME

If one admits that clothing has to do with covering one's body, and costume with the choice of a particular form of garment for a particular use, is it then permissible to deduce that clothing depends primarily on such physical conditions as climate and health, and on textile manufacture, whereas costume reflects social factors such as religious beliefs, magic, aesthetics, personal status, the wish to be distinguished from or to emulate one's fellows, and so on? Must we also envisage a process of emergence, which might place clothing before costume or costume before clothing?

This last point has given rise to diametrically opposed opinions. The Greeks and the Chinese believed that Man first covered his body for some physical reason, particularly to protect himself from the elements, while the Bible, ethnologists and psychologists have invoked psychological reasons: modesty in the case of the ancients, and the ideas of taboo, magical influence and the desire to please for the moderns.

Clearly we have insufficient information to assess the relative soundness of these theories.

While ethnologists in the last hundred years have collected precise data about the role of costume among present-day primitive peoples, archaeologists have not succeeded in compiling an equivalent corpus of information about the human groups of the various Prehistoric periods: as a result one must be wary of accepting questionable analogies.

We may at least surmise that when the first men covered their bodies to protect themselves against the climate, they also associated their primitive garments with the idea of some magical identification, in the same way that their belief in sympathetic magic spurred them to paint the walls of their caves with representations of successful hunting. After all, some primitive peoples who normally live naked feel the need to clothe themselves on special occasions.

Costume, at any rate, must have fulfilled a function beyond that of simple utility, in particular through some magical significance, investing primitive man with the attributes, such as strength, of other creatures, or protecting his genitals from

9

3 *Polish Tailor's Shop*. Illumination from *Cracow Customs* manuscript. Early sixteenth century. Cracow, Jagiellonian Library

4 *Italian Tailor's Shop*. Illumination from *Tacuinum Sanitatis*. Late sixteenth century. Paris, Bib.Nat., Ms N.A.L. 1673, f. 95 (Photo Bibliothèque Nationale)

evil influences. Ornaments identified the wearer with animals, gods, heroes or other men. This identification, actual for primitive people, remains symbolic in more sophisticated societies; we should bear in mind that the theatre, which is a basic expression of this feeling, has its distant origins in sacred performances, and in all periods children at play have worn disguises, so as to adapt gradually to adult life.

Costume also helps inspire fear or impose authority: for a chieftain, costume embodies attributes expressing his power, while a warrior's costume must enhance his physical superiority and suggest that he is superhuman. In later times, professional or administrative costume has been devised to distinguish the wearer and to express personal or delegated authority; this purpose is seen as clearly in the barrister's robes as in the policeman's uniform.

Costume denotes power, and as power is more often than not equated with wealth, costume came to be an expression of social caste and material prosperity. On this level, costume becomes subject to politics: the revolutionary defiance of the *Sans-Culottes* in 1789, the sartorial simplicity affected by the leaders of totalitarian regimes, the proletarian uniformity of the Chinese under Mao tse-tung, all contrast with the preening extravagance of exotic 'parvenu' dictators – even today.

Military uniform also denotes rank, and is intended to intimidate, to protect the body and to express membership of a group: at the bottom of the scale, there are such compulsory costumes as convicts' uniforms.

Contrary to widespread belief, it is probable that only latterly did primitive man's costume express a desire to please; clothing only gradually became a means of seduction by enhancing natural or adding artificial attractions.

Finally, costume can possess a religious significance that combines various elements: an actual or symbolic identification with a god, and the desire to express this in earthly life, the desire to increase the wearer's authority. Sometimes religious associations may even lead to the wearing of garments for reasons of respect: among primitive peoples recently converted to Christianity, the adoption of clothes recommended by missionaries often leads to the formation of taboos of modesty, whereas modesty in itself does not automatically lead to wearing clothes.

When and how did these various functions of costume make their appearance? It is very probable that they followed and were determined by the development of civilizations, allowing that the two evolved at different rates.

When we consider the causes of emergence of these functions of costume, we see that they appear as the result of essential elements of these civilizations, which gradually took shape out of an interplay of opposing forces, progress on the one hand, and on the other, reaction or simply stability. Can we not cite the religious and static character of Indian civilization as the chief reasons, along with climate, for the adoption of draped costume, which still shows no signs of losing popularity? And in the ferment of ideas and beliefs, the constant exchanges that mark the development of the general economy of western Europe, can we not see the principal causes behind the rapid, diversified development of its costume?

DEVELOPMENT

The study of costume and its development cannot be based on isolated scraps of information. By giving the term *fashion* – or

EMBROIDERY

2 In the Middle Ages the most highly prized embroidery came from England and Germany

EMBROIDERY AND KNITTING

5–7 Embroidery was work for craftswomen as well as for ladies (plates 5 and 7). A rare example shows a woman knitting with four needles, a technique which was only later to become widespread

5 FRANCESCO COSSA: *Women at Work*, 1460. Ferrara, Palazzo Schifanoia. (Photo Villani)

6 MASTER BERTRAM: *The Virgin Knitting*. Late sixteenth century. Detail of the Buxtehude Altarpiece. Hamburg, Kunsthalle. (Photo Kleintempel)

7 *Woman Embroidering a Cushion*. Early sixteenth century. *Courtly Life* tapestry. Paris, Musée de Cluny. (Photo Flammarion)

8 J. AMMAN: *The Tailor*. Late sixteenth
century. Paris, Bib. Nat., Cab. des Estampes
Ec 7 h. (Photo Bibliothèque Nationale)

9 JEAN DE BRAY: *Tailor's Workshop*.
Mid-seventeenth century. Collection F. Lugt.
(Photo Lemare)

10 C. N. COCHIN; *Women's Tailor*.
Eighteenth century. (Photo Flammarion)

11 R. DESTONENTE: *Shoemaker's Shop*. Fifteenth century. Detail of
the retable of Saint Mark. Manresa, Cathedral. (Photo Mas)

12 A. BOSSE: *The Shoemaker*. Seventeenth century.
(Photo Flammarion)

mode – the narrow sense of variations entrusted to the fantasy of creators and the caprices of wearers, we have, most often involuntarily, ignored the complex nature of this development, which can only be explained in terms of very different formative factors and influences.

Over almost ten millennia of history, the manifold creations of costume, stripped of all accessory elements, can be reduced to five archetypes: *draped costume*, obtained by wrapping a skin or a piece of material round the body, from the Egyptian *shenti* and the Grecian *himation* to the Tahitian *pareo*; *slip-on costume*, made from one piece of skin or cloth, pierced with a hole for the head and worn hanging from the shoulders, a type related to the Roman *paenula*, the medieval *huque* and the South American *poncho*; *closed sewn costume*, made of several widths of light stuff, fashioned round the body and fitted with sleeves, developing into the Grecian *chiton*, the Ionian *tunic*, the *gandourah*, the *blouse*, the *chemise* and the *shirt*; *open sewn costume*, made of several widths of material assembled lengthwise, worn over other garments and crossed in front, represented by the Asiatic *caftan*, the Russian *tulup* and the European *topcoat*; lastly, *sheath costume*, fitting closely to the body and limbs, particularly to the legs, which gave the breeches of the Nomads and the Eskimos, but which was always complementary to the caftan. It is only in modern times that composite types of clothing have been obtained by various combinations of these archetypes, which did not appear successively, but coexisted in different parts of the world from the most ancient times.

Basically, the fundamental differences between the various types of costume were determined by climate. The inhabitants of cold regions have always worn clothes to help them withstand the rigours of low temperatures: for them this was a necessity, rather than a matter of choice. The choice of covering and ornament in tropical regions is conditioned by the exhausting heat. Peoples in temperate zones, freer from the dictates of climate, could vary their costumes at will in accordance with religious or social demands, or out of sheer caprice.

Nonetheless, the development of the costume of any period must be related not to one, but to all outside factors, and the

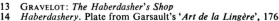

13 GRAVELOT: *The Haberdasher's Shop*
14 *Haberdashery*. Plate from Garsault's '*Art de la Lingère*', 176

15 JAN STEEN: *Young Girl taking off her Stockings.*
Seventeenth century. Amsterdam, Rijksmuseum. (Photo Ciba)

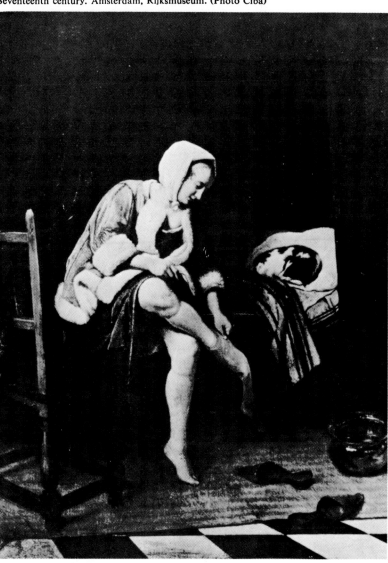

relative importance of these influences is bound to differ between periods and places.

Such an examination demonstrates that basic differences in costume are not determined solely by race or ethnic type, by political regime or artistic gifts, but rather by the overall nature of the civilization and the people's way of life.

Since economics most often determined the development of the civilizations in question, the study of costume obviously cannot neglect this aspect of the environment.

In ancient times and up to the end of the Middle Ages, the instability of the human masses indubitably had a strong influence on costume as a result of the wars and population movements it caused. The extension of the Roman Empire and the Dorian invasion, to name only two examples, imposed the victors' styles and customs on the defeated peoples; the advance of the Steppe Nomads towards the west of Europe and the adventure of the Crusades furnish equally typical examples.

Throughout the general fluctuation of civilizations, the development of costume never ceased to depend on one predominant factor: the human wearer. At the various stages of his development, Man was obliged to make successive modifications to his clothing in order to adapt it to the progress that had taken place around him. If we were to simplify to the utmost the development of European costume, it would be possible to divide it into three broad phases.

The first stretches from the earliest antiquity to the fourteenth century. In most civilizations, in spite of their diversity, costume underwent little change in this period: it had no definite national characteristics and remained uniform in each social class; generally long, loose and draped, its various forms reflect the remains of the magical and religious functions that had run through its earliest origins.

The second phase lasts from the fourteenth century, when costume in general became short and fitted, to the period of great industrial expansion in the nineteenth century. It was in the fourteenth century that clothing acquired personal and national characteristics; it began to undergo frequent variations in which we must recognize the appearance of fashion in the modern sense of the term. Costume depended more and more

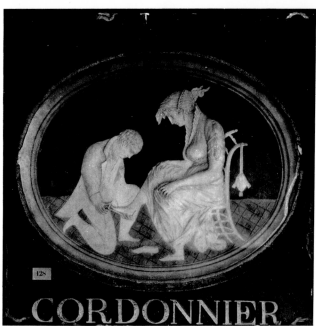

CORDONNIER

closely on political and commercial organization during this period: each nation formed its own style of costume, but each individual adapted it to his personal tastes. The creation of 'civilian' costume must be dated from this period.

The third phase, which began in the middle of the nineteenth century and which continues to the present, is marked by the appearance of a costume that is increasingly less personal and more international, under the influence of industrial mass-production and European expansionism in the world as a whole. As if to counteract this tendency, *Haute Couture*, which also appeared first in the mid-nineteenth century, combines the preservation of 'personal' costume and the imperatives of more rapidly changing fashion with class privilege based on uniform wealth. The outline of this succession of dominant factors – at first religious and mystical influences, then strivings towards spiritual and social emancipation, lastly the concentration of economic interests – must constitute the basic framework of any historical study of costume. And indeed, it has determined the structure of this book.

17 FRENCH SCHOOL: *The Ribbon Vendor.* Late eighteenth century Paris, Musée Carnavalet. (Photo Flammarion)

NINETEENTH-CENTURY MILLINERS

18–19 The *modiste* or milliner did not appear until the nineteenth century, when the vogue for hats placed women employed in their manufacture in a privileged position

18   MALO RENAULT: *The Milliner*, 1911.
Paris, Bibliothèque Nationale, Cabinet des Estampes.
(Photo Flammarion)

19   E. DEGAS: *At the Milliner's.* (Courtesy Mr and Mrs Robert Lehman, New York. Photo Archives Durand-Ruel)

15

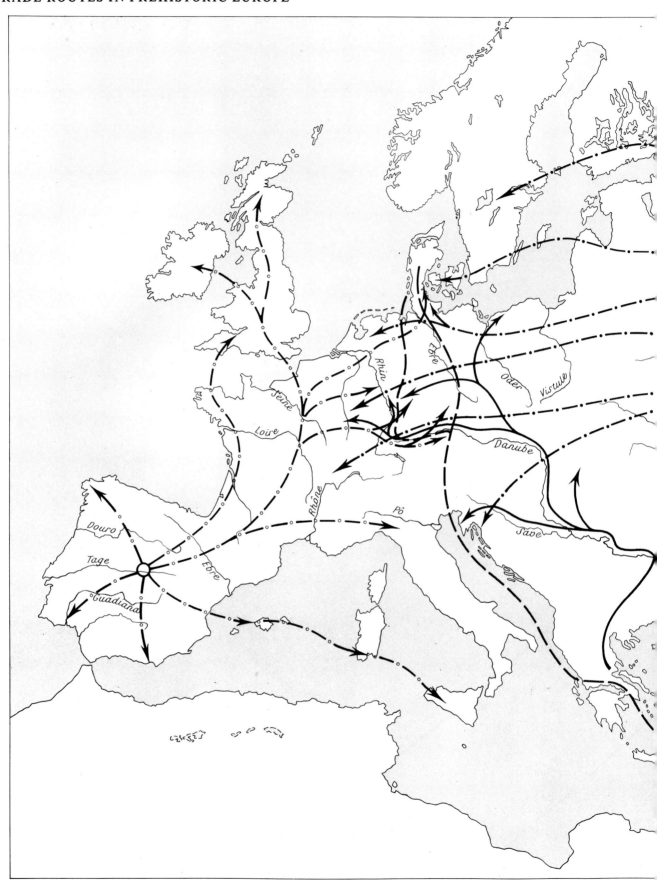

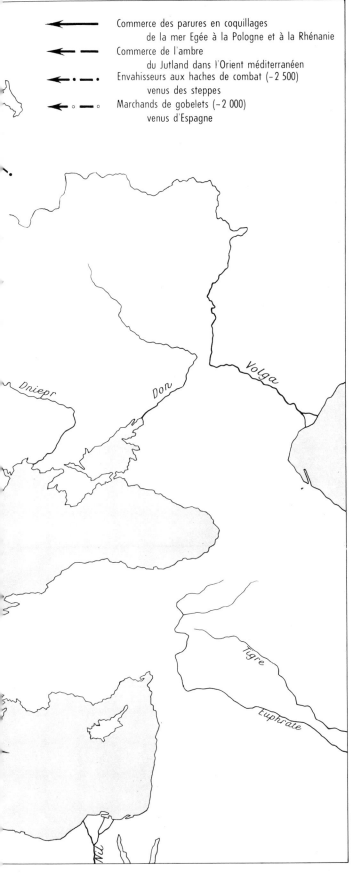

Chapter I

Prehistoric Costume

The present state of knowledge about prehistoric times enables us, with all the necessary reservations, to assess the little data we possess about costume in the quaternary period of about six hundred thousand years, covering the history of tool-making man.

It is as well to remember from the outset that the development of prehistoric civilizations is influenced by the geography of the continents, which, though broadly as it is today, had numerous differences in detail, such as the land link between Britain and the continent of Europe.

The information we possess about prehistoric costume for the whole of the quaternary age is divided between the earlier, longer period (until about 10,000 BC) known as the Palaeolithic period, and the shorter, more recent Neolithic period, which lasted for a few thousand years and was followed by the Bronze and Iron Ages.

In spite of glacier movements, the general climate in the greater part of the ancient world was fairly constantly tropical or sub-tropical, comparable to the climate of present-day Africa or central Asia, and favouring a fauna of hippopotami, elephants and rhinoceros. Only after the last Ice Age (100,000 to 10,000 BC) did the temperature of the northern hemisphere fall, causing changes in fauna and flora.

The various ways of life of these first men changed according to these climatic conditions, which also influenced costume; men in tropical regions lived in forests or on plains, in camps or shelters, and left traces of their clothing industries in the valleys and steppes; men in the areas affected by the last glaciation took refuge in grottoes and caverns, where the vestiges of their primitive clothing are to be found.

Palaeolithic man lived by hunting and food collection; for him, the search for food entailed defending himself against animals, at first in tropical regions, and then in glacial conditions. Only towards 10,000 BC, when Europe was once more freed from ice and became covered with forests, was Neolithic man to find his food by agriculture and stock-breeding; this revolutionary change appeared first in the centre of the New World and in the Middle East, from where it spread through Asia.

Prehistoric civilizations therefore show a succession of changes of level, influenced by the prevailing climatic conditions, by increasing technical skills, and perhaps by changes in the physical type of primitive man.

These are the dominant factors which, in conditions that are often difficult to establish and are complicated by overlapping and mixture, influenced the evolution of prehistoric costume.

17

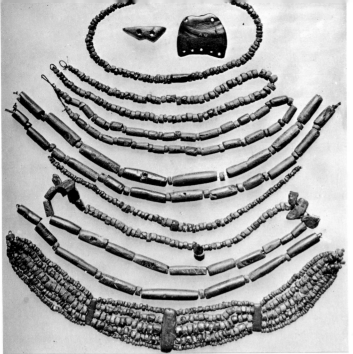

20 Amber ornaments, *c.* 2500 BC
Copenhagen, National Museum. (Museum Photo)

21 Women wearing fur skirts. Reindeer period. Cave painting, Kogul
(From copy by M. Almagro. Photo Museo Arqueologico, Madrid)

Races and Civilizations

While we are now entitled to speak of 'prehistoric civilizations' it is still difficult to establish relationships between cultures widely separated in time and space, with no perceptible link between them. On the grounds that in our own times ethnic groups living in some little-explored areas use objects similar or identical to those used by prehistoric men, one is tempted to compare these surviving primitive societies with known prehistoric civilizations and then to conclude, where costume is concerned, that rigorous parallels hold good; but it is impossible to affirm that some characteristics of the costume of contemporary primitive peoples, such as the Pygmies, also belonged to them in the past.

Analogies between the present costumes of primitive races in Africa, South America or Oceania and some prehistoric costume elements must therefore be considered with circumspection. We shall limit ourselves to observing that some techniques have persisted to the present day: the techniques of the Mousterian period were still used in about 1860 by the natives of Tasmania, whose technical knowledge was scarcely more extensive than that of Mousterian Man; the Tasmanians knew nothing of metals, and used scrapers, borers and arrow-heads identical with those of the earlier period.[1]

The study of the races and civilizations of prehistoric Africa has demonstrated the existence in that continent of the same Stone Age civilizations found in Europe and the Middle East: from Upper Senegal to Abyssinia, from Morocco to Uganda, from Egypt to the Congo, from Morocco to South Africa, the excavations undertaken in the last forty years prove the existence of more recent civilizations from the Neolithic and Mesolithic periods.

By making a closer association than has hitherto been attempted between the history of prehistoric costume and the study of currents of civilization, we arrive, in terms of the present state of knowledge, at the following hypotheses, which are valid mainly for the Aurignacian civilization (between 40,000 and 10,000 BC).

Firstly, a current of civilizations from South West Asia, passing through the Bosphorus, Transylvania, the Ukraine and Moravia, deflected westward along the old glacier line, apparently turned in Poland towards Bohemia and Bavaria, ending on one side by the North Sea in Jutland, and on the other, in the centre of Western Europe.

Then another current, from the south this time, passing simultaneously through Italy and Spain, reached Western Europe, where it continued influenzing the previous drift; but its original source may have been in Africa or even in Asia for, according to Menghin, backed by the Abbé Breuil, some of the forms of the Aurignacian in Europe are very close to those of Asia Minor, and may have penetrated to North-East Africa through Syria. Not only would this current have touched the entire perimeter of the Mediterranean, but it would naturally have penetrated into the African continent, crossed the Sahara and introduced the tools of this Palaeo-Mediterranean civilization into the Sudan; however, it has not been proved decisively that it went beyond the Gulf of Guinea to reach the South African coast through Chad.[2]

It must be remembered that in a more recent period there were perceptible relationships between some aspects of a Neo-Sudanese civilization and the old Oriental civilizations of Arabia, Syria, Mesopotamia and, most of all, India. We can trace links with the distant south of Asia in many costume decorations: punched work, openwork, dyes and appliqués.[3]

Trade in Prehistoric Times

After the early Palaeolithic period, these currents of primitive civilization produced the trade routes which were extended and took precise shape in the Bronze and Iron Ages; weapons and

20 Amber was one of the oldest prized personal ornaments; numerous amber necklaces have been found in Stone Age tombs; no doubt these were bartered for the gold and bronze of Mediterranean countries

FUR SKIRT

21 The women shown in this ritual scene are wearing skirts with rounded fronts, a form which reappears in the Sumerian *kaunakès* (Cf. the Hagia Triada sarcophagus, plate 97)

WOMEN'S LOINCLOTHS

22 The striations on the thighs of this statuette suggest a sort of loincloth made of woven bands and edged with a fringe. Examples of skirts of this type are to be found in Denmark (see plate 23)

22 Statuette known as the Venus of Lespugue. Aurignacian Period. Paris, Musée des Antiquités Nationales. (Photo Flammarion)

23 Clothing found in the Egtved tomb. Early Bronze Age. Copenhagen, National Museum. (Museum photo)

tools flowed along these routes, and so did costume and accessories.

Numerous discoveries have established beyond doubt that Bronze Age objects (e.g. heeled and two-edged axes)[4] then followed a great trade movement which started from the Iberian peninsula, and reached Great Britain to the west and, to the east, north-west Germany by means of the rivers of France and Belgium. But the trade currents which fostered exchanges of shells and amber in Central Europe have been even better defined.

The importation of Nordic amber into the Eastern Mediterranean provides proof of regular trading between the two zones (then inhabited by races whose civilizations were presumably very different) throughout the Early and Middle Bronze Age, during which the amber deposits of West Jutland were worked. The high point of this trade was reached during the first phases of the Mycenaean period (fifteenth century BC).

Supplies were carried in many directions, through the region of Saxony and Thuringia, which seems then to have been the crossroads of the great amber routes as well as the main source of metals. Trade was definitely organized by merchants like those who deposited the Dieskau (near Halle) treasure: there is no doubt that traders, for example those of Aunjetitz, or intermediaries bartered amber for decorative objects such as Pontic pins, or for raw materials like tin from Vogtland or metal ingots from central Germany. Finally the amber was sent south towards the Mediterranean, generally following rivers as far as the Brenner, then beyond towards the Po and the Adriatic. To the west, it was sent either to southern Britain, where it has been found in the Wessex graves, or to Brittany and the Pyrenees.

Similarly, we know that the distribution of shell ornaments from the Black Sea, the Sea of Marmara and the Aegean reached all along the Danube, as far as Poland and Germany.

These trade currents were superimposed on the main streams of civilization: it is not unreasonable to suppose that, from the Stone Age on, furs used for clothing may have constituted an exchange currency between the hunting and fishing peoples and the first settled societies.

Prehistoric Costume

The elements of prehistoric civilization today revealed by archaeological excavations provide a certain amount of information, if not about the actual costume worn by the people, at least of the state of their material culture at particular periods and of its development.[5]

Our knowledge of this costume is in fact limited to a small number of objects that have survived because of their durable materials (stone, bronze, bone, etc), while more perishable materials (fibres, bark, hide, etc.) are only rarely found, either in former inhabited zones, mainly lake-dwellings or in tombs. This is the case with cloth made from vegetable fibres: linen, tow, rush, etc.[6] From the objects used in everyday life which have thus come down to us, it is possible to deduce certain characteristics of costume and its distribution in the then inhabited areas.

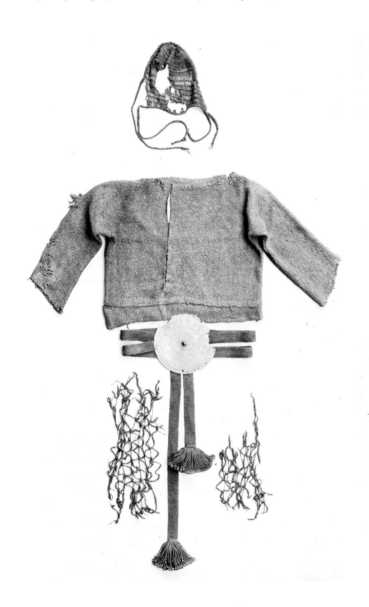

24–26 Clothing found at Skrydstrup and Borum Eshöj. Early Bronze Age. Copenhagen, National Museum. (Museum photos)

27 Dress found at Trindhöj. Early Bronze Age. Copenhagen, National Museum. (Museum photo)

28 Gold gorget found at Glininsheen, Co. Clare. Halsatt Period. Dublin, National Museum of Ireland. (Museum photo)

29 Bronze statuette from Faardal. Early Bronze Age. Copenhagen, National Museum. (Museum photo)

We can fill some gaps thanks to the increasingly rigorous methods and techniques used in archaeology, for there is now a happy tendency to approach a wider field of discoveries with scientific methods capable of extracting the fullest information about the materials used and the manufacturing techniques employed. The excellent studies made in Scandinavia and Switzerland[7] on prehistoric textiles bear witness to the results that can be obtained by the methodical application of chemical and spectrographic analysis.[8]

While it seems possible to imagine fairly exactly what pre-historic costume must have been from surviving specimens, it is more difficult to determine the limits of space and time within which this costume was worn, the modifications it underwent and the causes that lay behind such changes.

The fact that, in more temperate regions, hunting peoples are adorned rather than clothed leads us to 'search for the origins of this behaviour in the wish to distinguish oneself from the other members of the group: the desire to attract attention or sympathy, to specify the age group, the tribal classification or the status of the individual, bachelor, married or widower. It is also possible to establish links with religious ceremonies, or rites connected with mourning and war.'[9]

We know the forms of magical costume that were developed to the north of Cantabria in prehistoric times: the strangest is shown by the sorcerer disguised with a horse's tail and stag antlers in the Trois-Frères cavern. A similar costume can be seen in a rock-wall drawing at Teli-Sahré, in Fezzan.[13]

It is very possible that in hot climates the skins and furs used in costume covered only the sexual organs, but this would have been in response to a religious idea of taboo rather than because of a physical need to protect. Originally in hide and later in cloth, this ancestral garment was respectfully preserved in the exercise of worship: on the Hagia Triada sarcophagus (*c.* 1500 BC) a striped skin, perhaps a panther skin, is worn by the offering-bearers and priestesses.[11]

SKINS AND HIDES

The raw materials used by prehistoric man for his clothing are necessarily related to the major demands of climate and the activities of everyday life.[12]

The dry, penetrating cold of the upper Palaeolithic (Aurignacian, Solutrean and Magdalenean periods) left cave-dwelling man only the two or three months of summer for hunting – herds of horses during the Aurignacian period, reindeer thereafter. These conditions led to the predominant use of animal skin for warmth.

Skins occupied an important place in the clothing, not only of Palaeolithic hunters and fishermen, but also of the farmers of the following Neolithic period in Northern Europe and in part of North-West Europe, including Great Britain.

We know the tools that were used for the preparation of these skins: scrapers and burins made of flint whose characteristic outline scarcely varies throughout the Palaeolithic, and flint knives for cutting leather; the reindeer horn combs used in the Neolithic period should be compared with the instruments used by the Eskimos in the preparation of their furs. Prehistoric man also used chemicals such as clay salts. The pieces were then assembled and sewn with threads drawn from animal ligaments, such as reindeer tendons, or with hair taken from horses' manes and tails, using punches and needles made of bone, ivory and reindeer horn, found as far afield as the

Palaeolithic caves of the Crimea. Sewing guides in the form of bone plates pierced with holes have also been found.

'Although little known, the garment worn during the upper Palaeolithic cannot have differed much from that worn by the Eskimos, including a set of bone buttons, perforated and often decorated with engraved motifs. A new representation discovered at Angles-sur-l'Anglin (Vienne, France) gives a fairly precise picture of this garment: a fur, opening in front over a richly worked plastron in the same carmine tone as the background, and a head-dress decorated with dangling bobbles.'[13]

The festoons of seal teeth found on female skeletons at Gotland (Sweden) suggest that women wore sealskin garments that drooped in front or were rounded like those of the Eskimos.[14] Under the Roman Empire, Tacitus, describing the German Barbarians, notes that tribes living far from the Rhine wore 'wild beasts' skins' which included 'striped skins of animals from the Outer Ocean and its unknown waters': these must have been seals.

Animal skins almost always kept their natural shape. 'The same tailed skirt worn by Kogul women in the Reindeer period still appears in Crete in representations of ritual scenes: rounded in front, it shows exactly the slit line, and the appendage that hangs from it is the actual tail of the animal.'[15] The statuette known as the 'Venus of Lespugue' (see plate 22) has decoration representing either an animal tail or a loincloth.

Furthermore, the cut of later cloth gowns found at Muldbjerg and Trindhöj clearly shows that the original model was made of fur: the shoulder straps obviously derive from animal paws and the measurements of these gowns correspond with the dimensions of skins.[16]

Another instance of the use of furs is to be found in the short 'Kaunakès' skirt worn in Sumer in the pre-Agadean period (c. 3000 BC), in which the knot at the back probably represents a survival of the animal tail.[17]

TEXTILES AND TECHNIQUES

In the more temperate regions, as we have said, hunting peoples were adorned rather than clothed. It is possible that weaving may have appeared there earlier than in glacial zones, and that it may have derived from basket-work, a technique of which it is in some ways a mechanized form. Loom weaving no doubt goes back to some stage of the Palaeolithic (hunting civilization) or perhaps, at the latest, to the end of the Mesolithic (beginning of settled civilizations).[18]

The perfecting of manufacturing technique is very noticeable in the various periods of the end of the Palaeolithic period.

During the Aurignacian period, objects made from bone included round-shafted pins, certain ornaments, and phials made from reindeer horn for powdered dyes used on the body (red ochre). The following Solutrean period brought a new implement for use in making garments, the eyed needle, which suggests a more delicate handling of the skins and the use of thread that was probably very fine, perhaps long horsehairs or split reindeer tendons. At the end of the Palaeolithic, in the so-called Magdalenean period, a new tool appeared: the bone sewing-plate (found at Laugerie-Basse in the Dordogne) which was used to push the needle. When the seam was finished, the thread was held across the plate and cut with a flint, which left a scratch on the edge of the plate each time.[19]

The development of tools went hand in hand with the use of

30 Boeotian terracotta statuette. Eighth century BC. Paris, Louvre. (Photo Flammarion)

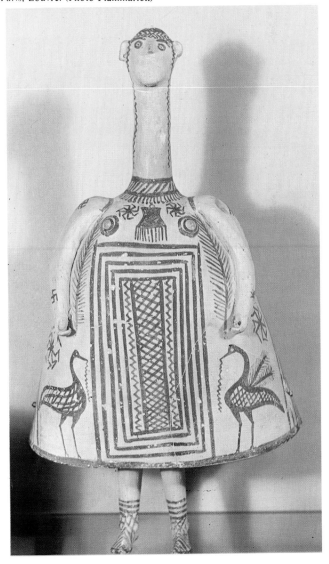

23

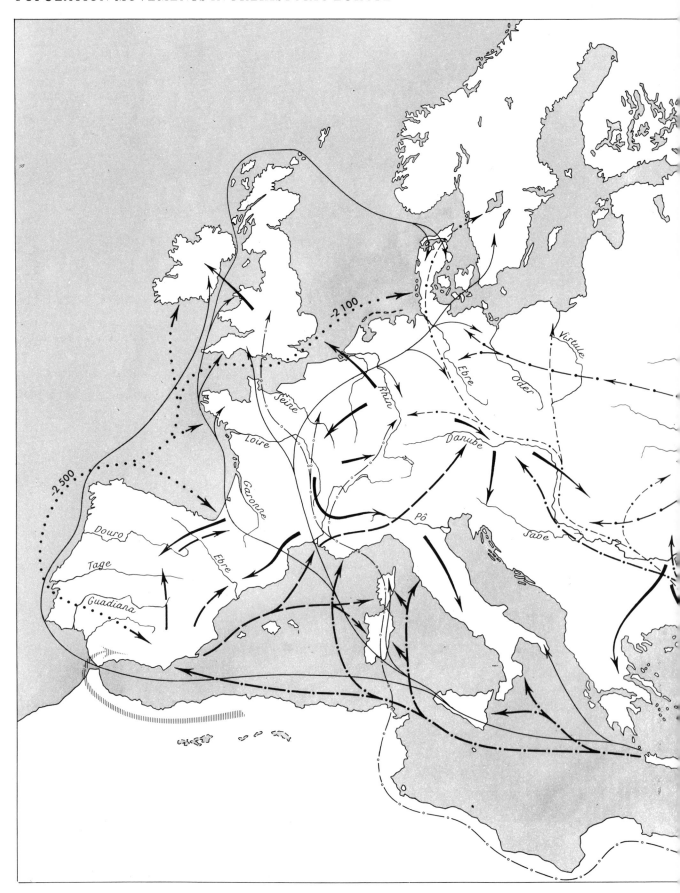

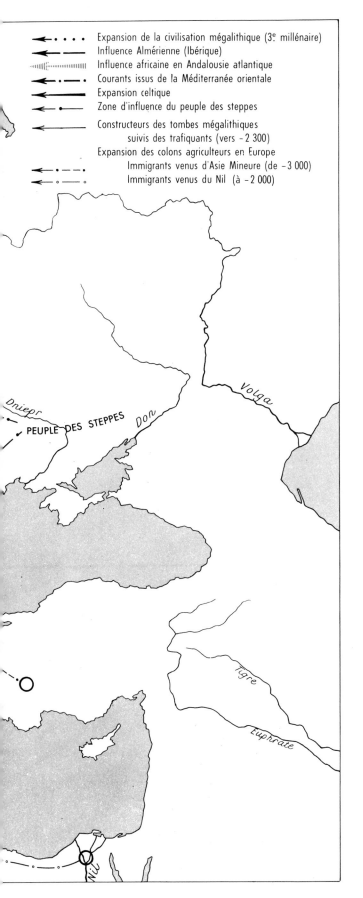

various fibres adopted to supplement animal skins. In the Stone Age, as well as birch bark which, when stripped off in the sap season, can be cut like soft leather (a girdle fragment was found at Frauenfeld in Switzerland), and the flax which was then the most widely used textile, wool was also used, though this fibre was really to be characteristic of the following Bronze Age and Early Iron Age. Discoveries at prehistoric centres in Northern, North-West and Central Europe have shown that sheep and goats began to occupy an increasing, sometimes dominating place in domestic herds.[20]

So far as Nordic woollen materials of the Bronze Age are concerned, it has long been known that the threads were apparently formed of different sorts of hair. Recent work, however, has shown that there were no mixtures of sheep wool and calf, reindeer and fawn hair, as was at first believed: the most detailed examination has established that only sheep wool was used, and that the wool came from an early breed whose fleece contained long, stiff hairs.[21]

The fibres in the textile fragments that have come down to us imply weaving on looms, which, as already mentioned above, certainly dates back to some period of the Palaeolithic (hunters and fishermen) or, at the latest, at the end of the Mesolithic civilization of settled breeders or tillers,[22] but it is impossible to decide whether linen or wool is more ancient. During these periods women were in charge of collecting fibres, and must certainly have seen to the weaving in addition to basket-making, as the two processes are so similar. Among modern Bushmen, the menfolk make the clothing.[23]

It has been stated that primitive cloth pieces are characterized by their small dimensions, whether the specimens are of Neolithic linen or Bronze and Iron Age woollens: people did not weave large pieces which could later be cut, but produced a series of small pieces which were joined by seams.

The complete garments found in Danish Bronze Age burials, on the other hand, were cut out of wider cloth. 'People had gone beyond the stage of the piece of cloth whose dimensions were strictly adapted to the garment that had to be made. In the Stone Age, in Switzerland as elsewhere, information is less precise. The relatively high number of edgings that have come down to us lead us to suppose that purpose-woven pieces were still frequent... We cannot draw conclusions about the cut of Neolithic cloth from that of Bronze Age woollens. At the most we can affirm that Neolithic weaving techniques were in no way inferior to those of the Bronze Age.'[24]

DYESTUFFS

The colorants used in costume – textiles or ornaments – must have been fairly numerous, though it is difficult to identify them by analysing surviving textiles. But we should not take the specimens' present faded state as implying an absence of colours; on the contrary, cave paintings from the Upper Palaeolithic attest their presence. Whole ranges of objects have been found: palettes and shells, bone tubes or hollow antlers, which also inform us about the natural or artificial colouring matters then in use. In North Africa we have palettes and stone grinders, with colorants belonging to the Capsian civilization, which is in some degree related to the Aurignacian.[25] The colours that have been identified are blue, red, lilac and yellow; violet-brown and green tones have also been found on plain woollen textiles with broad and narrow stripes, found in the saltmines at Dürrnberg, near Hallein (Austria).[26]

The blue that is frequently to be seen was obtained from the dwarf alder or bloodwort berries, or else from woad, also known as dyers' pastel: if the presence of woad blue has really been observed in a French centre, its appearance in so early a period is particularly curious, since this colour is produced by the oxydizing effect of the air, only when the dye has been exposed for some time.

The plants already mentioned also furnished other dyes. Lilac colour could be extracted from myrtles, yellow from weld, a type of reseda, or the artichoke. For red, the white orach could be used, and for orange-yellow, marsh-bedstraw. Red chalk was principally used for cave paintings and in the cult of the dead; skeletons have been found lying on layers of pulverized red ochre which may originally have also covered their garments.[27]

ORNAMENT

It is extremely difficult, at the present stage in the discovery of prehistoric textiles, and in the techniques of examining them, to imagine their decoration. This may, however, have been by cording in the weaving or by brocading: we know that in the Stone Age the latter process was extraordinarily well developed. But while the most famous, most splendid specimen of brocaded textile is a cloth found at Irgenhausen in the canton of Zürich and preserved in the National Museum in Zürich, we cannot be sure that it is not a wall hanging, like the one shown in the engraved scene on the great stone sarcophagus from Göhlitzsch (Merseburg district, Germany). A woollen cloth brocaded with yellow, green and brown threads, found in the Dürrnberg mines and probably dating from the end of the Bronze Age can reasonably be considered as part of a garment: it would then constitute one of the rare documents in prehistoric costume, in which woven ornament played a more important role than needlework.[28]

THE COMPONENTS OF COSTUME

In the famous female statuette discovered at Lespugue in 1922 (plate 22), we can see an example of a textile at the back of the legs, where there is 'a singular garment consisting of a series of long, narrow bands, crossed at first by horizontal striations which seem to indicate thongs; then each band is divided into simple vertical lines that reach to the feet; on the upper part, the bands are attached to a horizontal cord which begins in short vertical striations. This representation seems to show a sort of loincloth composed of a series of plaited bands each of which ends in a fringe at the foot.' The costume must have been made of plaited fibres, like that worn by the Late Bronze Age woman represented in the Faardal bronze.[29]

This sort of *pagne* or loincloth is to be found at widely scattered points throughout prehistoric Europe. In Catalonia the cave paintings of Kogul, near Lerida (plate 21), show a dance scene with nine bare-breasted women wearing bell skirts attached at the waist, which stop above the knee as if they were hitched up in front, and fall at the back and on the sides; one of these skirts is in red and black stripes (we find the same short skirt at Alpera). While it is scarcely possible to speak of 'form' in connection with prehistoric costume, we can note a curious analogy between this flared skirt and the garments represented on the famous urn from Oedenburg (Western Hungary) which

31 The Brassempouy Lady is the oldest known representation of a human being. The hair, which was probably braided, seems to be held in a hairnet

32-5 Menhir carved with figures show, despite their extreme stylization, the presence of a cloak with vertical folds, held in by a double belt, or fringed girdle with ends hanging down the front. The female idol wears a heavy necklace and the male idol a baldrick fastened on the shoulder with a fibula

31 *The Brassempouy Lady. c.* 36,000 BC. A small mammoth-ivory figurine found at Brassempouy (Les Landes). Paris, Musée des Antiquités Nationales. (Photo G. Papo)

recall the immense skirts of present-day Hungarian costume. According to the Abbé Breuil, this model evokes the costume of modern Eskimo women. Looking at these curious paintings, we may think of certain Minoan figures; but in the absence of more precise classifications, such a comparison remains too bold.[30]

Exceptionally interesting excavations in Denmark have revealed actual examples of Early Bronze Age costume that come close to those represented. In two burials (plate 23) and at the Olby tomb, the excavators found skirts made of vertical cords, about eighteen inches deep and almost five feet in length, attached to a woven girdle ending in fringes, carrying a circular disk in decorated metal which was worn on the front of the body: a dagger and a horn comb were still fastened to this girdle.[31] This type of skirt disappeared completely at the beginning of the Iron Age.

No doubt this style of skirt should be related to the various forms of loincloth, some of which are still worn to this day by numerous African peoples; some seem to have kept this garment since the Palaeo-Mediterranean period.

The Danish excavations also brought to light a garment for the upper body (plates 23, 24, 26), which is not to be found on painted or carved figures: a sleeved jacket in plain wool, woven in one piece, the cut parts being hemmed together.[32]

The similarity of all the pieces discovered makes it possible to speak of the current use of the following garments in this Nordic region during the Bronze Age: for women, jacket and skirt, girdle, shoes and a decorated cap or hair-ribbon, and for men, cloak, tunic-gown, shoes and cap.

In Southern Europe, this sort of loincloth is to be recognized in the rock-paintings of the Iberian peninsula along the coastal mountain ranges. Further proof is provided by certain decorative elements, notably shells and pierced teeth, which played a very important role in the arrangement of costume, from the middle Palaeolithic period on. 'The thousand or so small *Nassa nerites*, deliberately pierced, found with burials at the Grotte des Enfants at Grimaldi near Menton, where they covered skeletons from the waist to the knees, can only be the remains

26

of thong or hair skirts, mounted on a girdle, and on which the shells must have been threaded.'[33]

In the Magdalenean period the wearing of a sort of cape is attested by the discovery of T-shaped 'toggles', whose presence in graves provides evidence that the dead were buried fully clothed. When both ends of a cord, each end fitted with a small wooden cross-piece, were passed through the hole in the toggle, a garment worn over the shoulders could be kept closed over the chest; toggles pierced with only one hole were worn vertically on the chest, while others, with several holes, were worn horizontally and enabled the wearer to leave the garment more or less open.[34]

This type of cape may well be represented by the woven wool cloak from the barrow burial at Trindhöj in Denmark; it was decorated with dangling threads on the outside, probably to direct rain water off the garment.[35]

Another garment from the Late Bronze Age, designed to protect the shoulders, was found in Ireland, at Armoy (Co. Antrim). To judge from the remains that were discovered in a peat-bog, it seems to have been a sort of scarf of black horse-hair, finished at either end with fringes made from tufts of hair held together by horse-hair spirals. Several strands of the fringes are finished with tassels. The textile itself has a zig-zag motif.[36]

The Stockholm Museum has a curious cape, probably from the same period, made from two-coloured serged wool; it is a single oval piece with a maximum diameter of almost eight feet, and was found at Gerumsberget (Västergötland).

The long cloak, several specimens of which have been found in Denmark, appears in the description by Posidonius (first century BC) quoted by Strabo, of the costume of the inhabitants of the Cassideridian Islands: it seems to have been identical with the heavy black *sagum* in coarse wool worn by the Celts.[37]

The men represented in the paintings of the Spanish Levant wear a sort of leather trousers (or breeches?) and are covered in numerous adornments, among them fringed girdles, garters (sometimes worn on only one knee), forearm and elbow bracelets, head ornaments of plumes, shells and teeth, caps flanked with standing appendages such as animal ears and crown-shaped rings.[38]

We know that at the end of the Bronze Age copper miners in the Austrian Tyrol wore leather jerkins.[39] At the same time the use of leather is attested by the presence of shoes held in place by thongs passed through holes round the upper edges, then wound round the feet and ankles (Jels tombs, Denmark).

The male costumes in the Schleswig-Holstein Museum, which were found in a marsh, must date from the Iron Age; they comprise long and short trousers, a tunic and some cloaks, which can be dated between 800 and 400 BC. These pieces of woven costume were found with shoes of soft leather and a short, oval fur cape for a girl of about thirteen, but no other women's costumes were discovered.[40]

From the Early Iron Age, we have shoes in calf from the Dürrnberg saltmines (near Hallein, Austria) and from the Amitlund peat-bogs (Denmark).

The hunting civilization must have been the first to use animal skins as foot protection, but only the tools used, bone needles and bodkins, enable us to deduce that such primitive shoes, whose origins are placed at the end of the interglacial period, were in fact worn. In Northern Europe, vestiges of leather shoes have been found in oak coffins in Jutland; they were similar to Indian mocassins, and date from the Northern Bronze Age (1900 to 680 BC).

HAIR AND HEAD-DRESSES

Women's coiffures in the prehistoric ages are known to us through various sculpted representations, like the female figures modelled in the round from Dolní Vestonice (Moravia), whose heads are covered with a sort of toque, or the mammoth-ivory figurine from the Brassempouy cave in the Landes (plate 31), which presents a sort of hood, in reality probably plaited hair held in a net. The woman from the oak coffin found in the Skrydstrup barrow in Denmark, of Bronze Age date, wears a fine net of horse-hair. A type of plumed head-dress has been observed in the rock-paintings of Eastern Spain.

From the Iron Age, we have a male head-dress in goat-skin from the Dürrnberg saltmines and a conical cap made of 'six pieces of hide with the furry side inwards' with a tassel of fine thongs attached to the crown, found at Hallstatt (Austria).[41]

This type of cap enables us to draw curious parallels between widely-separated points in the prehistoric world. At Trindhöj in Scandinavia a cap woven from thick wool has been found, covered on the outside with bristling threads ending in knots; in Crete, a cap with a lock or curl of hair has been mentioned; a cap with 'dangling olive-shaped pendants' has also been discovered.[42]

ORNAMENTS

It is unnecessary to recall that in the primitive state of humanity the first men seem initially to have worn, before or for lack of true 'garments', only ornaments such as necklaces and arm or ankle bracelets.

Personal ornaments proper consist of pectorals, frontal nets, girdles, necklaces and bracelets made of shells (Grotte des Enfants at Grimaldi, Barma Grande and Cavillon caves near Menton), and also of multicoloured stones, fish vertebrae, pierced teeth, animal paws and claws.[43] Men wore more ornaments than women, who often wore only a simple bone pendant (Barma Grande); amber, worked on the spot, was also used for necklaces (plate 20), and ivory for bracelets.

These objects are known to us through funerary customs: the body was buried in its finest trappings and the decorative elements were durable, whereas the garments, loincloths and caps to which they were sewn, perished.

Comparative Study of Prehistoric Costume

The wide disparities between the various civilizations in the same period, whether Palaeolithic or Neolithic, make it very difficult to carry out a comparative study of costumes in different geographical zones.

The terms of comparison cannot be the same, for instance for the Babylonian civilization towards 3000 BC, which was

32–3 Menhir carved with a male figure from Les Maurels, seen from front and rear. Neolithic Period. Rodez, Musée Fenaille.

34–5 Menhir carved with a female figure from Saint-Cernin, seen from front and rear. Neolithic Period. Rodez, Musée Fenaille. (Photos Louis Balsan)

the most advanced of the Bronze Age, and that of Polar Europe, where the Arctic Stone Age continued over a long period. Comparisons can be valid only if they are based on cycles of civilization observed in each of the four geographical zones that are today almost universally acknowledged: the Ancient East, Mediterranean Europe (East and West), temperate Europe (West and Eastern Central) and the Polar regions of Europe.

But taking into account the differences implied by this classification, as Clark does, if we are to understand the causes behind the evolution of primitive costume, we must be able to appreciate the importance of the links, in particular trading links, established between the various civilizations, and the scale of migrations. While it is admitted nowadays that the process was not so much a development, more an interpenetration between the various periods of prehistoric civilizations, the migratory element must have played a determining role in causing the spread or transformation of some characteristics of costume. Furthermore, it has been proved that the arrival of a more advanced people always led to the regression of the indigenous people.

It is therefore permissible to conclude, from certain resemblances in materials, techniques and forms, that in the Palaeolithic periods, people must have dressed in almost the same way in Western Europe, in the Mediterranean basin and in Africa, due allowance being made for the different demands of climate and way of life. This similarity must date from well before the Bronze Age.

But the appearance of similar costumes in these widely separated geographical zones cannot yet be presented as more than a hypothesis; the mere fact of formulating it, however, allows us to glimpse the important contribution the history of costume is liable to receive from the study of migrations and primitive economies – and of course, the contribution is reciprocal.

The elements of prehistoric costume we know seem pitifully few by comparison with the vast fields which would be opened up by a comparative study of this order: such an undertaking cannot hope to produce quick results, but it must be begun. It is strange to note how little research has been carried out along these lines on the basis of the discoveries of the last half-century.

Such a study of prehistoric costume, even applied to its most distant known origins, must always be linked closely with the general study of human development.

Because of the difficulties of comparing prehistoric costume, this general introduction is expanded in three separate sections, covering the Ancient East (Chapter II), Crete (Chapter III) and the Mediterranean countries (Chapter IV).

Notes

1 Goury; Claugh; Varagnac: *L'Homme avant l'écriture, passim*.
2 Goury, pp. 194, 197; Baumann, pp. 15, 17, 71, 82, 83.
3 Baumann, p. 74.
4 Clark, p. 401.
5 Goury, p. 142; Clark, pp. 324–329; Lantier, pp. 99–100.
6 Vogt.
7 Geiger and Ljungh; Vogt, *Ciba* 15, pp. 507 ff.
8 Clark, p. 12.

9 Lantier, p. 99.
10 Goury, p. 350, fig. 192; Baumann, p. 44 fig.
11 Glotz, ch. 11, pp. 81 ff.
12 Goury, p. 142; Clark, pp. 324–329; Lantier, pp. 99–100.
13 Lantier, pp. 99–100; Leroi-Gourhan, pp. 112–113.
14 Clark, pp. 324–329.
15 Glotz, pp. 85 ff.
16 Broholm, pp. 73–74.
17 Parrot, p. 114.
18 Vogt, *Ciba* 15, p. 253.
19 Goury, pp. 150, 205, 227, 228 and fig. 90.
20 Clark, p. 185.
21 Vogt, *Ciba*, 15, p. 323.
22 *Ibid.*, pp. 523–533.
23 Baumann, p. 98.
24 Vogt, *Ciba* 15, p. 538.
25 Baumann, p. 16.
26 Clark, pp. 355–357.
27 Vogt, *Ciba* 15, pp. 537–540.
28 *Ibid.*, pp. 531, 632 (repr.), 511–512 (repr.), 532–533 (repr).
29 Lantier, p. 69; Broholm, p. 38 and fig. 23.
30 Breuil, p. 15.
31 Broholm, pp. 29 ff.
32 *Ibid.*, pp. 29–36.
33 Lantier, pp. 99–100.
34 Goury, p. 231 and fig. 92, after a T-toggle in the Périgueux Museum.
35 Vogt, *Ciba* 15, p. 519; Broholm, pp. 43 ff.
36 Vogt, *Ibid.*, p. 540.
37 Déchelette, II, p. 309.
38 Clark, p. 324.
39 *Ibid.*, p. 328.
40 Schlabov; Salin, I, p. 105 and fig. 8, mentions these garments as Germanic from the sixth-seventh centuries.
41 Clark, pp. 324–329 and fig. 122.
42 Demargne, p. 192.
43 Lantier, p. 100; *Appelgren*, passim (on Bronze Age ornaments).

Bibliography

GENERAL

J. G. D. CLARK: *Prehistoric Europe*, 1955.
G. GOURY: *Origine et évolution de l'homme*, 1927.
H. BAUMANN and D. WESTERMANN: *Les Peuples et les civilisations de l'Afrique*, 1948.
R. LANTIER: *La Vie préhistorique*, 1952.
A. PARROT: *Mari, une ville perdue*, 1936.
G. GLOTZ: *La Civilisation égéenne*, 1923.
ABBÉ BREUIL: *Les Peintures rupestres schématiques de la Péninsule ibérique*, 1933–35.
DÉCHELETTE: *Manuel d'archéologie préhistorique*, 1908–1917.
P. DEMARGNE: *La Crète dédalique*, 1937.
G. CONTENAU: 'La Vie en Sumer', in *Histoire de l'Orient ancien*, 1936.
C. LEGRAIN: 'L'Art sumérien au temps de la Reine Shoubad', in *Gazette des Beaux-Arts*, July 1931.
L. DELAPORTE: 'Le Proche-Orient asiatique', in *Les Peuples de l'Orient méditerranéen*, 1938.

COSTUME

A. GEIJER and H. LJUNGH: *Die Kleider der Dänischen Bronzezeit*, 1937.
H. C. BROHOLM and M. HALD: *Bronze Age Fashion*, 1948.

TEXTILES

E. VOGT: *Geflechte und Gewerbe der Steinzeit*, 1937.
E. VOGT: 'Vanneries et tissus à l'âge de la pierre et du bronze en Europe' *Les Cahiers Ciba*, No. 15, February 1948.

Prehistoric Chronology

PALAEOLITHIC	EARLY	Abbevillean Acheulean	600,000 to 160,000 BC	Hunters of mammoth and reindeer
	MIDDLE	Mousterian	160,000 to 40,000 BC	Fur garments
	LATE	Aurignacian Solutrean Magdalenean	40,000 to 8000 BC	
MESOLITHIC			8000 to 3000 BC	Hunters and fishermen Hide garments
NEOLITHIC			3000 to 1000 BC	Farmers and shepherds Flax cultivation Hide garments Early weaving
BRONZE AGE			2100 to 1000 BC	Sailors and artisans Early use of wool Woven, decorated garments
IRON AGE	HALLSTATT PERIOD		1000 to 500 BC	Woven, decorated garments
	LA TÈNE PERIOD		500 to 50 BC	

Note: Adapted from A. VARAGNAC: *L'Homme avant l'écriture* and A. LEROI-GOURHAN and J. NAUDOU: *Préhistoire et Proto-histoire (Histoire Universelle de l'Encyclopédie de la Pléïade)*.

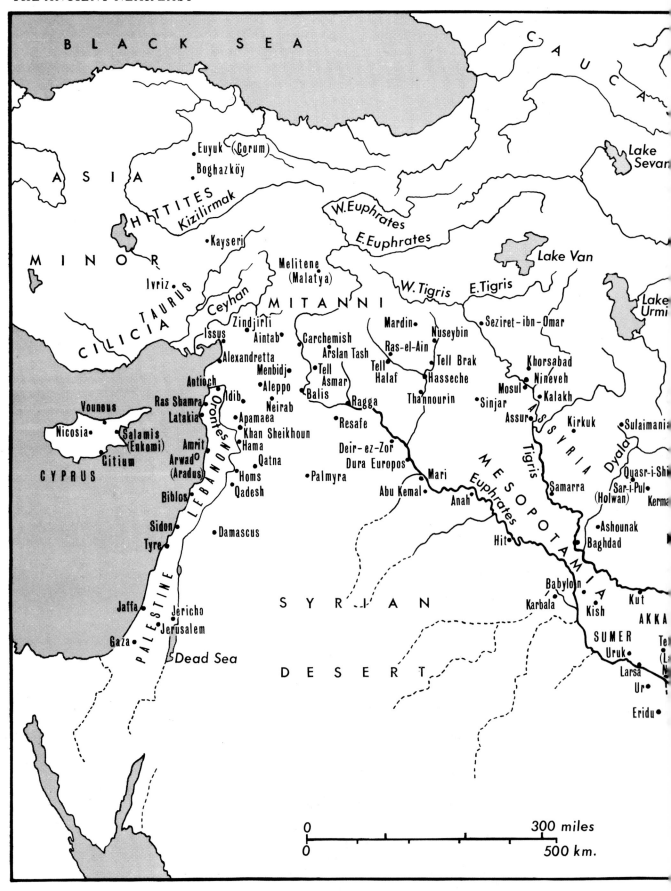

Chapter II

Costume in the Ancient East

General Conditions

In the present state of archaeological discoveries and our knowledge of migrations in the Middle East from the fifth millennium to the Christian era, it is very difficult to pin down precisely the influences exercised by successive autochthonous and invading civilizations on the costume worn by the different peoples of ancient Asia, from the Indus and Arabia to the Bosphorus, from Palestine to Turkestan. Indeed, many widely differing factors must be borne in mind if we are to understand the elements that determined the development of costume in this immense section of South-West Asia where the first human civilizations took shape.

Physical characteristics enable us to propose three zones: regions of plains and valleys, of low or medium altitude (Mesopotamia, Arabia, Palestine and Western Syria), coastal regions, of varying altitude (Eastern Mediterranean and Black Sea) and high plateau and mountainous regions (Anatolia, Armenia, the Caucasus, Persia, Afghanistan and Baluchistan).

Political economy shows that the most ancient fixed civilization in this part of Asia – Mesopotamian civilization – grew up in essentially agricultural areas, which the mountainous terrain sharply separated from the two other civilizations of the time, those of China and India.

'Thus from prehistoric times there grew up a "classical" Orient which presents itself to us as a whole because on one side, Mesopotamia had infinitely more contacts with the Mediterranean area (Syria and Anatolia) and Egypt than with India and China, and on the other, because Iran, though dominating the Indus from the heights of the Afghan valleys, gravitated more naturally down to Babylon and Baghdad by the cols of Zagros.'[1]

Where history is concerned, we are told that from about 2500 BC a series of migrations and invasions, stemming first from the steppes of Central Europe and Asia, then from the high plateaux of Western Asia, led to a converging rush of various peoples who swooped down in rapid succession to pillage the rich civilizations of Mesopotamia and Syria. Most important of all is the second wave, which originated around the Bosphorus and the Caspian Sea about 2000 BC, covering Western Asia and Central and Eastern Europe, pushing the inhabitants of the mountains and high plateaux further south into Asia, just as it displaced the Achaeans in Europe, who in their turn invaded Hellas.

Nowhere more than in the Middle East do we see the importance of migratory movements and invasions, but at the same time we cannot lay too much stress on the continuity of civili-

33

zations and the maintenance of certain values – or cultural elements such as costume styles – represented or preserved by the defeated peoples.

The Middle East also shows characteristic features and patterns of development that, while there is seldom any real link between them, correspond to climatic, environmental and economic conditions and dominant or dependent political situations.

Under those dominating conditions, we see the emergence of the first type of primitive drapery, which appeared in the costumes of the Mesopotamian valleys in the early millennia, then of a later style, from the middle of the third millennium BC on, characterized by additions made by invading peoples, and lastly, a mixed type which was fairly generally worn but tended to be localized on the plains and round the coasts.

It is probable that the prehistoric inhabitants of the Middle East wore simple garments, analogous to those found in Europe and the Mediterranean region. The most recent excavations enable us to glimpse similarities between the Stone Age civilizations of Europe and the Syrio-Palestinian countries.

From the middle of the third millennium the development of costume in the Middle East showed dual tendencies characteristic of costume in all times: draping (in the costume produced by the natives) and cutting and sewing (in the hemmed garments brought by invaders). But these two types of costume did not maintain their identity intact, and their principal elements became intermingled during the second millennium so as to form a composite costume in certain regions of this vast zone, as a result of successive accretions from more or less neighbouring civilizations.

In the Middle East we are thus confronted with a varied, complex situation in costume,[2] whether different modes succeeded one another or existed simultaneously, for the older styles were not always completely superseded by the new.

Costume in the Valleys and Plains

THE GEOGRAPHICAL SETTING

'All the regions of the Middle East were grouped round Mesopotamia, where wide waterways and the Persian Gulf gave them access to the Indus valley and the Arabian peninsula.'[3]

The Mesopotamian basin, bordered on the east by the Elam and Zagros mountains and on the north by those of Armenia, opens to the west on to the Syrian desert. From the very beginning two rivers, the Tigris and the Euphrates, stimulated commercial contacts which soon developed into an important international trade network.

These active exchanges, whose principal axis was Mesopotamia, explain all the urban development of the Middle East, its civilization and the development of its costume, which can be perceived from the fourth century on in the two population groups inhabiting the country: the Semites in Akkadia, an agricultural people to the north, and towards the sea in the south, the Sumerians, a trading people. The latter civilization

spread more rapidly and was adopted by the Akkadians, expanding through the whole of the Middle East.

This situation made Mesopotamia an ideal land for migration, and led to successive, repeated enrichment and plundering by nomads who came down into the valleys from the mountains of the east, the Caucasus and Asia Minor, attracted by the mirage of Oriental wealth.

The fluctuating evolution of this region, incessantly interrupted by floods and wars but always rebuilt on the basic prosperity of reviving trade, explains the changes, relationships and influences that can be observed in the history of its costume.

Sumerian Costume

In its earliest stage, the Al'Ubaid period in the fourth millennium BC, the Sumerian civilization was that of a people clad in skins and hides worn furry side inwards, then in woven clothes, sheep and goats providing the raw materials for these first garments. As such, it was well in advance of the contemporary civilizations of hunters and fishermen of the Palaeolithic and Neolithic periods in Europe and Africa.

We have extremely important sources of costume information in the numerous statues, bas-reliefs, etc. discovered in recent years. The economically advanced nature of this civilization is also shown by its production of woven cloth, many excellent specimens of which survive, and by the spread of these garments and textiles through a large part of Central Asia.

It is extremely curious that a vestimentary problem was raised immediately by the first archaeological finds which revealed the various periods of Sumerian civilization.

SKINS AND WOVEN CLOTH

In the oldest representations of humans, which date from the third millennium, the skins of various wild animals, formerly worn over the shoulders, were now draped round the hips like a skirt; these garments were made from long-haired skins, particularly sheepskins whose texture is represented by hatched patterns, from 2900 to about 2500 BC in Mesopotamia (Sumer and Akkad). Then, towards 2500 BC, in Telloh, skins sewn together are represented by bands of straight and wavy stripes on representations of the skirts and cloaks worn throughout Sumer. The fashioning of these skins made it possible to adapt them into garments such as gowns.

These skins were used in skirts and cloaks from about 2885 BC to form complete garments; then, towards 2500 BC, they were made with sleeves, which may have been simple unsewn flaps of skin folded over the arm. Vertical fringes along the foot of garments, perhaps made of leather thongs, seem to date from the beginning of the third millennium.

During the third and second millennia the term *kaunakès* was still applied to this garment, and thus referred not to a material but to a form.[4]

From 2700 BC at the earliest and until about the fourth century BC, the hides originally used for these skirts and gowns were replaced by kaunakès cloth, a textile imitating goat-skin, while short capes were still made of skin or hide. By the fifth

36–8   Representation of the Sumerian pagne-skirt of fur or long-haired cloth, stylized into cross-hatched decoration, curled tongues or frill-motifs. The crimped beard of Ebikhil (plate 37) may be false

36   Limestone votive plaque of Ur-Nanshe from Lagash. Third millennium BC. Paris, Louvre. (Photo Flammarion)

37–8   Ebikil, superintendent of the Ishtar temple at Mari. Paris, Louvre. (Photos Flammarion)

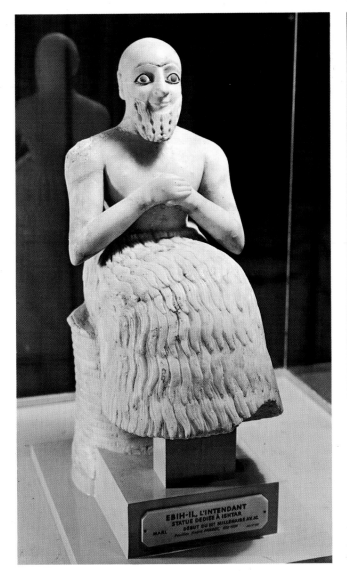

35

century BC a thick, heavy cloth was used, made of large quantities of wool or hair, from which a garment in the Persian style was made; this garment was probably semicircular and worn over the shoulders, like the *cappa floccata* of modern Greek shepherds. The term kaunakès is then used, by confusion, for cloth of any sort, whether coarse or fine, woven or not, as well as retaining its original meaning of 'skin'. The cloak, too, gradually came to be made of cloth.

Finally, from the mid-sixth century BC (*c.* 558 BC) we see the emergence of loose garments with generous folds, following the lines of the body, in Susa under obvious Grecian influences.

Kaunakès cloth, which is still made in modern times by some peoples in Asia Minor and even in the mountainous region of the Pindus, was in practice generally abandoned and was later used only for the symbolic costume of gods and goddesses, as in the case of the god Shamash on the Hammurabi code stele.[5]

The other type of cloth, which appears on two monuments in the Jemdet-Nasr period and even at the end of the Uruk period, is smooth, with or without fringes and decorated with patterns such as lozenges or checks: these textiles are entirely woven, and are not kaunakès. Traces of woven cloth have been found on metal axes in tombs from the Susa necropolis, at the end of the Al'Ubaid period; oxidization preserved the prints and chemical analysis has shown that these cloths were fairly fine in texture.[6]

Cloth was woven in rectangular pieces on vertical looms; wearers simply swathed them in various ways round their bodies.

TRADE AND COSTUME

These observations are in accordance with what we know of Sumerian trade after the fourth millennium.

In the Tigris and Euphrates delta, Sumerian towns had become centres of international trade; originally they had turned towards the rich cities of the Indus and the Persian Gulf and the Pre-Aryan civilization, which is confirmed by the Mohenjo-daro excavations. Later, following the two river-courses, they entered into contact with the regions of the Caspian Sea, Cappadocia and the Mediterranean coast, and received and transmitted the produce of Armenia, Syria and even Egypt by means of caravans. Objects in obsidian provide proof of regular contact with the Caucasus.[7]

Under Hammurabi (2003 to 1961 BC) Cappadocian tablets reveal the economic history of Asia Minor and mention Akkadian merchants engaged in the wool trade.[8]

Commercial relations had been established with India since the Pre-Aryan period, and artistic influences from the Indus valley affected Sumer and Akkad, as we see from the proto-historic painted ceramics from Sind, some of those motifs recall similar work from Al'Ubaid (*c.* 3400 BC) and Mesopotamia (late sixth millennium BC).[9] One may suppose that these influences left their mark on weaving and textile decoration.

Numerous Sumerian features can be found in the Kuban during the Copper Age and Armenian wealth fostered its trade with Asia Minor and Pontis.[10]

COSTUME

The costumes of the most ancient Pre-Aryan civilizations of the Middle East (Pre-'Ubaid, 'Ubaid and Ur) were, in their purest form, the same as those of Sumer and Akkad; this form was very widespread before the third millennium and was no doubt worn from the Persian Gulf to the Mediterranean. Designed to cover the hips, it was generally made of skins and pelts, then of pieces of woollen material cut and roughly assembled by means of a few seams.

This very characteristic 'original nucleus' can still be traced in even the most complicated later costumes when added elements, easily recognized by their cut and mounting, are removed. In this way the 'primitive form' of Sumerian costume can be seen in garments from more recent civilizations.

The oldest representations of this Sumerian 'primitive form' take the form of calf-length skirts; the inlaid panels decorating the harp found in the royal tombs at Ur (plate 51), dating from the reign of Queen Shub-ad (3500 or 3200 BC, British Museum), the bas-relief of Ur-Nanshe (*c.* 2900 BC, Louvre), the votive mace-head from Telloh (*c.* 2800 BC, British Museum) and the limestone statuettes in the Louvre and the Berlin Museum show various male figures wearing this skirt with several tiers of kaunakès decorated with a tassel at the back, gathered at the waist and held tightly round the hips by tucking a corner through the girdle; the knot, forming what almost amounted to a bustle at the back, was doubtless the tassel of this girdle, a survival from the tails of the animals whose fur had been used in former periods.[12]

The long woollen shawl also represents one of the most ancient pieces of Sumerian costume, and derives from the classical Indian model. It is possible that at the beginning of the third millennium ordinary people swathed a coarse, fringed shawl, narrower than the Indian original, round their hips 'either leaving its full width to form a long skirt, or folding it in half several times'; in this case, they gave it the appearance of the Egyptian *shenti*, a sort of cotton loincloth, similar to the *farous* worn by Iraqi workmen.[13]

To judge from the varied representations (e.g. the Ur-Nammon Seal, British Museum, and the 'Stele of the Vultures', Louvre, plate 39) this shawl was composed of skins or furs or smooth or deep-piled cloth.

Later (*c.* 2400 BC) statues of Prince Gudea represent him wearing a skirt probably made from a shawl which, when shortened, showed the left leg to above the knee, but as its two edges overlapped it had the general appearance of a closed skirt, which was always worn by men of the people and servants.

The same shawl could also be rolled and wrapped round the body, with the end thrown over the left shoulder. Sometimes worn by men (the Elamite and Suppliant with Kid, Louvre), it seems generally to have been the costume worn by women, in the form of a short skirt, or else draped so as to leave the right arm free (the Ur-Nanshe bas-relief, Louvre, plate 36).

Draped in this way, the Sumerian shawl fulfilled the role of a separate garment (*cf.* the 'Stele of the Vultures'), particularly among the wealthy classes, or of a gown forming a half-cape over the left shoulder, the whole being in one piece. It seems that Cherblanc, in his study of the kaunakès, interpreted this drapery wrongly and imagined the half-cape to be an independent part of the costume, despite Heuzey's admirable explanation.

It is very likely that the shawl was thus contemporary with the whole gown which appears only on female figures; the bust of a Sumerian woman, plate 44 (2700 BC), the goddess Inanna (*c.* 2500 BC), the praying woman with the aryballos, plate 41

SHAWL IN KAUNAKÈS

39 King Ennatum at the head of his troops wears, over his pagne-skirt, a flowing shawl in kaunakès which probably served as protection; the helmet, with the knot of hair at the nape of the neck, and the false ears, is very similar to the royal helmet discovered at Ur. The soldiers wear helmets without chignons or false ears, probably made of copper; they wear shawls diagonally over their torsos

40 A rolled girdle holds the pagne, edged with a long-haired flounce; the hair and beard are probably false

39 Fragment of the 'Stele of the Vultures' from Lagash. Early third millennium BC. Paris, Louvre. (Photo Flammarion)

(Telloh, *c.* 2500 BC), the group of two divinities (*c.* 2500 BC); these are the first representations known in Sumer and Akkad of this type of garment, which is characterized by its round neckline, the sleeves covering the forearm, and the seams joining the widths of kaunakès (fur), sometimes arranged in tiered flounces.

The same type of gown can be found in a more recent period-without sleeves and made of plain material, on the diorite statue of Gudea (twenty-fourth century BC) and on the Hasha-mer cylinder (twenty-third century BC); it seems that the former is covered by a long fringed shawl draped over the left shoulder, and that in the latter case, the shawl covers both shoulders.

The use of hard materials, alabaster, diorite and bronze, in the representations of the costumes of Ur-Ningirsu (twenty-fourth century BC) and Queen Napirasu (mid-second millennium, Louvre), made it possible to give exact definitions of the textiles and forms employed: the representations of the goddess Ishtar and Prince Ishtup-ilum show long fitted gowns following the shape of the body, worked on the bias or in criss-cross bands.[14]

The small number of documents provided by excavations and their still approximate dating and attributions do not enable us to say firmly whether or not they represent divine costumes or merely short-lived fashions.[15]

Costume made no clear-cut distinction between the sexes except in the details of its arrangement; this aspect of costume shows more particular efforts to achieve elegance in the Susa region, where the richness of the shawl as an outer garment is brought out (plate 48). Gradually sumptuous cloths and complicated arrangements make their appearance; some monuments represent materials with trellis patterns, or covered with small engraved circles marked in the centre with a small concavity, which may have corresponded to paillettes or beads of gold, lapis, agate or cornelian sewn to the garment.[16]

Plain and tasselled fringes appear from the twenty-second century BC, embroidery a little later; but both decorative devices are used until the end of the Persian period (330 BC).

No ancient textiles have been discovered in excavations, but this is because in Sumer the dead were buried naked, apart

40 Statuette of Abu from Tel Asmar. Early third millennium BC. Iraq Museum, Baghdad. (Photo Flammarion, after Frankfort: *The Arts of the Ancient Orient*)

37

42 Figure of a female suppliant discovered at Mari. Twenty-eighth century BC. Paris, Louvre. (Photo Flammarion)

43 Woman with aryballos, discovered at Telloh. Twenty-eighth century BC. Paris, Louvre. (Photo Flammarion)

SHAWL DRAPED AS A GOWN

41 This figure shows how the decoration of knotted, curled fringes enriched the Sumerian shawl; the fringes also make it possible to give a precise interpretation of the complex drapery of royal costumes

FEMALE COSTUME – ROBE AND MANTLE IN KAUNAKÈS

42–3 These two women wear over their robes another garment, also in kaunakès, covering the shoulders and arms; it envelops the entire body in the Mari figurine, like a cape whose flat edging and tapes can be seen on the front of the body. The bodice of the woman with the aryballos is either a sewn garment or a draped shawl

FEMALE DRAPED COSTUME

44–5 Two ways in which women arranged the rectangular shawl: the fringe trimmings allow one to trace the drapery of the cloth, from which the sculptor has suppressed the folds. The Lagash figurine's coiffure is a chignon tied inside a scarf, while the spinner has bands wound round her hair, which is perhaps false

41 Idi-ilum, Governor of Lagash (Telloh). c. 2350 BC. Paris, Louvre. (Photo Flammarion)

38

44 Woman with a scarf, discovered at Telloh.
Twenty-fourth century BC.
Paris, Louvre. (Photo Giraudon)

45 Bas-relief of the Spinner, discovered at Susa. *c.* 1000–540 BC.
Paris, Louvre. (Photo Flammarion)

from members of the royal family (tombs of Ur): on archaic monuments, the priest is always shown naked, to avoid sacralizing his garments and thus displeasing the god.[17]

HAIR AND HEAD-DRESSES

Statuettes of men represent some as beardless and shaven-headed, others as wearing long hair and beards. It is unlikely, contrary to what has been thought, that the former were Sumerians and the latter Semites: the choice of styles depended on fashion and not on racial customs.

Originally the Sumerians probably wore beards and long hair; the hair was tied on top of the head with a ribbon or else held by a bandeau over the brow, falling in a mass over the shoulders. The lips and chin were shaven and the beard was square-cut or allowed to grow in long locks at cheek level to form sideburns, or even grown long in a wavy screen over the chest. Prince Ishtup-ilum is shown with a flourishing moustache. Later the Sumerians shaved their heads and were often beardless, but gods were still represented with the hairstyles of the ancient Sumerians.[18]

It is possible that the King of Mari, shown with a beard and his hair in a large chignon at the back of his head, was in reality wearing a wig, and perhaps also a false beard held in place by a narrow band, perhaps an ornament worn by gods (Ningirsu on the Stele of the Vultures); princes (Mes-kalam-shar at Ur), and kings (Eannatum at Telloh [Lagash]); Woolley has found remains of wigs in a man's tomb in the royal cemetery at Ur. Furthermore, out of four Mari dignitaries, three are bearded and only one clean-shaven. Their hair falls well down their backs and is dressed smoothly, ending in a neatly rolled curl.[19] Apart from any consideration of fashion, the way hair was worn was dictated by protocol.[20]

For men, head protection consisted generally of a small pleated toque or a scarf made of a piece of cloth folded and rolled round the temples, a style still to be found in the East. Strabo mentions a light piece of linen. Dignitaries wore a low toque with projecting ends.

The scarf worn in this way was what the Greeks called a 'mitra'. We do not know what colour this scarf was, but we can tell that it was also used as a girdle. Ancient authors use the term *mitrati* to designate certain head-dresses worn by the people of Susa, the Arabs and the Kings of Cyprus. Chaldean statues show similar headdresses decorated with relief ornaments, giving the impression of a deep-piled, curly material: this is a type of long-haired cloth.[21]

On the Hammurabi Code Stele, the god Shamash is shown with the features of a Sumerian god of the archaic period, clad in a flounced kaunakès-cloth. On his head he wears a tall tiara which latterly becomes a cylindrical tiara crowned with a row of plumes.

Women's head-dresses present a fairly wide variety. Most often their long hair was knotted into a heavy chignon held in a sort of net or a piece of pleated cloth. In the most elegant class of citizens, the hair was rolled over the ears, with a high, raised chignon and plaited bands arching on to the top of the head. Another type of hairstyle, short and knotted and finely curled on the top of the head, carried the hair forward in festoons over the temples, leaving the ears uncovered; the waves were held in place by two bandeaux, one round the front of the head, the other passing transversally over the top; the hair was bouffant at the nape and fell freely over the shoulders.[22]

In certain instances the hairstyle comprised two separate pieces, similar to the *kaffiyeh* and the *agal* of the Arabs.

The goddess Ishtar is alone in wearing a sort of helmet-wig with a row of horns.

ORNAMENTS

A head ornament like the one found in the tomb of Queen Shub-ad remains exceptional (plate 49): formed of numerous mulberry leaves in gold, it was held in place by tall combs, also in gold, flattening at their leaf-shaped tips and ending in small globes of lapis.[23]

Necklaces with several strands of beads, and from three to

39

46 Warriors, mosaic inlay from Mari. Third millennium BC.
Paris, Louvre. (Photo Flammarion)

47 Head of the statue of Prince Gudea, from Telloh. *c.* 2350 BC.
Paris, Louvre. (Photo Alinari-Giraudon)

SUMERIAN MILITARY COSTUME

46 Over the pagne soldiers wore a leather stole reinforced with metal studs

CURLED TURBAN

47 The cap worn by the *Pathesi* is probably a sort of turban formed of a swathed scarf of curly-textured material

FEMALE CEREMONIAL COSTUME

48 This large statue shows a complicated costume: a tunic edged at the foot with long fringes that spread out on the ground, and over it, a swathed shawl, perhaps picked out with metallic embroidery. The short, close-fitting sleeve comes to above the elbow, and a fibula on the shoulder holds the neckline in place

SUMERIAN JEWELS

49 Pearls, fragments of lapis and cornelian are set in gold; rings, mulberry leaves and a comb adorned with flowers were set in the wig; crescent-shaped earrings completed the *parure*, which is presented here on a mask reconstructed on the basis of the skulls found in the royal tombs at Ur. Queen Shub-ad also wore a plastron covered with tubular beads and held in place by long gold pins

50 The golden helmet, with its false knot of hair and false ear is a ceremonial helmet, like the one that can be seen worn by King Ennatum on the 'Stele of the Vultures' (plate 39)

48 Queen Napirasu, bronze statuette discovered at Susa.
c. 1500 BC. Paris, Louvre. (Photo Flammarion)

49 Head-dress of Shub-ad (Pu-abi), Queen of Ur. Fourth millennium BC. Philadelphia, University Museum. (Museum photo)

50 Golden Helmet of Prince Mes-kalam-shar from Ur. Third millennium BC. Iraq Museum, Baghdad. (Museum photo)

six bracelets constitute the most usual range of ornaments worn by women. Men do not seem to have worn jewellery.[24]

FOOTWEAR

The Sumerians went barefooted, according to the Old Testament, as did the Égyptians: however, sandals are worn by one Sumerian, Naram-Sin, on a triumphal stele (*c.* 2500 BC).

Syrian excavations have also yielded a clay model – probably a religious offering – which may have been in use around 3000 BC, in the form of a shoe with a slightly upturned point; seal cylinders show similar shapes in the Akkadian period (*c.* 2500 BC). This form, with the upturned point, originally reserved for the king, then becoming an accessory of formal ceremonial costume, may have come from mountain peoples who introduced it into Mesopotamia, whence it spread into central Asia, the Eastern Mediterranean and as far West as Etruria.

BATTLE COSTUME

In Sumer there was no specifically military costume, but it is interesting to note certain characteristics in warriors which mark one of the first instances of specialization by a group, a phenomenon unknown among the contemporary prehistoric men of Europe and Africa.

The warriors – perhaps Semites – represented in the celebrated Mari shell-mosaic panel (plate 46) are never clad in the kaunakès skirt, but wear a more or less long, fringed gown, leaving the right arm free, with a thick knot at the back. Sometimes this tunic-gown completely envelops the body and falls to mid-calf; at other times it is split and stops at knee-level. The most curious characteristic, however, is the wide band of nailed leather which, protecting the chest and back, is thrown over the left shoulder and reaches down the back: it must be compared with the similar band of nailed leather which hangs over the left shoulder of dignitaries of Mari and Gudea (*c.* 2400 BC), perhaps constituting a badge of authority.

These Sumerian warriors wore rawhide caps or else copper helmets protecting the ears and the nape of the neck, sometimes fitted with chinstraps; both types of head-dress were padded with wool and leather.[25]

Naram-Sin, King of Agade towards 2700 BC, is shown as the conqueror of mountain communities, on a stele in the Louvre, with a metal helmet decorated with horns, an attribute reserved for gods and deified princes.

THE SPREAD OF SUMERIAN COSTUME

In reconstructing the spread of Sumerian costume, we are led to observe that the study of the kaunakès takes on more importance than the simple study of a garment, if we place the question in the context of its relationships with other civilizations: only this type of study enables one to offer not merely conjectures, but new observations about the links between peoples and their economies in the fourth millennium BC.

Various authors, among them G. Contenau, C. Legrain, A. Parrot and E. Cherblanc, have taken an interest in this question and their works, which complement one another, pinpoint one of the first problems of prehistoric costume.

From their various contributions it appears that the term *kaunakès* originally referred to a sheep fleece or goatskin with long tufts of hair on the outside, worn as a garment in Sumer at the beginning of the Pre-Agadaean period. According to representations discovered, this garment was worn in part of Central Asia during the period from 3400 BC to 2400 BC. We then find textiles imitating goatskin and fleece, with tufts arranged more regularly than those on real skins, often even placed in rows like flounces; this arrangement of tufts is found at Mari in the tiered gowns worn by women (plate 42) and the long robes of men, like those worn by the King and the Superintendent Ebikhil (plates 37–8), about 2900 BC.

It now seems beyond doubt that animal skins were replaced in prehistoric Europe by woven material during one of the last stages of the Palaeolithic or, at the latest, at the end of the Mesolithic period, towards 5000 BC. This cloth must have been

41

51 The 'Royal Standard', mosaic from Ur. The 'Peace' side. Early third millennium BC. British Museum, London. (Museum photo. Courtesy of the Trustees)

the same as that still worn by the Celts, a coarse wool 'resembling goat hair', as Diodorus says. Moreover, this is the type of cloth, with dangling strands, which was found in 1865 in the Jutland and Scandinavian (Trindhöj) excavations, used in both cases for cloaks; observers compared this weaving with the skin of a longhaired animal and dated it to the Middle Bronze Age (c. 1440 to 1150 BC). Some prehistoric weaving, with hairy, corded strands, must also be compared with these Nordic textiles, some of which may have been used as blankets; today, similar plush-piled cloths are still produced in Africa by the Gurmos, in the south-east of Haute-Volta.

These curious resemblances, noted in two very widely separated geographical zones (Northern Europe and Central Asia) in periods separated by almost two thousand years (3200 and 1200 BC respectively) allow us to suppose that an analogous type of cloth must have been used in prehistoric costume in very different civilizations. If this sort of weaving can be explained in the northern zones by the need to make the outer garment (cloak) shed rain, in the Middle East, on the other hand, it seems never to have been more than a type of decoration. Indeed, we can trace the use of kaunakès by the Sumerians in women's gowns as well as in the 'shawl' which men wore rolled at the waist, leaving the upper torso bare. It seems indubitable, however, that in both zones this very special weaving derived from the same earlier use of animal skins: it must therefore be admitted that the sheep and the goat, which occupied an increasingly important place at the end of the Bronze Age and in the first Iron Age in Northern Europe, were already widespread two centuries before in Asia.

A hypothesis of another kind might enable us to explain these similarities in prehistoric costume and could resolve the double problem, on the ethnological and geographical levels, which they pose. This is envisaged by Clark: 'The Danubian people', he says, 'rapidly made their way across the loess in successive waves. From Moravia, they spread out in one direction towards the east, in Galicia and Poland as far as the lower Vistula, and in another to the north and west, to Germany; they penetrated into Silesia by the Oder, into Saxony by the Elbe, into Bavaria by the Danube, finally colonizing the lands

to the west of the Main, the Neckar and the Rhine, and reaching as far as Hesbaye and the north-west of France by the valley of the Meuse.'

The directions followed by this current seem clearly established and can be recognized at several points (for instance at Vitonico, on the Don), although we cannot gauge the time taken to cover such distances. Thus it would have introduced the so-called Aurignacian civilization into temperate Central and Northern Europe. The costume with dangling strands worn by Bronze Age men in Jutland, the descendants of huntsmen led there by this early Palaeolithic current, would then represent the distant, transformed continuation in Northern Europe of the tufted garment worn in Ur and Mari.

This example demonstrates that the study of costume can throw appreciable light on the problem of the penetration of prehistoric civilizations.

Costume in Babylon from 2105 to 1240 BC and in Assyria from 1200 to 540 BC

The decline, towards the end of the third millennium, of the Sumerian empire of Ur had, from the twenty-first century on, enabled Babylon to assume increasing importance: the reign of Hammurabi (2003 to 1961 BC) made the city the centre of a new Mesopotamian empire which gathered together the legacies of the ancient Sumerian cities of Mari and Lagash (Telloh).

It was, however, the commercial activity of these cities that gave rise to the new civilization by organizing, in the fourth millennium, international maritime and caravan traffic on the delta of the Tigris and the Euphrates: if Babylon took on a leading role with the reign of Hammurabi, it was because

52-3 Male costume was formed of a long tunic with narrow sleeves to the elbow, often made of patterned or embroidered cloth, edged with a fringe at the foot; a scarf with long fringes was swathed over the tunic so as to cover the right shoulder. Sandals had uppers at the heel, and a ring to hold the big toe. Hair and beards were crimped. The King wears a tiara in the form of a truncated cone topped with a point. Behind him, his guards carry flywhisks, and a soldier in a cuirass of metal scales, with shinguards and front-laced high boots, pushes the chariot wheel

52 Ashurbanipal in his chariot, relief from Nineveh. Seventh century BC. Paris, Louvre. (Photo Flammarion)

Sumerian merchants had already established the meeting point between the rich lands of the Indus and the coastal regions of the Caspian, Cappadocia and the Eastern Mediterranean. When the sanding-up of the delta deflected traffic towards the north, Babylon benefited from this by becoming an important stage on the new caravan routes to Arabia, prolonged to the north along the Euphrates.

The Akkadians of the Babylonian empire, who belonged to the Semitic race and spoke a different language from the Sumerians, had from the beginning adopted the civilization and styles of clothing of their neighbours; they made certain modifications to their costume, corresponding to the hegemony of their new empire and their economic enrichment.

Babylonian costume, formerly identical with Sumerian costume, became differentiated from then on by a development which the bas-reliefs of Kassite art enable us to follow throughout the second millennium, but it remains difficult to attribute these changes with precision to particular invaders – Hittites, Kassites or Hurites – all of them mountain peoples.

After the ruin of Babylon, the costume worn in the Assyrian empire was only a continuation of the preceding style, and its particular features can be explained in terms of new influences.

TEXTILES

The fashion for thick, richly-decorated garments, which had already been widespread among the Sumerians, developed in Babylon and Assyria at the same time that the process of woollen weaving was being perfected. On the so-called 'Cappadocian' tablets, woollen stuffs and garments are mentioned frequently, and in Babylon there were guilds for linen and woollen weavers, who produced quantities of cloth. Unfortunately the soil of Mesopotamia, less dry than that of Egypt, has not preserved any examples. The use of cotton and linen cloth was more limited; Phoenician purple stuffs were highly esteemed and the embroidered textiles that are easily recognizable on bas-reliefs reveal a pronounced taste for sumptuous clothes and coloured ornament.[26]

53 Two officers of the retinue of King Sargon, relief from Khorsabad. Seventh century BC. Paris, Louvre. (Photo P. J. Oxenaar)

54 Ashurbánipal at table, relief from Nineveh. Seventh century BC. British Museum, London. (Museum photo. Courtesy of the Trustees)

From the relief representations that have been found, textile designs seem to have been very varied; the most common pattern consisted of regular circle or rosette motifs surrounded by narrow friezes which were probably woven for royal ceremonial robes. The assymetry of secondary ornamental motifs leads us to suppose that they were embroidered separately, then appliquéd on, while in Egypt the ornaments were woven, as on the ceremonial robe of Tutankhamen.

Only ceramics now give any idea of the richness and colour of luxury garments in the Assyrian period: faience shows green costumes with red or yellow edging, trimmed with fringes in these two alternating colours. Various shades of red seem to have been the tints most widely used, but there are mentions of blue, red, brown and dark purple woollens, and of blue-purple and dark red garments.

COSTUME

On the whole, the simple forms of Assyric-Babylonian costume met the needs of a primitive, patriarchal way of life in a hot climate: the basic principle of dress resided less in the ways of cutting and sewing cloth than in the art of arranging it round the body.

In sculptures and bas-reliefs this costume is represented as a sheath, fitting closely to the body, since the artist suppressed all folds so as to show more easily the design of rich embroidery, which sometimes forms whole figurative compositions.

In the various classes of society the long Sumerian type of robe, which left the forearms free, remained in use right up to the period of Sargon who, with his highest dignitaries (plate 53), continued the style. Women of the people wore it fastened at the waist with a roll belt, as we see from the Nimrud bas-reliefs, drawn by Layard.

Gradually, however, for men the gown was supplanted by the long or medium length tunic, generally with wrist-length sleeves: this was probably an innovation brought by the mountain peoples, whose original climate had made them necessary. The garment survives in the East today in the form of a shirt

55 The Siege of Lachish by Sennacherib, detail. Seventh century BC. British Museum, London. (Museum photo. Courtesy of the Trustees)

56 Soldiers leading captives. Relief from Nineveh. Seventh century BC. Paris, Louvre. (Photo Flammarion)

worn for considerations of decency. This tunic, with three openings for the head and arms, had also a slit on the chest, fastened by two cords with woollen tassels.

Over this long garment a sort of one-piece cloak was draped, fastened at the top on the right of the chest, then thrown over the left shoulder to fall to the ground. This cloak is the Sumerian fringed shawl, often very voluminous, which was passed under the right arm and thrown over the left shoulder but which, later, on seventh-century royal effigies, was also drawn over the right shoulder so that it almost completely covered the chest.

The large draped shawl was reserved for the king and gods;[27] high court officials wore the shawl folded into a band over the long or short tunic, the grand vizier being distinguished by the length of his fringes.

Royal costume, the most frequently represented in sculptures, shows increasing richness in Babylonia and Assyria, though it retains certain archaic features. Although in the twelfth century BC, the costume of King Melishipak of the Kassites (c. 1200 BC) was not embroidered or decorated, that worn by one of his predecessors at the end of the thirteenth century BC, King Marduk-Nadim, departs completely from the ancient costume of Gudea and even that of Hammurabi, with its three superimposed garments made in a variety of stuffs richly decorated and embroidered in several tones, indicating increased refinement and in sharp contrast with the Assyrian military spirit.[28]

Assyrian court costume, with its daggers passed through the belt, can be compared with certain costumes of contemporary India.

Primitive Sumerian costume[29] certainly remained the normal dress of Babylonia and Assyria over a long period; however, we know of an Assyrian law which towards 1200 BC compelled free and married women to wear veils whenever they went out; this is the most ancient known allusion to the custom, which still persists in Eastern countries.[30]

Beside the conventional type of simple open sandal, laced at the ankle and holding the big toe in a ring,[31] we also note the closed shoe, introduced into the Mesopotamian valley by the mountain dwellers.

HAIR AND HEAD-DRESSES

In Assyria, men wore their hair thick and flowing over the shoulders and curled with curling irons; the King's hair was adorned with gold threads, no doubt arranged in a sort of net.

The headgear worn by the kings of Babylon consists either of a curious conical cap with a long tassel falling to waist level, following Syrio-Hittite styles,[32] or a tall cylindrical tiara crowned with a row of short plumes, no doubt made of metal. While the latter head-dress seems to have been reserved for divinities and kings, the conical cap seems to have been commonly worn among non-'Sumero-Akkadian' populations surrounding Mesopotamia.[33] The Assyrio-Babylonian divine head-dress, the horned tiara, derived from the ancient head-dress of Sumerian gods, with plumes or palm-leaves, and points the contrast between traditional costume and the more elaborate styles to which it is related.[34]

57 King Ashurbanipal II, from Nimrud. 883–859 BC. British Museum, London. (Museum photo. Courtesy of the Trustees)

57 Royal costume for religious ceremonies, with the shawl arranged in a special way, folded in two lengthwise, so as to form two tiers of fringes, then wound round the body like a skirt and held on the left shoulder. The King holds the sceptre and mace

58 Two soldiers carrying a war chariot, relief from Khorsabad Seventh century BC. Paris, Louvre. (Photo Flammarion)

59 Army on the march. Seventh century BC. Paris, Louvre. (Photo Flammarion)

ORNAMENTS

The Assyrians, who prized rich jewels, wore long ring- or walnut-shaped ear-rings, and on their hair bandeaux covered with metalwork rosettes; at the neck, necklaces of several strands, composed of talismanic motifs, while on their arms they wore wide bracelets, generally decorated with rosettes.[35]

BATTLE COSTUME

The Assyrians' warlike nature manifested itself in military costume. From the tenth century BC on, infantry and cavalry soldiers were dressed with comparative uniformity: short, fringed tunics, wide belts, conical helmets lined with leather (plates 55, 58–9). Horseback archers, who fought in pairs, wore helmets or round caps; those of Tiglath-pilesar III are represented in long garments reaching to the ankles, their heads protected by round caps covering the temples and reaching over the nape of the neck; chariot archers wore long tunics covered in metal scales, belted at the waist, and hooded helmets.

After the seventh century BC we can note the extension to cavalry and heavy infantry of the scaled cuirass, completed with trousers and shin-guards worn inside high boots (plate 60). Light infantry replaced the cuirass with a metal disk fixed to the front of the chest; archers, used in dispersed order, protected their chests with a folded cloak and wore only a short skirt and an ordinary scarf rolled round their heads.

To sum up; in most of the countries of the valleys and plains of Central Asia, a first transformation of costume took place when prehistoric skins and pelts were abandoned, probably towards the middle of the third millennium; the use of cloth, originally reserved for the skirt, spread to the shawl and cloak, but the form of garments, which remained primitive, was not modified. This was the type of Sumerian clothing which was most generally adopted in other regions.

The period which followed was marked by the appearance of the robe in the middle of the third millennium, along with better produced, more sumptuous textiles and the introduction of the tunic of varying length with narrow sleeves, borrowed from the mountain peoples.

Sumerian styles spread not only down the valleys of the Tigris and the Euphrates, but also into the higher regions to the north and east, from the Persian Gulf to the Black Sea and the Mediterranean. However, this extension did not take place without the appearance of important transformations, adaptations to the climatic conditions of the mountains and high plateaux. It seems, as we shall see later, that the styles were reintroduced, with these modifications, into their original regions in the course of invasions during the second millennium.[36]

60   Musicians of the Babylonian army, from the palace of King Ashurbanipal, Nineveh. Seventh century BC.
Paris, Louvre. (Photo Archives Photographiques)

61-2 Bronze plates from Björnhofda in Torslunda. Stockholm, Nationalmuseum (Photo ATA)

63 Mosaic. Eleventh century. The Monastery Church, Daphni, Greece. (Photo André Held)

SHEEPSKIN GARMENTS

61-2 The men shown fighting wild animals wear, in one case, a sort of sleeved smock with the hairy side out, and in the other, *braies*

63 The shepherd wears a sleeved tunic of goat- or sheep-skin, the normal garb of shepherds; in Western iconography this was to become the traditional costume of Saint John the Baptist

Survivals of the Kaunakès

The ancient fleece or goat-skin with long tufts of hair on the outside, known as *kaunakès* in Sumerian civilization, continued under this form or as a cloth imitating skins until well into the Middle Ages.

This tuft arrangement is to be found during the first centuries of the Christian era in various representations of popular or military costume, and also, particularly after the Roman period, in the representation of people from distant, little-known lands (plate 67); it continues even up to our own times as an attribute of Saint John the Baptist (plate 64), of whom it became an almost inseparable symbol in religious iconography.

49

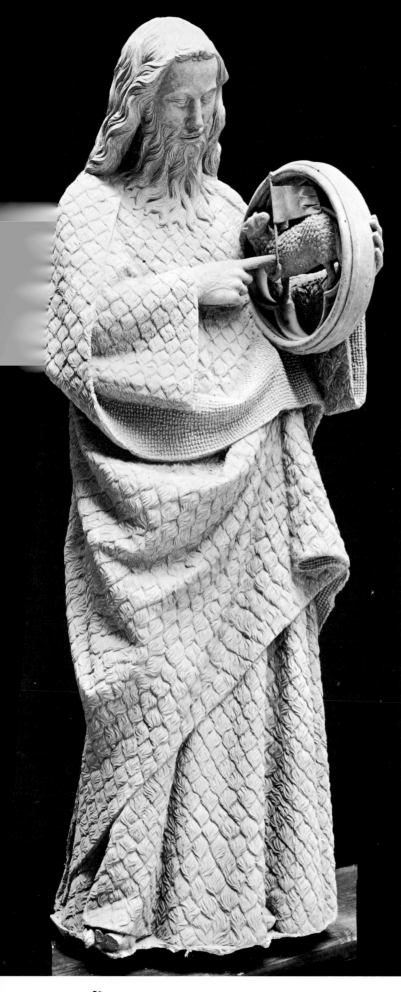

64 Saint John the Baptist. Early thirteenth century.
Church of Saint-Urbain, Troyes. (Photo Giraudon)

65 SIMONE MARTINI: Fresco of the Triumph of the Church,
c. 1355, (detail).
Spanish Chapel, Cloister of Santa Maria Novella, Florence.
(Photo Anderson)

64   The camel-hair garment is represented by tufts of hair arranged in a checkerboard pattern

65   One of the onlookers, probably a pilgrim, whose hat is pinned with crests, wears a sheepskin surtout with short sleeves

66   The big-eared man, who seems to be an allusion to a legendary people, wears a kaunakès, represented by tufts of hair similar to those found on Sumerian statues

67   To evoke the strange costumes of distant lands, the dancers wear tufts of wool attached by pitch to a close-fitting garment evoking the kaunakès mentioned in travellers' tales

66   The Scythians, lintel of the Church of Sainte-Madeleine, Vézelay. Twelfth century. (Photo Giraudon)

67   *The Ball of the Savages,* French tapestry. Mid-fifteenth century. Notre-Dame de Nantilly, Saumur. (Photo Flammarion)

68 Asiatic family arriving in Egypt, painting from the tomb
of Khumhotep, Beni Hassan, *c.* 1900 BC.
Bibliothèque Nationale copy. (Photo Flammarion)

69 Syrians bearing tribute to Egypt. Egyptian tomb painting from
tomb of Sobekhetep, Thebes. British Museum, London. (Museum
photo. Courtesy of the Trustees)

SYRIAN COSTUME

68 The garment worn at this period by Semitic traders was formed
essentially of a square or rectangular piece of cloth; according to its
size this was arranged as a skirt or as a tunic fastened on the shoulder.
It was also worn by women, who wore coloured shoes whereas men wore
sandals. These peoples are characterized by their taste – which was to
survive – for varied dyes in vivid patterns which contrast with the whiteness of Egyptian costume

SYRO-PHOENICIAN COSTUME

69–72 The costume worn by the Syro-Phoenicians was composed of a
tunic over which the wearer swathed one or several multicoloured shawls.
The Barbarian prisoner (plate 71) seems to be wearing trousers. We also
see (plate 69) a white costume with some red and blue bands: a shawl is
wound several times round the waist, forming flounces over a long-sleeved
tunic, slit at front and back, and inspired by the Orient

Costume in the Coastal Countries

(Mesopotamia, Syria, Arabia)

THE GEOGRAPHICAL AND HISTORICAL SETTING

In the third millennium the Sumerian civilization, which had been formed several centuries before and dominated all the Middle East, spread as far as the Cappadocian coast to the north and the Cilician coast, in Asia Minor, to the south; as the result of the proximity of the Upper Euphrates to the Gulf of the Orontes, it had become firmly implanted in Syria, opposite Cyprus, which in turn brought it into contact with Crete and the Cyclades. Further south, around Byblos, under Sargon I, it existed close to the Egyptian civilization which the Pharaoh Pepi I had extended thus far. On the western coasts of Asia Minor, from the Hellespont to Rhodes, Aegean influence was to be shaken by the arrival of the Achaeans.

All these coastal regions, whose altitude varied, were close either to south-east Europe or to the Middle East, and this proximity destined them to become a real crossroads of civilizations, to become 'the boulevard serving the transit of the peoples of all lands.'[37]

The great Aryan invasions of the year 2000 BC were to sweep away Sumerian trading posts in Cappadocia and Cretan centres on the coasts of Asia Minor, while only Egypt maintained its zone of influences until, towards 1700 BC, it was invaded in its turn. However, more or less everywhere the vanquished peoples slowly absorbed their conquerors. The coastal countries regained their prosperity in Asia Minor with the development of Troy, the Carian and Aegean colonies and, from the Orontes to the Nile, the international markets of Byblos, Tyre and Sidon in Syria, the country through which the Pharaoh Ahmosis I carried forward the frontiers of his empire as far as the Upper Euphrates. The entire Syrian and Palestinian coast underwent successive Egyptian, Cretan, Cypriot and Hittite invasions, besides the new incursions of other sea-going peoples and the maritime expansionism of the Phoenicians.

At the end of the second millennium an Aramaean kingdom took shape around Damascus and an Israelite kingdom in Palestine. Annexed in turn by the kings of Assur, Babylon and Persia, these states were then dominated by the Greeks under Alexander and bowed to Greco-Roman supremacy.

All these changes gave rise to 'a succession of styles taken from the various Eastern civilizations of antiquity as they passed the zenith of their histories'[38]; therefore we must not be surprised to find the populations of this long, wide coastal strip borrowing elements from Cretan, Hittite, Mesopotamian and Greco-Roman costume, while elements from Sumerian and Egyptian dress persisted, never entirely extinguished and sometimes very flourishing.

TRADE IN THE COASTAL COUNTRIES

The coastal region extending from Cilicia to Sinai has always been an area of transit and meeting between very varied ethnic

70–1 Barbarian captives. Paris, Louvre. (Photo Flammarion)

elements: from the third millennium on, its inhabitants were engaged in trade and transport, both serving as intermediaries and producing textiles on their own account. Later the Phoenicians, who seem to have occupied much of this area from the sixteenth century BC, created the first urban centres of trade and communications.

From then on we see the growth of a traffic which radiated over the entire Mediterranean basin, and inland as far as Armenia and Mesopotamia. These are the first links of a purely peaceful nature we find, and were oriented exclusively towards material gain. After this, urban life raised the standard of living and engendered luxury, while the use of larger ships fitted with tillers facilitated the development of maritime exchanges, particularly of textiles and dyes.

This maritime expansion all along the coast of Asia in the second millennium, with its consequent multiplication of commercial contacts, brought innovations that we can well imagine in the richness of fabrics, the colour of ornaments, and the type of jewellery, thereby contributing to the development of costume and the diffusion of styles.

TEXTILES AND DYES

When it relates that Adam and Eve were provided by the Lord God with 'coats of skins', the Bible joins with history: furs and hides were indeed worn as winter garments, and also used for tent-coverings and water-skins, by the ancestors of the Jewish people in the Neolithic period at the latest. Manufacturing processes exposed one to ritual defilement and were looked at askance by the Israelites, who never mentioned them; there is no Hebrew word for 'tanner', yet it is certain that the same tanning processes used in Egypt must have been practised by the Israelites.

It is through the Bible that we know of the weaving techniques of the Hebrews, for textiles from Archaic periods have completely disappeared. This information about weaving at its origins can be applied to the whole of the Middle East.

We know that among the Israelites wool was shorn in the course of a ritual feast mentioned several times in the Bible, and was then spun by women, for whom this was the normal home occupation. Different varieties of weaving made it possible to produce cloth with leaf motifs, using a loom similar in type to the model found in Egyptian tombs.

Apart from woollen cloth, linen imported from Egypt was the only textile used in Palestine: from there it spread next to Syria, then to Caria. Before the Hellenistic period (third century BC) it was a luxury product, reserved for fine garments and priestly vestments; there was only a small native output and generally people wore the white Egyptian linen or the Syrian flax cloth which were sold in the markets of Tyre.

Bright colours were widely used in costume in the coastal regions, as we see from the texts; the dyeing industry was important, as is proved by the dyeing workshop discovered at Tel Beit Mirsim. Blue tints were obtained through the use of woad, as indigo was then unknown, yellows were extracted from saffron, red from madder and henna; to these we must add a luxury dye, scarlet, often mentioned in the Bible in references to ritual accessories; purple, an essentially Phoenician product, came from Tyre.

Although it is difficult to imagine such a thing today, it was the scarcity of colouring agents for dyeing textiles in the Mediterranean area that induced Carthage to undertake its campaign against Southern Spain in 530 BC and close the Straits of Gibraltar. The industrial wealth of the Phoenicians – and later of Carthage – was based on the manufacture of glass, precious metalwork and, above all, the renowned Tyrian purple with its full, glowing tone.

At first Tyrian chemists doubtless used a dye, also used by the Greeks and Cretans, which was extracted from a shellfish found in eastern Crete. But this marine source involved a method far too costly and complicated for large-scale production; each shellfish provided only a few drops of liquid and this liquid had to be reduced to one sixteenth of its original volume, under constant, close supervision if the dye was to be perfectly uniform. Indeed, the liquid extracted from this shellfish, the *Murex brandaris*, is milky white when first isolated; exposure to light makes it turn to yellowish green and green, then to violet and finally red. By carefully timing the exposure, it was possible to obtain colours right up to a deep, almost black purple, the tint most highly prized.

The procedures were lengthy and laborious, and the price of this purple was extremely high, so that we can imagine the delight felt in Phoenicia at the discovery of islands in the Atlantic beyond Gibraltar, the Azores, with ample sources of the dye for which Tyrian chemists had been searching so long: the *rocella tinctoria*, a lichen from which *orchil* is extracted, and the dragon tree, whose intense red resin equally provided an excellent dye – a huge tree whose most famous specimen, the giant tree of Orotova, on the island of Tenerife, was believed to be six thousand years old by the time it died in 1868.

For the Phoenicians these two dyes were of the highest industrial and commercial importance, and it was doubtless to ensure a continued monopoly that Madeira and its colonies were annexed by Carthage.

As manufacturers of purple and salesmen of cloths from various lands, the Phoenicians played an important role in the history of costume in the Western world; and as creators of textiles, particularly those of Sidon, praised by Homer and Ezekiel, they may well have influenced the geometric art of the High Orientalizing period.

COSTUME

Mycenaean influence only touched the central part of the coast of Asia Minor and nowhere did it penetrate the continent. It was later, during the migrations provoked by the Dorian invasion, that Ionian colonies gradually began to form a powerful group, leading the Assyrians and Palestinians to describe Greeks by the generic name of Ionians.

From the twelfth to the ninth century BC Achaean and Ionian emigrants were certainly few in number among the artisan class in these colonies, while the social élite was almost entirely Greek and dominated the cities where it established itself. Since it included merchants it gave a new impetus to colonial, commercial and maritime expansion.

The costume of the coastal populations from the Black Sea to the Orontes seems originally to have been Sumerian-inspired, and its development appears to follow the evolution of clothing in the Mesopotamian regions, with influences from the mountain races and, occasionally, from the Hittites.

Thus, between 1700 and 1300 BC, Troy and its circle of allied peoples from Phrygia to Caria, while wearing Greek styles, also adopted costumes more specifically imported from

72 Enamelled panels representing the captives of Ramesses III, *c.* 1180 BC, from Medinet Habu, Thebes. Boston, Museum of Fine Arts. (Museum photo)

the plains of Mesopotamia or, as in the case of long sleeves, from pastoral countries. From the twelfth century BC, Achaean costume was increasingly influenced by the East, as a result of the intense commercial activity along the route from Babylon to Ephesus, through Sardis.

The mixture of Grecian and Oriental customs was made easier by the greater freedom enjoyed by Asiatic women, who shared men's lives and took meals with them, customs which were not without repercussions on clothing, which took on a predominantly Asiatic note. In the great towns of the coast, women of the higher social classes might wear sumptuous almost transparent pink stuffs, and traders tunics of purple embroidered with gold: all this luxury was made possible by the raising of the celebrated sheep of Miletus and the development of weaving industries working with wool, flax and purple stuff. Ionia gave the Greeks the habit of pleating linen as the other Asiatic peoples did.

Men were dressed in the short tunic, an undergarment of linen, closed with a seam down one side, and so without fibula. Transmitted to the Carians by the Phoenicians, this garment became widespread throughout Asia Minor. It was the Greek *chiton*, and it must not be forgotten that this term is Semitic in origin, related to the Aramaean *kitoneh*, referring to linen material.[39] This tunic could be long for ceremonial wear: Homer talks of the Ionians 'trailing their tunics'.

Ionian women wore this long linen tunic with a shawl draped like a cloak, pinned either on the right or on the left.

From the earliest times Cyprus had been the intermediary for Asiatic and perhaps also Egyptian influences moving towards Aegea, and vice versa. Ras Shamra was the Cypriot outpost on the Syrian coast.

During the third millennium BC, the clothing worn by the coastal peoples was closely related to the costume of Sumer – the large archaic fringed shawl, swathed or draped; this was worn with a short skirt or loincloth, a short or long gown covering the left shoulder and often trimmed on its long edges with a very thick semi-cylindrical roll, perhaps of fur and probably of Mitanian origin. A separate scarf, a sort of tippet crossed on the chest, was also worn.

In Palestine this costume survived until the first millennium and the cloak worn by the Israelites is none other than this ancient shawl. Perhaps we may see in the permanence of this sartorial tradition one of the characteristics of the Semitic people, and at the same time, the effect of the long tribulations of the Israelites who, tributaries and prisoners throughout their migrations and persecutions, were unable to enrich themselves and adopt luxurious costumes as did the other peoples of the Middle East. Sumptuous costume appeared among the Israelites only in the last centuries of the monarchy, during Egyptian domination; the Egyptian princes of Palestine sometimes wore the Pharaonic garment.

Particularly in Syria and Phoenicia, this costume was characterized by bold stripes and mixtures of colours, blues and reds, used either discreetly as a border or in alternate panels enlivened with a sprinkling of flower motifs or rosettes.

In the second millennium BC the loincloth-skirt for men was generally adorned with fringes, tassels and bands of relief decoration, in the spirit of the Aegean costume of the period; it is also, under the influence of Egypt, crossed and held up in front with a central point which presumably belonged to a separate garment, perhaps a cache-sexe.

This simple knee-length loincloth, draped round the hips to form its own girdle, is worn by the Asiatics shown in the Beni Hassan tomb painting (plate 68; Eleventh dynasty, 1700 to 1600 BC). While the Egyptians wear a loincloth of white cloth, the Asiatic variety is dyed and embroidered in combinations of red. white and blue. It can also be seen on the Ras Shamra statuettes.[40]

The robe leaves most of the arms bare, and could be short and made of thick cloth with fringes, in the style of the Sumerian shawl-scarf, or long and in fine-pleated stuff, in the Egyptian style: thus we have the long robe with very wide sleeves represented on the sarcophagus of Ahiram, King of Byblos, clad in Egyptian style, as are the other figures.

Male head-dresses include the rolled turban, similar to those worn by Mesopotamian kings in the last centuries of the third millennium BC, as well as the low cap with rounded crown or the light Sumerian turban.[41]

73–6 The bas-reliefs of Assyrian military triumphs show us the costumes of the conquered peoples: fringed cloaks and the shoes with upturned toes worn by the Hebrews and the fur capes worn by other peoples. However, plate 76 shows that it is possible to find examples of strictly Babylonian costume in Syria

73 Obelisk of Shalmaneser III (858–824 BC) receiving tribute from Sira the Gilzanite and Jehu, king of Israel. British Museum, London. (Museum photo. Courtesy of the Trustees)

Women's dress in the second and third millennia was still essentially the long tunic-gown whose fullness was represented in sculpture by vertical striations; it was made of cloth which was striped or finely pleated in the Egyptian tradition. The head-dress consisted of a high, cylindrical tiara, in the case of married women covered at the back by a full, very enveloping veil.

In the Rekhmire tomb paintings, however, we see curious balloon skirts divided by two girdles into three tiers and recalling the line of certain Cretan costumes. Other examples of 'Aegea-Syrian' skirts are represented in the bas-reliefs in the Leyden Museum and on the El-Amarna paintings. Various explanations have been advanced for these: crude approximations to a Sumerian kaunakès skirt? an artistic convention repeated mechanically? tunics held in at several levels by girdles? flounced gowns? The last hypothesis seems the most probable and the presence of such gowns in Syria towards 1400–1200 BC can be explained by the country's regular relations with Crete. We know that the Cretans, settling in Syria, kept their Aegean styles and made them known to others. On a tomb of the fifteenth century a Syrian princess is shown with the short-sleeved bodice and flounced gown worn in Crete. Now the fifteenth century corresponds to the apogee of the expansion of Cretan civilization which had, from the sixteenth century on, developed not only in the Cyclades but also towards Cyprus and the coast of Asia, and Aegean models were adopted in particular by great Phoenician ladies, dressed like the fashionable women of Knossos.[42]

A tunic in a clinging fabric, shown on a cosmetic spoon decorated with the figure of a foreign woman (?) with a hairnet and a heavy figured girdle (Louvre), presents the characteristics of Babylonian weaving. Stuffs made according to this technique were probably introduced into Egypt in particular after the victorious campaigns of Thutmosis into Syria as far as the Euphrates.

In the first millennium BC women's costume consists, like men's, of two contrasting types; on one hand, the draped Sumerian garment, with a veil covering the head, and on the other, the sewn garment, generally a short tippet (or tunic) open down its length.

The crown of rolls highlighted with beads worn by women reveals the influence of Cypriot art, as do their necklaces of several attached strands (choker or dog-collar).

When Assyria extended its dominion from Cilicia to Upper Egypt, in the eighth and seventh centuries BC, Syria, Phoenicia and Palestine borrowed some characteristics of its costume for their richer classes: the full tunic, open down the front with the two edges brought together at the waist by a heavy jewel, a garment of the sewn type which frescos show to have been in blue and red, or black on a white ground. This tunic should not, in my opinion, be classed as a caftan, like the backed garment in Assyrian styles of the period, since the caftan, originating in the Steppes of Central Asia, became widespread only later, after the migration of the Scythians and the Sarmatians.

Assyria also gave the world the long, fine gown that recalls at once the Persian tunic and the Egyptian calasiris; 'its fullness, held in to the body by a tight girdle, broke into numerous folds which were lifted and held mostly on the front of the body.'[43]

A Phoenician cylindrical cap, sometimes slightly flaring and lower in front than at the back, recalled 'not only the Achaemenid tiara but also the low crown of Pschent cut short at the back.'[44]

74　Prisoners taken after the capture of Lachish. Seventh century BC. British Museum, London. (Museum photo. Courtesy of the Trustees)

JEWISH COSTUME

From the first millennium, the documentation on Jewish costume is sparse: Jewish documents are virtually non-existent and the names for clothing in the Bible, though abundant and varied, give us scant grounds on which to reconstruct it. For the periods of subjection of the Israelites, however, some indications are supplied by Egyptian sources (Bronze Age II and III) and Assyrian material (end of the kingdoms of Israel and Judah), but we have no information for the period of the entry into Canaan, nor for the post-exile period, and especially, virtually nothing concerning women's clothes.

During the Bronze Age III period (900 to 800 BC) the tunic, probably made of linen, appeared and tended to replace the loincloth among the upper classes; represented as close-fitting but doubtless full in reality, it reached to the calves or ankles, with long or half-length sleeves, and was embroidered at the hem; later we see fringes (Early Iron Age, 900 to 700 BC).[45]

During this period we find mention of a sort of 'plaid' worn over the skirt and pinned on one shoulder; this can be interpreted as the Sumerian shawl, which becomes longer for women, drapes over the chest and leaves one shoulder bare. It was either plain white or embroidered with red.[46]

At the end of this Bronze period, under the eighteenth and nineteenth dynasties of the New Empire, the long tunic predominated but was complemented by this woollen shawl, probably worn as a cloak, wound several times round the body and girdled at the waist, a novelty which we find introduced into Mesopotamian costume by the Hittites. The last swathes draped over the shoulders formed a sort of cape. The garment may, on the other hand, have been in two pieces, with the cape separate like the short Syrian tippet. The Egyptians mocked this Hebrew costume, heavy and enveloping, which figures on several documents from the reigns of Ramesses II and Ramesses III.[47]

However, Jewish women on reliefs of the capture of Lachish by Sennacherib (705 to 680 BC) wear the plain tunic and a long, light fringed cloak (plate 74). It seems that they went bareheaded with a ribbon in their hair and with their faces un-

75　Tribute bearers leading horses, relief from Khorsabad Sixth century BC. Paris, Louvre. (Photo Flammarion)

76 Stele from Neirab, Syria. Late seventh or early sixth centuries BC. Paris, Louvre. (Museum photo)

covered;[48] but in the third century AD Tertulian, recommending the Christian women of Carthage to wear veils outdoors, quotes as examples Jewish women, who by then were veiled all the time. The Christian bride was veiled when presented to her future husband. In Deuteronomy (XXII, 5) women are forbidden to wear men's clothing, and vice versa. The effeminate styles of Egypt, with the transparent pleated stuffs worn by Eighteenth dynasty citizens, were similarly prohibited by the Torah.[49]

From the eighth century on, the Bible ordered the Jews to make a fringe[50] (*sisith*) round the hems of their garments and to place a blue cord over them. Christ speaks of the ostentatious tassels worn by the Pharisees; the paintings of Dura Europos show the Jews in Greek costume, with the *chiton* and the *himation*, with, at the corners of the latter garment, a fringe and some loose threads hanging free or attached to their base; this type of himation with pompoms at the corners is to be found in the statuary of Palmyra (first to third centuries AD) and this Jewish style spread elsewhere.[51]

Footwear consisted of flat Egyptian-style sandals which were also found in ancient Mesopotamia in the third millennium BC.

It is possible that in winter people wore garments lined with dog or sheepskin.

Jewish kings wore a flat crown or diadem of precious metal decorated with precious stones and placed over a cloth turban. They also probably wore cloth caps adorned with embroidery and gems, analogous to the Assyrian tiara.

As for Jewish priestly costumes, it is impossible to find definite evidence concerning this question in spite of the elaborate description in Exodus XXVIII. Mention is made of 'linen breeches' for all 'the sons of Aaron'. We gather that the pontiff wore a tunic of fine linen, held at the waist by a girdle decorated with needlework, and a head-dress of the same cloth, no doubt in the form of a turban; he added to this a gown of blue material adorned with small bells and vari-coloured pompoms in the form of pomegranates, and the *ephod*, a kind of cuirass held in place by a belt and shoulder straps. Over the breastplate was hung a rectangular piece of material adorned with twelve gems representing the Twelve Tribes of Israel. The turban or mitre was decorated with a panel of gold, held in place by blue cords and carrying the engraved phrase 'Holiness to the Lord'.[52]

Throughout these variations of costume among the coastal populations, it is interesting to notice that for long the ordinary people continued to wear the old Sumerian type of loincloth-skirt. Very ancient arrangements of garments are represented in images of gods and, piously perpetuated, become ritual, all the more so as certain peoples, among them the Canaanites, always showed a certain unwillingness to invent the form of their own gods.

Heuzey wondered if this archaism, prolonged by religious conservatism and foreign influence, could explain the difference that can be observed between Asiatic documents representing divinities and the frescos in which Egyptian artisans tried to reproduce real ethnic types and costumes. This must surely be taken into account in the interpretation of the representations.

Phoenicia, as we have seen, played a very special role in spreading costume styles throughout the coastal countries of the Middle East, a role which fell to her as the result of her artistic dominance and her exceptional trading position. Phoenician art of the second millennium was the 'offshoot of a great Syrian art which at all times served as intermediary between the Aegean and the Middle East'.[53] However, her art gained from the far-flung explorations of her navigators and the numerous trading posts founded by Tyre and Sidon, not only in southern Italy and Carthage, but even further afield.[54]

Phoenician supremacy, which after the fall of Minoan power dominated the Mediterranean, from 1100 to 800 BC approximately, contributed greatly to the spread of Middle Eastern costume, more even than did the supremacy of Knossos for Cretan costume.

Costume in the Mountain Countries

(Cappadocia, Armenia, Caucasus, Iran, Turkestan)

THE GEOGRAPHICAL SETTING

The region of high plateaux and mountains which, from Cappadocia to the Indus, form an immense semicircle to the North of the plains of Syria and the Mesopotamian basin, were inhabited by peoples whose original costume was doubtless that worn by the prehistoric races, adapted to suit an extremely rigorous climate.

At the beginning of the second millennium Steppe peoples, whose civilization, though simple, was already moderately advanced, left their Russian and Asiatic homes, and armed with new weapons and mounted on horses (still unknown in the West), they swept down on the Middle Eastern countries, driving the indigenous peoples before them and forcing them to settle in the plains. While the Achaeans established themselves in Greece and at certain points on the coast of Asia Minor, other invaders, Hittites, Hurites and Mitonians in the north and Medes and Persians to the east, settled in their turn in the mountainous regions, and then came down into the plains. This Aryan invasion pushed forward peoples like the Kersites, semi-nomads from the high plateaux, expelling them from Cappadocia and the Pontic coast-lands, so that they surged down the valley of the Euphrates, overran Chaldea, and in 1875 BC captured Babylon, soon to collapse under a second attack in 1745 BC. This thrust forward continued in successive waves until the period of the Aegean migrations (1200 BC), a further consequence of the great Aryan movements.

A Hyksos empire, in which the Mitannian military aristocracy seems to have played a preponderant role, then formed between Babylon and Tyre, and soon expanded to conquer Egypt. During over one hundred and fifty years of rule, its influence slowly disintegrated, as it was gradually absorbed by its vassals, in the classic process of assimilation.

Later, after the fall of Niniveh in 612 BC and the destruction of the Assyrian empire, the Persians in their turn left the mountains of Kurdistan and spread through the plains of Susiana.

We are only now coming to know the discoveries made since 1938 in Armenia. At Karmir-Blur near Erevan, Soviet archaeologists have discovered jewels and textiles which make it possible to give precise dates for the costume of this civilization before its ruin by the Scythians in the sixth century BC, and to establish its relations with its neighbours in Southern Russia and Central Asia.

77 The Great God of the Air, carving from Tel Asmar. Twelfth-eleventh centuries BC. Paris, Louvre. (Photo Archives Photographiques)

We have very little evidence that definitely relates to Iranian textiles, so that it is difficult to determine their use, particularly in Sassanian Persia.

Between the first quarter of the third century AD and the middle of the seventh, when it collapsed under the thrust of Arab invasions, the Sassanian dynasty preserved in its civilization ancient art forms and symbols inherited from the old peoples of the Middle East.

Sassanian towns such as Samarkand and Bokhara – great silk markets whose caravans came bearing the precious textile from the Far East or carrying supplies of finished cloth to the West – and probably other cities as well, possessed looms on which silk was woven in accordance with processes borrowed from China.

It seems that Persia must have known this industry at least two centuries before Byzantium.

Sassanian textiles, fragments of which have shown the technical virtuosity of the weaving as well as the decorative richness, were adornments worn by the upper classes. We find in them the taste for scenes of action to be noted in sculpture and metalwork: horsemen at the gallop turn in their saddles to fire arrows, a characteristic theme among the Parthian, Medean and Turkish peoples. This hieratic decorative style invariably used facing or addorsed animal or human figures, sometimes enclosed in circles or rowels, and with a variety of other motifs.

We know that textiles of this kind, the rare surviving specimens of which are generally preserved in European church treasuries, were used as shrouds and religious vestments. But above all they provided cloaks and mantles, as we learn from such sources as the rock carvings of Taq-i-Bustan, where court costumes dating from about AD 600, shortly before the fall of the Sassanian Empire, are represented. The cloth used for ceremonial robes generally incorporated woven portraits of kings or signs symbolizing royal dignity.[55]

The stylization of Sassanid textiles had a great influence on Byzantine weaving, and this influence is also apparent in a Chinese cloth taken to one of the temples of Nara, in Japan, by a Korean embassy in 622. In Byzantium, where the influence of Chinese art made itself felt in luxury textiles, decoration followed the Sassanian arrangement of isolated or linked wheel motifs, and also horizontal bands or geometrical patterns: cloth decorated in this way was called either *rotata* (in wheels) or *scutalata* (in squares).

After the Arab conquest, which threw the industry of the defeated Sassanians into temporary confusion, the Persian manufactures resumed their activity, to meet the customary sartorial needs of the country and satisfy a new Moslem clientele which, on this point at least, soon forgot the rulings of primitive Islamism.

By modifying the forms of its traditional decoration, Sassanian production thus remained at the centre of the silk trade network, which soon covered the middle east with the extension of Arab power. The proverbial luxury of Asia became that of most Moslem princes and caliphs, Abbassids, Ommayads, Fatimites, etc., who wore silk in their palaces and tents. As the textile industry developed among the Islamic peoples, it abandoned its former Sassanid motifs, but the silks taken in quantity by the Crusaders in the course of their conquest of the Holy Land have their distant origin in the textiles of Sassanian Persia, as did the textiles of the Byzantine Empire.

It was probably as the result of these successive waves of peoples, invaders and invaded, that towards the middle of the second millennium the *sewn costume*, whose typical element is the tunic with sleeves that fit closely to the arms, was introduced into the countries of the Middle East. In the case of the old zone of the Tigris and the Euphrates, it was brought by peoples who came down from the mountainous regions to the north and east. It seems that in Mesopotamia these invaders brought only modified versions of costumes which had formerly been spread among them by Sumerian fashion, probably through trading caravans. A similar 'backlash' can often be observed in the history of costume; it must be traced carefully, as it can explain certain modifications in costume which would otherwise remain incomprehensible.

We know from Herodotus that this sewn costume was worn by the Aramaeans, the Scythians, the Sacians and the Afghans, and that it might be made entirely of leather, as in the case of all the Northern peoples, from the Caspian to the Atlantic.[56]

The costumes worn by both sexes were brightly coloured, particularly blue and yellow.

In the present state of archaeological excavations, it is still fairly difficult to assign the new costume elements introduced to particular population groups; for this reason I have attempted no classifications which would run the risk of invalidation in the near future.[57]

The main contribution of the mountain peoples, who were obliged to dress for warmth, was the tunic fitting closely to the body. As Strabo remarks, it was suitable for the coldest regions of Asia, the Middle East and, most of all, for windswept countries like Medea. A skirt similar to that worn in Sumer, often enriched with ornament, was still worn on its own.[58]

Both the shape and the construction of this tunic, a sort of shirt of varying length, closed down the front and including short or long flaring sleeves, make it a new type of garment. It was cut full in fact, though in sculpture it is represented as being tight-fitting; it was generally short for men and long for women, and it was accompanied by the large Sumerian shawl, edged with a roll-shaped trimming, which had served as a cloak from the early periods of Ur and Mari. Women of the common people wore the narrow Chaldean scarf.

For women, whose costume is seldom represented, this tunic-gown could have very short sleeves and fall heavily to the ankles, or else trail on the ground and have wrist-length, flaring sleeves. A skirt in fine material with numerous pleats may have been worn as a summer garment; in the Greco-Persian period, women wore a full tunic of fine, pleated stuff, the *serapis*, which the Greeks of Asia borrowed from the Lydians.

It seems that the Persians, gaining refinement in contact with the more sophisticated Assyrian civilization, added other elements – perhaps taken from peoples that had fallen under their domination – to the tunic which was common to all mountain-dwellers. Strabo noted that they adopted a style in keeping with the 'dignity and majesty of a kingdom' and better suited to the luxurious, sedentary life of a court in a hot climate. It is possible that they gave the tunic more fullness and length, as well as the open, loosely falling sleeves.

We can perhaps attribute to the Persians the spread of the long under-tunic or caftan, known as the *candys*, often worn with hanging sleeves, which seems to have been a development of the large Sumerian shawl; with more certainty we can credit

MALE COSTUME

77 The typical features of costumes worn by mountain-dwellers are the tunic, with short or long sleeves, and shoes with upturned toes. Tall headdresses are also characteristic

FEMALE COSTUME

78-81 These various female images emphasize the widespread normal wear of a long tunic, generally cut quite narrow. The tufted cloth of fur of the gown worn by the goddess (plate 78) is doubtless ritual. The open bodice reminds one of Cretan figures. The roll is to be found in other regions. A fringed veil is worn by the nurse (plate 81), whose braid-decorated sleeves also evoke Crete

78 Goddess from Ras Shamra, ivory box lid.
Nineteenth-eighteenth centuries BC.
Paris, Louvre. (Photo Flammarion)

79 Seated Phoenician goddess.
Fifteenth-fifth centuries BC.
Paris, Louvre. (Photo Flammarion)

80 Seated Phoenician goddess.
Fifteenth-fifth centuries BC.
Paris, Louvre. (Photo Flammarion)

81 Young prince with his nurse, Neo-Hittite art. Ninth-eighth centuries BC.
Paris, Louvre. (Photo Flammarion)

83 Model shoe, found in a tomb at Azerbaijan.
Thirteenth-twelfth centuries BC.
Schoenenwerd, Switzerland, Musée Bally.
(Museum photo)

SHOES WITH UPTURNED TOES

82–3 Shoes with upturned toes were to become widespread throughout
Syria and Phoenicia; from Phoenicia they passed to Etruria

SCYTHIAN INFLUENCES IN COSTUME

84, 87 The Persians adopted the trousers worn by warlike peoples, made
of soft stuff and worn loose on the leg; they also wore the *kandys*, a cloak
with a collar, perhaps of fur; on their heads they wore a soft tiara fitting
round the head like a hood

82 Hittite hoplite, carving from Gendijerli. *c.* 1200 BC.
Berlin, Museum of Asiatic Antiquities. (Museum photo)

84 Silver statue of a man. Achemenid period.
Berlin, Museum of Asiatic Antiquities. (Museum photo)

them with the introduction in the Middle East of long trousers, called by some sources *anaxyrides*, which are represented on the Apadena reliefs at Persepolis (approximately 400 to 360 BC) and whose origins are to be sought among the Steppe nomads.

FOOTWEAR

Another characteristic contribution of the mountain-dwellers is the shoe with upturned toe (plates 82–3), coloured leather uppers and a high heel, whose particular form reveals familiarity with rough hilly country. This type of footwear, which passed into Cypriot fashion, is still worn today in Anatolia and Syria. The Persians fastened their low, open-cut shoes with triple laces.

HAIR AND HEAD-DRESSES

Felt caps in various shapes were worn by the peoples living in mountainous regions.

In the first millennium, Hittites of both sexes wore the tall cylindrical cap over a rounded or conical skull-cap, a close relative of the Phrygian or Cypriot cap: to this women added a long veil placed on top of the cap, sometimes drawing it forward over the face. A plait ending in a spiral, emerging from the cap or tiara, Chaldean in origin, seems to have been an attribute of divinity before becoming a general fashion: it must be compared with the lock of hair worn by royal children in Egypt, the long hair of Greek children which was cut off in adolescence, and the lock of hair which enables the Arabs to be lifted to heaven by the angel Azrael, all embodying the same religious and symbolic meaning.[59]

Among the Persians, the most common head-dress consisted of a sort of round cap in soft felt, covering the hair and fastened by a strap; from this important personages hung on either side long bands of cloth covering the ears, the cheeks and the nape of the neck. The hair was parted and curled, at first in numerous curls, then in a single row framing the face to meet the beard, which was also crimped.

Kings often wore either a tall cylindrical head-dress, a sort of tiara slightly flaring at the top, rather similar to the one worn today by Orthodox popes, a circular diadem or even a crenellated crown.[60]

It has already been pointed out that the conical cap seems to have been commonly worn among 'non-Sumero-Akkadian' peoples.

ORNAMENTS

The Hittites and Persians must have taken from the Assyrians the style of their wide necklaces and bracelets, and the eighth-century Greeks must have provided the wide arc-shaped fibulae used for fastening one corner of the shawl on the left shoulder – as Indian women still fasten their saris in place; this use of large pins was in fact known in Mycenae as early as the seventeenth century BC.

The Sassanians inherited from the Persians a pronounced taste for large jewels: there were head-bands, sometimes trimmed with gems and beads, chest ornaments, necklaces, pectorals and chains, and girdles.

85 Archer of the Royal Guard, frieze from Susa. Early fourth century BC. Paris, Louvre. (Photo Flammarion)

85 The archers wear tunics held in at the waist by a piece of cloth of the same colour as the hanging parts of their wide sleeves. The flowered materials are in variegated colours; they wear coronets on their heads, and their hair and beards are crimped. Some archers wear high-crowned hats. This costume scandalized the Greeks

86 This example demonstrates the mixture of drapery with the costume of the Steppe horsemen

86 The Kacyapa brothers and their families venerating the Buddha, bas-relief from Begram. Kabul Museum. (Photo Flammarion)

87 Battle of Darius and Alexander, mosaic found in Pompeii. Third-second centuries BC. Naples, Museo Nazionale. (Photo André Held)

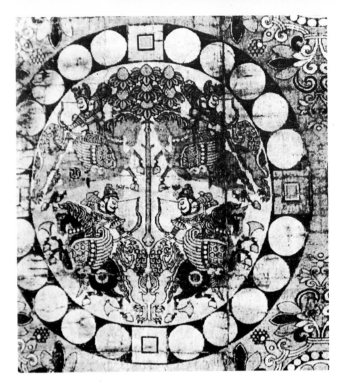

88–9 The Persian taste for rich colours survived in the Sassanian period in silk materials with stylized motifs, often representing hunting scenes in a more or less symbolic manner. These stuffs were imitated in Byzantium and even in China. Persia also produced the wheel-shaped motifs used in textiles

88 Chinese woven cloth. Tokyo, Museum.
(Photo Ciba)

89 Byzantine silk cloth. Seventh century AD.
Berlin, Schlossmuseum. (Photo Giraudon)

BATTLE COSTUME

Hittite battle costume consisted of long tunics, probably made of leather, at least initially, and with wide belts. During the second millennium, the conical helmet with ear-guards and a plume falling down the back appeared, and in the first millennium it acquired cheek-guards and a crest of plumes or horse-hair. This type of helmet was transmitted by the Hittites to the fifteenth-century Mycenaeans, and it later became the head-dress of light cavalry in Assyria in the eighth century BC, and later still the original inspiration of the Ionian helmet. Hoplites are shown wearing conical caps (plate 82).

Among the Persians, the friezes of the palace of Darius (about 500 BC) show long tunics with flaring sleeves, ribbed caps with fluted edges, swathed turbans and the nailed boots worn by the royal archers. Other soldiers are represented with stiff, almost hemispherical caps whose front parts are straighter and project slightly forward.[61] Charioteers wore a cloth cuirass with black trellis patterns and white edgings, and a red and yellow head-dress.

The Persepolis reliefs clearly show the trousers worn by certain Persian or Hittite warriors and the short tunic held in by a belt through which long-handled daggers are slipped.[62]

Among the Persians certain war costumes present the same fashionable colours used in everyday costume: yellow for the head-dress, red for the cloak and tunic; shoes and boots are black with red laces, and trousers are purple. Philoxenos of Eritrea, who painted the portrait of Darius at the Battle of Issus, showed him in a purple tunic crossed by a broad white band with two rows of golden stars, and a cloak trimmed with panther skin.[63]

Costume in the Irano-Indian Regions

The expeditions and immense conquests of Alexander (334–325 BC) brought new opportunities for contact between the peoples of the West and the Middle East. The kingdom of Bactrians, formed about 250 BC, perpetuated Hellenism in eastern Iran for over two centuries, and extended into the regions of Kabul (then Kapiça) and Peshawar (then Gandhara), and later as far as the Indus basin. Just then, however, the rebelling Parthian kings invaded Iran and Babylonia and restored the Iranian empire which Alexander had destroyed.

This new invasion of mountain peoples in the Middle East does not seem to have had repercussions on costume, but then, the Parthians were only one tribe of the peoples settled in Khorassan and wore similar clothes.

In the new empire of Bactria and Gandhara, where at the end of the third century the court of the Indo-Grecian kings saw the formation of a Greco-Buddhist art whose influence was considerable in Central and Western Asia, it seems that on the whole costume retained the archaic characteristics of its Sumerian origins.

This can be observed most of all in the easternmost part of Bactria, Gandhara, where the clothing of the common people consisted of a simple Indian type of loincloth, which was very short, and a piece of cloth wrapped round the head: this loin-cloth, hitched up on the hips in the classic style, could also be draped like the Indian languti.

Costume for the middle classes was made of two rectangular pieces, partially cut and sewn: a loincloth, the paridhana (now dhoti) and a cloak or shawl, the chaddar or uttariya. The cloak was wide and covered the shoulders. For women, costume consisted of a sleeved tunic or chemise, a draped skirt and a shawl worn as a scarf, sometimes with one end fastened to the girdle. The tunic, shaped and sewn, could be worn inside or outside the draped skirt.

The paridhana, common to both sexes, was a rectangular piece of cloth wrapped round the hips as a long, straight skirt, rather like the Malayan sarong: one of the ends, brought forward between the legs and tucked into the waistband, gives the knee-length Indian dhoti or the Cambodian sampot, which resemble baggy trousers. This garment could also be long enough to reach over the upper part of the body, like the costume worn today by women in the Dekkan.[64]

The colder climate of northern India led to the paridhana being supplemented by a tunic in warmer material, probably wool.

A metalwork belt was made of chains and panels with tiny bells, and was worn from the Ganges to Turkestan and in Northern India.

We may suppose that among the richer classes costume benefited as a result of the extraordinary commercial progress in the second half of the first century AD, with its apogee in the second century: the exchanges which then multiplied attracted craftsmen and artists from Alexandria, Syria and Seleucia.[65] This would explain the differences between the costume of the common people and that of the wealthy classes.

Indeed, the aristocracy of the Indo-European race had been Iranianized in costume and material culture as it had been Indianized in religion and literature, so that we are not surprised to find features taken directly from Iranian costume represented until the early seventh century, as in the Sassano-Brahmanic sculptures discovered by Hackin at Khair-Khaneh, near Kabul, in the Sassanian frescos of Dokhtar, on the road from Kabul to Bektres, or those of Quizil, or in the stuccos of Fondukistan. These Iranian features comprised essentially a jacket belted tightly at the waist and decorated with wide revers at the collar (from the Kuch area, found at Bamiyan), long trousers and high boots. Until the Arab conquest in AD 170, Irano-Buddhist Afghanistan was to continue to provide the inspiration for fashionable upper class male costume under the Indo-Scythian Kuchean dynasty.

We find the same influences in battle costume.

A few days ride away from the Turco-Mongolian hordes, the costume of the Kuchean knighthood seems to foreshadow the Persian miniature, recalling Saracen knights and Sarmatian cavalry. Everything is already Iranian in the physical type, with the long, slim bodies and the faces ornamented with faint moustaches. But court costume accentuates the resemblance: long, straight coats held in at the waist by metal belts, opening on the chest with the wide lapels already noted in Afghanistan (Bamiyan frescos) and decorated with passementerie, bead embroidery and florets borrowed from Iranian decoration. Women wore tight-waisted bodices and full gowns.[66]

This Iranian type also covered the region of the Indo-European oases of Taris which, until they were conquered by the Turco-Mongolians in the second half of the seventh century, depended culturally not on the Altai and the Steppe civilizations that dominated in Upper Asia, but on the great civilizations of Iran and India.

Broadly, Iranian costume of the Achemenaean period was originally a development of the dress of mountainous countries, and spread rapidly across the Middle East. It constituted the basis of costume throughout these vast regions, and passed through three successive phases: first, as a primitive costume of the common prehistoric type, made originally of skins and later of cloth, and comprising a loincloth and cloak; second as a costume of the closed type with trousers, taken from the Steppe peoples; third, as a fitted, sewn costume, representing a mixed type, an improved version of the preceding style, worn chiefly by the upper classes and warriors, while ordinary people continued to wear the original costume.

Steppe Costume

For a long time all the Steppe nomads – Huns, Scythians, Alans and Sarmatians – wore the same fur and leather clothing, composed of a tunic, long trousers with or without boots, and a tall fur or felt cap.[67]

It would be dangerous to attribute the invention of any given element to any one of these peoples, as similar garments were probably worn by the race that originally inhabited these regions.

The ethnic distinctions that may be drawn between these peoples are of interest here only in enabling us to follow the spread of the most characteristic elements of their costumes, linked to their various population movements.

THE RACES AND THE SETTING

The Huns, ancestors of the Turks and Mongols, seem to have been at the centre of these movements in the Steppes of central and eastern Mongolia. From the earliest times they had been tribes of warlike herdsmen, who had remained very savage and endlessly migrated to and fro in the immense plains. They wore a long tunic-robe reaching to mid-calf, slit down the sides and belted at the waist with a girdle whose ends hung down in front; for better protection against the cold, the sleeves were tightly closed at the wrists. Fur was used for short capes and caps. Wide trousers were fastened with straps at the ankles above leather shoes very similar to European shoes.[68]

It is probable that the Huns – or Hsiung Nu, 'the cruel men' – were at the origin of the first migratory movement which, from the early ninth to the late eighth century BC, led the Scythians, closely followed by the Sarmatians, towards the Manai. For a long time they continued to wear their riding costume from the Steppes. Ammianus Marcellinus noted that in the fourth century BC they wore a cassock of rat-skins over their tunic-shirt, helmets or caps on the back of their heads, and wrapped buckskins round their legs; their shapeless, unfitted shoes prevented them from walking. Following their example the Chinese, attacked by them, reorganized their cavalry, from 300 BC on, by adding to their chariot troops equal numbers of horseback troops; this led to an important modification in Chinese costume, with the adoption of trousers in place of the gown and perhaps also the introduction of certain ornaments: pins, harness-plates and equipment plates.

Towards the west, this Steppe costume was transported to the Middle East and South-East Europe by the Scythians and Sarmatians.

The origins of the Scythians and Sarmatians and the causes behind their expansion still remain obscure, despite recent research. Going beyond the bounds of ethnography, the problem touches on the political history and geography of this immense Steppe empire, all of whose elements are difficult to define because of the absence of distinctive civilizations and the scarcity of documentation concerning them. However, Scythian and Sarmatian costume is of considerable interest in showing us the influences exercized by the Steppe peoples on the costume of the Middle East and Central and Western Europe. The animal motifs characteristic of this so-called *Gandharan* art of the nomadic huntsmen are known to us through sources which include numerous costume accessories (bracelets, pins, plates, etc.) and through clothes decorated with stylized motifs. Their discovery in the last thirty years has suggested hitherto unknown relationships between costumes in a considerable part of Eurasia, the results of migratory and trading movements.

The northern barbarians who remained in the Steppes of their original Iranian native land – called Scythians or Sarmatians by Greek historians, Kuchus or Kuchuanas by the Chinese, and Sakas or Arsis by the Iranians – were basically Iranian themselves, attached to a Togar tribe from which we derive the name *Tocharian*. They seem to have occupied central Siberia towards the middle of the second millennium; then, towards the twelfth century BC, to have reached western Siberia and the regions of the Kuban, Russian Turkestan and Kurdistan, then known as Manai, thus largely escaping the influence of the civilizations of Assur and Babylon, which was to be so strong on their Medean and Persian brothers who had long been established on the Iranian plateaux to the south.

MIGRATORY MOVEMENTS

The Scythians, apparently preceding the Sarmatians who later fought against them, made contact through the occupation of Manai with the old civilizations of the Middle East, between the early ninth and the late seventh century BC, that is, between the beginning of the greatest Iranian immigration and the date of the latest known objects in Scythian style. They also became customers for Manaean art, as the Medes and Persians were for Assyrio-Babylonian art.[69]

Continuing their thrust towards the Black Sea, the Scythians reached Georgia – where between the twelfth and tenth centuries there was already a civilization known as Lelvar – and appeared between 750 and 700 BC in southern Russia, whence they chased the Cimmerians down towards the Middle East. Descending through Pontus Euxinus, they then came into contact with the Assyrians whom they attacked about 678 BC; after joining forces with them to dispose of the Cimmerians, they were repulsed by the latter and forced back into southern Russia. This civilization had left some curious bronze belts with geometric animals and human figures; it apparently covered the Northern and Black Sea regions, Rumania and Hungary, from the twelfth century BC.

The Scythians were then, to quote Grousset, 'Barbarians

90–91 The King wears long trousers and a scarf, probably made of goffered silk. Women's clothes are similarly made of goffered silk

90–91 Sassanian dishes representing a king hunting and various male and female figures. Paris, Bibliothèque Nationale, Cabinet des Médailles. (Photos Flammarion)

92, 94 Bas-relief from Nakshi-Rustam: Scenes from the investiture of the king Narsh. Third century BC. (Photos Inge Morath-Magnum)

with a smattering of Hellenic culture', and occupied not only Kuban[70] and the Ukraine from 550 to 450 BC but also, from 350 to 250 BC, the lower Dniepr area. In the second half of the third century BC, repelled by the Sarmatians, who belonged to their own race, they met the first Germanic forces in the Crimea and probably forced them back. During these three centuries, they carried out raids into the very heart of Central Europe and also reached the frontiers of Syria; there they found themselves close to the Ionian influence which was already represented in the sixth century by the Greeks of Pontus Euxinus.

As far as experts on Central Asian migrations and art have managed to establish the migratory movements of these peoples, it seems that the second wave of Indo-European invasion can be recognized as the Sarmatian wave, whose movements seem to have followed several directions. Some moved towards the west and, as we have seen, expelled the Scythians from the Crimea towards 250 BC. Others moved north-east towards Siberia, where they seem to have reached the centres of Pazyrik on the Ob and Minusinsk on the Yenisei, while to the east towards the oases of the Taris basin, they appear to have reached the towns of Quizil, Kucha and Karachar, perhaps even the Gobi Desert. Lastly, it is not impossible that the elements of a last group may have moved south-west of Turkestan, towards Bactria and the Indus.

It is useful, from the standpoint of costume history, to observe that three contacts were thus established by the Scythians and Sarmatians: first by the Scythians, then by their rivals the Sarmatians, with the civilization of Pontus and Southern Russia; then by the Huns and the Chinese with the civilization of China; and lastly, by the Sarmatians and the Tocharians with the Greco-Buddhist civilizations of Bactria and the Indus.

COMMERCIAL LIFE IN CENTRAL ASIA

Having thus made contact with the Assyrian and Aegean civilizations in the course of their migrations, the Scythians and

93 Stele of Maliku from Palmyra. Second-third centuries AD. Paris, Louvre. (Photo Flammarion)

later the Sarmatians increasingly played the role of intermediaries on the great trade routes between Western Europe and Central Asia, and these two outlets enabled them to spread their art with its animal motifs and, no doubt, certain elements of their luxurious clothing, towards China on one hand and, on the other, beyond the Dniepr and the Danube.[71]

We know the importance of the exchange colonies (emporia) established at the mouths of the Don and the Dniepr, at Tanaia and Olbia, by the Greeks of Pontus Euxinus, Trebizond, Sinope and the Caucasus; we also know that the Scythians of Southern Russia were in constant contact with them, for furs from the Balkan peninsula, for instance. At the beginning of the first millennium, regular, substantial exchanges also took place between Pontus Euxinus and the towns of Western Siberia, the home of the Scythians and Sarmatians; Herodotus speaks at length of a trade route which, from the Black Sea, followed the Volga, crossed the Russian Steppes through a col in the Urals and ended on the high plateaux of Central Asia by the Dzungarian Gate. This account was confirmed in 1922 by the discovery near Yekaterinburg-Sverdlovsk of about forty silver objects from the Greek workshops of Pontus Euxinus. Some years later, the Koylov mission at Noin-Ula, near Urga, the capital of Outer Mongolia, discovered precious Han Dynasty (c. 200 BC) Chinese silks, but also a whole assortment of figured woollen cloths showing the same inspiration as Scythian bronzes and incontestably made on the shores of the Black Sea – in particular a Greek cloth representing a moustached figure, probably the work of some artist from the Cimmerian Bosphorus.[72]

COSTUME

Steppe costume possesses a characteristic element whose appearance in the Middle East constitutes an innovation of capital importance: trousers, a garment essential to nomadic horsemen, indissolubly linked with the use of the horse in the Steppes. We know that a primitive form of horsemanship was probably introduced from South Russia into Central Europe before the end of the Stone Age, towards 2500 BC.[73]

In place of the Mediterranean and primitive Chinese gown, the Scythians adopted the pointed hood, the jacket, the tunic and trousers which were better adapted to their native climate and their way of life and fighting: to this they added the long, and long-sleeved garment, fastened with a belt, which survived for over three thousand years to become the caftan. This coat was sometimes cut like an apron and fell to the knees. Trousers were tacked into boots that rose to mid-calf.[74]

The long coat already figures on a pottery fragment from Kansu from the middle of the second millennium, where it is decorated with a trellis pattern. The sleeves are made of heavily stuffed or padded rings or rolls seamed together, and the body of the garment is a coat of mail, covered with metal plates. Men wore it flat over their shoulders, with fastenings underneath.

While long trousers were adopted by the Greeks round the Black Sea as the result of their contact with the Scythians, as was the case with the Persians, we must note that Occidental antiquity always considered this garment very indecent, and Greek literature contains many remarks on the subject: this aversion can be explained by the memory of the defeats inflicted on their ancestors by these Steppe horsemen. However, when Alexander the Great created his cavalry, he equipped them

not only with bows and arrows, but also with long Scythian breeches.

The tunic was very tight-fitting with long sleeves and sometimes deep revers. Men wore a belt of disks with it, women an edging of beads (Fondukistan stuccos).[75] It reached to above the knees and seems to have been worn in winter by the middle classes; we have also discovered a type of apron-style tunic, rounded for the king and incurved for courtiers. A sort of jacket with revers is represented on the Quizil frescos.

BATTLE COSTUME

It is difficult to distinguish the representations of Scythian and Sarmatian battle costume from everyday civilian clothing.

In hunting and fighting scenes the Scythians, always shown with long hair and long moustaches, wear pointed head-dresses and the coat of mail from the nomadic world of the Eurasian Steppes, with trousers and leggings indicated by incisions.[76]

In 179 BC Polybius mentions this coat of mail in connection with Scythian cavalry, who then wore conical helmets.

ORNAMENTS

Ornaments and ornamental accessories found at Begram, the summer capital of the Kucheans, present close links with Sarmatian art and reflect the North Iranian style of the Steppes, as do Hun tombs of the Middle Yenisei and the Altai.

The Sarmatians' use of cornelians, garnets and coral from Siberia and the Urals, and the Kucheans' use of rubies and lapis lazuli from the mines of Badakhistan show that they had learned the technique of extracting these gems.[77]

A particular feature of their ornaments is the use of metal plates fixed to the cloth of garments by means of threads passed through small holes. This type of ornamentation was doubtless transmitted to the Persians by the Kucheans, and is probably the origin of the sewn decoration on their textiles; it continued in the custom of sewing coins on to garments, which might in turn explain the use by Sassanian weavers of gold and silver thread, precious stones and brocades with geometric, floral, animal and human motifs.

In the tombs of Southern Russia, thousands of these plates have been found. They are generally fairly large and decorated with repoussé scenes of animal or human subjects, whereas the Sarmatians and Kucheans preferred geometrical and floral motifs and polychrome pastes.

The Scythian costume described above, common to all the groups of this region, and also the best known, spread throughout the whole of Iran and Syria.[78] With the exception of the pointed cap, it became the costume of the Parthians, who adopted the same weapons and tactics. Naturally, it is to be found in countries that were occupied by the Scythians and the Sarmatians; the excavations of Voronecj (fourth century), the Solokha tumulus (sixth to third centuries BC), the Kul Oba tumulus at Kertch and the Taman Peninsula (second century BC) yielded various objects on which Scythians are shown in short, belted tunics, pointed caps, long trousers and closed boots. At last the Sarmatians, spurred on by the Goths, carried the costume as far as Austria, Italy, Normandy, Britain, Spain and North Africa.

Moreover, the Iranians of Central Asia communicated this style to their Hun and Chinese neighbours.

95 Fresco from the synagogue of Dura Europos. Third century BC. (Photo Yale University)

The General Development of Costume in the Ancient East

The general development of costume in the ancient Middle East consisted essentially of progressive movement from the original draped or swathed type of garment (loincloth, shawl and cloak) that evolved from prehistoric costume, towards the flowing, fitted type (tunic and gown over trousers) gradually introduced by mountain dwellers, then by invaders from the Steppes of Central Asia.

This part-fitted type of garment – which underwent modifications, particularly in the coast countries, under the more or less distant influences of India, Crete or Egypt – did not, however, force the old draped, swathed type out of existence: both remained in current wear, the older form remaining the costume of the poor classes, while the new became the mark of warriors, or of the wealthy or governing classes.

It was by this process that the settled population groups of the Middle East progressively adopted a garment developed by peoples of herdsmen and nomads; later it spread to Europe, where some elements took particularly flourishing root in the region to the east of the Oder.

With various modifications of detail in cut and decoration, this type of semi-fitted costume – in some cases derived from the cloak – then spread throughout Asia, developing into the caftan, a loose, backed costume, simply cut, characterized by sleeves and an arrangement of two panels crossing in front, slit to facilitate riding.

Thus from the end of the prehistoric period the Middle East presented the simultaneous use of two costume archetypes; but while the development of one of them can be followed there for over three thousand years – the fitted costume – it is elsewhere, around the Mediterranean and particularly in Egypt, Greece and Rome, that we must study the career of the older type, the draped costume.

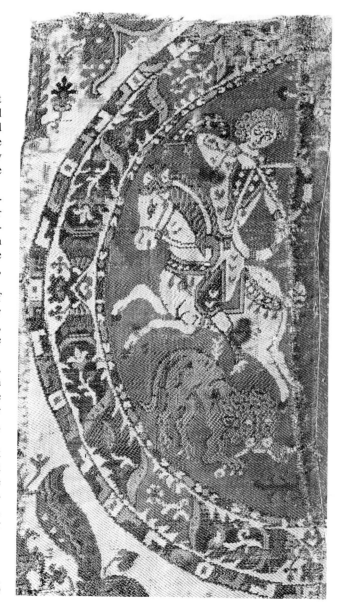

96 Byzantine silk cloth. Sixth-seventh centuries BC. Maastricht, Church of Saint Servais. (Photo Giraudon)

Notes

1 Grousset, *Asie*, p. 9.
2 Heuzey, pp. 114, 115.
3 Pirenne, *Civ. ant.*, p. 9.
4 The question was remarkably well presented by L. Heuzey, then taken up again and completed by J. Heuzey (Cf. *Costume dans l'Antiquité*) and covered once more by Cherblanc (cf. *Kaunakès*), whose conclusions have been adopted here.
5 Contenau, p. 227.
6 *Ibid.*, p. 186; Delaporte, p. 81.
7 Pirenne, p. 9 ff.
8 Contenau, p. 219.
9 Grousset, Auboyer, Buhot, pp. 13–15.
10 Tallgren, p. 222.
11 Glotz, Pottier, Heuzey, *passim*.
12 Legrain; Heuzey, p. 45.
13 Heuzey, pp. 47–52, specifies the ways this shawl was draped.
14 Parrot, pp. 102, 111. Cf. the gowns shown on the seal-cylinders from the reign of Shubad (Legrain, p. 19, fig. 24).
15 Parrot, pp. 114, 119.
16 Heuzey, pp. 58–61; Contenau, p. 158, mentions that it was forbidden to wear new clothes on certain days.
17 Contenau, *Civilis*, pp. 95, 99.
18 *Ibid.*, p. 260.
19 Parrot, p. 129.
20 Contenau, p. 186.
21 Heuzey, p. 52.
22 Parrot, pp. 112–113.
23 Legrain, pp. 321–338 and fig. 8.
24 Parrot, p. 192.
25 Parrot, p. 127.
26 Contenau, p. 316; Heuzey, pp. 45–46.
27 Heuzey, pp. 68–70.
28 *Ibid.*, pp. 63–65.
29 Contenau, p. 95. On a stele from Ur the sacrificer is shown wearing a short tunic tightly belted at the waist.
30 Contenau, p. 310.
31 Also found at Dura-Europos. Cf. Cumont.
32 Worn by the King of Babylon, Marduk-Balinddin (eighth century).
33 Contenau, p. 260.
34 Heuzey, pp. 64–65.
35 Contenau, *Asie*, pp. 294–295.
36 Heuzey, pp. 86, 114–115, 93–97.
37 Dussaud.
38 Cf. the excellent table by L. and J. Heuzey, pp. 99–100.
39 Heuzey.
40 *Syria*, 1933, plates XVI and XVII.
41 Heuzey, pp. 111–114, 130–131.
42 Glotz, p. 250; Bossert, pp. 261, 264; Pirenne, p. 48.
43 Heuzey, p. 109.
44 According to Cumont, the Phoenicians introduced into Italy the cap which became the Roman *pileus*.
45 Barrois, vol. 1, pp. 475 ff.
46 *Ibid.*, p. 479.
47 *Ibid.*, p. 480.
48 *Revue Biblique*, 1935.
49 Barrois, p. 483.
50 The tunic was already decorated with a fringe in the Iron Age (*c.* 1300 BC). Cf. Suscham.
51 This treatment of the himation worn by the Geneva Zeus Serapis (Hellenistic period) is no doubt simply the attempt by a Jewish sculptor to convert Zeus to fit Jewish ideas. Cf. du Mesnil du Buisson, pp. 244–250. Only the modern costumes of the Druses and Lebanese enable us to imagine this costume.
52 Barrois, pp. 54, 421.
53 Demargne, p. 43.
54 It is significant that the word *phoenix* refers equally to Phoenicians and to purple.
55 Christensen: *L'Iran sous les Sassanides*.
56 Herodotus, *Histories*; Heuzey, p. 83.
57 Heuzey, pp. 90–97; Pottier: *L'Art Hittite*, pp. 18–19.
58 Cf. the warrior god on the outer wall of Hattusa, the Hittite capital (fourteenth century BC).
59 Pottier, pp. 60 ff.
60 Pottier, pp. 18–19; Heuzey, pp. 90–97.
61 Cf. the Hittite warriors of Hattusa and the archers on the Susa friezes.
62 Heuzey, p. 85, and notes plate XLV.
63 Cf. mosaic from Pompeii (Naples, Museo Nazionale).
64 Foucher, vol. II, fasc. I, pp. 72, 90.
65 Grousset; *Steppes*, p. 87.
66 Cf. the frescos on wood from Dandan-Uilig (north-east Khotan) and the frescos of Kertch-Ponticapaea (Crimea).
67 Grousset: *Steppes*, pp. 13 ff.
68 Wieger, vol. I, p. 283.
69 Grousset: *Steppes*, pp. 34 ff; Dussaud, p. 159; Godard, *passim*.
70 Tallgren, *passim*, who shows that the Grecian fibulae found at Kouban reached there by way of Asia Minor as well as by the Black Sea: numerous Sumerian traits can be traced in the Copper Age of Kuban.
71 Rostovzeff, *passim*.
72 Hermann, p. 108; Grousset: *Steppes*, p. 60.
73 Clark, *passim*.
74 Bachoffer, Rostovzeff, Hackin, Ghirshman.
75 Hackin, *passim*.
76 Ghirshman.
77 *Ibid.*
78 Seyrig, *passim*.

Chronology of Western Asia

SUMER AND AKKAD	Pre-Obeid Period	5000 BC
	Obeid Period	4000 to 3400 BC
	Ur Period	3000 BC
BABYLON	1st Dynasty	2105 to 1806 BC
	2nd, 3rd, 4th, Dynasties	1949 to 1039 BC
	5th to 11th Dynasties	1038 to 539 BC
HYKSOS		1180 to 850 BC
ASSYRIA		2134 to 1250 BC
PERSIA		540 to 330 BC

Adapted from G. CONTENAU: *L'Asie occidentale ancienne.*

Bibliography

GENERAL

R. GROUSSET: *Histoire de l'Asie*, 1941.
J. PIRENNE: *Civilisations antiques*, 1939.
G. CONTENAU: *L'Art de l'Asie occidentale*, 1928.
C. DELAPORTE: *Le Proche Orient asiatique*, 1938.
GROUSSET, AUBOYER, BUHOT: *L'Asie Orientale des origines au XVe S.*, 1941.
A. TALLGREN: *Eurasia septentrionalis antiqua*, VIII.
G. GLOTZ: *La Civilisation égéenne*, 1923.
E. POTTIER: *Le Palais du roi Minos*, 1902.
C. LEGRAIN: 'L'Art sumérien au temps de la reine Shoubad' in *Gazette des Beaux-Arts*, July 1931.
A. PARROT: *Mari, une ville perdue*, 1936.
G. CONTENAU: *Civilisation d'Assur et de Babylone*, 1937.
F. CUMONT: *Fouilles de Doura Europos*, 1926.
H. T. BOSSERT: *Alt Kreta*, 1921.
BARROIS: *Manuel d'Archéologie biblique.*
VON SUSCHAM: *Meissner Babylonien nord Assyrien*, I.
DU MESNIL DU BUISSON: 'Le Sisite de Sérapis', in *Bull. Soc. des. Ant. de France*, 1948.
P. DEMARGNE: *La Crète Dédalique*, 1937.
E. POTTIER: *L'Art Hittite*, 1926.
A. FOUCHER: *L'Art gréco-bouddhique du Gandhara*, II, 1951.
WIEGER: *Textes historiques*, 1922.

M. ROSTOVZEFF: *Animal Style in South Russia and China, Iranians and Greeks in South Russia*, 1922.
P. E. HERMANN: *L'Homme à la découverte du monde*, 1954.
L. BASCHOFFER: 'On Greeks and Sakas in India', in *Journal of the American Oriental Society*, vol. 61, 1941.
J. HACKIN: 'Fouilles françaises en Afghanistan' (1938) in *Revue des Arts Asiatiques*, 1939 and 1948.
R. GHIRSHMAN: *Begram: Recherches sur les Kouchans*, 1946.
H. SEYRIG: 'Antiquités syriennes', in *Syria*, XVIII, 1937.
R. DUSSAUD: 'L'Art phénicien du IIe Millénaire', 1949. *Syrie*, vol. XX.
G. CONTENAU: *Histoire de l'Orient ancien: La vie en Sumer*, 1936.
R. GROUSSET: *L'Empire des steppes*, 1939.
O. VON FALKE: *Kunstgeschichte der Seidenweberei*, Berlin, 1913.
A. CHRISTENSEN: *L'Iran sous les Sassanides*, 1936.

COSTUME

L. and J. HEUZEY: *Histoire du Costume dans l'Antiquité, l'Orient*, 1935.
J. HEUZEY: 'Le Costume en Mésopotamie', in *Gazette des Beaux-Arts*, 1955.

TEXTILES

E. CHERBLANC: *Le Kaunakès*, 1937.
R. PFISTER: 'Etudes textiles', in *Revue des Arts Asiatiques*, 1934.

97 Painting on a sarcophagus from Hagia Triada. Late Minoan. Heraklion Museum. (Photo André Held)

RELIGIOUS COSTUME

97 The priestess walking at the head of the procession wears a costume reminiscent of the ancient kaunakès, with a tail at the back, while her two companions wear the specifically Cretan embroidered, close-fitting garment

BELL SKIRT

98 The width of this skirt, which fits very closely at the waist, can only be explained by clever cutting; the head-dress is a sort of large striped beret

DECORATED LOINCLOTH

99 This large-scale painting shows the multicoloured material of the outer loincloth worn over a plain pagne, falling to a point in front

98 Terracotta figurine from Petsofa. Middle Minoan. Heraklion Museum. (Photo Androulaki)

Chapter III

Crete and its Costume

The Setting and the Civilization

Uninhabited, it appears, before the sixth millennium of the prehistoric period, Crete reveals traces of civilization after 3400 BC. Then, at the beginning of the third millennium, the new populations that occupied the Cyclades penetrated into Crete and introduced their systems of navigation, which were unknown to the ancient Cretans, and now enabled them to establish permanent trade links with Egypt and, through Syria, with Mesopotamia – that is, with the two other groups of people who created the source civilizations of the Eastern Mediterranean. Jewels executed with a sure taste, indicating a developed art, constitute the first specimens of ancient Cretan costume.

Originally strongly influenced by the two civilizations of Egypt and Babylon, Cretan civilization became increasingly distinctive at the end of the third millennium and the beginning of the Bronze Age (*c.* 2100 BC). The manufacture of bronze objects developed on a vast scale and supplied all the peoples on the coasts of the Eastern Mediterranean; the rapid growth of Cretan wealth and art placed it on an equal footing with Egypt and Babylon.

However, towards 2000 BC, following on the first Aryan migrations, mainland Greece was invaded by the Achaeans, and although Aegean civilization on the islands was untouched, it was nonetheless shaken by the disorganization of trade: in Crete this led to an economic crisis, generally dated to around 1750 BC, which marks the end of the first Cretan hegemony, which had lasted almost four centuries.

A second period of prosperity soon opened up, and lasted about three and a half centuries, from 1750 to 1400 BC. This was the most important period for Cretan costume, the period of the building of the palace at Knossos (Middle Minoan III and Late Minoan I), whose discovery revealed the extraordinary richness of the dress of kings, the Cretan's pronounced taste for clothes and jewels and the astonishing variety of their costumes.

The development of the minor arts and the diffusion of the various forms of luxury, closely interlinked, affected all the objects that clothe and surround men and, still more, women; there began a quest – carried to excess perhaps – for luxury in costume and toilette in which women played their part, for Cretan women occupied an important place in society and did not live shut away in their quarters. Cretan art represents Minoan feminine beauty in a lively, realistic form – very unlike

99 Vase-bearer, fresco from Knossos. Late Minoan. Heraklion Museum. (Photo Flammarion)

the masculine style that fifth century Greek art had forced on it – and owed much to the varying modes worn by the fashionable women of Knossos.

During the second period of prosperity, Cretan civilization conquered the Cyclades and Greece, penetrated into Cyprus and reached Syria, bringing about the universal adoption of the fashions of Knossos: the hegemony of Cretan costume went hand in hand with the island's maritime, commercial and artistic supremacy.

The invasion of the warlike Achaeans, the destruction of Knossos and the ravages wrought in the surrounding country side marked the end of Cretan supremacy: the island became a vassal of distant Mycenae. But in Argolis everything was 'Cretanized', although the Achaeans retained certain peculiarities of their costume.

The Cretan civilization of this last Bronze Age (Late Minoan III, from 1400 to 1200 BC) cannot be included among the civilizations of the Middle East, even when its individual flavour is weakest; Eastern influence became more marked, but without being absolute, and just before the Dorian migrations at the beginning of the Iron Age (1200 BC) we find a mixed civilization, a result of reciprocal interpenetrations in the Eastern Mediterranean, in which we must recognize a large Cretan contribution, noticeable particularly in Mycenaean art, whose origins remained Cretan.

Towards 1200 BC, the Dorian invasion of Greece created a powerful current of emigration in the Aegean, towards the neighbouring coasts of Ionia and Asia Minor, whose civilizations were to be profoundly marked by it. However, this Creto-Mycenaean influence remained predominantly Cretan following the earlier penetrations by the Phoenicians along the coasts of Asia: so 'Mycenaean civilization itself only brushed over the edge of Asia in Ionia, while it was to put down its deepest roots in the land that was to be Dorian'.[1]

In the ninth, eighth and seventh centuries BC, a new flowering of Cretan art took place, a renascence in which Crete became a vital artistic centre, poised between the East and Greece proper.[2] The sixth century saw its decline, with the complete transformation of trade relations, the shift of the economic centres and the main lines of communication, and the political weakening of the country as the result of internal discords. The distinctive Cretan costume was fated to disappear, and one of its last appearances is on the Dipylon Vase.

The evolution of Cretan costume during these different periods of the Cretan and Aegean civilizations is particularly well documented, with abundant texts and archaeological discoveries of extremely high artistic quality.[3]

arts and industries begins in Crete and finishes in Mycenae';[5] we know that Mycenaean women not only dressed in Cretan styles, but also sought after the luxury fabrics woven on the island.

Where Egypt is concerned, it is established that there was a continual flow of merchandise from the Nile Delta towards the Aegean islands until the end of the Sixth dynasty (Old Kingdom, 2390 BC, or Early Minoan II) and again in the Middle Kingdom that this current exercized a certain influence through the introduction of numerous toilet articles. There can be no doubt that there was a similar current in the other direction: from the sixteenth century the Cretans, known as *Kefti* in Egypt, are recognizable in tomb paintings by their physical traits, their vividly striped skirts and high laced boots; they are shown bringing their produce to the land of the Pharaohs, particularly textiles, some lists of which have survived.[6]

In the East itself, for instance in Syria, Aegean styles were known through Cretans established in these countries, and were also introduced by merchants who, on their return, spread Syrian costume in the island.

We know precisely the sea trade routes, direct and indirect: from Naukratis in Egypt to Rhodes, then by the south coast of Asia Minor towards Cyprus and beyond, towards the Syrian coast; from Rhodes to the north west by Melas, towards Aegina, Megara and Argos; from Rhodes to Sidonia by Crete (the Cyrene route); and lastly, from Cyrene towards Taranto and Cybaris and, to the north west, to Megara and Selinunte.[7]

This far-flung network, spreading to the east and west as well as north and south, led to abundant exchanges which enabled Cretan costume to exercize a very strong influence, and also to acquire new enrichments.

Cretan Trade

External trade played a considerable role in the spread of Cretan costume: the most remarkable Cretan artifacts are often known from finds on the mainland.[4]

Dyed cloth and jewels held an extremely important place in these exchanges; but we must not forget the mass of objects in fragile or perishable materials that have not come down to us.

It is in the broader framework of Aegean civilization that we must consider Cretan trade, for 'the history of all Aegean

Cretan Costume

The discovery of Cretan civilization, predicted by Schliemann and realized by Evans from 1894 to 1920, revealed the originality of costume from the second millennium on ward. Statuettes, vase paintings, intaglios yielded fairly sure information, but the same cannot be said of the paintings that have been brought to light, for most of them have been restored and some reconstructions must, in all prudence, be treated as interpretations rather than as original sources.

100–102   The Tiara Goddess, polychrome terracotta figurine
from Knossos. Late Minoan. Heraklion Museum.
(Photos Maraghiannis and Androulaki)

The search after elegance of line, one of the characteristics of Crete, particularly after the second millennium, is reflected in a conscious geometric stylization;[8] this style also complements to perfection a short physical type with long, slender legs.[9]

From 2100 to 1900 BC, (Middle Minoan I), the terracotta figurines from Petsofa (plate 98) show the main features of costume already developed; the upper part of the body is bare, completely for men and partially for women, which relates this costume to that of several prehistoric Middle Eastern peoples; the waist is close-fitting, echoing the loincloth once tied round the waist. We must see an inheritance from prehistory in this Cretan habit of leaving the torso bare, acquired from their Stone Age ancestors and not from Mesopotamia, where it has similar origins.

But it is with Middle Minoan III, from 1750 to 1580 BC, and under Late Minoan I, from 1580 to 1450 BC, that various pieces of sewn costume using rich textiles begin to appear: gowns whose forms and trimmings vary, aprons, bodices, culotte-skirts, several types of hat. For clothing, this period is the most luxurious and the most curious.

GARMENTS OF SKINS

In the Neolithic period (6000 to 300 BC) when Crete is first known to have been inhabited, its original inhabitants sheltered in caves or under rocks as did their relatives on the mainland, and, like them, wore animal skins. The skins depended on the climate of the period and, presumably, as happened elsewhere, continued to be worn until the appearance of weaving, which apparently was invented at the same time as permanent dwellings, round wattle and daub huts or rectangular houses in hewn stone. Working the skins seems to have been employment for women.

It is likely that these costumes of skins and furs had common characteristics among the various peoples of the cold Neolithic and Palaeolithic periods, and it is most probable that the first woven costumes all belonged to the same general type in the milder Neolithic periods; this may hold for all the regions then inhabited and, in any case, is particularly likely for the Mediterranean basin.

The memory of these skin garments from Palaeolithic times persisted in Crete, as elsewhere, in the form of chasubles and other skin costumes for priests and priestesses, shields for soldiers, gauntlets for athletes, shoes and belts for the public at large.

TEXTILES

'As far back as evidence exists,' writes Glotz, 'we see that the inhabitants of Crete spun wool. Textiles have not been preserved in the Aegean lands as they were in hot, dry conditions and in peat-bogs, and only a few scraps of cloth have been found in the tombs of Zapher Papoura and Mycenae. It is no less certain that spinning and weaving were already known in Neolithic communities: proof is furnished by the discovery of numerous spindle-weights.'[10]

The Cretans also used flax, the cultivation and preparation of which appeared in Europe after the end of this advanced civilization.[11]

Spinning and weaving were family industries in Crete as elsewhere, and differed in this from dyeing. From sheep-shearing to cutting the cloth, everything connected with clothing was a domestic occupation. Carding combs, distaffs, spindles and spindle-weights, bobbins with notches, pierced along their axis, pins, punches and awls have been found: the palace at Knossos included a spinning and weaving workshop, and a distaff was represented above the entrance to the Queen's apartments. Around Mocklos there was probably a textile industry which worked for the general public.

Textiles became increasingly loaded with embroidery: Cretan terracottas, vases and statues represent garments whose rich, embroidered decoration is incised with a sharp point or traced with fine brushes, or may even appear in relief on the clay.[12]

103 Marble statuette of a goddess. Late Minoan.
Fitzwilliam Museum, Cambridge. (Museum photo)

DYES AND COLORANTS

Dyes, the preparation of tints and the actual colouring of textiles, could scarcely have been a family occupation. The industry used vegetable pigments as well as the purple extracted from shellfish, large deposits of which have been found in eastern Crete; this purple industry had already a long history under the middle Minoan period, and made it possible to dye fine materials with three or four colours in varied patterns, as can be seen from frescos and pottery.

It may appear too bold to praise the astonishing elegance of textiles when representations are all the evidence we have: the bell skirt of the goddess in faience or the divided skirts worn by palace beauties. But the faience replicas of skirts hung as votive offerings in the temple at Knossos are models whose exactness cannot be doubted and whose taste and elegance are undeniable: motifs in purplish brown, light sprays of flowers or rows of crocuses stand out against a greenish white background divided by a wavy line. At Phylakopi, between white, red and yellow boughs, two swallows with outspread wings form the magnificent decoration of a skirt.

MALE COSTUME

The loincloth common to all Eastern Mediterranean peoples was generally worn; most often it took the form of a cache-sexe hung from the belt, but loincloth and cache-sexe could also be worn together.

The Egyptian *shenti* was a simple loincloth; that worn by the Cretans, by workmen and warriors as well as by princes and high-ranking dignitaries, varied in cut according to the material used, which could be soft cloth (probably linen), a stiffer cloth (perhaps thick wool), or even leather. Often arranged like a short skirt or even as a double apron, it generally finished at the back in a point that was sometimes lengthened and upturned like an animal's tail. Exceptionally two loincloths worn one on top of the other could form flounces and reach to mid-thigh with a double point at back and front.

This loincloth, worn 'in Cretan style' in the Cyclades, was closed and converted into short trousers on the mainland, where the development of cutting and sewing perfected the principle of a piece of stuff passing between the legs and tucked into the belt at back and front. On a criophorus in the Berlin Museum, dating from the end of the Daedalic period (*c.* 800 BC), we see a pair of shorts with a triangular front leaving the upper thighs bare.[13]

Objects show tight shorts which, it has been alleged, were worn by foreigners or by demons, who had to be represented in some strange form: but could this not be the same type of flattening stylization employed by Egyptian artists? The Cretans depicted on Egyptian tombs of the Eighteenth dynasty (fifteenth century BC) show on their multicoloured loincloths a band stiffened with bindings and embroidery which descends obliquely towards knee level.

Loincloths and shorts were held at the waist by a tight belt, probably made of cloth more or less heavily decorated with metal; the belt worn by the vase bearer (plate 99) seems to be composed of a roll with metal edges. Others, which must have been very costly, were decorated with rosettes and spirals depicted in white and yellow, in reality made of silver and gold, or even of plates of copper. On one bronze, a wide band of

104-5 Serpent goddess, polychrome terracotta figurine from Knossos. Late Minoan.
Heraklion Museum.
(Photos Xylouris and Percheron)

deep-piled stuff is wound twice round the waist; in Egypt, a *kefti* belt was made of two long, stiff ribbons with large loops on the hips.

The bodies of some figures are protected by a sort of cassock, sometimes showing joints like the one between the metal plates of the cuirass: this cassock[14] which was often wide enough to cover the arms, appears only in religious scenes and seems to have been a sort of ritual cape.

Also for ceremonial wear there was a long, one-piece gown made in bright colours with rich embroidery. It was worn only by princes, high dignitaries and priests: it clothes the official figures in processions and, on the Hagia Triada sarcophagus (plate 97), takes the form of a tunic descending from neck to calf or ankle for flute and lyre players, exactly as for the women who take part in sacrifices or for the deceased to whom the funerary offerings are made.

Presumably for warmth, a long garment was added to the loincloth. The Cretans and Aegeans covered themselves with a cloak in animal skin and the thick wool *diphtera*. Charioteers wrapped themselves in long cloaks similar to those worn later by *aurigae* in Greece. On a figurine from Petsofa we can see a sort of short cape which has been compared with a Scottish plaid and recalls certain Middle Eastern garments.

Though they were bareheaded for most of the time, and wore their hair long, perhaps in plaits,[15] the Cretans nonetheless had several types of head-dress, generally turbans or caps, apparently made of skins; they recall some women's hats from Petsofa or, still more, the Grecian *petasos*. Tiered hairstyles are characteristic of the seventh century BC.

Cretans wore shoes only to go outdoors. Indoors and in sanctuaries they went barefoot; in palaces the steps of outdoor stairs are badly worn, whereas interior stairs and all floors, even the pink-tinged plaster, are still in a good state of preservation. In Homer too, the heroes only put on their 'fine shoes' to travel or fight and in the late fifth century, long after the period of the *Iliad*, the Victory from the Temple of Nikè Apteros in Athens is shown untying her sandals when withdrawing from action.

Men wore half-boots reaching to the calf. On the Petsofa

statuettes these types of footwear are represented as white; they must have been made of some white leather or pale chamois skin, similar to the skin from which the Cretans of today still cut their boots. They can also be red, like Russian leather, on a fresco at Orchomenes, with thongs tied seven times round the leg.

While fishermen and pugilists went barefoot outdoors as well as in, great court personages never showed themselves in public without shoes or sandals.[16] The latter were finely worked and attached above the ankles with thick thongs; sometimes these thongs were decorated with beads, but this was the height of luxury.

The wearing of high, closed boots in Crete can be explained by the uneven nature of the terrain, as can the wearing of a similar type of shoe in the mountainous parts of the Middle East, whence it spread to other regions. This type of shoe, with upturned toe, is to be seen in frescos of the Pre-Hellenic period representing games and ceremonies at the royal court.

WOMEN'S COSTUME

Before the eighteenth century BC (Middle Minoan III, 1750 to 1580 BC) Cretan women seem to have worn the loincloth common to both sexes, but no doubt arranging it in the form of a skirt more often than men did; the skirt itself is only a longer form of this garment, and probably did not become distinguished from the loincloth before the development of weaving.

A long dagger slipped through the belt can be seen on the terracotta figures of women from Petsofa (Middle Minoan I, 2100 to 1900 BC); it is interesting to note here that Bronze Age women in Denmark always carried a comb and a dagger in the girdle of their loincloths.

Towards the beginning of the eighteenth century BC, the usual costume for women included a more or less decorated skirt, a bodice of varying forms, an outer garment, which could be a long cloak or a short cape, and a head-dress. By an inevitable, almost 'biological' process of evolution, to these various pieces were added new elements (pleats and flounces) or details (embroideries, multicoloured decoration), all in contrast with the costume of the Middle East, which was swathed round the body.

In Crete the skirt was treated as a separate part of female costume, supported at the waist and reaching to the ground; it was always tightly belted and fitted closely over the hips, but otherwise presented very varied forms. The oldest model, already represented on seals from Early Minoan III (2400 to 2100 BC) and better still on a Petsofa figurine (c. 2000 BC), is *bell* shaped, made in broadly striped cloth; later it became narrower (plate 107). Its fullness was supported on horizontal hoops which helped to stiffen the garment. It has even been advanced that later 'these embroidered bands on the skirt form a cone so wide and stiff that we must imagine them as stretched over switches of rush or metal plates, genuine boned skirts of crinolines.'[17]

However, though the skirt included sewn trimmings, nothing has yet proved the existence of an independent support like the crinoline of nineteenth-century Europe. Figurines from Palaikastro prove that this fashion for stiff skirts persisted in provincial towns until Late Minoan times (early sixteenth century BC).

The skirt decoration itself is extremely interesting. The material could be divided into a score of horizontal bands, em-broidered or left plain, by hoops of braid bordered with cross motifs, trellis patterns or lozenges (seventh century BC), or a vertical line of braid might run down the centre of the gown (possibly a button braid).[18] The so-called 'geometric' style of Crete can be seen in the decoration of gowns.

Above all, we note the use of flounces sewn to the skirt from the hips to the foot. These flounces might be of equal or of graduated depth, and might form a checkerboard pattern in brown and beige or brown and light blue (plates 104, 105). From the Early Minoan period, the two-tiered skirt predominates, with flounces that leave the body of the skirt visible and form a point in front; in the palace at Knossos, a more restrained fashion placed these pointed flounces only on the lower part of the skirt. A fresco at Hagia Triada illustrates one of the most curious and richest examples of this fashion: two tiers of flounces with white, red and brown rectangles were attached with red and white binding on to a skirt on which white and red crosses alternate with blue.[19]

The extremely detailed information we have gained from Knossos concerning these flounced skirts[20] has suggested various hypotheses about their origin. For E. Pottier, as for L. and J. Heuzey,[21] this arrangement derives from the Sumerian kaunakès, and the distant links maintained between Sumer and the Aegean support this argument. The long, tiered strands of this cloth could have inspired the Cretan inventors of the flounce, which then spread throughout the Eastern Mediterranean. It is interesting to note skirts with three tiers of flounces (or pleats) in the paintings of Rekhmire, in Syria, and in countries situated on the route between Sumer and the Aegean.

Could the rounded apron covering the upper skirt have derived from the same source? It seems more likely that it originated in the primitive loincloth common to all prehistoric Palaeolithic and Neolithic peoples, which might have been ritually preserved in religious costume.

While the elegant women of the Minoan court did not show the whole of the upper part of their bodies, as goddesses and priestesses sometimes did, the bosom was completely, or almost completely exposed. At the end of Middle Minoan (1580 BC) the bodice, which was open down the front to the waist, rose behind the neck in a Medici collar. From the eighteenth century onwards, the collar disappears and the décolletage remains, for the bodice was laced only below the breasts. Gala costume in this 'Belle Epoque' was completed by a short, transparent shift: the bodice of the 'Parisienne' (plate 109) is held in place by a ribbon passing under the arms and decorated at the nape of the neck with a large falling bow, while its transparent front is trimmed with narrow red and blue ribbons. The 'Dancing Girl' has her breasts held in a yellow bolero with an embroidered border worn over a shift with a high, round-cut neck. Forearms were universally bare in all periods; sleeves were short, sometimes tight and sometimes puffed or leg-of-mutton shape, and appear to have been held in place by light ribbons at the neck or by crossed shoulderstraps over the back.

The slim waist, accentuated by this type of costume, was sought after by women even more keenly than by men, and most often stressed further by a belt. Cretan women of Middle Minoan I wound the girdle twice round the waist,[22] letting the ends fall in front[23] to the foot of the skirt. The bouffant shape of certain primitive costumes around the lower part of the hips has suggested to some a survival of the steatopygy of female sculptures of the Palaeolithic period. The double belt with two tabs mentioned above recalls the Danish Bronze Age and the

106 Bronze figurine from Hagia Triada. Early Minoan. Heraklion Museum. (Photo Androulaki)

Sumerian models. Another type of belt, with two rolls but without tabs, remained in vogue over a long period and has been found in faience votive objects. There was also a simpler style with only one roll.

The most surprising garment is the corset apparently worn by the 'Serpent Goddess' (plate 107) and the fashionable women of the Tiryns and Thebes frescos, who have no belt. This corset, which made the skirt lie flat on the hips and accentuated the slimness of the waist and the prominence of the bare breasts, must have been formed of a framework of metal plates: it was certainly not known to Neolithic peoples, for it presupposes the use of copper at least. This, in the eighteenth century BC, represents one of the first applications of metalwork to costume.[24]

Like men, women wore a long cloak for riding in chariots; in other circumstances, they threw a short, sleeveless cape or tippet over their shoulders.

From what we know of their way of life Cretan women, without leading a cloistered existence, stayed at home more than did their husbands. Painters represented them with white skins and men with dark complexions: at first the Greeks called Cretan men *Phoinikès* or 'redskins'. Cretan women thus wore shoes infrequently, but had sandals, slippers or high boots, and sometimes shoes with heels.

Women's hair, which was almost always covered by some sort of ornament, seems to have been plaited, but it was characterized most of all[25] by one or two curls separated above the ear and falling to the neck, recalling the side-curls of Syria. All figures were drawn in profile, as in Egyptian art, and we presume, though we cannot be certain, that there was a matching curl on the other side. The hairstyle was quite high and was held in place by a ribbon. Towards the seventh century BC, tiered hairstyles were characteristic: the Gazi goddesses have their hair arranged in a point on the top of the head, held in place by a band with three flowers on the forehead, passing above the ears and round the back of the neck. In other cases, the hair is flat on top of the head and falls freely on either side.[26] We also find an enormous horn-shaped hairstyle.

Cretan women's costume furnishes the first models of hats in the history of fashion.

107 Serpent Goddess, statuette in gold and ivory. Late Minoan. Museum of Fine Arts, Boston. (Museum photo)

HEAD-DRESS

108 Example of the arrangement of the tall headdress with headband

109 The upper part of the dress is finished with a bow at the back. The hair is dressed in ringlets falling over the neck

MYCENAEAN COSTUME UNDER GREEK INFLUENCE

110–12 This unusual group shows different aspects of a typically Cretan costume: a wide, open corselet with short sleeves and seams picked out with braid; a skirt in checked material trimmed with groups of three flounces, showing the foundation cloth at knee height. These flounces slant to a point in front (cf. plate 106), giving the appearance of a culotte skirt. It is impossible to be certain of the exact nature of the wide scarf edged with short fringes

108 Small terracotta head from Piskocephalo. Late Minoan. Heraklion Museum. (Photo Androulaki)

109 *The Parisienne*, fresco. Late Minoan. Heraklion Museum. (Photo André Held)

In Crete at the beginning of Middle Minoan, we find the most varied and bizarre hats: high caps, pointed hats, berets and turbans and even tricornes, perhaps with ritual significance, decorated with rosettes and crowned with a curled plume or ribbon. Certain hats have white trimmings, while others are black. We also discover, not without surprise, the *polos* worn by Tanagra women in the times of Pericles, already worn in Daedalic Crete in the seventh century; in the latter period, women also wore tall caps recalling the plumed cap of primitive times.[27]

In general, Cretan women's costume shows a pronounced taste for vivid colours, their brilliance and variety enhancing the richness of the decoration. The harmonies and dashes of reds, yellows, blues and purples have been preserved almost unchanged in palace frescos. Sometimes the effect was heightened by the application of gold leaf.

Lastly, the celebrated Toreador Fresco shows a young woman wearing tight shorts, holding out her arms to catch a jumping athlete. Perhaps male costume was customarily worn by women gymnasts in Crete, but this is the only example we have.[28]

ORNAMENTS

Large numbers of sumptuous ornaments and jewels have been found in the graves of both men and women: they consisted of rings, necklaces and bracelets.

Several bracelets were often worn on both arms. The Mycenae excavations yielded carved bracelets like those shown in the frescos.

For ordinary people, necklaces were made of common stones threaded together: for the wealthier classes there were beads of blue steatite, of blue paste imitating lapis lazuli (*Kyanos*), agate, amethyst, cornelian or rock crystal, or metal plates. Mixed with these beads were pendants bearing animal, bird or human motifs.

Hairpins were made of copper or gold. The simplest kind had spiral heads, while examples with flower heads were found

110–12 Ivory statuette from Mycenae. *c.* 1500 BC. National Archaeological Museum, Athens. (Museum photos)

at Mochlos. At Mycenae, pins appear to have been much richer, decorated with engraved gold, plates, quartz or rock crystal globes or animal heads modelled in the round. Although women's tombs generally yielded the finest specimens, at Isopata a gold headed pin was found in the royal tomb, together with a number of others engraved with hunting motifs.

Head ornaments were usually worn only by women, though at Hagia Triada the Chief has a jewel set with large pearls in his hair. Elegant women decorated their hair with gold bands or diadems, which were sometimes of gold, or else wore leaf-shaped, hinged gold plates.

The celebrated head ornament from the 'Treasure of Priam' at Troy consisted of sixty-four fine gold chains hanging over the brow and shoulders and ending in the same number of small medallions with idol motifs.

Pendants and ear-rings were very wide-spread in Crete; they have been found in even the simplest tombs, made of wire, thin strips of metal rolled into spirals, or metal plaques decorated with rosettes.

Among these various ornaments the fibula is strangely absent. And indeed, the fibula, the characteristic fastening of Greek and Roman draped costume, could serve no function in the sewn, fitted costume of Crete.

BATTLE COSTUME

The helmet was occasionally worn in Crete, by warriors and huntsmen, and sometimes by athletes. There were four types:

First: a cone of plaited thongs, in horizontal rings held together by a lattice, with a tassel at the point.

Second: a metal casque divided by groups of circles, also conical but less tall than the preceding model, topped by a large metal boss and held in place by a wide chin-strap that also served as a cheekguard; the spaces between the rings were often decorated with boars' tusks. This type of helmet is shown on the carved ivory heads from Sparta, Enkomi and Mycenae, and in bronzes distributed from Crete to Phoenicia, Argos and Thessaly.

Third: a helmet with a shell made entirely of metal, with a crest and long horse-hair plume, fitted with cheek- and neck-guards of rivetted plates, one of which projected forward to form a visor. This type appeared at the end of Minoan II, and was worn by officers and lancers.

Fourth: a low, round helmet, fitting closely to the skull, bristling with spikes, or an oval helmet, pointed at back and front, or with a long plume hanging behind. These last two varieties, seen on the Middle Minoan 'Warrior Vase', were worn at the end of the Mycenaean period, about 1200 BC.[29]

RELIGIOUS COSTUME

Examination of divine costume reveals some curious facts about Cretan costume in general; the two types of goddess which have always existed side by side, the naked and the clothed, are particularly significant.

The religious idea was that the magical emanations of the divine body kept their powers and virtues better when protected against continual depreciation; the costume of women, who were symbols of motherhood, fecund and beneficent, is consequently explained. Yet the emanations of the goddess could more easily produce the desired effect if nothing was placed between her and the person to be made fertile. 'It is enough,' says Glotz, 'if not all the sources of fertility are intercepted, if not all signs of sex are hidden... The Cretan fashion for the bodice that left the breasts bare could not have become established nor lasted so long had it not corresponded to some religious idea; it was created for the goddess, and this ceremonial costume was at first a *ritual costume*. As from Early Minoan III, the goddess has her bust held in a piece of cloth pierced with two openings through which her breasts pass. Later, she wears the deeply décolleté bodice which passes from her to the ladies of Knossos, unless she had breasts entirely naked above her flounced skirt, by a compromise reserved exclusively for her.'[30]

We must note the curious resemblance between the famous Serpent Goddess of Crete (plate 107) and a clay image repre-

85

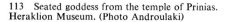

senting a goddess invoked against snakes among the Ibisios of Southern Nigeria: this goddess' breasts are also bare and snakes twine round her arms and breasts.[31]

We can also trace the influence of religious rites on other items of Cretan costume. It is certain that priestly service imposed on men and women alike the wearing of special garments, long gowns or divided skirts, stiff and often full, made of cloth spotted to imitate animal skins and ending in a point like a tail, or some similar appendage: a clear evocation of the prehistoric garment, perpetuated by religious tradition. A stole completed the costume.

In general, however, those present at religious ceremonies wore the ordinary costume of the time.[32] Sometimes we find a special head-dress, a tiara, a toque or a round, flat hat; a seventh-century goddess also wears a *polos*.

The religious associations of a long, one-piece gown worn by men and women alike depend simply on the fact that it was worn only for certain ceremonies. It figures on the Hagia Triada sarcophagus (plate 97), where women carry out ritual acts, and in an engraving where the goddess seated between lions is wrapped in this garment, which even covers her arms.

113   Seated goddess from the temple of Prinias. Heraklion Museum. (Photo Androulaki)

Cretan Costume: Reciprocal Influences

The exceptional originality of Minoan costume not only gave it a special place in the development of clothing, but also won it a remarkable degree of influence through the entire Mediterranean, aided by the spread of Cretan civilization and the expansion of the island's trade.

Either directly or indirectly, through Mycenae, whose art came from Crete, Minoan styles were increasingly adopted in all the countries with coasts on the Black Sea and the Eastern Mediterranean, and even in some countries of inland Asia. Weak in Cappadocia, Rhodes and Cilicia, its influence was stronger in Cyprus and on the Syrian coast; it was pronounced in Egypt and could still be traced in Assyria. It is not surprising that it was active above all in the places where, after the destruction of Knossos by the Mycenaeans towards 1400 BC, and after the Dorian invasions of 1200 BC, Cretan and Achaean refugees carried Minoan civilization into Asia, where it was continued by the Achaeans. These movements of peoples and trade relations in turn introduced foreign elements into Cretan styles.

Towards the end of the seventh century BC in Greece, everything became 'Cretanized'; an exception, however, was a detail of male costume. Achaean men continued to declare their northern origins by wearing beards, and a costume composed of short trousers and a sleeved *chiton*. Frescos in the temple at Thebes, erected between 1600 and 1400 BC on the Cadmean, show figures in Cretan costume.[33]

Similarly, the Mycenaeans adopted Cretan footwear, but like the Achaeans omitted from their costume an essentially Cretan element: instead of a skirt they wore short trousers and the short-sleeved chiton belted at the waist and falling to mid-thigh in stiff folds. This difference in male costume provides a clear demonstration of the separate nature of the Cretan and mainland peoples.

Pre-Hellenic women, on the other hand, enthusiastically adopted the styles of Knossos. A contrast can be observed between the Pre-Mycenaean period and the one following: 'the third trench tomb in Mycenae, where some dowager faithful to past fashions had been buried, held jewels without equal in Crete, pins which, with their enormous length and heavy rock crystal heads, could not have been worn in the hair and must have fastened a costume of the peplos type.' The new generation of Mycenaean women, on the other hand, took as their own the flattering fashions of Crete, the close-fitting bell skirt, with the same varieties of shaping and ornament to be found in Knossos. In Argolis, women preferred the skirts with curved flounces, heavily boned, and even wore a type with multicoloured ribbons alternating with bands of cloth, which was rare in Crete;[34] they sometimes also added an enormous 'bustle'. They showed the same enthusiasm for the Minoan bodice laced below the breasts, with a roll belt; on a ring from Mycenae we can even discern a triple roll.

We know that in all periods Cyprus was the great clearing house for Asiatic and perhaps Egyptian influences towards the Aegean and vice versa; it was there that the Achaeans created the curious mixed civilization known as Cypro-Minoan, which in its turn spread out in all directions: Ras Shamra was only a first outpost of Cyprus on the Syrian coast. Consequently we are not surprised to find the Seated Goddess from Ras Shamra (plate 78) with entirely bare breasts, clad in a well-known type of Mycenaean gown with flounces and entwined Cretan decoration; like Mycenaean women she wore the mass of her hair swept on top of her head and held in place by a bandeau under which small, regular curls show; a higher curl is seen on her brow and a wavy lock of hair falls from the top of her head. All these details are also to be seen in the Knossos 'Ladies in Blue' fresco reconstructed by Evans.[35]

Egyptian influence, which reached Crete by way of Cyprus, was noticeable first in toilet articles.

At this period when the Empire extended as far as Syria and the Upper Euphrates, there appeared among the Pharaohs the more elaborate draperies of Syrio-Phoenician fashions influenced by those of Crete. The statue known as the *Auxerre Goddess* (plate 114), on the other hand, shows the penetration of Egyptian elements into Minoan clothing. But above all it was by trade in cloth and through the Phoenician sea-routes that Egyptian art exercised some influence on Cretan costume: on their way to Greece the traders of Tyre brought not only their own textiles but also cloths from Egypt, Mesopotamia and Arabia, and these textiles, decorated with flowers and real or fantastic animals, provided Cretan artists (and those of Cyprus and Rhodes) with new motifs which softened the severity of geometric style.[36]

In return, after the Eighteenth and Nineteenth dynasties, from 1580 to 1320 BC, we can follow the penetration of Aegean elements into Egyptian art, still through the intermediary of the Phoenicians.[37]

115 Greek black figure vase painting. Vatican Museum. (Photo Flammarion)

We shall probably never know precisely the routes by which the countries of the continental Middle East, such as Mesopotamia and Assyria, introduced the elements of their costume into Cretan dress. Loincloths and roll belts are part of the common heritage of Neolithic and perhaps even Palaeolithic peoples, but, 'trade relations between Sumer and the Aegean, often clearly demonstrated, may have made known the luxurious Sumerian kaunakès cloth and led to its adoption in places as distant as Crete.'[38] This may also have been the case for the high, closed footwear of the mountain-dwelling Hittites, which probably inspired Cretan shoes of the second millennium by way of Syria and Cyprus, where they were worn in the same period. But the great caravan route from the Mediterranean to the Tigris passed through inland or *Hurite* Syria, a land where old Mesopotamian influences met those of the Creto-Aegean world.[39]

In all this exchange of ideas, tastes, raw materials and artists, the principal influential role remains indubitably with Cretan costume.

Notes

1 Demargne, pp. 263, 309.
2 *Ibid.*, p. 321.
3 Evans.
4 Glotz, p. 231.
5 *Ibid.*, p. 228.
6 *Ibid.*, p. 239.
7 *Ibid.*, p. 326.
8 Deonna, pp. 380–401.
9 Glotz, p. 74: between five foot three and five foot five inches tall, a mixture of dolychocephalic and brachycephalic types, probably Asiatic in origin. Pottier, p. 842.
10 Glotz, pp. 81 ff.
11 Clark, p. 354.
12 Demargne, p. 121.
13 *Ibid.*, p. 270, fig. 44, p. 256, plate XVI, for an example in Mycenae in the seventh century.
14 *Ibid.*, fig. 36.
15 *Ibid.*, p. 256, plate XVI.
16 According to Glotz the word for sandal is not Grecian, but of Pre-Hellenic origin.
17 Glotz, pp. 85–95.
18 Demargne, pp. 258, 262, plates XIV, XV (Berlin criophorus) and pp. 97–98.
19 On an engraved stone a woman, wearing a sort of culotte skirt, holds a flounced skirt in her hand; similar flounced trousers are to be seen in a Hagia Triada fresco.
20 A fashion also found in the seventh century. Demargne, pp. 192, 270, fig. 44.
21 Pottier, p. 842; Heuzey, p. 130, p. 113 note.
22 Recalling the curious stone carving from Aveyron, cf. Solomon Reinach.
23 Cf. terracotta statuette found at Siteria (Crete).
24 Demargne, p. 276 and fig. 49.
25 Cf. 'Ladies in Blue Fresco', partially reconstructed. Demargne, pp. 246, 249, plate XIII.
26 Demargne, pp. 246, 259, plate XIII; pp. 258, 262, plate XIV.
27 *Ibid.*, p. 279, fig. 49 (Louvre terracotta); p. 280, fig. 51; pp. 248, 126, plate VI; Glotz, pp. 81–95, supposes that the tiara and turban were worn by women before being reserved for divine or priestly images.
28 Glotz, p. 341.
29 The Late Minoan I (1580 to 1450 BC) helmet was also worn in seventh-century Mycenae.
30 Glotz, p. 282, figs. 37, 40, 43.
31 Baumann, p. 85, fig. 26.
32 Glotz, pp. 307, 308 ff.
33 *Ibid.*, pp. 55, 59.
34 Cf. Thyrintes and Thebes frescos.
35 Dussaud and Schaeffer, p. 56, plate 6.
36 Demargne, pp. 120–121. Cf. above 'Aegean Costume' concerning the Rekhmara three-tier skirts.
37 Cf. 'Iberian Costume' for Oriental and Greco-Phoenician influences.
38 L. and J. Heuzey, p. 130, p. 113 note.
39 Demargne, pp. 58–74.

Bibliography

GENERAL

J. PIRENNE: *Les Civilisations antiques*, 1951.
P. DEMARGNE: *La Crète dédalique*, 1937.
SIR ARTHUR EVANS: *Annual of the British School in Athens*, 1902–1903.

CRETAN INFLUENCE ON DORIAN COSTUME

115 This costume is a compromise between the soft, draped costume of the Greeks and the fitted, sewn costume of the Cretans; the richly-decorated material and the way the top of the sleeve is covered by a special arrangement of the peplos, attached to the front of the bodice with long pins, reveal Cretan influence

116 Prince with Fleur-de-Lys. Late Minoan. Fresco (restored). Heraklion Museum. (Photo André Held)

117 Weeping woman, from Tanagra. Seventh century BC. Paris, Louvre. (Photo Flammarion)

G. GLOTZ: *La Civilisation égéenne*, 1923.
W. DEONNA: 'Quelques conventions primitives de l'art grec', in *Revue des Etudes Grecques*, 1910.
— *Les Toilettes modernes de la Grèce minoenne*, 1911.
P. POTTIER: *Le Palais du roi Minos*, 1902.
SOLOMON REINACH: 'La Grèce avant l'Histoire', in *Anthropologie I* 1908.
H. BAUMANN and D. WESTERMANN: *Les Peuples et les civilisations d'Afrique*, 1948.
R. DUSSAUD and SCHAEFFER: 'Ivoires d'époque mycénienne', in *Gazette des Beaux-Arts*, July 1936.
SIR ARTHUR EVANS: *The Palace of Minos at Knossos*, 1911.
R. DUSSAUD: *Les Civilisations préhelléniques dans le bassin de la mer Egée*, 1914.
H. T. BOSSERT: *Alt Kreta*, Berlin, 1921.
A. MOSSO: *Escursioni nel Mediterraneo e ... Creta*, 1957.
A. J. B. MACE: *A Cretan Statuette in the Fitzwilliam Museum*, 1927.
— *Catalogue of the Benaki Museum*, Athens, 1936.

Chronology of Crete

EARLY MINOAN	I	3000 to 2800 BC
	II	2800 to 2400 BC
	III	2400 to 2100 BC
MIDDLE MINOAN	I	2100 to 1900 BC
	II	1900 to 1750 BC
	III	1750 to 1580 BC
LATE MINOAN	I	1580 to 1450 BC
	II	1450 to 1400 BC
	III	1400 to 1200 BC

After Glotz: *La Civilisation égéenne*.

118 Women bearing offerings, painted bas-relief from the mastaba of Akht-Hetep. Fifth dynasty, *c.* 2563–2423 BC. Paris, Louvre. (Photo Archives Photographiques)

Chapter IV

The Mediterranean Countries

Egypt

The prehistory of Egypt, clarified by the work of Breuil, Leakey and Menghin, reveals the presence of objects from Palaeolithic civilizations, with Aurignacian forms very close to those of Asia Minor, which seem to have penetrated into Africa through Syria.

In the Neolithic period the civilization of herdsmen and farmers which had lasted four thousand years in the Delta and in Upper Egypt presented certain similarities with the civilization of Susa.

The inhabitants of North-East Africa contemporary with the Pre-Dynastic Stone Age civilizations of Egypt and Nubia may have come, at least in part, from the Middle East, though this cannot be stated with certainty. Could they have been ancestors of the Ethiopian and Bushman races that must have been dominant throughout the length of Africa and belonged to the Palaeo-Mediterranean civilization?

In any case, it is probable that the huntsmen and stock-breeders who were the first occupants of the Nile valley and its delta wore a garment close to the prehistoric type worn generally in the Middle East and the Mediterranean: a loincloth/blanket initially made of leather and hide, and later of cloth.

The fluctuations of Egyptian civilization and costume

We are well informed about Egyptian civilization through the many documents recovered, and we are equally fortunate in the number and variety of representations of costume in Egyptian art.

We know that Egyptian civilization benefited from the period of peace and authority established over the entire country from 3200 BC, and especially between 2800 and 2400 BC. This period is characterized by organization of the state, progress in the arts and economic prosperity. Then from about 2400 to 2000 BC, unwise use of the country's resources led to a decline in the powers of the Pharaohs and a decrease in trade, while manufacturing techniques continued unchanged. Towards 2000 BC, the kings of Thebes restored order and the unity of the state, bringing back a prosperity which was to last for two centuries.

But a new period of political and economic disintegration set in, during which, from *c.* 1680 to *c.* 1580 BC, Egypt was invaded, overrun and mastered by the Hyksos or 'shepherd kings', probably Syrians led by Hittites or Aegeans. Before their

91

expulsion by the King of Thebes in *c.* 1500 BC, they had introduced the horse and chariot. Under the Pharaohs of the Eighteenth dynasty, from 1580 to 1350 BC, the Egyptians in turn attacked their neighbours and subjugated Palestine and Nubia, perhaps even forcing Crete to pay tribute.

The new period of economic expansion, accompanied by a renascence in cultural life, ended about 1350 BC; then a new decadence swept over Egypt once more, and the country, invaded by the Nubians, became an Assyrian province. In 525 BC it fell under Persian domination; it was conquered by Alexander the Great in 332 BC and became a Roman province in 30 BC.

Did Egyptian costume reflect this series of oscillations in political history and economical development?

On the contrary, there is a striking contrast between these changes and the continuance of costume styles during the first sixteen centuries, from about 3200 to 1500 BC. The exclusive use of draped costume, the use of linen and the wearing of very similar styles by men and women maintained almost unaltered the main features of costume established under the first Pharaohs.[1]

Egyptian garments always remained simple, despite the luxury afforded by foreign conquests. The long robe common to both sexes accentuated the squareness of the shoulders, the narrowness of the waist and hips, and the general elongation of the figures.

From the sixteenth century we see the appearance of a new type of costume, the sleeved tunic or *calasiris*. This date corresponds to the liberation of the territory occupied for one hundred years by the Hyksos, and at the same time, to the new contacts established by the wars with the Semitic peoples, for whom it was the rule to cover the body completely.

Under the New Kingdom, we find a wider range of colours and the simultaneous wearing of costumes from very different periods. We also note, later, under the Twenty-second dynasty (817 to 730 BC) an archaicizing tendency with the reappearance of certain characteristics of the Fifth and Sixth dynasties (*c.* 2500 BC); statues from the region of Memphis represent figures in wigs and the robes of these periods.[2]

TEXTILES

The textiles which appear in paintings and sculptures of the earliest periods are well adapted to draped costume, and present certain characteristics that have remained constant from the Old Kingdom to our own times.

The Egyptians used cloth woven from vegetable fibres, particularly flax which was grown in Egypt from ancient times. Linen offers the advantages of lightness, coolness and easy laundering, so that it is suitable for working clothes in a hot climate, and in particular, appealed to a people interested in personal grooming, a fact attested by the innumerable toilet articles and variety of perfumes and cosmetics that excavations have brought to light: boxes, cosmetic pots, mirrors, razors, etc.

Wool, the material preferred in most ancient countries of Asia, was considered impure by Egyptian religion, and although at least woollen cloaks were tolerated by the first century BC, they remained forbidden in temples and for burial.

Linen no doubt also owed much of its popularity to its natural whiteness. White was a sacred colour, and we know that Egyptian religion laid down rigorous rules in such matters. In art, we are struck by a uniformity of conception and treat-

118–21 All these figures wear the tight gown held over the shoulder by wide shoulder-straps and gathered over the breasts (plate 120). The white gowns worn by the offering-bearers (plates 119, 121) are covered with a net, no doubt made of multicoloured cut leather. Bead nets giving a similar effect have been found on mummies of the Saitic period

119 Women bearing offerings, from the tomb of Meket-re, Thebes. Wood and plaster. Eleventh dynasty.
New York, Metropolitan Museum. (Museum photo)

92

120 Ivory statuette of a woman. Early twelfth dynasty,
early second millennium BC. Paris, Louvre. (Photo Flammarion)

121 Woman bearing offerings, made of wood and plaster.
Eleventh dynasty. Paris, Louvre. (Photo Flammarion)

ment stemming from the artists' reluctance to change any traditional detail for fear of jeopardizing the well-being of those depicted.[3] Gold and colours were used most for girdles, scarves and jewels.

During the whole of the third millennium, linen weaving seems to have been carried out on horizontal looms. The vertical loom, which in any case did not completely supplant the earlier model, appeared only towards the second millennium. The pieces of cloth found on mummies are generally small in dimensions.

A characteristic of Egyptian costume was that it covered all the lower part of the body while leaving parts of the upper body bare – hence the use of light, transparent stuffs. Complete nakedness was another matter, and was considered a sign of lowly condition for anyone except children. Egyptian statuary has few unclad figures, for people of good families who allowed nakedness in their effigies would have run the risk of being confused with common people and losing caste in the after-life. Particularly in the statuary of Memphis, women are always clothed; occasionally young boys and men, free or slaves, are not, but this exception may have corresponded to some religious dictate.[4]

It was thanks to the conquests of Tuthmosis III that the art of weaving was perfected in Egypt. Numerous foreign weavers came to settle there: the name *Syrian* even became a synonym for weaver. It was this improvement in textile production, linked with the introduction of Asiatic styles, that brought about a change in Egyptian clothing. We can appreciate the progress when we study the textiles found in the tomb of Tutankhamen (Eighteenth dynasty).

The period of Ramesses (thirteenth–twelfth centuries BC) introduced the taste for light materials, finely pleated or slightly gathered. Egyptian painters of the New Kingdom rendered the transparency of women's garments by dimming, with a mixture of colours, the tint of the flesh seen through the material: modelling and the relief of folds were rendered by shading in white and black.[5]

We must not forget that it was an Egyptian artistic convention to mould the costume over the body in sculpture, and in painting to represent it as a sheath. The body is shown facing the spectator, but with head and limbs in profile. In reality the costumes were always loose and flowing, for ease of movement.

WOMEN'S COSTUME

Over thousands of years the few elements of Egyptian women's costume remained almost completely unchanged, modified only in one or two details.

One type of gown worn during the Old and Middle Kingdoms for almost fifteen centuries (c. 3200 –1500 BC) was composed of two separate pieces: a short, tight bodice with long, close-fitting sleeves, with openings back and front fastened by thin cords, and a wide skirt sewn to the bodice, with horizontal folds. Some bodies are decorated with narrow panels under the arms and along the sleeves.

Gowns of this type, recalling the robe worn by modern fellahin (*galabijeh*), are found represented in the tombs of the Fifth dynasty (Old Kingdom, 2563–2423 BC). We should remark at this point that fashions may be represented on monuments only 'with a delay and arbitrariness that are impossible to gauge', and that, on the other hand, some arrangements of clothing would still be reproduced by artists in periods when they had disappeared altogether from current wear or had become limited to specific occasions dictated by protocol.[6]

'Under the New Kingdom, wall-paintings furnish some examples of gowns with long, tight sleeves, decorated with braids along the hems and seams, worn generally by male Asiatic-type figures or by women of low social rank.'[7]

During the New Kingdom (1580–1090 BC) the tunic-gown or *calasiris* became more widespread; indeed, with an increase in luxury, it was worn as an outer garment over a loincloth (*shenti*). It was always made of very fine, light linen, diaphanous and pleated. Its edges were seamed, with slits for the head and arms, and a narrow cord served as girdle. The parallel horizontal pleats were probably obtained by starching with gum: 'the same preparation was also used for Ionian tunics, and we find a survival of this process even today in priests' surplices... We should note the existence of cloths with a waved, almost crimped appearance, which appear on Theban wall-paintings towards the period of the Tuthmoseid kings and are perhaps of Oriental origin.'[8]

The gown could be worn hanging loosely or swathed. In the former shape, it was quite narrow, a sort of sheath beginning below the throat and held on the shoulders by straps, sometimes narrow, at other times wide enough to cover the breasts. Among women of the common people, this gown resembled a loose smock of plain white or natural cloth, and was worn with a belt and snood of black cut-out leather or coloured beads. Women of rank chose coloured or golden straps, knotted on the collar-bones: the material could be saffron yellow or bright red, or decorated with a variety of designs in different colours, woven or appliquéd to imitate the plumage or wings of birds folded and crossed round the body, evoking the wings of Isis. Long ribbons of all colours were knotted round the waist, with the ends hanging down in front, during the Eighteenth dynasty (1520–1320 BC).

The swathed gown, worn during the reign of Tuthmosis III (1505–1480 BC), consisted of a large piece of pleated or striped muslin forming a short skirt tightly belted at the waist then wound over the chest, in the fashion of the *royal haïk* worn under the New Kingdom (*cf.* p. 97), but with less fullness and fewer turns round the body. The use of this swathed gown corresponded to the period when the Empire extended as far as northern Syria and the upper Euphrates, thus coming into contact with Asia. Egypt seems then to have welcomed styles of drapery and swathing that were less primitive than its own and related to Sumerian or Syrio-Phoenician modes.[9]

Contrary to what a superficial examination might suggest, the variety of ways in which female costume could be draped was very great;[10] it is impossible to give a detailed list here. A typical formula for one of these styles could lead us to expect a tunic, a scarf and a cloak,[11] and this is not out of the question; yet, as with the *royal haïk*, it is possible to obtain the same effect by draping, covering the legs and yet leaving them greater freedom of movement. In Greek and Roman times, we find gown and shawl swathed in a similar way.[12]

The classic shawl, as fine as Arachne's weaving and white or saffron-coloured, was worn by women to protect them from the coolness of the air and the heat of the sun. It lent itself to many combinations with the tunic or gown. When it was placed flat over the shoulders without draping, it became a ritual garment, religious and funerary, hiding the arms but leaving the hands free.

Servant-girls, such as flower-pickers, are represented naked; female musicians are clad in muslin gowns.

122–5 Examples of a light linen garment, more or less transparent, finely pleated and swathed several times round the body. In the fresco with musicians (plate 124), the small cones on top of the heads were probably made of perfumed grease which melted in the course of the feast. The vast cape-necklaces were perhaps edged with a row of lotus petals. The dancing-girls, like the slaves, are naked, wearing girdles. The realistic Saite torso (plate 123) shows the shawl knot on the chest, over the tunic

122   Woman at her toilet. Paris, Louvre. (Photo Giraudon)

123   Woman's torso draped in Grecian style, Saite statue of limestone. Paris, Louvre. (Photo Flammarion)

MALE COSTUME

Certain elements of Egyptian costume (gown, tunic, wig) are common to both sexes; others are reserved for men.

The loincloth (*shenti*)[13] is a long, straight piece of white cloth, similar to the zôna, the ancient Greek girdle, or the modern loincloth of Africa or India. Workers held it in place with a girdle as wide as the hand, with no ornament, in Asiatic style (plates 129–130).

With the reign of Tuthmosis IV (1425–1405 BC), the tunic with sleeves and pleated skirt (also worn by women) made their appearance. Under Amenophis IV (1405–1375 BC), the fringed panel that can sometimes be seen earlier in the opening of the skirt emerged to be worn outside, and progressively developed into the wide, triangular, pleated front-panel (plate 127) characteristic of the Nineteenth dynasty (1320–1200 BC).

The cloak of linen or, more often, of wool, swathed round the waist like a skirt, was in fact almost a double of the shenti, only longer; when it was made of linen the Greeks called it a *sindon*. It seems to have been worn only in a late period, after the New Kingdom.

HEAD-DRESSES AND ORNAMENTS

While men's heads were often shaved, women usually dressed their hair in coils or plaits, spiked with huge knobs of embossed gold (examples in the Leyden and Cairo Museums). When women wore wigs, they often allowed their own hair to show underneath; their wigs had braids falling to the breasts and attached by ribbons, or curled or waved hair.[14] We also find the hair dressed close to the head and decorated with flowers. Texts tell us of many different ways of dressing the hair.

The wig (which was common to both sexes, but which men seem to have used most often in religious feasts and ceremonies) could be in various styles. Under the Middle Kingdom (1580–1090 BC) it was short and square-cut; it was transformed under the Eighteenth dynasty, acquiring fringes and then lengthening at back and front until it became the classic type of Nineteenth

124 Wall-painting from the tomb of Neb-Amon, from Thebes. Eighteenth dynasty. British Museum, London. (Museum photo. Courtesy of the Trustees)

125 Inside of the back of the throne of Tutankhamen. Eighteenth dynasty, 1350–40 BC. Cairo Museum. (Photo Percheron)

dynasty wig.[15] To maintain their complex arrangement, wigs were placed on stands after wearing, to be dressed by slaves.

Light crowns could be placed on the hair, which was arranged in fringes or bands. In the Dashhur treasure, the diadems of the princesses Ita and Khnumet are made of gold wire scattered with minute florets or with a combination of lyre-shaped ornaments and buttons.

Both amulets and personal ornaments were believed to have beneficient powers; the goddess Hathor (plate 127) therefore holds out to the King her *menat* necklace imbued with a protective power (early Nineteenth dynasty). Decoration was sometimes purely symbolic.

Earrings and pendants, which appear on monuments of the Eighteenth dynasty (1580–1320 BC), are often enormous and heavy, perhaps under Asiatic influence;[16] the influence of Greek art only began to make itself felt at the end of the Saite period, in the fourth century BC.

For the common people necklaces were made of glass beads in the sacramental colours: lapis blue, turquoise, jasper red and yellow; for women of the higher classes, they were made of precious stones.

A very special ornament, the wide necklace of two or four rows of metal disks, was an invention of the Eighteenth dynasty, when expeditions into Asia brought plentiful supplies of gold into Egypt.

Worn on the bare throat or over the gown, it was threaded either on the ancient cloth neck-piece inherited from the austere styles of the Old Kingdom, or on the necklace: it could be decorated with tear-shaped pendants or even (as the Louvre statuette, plate 135) with a serrated border that cannot have been metalwork. We see, under Tuthmosis III (1505–1480 BC), young servant girls fastening cloth collars of this type round guests' necks, with a series of tongue-shaped ornaments of different colours. This accessory, reserved for special festive occasions, must have been made of lotus petals fixed to spangled or multi-coloured stuff; these would have been the 'flowers around the neck' mentioned in texts, which are sometimes curiously represented as blowing in the breeze.[17]

Bracelets, made of networks of beads or beaten gold, were worn in groups on the forearms. Inspired by the Asiatic reper-

tory of ornament, they used all the varieties of colour provided by lapis, turquoise and cornelian.

In the period of Tuthmosis IV, men are represented adorned with metal armlets in traditional shapes. This ornament, never worn by women, was the mark of royal favour, and disappeared under Amenophis IV.[18]

The head-dress commonly worn by men was made of a square of material, simple but thick and richly decorated with stripes, fitting closely round the temples and falling in square folds behind the ears. For the Pharaoh and the gods, it was knotted in a particular way and given the name *klaft*.

Egyptian women painted their eyes and lips (plate 122) and their finger- and toenails; only women of the middle classes were tattooed.[19]

FOOTWEAR

Footwear did not differ according to sex. Sandals in plaited leather had been worn from the earliest times. For priests they were made of papyrus. The main thong passed between the big second toe and joined other straps on the instep to form a stirrup and tie behind the heel. These sandals were treated with care, and most often were carried in the hand, to be put on on arriving at the destination.[20]

ROYAL COSTUME

The Pharaohs wore the same shenti as their subjects, but it was made of rich cloth and supported at the waist by different kinds of girdles. In primitive Egypt and even in the time of the Old Kingdom (fourth and third millennia), the sovereign was clad only in this simple loincloth with a lion's tail at the back indicating his chieftain's role.

From the Eighteenth dynasty (sixteenth century BC) princes appear clad in an elegant and elaborate costume to which the name *royal haïk* has been given. This was a large veil, similar to the Arab haïk, held only by one knot at the base of the neck; however, by means of a roll over one shoulder, then

ROYAL COSTUME
127–8 Akhenaton (128) wears the shenti loincloth, the traditional garment for men in all classes of society, here made of fine white cloth pleated at the front like the gown worn by Queen Nefertiti, rolled into the royal haïk which was knotted at the waist with the two ends hanging free. Both wear blue head-dresses with the protective serpent Ureus, and sandals with a thong passing between the toes. Seti I (127) wears the royal haïk swathed three times round the body; this was now worn as a male garment, with over it a triangular front-piece decorated with embroidery and goldsmith's work. Hathor has kept the narrow sheath, covered with beads and embroidery, with many jewels

127 Seti I and the Goddess Hathor,
painted relief.
Nineteenth dynasty.
Paris, Louvre.
(Photo Flammarion)

128 Akhenaton and
Nefertiti, painted relief.
Eighteenth dynasty.
Paris, Louvre.
(Photo P. J. Oxenaar)

round the hips and over the other shoulder, it gave the impression of a costume composed of a short kilt, a tunic with flaring sleeves and a flowing cloak.

Coloured girdles, multicoloured ribbons, ornaments and jewels of gold and enamel all enhanced the royal dignity of the Pharaohs, as did the tiered head-dresses symbolizing their power. This tiara or truncated conical cap, the *pschent*, which King Akhenaton (Amenophis IV) and Queen Nefertiti wear (plate 128), fitted very closely to the head, was white in Lower Egypt and red in Upper Egypt; none of the texts allows us to specify its material.

The discovery in 1922 of the tomb of Tutankhamen brought to light the remains of at least seven royal garments found in a chest, which showed the use of cloths embroidered with multicoloured glass beads and gold plates. Similar embroidery was seen in Mycenae. The finest of these garments is a gown decorated in front with a stirrup-cross, symbol of immortality.

This tomb also yielded gloves decorated with a plaited, scale-motif design, probably worn for archery, as well as several pairs of sandals embroidered with beads or decorated with designs in different coloured leathers.

Altogether, Egyptian royal costume shows a search for religious and temporal symbolism.

RELIGIOUS COSTUME

To judge from certain statues, priests wore a tunic with goffered sleeves, two superimposed skirts in similarly goffered material, one of which fell to ankle-level while the other, draped round the hips, showed a fringed panel through the front opening. A scarf was tied tightly round the hips and one of its ends fell down on the right.[21]

The most distinctive element of this costume is a leopard-skin thrown over the right shoulder, with the beast's head falling on the belt: a specifically priestly attribute, it seems. This fur appears to have been compulsory wear in certain ceremonies for the priests who represented the Pharaoh (plate 135).

On a bas-relief showing lily-gathering, a priest wears a cloak edged with regular notches; this border appears only towards

129–30 Sandal-makers, copies of wall-paintings. New York, Metropolitan Museum. (Museum photos)

COPTIC TUNIC

131 Talaris tunic woven in a single piece and decorated with multicol-oured woollen motifs. The arrangement of these motifs was dictated by certain rules: it could be in vertical bands, at the neck, or in squares on the knees, at the foot of the tunic and on the sleeves. This garment be-came widespread in Syria (cf. Dura Europos fresco, plate 95) and in the Byzantine Empire (cf. plate 151), and appears again in the liturgical dal-matic worn by deacons

SOURCES OF COPTIC TAPESTRIES

132–3 It is not possible to provide a definitive chronology of surviving pieces nor of the variety of influences shown in Coptic tapestries. Alexan-drian taste figured in some (plate 133), and in others, Byzantine natura-lism; Sassanian style with horsemen and hunting scenes is found in silks (plate 132). These various influences are closely intertwined

In battle the Pharaoh wore either a coat of cloth or leather trimmed with bone or metal scales, or a corslet decorated with bands of varying colours, for example linen ornamented with animal figures woven in cotton and gold thread. On his head he wore the tiara (*kepresh*), painted blue in Lower Egyptian paintings, often white and red in Upper Egypt.

'By combinations of textiles and various types of plates, the Egyptians created a sort of light armour, offering only moder-ate protection, in keeping with the primitive character of their weapons and well suited to the climate of the country.'[22]

the sixth century, in the Saite period, with the first Greek colonists, and remained in fashion until Roman times.

Lastly, priests are represented with broad necklines, but only in ceremonies not connected with funerary rites; they also wore square cut wigs.

It is possible that the cape which women wore undraped over their shoulders may have had a ritual significance. Only linen cloaks were permitted in the temples.

MILITARY COSTUME

Soldiers generally wore the white loincloth, but it was some-times coloured or striped, particularly for the troops of tribu-tary nations. During the Middle Kingdom, this loincloth was reinforced with a sort of leather apron, with a belt of coloured cloth or leather. The head was protected by a padded wig or a war-cap in thick cloth: the Egyptians had no helmets.

Officers wore a wide *calasiris* tunic, which during campaigns was completed with a sort of jacket or cuirass made of leather or linen.

The Shardana guard of Ramesses II (1298–1232 BC) was exceptional, with helmets, cuirasses and shields.

Egyptian Costume from the Third Century BC to the Sixth Century AD

After Egypt was conquered by Greece, her art reflected very varied influences in the Greco-Roman and Copto-Byzantine periods: Hellenistic and Alexandrian at first, Syrian and Sas-sanian later. We find motifs that can be traced back to the times of the Pharaohs alongside others borrowed from Chris-tian iconography. These multiple influences formed the art known as Coptic, which was at the origins of Byzantine art, and thus of early Christian art.

Egyptian costume, too, reflected the composite nature of this new civilization.

Our knowledge of this costume, from the beginning of Alexander's conquest to the eve of the Arab invasion, is due to the excavations carried out in Egypt by Maspero around Saqqara, in the Fayum and at Ashmin in about 1884, and by Gayet and Guimet at Antinoë from 1896 to 1905; in these burial grounds were discovered vestiges of garments, very varied in origin, and astonishingly well preserved, thanks to the dryness of the Egyptian soil.

Everyday and religious costume of the so-called Antinoë period included, for men, a shirt – also called a tunic – with

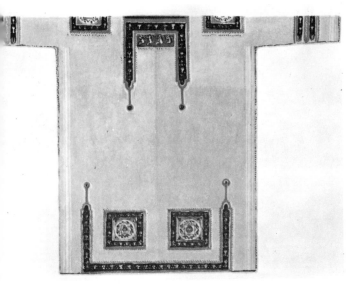

131 Yellow woollen tunic. Berlin Museum. (Museum photo)

132-3 Tapestry fragments from the decoration of Coptic tunics. Lyons, Musée Historique des Tissus. (Museum photos)

sleeves closed tightly at the wrists, leather or cloth leggings with embroidered or woven motifs, and a long, more or less draped cloak recalling the toga.

Women's clothing comprized the fine linen shift, with a high neck still trimmed with rich embroidery, the gown of natural wool, made of two widths of cloth joined with welted seams, with tight sleeves and often a square neckline with no slit on the chest. The rectangular frieze cloak had a roll framing the face and sometimes long sleeves. A net covered the hair.

Decorative elements were placed on the wool or linen tunic, at least before the reign of Justinian; the fineness of the stitching won the later sobriquet 'Gobelins' for these Coptic embroideries in wool or silk, executed directly on to the garment or prepared separately and then inset (plates 132-3). The subjects, drawn from Nilotic decoration or inspired by Syrian or Sassanian themes, were very varied; among them we find winged cupids, snakes playing in the Nile (an ancient Egyptian tradition), children playing in water (an Alexandrian motif) or gushing water.[23]

The profusion of these ornaments and figures seemed incompatible with Christian sobriety once Christianity had become the official religion; Bishop Asterius of Amaesa reproached his fourth-century compatriots for wearing scenes from the Holy Scriptures on their clothes rather than carrying them in their hearts.

Because of the skill of Coptic workers, the art of weaving represented one of the most flourishing industries of this period in Egypt. They also stimulated important progress in dyeing techniques, for the costumes present an extraordinary and increasing richness of colour. Linen was scarcely ever dyed, but the woollen cloths discovered have all retained their colours, allowing us to recognize the probable use of madder, or 'poor man's purple', indigo, which was not in use before Roman times, and an iron oxide producing tones of yellow.[24]

Sassanian influence on costume in the Antinoë period is typified by very high leggings, widening towards the top and probably fastened on the thigh, very probably worn outside the trousers; this influence is also noticeable in textiles and textile decoration, and sometimes in the cut of garments (plate 131).

134 Selkit, one of the guardian goddesses of the canopic chest of Tutankhamen. Eighteenth dynasty, 1350–1340 BC. Cairo Museum. (Photo Percheron)

135 The priests of Ptah wear roughly the ancient royal costume, with the frontal of coloured beads hanging from the girdle. The added baldrick and *sah* necklace are priestly emblems. The priest is dressed in a tunic and baldrick of panther skin, perhaps replaced by a piece of cloth or hide decorated with embroidery and cut-work. Several necklaces are worn over a cloth collar, whose lower band appears to be trimmed with lotus petals on a multi-coloured ground. An armlet is worn on the upper arm

The Sassanian contribution can be explained by the intermediary role played by Byzantium, which had adopted Eastern styles, at first for military uniform, then for court costume. No luxurious Byzantine costumes were found at Antinoë, but only some fourth and fifth century Persian costumes, brought by officers and officials.

Influences between Byzantium and Coptic Egypt were, in any case, mutual. On the one hand, some Coptic textiles are directly influenced by Byzantine art in their interpretation of the human figure, borrowings from the sacred repertory and the taste for striking or unusual colours; on the other, the Copts wove and embroidered a good proportion of the decorative pieces which the Byzantines used to enrich their costumes. Coptic art, which was at the origins of Byzantine art, may, by the intermediary of the latter, have contributed to the birth of Romanesque art in the West.[25]

These particular features of Egyptian costume were to disappear with the Arab invasions of AD 641, which broke all commercial links with Byzantium.

Chronology of Egypt

Prehistory	before 3000 BC
Thinite Period (First and Second dynasties)	3000 to 2800 BC
Old Kingdom (Third and Fourth dynasties)	2800 to 2420 BC
Late Old Kingdom and First Intermediate Period (Sixth to Eleventh dynasties)	2420 to 2065 BC
Middle Kingdom (Eleventh and Twelfth dynasties)	2065 to 1785 BC
Second Intermediate Period (Thirteenth to Seventeenth dynasties)	1785 to 1580 BC
New Kingdom (Eighteenth to Twentieth dynasties)	1580 to 1085 BC
Late Period (Twenty-first to Twenty-seventh dynasties)	1085 to 525 BC
Persian Domination (Twenty-eighth to Thirty-first dynasties)	525 to 333 BC

Adapted from E. Drioton and J. Vandier: *L'Egypte*

135 Second priest of Onouris. Eighteenth dynasty. Paris, Louvre. (Photo Flammarion)

Classical Costume in the Central Mediterranean

General Characteristics

Ancient Greek and Roman costume is essentially draped, and presents a traditional stability and permanence. While it received certain fashions over the centuries, it never underwent any major transformation.

Léon Heuzey, the pioneer of the study of classical costume, set forth with exemplary clarity its two basic principles: the first is that Classical costume has no form in itself, as it consisted of a simple rectangular piece of cloth woven in varying sizes according to its intended use – tunic or cloak – and the height of the customer, without differentiation between the sexes; the second is that this cloth is always draped, never shaped or cut, and was worn round the body in accordance with definite rules. Thus it was always fluid and 'live'.[26]

It is notable that we find no evidence in Classical times of tailors or dressmakers: the word itself barely exists in Greek or Latin. The *vestifex* made *vestes*, that is, pieces of cloth of various sizes.[27]

Heuzey brings out the persistent fidelity of the Greeks to simple, sharp, elementary forms, as well as their reserved attitude towards the fanciful, sumptuous textiles of the East, with leaf and flower patterns. The Romans looked for greater variety and richness.

The Greeks transposed into costume the dominant ideas of their architecture, particularly until the end of the fifth century BC. Thereafter, however, the state of the marriage market, and the reign of the courtesans, brought, with the over-riding importance attached to money, a passion for luxury and a relaxation of taste, which was expressed in an increasing receptivity to the foreign fashions which Rome was to accept shortly after.[28]

We should note the small number of types of costume in ancient Greece and Rome, but at the same time appreciate the very large number of draped arrangements that could be achieved with the same piece of cloth. As Heuzey has established, the incredible variety of forms is due entirely to the artistic imagination of the Greeks. Thus the drapery on the metopes of the Temple of Zeus at Olympia and that on the Parthenon metopes owe their differences only to the different personalities of the sculptors who gave these accounts.

Beside admirable representations of architectural drapery in the works of Polycleitus, Phidias and Praxiteles, the interpretations provided by Tanagra statuettes (fourth century) emphasize further not only, as L. Heuzey justly pointed out, the predominant role of the pictorial sense, but also the influence of Asiatic schools of sculpture, committed to mobility and lively exuberance. The Tanagra figurines' charming grace (plates 144, 146) must not lead us to forget that these popular productions capture transient fashions for us in all their detail and variety.

136 The Delphi Charioteer, bronze. *c.* 475 BC. Delphi Museum. (Photo Percheron)

137 Fragment of the Parthenon frieze. British Museum, London. (Museum photo. Courtesy of the Trustees)

138 Replica of a relief representing Orpheus, Eurydice and Mercury. Fifth century BC. Paris, Louvre. (Photo Flammarion)

139 Fragment of the Parthenon frieze: horsemen. c. 445 BC. British Museum, London. (Museum photo. Courtesy of the Trustees)

THE MALE LONG TUNIC

136 Here the long tunic, a ceremonial costume, is held in by bands so as not to hamper the charioteer's movements. A band also holds his hair

THE SLEEVED TUNIC

137 The short chiton with long narrow sleeves was of Oriental origin. A young slave is knotting his master's belt as he prepares to mount his horse

THE MALE CHITON

138 The tunic worn by men was a rectangle, first of linen, then of wool, originally without cutting or shaping, later with a seam at the side. It was fastened on both shoulders, and held at the waist by a double belt which caught up a fold of the material called the *kolpos*. Mercury wears strong boots, and Orpheus shin-guards. Both wear the chlamys, the short cloak fastened on the right shoulder, borrowed from military costume

THE HIMATION

139–41 Various examples of the way in which Greeks wrapped themselves in the himation, a large rectangle of cloth, often worn as an undergarment, but also sometimes worn alone – either for austerity or for economic reasons

FOREIGN INFLUENCES

The influences exercised on Classical costume in Greece and Italy, as in Asia previously, are too often classed as 'barbarian'; they emanate from peoples whose lives and customs were comparatively simple, living for the most part in desert or mountainous countries, rather than from genuinely backward, savage peoples.

The successive invasions from Central Asia gradually, in various periods, introduced to the coastal peoples the elements of special costumes adapted to particular ways of life, mountain or nomadic; recent archaeological discoveries have revealed an Asian civilization that, if not identical, was at least very advanced. The way of life and climate are often the primordial factors in the evolution of costume, far more than ethnic elements. Proof of this is found in the resemblance between the costumes of peoples in high plateaux and mountains, whether in Europe or in Asia Minor.

The elements imported from abroad, most often from Asia, were mainly the thick cloak, the hood (*lacerna* and *caracalla*), breeches held to the legs by criss-cross bands of linen or some other cloth, ornamental braid (*patagium* or *segmenta*) with geometric figures and later iconographical scenes. Towards the end of the second century AD, the *dalmatic* worn by the Emperor Commodius (AD 180 to 192), characterized by wide, flowing sleeves, came from the East to Rome. Gloves were also foreign imports, the product of cold climates, as were the Phrygian cap, originally Anatolian, the *petasus* or Grecian hat, the *cucullus* or cowl and the Gaulish *gallicae*.

Between Athens and Rome there was virtually no reciprocal influence in costume: Athens only influenced Roman costume indirectly, by agency of Imperial officials who, sent to the East where they dressed in Greek style, kept this costume on their return to Rome. Soldiers and certain foreign-born emperors contributed to the popularization in Rome of some of these costume elements brought from distant countries.

These importations increased with the commercial development of the Roman Empire which was the work of Augustus; over land pacified by Roman armies, and seas from which

Roman ships had swept the pirates, an increasing wave of exchanges spread. Roman traders reached Ireland, the coasts of the Baltic, the Chersonese and the Stone Tower of Tashkurgan as well as India and Ethiopia. But it was above all from the Orient – and this phenomenon was to be repeated later – that Greece and Rome drew new or more abundant materials and elements (linen, silk, jewels) and, above all, the taste for luxury and elegance that they transmitted in turn to the Western nations with the progress of their own civilization.

Greece

THE GEOGRAPHICAL AND HISTORICAL SETTING

The civilization of the countries of the Aegean, whose affinities with Mesopotamian and Egyptian civilizations need not be recalled again, shows in costume from the early third millennium some essential elements received from the original centre of Crete. Primitive weaving provided the cloth for the loincloths and short cloaks common to all prehistoric peoples.

We must suppose that the first Aryan migrations, which led to the invasion of Greece by the Achaeans in *c.* 2000 BC, stabilized the basic elements of primitive costume, and prevented it from evolving as it did in a Crete that was still sheltered from the barbarian requirements of the Achaean aristocracy and its feudal organization.

With the seventeenth century BC, when Crete conquered the Cyclades and Greece, certain styles from Knossos were adopted by women on the mainland.

In Greece, then, costume had remained stable, while in Knossos during the Middle Minoan and Late Minoan periods

142 Dancing girl, from Herculaneum. Naples, Museo Nazionale. (Photo Alfredo Foglia)

143 Archaic Kore, marble. Sixth century BC. Athens, Acropolis Museum. (Photo Percheron)

(approximately 2000 to 1400 BC) a relative security provided favourable conditions for extraordinary fashions in clothes.

Towards 1200 BC, the second wave of invasions, that of the Dorians from Illyria, expelled the Achaeans in their turn from Greece and from Crete, where they had been settled since 1400 BC. It is probable that here again the uprooting of Achaean or Mycenaean civilization, which was then transplanted to the shores of Asia Minor, must have had the effect of temporarily stabilizing costume, as with all forms of art already penetrated by Cretan influence. During more than four centuries, a new civilization was to take shape in Greece, and the elements of its former culture were only to be restored to it by Ionia.

The importance of Ionian costume in the study of the dress of mainland Greece comes, strange as this may appear, from the borrowings that Greek settlers in Asia Minor made from the natives of the coastal regions, and which they then transmitted to Greece. Their inability to extend their possessions inland, where they came up against hostile tribes, had led them to specialize in certain products, particularly textiles. So they took from their adversaries textiles and certain forms of clothing as well as techniques that had originated in Egypt and Mesopotamia.

This general development of Ionia affected mainland Greece in turn, both by stimulating a greater extension of the textile industry and by spurring the mainland Greeks to undertake their own exchanges with Asia Minor. There followed an emigration movement which installed colonies in Sicily, Southern Italy, Gaul, Egypt and Libya and on the shores of the Black Sea during the eighth and seventh centuries BC.

It is easier then, to understand how during the great period of its civilization, from the sixth century BC to the fourth, Greece owed some of the elements of its Classical costume to these currents of trade, to the riches amassed and the foreign techniques acquired as the result of this expansion.

We may also legitimately conclude that the confrontation of the unsophisticated costume of the Achaeans, and later of the Dorians, with the strange forms and vivid colours of the more refined Cretan styles adopted in Greece, gradually gave rise to the Classical costume of that country, and later of Rome.

MATERIALS AND COLOURS

Although little is known about the details of Dorian costume, we do know from Herodotus that it used woollen cloth. This served mainly for the wide cloak, the *himation*, and for its military derivative, the *chlamys*. In the time of Herodotus (fifth century BC) country people wove their own garments from the wool of their own sheep. This use of wool was evidently due to the Dorians' origins as mountain dwellers.

At the time of the great development of Greek industry, towards the middle of the first millennium, the handling of wool showed a considerable degree of specialization; at the end of the fifth century BC, the division of work between particular workers was widespread, some being assigned to shearing the animals, others to washing and carding, spinning and weaving, fulling and dyeing the wool.

Linen was introduced into Greece by the Ionians, who had received it from the Carians, who themselves had obtained it from Egypt by way of Palestine and Syria. One of Plato's characters tells us that it was also brought from Sicily.[29] Its fineness and lightness led to a curious system of pleating, consisting of

144, 146 Draped women, Tanagra figurines. Hellenistic period. Paris, Louvre. (Photos Flammarion)

145 Draped woman, Peloponnesian style. Sixth century BC. Paris, Louvre. (Photo Flammarion)

first setting the pleats by hand, then holding the material twisted and tied at either end for several hours; 'thus one can obtain a lively, springy pleat that harmonizes wonderfully well with the natural effect of drapery.' Imported by the piece or by the bale and sold in these forms by 'linen criers' in the streets, it was probably used to make the first tunics. As in other cases the term *chiton*, applied first to a certain textile, later came to designate a piece of clothing, whatever its material.

The use of wool kept most garments in a tonal range of off-whites, but ordinary people seem to have worn cloaks in dark colours, rust-reds or reddish browns according to Herodotus. An Athenian edict forbidding the wearing of this type of cloak in theatres or public places adds weight to the supposition.

However, vivid colours were not always excluded from Greek clothing, and we know from Pliny that the painter Polygnotus was the first to introduce, in women's costume, the brilliant colours which his contemporaries called *flowered colours*. A painted statue has retained traces of a green tunic.

Colour distinguished the costume of warriors, and according to paintings, the *chlamys* was generally decorated with bands of colour, either along the upper edges on the neck and shoulders, or down the side seams. For youths it was at first black, then latterly white.[30]

MALE COSTUME

The primitive type of Greek costume worn by men[31] was the rectangle of seamless cloth, forming a tunic when fastened on the left shoulder to leave the right arm free, and belted at the waist, or, when it was draped round the body, providing a cloak; this *exomis* was thus the same type of garment as the Mesopotamian and Indian shawl. Made at home with wool from the family flock, it still served as a blanket at night, as did the cloak of Homeric shepherds and warriors, the *chlaine*.

Usually the opening over the right thigh was enclosed by a few stitches and the shoulder was fastened, not by a pin, but with ribbons, which hung over the chest and back, or by some threads of the cloth, which formed natural, strong fastenings; or the two upper corners of the rectangle of cloth might simply be knotted together.

This primitive exomis worn by men gave the short, belted tunic, or *chiton*[32] which was 'essentially an undergarment closed down the side by a seam'. It may be that the original chiton was made of wool, if we are to believe Herodotus, and Aristophanes mentions a 'chiton of hairy wool'. The chiton could be pinned on the left shoulder, with one arm-opening on the left, or on both shoulders, in which case there were two arm-holes. The pins could be replaced by cords. A second belt, wider and worn on top of the first, made it possible to create a wide tuck of cloth between the two.

Without a belt, this tunic hung loosely and served as a night garment; it was also easy to slip a cuirass over it. Lengthened, the male tunic was worn as a ceremonial costume by important

147 Funerary stele of the warrior Ariston. Sixth century BC. Athens, National Museum. (Photo Alinari-Giraudon)

personages and, in festivities, by musicians and charioteers. It also replaced the short tunic in winter. Like the short tunic, it could be worn tucked up with an extra fold at the waist.

Finally, the chiton could sometimes be made of two pieces of cloth sewn together lengthwise. It could then be very narrow and fit more closely to the body. This form made it possible to add sleeves of varying lengths, worn widely from the fifth century on; the Parthenon friezes show youths and men wearing them (plate 137).

Another male garment developed from the early exomis: the cloak, made of a single large (six by nine feet) piece of cloth, called the *himation*, which was swathed round the body without fixed fastenings. While in many ways it resembled the original shawl, in Greece it differed by the absence of fringes. It was still called a *chlaine* (see above) although it was more elegant and made of finer woollen cloth.

This cloak could be worn alone (plate 141), baring the right shoulder and arm and the upper chest – either following the Spartan style or simply for reasons of economy, as in the case of Socrates; but in the first century BC the cloak worn without a tunic was so unfashionable as to provoke public mockery.[33] With this type of cloak, one could wrap oneself up to the chin, entirely covering the arms and hands and even the head, or use it folded at night as a blanket as in primitive times.

WOMEN'S COSTUME

Since the earliest times, women's costume had been formed of the primitive rectangle of cloth.

From the very precise information given by Herodotus, confirming Homer after several centuries, we know that the Dorians had a female costume known as 'Dorian', the Homeric *peplos*, which had formerly been the costume of all Greek women. In Athens this Dorian style retreated to make way for Ionian costume, represented by the linen tunic. According to Herodotus, this particular feature of Athenian women's costume arose as the consequence of the Aegina disaster (558 BC), for the Athenians then imposed Ionian costume on their women to punish them for having killed the only survivor of the battle by stabbing him with their fibulae.

The old peplos, a gown or outer garment worn by women, remained basically a sort of shawl with two fibulae, completely open down one side, usually the left; this *open peplos* was not normally belted at the waist. However Greek women, who attached great importance to personal modesty, seamed together the two free edges of the garment, instead of leaving them open on the thigh: this gave the *closed peplos*.

It was simple to fold up the edge of the garment, shortening it to waist-length, and use the flap to cover the head or to veil the face. And with or without a belt on the fold, the open or closed peplos lent itself to arrangements very similar to those of the tunic: it is easy to confuse it with the chiton. The 'Minerva with necklace' in the Louvre is represented in this garment.

The long, linen gown, Ionian in origin, also described as a tunic but properly called a chiton, consisted of a piece of cloth whose side edges were seamed together; a series of fibulae joined the upper edges on the shoulders and along the arms, leaving an opening for the head. The piece of cloth used could measure as much as nine feet wide; the chiton, with or without its extra fold (see above, *Male Costume*), was worn at the same time as the Dorian peplos.

148 Pericles, replica of an original by Kresilas. Second half fifth century BC. British Museum, London. (Museum photo. Courtesy of the Trustees)

149 Stele of a running hoplite. Athens, National Museum. (Photo Roger-Viollet)

109

Over the tunic women wore the male cloak, the *himation*, pinned on one shoulder, with the end falling down the front. Ionian costume also included a linen cloak, the *pharos*, and a long 'scarf' formed of a fold of the shawl arranged diagonally across the body. The shawl might either be pinned to form this scarf, or swathed round the body, or arranged to protect the head in cold weather.[34]

The belt was generally simple, but was gilded for courtesans.

HEAD-DRESSES AND FOOTWEAR

Greek women covered their heads either with a bulbous hat similar to the Lacedaemonian *caissia*, or with a hat like the modern head-dress of Nice, the *tholia*. This latter type of head-gear (plate 146) is often represented on Tanagra figurines.[35]

Sandals, worn by both sexes alike, were fastened in very varied ways, as we can see from the marble models that served to advertise ancient shoemakers. The straps were very light and elegant, leaving the foot almost bare; some were purple with piped edges, attached to a fleuron-shaped clasp elongated by short cords of plaited leather; others were simpler, with a fan-like spread of straps passing between the toes.

Soles were studded with nails. We know of a sandal from Lower Egypt, probably close to the type worn by the Greek courtesans of Alexandria, whose studs print the message 'follow me' on the ground.[36]

The Greeks scarcely ever wore the closed shoes with upturned toes found in the East.

MILITARY COSTUME

In military life, mounted and foot soldiers and youths in training wore the *chlamys* (plates 150–51), originally called the chlaine, which corresponded to the civilian *himation*. The term referred to the garment as well as to the material, a thick, warm woollen cloth made of a strong, tightly warped yarn.

The piece of cloth was rectangular in shape, narrower than the himation but as long. The Macedonians cut away the corners so that the lower edge of the cloak hung evenly.

The chlamys was fastened on the right or the left shoulder, or even on the back so as to cover both shoulders. It could be worn rolled round the left arm to parry blows.

From being a military garment, the chlamys fairly naturally became a royal vestment, with the dyework becoming more careful and the ornamentation richer under Oriental influence. Alexander wore purple, and Demetrius Poliorcetes a darker shade, with golden stars and signs of the zodiac.

The Greek helmet has been the subject of several studies.[37]

The Mycenaean helmet, which has been described as of leather with shaped metal plates, would most probably have been made of some plaited material, but not leather, which would have been too hot and heavy. If there appears to be some similarity between the Hallstatt helmets and those of Olympia, we must remember that there are three or four centuries separating Mycenaean civilization (1000 BC) from that of Hallstatt (600–500 BC). From its origins, the Greek helmet seems to have been different from that worn by the peoples of the Middle East, with its hemispherical crown, nose-guard and horse-hair crest. Cheek-guards are already mentioned in Homer. The helmet represented in the seventh century on black-

figure vases from Rhodes and Knossos developed from this type. In the fifth century, we see from red-figure vases that cheek-guards are winged, the nasal piece no longer exists and the front is reinforced by a projecting band. Certain bas-reliefs show helmets in the shape of the felt cap known as the 'Phrygian cap'

According to Herodotus, all nations owing allegiance to the Hellenes wore the Greek helmet at the beginning of the fifth century BC: Lydians, Carians, Cypriots and even Phoenicians. In fact, Cypriot terracottas show that both Assyrian and Greek helmets were worn.

Instead of helmets the Greeks sometimes wore the leather cap or *kyne* current among the lower classes and apparently of Boeotian origin.

Greek horsemen protected themselves with a sort of leather jerkin strengthened with bronze disks, shoulder pieces and leather leggings. For hoplites or heavy infantry, the cuirass was made of metal scales sewn or rivetted, while light troops wore woollen leggings and a tunic made of twilled, padded cloth held in at the waist by a bronze belt.

RELIGIOUS COSTUME

In Greece there was no specialized religious costume. In representations of religious ceremonies we note certain types of everyday garments worn by the figures exercizing priestly functions. Thus, on the Parthenon frieze, the High Priest holding up the goddess' peplos wears the ordinary long chiton; similarly, the young girls shown at the head of the Panathenaic procession are clad in the closed peplos.

THEATRICAL COSTUME

When the theatre of antiquity reached its definitive form, initially in Greece, its costume soon became fixed and codified.[38]

Tragic actors wore under their garments the appropriate padding, and also tall wigs, or at least tufts of hair stuck to their masks. The very thick-soled shoes struck the Romans as so characteristic of tragedy that their name (*cothurna*) came to designate the tragic genre itself.

Tragic kings and queens wore sleeved tunics reaching to their feet, sometimes with trains for women. These tunics were decorated with bands of very bright colours for happy characters, grey, green or blue for fugitives or luckless figures; characters in mourning were dressed in black. Over the chiton, performers wore a garment similar to a shawl, generally brightly coloured, or else a coarse cloak or even a goat-skin.

Gods and goddesses were distinguished by their insignia; seers were clad in a knitted woollen garment over the chiton; huntsmen rolled a purple shawl round their left arms.

The members of the chorus did not wear cothurnes and their chitons were shorter than those worn by actors: they also wore square or oblong shawls.

Slaves were given leather jackets and tight trousers, perhaps to indicate their Barbarian origins.

In Rome, in the *praetexta* tragedy whose subjects were drawn from Roman history, actors wore the *toga praetexta*. In the *palliata* or comedy genre whose action took place in Greece, they wore the *pallium*; and in the *togata*, whose scene was set in Italy, the toga.

THE CHLAMYS – MILITARY COSTUME

150–51   The short military cloak was decorated with vivid coloured embroidery. The soldier in plate 151 wears shoes which continue well up the leg and are very open, and a hat with a wide brim (*petasus*). The corners of the cloak worn by the young man in plate 150 have been cut to round them off

150   Tanagra figurine. Hellenistic period.
Paris, Louvre. (Photo Flammarion)

151   Cup by Pistoxenos, *c.* 500 BC. Paris, Louvre. (Photo Flammarion)

152   Young girls dancing, relief on a funerary urn from Chiusi. Late sixth-early fifth centuries BC. Chiusi Museum. (Photo Flammarion)

153   Statue of seated young man, terracotta from Cerveteri. Late seventh century BC. Rome, Museo dei Conservatori. (Photo Bulloz)

154   Bronze statuette discovered in the Vix tomb. Probably end of the sixth century BC. Châtillon-sur-Seine Museum. (Photo Chambon)

Etruria

ETRUSCAN CIVILIZATION

In Italy it is not until the second millennium that we see the rise of relatively advanced civilizations.

In the Copper Age, which marks an important stage in the development of the prehistoric peninsula, it seems that a certain linguistic unity existed round the Mediterranean. From this we can deduce that, before the second millennium, Italy was inhabited by groups who not only were attached to the primitive race of the entire Mediterranean basin, but who also wore their costume.

In this first civilization, the techniques of bronze make their appearance towards the middle of the second millennium, while the first waves of invaders brought with them the Indo-European languages. While bearing in mind that discussion is still open concerning the origins of the Etruscan people, it is possible to suppose that the enigmatic Etruscan migration from Asia into northern Italy lasted for centuries, either from the thirteenth to the eighth, according to some,[39] or, as others claim, from the ninth to the seventh. However, it is equally admissible to consider the Etruscans as the residue of an ancient pre-Indo-European ethnic stratum of the central and eastern Mediterranean.

Since either of these two theories of Etruscan origins may be correct, it is impossible at present to advance a definite opinion as to the origins of Etruscan costume. It could be of Eastern origin, or be a sophisticated survival from the primitive Mediterranean civilization, or it might be partly both.

We can do no more than observe, from objects discovered in excavations, a distant Mycenaean influence,[40] attested in Italy by the presence of bronze fibulae which indicate the use of draped costume. Between 750 and 700 BC, the period of the Villanovan civilization, Aegean influence showed itself principally in military costume. This was followed by an Orientalizing period between 700 and 575 BC, while Phoenician and Cypriot

155 Woman with offerings, bronze statuette from Monteguragazza. Early fifth century BC. Bologna, Museo Civico. (Museum photo)

FEMALE COSTUME, ORIENTALIZING PERIOD
152 The long, low-belted tunic, the cape covering girls' shoulders, the cloak with two tabs on the shoulders recalling the *kandys* of Persia, the Phrygian cap and shoes with upturned toes (see also plate 154) all show marked Oriental influences

MALE COSTUME, ORIENTALIZING PERIOD
153 The costume, Eastern-influenced like the head-dress, is composed of a long tunic and cloak fastened on the right shoulder by a square fibula. The engraved decoration suggests cloth, probably multicoloured

154 Although it was found in France, this statuette is undoubtedly of Etruscan origin. We see the shoes with upturned toes, the long tunic which here widens at the foot with the addition of a gathered panel, and the cloak worn over the head and falling to the calves

FEMALE COSTUME UNDER GREEK INFLUENCE
155, 162 The first figure wears a costume similar to that of the Ionic Khore on the Acropolis (plate 143), here translated rather heavily, whereas the material should be light and transparent.
Aphrodite (plate 162) wears a richly ornamented tutulus on her head; her embroidered tunic is fastened on the shoulders and the upper arms by lion-headed fibulae. The shoes with upturned toes are in the Etruscan tradition; elegant women wore them in red

156   Fresco from the Ruovo tomb. Fifth century BC. Naples, Museo Nazionale (Photo André Held)

156   The dancing girls wear the dark-coloured cloak decorated with bands of light colours and falling into a cape over the shoulders, a form derived from the original cloak of Mediterranean peoples

157   The draped, round-cut cloak, the embroidery on the tunic and cloak and the thick-soled shoes are typical Etruscan details

157   Bronze statuette of an Etruscan priest. Fifth century BC. Paris, Bibliothèque National, Cabinet des Médailles. (Photo Bib. Nat.)

GOLD JEWELLERY

158–61 The wealth of the Etruscans showed in their jewels, in which the combination of repoussé, filigree and granulated techniques gave an impression of refinement and variety. Decadence was rapid after the Orientalizing period, when the style became dry and impoverished

158 Gold bracelet. Mid-seventh century BC. Vatican Museum. (Photo Flammarion)

159 Gold disk fibula. Mid-seventh century BC. Vatican Museum. (Photo Flammarion)

160 Small necklace with gold pendant, the head of Acheloüs. Late sixth century BC. Paris, Louvre. (Photo Flammarion)

161 Gold fibula, typical male form. Seventh century BC.
Florence, Museo Archeologico. (Photo Flammarion)

162 Aphrodite, bronze statuette. Early fifth century BC.
Paris, Louvre. (Photo Flammarion)

influences were visible mainly until about 625 BC. During this period, from the seventh century BC to the fifth, we also see Etruscan civilization expand southwards in the peninsula; from the sixth century to the fourth it was to expand towards the plains of the Po and to the north, as the result of the growing strength of the Greek colonies in southern Asia and Sicily and the ascendancy of the kingdom of Carthage.

CIVILIAN COSTUME

The development of Etruscan costume corresponds to the two phases described above.

During the Orientalizing period, between 700 and 575 BC, when various influences, Daedalic Cretan and Peloponnesian, Phoenician and Cypriot, appeared in art, the principal elements of Etruscan costume resembled their equivalents in the same period in the Middle East.

Men and women represented in sculptures and bas-reliefs then wore tunic-gowns in varying lengths, with half-sleeves, fastened on the right shoulder with a rectangular fibula. Men were sometimes shown in long cloaks, while women wore short round capes or a sort of cloak reaching down to the back of the knees with two panels falling down in front (plates 152, 153): this cloak recalls the persian *kandys* whose sleeves fell from the shoulders. Men and women also tended to wear fairly wide belts.[41]

For the early fifth century, the paintings from the Triclinium Tomb in the Tarquinia necropolis, among the few coloured representations of Etruscan costume in existence, enable us to realize how far art was then subject to Greek influence; however, this seems less certain for costume. Adolescents are shown wearing the toga cut in a semi-circle, similar to the toga worn in Rome during the historical period,[42] which seems to have been taken from the Etruscans. The dark-coloured cloak, sometimes completed with a cape, worn by female figures seems clearly to derive from the original cloak of the Mediterranean peoples, which became the *tebenna* of the Etruscans.

On some Etruscan monuments we find representations of a low-cut shoe, with an upturned point (plates 152, 154), which must have been worn in very ancient periods in the north of Italy, from where it was presumably introduced into Rome: it should be compared with the full-cut Persian shoes of the sixth century BC which we can see on the red-booted *kore* in the Athens Museum.

On the other hand, the high laced shoe with upturned toe is reminiscent of the shoes worn by mountain dwellers in the Middle East; the shoes worn by the Greeks and Romans were always of the closed brodequin type, with round or pointed toes.

During the Ionic-Etruscan period of the sixth and early fifth centuries BC, male costume scarcely underwent any modification: the original long cloak became the short Etruscan toga, the *trabea* (plate 156), worn with the tunic, which kings draped elegantly over the left shoulder. This toga was decorated with sewn or embroidered motifs, and could also be painted or embroidered itself: it was copied by the Romans, who turned it into a more elaborate garment.[43]

In women's costume the development was much more noticeable: the tunic-gown apparently underwent the influence of softer, probably originally Ionian styles, and became lighter.[44] Thus we see very fine, short-sleeved chitons worn by the dancing-girls in the Lioness Tomb at Tarquinia. Some sculptures

163   The Mars of Todi. Early fourth century BC. Vatican Museum. (Photo Flammarion)

show gowns with decoration that appears to have been paint-ed.[45] Hair was often plaited, hanging down the back, or brought round over the chest, with the round cap or *tutulus*.[46] The flat-crowned, broad-brimmed *petasus* of Greek origin was the most widespread type of hat. We also see ribbons decorated with feathers worn in short hair. Fashionable women wore red shoes with pointed toes and covered their shoulders with a loose red cloak with revers.

In the fifth century we see certain changes: the tutulus dis-appeared, and pointed shoes were replaced by sandals. In the second century we note the use of slippers made of yellow leather or cloth.[47]

Objects from excavations and the reclining figures from Etruscan tombs show the great importance attached to personal ornament by the upper classes in Etruria. In the seventh cen-tury BC, for instance, economic prosperity and an Orientalizing refinement of luxury in dress were evident [48] in necklaces, pen-dants, decorated fibulae (plates 159, 161), bracelets (plate 158), rings and disk ear-rings, all revealing very advanced repoussé, filigree, engraved and granulated techniques. We should also note the wearing of several rings on the left hand, a style also seen in Cyprus and Spain, where the Phoenicians had perhaps first introduced the fashion.[49]

MILITARY COSTUME

Warriors are shown in short, tight trousers – *perizoma* – similar to those worn by Hittite hoplites (plate 164), and wear round helmets with neck- and cheek-guards.[50]

The main protective garment was a plated cuirass, worn over a short tunic, as can be seen from large fourth century Italic bronzes such as the Todi Mars (plate 163).[51]

RECIPROCAL INFLUENCES

It would be extremely interesting to undertake exhaustive research on Etruscan costume and in particular on the strong

117

164 Bronze statuette of a warrior, from Brolio. Seventh century BC. Florence, Museo Archeologico. (Photo Alinari)

164 He wears short, tight trunks, influenced by Crete, known as *perizoma*, and a bronze helmet with cheek- and neck-guard

Ionian influences in women's costume, which seems to derive far more directly than has been indicated from certain Hittite or Syriac styles.

Other astonishing resemblances, which until now have not been pointed out or studied, exist between Etruscan and Iberian costume: the short cape worn by Etruscan women in the first half of the fifth century BC is the same shape as that worn by Iberian men in sixth and fifth century bronzes. Etruscan warriors from the sixth century, and sixth and fifth century Iberian soldiers wear the same tight shorts or *perizoma* that can also be seen among the Hittites.

These similarities enable us to suppose that, through certain commercial relations, there was a penetration of Etruscan styles into Iberia at that period, as there had been from Ionia and the Middle East into Etruria. Cyprus and Crete had been the main stages in the spread of primitive civilization.

Rome

CIVILIAN COSTUME

The Romans wore a wide variety of costumes after the end of the Republic (we have very few documents for the preceding period). They distinguished between two types of garment: those which were slipped over the head (*indumenta*) – undergarments removed only for sleeping, as is still the case in the East – and those which were wrapped round the body (*amictus*). This division, based on function, corresponded to that made by the Greeks.

165 The master of the house, on the point of offering a sacrifice, indicates his priestly function by throwing over his head a fold of his wide toga with a band of purple woven into the cloth – the *toga praetexta*

165 Painting from the House of the Vetii, Pompeii. First century AD. (Photo Alfredo Foglia)

MEN'S COSTUME

The Indumenta

The *indumenta* comprised the *subligaculum* and the *tunica*. The *subligaculum*, or *licinium*, was a linen loincloth knotted at the waist, originally the only undergarment. Under the Empire, only athletes wore nothing else in public; workmen wore a tunic on top.

The sewn linen *tunica*, another version of the Greek *chiton* but given a name with a Semitic or Phoenician derivation, had come originally from the East, while the primitive woollen shawl woven by women from the wool of their own flocks bespeaks the mountain origins of the Hellenic people.

The tunic was introduced into Italy by the Greek colonists, and in Rome as in Greece it was worn chiefly by men. It was made of two pieces of linen or woollen cloth sewn together, slipped over the head and tied at the waist so that it was a little longer in front than behind, where it reached the knees; it was also the costume of the common people. When it had wide sleeves it was known as the *dalmatic*.

Under the Empire men wore two tunics, the *subucula* underneath and the *tunica exteriodum* on top; people who felt the cold might wear two under-tunics. Both outer and under tunics had short sleeves, and were worn with mitts – only under the Late Empire was the sleeve length increased without appearing incorrect. When the tunic was slit in front, a hood was often added. Under the name of *caracalla*, this outer tunic lengthened to ankle level at the beginning of the second century BC, to be worn throughout the Empire in the early fourth century AD.

Lastly, the *femoralia*, also called *feminalia* although apparently not worn by women, consisted of half-length trousers worn under the toga particularly by emperors in winter. They were adopted by soldiers from the second century on and entered civilian costume under Trajan (late first century).

The Amictus

The *amictus* was essentially the toga, a specifically Roman cloak during the Republic and in the early Empire: originally it was the only outer garment for both men and women, and at night it was spread over the bed to serve as a blanket.

Historians do not seem to have investigated when the Romans gave up their original cloak, made of a vast piece of cloth cut as the segment of a circle about eight feet in diameter, common to Greeks and Romans alike. They have generally contented themselves with explaining that 'while the Greeks remained faithful to this versatile early type, the Romans soon sought after a more complicated cut'. In the middle of the first century BC it was already cut in a semi-circle, as we learn from Denys of Halicarnassus; at that time it was said that the shape came originally from Etruria, but we know that it was also worn in Macedonia.

However, nobody seems to have thought of comparing it with the similar type of cloak found in most European countries, thereby pointing to its origin as the garment of mountain dwellers. The Gauls seem to have received it from the Celts, but it is also to be seen in the entire Mediterranean area.

The Romans took the short toga or *trabea* from the Etruscans; this seems to have been a rounded garment similar to the rounded Hellenic chlamys.

Among Romans during the early centuries, the toga was cut straight and could envelop both shoulders, wrapping the left hand against the chest and leaving only the right hand free.

During the last century of the Republic and at the beginning of the Empire the toga became extremely wide and complicated, especially when it served as a ceremonial garment.[52] It was difficult to drape oneself in it without the help of one's wife or a slave: in his treatise *De Pallio* Tertullian wrote, 'It is not a garment, but a burden.' It could easily be drawn over the head, in imitation of the Greek peplos, and its end, rolled round the left hand, served as protection in the brawls of the Forum.

The Romans gave the name *praetexta* to a toga which bore a band of purple woven into the cloth along its upper, straight edge, *prae-texta*, but never on the rounded edge which had to be shaped with scissors. We know that purple was considered a symbol of power: Roman laws, which strictly controlled etiquette, had reserved the *toga praetexta* (plate 165) for Curule magistrates and priests, offices which gave the bearer the right to the ivory chair. Tribunes could wear only the plain white

119

166 Shoemaker and ropemaker, bas-relief from Ostia.
Second century AD. Rome, Museo Nazionale.
(Photo Alinari-Giraudon)

167 Augustus. First century BC.
Paris, Louvre. (Photo Archives Photographiques)

toga, called *toga pura* or *toga virilis* because ordinary citizens were only allowed to wear it on reaching the age of political majority. Magistrates arranged their togas to obtain a band on the centre and left of their chests, formed of several folds of cloth showing the red edging of the *toga praetexta*. The edging along the bottom of the garment was more restrained here than in the Middle East: Julius Caesar attracted attention by wearing borders on the sleeves of his tunic.

In the ceremonial costumes imposed by Imperial edicts, triumphal magistrates wore a toga decorated with embroidery or palms, a mantle of gold and purple which formed part of the sacred costume of Jupiter on the Capitol or the Palatine. Various arrangements enabled the wearer to obtain subtle effects of slanting or crossed drapery, to which the bands added an imposing character.

For meals, the Romans wore the *synthesis*, which combined the simplicity of the tunic in its upper half with the fullness of the toga below. The true toga was used to dress a dead Roman on his funerary couch.

In the second century, Romans of the lower classes gave up wearing the large toga, whose cumbersome dimensions no longer suited the practical needs of everyday life. They preferred the *pallium*, imitating the Hellenic *himation*, or the Gaulish *saie*, both garments of the cloak type borrowed from the costume of neighbouring peoples.

The Romans added other more or less related garments to these various types, but it is difficult to assign definite names to the sculpted representations that have come down to us. There was the *paenula*, a sort of hooded blouse which was slipped over the head, somewhat like a *poncho*, and the *lacerna*, which some authors have identified as a long, draped scarf with openings for the arms, and others as a fairly wide cloak to be worn over the toga.

WOMEN'S COSTUME

Several garments were common to men and women, and it seems that their variety stemmed more from the diversity of

168 Aedile. Third century AD. Rome, Museo dei Conservatori. (Photo Alinari)

names applied to them than from any genuine differences.

The specifically feminine garment was the breast-band (*strophium* or *mamillare*) which was added to the fitted loincloth as an undergarment (plate 170).

The woollen *subucula*, worn next to the skin, and the *stola*, the long *talaris* gown reserved for matrons, generally with sleeves, lengthened by a pleated train (*insita*) corresponded to the male tunic and toga; the stola was held on the hips by a wide, flat belt called a *succincta* and below the breasts by another girdle, the *cingulum*.[53]

Noble Roman ladies wore a short tunic of luxurious silk, decorated with gold fringes. They covered this either with the half-sleeved linen *sapparum* (plate 171), which seems to have been a short outer garment, or with the *palla*, a large square or rectangular piece of cloth, folded lengthwise and held on each shoulder with a fibula. It seems that they also wore the *olicula*, a cape covering the upper arms. From the second century on, a silk scarf, a kerchief, a fan and a sunshade in fine weather completed the toilette of an elegant woman.

Among the lowest classes, men and women alike wore the *bardocucullus*, a cape whose origins were probably Illyrian, similar to the *paenula* of the wealthier members of society, but made of coarser stuff, with a hood and sleeves.

Foreign influences, and probably the importing of Oriental fashions led, during, the last centuries of the Republic, to the multiplication on textiles of the applied ornament known as *segmenta*: braid, fringes, embroideries of every sort, even representing figured scenes, particularly on clothing worn by women.

Materials and colour, rather than form, distinguished women's costume from men's. Instead of linen and wool, women preferred lighter, softer materials, cotton stuffs from India and, most of all, silks, which reached Rome by the land routes of the Empire or through Indian and, later, Egyptian traders. Dyers coloured them in light or dark blues, yellows or reds: Ovid recommended sea-green, azure blue or flesh pink.

Some special occasions demanded particular modifications to certain parts of the costume: on marriage the young woman,

169 Tiberius. Paris, Louvre. (Photo Giraudon)

UNDERGARMENTS

170 The astonishing clothes worn by the young women shown in these mosaics must be the garments mentioned in texts, the *strophium* and the *pagne*

FEMALE COSTUME

171 The woman is dressed in Greek style, with a chiton folded over at the top, fastened on the arms with fibulae and covered with a shawl, the *supparium*. Her hairstyle is still simple; on her feet she wears *soleae*

170 Mosaic from the Piazza Armerini villa, Sicily.
Third-fourth century AD. (Photo Scala)

171 Agrippina. Imperial period. Rome, Museo del Campidoglio. (Photo Anderson)

172　The Marriage of the Aldobrandi. Imperial period. Vatican Museum. (Photo Alinari)

173　Woman Initiate, painting from the Villa of the Mysteries, Pompeii. (Photo Alinari)

BRIDAL COSTUME

172　The bride, seated on the bed, wears the loose saffron cloak and the veil, *flammeum*, worn over six pads and hiding the brow

174　This fresco shows various ways of arranging the shawl and gives an idea of the rich colours and embroideries; hairstyles and jewels are very varied

174　Slave dressing a young girl's hair, painting from Herculaneum. Naples, Museo Nazionale. (Photo Alfredo Foglia)

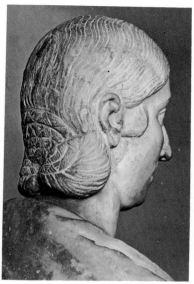

175–8 WOMEN'S HAIRSTYLES:
175 Bust of Plautilla. Imperial period. Paris, Louvre.

176 Roman lady. Third century. Paris, Louvre

177 Roman lady. Third century. Paris, Louvre

178 Head of Roman lady. Second century. Paris, Louvre.

who had dressed her hair in a red net the night before, put on first an unhemmed tunic held by a double-knotted woollen girdle, then a saffron cloak, sandals of the same colour and a metal necklace; on her head, which was protected by six false rolls, she placed an orange veil or *flammeum*, hiding the upper part of her face (plate 172), and a wreath of marjoram and verbena, later of myrtle and orange blossom. The Christian Church made this modest veil a permanent feature of bridal costume.

HAIR, HEAD-DRESSES AND ORNAMENTS

Dressing the hair constituted one of the main activities in a Roman woman's morning toilet. The old simplicity of a centre parting and chignon or the rolled plaits of Livia and Octavia had been abandoned under the Empire in favour of the more complicated curls and waves launched by Messalina. These arrangements, often enormous, required the work of a hair-dresser (*ornatrix*), who often figures in the Epigrams of Juvenal: it was she who adjusted false switches or whole wigs, dyed blonde or ebony black. Otherwise the Roman woman bound her hair with a simple red or purple band (*vitta*) or built it up into a conical shape or *tutulus*.

In the second century AD the Roman man too, on rising, gave up much of his time to his toilet; first, he gave himself over to his *tonsor*, who arranged his hair in imitation of the emperor's style, which was initially simple and careless but, after Hadrian's time, crimped with curling irons, even for those of mature age. He perfumed himself and painted his face, decorating it if need be with patches, which drew the mockery of some authors. He bathed in the evening rather than in the morning.

In Rome as in Greece, beards were worn over a long period; they first began to be shaved off in the second century BC, and this practice became general in the following century, although the fashion for beards returned with Hadrian.

People are shown bareheaded by convention, but never-theless we know of several types of headgear. The *galerus* was an ancient style of cap fitting closely to the head;[54] the *petasus*, Greek in origin, was sometimes made of straw and was adopted in the time of Augustus, particularly by women: senators were authorized to wear it at the Circus from the time of Caracalla. Its very wide brim could be raised or lowered, while the hat itself varied in shape and height. The Phrygian cap, which came originally from Anatolia, was little worn. To this list we must add for men, the *pileus*, a cap made of felt like those mentioned above, but differing from them in being round and brimless, encircling the head.

We have already seen that the *cucullus* was nothing more than a hood, sometimes independent and sometimes attached to the cape.

Jewels – necklaces, pendants, trinkets, bracelets, rings, arm-lets and anklets – were worn by both sexes, but most of all by women.

Among ornaments, particularly those worn by women, we must include belts inset with gold or silver and others, excep-tionally, set with crystal or ivory, Specimens have been found decorated with the most varied techniques: enamelled, damas-quined or plated. The *cingulum*, worn by men and women alike, served mainly to shorten the peplos or tunic.

This luxury in jewels corresponded to the periods of conquest and commercial expansion, during the last two centuries BC and the first two of the Christian era. While Rome was then an important manufacturing centre, Antioch and Alexandria rivalled her in the execution of fashionable ornaments in the Oriental taste; gradually her artisans introduced not only their techniques (filigree and granulation) but also their decorative motifs and habit of piling on precious stones.

The bestowal of gold rings as marks of distinction under the Empire was followed by the widespread and lavish wearing of jewelled rings by both men and women.

These tendencies towards luxury became more marked in the third and fourth centuries AD, with a predominance of Syrian styles represented by large gems: heavy pendants were hung

124

179   The actor is preparing to perform in a play whose action, situated in Greece, is said to be *palliata*: that is, performed in a wide *pallium*, worn over the chiton. The special part of his costume is the large mask which is being held out by a servant clad in a simple tunic

FOOTWEAR
180–82   These well-preserved examples show the suppleness of sandals cut out of a single piece of leather and held in place by numerous thongs

179   Bas-relief. Imperial period. Rome, Villa Albani. (Photo Alinari-Giraudon)

from necklaces made of massive cylindrical pieces, or ear-rings (*crotalia*) composed of three of four beads – criticized by Ovid – were hung with heavy pendants, while bracelets developed into multiple convolutions.

FOOTWEAR

There was little noticeable difference between the footwear of Greece and Rome, the latter having adopted the essentials of Athenian styles. Among both peoples there was a marked difference between right and left shoes. But whereas in Greece and the East, to go barefoot signified neither caste nor poverty, in Rome some types of footwear became the distinctive mark of social classes.

The most primitive and commonest model, worn in Rome over a long period, was the *carbatina* (plates 180–182), made, it seems, from a piece of ox-hide wrapped round the foot and laced on over the instep.

The usual outdoor shoe worn by men and women was the *calceus*, a low-cut shoe with a leather sole and thongs crossed tightly over the foot and up part of the leg; it was characteristic of the Roman citizen, for slaves were not allowed to wear it.

A light boot reaching to the calf and laced all its length was worn in the country; it was called the *pero* and was made of raw, natural hide. The *campagus* was derived from this, low and leaving a large part of the top of the foot bare.

In Rome, the *calceus senatorum* was probably black at first, then became white under the late Empire. Its leg was quite high, slit on the inside and fitted with a tongue. Its fastening was complicated, with criss-cross thongs and dangling tabs. The *muleus* with its red leather thongs was reserved for the Emperor.

The *gallicae*, originally from Gaul, which appeared in Rome in the last century of the Republic, seem to have been entirely closed boots, although some authors place them midway between the sandal and the shoe.

In the house, Romans simply wore sandals, either the *solea*, whose sole was fastened on by cords over the instep, or the

180–82   Roman sandals discovered in London. First century AD. The London Museum. (Museum photo)

183 The Emperor Trajan. Second century.
Paris, Louvre. (Photo Archives Photographiques)

184 Bas-relief from Trajan's Column. Second century AD.
Rome. (Photo Alinari-Giraudon)

183–4 Trajan wears a cuirass formed of two metal plates decorated with bas reliefs, protecting his torso, completed by leather tabs trimmed with metal over his shoulders and abdomen. His soldiers wear, over *femoralia* (long drawers), either the cuirass of several layers of leather straps, or a sort of short tunic with dentate scalloping at the hem. On their feet they wear a type of *calceus* covering the ankles. Helmets have smooth crowns, cheek-guards, neck-guards and hinged visors

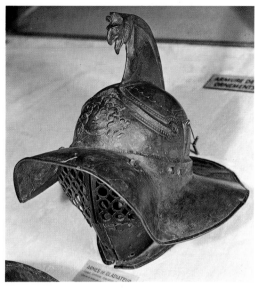

185–6 Gladiator's helmet and shin-guards decorated with Gorgon masks, from Herculaneum. Paris, Louvre. (Photo Flammarion)

crepida, which were leather espadrilles held on by a strap passing through eyelets, with a wide range of fastenings. Greek sandals were particularly fashionable.

Women most frequently wore the *soccus* indoors, a sort of fairly richly decorated slipper, or the *calceoli*, a term which seems to have been applied specially to shoes worn in the house.

All these types of footwear reached the ankle, and had flat soles. They might or might not have cords; when there were cords, these passed through slits made on the instep. The upper of women's shoes was not divided into two pieces, as was usual for men's footwear, and women's shoes were made in red, green or yellow as well as white.

Emperors wore shoes in the current styles, but made of richer materials. Gallienus launched the *campagus* and the *zancha*, the latter being a high leather boot fitting closely to the leg; it was supposed to have originated in Armenia or the Crimea, and indeed it may have been a style disseminated by the Scythians.

RELIGIOUS COSTUME

Religious costume was generally much the same as civilian costume, though the differences in function and ornament were more marked than in Greece.

While in Athens the priests presented themselves bareheaded to the gods, in Rome they veiled their faces during prayer and sacrifice with the free fold of their togas; Vestal Virgins wore an edged white *amictus* called a *suffibulum*, which they could wear over their heads and fasten at the throat. Some colleges of priests wore the high conical cap called the *tutulus*.

Among the Romans, fringes – which disgusted the Greeks – adorned the lower edges of the garment as a sign of religious dignity; the priests of Isis wore them.

MILITARY COSTUME

The toga worn during campaigns could also play a protective role. Roman soldiers wrapped it round their waists, fastening

187 Treading linen, painting from Pompeii. First century BC. Naples, Museo Nazionale. (Photo Alfredo Foglia)

188 Bas-relief from the Column of Marcus Aurelius. Rome. Imperial period. (Photo Anderson-Giraudon)

it firmly enough to wear it on horseback. One of these ways of wearing it acquired the name *toga gabiana*, and its tradition continued until the late Empire.

The legionaries wore garments of civilian type: the tunic and, occasionally, the cloak (*sagum* or *paenula*), forming a hood. They also adopted the *lacerna*, a short cloak of coarse wool reaching to the thighs, pinned at the top and frayed out along the lower edge. The *feminalia*, half-length tight trousers worn by Augustus, were worn by soldiers before civilians began to wear them.

Like Greek soldiers, the Romans wore sturdy boots (*caligae*) with thick soles and numerous leather thongs, reaching over the ankle but leaving the toes bare. Greaves (shin-guards), worn during the Empire in imitation of the Greek *cnemides*, were part of the centurions' ceremonial equipment.

The helmet, originally of bronze, then of iron, had a smooth crown, a neck-guard, and in some cases, a fixed or moveable visor and cheek-guards; sometimes there was a plume of feathers.

The cuirass took various shapes. In Republican times it might be made of layers of leather straps (plate 184), or of two separate plates of brass, or it might be a corselet of small metal metal plates. Under the Empire, it consisted of two large metal plates covering the chest, and long bands of steel over the shoulders and round the waist. The coat of mail worn by lance-bearers under the Republic was still worn during the Empire.

Finally, as distinguishing accoutrements soldiers had a broad belt of soft leather with a buckle, or of stiff leather with metal plates. An apron of leather thongs might be attached to this belt. Emperors and higher officers tied a sort of scarf round their waists as an emblem of command.

FOREIGN INFLUENCES
188 The Germans wear long and loose braies (or breeches), and fringed cloaks, as well as coats of mail

189–91 Bronze statuettes. Nuragic period. Rome, Museo Preistorico, and Cagliari Museum. (Photos Alinari-Giraudon)

Sardinia

Prehistoric Sardinia is still mysterious, and a variety of hypotheses have been advanced concerning the origins of its civilization, which has been attributed successively to Mesopotamia, Greece, the Aegean, and even to the Hittites. Immigrants from Liguria, North Africa, the Eastern Mediterranean and Iberia are said to have peopled the island gradually, but it seems that towards the end of the third millennium it was invaded by a mixed Cretan race.[55]

MALE AND FEMALE COSTUME

We have no indication of the way Sardinians dressed in the Neolithic period (2000 to 1500 BC): the few representations that have come down to us are all of naked figures. However, weaving must have been known, since spindle weights dating from this period have been found, though we have no fragments of cloth.[56]

For the Classical Nuragic period (eighth to sixth centuries BC), when the island was penetrated by Phoenician civilization and established trade links, bronze figurines represent men wearing loincloths that fit closely over the hips and generally, but not always, cover the upper thighs. These small bronzes suggest a variety of shapes of loincloth, presumably cut out of stiff materials or leather and then sewn. They sometimes have two short knee-length panels which may indicate two garments of different lengths, worn one on top of the other. This loincloth is fastened at the waist by a narrow belt or roll.[57]

During the cold seasons or at night, people wore thick woollen cloaks, perhaps fringed, or, according to Nymphodorus, made of goats' hair, similar to the Aegean *diphtera*. The Sardinians seem to have worn this with the hairy side inwards during the cold season and turned it the other way out in warm weather.

These bronzes always represent men and women barefoot, probably because of the religious significance attached to these statues, as in Crete (it was the custom to go barefoot in sanc-

tuaries). On the other hand, leggings often protect the legs. These could have been made of wool or of plaited, sewn cords or leather thongs.

For head-dresses men wore forward-tilted toques or a type of beret.

Chiefs wore, besides a short, narrow tunic, a thick rectangular or rounded cloak and a baldrick over the right shoulder. They tied a band of cloth over their brows.

Women were very simply dressed in a single piece of cloth tied round their hips. A statuette of a female musician (plate 195) shows a sort of jacket composed of vertical bands, perhaps woven into the cloth: a roll that can be seen round the legs may correspond to the foot of tight trousers or anklets. About ten figures show musicians and priestesses in very tight-fitting gowns (plates 192–3), no doubt sewn, without sleeves; there are no signs of fibulae or buttons. This gown includes three flounces, perhaps corresponding to three gowns worn on top of one another. Women's costume was completed with a sleeveless mantle; the head was normally left uncovered.[58]

Ornament in Sardinian costume may have played a role of protection against evil spirits, or have had some tribal significance, or else may have aimed simply at attraction.

Amulets in great numbers were placed in tombs, arranged over the body. They might be necklaces and pendants of bone or ivory, shells, fishbones or pierced bronze beads. Shellfish were associated with the idea of fertility from Palaeolithic times on. Some bracelets are of flint, very inferior to the Egyptian type; others are of copper, and a very few of bronze. Fibulae are rare, but some buttons have been found.

192–3 Bronze statuettes. Nuragic period. Rome, Museo Preistorico. (Photos Alinari-Giraudon)

FEMALE COSTUME
192–3, 195 Priestesses' costumes seem to have included three superimposed tunics, each one shorter than the one beneath, covered with a cloak. The female musician (plate 195) has a circular head-dress, a short, apparently quilted garment, and anklets

BATTLE COSTUME
194 Warriors wear a pleated pagne and a padded cuirass, leg-guards and horned helmets, examples of which were found throughout all Western Europe in the Bronze Age

MILITARY COSTUME

The bronze figurines in the Cagliari and Sassari Museums (plate 194) in Sardinia, like those in the Cabinet des Médailles of the Paris Bibliothèque Nationale, represent warriors – generally archers – clad in tunics that are generally short and fastened at the neck, sometimes vertically striped. Some of the figures have cloaks over their shoulders, while some archers wear long, pointed aprons [59] or a plastron of two wide bands forming a cuirass over the chest.[60]

Warriors wore either leather or cloth or, following a Cypriot model, bronze leggings, or else thongs wound round their legs. The helmet, whose shape varied considerably, was decorated with two horns or a plume at the front.

RELIGIOUS COSTUME

Numerous statuettes reveal the costume worn for religious ceremonies.

The High Priest – or chief assuming this function – was clad in a tight tunic and a cloak; priestesses (plates 192–3) wore light tunics, over which they had other, tight tunics showing the foot of the gown; the cape was sometimes worn in a curious way on only one side of the body, apparently the left.

Men wore a tunic and cloak made of sewn animal skins.

RECIPROCAL INFLUENCES

On the whole, at its origins Sardinian costume resembled that worn by the primitive peoples of the Mediterranean: ornaments are related to those found in North Africa, Sicily and southern France.

Even if, as we suppose, commercial links between Sardinia and the outside world were weak for a long time, contact was certainly established later on with the Eastern Mediterranean regions. The hypothesis according to which the eleventh century BC 'Shardana' came, like the Etruscans, originally from Asia Minor could explain certain analogies between Sardinian costume and that of Phoenicia or the Aegean during the first millennium; but it throws no light on the resemblances which representations, though few in number, allow us to glimpse with Iberian costume of the same period.

194 Bronze statuettes. Nuragic period. Cagliari Museum. (Museum photo)

195 Female musician, bronze statuette. Nuragic period. Rome, Museo Preistorico. (Museum photo)

196 Statuette of woman making offerings, from Despeñaperros. Fifth-fourth centuries BC. Madrid, Museo Arqueológico. (Photo Mas)

197 The Dama de Elche. Madrid, Prado. (Photo Giraudon)

The Iberian Peninsula

Situated as it is close to North Africa at the western end of the Mediterranean, the Iberian Peninsula provided the most natural route into Europe for influences from the east during the prehistoric period.[61]

Of the costume worn by the original Neolithic inhabitants we have only shell ornaments and stone buttons, some with stems, others conical and prismatic.[62]

The civilizations of Phoenicia, Crete, the Middle East, and those of Greece, Carthage, Etruria must definitely, making allowance for the hazards of primitive trade, have brought certain characteristics of the clothing indicated by Iberian bronzes after the tenth century BC.[63]

COSTUME

Particularly towards the sixth and fifth centuries, men wore a type of tight shorts, a short tunic like a singlet belted at the waist, and a short cape. Women wore long gowns, sometimes high-cut and fitted (plate 198), at other times leaving the left shoulder bare, decorated at the arm-holes and above the waist. Some wore capes with very pointed hoods, while others were enveloped from head to foot in a veil draped over the hair and edged with braid, and yet others wore cylindrical caps from which short veils hung down. Finally, an astonishing statue of a woman making an offering (plate 196) shows a very tall head-dress in the form of a pointed tiara, covered with a sort of cowl (like a *caracalla*) swathing her shoulders and open from the waist, lying in oblique folds over the chest: this arrangement shows only the oval of her face.

This type of clothing presents striking similarities of detail with costumes worn in other Mediterranean countries. The shorts worn by men recall those of Etruscan military costume, the *perizoma*, and also those of the Hittite heavy infantry. The short male cape is echoed in Etruria, and the hooded cape is also to be seen among the Scythians and on Gallo-Roman bronzes. The tall, tiara-shaped head-dress can be related to numerous conical caps of varying heights, examples of which are seen in Etruscan bronzes of the sixth century BC, in figures of Cretan goddesses from the second millennium, and in bronze statuettes of the Syrio-Hittite style from the second half of the second millennium BC.[64] The tall cylindrical cap can be related to that worn by the Hittites during the first millennium.

198 Bronze statuette from Collado de los Jardines. Fifth-fourth centuries BC. Madrid, Museo Arqueológico. (Museum photo)

199 Statuette of a woman with offerings, from El Cerro de los Santos. Fifth-fourth centuries BC. Madrid, Museo Arqueológico. (Photo Mas)

200 Statuette of a woman making offerings, from Despeñaperros. Madrid, Museo Arqueológico. (Photo Ramos)

RECIPROCAL INFLUENCES

These analogies permit us to suppose, until fuller research has been carried out, that the various streams of Mediterranean trade and civilization gave Iberia styles borrowed from Eastern and Central Mediterranean costume, perhaps as early as the second millennium, but more probably in the course of the first. The fragmentary nature of the evidence so far discovered suggests that they were introduced by small groups reaching Iberia either over land or by sea. This hypothesis fits in with what we know of Iberian trade relations during prehistoric times.[65]

Several of the Visigothic kings and queens of Leon depicted in the *Codex Aemilianensis* in the Escurial, Madrid (plate 201), are represented with a garment (long tunic or gown) with several flounces, recalling the style of Cretan gowns; however, it is difficult to conclude that Minoan styles had been introduced into Iberia and maintained there under Arab domination, and had then been driven into the northern region with the Visigothic kings of the tenth century. But we may suppose that these tiered garments were introduced into Spain during the Moslem occupation by merchants from Syria, where we know that the women wore skirts of this type, inspired by Cretan elegance.

201 *Codex Aemilianensis.*
Visigothic Manuscript. Madrid, Escurial Library

202 Dice players, mosaic from El Djem. Tunis, Bardo Museum. (Museum photo)

203 Punic woman from Masra. First century AD. Tunis, Bardo Museum. (Museum photo)

North Africa

During one-and-a-half millennia, the coastal lands of North Africa saw several successive civilizations, whether they were conquered by military forces or occupied administratively by foreigners: Phoenicians, Romans, Vandals, Byzantines and Arabs all introduced their customs and, to some extent their dress.[66]

When they were supplanted in the Eastern Mediterranean by Greek trade, the Phoenicians settled in North Africa and founded Carthage (814 BC). The new civilization that developed there retained the characteristics of its Eastern origins in its costume.

CARTHAGINIAN COSTUME

Like the Phoenicians, Carthaginian men dressed in the traditional clothing of the coastal peoples of the Middle East: a loose tunic, usually reaching to the feet, sometimes hanging freely, sometimes belted at the waist, and with long sleeves, or more rarely, short sleeves which left the forearms bare.

Men generally wore no other garment over this tunic; but Tertullian indicates that in cold weather they wore the large, rectangular cloak, the primitive type of *pallium*, fastening it with fibulae on the shoulders and letting it hang on either side.

On a stele in the Carthage Museum we see a man, probably a traveller or a country dweller, clad in a tunic reaching to his knees and a short cloak fastened on the shoulder. A sort of cape, formed of several parallel bands one above the other, seems to have been worn occasionally by both sexes.

As in Asia, the male head-dress remained the conical cap or the round felt or cloth skullcap.

Women's costume reveals a pronounced Cretan influence. In the second half of the third century BC, at the time of the Punic Wars, Carthaginian women of the wealthier classes probably dressed in Greek styles, in the long, fitted linen tunic,

202-3 Carthaginian women appear to have worn a sort of Greek peplos, probably completed by a sort of cape (plate 203) until the Christian era, while with men, the ancient Punic tunic only latterly showed Roman influence (plate 202)

fastened above the arm-holes with fibulae, and for outdoor wear, the *himation*.

Men were bearded and wore their hair cut short.

A characteristic Carthaginian ornament is the nose-ring worn by men and women; we know also of their taste for necklaces made of glass beads.

Priests wore a special costume, at least for ceremonies; it was often purple, with narrow tabs. They also wore flowing linen robes, and caps on their heads.

COSTUME AFTER THE ROMAN OCCUPATION

The victorious Romans do not seem to have made much impression on the basically Eastern style of costume which made the Carthaginians instantly recognizable in Italy and Greece. Probably only people in positions of authority assimilated by the conquest wore Classical costume. It does not seem that the Empire's auxiliary troops – including the Pannonians – who were stationed in North Africa brought any characteristics of their military dress, any more than did Genseric and his Vandals, whose arrival in AD 429-30 marked the end of the Romanization of these countries.

The rule of Byzantium (AD 534) only affected the coast and we cannot say that native costume, with the exception of that worn by members of the administration, was influenced by that of the Eastern Empire.

As with Egypt, the Arab invasion of North Africa in AD 647, followed by the capture of Carthage fifty years later (698), was to cause profound modifications in costume.

Notes

1 Pendlebury, *passim.*
2 Bénédite, p. 32.
3 Maspero, pp. 303–309.
4 *Ibid.*, pp. 304, 79.
5 Bénédite, p. 40.
6 J. Heuzey, *Gazette des Beaux-Arts*, p. 22.
7 L. and J. Heuzey, p. 119, p. 13, note.
8 *Ibid.*, p. 15, note 119.
9 J. Heuzey, *Gazette des Beaux-Arts*, pp. 21–34. Cf. p. 17.
10 Bénédite, p. 33.
11 Cf. certain statues (Queen Nefertiti, Luxor). L. and J. Heuzey give a perfect explanation of the way this costume is arranged.
12 J. Heuzey, *Gazette des Beaux-Arts*, pp. 26–28.
13 This term has often been applied to the royal loincloth. For the arrangement of the shenti, cf. L.Heuzey and L. and J. Heuzey.
14 Maspero, figs. 325, 326.
15 Drioton, p. 113ff.
16 Maspero, figs. 404–406.
17 Drioton, *passim.*
18 *Ibid.*
19 Capart, p. 70.
20 Montet, ch. IV.
21 Drioton, p. 113ff.
22 L. and J. Heuzey, p. 25.
23 Cf. the numerous anthoritative publications of R. Pfister on this subject.
24 Pfister, *passim.*
25 Vandier, *passim;* d'Hennezel, ch. I.
26 L. Heuzey, pp. 1–36.
27 Chapot, pp. 37–66.
28 Glotz, pp. 345, 365.
29 L. Heuzey, p. 169.
30 *Ibid.*, pp. 18, 199, 203.
31 Chaineux, *passim.*
32 From the Aramaean 'kitush'.
33 L. Heuzey, pp. 93–94.
34. J. Heuzey, *passim;* L. Heuzey, pp. 220–225.
35 L. Heuzey, p. 134.
36 *Ibid., Chaussure antique*, p. 35.
37 L. Heuzey, *Casque*, p. 145; Benton, pp. 78–82; Reinach, *passim.*
38 Gow and Reinach, pp. 218, 220.
39 Demangle, p. 92.
40 Bloch, pp. 8–10, figs. 3, 4 (fibulae with engraved decoration).
41 *Exp. Art. Etr.*, No. 7, 11, 14, 20, 23, 75, 415.
42 L. Heuzey, p. 231, fig. 120.
43 Richardson, pp. 125–135.
44 Bloch, fig. 5 (gown with collar and tiered bands cut in swags, cap tightly covering plaited hair).
45 Pallotino, p. 47.
46 *Exp. Art. Etr.*, No. 224.
47 Pallotino, p. 121.
48 *Exp. Art. Etr.*, No. 92, 93, 104, 112.
49 L. Heuzey, *Stat. esp.*, *passim.*
50 *Exp. Art. Etr.*, No. 27, 74, 221.
51 *Ibid.*, No. 231.
52 L. Heuzey, p. 237ff., who carried out its reconstruction with materials eighteen feet long and six feet wide.
53 Rich, p. 604.
54 Term referring to wigs of false hair and the hairstyle of athletes.
55 Childe, p. 225.
56 Zervos, *passim.*
57 Cf. Sumerian and Cretan costume.
58 *Exp. Bronzes Ant. Sard.*, No. 70 (woman draped in cloak, with pointed hat).
59 *Ibid.*, No 68 (Oriental feature).
60 *Ibid.*, No 102. The cuirasses may have been made of cloth or sheepskin.
61 Pidal, Book I, vol. III, figs. 316ff.
62 Childe, pp. 296, 298.
63 Pidal, figs, 316ff; Paris, *passim.*
64 L. and J. Heuzey, plate IV. Cf. Dura Europos frescos (Damascus Museum).
65 L. Heuzey, *Stat. esp.*, pp. 95–114: Bernis Madrazo, *passim* and p. 60, No. 11.
66 Gsell, IV, pp. 184–188.

Bibliography

GENERAL

Chanoine Drioton: 'Un Deuxième prophète...' in *Mélanges Picot*.
G. Maspero: *Egypte (Ars Una)*, 1922.
J. D. B. Pendlebury: *Les Fouilles de Tell-el-Amarna et l'époque Amarnienne*, 1936.
J. Capart: *La Beauté égyptienne*, Brussels, 1949.
P. Montet: *La Vie quotidienne en Egypte*, 1946.
J. Vandier: *Les Antiquités égyptiennes au Musée du Louvre*, 1948.
G. Glotz: *La Cité grecque*, 1953.
S. Benton: *Annual of the British School in Athens*, 1939–40.
J. Gow and S. Reinach: *Minerva*, 1905.
R. Bloch: *L'Art et la civilisation étrusques*, 1955.
Catalogue: *Exposition d'Art étrusque*, 1955.
E. Hill Richardson: 'An Archaic Libation-Bearer', in *Art Quarterly*, Summer, 1954.
Massimo Pallotino; *L'Art des Etrusques*, 1955.
— *La Civilisation étrusque*, 1950.
— *La Peinture étrusque*, 1952.
L. Heuzey: *Statues espagnoles de style gréco-phénicien*, vol. II, 1888.
Christian Zervos: *La Civilisation de la Sardaigne*, 1956.
Catalogue: *Exposition de bronzes antiques de la Sardaigne*, 1954.
R. Menendez Pidal: *Historia de España*, Book I, vol. I, 1954.
Pierre Paris: *Essai sur l'art et l'industrie de l'Espagne primitive*, 1903.
G. Gsell: *Histoire ancienne de l'Afrique du Nord*. vol. IV, 1913.

COSTUME

R. de Vaux: 'Sur le voile des femmes dans l'Orient ancien', in *Revue Biblique*, 1935.
J. Heuzey: 'Le Costume des femmes dans l'ancienne Egypte', in *Gazette des Beaux-Arts*, July-August, 1936.
L. and J. Heuzey: 'Le Costume oriental dans l'Antiquité', in *Gazette des Beaux-Arts*, September-October, 1926.
H. Seyrig: 'Costumes et armes iraniens à Palmyre', in *Syria*, 1937.
V. Chapot: 'Propos sur la toge', in *Mem. Soc. Antiq. de France*, 1937.
Lilian M. Wilson, *The Roman Toga*, Baltimore, 1924.
J. Heuzey: 'Le Costume féminin en Grèce à l'époque archaïque', in *Gazette des Beaux-Arts*, March 1938.
D. Chaineux: 'Le Costume préhellénique', in *Mem. Acad. Inscr. et Belles-Lettres*, 1908.
L. Heuzey: 'Une Chaussure antique à inscription grecque', in *Mem. Soc. Antiq. de France*, 1877.
L. Heuzey: 'Sur un petit vase en forme de casque', in *Gaz. Arch.*, 1877.
S. Reinach: 'Casques mycéniens et illyriens', in *Amalthee*, 1930–1931.
C. Bernis-Madrazo: *Indumentaria medieval española*, Madrid, 1956.

TEXTILES

R. Pfister: 'La Décoration des étoffes d'Antinoë', in *Revue des Arts Asiatiques*, 1928, 1932, 1934.
— *Textiles de Palmyre*, 1934.
H. D'Hennezel: *Pour comprendre les tissus d'art*, 1930.
A. Gayet: *Etoffes d'Antinoë*, 1904.
O. Wulff and W. Volback: *Spätantike und Koptische Stoffe aus ägyptischen Grabfunden*, Berlin, 1926.

Chapter V

Europe from the Fifth Century BC to the Twelfth Century AD

The Peoples of Northern and Central Europe

The La Tène Civilization and the First Centuries of the Christian Era

Like Asia, Europe was affected from the earliest times by incessant migratory movements. It is as difficult to establish the various directions of these movements as to determine the original homelands of the peoples involved; it is even more problematical to determine what effects these movements had on costume in Central and Western Europe from the La Tène period until the great invasions of the fifth century AD.

'An exodus, in prehistoric times, of the ancestors of the Germans towards Scandinavia seems very probable: the appearance of a German vanguard in the Pontic region in the second century BC, the exodus from Scandinavia and massive appearance of the Goths in the same region in the third century AD are certain.'[1] If we could ascertain what were the main features of the costume of the various peoples living in this immense region during this long period, we should be able to relate them to those later found in the Merovingian and Carolingian periods, when the wave of invasions came to a halt and Charlemagne tried to weld the peoples juxtaposed in his empire into a political unit.

In the last centuries before the Christian era, Germanic tribes from Scandinavia and Denmark forced back the peoples between the Elbe and the Oder, the Saale and the Vistula, and in the first century AD settled in the entire German territory. Further south, in Central Europe, the Illyrians were scattered between the Baltic and the Adriatic, but were concentrated mainly in the Eastern Alps. To the east, between the Vistula and the Dniepr, we find the original habitat of the Slavs, then known as the Vanedes, who were linked with the Scythians from the eighth century BC. Lastly, in west and south-west Germany, in the triangle between Cologne, lower Bohemia and Bavaria, the advanced civilization of the Celts set them apart from these nomadic peoples.

204 Hunting god from Mont Saint-Jean (Sarthe).
Second century AD.
Paris, Musée des Antiquités Nationales. (Photo Flammarion)

205 The toilette. Third century AD. Trier Museum. (Photo Flammarion)

206 Treading and shaving cloth. Third-fourth centuries AD. Sens Museum. (Photo A. Boivin)

207 Daniel in the Lions' Den, sarcophagus from Charenton-sur-Cher, France. Sixth-seventh centuries AD. Bourges Museum

When, from 1100 BC to the fifth century AD, the Celts began their broad expansion towards Western Europe, they seem to have split into two groups, one of which, the Goidels, certainly moved from north-west Germany (Hanover and Westphalia) to Great Britain and Ireland, while the other, the Brittons, advanced into Gaul, Iberia and Liguria. In the fifth century AD the Celts turned towards the east and, penetrating the territory of the Illyrians, who were forced back to the Adriatic, passed down either side of the Alps into the lower valley of the Danube; they were accompanied by Germans from the north, themselves replaced in their original regions by other Germans from Scandinavia.

We know that in the course of their advance, the Celts came into conflict with the Romans at Rome in 300 BC, occupied the valley of the Po and were forced out of Milan only in 222 BC. Some Celtic and Germanic tribes reached the shores of Pontus Euxinus and founded a kingdom there; others arrived in Asia Minor and created a Galatic state. But towards the middle of the second century BC, under the onslaught of the Huns and other Asiatic peoples, the Eastern Celts moved back westwards towards Gaul.

In the middle of this general post of migratory movements, the La Tène civilization finally imposed itself over the whole of this considerable zone. This civilization took shape during the Hallstatt period (900 to 500 BC) during which we find the first use of iron in Europe. In the great mingling of nomadic peoples which then took place – Goths, Slavs, Germans, Celts, Illyrians – costume was essentially that of the advance guard of the immense reserve of nomads spread out to the north of the Alpine-Himalayan fold, from the Atlantic to the Gobi Desert.

The Celts and their Costume

We have little precise knowledge of the costume worn by the Celts, who were at the western edge of this expansion area.

While in Scandinavia and Jutland tombs have revealed many curious woollen costumes for men and women, in Gaul neither tombs nor lake-dwellings have yielded clothing fragments of the Bronze Age. It seems, however, that from the middle of the Hallstatt period the side-seamed tunic and the cloak constituted its main elements. At that time Celtic costume was not differentiated from the general primitive costume of Northern Europe, and we can reasonably suppose that it was mainly as the result of their contacts with the Scythians and Persians that those Celtic tribes who advanced down the lower Danube and to the east came to know the trouser style and adopt it, probably in the third century BC. When they retreated westwards in the second century BC, they must have spread this garment widely in Germany and Gaul. Although d'Arbois de Jubainville claims that the garment originated with the Persians, who then passed it on to the Scythians, it seems that the reverse took place.[2]

INFLUENCES

In the jewels and ornaments so far discovered (bracelets, rings, torques, ear pendants, pins, fibulae, belts and buttons), specimens from the First Hallstatt period (900 to 700 BC) already show the influence of the Italic peoples: by then the fibula had replaced the pin for fastening the cloak. Later, in the Second Hallstatt period (700 to 500 BC), a close link with Etruscan art is apparent. Through the intermediary of the Etruscans and of those tribes which had come into contact with the Scythians on the lower Danube, numerous European ornaments of this period have elements borrowed from the Scytho-Sarmatian and Siberian Steppe figurative repertory, and others from the art of the Near East.

It was not only in Central Europe that ornaments showed Mediterranean or Asiatic influences in the last years before the Christian era: the northern Germans, of whom the Scandinavians were the last representatives, seem also to have received models from the south for their jewels. Later, when the Church made lavish use of gold and metalwork, the Scandinavians

136

208–9 Children (?) in cowled cloaks. Second-fifth centuries AD. Paris, Musée des Antiquités Nationales. (Photos Flammarion)

adopted models that had already passed through Roman hands. But it must be remembered that for all the Germanic peoples (Franks and Alemans in the west, Visigoths in the south, Scandinavians to the north), the fibulae – important for archaeological dating and classification – originate among the Goths of southern Russia.[4]

These foreign decorative contributions later left a clear imprint on costume in the Merovingian period, when the amalgamation of the European peoples began to take effect. At that period, industry and commerce began to revive, though still in the framework of a limited economy. On the foundation of ancestral customs, a new civilization was to create the archetypes of a new form of clothing, deriving from both Greece and Rome.

Gaulish costume[5] from before the Roman conquest, like Celtic costume, and the Central and Western European costume described above, was designed principally to protect the body from inclement weather without restricting movement.

After the Roman conquest the style of Gallo-Roman costume remained pronouncedly Gaulish, since the Roman and Italic occupiers promptly adopted its main elements, which were perfectly suited to the climate: the slightly-shaped *tunic*, longer than its Roman equivalent, the *cloak* and *breeches*.

Gaulish and Gallo-Roman Costume

CIVILIAN COSTUME

Worn by men and women alike,[6] the semi-fitted tunic with long or short sleeves was slipped over the head, and worn long with a belt, or short and unbelted, perhaps according to the sex of the wearer. It was the basic element of primitive costume adopted in the Nordic and Mediterranean world. On some sculptures it appears to be pleated, which indicates at least partial fullness. Decorated with fringes or toothed work along the lower hem, lined with wool or fur which showed round the edges, it generally had tight, wrist-length sleeves. The neck was trimmed with a sort of roll resembling the turtle-neck of modern sweaters. Tunics could be worn singly or two at a time, in which case the longer one served as an undergarment. Another garment worn by both sexes, probably for similar uses, was a sort of long-sleeved vest with broad, parallel bands.

Derived from the tunic, the shirt or chemise worn only as body linen appears in the fourth century AD under the name of *camisia* (a word of Celtic, or rather, Germanic origin) and supplants the loincloth originally worn under the tunic.

The outer garment, again common to both sexes, was made of a piece of coarse wool and existed in several forms. The *saie* or *sagum*, a short garment covering the shoulders and fastened on the chest, and the *rheno*, a wide cloak generally made of reindeer hide, were specifically Gaulish or Frankish. Latin imported models were related to the *paenula*, a sort of fairly long, hooded cape, and the *lacerna*, a full cloak worn over the tunic, both cut in a circle. The *cucullus* was a hood, and the *bardocucullus*[7] was a cloak with attached hood. Another type of hooded cape, with slits for the arms, went by the name of *birra*, but it seems to have been differentiated only by its material, a stiff, long-haired stuff.

The Gaulish forms of the bardocucullus enjoyed a great vogue among the Romans and, under the name of *caracella*, gradually penetrated throughout the Empire.[8]

Gaulish women wore as cloaks either a long, swathed shawl, or, after the conquest, Roman-style draperies fastened at the shoulders.

The most characteristic piece of Gaulish male costume were the *breeches*,[9] long, wide-seated trousers, neither tight nor loose, but full enough to make folds round the legs and narrow enough to resemble breeches rather than modern trousers. Some documents lead us to suppose that the Gauls wore tighter, even skin-tight breeches after the Roman conquest, whereas the peoples to the north of the Danube kept a degree of fullness. Breeches themselves – perfectly depicted on a bronze panel discovered at Alesia, representing a dead Gaul – opened in

210 Funerary stele of a blacksmith. Third-fourth centuries AD. Sens Museum. (Photo A. Boivin)

front, reached to the ankle and were sometimes fastened above the shoes. Polybius mentions them among the Gauls in 325 BC, under the Greek name *paison*, for Persian trousers. They are represented on coins of the Santones and Pictones, and on the triumphal arch at Orange. The Romans adopted them for their troops, after first having found them so strange that they named *Gallia Narbonensis* 'Gallia braccata', and they called any tailor a '*bracaricus faber*'.[10]

But, it is useful to recall, these breeches were not an invention of the Gauls: they derive from the long trousers worn by the Steppe nomads, adopted by the Scythians and introduced by them to the Germans and Celts, from whom the Gauls acquired them. Cut more tightly and noticeably shorter, they took the name of *femoralia*, and legions stationed in the northern countries followed the example of the Emperor Augustus in wearing them. Despite their contacts with the Scythians, who spread long trousers throughout Europe, the Greeks did not adopt this garment, except for Alexander who used them for his cavalry (394–324 BC). The Romans received them from the Gauls, after a long detour through Germany, towards the second century BC.

Head-dresses were rare in Gaulish civilian costume: the round cap (*pileus*) was still worn by freedmen. The boatmen of the Seine seem to have worn a sort of two-tiered cap. Women may have worn very wide-brimmed hats, probably made of felt, like those of mother-goddesses. They had a sort of veil falling over their shoulders or a band of cloth over the front of the head, to hold the hair in place.

Footwear was of various kinds, but always without heels and round-toed. The most widely worn were sandals (*gallicae*) common to men and women, of a specifically Mediterranean type, with the sole fastened to the foot by very varied arrangements of thongs. Knee-high gaiters seem to have been a special feature of the south-west; short woollen socks were sometimes worn inside the shoe, with a rolled edge. The various types of footwear current in Rome were also adopted in Gaul.

Although after the conquest women tried to imitate Roman hairstyles, men remained faithful to their beard and moustache, which were then unknown in the Imperial capital.

COSTUME MATERIALS

Among the peasantry, many wore the *colobium* (sleeveless tunic) and breeches in goatskin, thus continuing the use of animal skins from prehistoric times.

Gaulish costume was made mainly of a more or less fine, extremely solid and hard-wearing regional woollen cloth,[11] which contributed to its success. Hannibal, crossing the land of the Allobrogi (218 BC), equipped his army with these warm woollen garments. While the best of these cloths were reputed to be made in Saintonge, Franche-Comté, Artois and the Langres country, textile production was general in regions where there was any degree of economic organization.

The Gauls seem to have known how to make felt, which was used for hats and cuirasses, as among certain Asiatic peoples.

Dyeing played an important part: the Gauls liked bright colours, and Strabo, Plutarch and Pliny all noted the curious, magnificent spectacle presented by the multi-coloured garments worn by Gauls: 'streaky, spotted, speckled and spattered'. Designs were endlessly varied, particularly on the tunics of Gaulish gods; they included cross motifs, leaf patterns, circles, lozenges and other ornaments. Vegetable dyes were used, many of which were already known to primitive peoples, extracting violet from the bilberry, purple from the hyacinth and blue-black from pastel. Plain-coloured outfits were reserved for slaves; priests wore tunics and cloaks of white material.

Skins and furs were still used by the rich or for war equipment; they provided belts and helmets among other things.

These garments were fastened either with buttons of bone, leather or enamel (which seems to have been very rare), or with fibulae.

ORNAMENTS

The Celts had found, penetrating into Gaul, the already highly-developed techniques of the Bronze Age (2500 to 1000 BC) and they certainly adopted ornamental objects whose abundance and variety equal their beauty. Certain jewels were made of gold.

211 A meal.
Trier Museum.
(Photo Flammarion)

They had also doubtless assimilated the ornamentation of these primitive adornments in which Bronze Age men had mingled elements received from the Mediterranean civilizations with whose of their old Neolithic repertory: the women's wide belts found in graves have one or more leaves of beaten bronze, with geometric ornament. The use of the fibula, invented towards the end of the Bronze Age, is general; torques for wearing round the neck, with hooked or knobbed ends, open or closed, are decorated with stylized faces, relief spirals, birds or cabochons, while bracelets in bronze or blue and white glass are sometimes highlighted with yellow enamel.

From the middle of the first millennium, the ornaments worn by the Celts of Gaul were enriched with an exuberance of motifs and by the increasing use of precious materials (gold, silver, coral and, later, enamel); fourth-century buckles have been found, decorated with facing pairs of animals.

From this prehistoric patrimony the Gauls under Roman occupation retained essential characteristics in the metal ornaments produced in their workshops: enamelled torques, anklets, rings which men wore on their left hands and women pushed only half-way on to their fingers, and, above all, fibulae with metal disks or openwork decoration, which became increasingly massive and were sometimes decorated with emblems.[12] We find once more a taste for geometric ornament and stylization with a pronounced fondness for strong colours.

The Gaulish preference for bronze ornaments, which they shared with all Celtic peoples, was combined with an unusual taste for coral and enamels: the first was often associated with lucky amulets and workers even tried to imitate its colour in enamel, a completely Celtic industry. Gallo-Roman craftsmen also made rings and bracelets from jet and lignite. Imported amber was used for beads and disks.

MILITARY COSTUME

We know of various costumes worn in battle by the Gaulish chiefs who placed themselves under Roman patronage: some wore armour (perhaps merely embellishment) in the shape of a long iron coat of mail, with broad shoulder pieces, tightly belted at the waist, and with a cloak that flowed behind (plate 225). Others might wear a fringed sagum fastened with a fibula on the right shoulder.

Primitive leather caps developed into similarly-shaped battle head-dresses (cones, domes, mitres), covered with metal; they later served as models for the first helmets (plates 223-4), some of which figure on the triumphal arch at Orange. This type, which was entirely of metal, with two horns, a rowel and cheek-guards, is to be found in other Mediterranean countries. Different models, likewise of metal, with crests, were perhaps only for parade wear.

The sculptures of the sanctuary at Entremont (Bouches-du-Rhône) provided the most complete evidence concerning Gaulish military costume in the last third of the second century BC; a kind of moderately tight tunic of skin or hide encases the torso, the chest being protected by a metal pectoral decorated with emblems, and the head was covered with a leather cap trimmed with metal and fitted with cheek- and neck-guards, like the model to be seen on coins from the reign of Vercingetorix.

The bronze leg-guards we see represented were very probably reserved for military chiefs; soldiers also wore gaiters recalling huntsmen's leggings, a type preserved to our own times among the Mongols.

RELIGIOUS COSTUME

There does not seem to have been a special religious costume in Gaul. Following Pliny, people have claimed that the druids wore white robes for gathering mistletoe or offering ritual sacrifices; no representations can be quoted in support of this, and in fact it was probably only the ordinary Gaulish tunic, completed with some special attributes.

213   Bracelet from Réallon. Bronze Age. Paris, Musée des Antiquités Nationales. (Photo Flammarion)

BRAIES (BREECHES)

212, 216   The two examples from Gaul show the Gaulish garment, which is represented in many Roman triumphal scenes. It is a long pair of drawers or trousers, of medium width, held to the leg by criss-cross bands or sometimes attached to the shoe

ORNAMENTS

213–5, 217–20   In all the various countries ornaments were of a sophisticated richness and refinement

212   Bronze figurine discovered at Alésia. First century AD.
Paris, Musée des Antiquités Nationales.
(Photo Flammarion)

214 Girdle with pendants, discovered at Theil. Bronze Age. Paris, Musée des Antiquités Nationales. (Photo Flammarion)

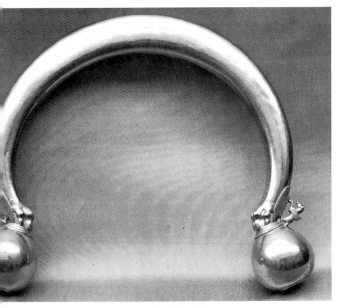

215 Gold diadem found at Vix. Late sixth century BC
Châtillon-sur-Seine Museum. (Photo Chambon)

216 Statuette discovered at Neuvy-en-Sullias.
Late sixth century BC. Orléans Museum.
(Photo Flammarion)

217 Solid gold torc found at Cavaret (Aisne). Fifth century BC. Paris, Musée de Cluny. (Photo Giraudon)

218 Bronze bracelet found in Banffshire, Scotland. Second century BC. Edinburgh, Scottish National Museum of Antiquities. (Museum photo)

219 Electrum torc from the Snettisham Treasure. First century BC. British Museum, London. (Museum photo. Courtesy the Trustees)

220 Roman gold bracelet and rings found at Zürich-Oetenbach. First century AD. Zürich, Schweizerisches Landesmuseum. (Museum photo)

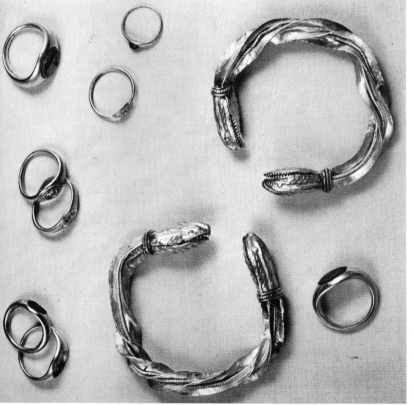

MILITARY COSTUME

221–2, 225 These rare specimens of Celtic and Iberian sculpture show that the equipment of a warrior consisted of a bronze cuirass formed of two pieces decorated with rosettes and chevrons, and a hooded helmet; the Vacheres warrior (plate 225) wears a coat of mail with laced sleeves, probably of leather

Costume and the Great Invasions of the Third to Sixth Centuries

CURRENTS OF CONQUEST AND TRADE

While the Gallo-Romans, safely installed in the *Pax Romana*, were introducing into their costume elements borrowed from their Imperial conquerors or from groups of foreign auxiliaries, among them Sarmatians, towards the third century AD, a new movement was beginning, across the Baltic region and slowly down towards Central Europe and the Rhine, forcing back the Celtic inhabitants of the countries in its path. In this way the Goths arrived near the Sarmatians who, particularly during the second half of the third century, had invaded Southern Russia, previously occupied by the Scythians. On the other side of Europe, new Germanic groups (Franks, Alemans, Saxons, Suevians, etc.) who had begun to threaten the Rhenish frontiers of the Empire, penetrated increasingly deeply into Gaul and prevailed on the Roman Emperors to grant them the title of Allies.

From the third century to the sixth a Nordic migration swept over Central Europe, from the Rhine to Spain across Belgium and Gaul, with the onrush of Alemans and Saxons; then another Eastern Indo-European flood of Huns and Sarmatians overthrew the Gothic Empire and opened the West to the period of great invasions.

The nomadic Huns from the Central Steppes first attacked the settled Chinese and Batrian Empires to the east; their western tribes reappeared towards 370 AD on the banks of the Don. Then, leaving their Steppes around the Aral Sea, they crossed the lower Volga, pushed back the Goths from the lower Danube, settled in Hungary and, under the command of Attila, crossed the Rhine at the beginning of 451. The victory of Aetius at the Catalaunic Fields finally halted their advance and forced them back over the Rhine.

After these fifth century invasions the Western Empire became divided into a series of states under hereditary dynasties. From Sicily to Scotland, from the Danube and the Rhine to Gibraltar and the coasts of North Africa, these barbarians – Alemans, Franks, Saxons, Burgundians, Visigoths, Ostrogoths and Vandals – were all Germanic. Probably representing less than five per cent of the population in the provinces they occupied, they lived side by side with their neighbours without modifying their customs and habits; often they formed only the military element in these societies.

It seems that the influence they exercised on Western European costume depended less on these profound political and territorial changes than on the degree of civilization of their respective groups, and the considerable imbalance then affecting the general economy. From the first pressure of barbarians on the frontiers of the Empire, elements of their costume penetrated with them, continuing the earlier contributions of the Celts, Scythians and Huns.

All writers between the fifth and eighth centuries, such as Sidonius Apollinaris (430–489) and Agathias (sixth century), agree on some essential points: tall and red-haired, with shaven necks, all the Barbarians of the great invasions dressed in sewn garments fitting closely to the body, short tunics and long or short breeches in various colours. These elements, after

221 Bust of a soldier, from Saint-Anastasie. Hallstatt period. Cast in the Musée des Antiquités Nationales, Paris, from the original in the Nîmes Museum. (Photo Flammarion)

222 Bust of a warrior from Grézan, Iberian art. Hallstatt period. Nîmes Museum. (Photo Flammarion)

undergoing varying degrees of modification, were to constitute the basis of costume in the true Merovingian period (seventh and eighth centuries) in Central and Western Europe.

The great invasions of the fourth and fifth centuries, by ruining the commercial economy of the West, had reduced the textile trade, which now transmitted only the rarest stuffs destined for princes and the wealthy classes. The silk routes were controlled by the Turks. Then in the seventh century the Arab conquest spread with prodigious speed from Syria to Spain, creating enmity and effectively severing all trade links between East and West. From then on it was by a new route, mainly following the Danube, that some textiles – and perhaps also some types of garment – were to travel from the Black Sea to Scandinavia, Britain and Gaul.

How much influence did these two streams of invasions have on Central and Western European costume in the fifth century? It was less, it seems, than we might imagine.

Indeed, as we have seen, the original costume worn in this vast continental zone had been influenced slowly by that of the semi-civilized Germanic peoples, or of the nomads from the eastern Steppes. The tunic and long breeches had already been adopted by the old, settled communities of Europe, and it is certain that the Scythians and Sarmatians in the pay of Rome, who settled in garrisons in Europe at the end of the fourth century, introduced no important new elements of clothing.

On the other hand these eastern influences revived the use of ornaments, for men and women alike. There were jewels of all types, but principally cloak pins and heavy belts worn with gowns.

The study of ornament – an important aspect of costume history – has made considerable progress with modern methods of archaeological excavation, which have assembled quantities of objects, for the most part precisely placed and dated. Funerary furnishings, in a very complex, composite style, reveal primitive, late Roman, Eastern or Pontic-Danubian influences. The ornamental finery which has been discovered informs us not only of fashions during several centuries, but also about the commercial exchanges of the time, and the population movement which motivated or accompanied them.[13]

Costume in Eastern Europe between the Fourth and Tenth Centuries

Byzantine Costume

In the East, the third century was marked by the decline of the Roman Empire, the retreat of Hellenism and the founding of the Sassanian Empire, accompanied by the re-awakening of Eastern nationalism. But Constantine, by creating a second capital of the Roman Empire in 324, began the transformation process from which an Eastern Christian Empire was to emerge. The Byzantine Empire under Justinian (AD 527–565) was to know a period of extreme brilliance, followed by a temporary decline; then, from the ninth century to the thirteenth, a new zenith, followed by a gradual weakening which ended in the capture of Constantinople by the Turks in 1453.

During these eleven centuries, Byzantium never ceased hostilities with neighbouring people or invaders from Asia, and was to experience periods of extraordinary development in the Eastern Mediterranean and the Middle East, as well as profound reverses and serious economic and political losses.

Byzantine costume reflected those diverse influences: it presented certain characteristics of ancient Classical costume, some of whose drapery it preserved, but it submitted mainly to Near-Eastern influences in its sumptuous nature and colour. Until the end of the Empire, court costume prolonged the fusion of these two elements.

In this, costume followed the evolution of all Byzantine art. Emile Mâle wrote: 'it was not born in the Byzantium which Constantine had transformed into Constantinople; it was prepared in the fourth and fifth centuries in the Greek towns of Egypt, Syria and Asia Minor and in the regions of Anatolia closest to Persia. A new architecture and decorative art were elaborated there, under the double influence of Greece and the Iranian world.'

THE ECONOMIC BACKGROUND

From the fourth century, while the Western Empire was invaded, weak and impoverished, the Eastern Empire possessed considerable riches as the result of intense commercial traffic, especially in luxury goods, from the Danube to Ethiopia and from Cyrenaica to Armenia. By virtue of its geographical position and its export policy, Byzantium maintained free relations with Asia and, as long as it held the keys to the great trade routes, it remained an important centre, attracting Venetians and Scandinavians when the Arabs cut off the West from the Orient.

It was through the intermediary of Byzantine trade that, from the fourth and fifth centuries, numerous Syrian and Alexandrian merchants established themselves in Italy, North Africa, Provence and even on the banks of the Rhine; thus, for many centuries, they became the best agents in the spread of textiles and garments from Byzantium and all the East.

In clothing as in the decorative arts (enamels, textiles and mosaics), colour 'gave an irresistible charm to everything from

226 The Tetrarchs, group in red porphyry. Venice. (Photo Percheron)

227 Stilicon, Serena and her son Eucher, ivory diptych. c. 395. Monza Cathedral. (Photo Giraudon)

228 Bas-relief from the obelisk of Theodosius, Constantinople. Fifth century AD. (Photo Faille-Giraudon)

229 Emperor's torso, porphyry. Fourth century AD. West Berlin, Staatliche Museen. (Photo Giraudon)

BYZANTINE COSTUME IN THE ROMAN PERIOD
226–9 Costume reflects Roman influences. Garments are simple in shape, loose and flowing: the tunic with long, tight sleeves; the military chlamys (plate 227) or the long pallium fastened on the right shoulder (plate 227); caligae as men's footwear (plate 226). Women wore superimposed tunics and draped scarves. However, engraved decoration suggests the new use of multicoloured silks which was to transform Byzantine costume

Constantinople', and from the ninth century to the twelfth, was 'the spell which fascinated all Europe'.

The silks woven with scenes which the emperors of Constantinople sent to Popes and sovereigns aroused lively curiosity; they introduced unusual colours and motifs into princely costume. We know that Constantine the Great (303–337) possessed a ceremonial robe patterned with flowers; in the Ravenna mosaics, Justinian is shown wearing a purple cloak decorated with a silk panel of blue ducks in red circles (plates 240, 242) while the garment worn by the Empress Theodora has a border with scenes of the Adoration of the Magi (plate 241). In the cathedral of Aix-la-Chapelle, on a splendid Byzantine cloth, yellow elephants harnessed in blue are set in medallions with a violet ground.

TEXTILES

Magnificent fragments of textiles patterned with flowers, real or mythical animals, quadrigae and races, circles and palmettes, have come down to us, revealing not only superior weaving techniques but also the exceptional importance of colour in all Byzantine textiles made in the capital.

In 333, shortly after the naming of Constantinople, Constantine issued an edict favouring cloths dyed with real purple or brocaded in gold, and placing strict controls on their sale. Luitpard, Bishop of Cremona, tried in vain to smuggle out some of these textiles, as did merchants from Venice and Amalfi.

The textile trade with foreign countries, Egypt, Chaldea and the Far East, was very important. Until the sixth century, caravans brought Chinese silk to Byzantium, then in 552 missionary monks brought back cocoons from Khotan and set up a flourishing industry. Weaving, tapestry and embroidery made use of varied techniques, some of which came from Persia or China.

The Eastern countries offered their very varied local products to Byzantium. Like Egypt, Syria manufactured tunics with geometrically-decorated woollen inserts; Palmyra imported Chinese silks similar to those found in 1924 in the tombs of Lu-Lan and Noïn-Ula; Tyre and Berites were famed for the silk garments they produced. Costumes found in the Ashmin and Antinoë graves show a wide variety of Oriental, Hellenic and Christian decorative themes.

Textiles made in or transmitted by Byzantium have survived in Western church treasuries, where they were often used to wrap relics or to make liturgical vestments. But contemporary texts establish that they were also used in the costume of the upper classes: Asterios of Amassis likened rich people to 'walking wall-paintings', and Theodore of Cyrus wrote that it was not rare to meet with the entire story of Christ woven or embroidered on the toga of a Christian senator.

During the period of prosperity from the ninth century to the thirteenth, the manufacture of textiles developed rapidly, especially in the Imperial workshops which worked for the exclusive use of the court. These textiles were dyed with dark red and violet purple, mixed with dark violet and yellow. The huge cloaks magnificently decorated with scenes were reserved for the Emperor. Sometimes the *basileus* sent these rich cloths as presents to foreign rulers, and we know that Theophanos, a Byzantine princess, brought textiles in her luggage when she married Otto in 972. Travellers, pilgrims and crusaders also contributed to their spread, but it was forbidden to export them, unlike inferior cloths, which could be exported on the delivery of a prefectorial bull.

The decoration of these textiles scarcely changed after the sixth century. Motifs were animals or human figures, and religious themes. The Sassanian influence became preponderant with the wars the Byzantine Empire waged against the Sassanians in the sixth and early seventh centuries.

COSTUME

Many costumes and ornaments came from the ancient East: the trousers are borrowed from the Huns or the Persians; the *tzitsakfon* from the Khazares; the soft boots, the *paragaudion*, the *kandys*, the collar and the *skaramangion*, the ovoidal tiara all came from the Persians; the Assyrians, by the intermediary of the Persians, gave the *cavvadior*, the *skaranicon* and the *granatza*, and the Medes gave the necklace. This diversity of origins explains the extremely complex character of Byzantine costume.[14]

CIVILIAN COSTUME

As luxury costumes far outnumber humbler examples in representations – and Byzantium is not unique in this – we have mainly to rely on the brief details supplied by various writers about ordinary civilian costume. We know only that in the sixth century the garments most generally worn were those of the Steppe peoples: blouse or tunic, trousers and footwear, inspired, according to Procopius, by the costume of the Huns.[15]

230 Two Saints, fresco in the monastery of Bawit (Egypt). Fifth-sixth centuries AD. (Photo Flammarion)

231–2 Saint Sisimos and Saint Phibamon on horseback, frescos in the monastery of Bawit (Egypt). Fifth-sixth centuries.

233 Oppian's Treatise on Hunting. Paris, Bib. Nat. ms grec, 2736, f. 5 v. (Photo Bibliothèque Nationale)

234 Zacchaeus watching Christ go by. Mosaic in the Church of Daphni, Greece. Eleventh century AD. (Photo André Held)

CIVILIAN COSTUME UNDER COPTIC INFLUENCE

230–32, 234–5 The arrangement of embroidered or woven motifs decorating the talaris tunic worn by men and women (plate 230) or the short tunics worn by men (plate 231) is dictated by Coptic weaving tradition: it appears in vertical bands, on the shoulders and at knee height. *Tablions* decorate cloaks at back and front; narrow breeches are sometimes tucked into high boots (plate 235)

TROUSERS IN BYZANTINE COSTUME

232, 236–8 Trousers, of the same type as Persian pantaloons, were originally narrow, made of rich material decorated with embroidery, sometimes arranged in bands round the leg (plate 233). The tunic was caught up in draped folds on either side for walking, and appears to have been fastened between the legs (plates 233, 236). Caps, including the so-called 'Phrygian' cap (plate 236) were also Persian in origin

235 Genesis: Joseph and Potiphar's wife. Sixth century AD. Vienna, National Library. (Library photo)

236 (*below*) Mosaic in the Church of Sant'Apollinare Nuovo, Ravenna. Fourth century AD. (Photo Alinari)

This everyday dress persisted over a long period, and still figured in eleventh-century miniatures.[16]

The trouser element of Byzantine costume is represented in the ninth century in the paintings of Mount Athos, in the form of tight, apparently skin-tight breeches, the lower part of which was tucked into boots rising to mid-calf. These Byzantine breeches seem often to have been cut from richly patterned or embroidered cloth (plates 233, 236–8).[17]

IMPERIAL COSTUME

From the fourth century to the sixth, the ceremonial costume of emperors – the best known Byzantine costume – was that we see in representations of Constantine: a gown woven of gold thread with multi-coloured decoration and a loose *chlamys* pinned on the right shoulder with a rich fibula. Imperial purple was reserved for the court and tributary kings wore a white chlamys. Justinian sometimes wore the toga of Roman consuls and the *trabea*, a wide scarf crossed on the chest, and the *paragaudion*, a gold-embroidered, sleeved tunic of Persian origin with a purple-dyed leather belt. The *tablion* was a rectangular piece of cloth inset in the front of the chlamys at waist height; it appeared in the costume of both emperors and empresses and in the dress of high court dignitaries.

The diadem worn by Constantine was made of a band of cloth decorated with gems and tied behind the head, at first called a *stephanos*. In the following century it became slightly flared, with pendants and chains hanging over the temples and cheeks in accordance with what appears to have been an Oriental mode, and it was called a *stemma* (plates 240–42). Over and above this, Theodora's crown was decorated with an aigrette of precious stones (plate 241). Hair was held in nets, sometimes decorated with pearls or beads.

A wide collar of Persian origin covered the shoulders of the Emperor and Empress: this was the *maniakis*, a band of cloth embroidered with gold and set with beads and precious stones.

Empresses wore the white tunic with a vertical band of embroidery, and a gown with elbow-length sleeves.

+SCS BALTHASSAR +SCS MELCHIOR +SCS GASPAR

237 King on horseback; silk cloth (restored). Late eleventh century
Bamberg, Cathedral. (Photo Ciba)

239 The Empress Ariadne, ivory.
Fifth-sixth centuries. Florence, Museo Nazionale. (Photo Giraudon)

238 Adoration of the Magi, ivory panel. Twelfth century.
Baltimore, Walters Art Gallery. (Museum photo)

IMPERIAL COSTUME

239–42 Imperial costume is enriched with precious stones and all kinds
of decoration: necklaces, the *maniakis* or gorget, a tablion inset in the
flowing purple chlamys worn by Justinian (plate 240), the *stemma*, a
crown widening towards the top, decorated with pendants, and, for
Theodora (plate 241), a long ornament of precious stones. Men wore the
short tunic or *paragaudion*, trimmed, like the long tunic worn by women,
with motifs woven in accordance with Coptic tradition. Women wore
bead-trimmed hairnets and earrings

On the Kershtsh shield, the basileus is represented in Eastern
costume: long trousers, a paragaudion belted at the waist, a
baldrick, a diadem, and low-cut shoes.

At court, boots followed the Persian model, and were soft,
red and embroidered.

In the tenth century, Imperial costume was completed with
a long scarf embroidered with gold thread and precious stones,
the *loros*, swathed and tied in a very special way, a revival of
an element of consular costume from the Late Empire. In the
eleventh century the ornament known as the *thorakion*, which
has often been described as a sort of shield, was in reality
simply the end of a scarf brought forward and hooked to the
belt.[18] Loros and thorakion were worn by both emperors and
empresses.

At the same period there was a long tunic lined with beaver
fur and belted at the waist; this garment derived from the fur-
lined, side-buttoned coat worn in parts of Asia.

In the twelfth century Byzantium similarly transformed the
loose caftan worn by Persian soldiers into an elegant garment.
A new coat, buttoned down the front, was in fashion. The Imperial crown was then completely closed, in the shape of a small
dome: the *camelaukion* (plate 243).

During the last centuries of Byzantium, the thirteenth, fourteenth and fifteenth, the Emperor was represented in a long,
stiff gown, the *saccoz*, which was purple or black, with sleeves
fastening tightly at the wrists. This also became the costume of
the kings and queens of Serbia. The *granatza* from Assyria was
long sleeved and of ground length. It was worn loose by the
Emperor, and belted by the archontes, who seem to have fixed

240–1 Justinian and Theodora, with their retinue, mosaics in the Church of San Vitale, Ravenna.
Sixth century. (Photos Alinari-Giraudon)

242 Justinian. Detail of mosaic in the Church of San Vitale, Ravenna. Sixth century AD. (See plate 240)

COSTUME IN GREECE

244–5 There are no longer any Byzantine characteristics in the garments worn here: short gowns with sleeves slit at the elbows, hoods, hats with pointed brims. Merchants wear Turkish costume, with caftan and turban

IMPERIAL COSTUME

243, 246–9, 251 Imperial costume is now long and increasingly adorned with jewels, with the long scarf or *loros* (plate 246), the shield-shaped *thorakion*, a fold of embroidered scarf (plate 249). The general use of silk materials gave costume a less flowing line.
The dancing-girls (plate 247–8) wear long skirts and short, fitted tunics. John Cantacuzenus (plate 243) wears the black *saccoz* with an embroidered *loros* and the dome-shaped crown or *camelaukion*. He is surrounded by monks and priests: behind them, we can see Cappadocians with their blue cylindrical head-dresses, and bodyguards with white, yellow-edged Tartar hats

243 The Emperor John Cantacuzenus. Fourteenth century. Paris, Bib. Nat., ms grec 1242, f. 5 v. (Photo Bibliothèque Nationale)

their sleeves to its back; empresses appear in the same costume in the Trebizond frescos.

In the thirteenth century, the head-dress of empresses became an oval tiara, following the Sassanian model. This was to become the *skiradion* worn by dignitaries in the fourteenth century. It might be scarlet, green or white, and was brocaded with gold and sewn with pearls. There was also a tiara, likewise of Persian origin, made of a circlet topped with a tall plume. The turban had the same Persian and, earlier still, Medean origins. The Emperor also wore the *calyptra*, in the form of an arched polygon. The *stemma*, which was still worn by the basileus, was in the shape of a flattened Persian tiara, its upper part turned slightly inwards, and was always trimmed with pendants and braiding.

There are certain obscurities and contradictions in the texts, but it seems that the *skaramangion* derived from the caftan of horsemen to become an official court garment, sometimes imposed and sometimes allowed as an honour. It finally became the gold-brocaded *skaranicon*, a riding garment.

CHARACTERISTICS AND INFLUENCES

The most noticeable innovation was the dominant use of silk among the Imperial family, the court and church dignitaries. Its brittle folds did not lend themselves to the broad drapery of wool, so generally Byzantine costume lost the softness of ancient drapery, some survivals of which remain in the chlamys and the sagum (short Roman cloak).

Oriental influence is revealed in the taste for coloured, sparkling ornaments, in the choice of decorative motifs and in the types of garment borrowed from the Huns, the Persians, the Khagares, etc. Thus, by means of very active commercial relations, the Byzantines received elements from the Persians which the latter had themselves received from the Assyrians or the Medeans. But most often the Imperial court received its Oriental fashions via the Barbarians; these became both court and military costume, and for prestige reasons were alleged to be Persian in origin.

244–5 Book of Job, executed at Mistra. Late fourteenth century. Paris, Bib. Nat. ms grec 135 f. 21 and 206. (Photos Bibliothèque Nationale)

These stiff shapes, rich cloths, striking colours and decoration were to be borrowed from Byzantium by the West, where they were adapted according to local tastes.

As a result of Byzantine civilization, Byzantine costume spread through the Balkans and Russia, influencing court costume for many centuries – until the sixteenth century in Russia – and persisting to the present in the liturgical vestments of the Orthodox Church. The adoption of Orthodoxy by the Southern Slavs in the ninth century and the submission of Bulgaria, Armenia and Georgia brought Byzantine influence to the north of Eurasia at the end of the ninth century.

In these various Balkan countries, the similarity between the national costume and that of Byzantium was most apparent in court and ceremonial costume.[19]

In the early ninth and tenth centuries the Bulgarians probably wore Avarian costume. As usual, we know well only the costume of the aristocracy. Its main element was the tunic[20] reaching to the knees or feet, decorated with braids and pearls, fastened on the right shoulder and worn as in Byzantium. The loose caftan or *skaramangion*, which could be long or short, had tight sleeves and was trimmed with a fur collar and braid edging. Sometimes it was slit in front to the waist, where it was belted, and it was decorated with plaiting, like the Persian, Bulgarian, Turkish and Russian caftans worn throughout the Middle Ages.

The sheepskin coat worn with the wool inwards was the typical garment of Bulgarian mountain dwellers. It was tight, reached half way down the legs, and was decorated with frogging on the front opening. The king, court and ordinary citizens all wore it. We find the same garment among the Huns, the Hungarians and the Cumanians.

Trousers, which were worn by both sexes, were tight and narrow and reached to the feet; they were worn with fairly high boots of black, red or yellow leather.

On the whole, Balkan costume presented a markedly Asiatic, Turanian character. Byzantine influence was very noticeable in the king's costume after the submission of Bulgaria in 1018. Popular dress, on the other hand, continued in an archaic style.

246 Christ crowning the Emperor Romanus IV and the Empress Eudoxia. Byzantine ivory cover of the gospel book of Saint John of Besançon. Eleventh century. Paris, Bibliothèque Nationale, Cabinet des Médailles. (Photo Bibliothèque Nationale)

247–8 Enamelled panel from the crown of Constantine Monomachos: dancing girls. Eleventh century. Budapest, Museum. (Photo Giraudon)

249 Saint Eudoxia: marble and coloured stones. Thirteenth-fourteenth centuries AD. Istanbul Museum. (Photo Flammarion)

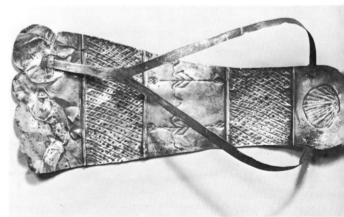

250 Silver sandal discovered in a tomb. Sixth century AD. Schoenenwerd, Switzerland, Musée Bally. (Museum photo)

251 NIKEPHOROS BORONIAT: Homelies of Saint John Chrysostom. Late eleventh century AD. Paris, Bib. Nat., ms Coislin 79 f. 2. (Photo Bibliothèque Nationale)

252 Bronze panels from Björnhofda in Torslunda, Oland. *c.* 600. Stockholm, National Museum of Antiquities. (Museum Photo)

253 Altar of Ratchis. Eighth century AD. Cividale, Church of Saint Martin. (Photo F. Stoedtner)

Costume in France under the Merovingians (481-752) and the Carolingians (752-987)

254 The Hornhausen Horseman, stele. Halle, Landesmuseum. (Museum photo)

Costume does not appear to have varied greatly between different peoples during the Merovingian period. Paulus Diaconus (born *c.* 720–25) informs us that the Lombards of the seventh century wore loose tunics decorated, like those of the Anglo-Saxons, with broad bands of various colours, while other chroniclers mention fitted tunics among the Franks. Precise documents are few; but the Merovingian France that was then taking shape provides us with more favourable conditions for the study of costume history, thanks to the custom of the Frankish and Alemanic newcomers of burying the dead fully clothed, armed and equipped, instead of cremating them, as did the Gallo-Romans.

It is fairly difficult to distinguish, not only from contemporary texts but also from modern studies made with more thoroughness than discrimination, whether the names applied to various garments during these three centuries refer to different pieces in each period, or if the terms simply changed according to the author's background or knowledge of clothing; it must not be forgotten that we have arrived at a period when the language was undergoing rapid development, and it is conceivable that a Vulgar Latin name may have survived alongside a Frankish term. Faced with two words, one is tempted to apply them to two garments which may differ only in some quite minor detail.

It seems most sensible, therefore, to confine statements to the broad outlines of clothing, in so far as figurative evidence permits us to establish them. These documents are rare for Merovingian times, but more abundant for the Carolingian period, and allow us to glimpse a development which was to

255 Statuette of a man, gold, found near Le Mans.
Late fourth or early fifth century AD.
Washington, Dumbarton Oaks Collection. (Photo Dumbarton Oaks)

256–7 Gilded bronze medallions from Alveschein.
Early ninth century AD.
Coire, Rätisches Museum. (Photos Caspar)

become more clearly defined in the Romanesque and Gothic periods.

A general feature of Merovingian and Carolingian clothing, some of which comes straight from Classical times through Byzantium, was that it was similar for both sexes. This was the case of the *camisia* or under tunic, the tunic itself, the *dalmatic*, which was an outer tunic with open or closed sleeves, the *colobium* or sleeveless tunic worn by peasants, and cloaks, whether rectangular like the *pallium* or circular like the *casula*.

MEN'S COSTUME

Men's costume reflects the military disposition of all the peoples of Merovingian Europe; the few representations and funerary objects that have come down to us do not enable us to differentiate – as we often can in other periods – between civilian and military costume.

Merovingian burial places, particularly in Lorraine, where methodical excavations have been carried out, have yielded fairly well-preserved fragments[21] of fine or strong linen cloth, loosely or tightly woven, proving clearly that corpses were buried fully clothed and that the finest stuffs were worn closest to the skin.[22]

As far as we can judge from the few documents of the period, the *gonelle*, a tunic with long or short sleeves, reached to the knees. Generally edged with braid and belted at the waist, it is often represented in the seventh and eighth centuries with fairly wide folds and, in the tenth century, with a thick roll at the neck, as in Gaulish costume. A stele from the Rhineland shows a warrior in an unusual type of long tunic.

Like all the preceding invaders, the Merovingians wore breeches: this is established by fairly abundant evidence. Sidonius Apollinaris describes the Franks of this period as dressed in a tight garment to above the knees, with bare legs; probably this tunic hid the breeches. A hundred years later, Agathias attributed to the same Franks the long breeches in linen or soft leather worn by the ancient Gauls, tied to the legs with the shoe-thongs.

258 Breviary of Alaric. Fifth century AD. Paris, Bib. Nat., ms lat. 4404 f. 197 v. (Photo Bibliothèque Nationale)

259 Chartres Gospel Book. Ninth century AD.
Paris, Bib. Nat., ms lat. 9836 f. 146 v.
(Photo Bibliothèque Nationale)

260 Antiphonary of the Cathedral of Léon.
(Photo Moreno)

261–2 Apocalypse. Ninth century AD.
Valenciennes, Bibliothèque,
ms 99, f. 23 and 31.

An object in the United States Dumbarton Oaks Collection (plate 255), so far unique of its type, has preserved for us the complete appearance of Merovingian costume.[23] This gold statuette, 11.4 cm. high, represents a standing, unarmed man, with medium-length hair combed to the neck, bare legs and feet; his knee-length tunic fits closely to the waist, implying sewn, fashioned construction, and is decorated all over with quadrilobed ornaments arranged vertically and in a horizontal band round the foot of the garment. The statuette, which was found near Le Mans, has been dated in the fourth or fifth centuries; it constitutes a precious document concerning clothing in a region traditionally peopled by Gauls and Gallo-Romans.

We find linen breeches once again in the Carolingian period, in the costume usually worn by Charlemagne. 'While the Gallo-Romans had kept their femoralia from the times of Trajan, most of the Franks had remained faithful to their long breeches: the great Emperor wore them in linen, covered, according to the fashion of huntsmen and country dwellers, with tibiales, a sort of gaiters held to the legs by the bands of his shoes.'[24] On some monuments these trousers are worn not only by horsemen and infrantrymen but also by workers. We can see a mounted soldier wearing tight breeches at San Pietro, in Tessino, and another, on foot, on the Niederhollendorf stele, both dating from the seventh century.[25]

In the ninth century trousers worn over linen underpants, shoes with long laces and bands tied round the calves are mentioned by the monk Abbon of St Gall as characteristic of 'Frankish workmen'. However, from the ninth to the eleventh centuries a certain number of miniatures show courtiers wearing either short trousers or long trousers like the old braies; everyone wears high boots laced half-way up the leg. It is possible that horsemen and soldiers may have preferred long trousers.

Men always wore the rheno, a cloak of animal skins with the fur side out, trimmed with narrow bands of other skins or fish-scales and fastened with a bronze pin.

Among the Franks, for whom weaving wool was a specialty, the saie, a small, short cloak covering only the shoulders, seems always to have been worn. Later, fitted with a hood, it seems to have become confused with the Gaulish bardocucullus.

157

263 Altar of Ratchis. Eighth century AD. Cividale, Church of Saint Martin. (Photo F. Stoedtner)

264 Bronze statuette of Charlemagne. Ninth century AD. Paris, Louvre. (Photo Giraudon)

265 Carolingian warriors resting, ivory panel.
Ninth century AD.
Paris, Louvre. (Photo Flammarion)

FEMALE COSTUME

259, 261-3 Female costume is composed of two tunics worn one on top of the other, or of a long tunic with a mantle fastened on the shoulder, sometimes covering the head. Embroidery is used, and a sort of mosaic work of different colours. The left sleeve is more richly decorated than the right, a custom which was to survive, as did the preference for tight folds (plate 263). The Whore of Babylon (plate 261) wears a costume which is a transposition of an Eastern model: such a style would never have been worn in France in real life

COSTUME IN THE CAROLINGIAN PERIOD

264, 269 These representations inspired by the naturalism of ancient models show with precise detail the short, full tunic, the *gonelle*, whose top hangs over to hide the girdle. A medium-length rectangular cloak, a survival of the ancient pallium, is fastened on the right shoulder (plate 270). The cloth *femoralia* are covered by *tibialia* (leggings) and high shoes or *brodequins* are laced up the front. The bishop's costume (plate 269) consists of a tunic, with over it an alb, a wide-sleeved dalmatic and a stole

MILITARY COSTUME

265-7, 270 Over the gonelle the guards (plate 265) wear a cuirass with a Roman-style leather and metal kilt and helmets decorated on top with a crest which may have been no more than the ridge where the two parts of the helmets were soldered together (plate 266). The Chamoson helmet (plate 267) is roughly the same shape but has applied decoration in gold. Legs are bare at the knee, with laced leggings that leave the toes exposed. The military cloak is short and round-cut like the Grecian chlamys. The circular shield is known as the *umbo*

SURVIVING PIECES OF COSTUME

268 The stocking, which is circular-knitted, is unique of its kind, as hose were generally tailored from cloth

266 Bronze helmet. Tenth century AD. Madrid, Instituto de la Historia de Valencia. (Photo IHV)

267 Chamoson helmet. Tenth century AD. Zürich, Schweizerisches Landesmuseum. (Museum photo)

WOMEN'S COSTUME

Though we have little information about garments worn exclusively by women in the Merovingian period, we know that in Carolingian times they generally wore the *stole*, a long gown pouched at the waist, with a leather belt, like the Roman *stola* but without the *instita*, and decorated round the neck with an embroidered band that continued down the front to the feet: this band, later separated from the gown, became the liturgical stole. This gown left the arms bare and the Salic Law ordered a fine to be paid by anyone who touched the arms of a free-born woman, although the fine was less if the offender touched only the forearms. Fibulae held these gowns at the shoulders; and another fibula, or a short chain with a hook, placed in front on the chest, enabled the wearer to raise the foot of her gown. A long, crossed scarf, the *palla*, held in place with a pin or a small fibula, was wrapped round the shoulders with one end falling down in front, the other behind; it could also cover the head, in the Byzantine style.

CEREMONIAL COSTUME

The costume of officials in the Eastern Empire became the cere-monial costumes of the Frankish aristocracy: the *chlamys*, also called by analogy the Byzantine slit toga, was an emblem of dignity worn by the king; the short tunic of purple had em-broidered sleeves and was tightly girdled with a scarf wound twice round the body; seamless hose (plate 268) and short trousers were also worn.

The excavations carried out in 1959 in the Basilica of Saint-Denis, outside Paris, brought to light much new information with the discovery of jewels (plate 271) and fragments of cloth in the intact tomb of the Merovingian queen Arnegonde (AD 550–570).[26] She was buried in a chemise of fine woollen stuff, no doubt knee-length like her overgown, which was in ribbed indigo-violet satin; her legs were clad in a kind of woollen cloth hose bound with crossed thongs: traces of garters were found. Over the gown, a long tunic of red silk lined with linen

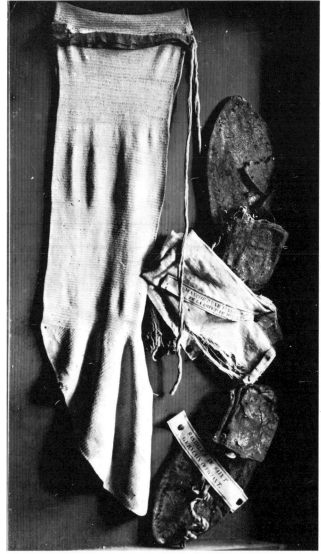

268 Hose and shoes alleged to have belonged to Saint Germain, abbot of Moutiers-Grandval (near Délémont, Switzerland). Seventh century AD. (Photo Musée Jurassien, Délémont)

269 Metz sacramentary: Coronation of an Emperor. Ninth century AD, Paris, Bib. Nat., ms lat. 1141, f. 2 v. (Photo Bibliothèque Nationale)

270 Bible of Charles the Bald. Ninth century AD. Paris, Bib. Nat. ms lat. 1, f. 423. (Photo Bibliothèque Nationale)

must have reached almost to the ground. It was completely open in front, with wide, long sleeves, and was fastened with round fibulae and a large gold pin, and a broad belt that passed twice round the waist, crossed at the back, and was knotted in front below the waist. On her feet she wore short black leather boots with laces joined to her garters. Between the tunic and gown, there was a wide baldrick fastened with a very large ornament formed of two plates. On one side she wore a veil reaching to the waist, no doubt fixed to the tunic with two gold pins.

This type of ceremonial costume can be related to royal ornaments, which are represented today only by the famous gold crowns of Guarrazar, belonging to the seventh-century Visigothic kings, proofs of the degree of technical sophistication reached under the Barbarian dynasties.

HAIR AND HEAD-DRESSES

We know of no headgear worn by men in the Merovingian period: their thick, red (natural or dyed), plaited hair was worn on top of the head, and the back of the neck was shaved.
˙ Kings may have worn beards, with their hair divided by a centre parting and flowing freely, curled or knotted above the shoulders, as they are shown on the Gundestrup Vase and on the oldest Merovingian seals. However, the King of the Alemans, in battle with the Emperor Julian (387) wore only a tuft of red hair, and Charlemagne was to have his hair cut short. It seems that the only head-dress worn was the narrow band holding in the hair and tied behind with the two ends falling down the neck in a survival of the Classical style.

We have no indication of how Merovingian women dressed their hair, except that young girls let their hair hang loosely, while married women had to tie theirs into a chignon. On the chests and skulls of skeletons archaeologists have found pins which may have been hair ornaments.

Under the Carolingians, miniatures show women wearing nets of woven beads or precious stones. Moreover, we know that for the sake of respectability they had to cover their heads

271 Earrings and pins from the tomb of Queen Arnegonde.
Sixth century AD. Saint-Denis, Paris. (Photos France-Lanord)

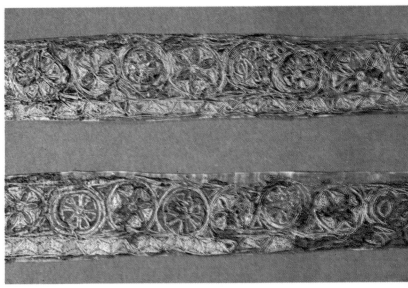

272 Sleeve embroideries with rosette patterns. Sixth century AD.
Tomb of Queen Arnegonde, Saint-Denis, Paris

with veils, generally the *ricinium*, draped like a turban. The
mafors was a large veil covering the head and falling like a
cloak over the shoulders and body, which it enveloped down to
the feet (plate 289).

FOOTWEAR

Men wore closed shoes of leather, more or less tanned and
dressed, often with the fur remaining. They are all described
as being slit on the top of the foot and held by laces over the
instep or by criss-crossed thongs, often very long and reaching
to the knees. Under Charlemagne, the term *brodequin* seems
to have taken the place of Roman names. The *heuse*, a high,
soft leather shoe, forerunner of the boot, appeared towards the
ninth century.

Women's footwear was more delicately made in leather decorated with patterns, with tongues fixed on the instep by a
tab or by light bands ending in tabs below the knees. Women's
shoes made of linen cloth have also been found.[27]

MILITARY COSTUME

For combat purposes the Merovingians probably wore a sort
of sleeved tunic, with iron scales, or a cloth jerkin with metal
plates, and a leather belt with an ornate buckle to which they
attached their weapons and other accessories. Their weapons
were the axe (*francisque*), the lance (*framée*), the shield or
buckler and the *angon* or barbed spear.

The head was protected only by the hair worn in a roll, which
explains why fighting men were so attached to their long hair,
loss of which was regarded as a sign of defeat or submission.
Moreover, their shaven necks, which they would have been
ashamed to show, forbade their taking flight in battle.

The helmet appears from about AD 800, but initially it was
apparently reserved for chiefs; it might have a conical framework (plate 266), or be a spherical crown composed of six
copper panels joined at the top by a round plate.

273 Cloisonné bronze
fibulae. Sixth-seventh
centuries AD.
Paris, Musée de Cluny.
(Photo Flammarion)

274 Buckle from
Tressan (Hérault).
Sixth-seventh
centuries AD. Paris,
Musée des Antiquités
Nationales.
(Photo Flammarion)

161

275 Necklace and sword and scabbard decorations. Fourth-fifth centuries AD. Stockholm, Historical Museum. (Photo Ata)

In the Carolingian period, the equipment of warriors was directly inspired by Roman tradition. Over the tunic, the soldier wore a cuirass or *broigne*, a sort of waistcoat covered with leather or horn. This broigne was accompanied by a *coiffe* which enveloped the head and was worn under a helmet or *heaume* (helm). With modifications in shape and material, this armour remained in use until the eleventh century. On their feet soldiers wore brodequins, and their legs were covered either with full-length hose or with socks cut off at the toe. A little later, they protected their legs with leather or metal shin-guards known as *bamberges*.

ORNAMENTS

The Merovingian period left its most noticeable mark throughout Europe in ornamental accessories; this was a new ornamental style brought originally by the Germans.[28]

The characteristic motifs, entwined and knotted serpents, appeared in the seventh century, at first in eastern Scandinavia (the so-called Vendal Style, named after the place where it was first discovered). At that period the strong influences previously exercised by the East on European art came to a halt; the Steppe style, continuing Pontic art, which included Hun objects with their rich animal and plant decoration, disappeared with the arrival of the Avars. After their entry into Italy the Lombards spread the new style, which reached as far as Ireland and survived longest in Scandinavia, undergoing constant renewal. Tombs have provided a wealth of ornaments of this period: women's tombs have proved particularly rich.

Necklaces were made of real or imitation amber, pearls, enamelled pottery or coloured glass paste, or more rarely of gold pendants. Ear-rings, which were very widely worn, were of two types: rings with pendants of bronze and amber, influenced by the East, and more sophisticated, geometrically shaped buttons set with glass or ivory, influenced by the Goths. Rings generally recall Roman forms, with intaglios which were often coarsely imitated. Bracelets, which seem to have been worn only by women and children, could be either of gold or

natural or gilded bronze, or else of glass, sometimes in the shape of wheat-ears. Pins, probably for the hair, were richly decorated.

Fibulae, derived from the earliest times, were indispensable for fastening garments and were the main jewel worn by women. They present the widest variety of decoration, while falling into two main categories: nursing pins and brooches.

The *spoked fibula*, decorated with a chequer pattern, perhaps Scandinavian in origin, was unknown among the Burgundians; it was worn on the abdomen to fasten an outer garment, or higher to drape an under-tunic. *Round* or *polygonal fibulae* were richer and more varied, recalling Byzantine fibulae in their cloisonné ornament. The small *zoomorphic fibula*, which was already made in Roman times but in a very different style, represented mainly grasshoppers, hook-billed birds of prey (plate 273) and two-headed serpents; it had been brought to Italy by the Ostrogoths and to Gaul by the Visigoths.

The *S-shaped fibula*, which resembled the Scandinavian serpent, evoked an Oriental theme: it developed into a closed, figure-of-eight shape. Lastly, the *handled fibula*, with a safety hook, was unadorned and worn in pairs, sometimes linked by a short chain. In the eighth century fibulae gradually disappeared.

The Merovingian girdle, worn by both men and women, provided very ancient motifs, sometimes single, sometimes composite, for buckles and plaques. The finest and most numerous buckles must have been used to attach a kind of baldrick on women's chests. Back-plates have been found, similar to the plaques themselves: these were generally rectangular, sometimes round or triangular in the case of wrought iron pieces, and were more complex when cast in white bronze imitating silver or in the more current red bronze. Some were made of a weak alloy of gold or silver, or they might be plated. Exceptional specimens in rock crystal, bone or imported ivory have been found. Several techniques were used: engraving, cloisonné or ordinary enamelling, damasquining and plating.

Men hung their weapons from their belts, and women fastened a small satchel to their girdles by means of a hanging rowel,

162

276 Penannular fibula in silver, Scandinavian work. Sixth century AD. Stockholm, Historical Museum. (Photo Ata)

277 Silver gilt fibula with polychrome inlays. Sixth century AD. Stockholm, Historical Museum. (Photo Ata)

a pierced circular or rectangular plate decorated with very varied motifs, ranging from geometric figures to mounted troops. A kind of leather or cloth alms-purse was used for carrying money, a custom foreign to the Romans, who had kept their money in their belts; men and women also used this purse to hold their combs, scissors, hair-tweezers and various other articles.

Bractiates, personal ornaments from the Nordic countries, were disk-shaped fastening plates, most often reproducing coins.

Among the Burgundians, decorative motifs seem to have been borrowed both from Scandinavian art and from Coptic sources (crosses, bands), while the Alemans wore all types of fibulae and every variety of jewel.

COSTUME TEXTILES AND TEXTILE DECORATION

The history of the textile industry during this early medieval age enables us to pin down exactly certain points in the history of costume.

Among the Merovingians, linen remained rare in costume and was generally imported, though flax had been cultivated in Gaul from the fifth century. It is possible that the introduction of these cloths, which were finer than any used by the Barbarians, was facilitated by Merovingian trading contacts with Italy. This linen was mainly used by the wealthy classes for the chemise, the light tunic and breeches.[29] Fragments of loosely woven cloth, like sackcloth, probably came from outer garments. Wool was used by the Merovingians for short and long trousers; breeches were often decorated with rosettes, trefoils, quatrefoils and spots, which seem to have been among the most widely used patterns.

For the Carolingian period, we know with certainty of the existence in Frisia, in the mid-eleventh century, of an industry, long established even then, producing cloth of various qualities used to make the *pallia* worn by monks and peasants. The Fri-

sians had certainly woven wool from the earliest times, taken from the sheep that grazed on their pasturelands, and texts inform us that in the eleventh century they made the *pallia fresonica* of high quality, which Charlemagne wore himself and sent as a gift to Haroun-al-Rashid. 'Louis the Pious gave them as gifts, on the great feast-days, to the second-class officers living in his palace while he presented silk stuffs to high dignitaries and common linen or woollen stuffs to the servants.'[30]

While coarse cloths made by local weavers served popular needs, fine, luxury grade, higher-priced goods, outstanding by virtue of their bright, varied colours, were exported (as far afield as Norway in the eleventh century). The Flemish Cloth trade was already highly developed and on the point of entering on its immense development of the following centuries.

The use of silk in costume of this period reveals Byzantine influence; it has justly been said that 'the bond between East and West was doubtless established by means of Byzantine silks, woven from the beginning of the sixth century'. We must recall here, however, that as early as 470 the Frankish prince Sigismer wore silk garments and jewels of gold and precious stone, though he was dressed in his national style. This luxury illustrates the adaptation of Barbarian chiefs to the Imperial civilization, at least as much as the penetration of personal ornaments of Byzantine and Oriental origin. But other Merovingians clung to their traditional costume of undressed animal-hides.

On the whole, the costume of the regions under the Merovingian and Carolingian dynasties retained certain Roman elements, but foreign elements introduced by the various occupying forces brought about a renewal, less by the introduction of altogether new types of garment than by the general diffusion of breeches, the tunic and the scarf, together with the habit of wearing several garments one on top of the other. In addition, this costume became richer, with the adoption of Byzantine textiles and the ornaments produced by an original art with decorative themes that were stylized and fanciful.

163

Costume in Central and Western Europe from the Ninth to Eleventh Centuries

Once Pope Leo III, reviving in 800 the concept of the Universal Empire in a new form, had conferred Imperial dignity on Charlemagne, a new international balance was reached: the Carolingian Empire was dominant in Central and Western Europe, the Baghdad Empire dominated the Middle East and Africa, and the Empire of Byzantium, astride Eastern Europe and Asia, ensured liaison between the two. However, neither the creation of the Carolingian Empire nor the advance of Arab civilization as far as Spain mark particularly important dates in the development of costume. The beginnings of a renaissance can be noted in the eleventh century.

If we leave aside certain Barbarian, and more particularly, Germanic details, clothing in the Carolingian Empire and among its tributary nations shortly before the Treaty of Verdun (843) remained much the same as that of the Merovingian period. But among the aristocracy of great secular or religious lords created by Charlemagne in Imperial and princely courts, a new costume developed, as splendid as it was solemn, matching the slow formation of a new style and spirit. Beside the costume of the primitive and developed Barbarian types, it bears witness to the strengthening of the influence of Christianity and the renewal of Mediterranean influences.

In the immense empire of Baghdad, established from the Indus to the Pyrenees by Arab conquests from Omar (634–644) to Haroun-al-Rashid (786–809) a new, unrivalled hegemony was imposed by Islam, showering its conquered peoples with riches, and spreading refinements and splendours in which Iranian influences dominated. However, as formerly during the Roman Empire, it was in the cities that the authority of caliphs, the opulence of viziers and their entourages, the activity of an administrative elite recruited from Persians and Greeks, were most in evidence. The occupied peoples (Asiatic Hellenes, Syrians, Mesopotamians, Iranians, Berbers and Iberians) kept their own styles of costume. In the Iberian peninsula, Visigothic costume survived in the midst of the immense development of textile industries established and run by the Moors.

The Asiatic influence of Byzantium covered a large part of the Italian peninsula: in the seventh century Rome was Byzantine. The main centres of influence were Ravenna and Venice in the north and Palermo and the abbey of Monte Cassino in the south, where splendid mosaics bear witness to the spread of the elements of Byzantine costume.

In general then, clothing in all Central and Western Europe from the Black Sea to the Atlantic and from the Baltic to the Straits of Gibraltar kept the principal features of the primitive Barbarian style of costume, influenced by the costumes worn on the marches of the Roman Empire and, among the princely and wealthy classes, with forms taken from Byzantine costume.

In the late tenth century, dominated by anxiety caused by the approaching Millennium, costume reached an apparent stability, similar to that equilibrium which political and economic Europe seems to have attained after numerous conflicts, out of the mixture of varied races and under dynasties spread between three empires. However, this stability was not long to resist the renewal that was beginning to shake the Western world.

LONG COSTUME AND ITS ORIGINS

During the first centuries of the Christian era Roman costume, in the conquered countries as in Rome, fell naturally into two principal types: long for the wealthy and cultivated classes, short for workmen and soldiers.

It is evident that this second type was to persist even after the invasions of the third and fourth centuries and was to be juxtaposed with the military costume of the Barbarians, as it were the 'occupying costume', which was also short.

From the third century on, in the Roman catacombs, merchants and workmen are represented in their short working costume; but other figures, and not only saints, are in long costume. No costume detail enables us to distinguish between men and women, laymen and priests.

It is particularly interesting to know with certainty that Saint Cyprian, on his martyrdom in 288, was wearing 'ordinary' costume: a shirt, a tunic or dalmatic and a cloak.

Texts inform us that in the increasingly Christianized Europe of the first centuries, costume worn by men and women scarcely differed. A decree of Diocletian in 301 mentions the dalmatic as a garment common to both sexes in the East. In the seventh century, Pope Agathonus, troubled by the possible inconvenient consequences of this similarity, tried unsuccessfully to impose distinctions in dress and hairstyles; moreover, at the end of the seventh century, Pope Celestinus I condemned the wearing of a special costume by the clergy. There was thus a general uniformity of clothing.

Representations dating from after the sixth century (frescos, sculptures, mosaics, miniatures) show the coexistence of two types of garment during the entire Middle Ages. Numerous examples are provided by manuscripts, as where the Apostles of Saint Bertinus appear clad in knee-length tunics or albs. Murals also prove a useful source; for instance the ninth-century scene of the stoning of St Stephen in the church of Saint-Germain in Auxerre (plate 287), or the figure of a saint in the Poitiers baptistery (plate 289).

The repercussions on costume of the two great events of the third and fourth centuries, the first Barbarian invasions and the

278 Mosaic, Santa Maria Maggiore, Rome. Fourth century AD. (Photo Anderson-Giraudon)

279 Saint Quirico, wall-painting in Santa Maria Antica, Rome. Eighth century AD. (Photo Alinari-Giraudon)

280 Three saints, wall-painting in Santa Maria Antica, Rome. Eighth century AD. (Photo Alinari-Giraudon)

281 The Good Shepherd.
Second–fifth centuries AD.
Rome. Catacomb of San Callisto.
(Photo Flammarion)

282 · The Good Shepherd.
Second–fifth centuries.
Rome, Lateran.
(Photo Alinari)

283 Saint Cecilia. Second–fifth centuries.
Rome, Catacomb of San Callisto.
(Photo Flammarion)

creation of the Eastern Christian Empire, were very different in the Western world.

The short Barbarian costume and that worn by the common people, also short, could coexist without great difficulty. Long costume, to which the invasions added little more than ornaments, spread considerably with the Christianization of Europe, of which the creation of the Byzantine Empire provided proof.

The Edict of Milan in 313 had consecrated the triumph of established Christianity as the religion of the Roman Empire, and this allowed Christian art 'born in the shadows, to open out magnificently in the light.'[32] Also, during the following centuries when Byzantine influence developed after Justinian's reconquest of the Empire, Christianity and the Church enjoyed an extraordinary expansion through almost the whole of Europe, from the Black Sea to the Nordic countries, and long costume gained in popularity in so far as it was identified with the clothing worn by the evangelists.

We should remember the importance and number of the great religious orders then created, whose monasteries were founded all over Europe after the sixth century. The monks of these regular orders adopted the rural costume worn at the time, including in particular the long frock or undergown, which has remained unchanged since then. This fact testifies to the persistence of long garments among the ordinary people in the sixth century.

This influence also penetrated with the progressive establishment of a regional network of bishoprics, which introduced the new forms of ecclesiastical costume to which writers begin to allude in the sixth century, and which in spreading conveyed the idea of a 'brotherhood'.

THE DEVELOPMENT OF LITURGICAL COSTUME

It is particularly from the sixth century on that a certain number of secular garments in current wear took on a religious and, to a certain degree, symbolic character, so creating a cos-

tume that became codified in its use and fixed in its form.

The tunic, dalmatic, alb, chasuble and cape became liturgical vestments while they were still widely worn; then, disappearing from everyday costume, they remained in use in religious contexts with modifications only in details of shape and ornamentation – among the most authentic examples of costume inherited from Classical times through the Early Middle Ages.

The *tunic*, which we saw appear in Syria in the second century and in Egypt in the third, was so widely worn in Africa that it was called '*discinti Afri*'; it was a short, straight-cut garment with wide sleeves, decorated with a key-pattern (*clavi*). Later considered effeminate, it went out of general fashion towards the fifth century, but became the garment of the under-deacon and the first garment of the bishop.

The *dalmatic*, often confused with the tunic, differed from it by its long, wide sleeves, covering the wrists: Dalmatian origins were attributed to it, but in reality it seems that it owed its name to its material, white Dalmatian wool. It had been launched by the Emperor Commodus (180–192) who wore it in public, and we have seen that in 301 Diocletian mentioned it as a garment worn by both sexes. Its vogue ceased towards the fifth century, but it remained the special attribute of deacons, replacing the *colobium* or short-sleeved tunic. Made of linen or silk, it was decorated with *clavi* from the shoulder to the foot of the front of the garment.

The *alb* is another variety of the Classical tunic, worn in civilian costume in the East from the first millennium BC. It presented two main characteristics: it was long, and it was made of linen. Like the dalmatic, it was decorated in front with a large embroidered panel, but in this case tight. In ancient texts it is called *tunica alba* or *tunica talaris*. The fact that the fourth Council of Carthage in 398 and that held in Narbonne in 589 forbade deacons and the lower clergy to wear it outside churches or ceremonial occasions, emphasizes its liturgical character.

The *chasuble* – *casula* or *paenula* – was likewise a civilian garment common to both sexes and remained so for a long period. It was a large piece of cloth cut in a circle with a central

166

284 Christian sarcophagus. Rome, Museo del Laterano. (Photo Alinari).

EARLY CHRISTIAN COSTUME

281–4 The first Christian paintings and carvings show costumes inspired simultaneously by Roman and Near-Eastern styles. The Good Shepherd (plates 281–2) wears shepherd's costume, and the praying woman (plate 284 left) the flowing costume of Roman matrons

LITURGICAL COSTUME

285–7 Liturgical costume consisted of long, flowing garments worn one on top of the other: the linen alb (*tunica alba*), the dalmatic with its wide sleeves decorated with clavi in purple, like the linen *tunica talaris*, and the circular chasuble

286 Dalmatic alleged to have belonged to Charlemagne. *c.* ninth century. Rome, Vatican Basilica Treasury. (Photo Alinari)

285 Mosaic in San Prassede, Rome. Ninth century. (Photo Alinari-Giraudon)

287   The Stoning of Saint Stephen. Fresco from the Church of Saint Germain, Auxerre. Ninth century. Paris, Musée des Monuments Français. (Photo Flammarion)

288   Life of Saint Quentin. Twelfth century. Saint-Quentin, Library. (Photo Tarascon)

289   Life of Saint Radegonde. Late eleventh century, Poitiers, Library, ms 250, f. 25 v. and 38 v. (Photo Mathias)

CONTEMPORANEOUS WEARING OF LONG AND SHORT COSTUMES

288, 290   Monks and ecclesiastics always wore long garments, but these scenes show short costumes also: the bliaud and the chlamys. Long garments are the tunic and the pallium which became general wear in the second half of the twelfth century. In plate 290 the shoes with long points 'like the tails of serpents' known as *pigaches* are an example of the extravagances condemned by Orderic Vital

COSTUME IN FRANCE IN THE ROMANESQUE PERIOD

289, 291–2   Female costume consists of a *chainse* with long fitted sleeves and a gown, sometimes short with long, flaring sleeves, known as a *bliaud*; embroidery and braid often decorate the foot of the gown and sleeves and the inset panel over the shoulders. As in the Carolingian period, the cloak is worn over the head; failing this a veil, the *mafors*, is wound round the neck. Radegonde wears a crown. Men always wear a short bliaud, full-skirted with the girdle usually hidden by the pouching upper part; a medium-length cloak is fastened on the shoulder or chest.

The child restored to life by Saint Radegonde's hair shirt (plate 291) is tightly swaddled, a custom which was to persist until the nineteenth century

opening for the head, shorter in front, and with slits at either side. It was a travelling cape which was adopted as a liturgical garment at the Council of Toledo in 636, first for members of the clergy. During the Carolingian period, it was reserved exclusively for priests.

The *cope* is also a civilian garment that goes back to Classical times and never ceased to be worn: as its alternative name, *pluvial*, indicates, it was designed to protect the wearer from rain, and it was for this reason that it was originally worn at outdoor religious ceremonies. Later it was embellished with ornaments and became a formal religious garment. Like the chasuble, it was cut in a circle, but was open in front, with a wide neck opening. The *chaperon* – a primitive hood – became a simple ornament fixed below the neckband.

Again, it was towards the sixth century that the stole, the maniple and the girdle were codified by the ecclesiastical authorities and took on the character of liturgical vestments. The stole, an adaptation of the Classical *loros*, had its origins in the decorative band on the Roman *stola*; the maniple was at first a sort of kerchief which became stylized into the form worn

290 Moralia in Job, Cistercian manuscript. Early twelfth century. Dijon. Library, ms 168, f. 4 v. (Photo Rémy)

291 Child restored to life by Saint Radegonde's hair shirt. Late eleventh century. (*cf.* plate 289).

292 Tapestry of Queen Matilda ('Bayeux Tapestry'). Late eleventh century. Bayeux, (Photo Le Monnier)

293 Poem by Donison in honour of Countess Matilda. Early twelfth century. Vatican Library, ms lat. 4928. (Library photo)

today. Of the *pallium* the large, draped Roman cape – all that remained in the sixth century was a long, scarf-like strip that narrowed progressively, then towards the eighth century became curved, to form a sort of woollen necklace in the tenth century, placed on the shoulders and continuing in long, straight bands down the front and back.

In this way the secular clergy maintained the traditional forms of Classical costume, while the costume of the lay citizens was gradually modified. At the same time, the new monastic orders submitted themselves to the Benedictine rule, and they too adopted the costume of everyday life of the time, which has been preserved unchanged to our own day. Originally the only difference between the elements of religious costume and those of lay clothing was the use of more sumptuous materials for the former. Meanwhile, the styles of a Christian Byzantium, where Classical costume had been preserved in Orientalized forms, penetrated liturgical costume, and thus the fashion for long costumes gained momentum.

294 The Miracle of San Clemente, wall-painting in the crypt of San Clemente, Rome. Late eleventh century. (Photo Anderson-Giraudon)

295 King Edward, tapestry of Queen Matilda ('Bayeux Tapestry'). Late eleventh century. Bayeux. (Photo Flammarion)

From the sixth century, it appears that Christian costume did indeed borrow from Byzantium ceremonial costume the elements to be seen in the mosaics of San Vitale in Ravenna, worn by members of Justinian's retinue (plate 240).

In quoting from Eginhard's text, where the usual costume of Charlemagne is described as being Frankish, writers too often omit the passage in which the author states that, while the Emperor preferred this style above others, he nevertheless, at the request of the Pope, allowed himself to be dressed 'in the chlamys, the long tunic and Roman shoes'[33] while he was in Rome. Alongside religious costume, garments for ceremonial or state occasions were inspired in Western Europe either by the Roman Empire or by models from the Byzantine Empire, adopted by Rome.

The fact that all Christians, lay citizens, priests or monks, wore the same long costumes must be stressed all the more insistently in that it lies at the basis of the history of costume from the beginning of the Christian era until the twelfth century in Western Europe.

The Christianization of Western Europe was thus accompanied by the expansion of a type of garment that we might call general; it could only be increasingly closely associated with the 'catholic' character of a community sharing one faith and one culture, faithful to an inheritance of the civilization of Classical Antiquity. The universality of Christendom and Christianity was thus expressed in the universality of the costume.

NEW STYLES

Modern historians of costume have claimed that they see an important general transformation in costume towards the middle of the twelfth century: remembering only the short clothes worn by the Barbarians and the common people, they consider the wearing of long costume as a 'revolutionary' innovation and attribute its spread to the Crusades.[34]

This thesis was based on texts which were interpreted without deeper investigation of the various circumstances in which they had been written, and at no time did historians envisage

the slow evolution we have just described; moreover, they failed to check the concordances they established between their texts and the events from which they drew their conclusions.

It must be recalled first of all that trade relations had never completely ceased between the Middle East and the West: as early as the sixth century, Syrian and Venetian merchants had established themselves in Gaul, Italy and even in England, under the general name of 'Syrians'. Their presence has even been noted in the Rhinelands, in the entourage of Charlemagne.

From the ninth century on, the Byzantium Imperial workshops exported silks to Western Europe; they had established a trading post in Pavia, which was supplied through Venice. After this, from the tenth century, silks made in Andalusia reached the court of the Franks through Spain, which had been conquered by the Omayyad dynasty (661–760). Thus the severe condemnations levelled by eleventh-century bishops against luxury in dress are aimed at the sumptuousness of textiles 'worn in imitation of the Saracens'. It is much more accurate to say that it was through the Byzantine East and the Iberian South-West that Eastern textiles and fashions penetrated into the West, since the reconquest of Sicily by the Normans dated only from 1090 and the First Crusade from 1096 to 1099, that is, after the first texts that we possess concerning the exaggerations of fashion.

While the Church was crystallizing the liturgical form of long costume, caprice, a new phenomenon, made its way into clothing and spurred Saint Bernard to reproach warriors in these words: 'You adorn yourselves with pomp for death... are your plumes the harness of a knight or the finery of a lady? You dress your hair... like women... You catch your feet in long, wide skirts. And accoutred thus, you fight for the vainest of causes.'

There can be no doubt that the Church was alarmed by the appearance of new fashions, in so far as she feared that the novelty and luxury of certain costumes might lead to a relaxation of morals and thereby a decrease in faith. But at no moment can we trace in texts any criticism of long costume, which would in any case have been inexplicable because lay and regular clergy had never ceased to wear it.

170

296 Herod and Salome, capital from the basilica of Saint Etienne. Second half twelfth century. Toulouse, Musée des Augustins. (Photo Archives Photographiques)

In 933 the third marriage of Robert the Pious, with Constance of Aquitaine, the daughter of William I, Count of Arles, brought, in the train of the new queen, Provençal courtiers whose strange garments astonished the Northern court; the chronicler Raoul Glaber notes the lively protests raised by Guillaume, Abbot of Saint Bénigne in Dijon, against the fashion for short hair and faces shaved 'like those of actors' and 'indecent shoes'.[35]

Costume historians have always referred to Orderic Vital (1075–1142) for support for their arguments: 'Tunics,' he said, 'were worn narrow but very long, with wide sleeves to the wrists and, like mantles, they had trains that trailed on the ground; men not only let their beards grow, but vied with one another to see who had the longest hair, like women, twisting and crimping it in various ways.' Furthermore, shoes were becoming longer and ended in points turned up 'like snakes' tails', a fashion that seems to have been introduced to the English court of William Rufus (1100) by a courtier named Robert; there is no evidence in this text that this Robert was Robert Courte-Hose, Duke of Normandy, as Enlart claims.

The curious part is that Orderic Vital, while giving these precise details, notes that people were now attracted only to Barbarian[36] ways, 'whether in way of life or fashion of dress.'

If we compare this text with the objurgations levelled in France against their contemporaries[37] by Sellon, Bishop of Séez (1122), Milon, Bishop of Térouane (1158), Geoffroy, Abbot of Vigeois (c. 1184), Maurice de Sully, Bishop of Paris (1196) and Pierre le Chantre (1197), we can observe that without exception what they attack is the *excessive* lengthening of tunics, gowns and cloaks with exaggerated trains or the fashion for over-long hair and curving-toed shoes, but not the normal long costume, which they themselves wore and whose simplicity for laymen and austerity for clerics accorded in their minds with a Christian ideal of humility and universality.[38]

This incursion of high fancy into secular costume is perhaps a first aspiration to liberation from a religious, spiritual conformism; but we must still wait for a century and a half before we see the appearance of clothing that expresses an independent lay individualism.

COSTUME IN EUROPE IN THE ROMANESQUE PERIOD

Before long costume became general wear, around 1140, the everyday costume of men remained much the same as in the preceding period. What some authors have called a *short bliaud* was probably the *gonelle* of the Carolingian period. The survival of the latter term in the English *gown* seems to imply that William the Conqueror, in the Norman Invasion of England, brought over this costume, which figures in the Bayeux Tapestry (plate 295). The word *bliaud*, from the Germanic-derived *blialt* (cloth) was gradually substituted for the term *gonelle*: the change can be explained by the influence of the Carolingian dynasty.

From this period on, costume for men and women alike consisted of the *chainse*, a long under-tunic with long sleeves, generally made of linen, and the *bliaud*, an outer tunic, also sleeved, wider for men, decorated with embroidery and braid and perhaps even with insets of cloth in different colours.

Apart from these two essential pieces, which are those most often represented, the *doublet* was worn under the bliaud; this was a short, fitted undergarment made of two thicknesses of linen. The *peliçon* was another undergarment, without sleeves, made of animal skin sewn between two pieces of cloth; the *gipon* or *jupe*, a short, very tight undergarment, was laced up one side, quilted and padded.

Initially the bliaud pouched over the belt, which it hid, but at the end of the twelfth century women wore it fitting so tightly that it outlined the torso, perhaps as the result of the use of silk. The girdle became visible, passing round the waist, then again round the hips to be tied in front, with the two ends falling to the feet. The sleeves of the *bliaud* worn by women began to be flared in elegant costume: they were to become so long that their ends were knotted to prevent their trailing on the ground.

As in the preceding period, rectangular and circular cloaks were currently worn: these are the *chape* (cape) and the *chasuble*. The term 'mantle' tended to replace the ancient names

171

'pallium' and 'chlamys', but referred principally to a garment reserved for the wealthier classes.

Women still veiled their heads with a corner of their mantles; their hair, which was generally dressed in long, dangling plaits, was concealed under a fine veil.

The only specifically male garment in this period was the breeches, *braies*, which were fairly long, wide trousers, generally coloured, worn under the *bliaud*.

Chausses, or hose, cover the legs; these were always made of tailored cloth, coloured and sometimes striped. Those worn by men often reached quite high; it is probable that women wore them too, though they are never visible below their long garments.

Footwear did not differ much from that worn in the preceding period, except at the beginning of the twelfth century, when shoes lengthened into a point, known as a *pigache*, mentioned by Orderic Vital. At the end of the century, we see brodequins whose moderately high legs are finished behind in long tabs, sometimes cut and festooned. The word *solers* appears during this century, applied to shoes in Cordoban leather (from which we derive the word cordwainer) which had recently been introduced. The use of wooden pattens seems to have spread during this century, for some specimens are found illustrated in contemporary documents.

The innovations introduced by Roman costume (less in the shape of garments than in their decoration) were characterized by the development of embroidery and ornamentation and by the taste for bright colours, both indicating a continuation of the influence of Byzantine costume.

Notes

1 Salin, p. 33.
2 d'Arbois de Jubainville, pp. 337–342.
3 Hubert, pp. 124, 135.
4 Salin, *Tierornament, passim.*
5 Cf. the finest study of this subject: Jullian, II, pp. 296–301.
6 Audollent, *passim.* An almost complete woman's costume was found in Puy-de-Dôme in 1851, but has unfortunately been lost.
7 Term of Celtic or Illyrian origin, giving the French *cagoule.*
8 Déonna, *passim.*
9 From the Gaulish *bracca:* the root of the word seems to have been the Indo-European *bragh.*
10 In 397 the Emperor Honorius still forbade their wear in Rome.
11 'Crossed' textiles similar to modern 'Merino' have been found. (Perron).
12 Particularly the S-shaped or the cross-bow types.
13 As it is impossible to give this study the space it deserves, the reader should consult Salin, Baum and Déchelette.
14 Cf. particularly Ebersolt, pp. 38, 142 and *passim.*
15 *Ibid.,* p. 38.
16 Cf. Greek psalter in the British Museum. (Add. ms. 19352).
17 Enlart, p. 15; Harmand, pp. 32, 14.
18 Jerphanion, pp. 71–79.
19 Ivanov, p. 325.
20 Cf. miniatures in a Greek psalter (early eleventh century, St. Mark's Library, Venice): Bulgarian chiefs are kneeling before Basil II, wearing tunics and chlamys.
21 Salin and Lanord, pp. 199, 227, 289; Lantier, p. 188.
22 Grégoire de Tours mentions 'honourable garments' for the dead of all classes.
23 Kuhn; Salin, pp. 113–115.
24 Harmand, p. 82.
25 Baum, figs. 16–17, plate IX, fig. 24, plate XII.
26 *Arts de France,* 1961.
27 Salin, *Lézéville,* p. 74.
28 Barrière-Flavy, *passim.;* Baum, *passim.*
29 Eginhard also mentions it later for Charlemagne.
30 Pirenne, pp. 55, 60 note 3.
31 Enlart, p. 315.
32 Mâle, *Histoire de l'Art,* p. 261.
33 Vita Caroli, chapter XXII.
34 Particularly Quicherat and even Enlart, and all their followers.
35 Glaber, IV, p. 9; Faral, pp. 20–21.
36 The term *barbarians* must be understood as applying to the non-Christianized peoples of Europe, rather than in the sense now attached to the word.
37 Bourgain, *passim;* Rathode died in 1038 in Bruges.
38 Enlart, pp. 318–341, entire chapter; Dom Cabrol, vol. II, *passim.*

Bibliography

GENERAL

CAMILLE JULLIAN: *Histoire de la Gaule,* vol. II, 1909.
EUNICE RATHBONE GODDARD: *Women's Costume in French Texts of the Eleventh and Twelfth Centuries.* Baltimore, 1927.
B. SALIN: *La Civilisation mérovingienne.* 1950.
J. BAUM: *La Sculpture figurale en Europe à l'époque mérovingienne.* 1927.
H. HUBERT: *Les Germains.* 1952.
B. SALIN: *Die altgermanische Thierornamentik.* Stockholm, 1904.
B. DÉONNA: *Du Télesphore au Moine Bourru.* 1955.
DECHELETTE: *Manuel d'archéologie préhistorique, celtique et gallo-romaine.* 1910–31.
B. SALIN and F. LANORD: 'Le Cimetière de Varangeville', in *Gallia* IV, 1946.
R. LANTIER: 'Le Cimetière wisigothique d'Estagal', in *Gallia,* I, 1943.
R. SALIN: *Le Cimetière barbare de Lézéville,* 1922.
H. PIRENNE: *Histoire économique de l'Occident médiéval.* 1951.
A. RICH: *Dictionnaire des Antiquités.* 1861.
C. DIEHL: *Manuel d'art byzantin.* 1930.
PAUL LEMERLE: *Le Style byzantin.* 1943.
JEAN EBERSOLT: *Les Arts somptuaires de Byzance.* 1923.
Gallia, vols I, IV, study by B. SALIN, F. LANORD, LANTIER.
ABBÉ L. BOURGAIN: *La Chaire française au XIIe s.* 1879.
E. FARAL: *Jongleurs de France au Moyen Age.* 1910.

COSTUME

F. CUMONT: 'L'Uniforme de la cavalerie orientale et le costume byzantin, in *Byzantion,* 1926.
D'ARBOIS DE JUBAINVILLE: 'Le Pantalon gaulois', in *Revue d'Archéologie,* 1913.
A. AUDOLLENT: *Les Tombes gallo-romaines de Veyre.* (Académie des Inscr. et Belles-Lettres). 1923.
KONDAKOV: 'Les Costumes à la cour de Byzance', in *Byzantion,* 1924.
P. DE JERPHANION: 'Le Thorakion', in *Mélanges Ch. Diehl,* vol. II, 1930.
JORDAN IVANOV: 'Le Costume des anciens Bulgares', in *L'Art byzantin chez les Slaves,* vol. V.
HERBERT KUHN: *Handbook of the Dumbarton Oaks Collection.* Washington, 1946.
A. HARMAND: *Jeanne d'Arc, son costume...,* 1929.
DOM CABROL: *Dictionnaire d'archéologie chrétienne.* Vol. IV, 1907, 1951.
M. FLEURY and A. FRANCE-LANORD: 'Les Bijoux mérovingiens d'Arnegonde' in *Art de France,* 1961.

TEXTILES

PERRON: in *Revue Archéologique,* 1882.
C. BARRIERE-FLAVY: *Les Arts industriels des peuples barbares de la Gaule, du Ve au VIIe s.* 1901.
C. CHARTRAIRE: 'Les Tissus du Trésor de Sens', in *Revue d'Art Chrétien,* 1911.

297 FRA ANGELICO: *Death of Saint Dominic*. Mid-fifteenth century. Paris, Louvre. (Photo Flammarion)

Chapter VI

Europe between the Twelfth and Four-teenth Centuries

Costume and New Conditions of Life

THE RELIGIOUS SPIRIT AND THE CRUSADES

New modes can be seen in Europe as early as the end of the twelfth century, but it was during the two following centuries that ideas and taste, as well as the material conditions of life, underwent profound transformations. The new religious spirit, the Crusades, trade relations and general economic progress all contributed more or less directly to the changes that took place in clothing, as also did the technical progress that we know took place then, although it cannot be precisely dated: the invention of the spinning-wheel and of carding, the introduction of more efficient looms and the standards laid down in cloth-making company rules.[1]

It must be said that these influential factors did not exist simultaneously from the twelfth century to the mid-fourteenth: the Crusades, which had begun in 1095, ended in 1270; the decline of Moslem sea-power dated from the tenth century and Italian maritime trade was in full swing at the beginning of the twelfth century. The most important, most spectacular aspect of this period was the immense upsurge in spiritual life, in mysticism and religious discipline, which generated the Crusades in which all the Christian peoples of the West took part. In this radiation of a common faith which began after the Greek schism of 1054 and broadened with Pope Urbanus' appeal in 1095 and the founding of the Order of Citeaux by Robert de Molesmes in 1098, we find a return to the spirit of the time of the Apostles. This is reflected in the common, impersonal character of costume, outwardly unifying Christendom as the Crusades united it in a single, indivisible surge of faith.

Most historians of European costume have notwithstanding recorded its length and fullness rather than its uniformity, and generally assigned these two features to the Crusades which allegedly brought to Europe clothing and costumes that were formerly specifically Eastern. The Crusades are said to have produced, not a pious detachment from the goods of this world, but an appetite for material enjoyment and refined luxuries. Yet is this theory not in contradiction with the irresis-

173

298 The cloth-merchants.
Thirteenth century.
North porch, Rheims Cathedral. (Photo Archives Photographiques)

299 Donation of Duke Richard, Mont-Saint-Michel Cartulary.
Mid twelfth century.
Paris, Bib. Nat., ms 210 f. 19. v. (Photo Bibliothèque Nationale)

tible current of religious enthusiasm and the ardent desire for knightly adventure that marked the period?

The influence of the Crusades on clothing showed itself much more in textiles than in the form of garments. It is difficult to find another explanation for the typically European phenomenon of the long costume well before the First Crusade, while Eastern styles had already penetrated into the West long before. On the contrary, the Crusades led to the penetration of Western costume into the East: the traveller Ibn-Jobaïr, describing a French wedding celebrated in Tyre in 1184, specifies that all the ladies present wore sumptuous gowns with trailing trains – 'in the French style'. Does he not thus emphasize their clearly foreign character in the East?[2]

In fact, all contemporary historians of the Crusades speak in very vague terms of the lengthening of gowns or the *barbaresque* fashions adopted in hair or beards. We have already seen that these caprices of European costume existed before the Crusades and were condemned as early as the tenth century, as excesses rather than as innovations in costume. Widely flaring sleeves had enjoyed successive vogues since the middle of the eighth century: it is difficult to see in them the importation of an Eastern style.

Some sources have also attempted to assign Eastern origins to the *amigaut*, a sort of fairly short slit placed in the centre or to one side of the neck of the surcoat. It does indeed recall a feature of Persian shirts or Kashmiri blouses, but we cannot base ourselves on the example provided by the famous 'bliaud of the Emperor Henri II' (1024, Bayerisches Museum), which was altered later.

Nor does any document prove that the North African *gandourah* inspired the mode for the sleeved surcoat which appeared towards 1220 and was adopted by King Louis.

From the various written sources we possess, we can gather the magnitude of the discovery the Crusaders made, coming on a whole Eastern civilization, steeped in essentially Eastern luxury, splendour and refinement. To these men, who had renounced their ancestral ways, who willingly underwent all the privations and dangers of their immense expedition, who had accepted prolonged exile, almost without hope of return,

the East offered, even before their arrival in the Holy Land, the charm of a legendary land, from the gardens on the Orontes to the rich palaces of Saint-John-of-Acre.

It is not surprising, then, that on their arrival in Palestine the Crusaders were won over by this seduction, and adopted, in civilian as well as in military costume, garments which were appropriate to the climate. Pilgrims and the colonists of the numerous feudal states of Asia Minor settled in Tyre, Antioch and Jerusalem, in dwellings whose decoration harmonized with their new dress; they sent for their families from Europe, or married Syrian or Saracen women, as once the Achaeans had done in Ionia. The chronicler Foucher de Chartres, who took part in the First Crusade, deplored these defections: 'the man who was Roman or Frankish is here become Galilean or Palestinian; the man who lived in Chartres or Rheims here becomes a citizen of Tyre or Antioch. We have already forgotten where we were born.'

There they discovered not only the long, wide-sleeved tunics and the wide Arab garments which are still represented by the *mashla* and *abbas* of Asia Minor, made of simple woollen or silken cloth decorated with gold braid and bead-embroidered; they also found new types of garment, like the fur-lined pellisses which were arriving, by the caravan routes, in the markets of the coast: ermine, then known as 'Babylon skin', dark marten or *zibeline*, *gros vair* and *petit vair*, Northern squirrels or red and white foxes from the Caspian.

Oriental textiles were still more appreciated and prized by the Crusaders: Guillaume of Tyre speaks of their first astonishment before 'these innumerable garments all in silk', captured as booty or received as gifts. The new masters of the Holy Land soon became used to wearing them. In 1138, at the siege of Caesarea, the Prince of Antioch and the Count of Rhodes were clad in these materials and wore pointed slippers or shoes on their otherwise bare feet. In 1161 the trousseau of Mélisande, the sister of the Count of Tripoli, sought in marriage by Manuel I Comnenius, Emperor of Constantinople, included 'gowns of rich, silken stuffs worked in many different fashions'.

In 1162 the Sultan Saladin presented Bohemond, Prince of Antioch, with ceremonial mantles lined with fur, and sent the

MONASTIC COSTUME

297, 299, 300 The bishop wears a mitre with the points on either side (plate 299). Monks wear peasant costume: a long, hooded gown known as a *froc*, a *coule frock* or a *cowl*

PILGRIMS

301 Saint James is always presented in the costume of pilgrims to Compostela, which varied little over the centuries: a long gown, a scarf (a bag carried on one shoulder), a staff (in this case broken) and a wide-brimmed felt or straw hat whose brim could be turned down as protection against the rain; the pilgrim always wore a prominent lead emblem or a shell picked up on the beaches of Galicia

CRUSADERS

302 The only feature that distinguishes the Crusader is the cross which seems here to be hung on the chest instead of being sewn into the garment. The Crusader's wife wears a wide-sleeved bliaud and a head-dress with a barrette and veil

300 Cistercian monk, manuscript from the Abbey of Cîteaux. Twelfth century. Dijon, Library. (Photo Rémy)

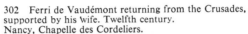

301 Saint James. Burgundian school. Fifteenth century. Paris, Louvre. (Photo Archives Photographiques)

302 Ferri de Vaudémont returning from the Crusades, supported by his wife. Twelfth century. Nancy, Chapelle des Cordeliers.

303 Column-statues on the portal of Chartres Cathedral. Second half twelfth century. (Photo Flammarion)

304   Miracle of Saint Giles, fresco from the Church of Saint-Aignan-sur-Cher. Late twelfth century. Paris, Musée des Monuments Français.

305   Sicilian silk cloth. Late thirteenth century. Lyon, Musée Historique des Tissus. (Photo Basset)

306   Coronation of Roger II, mosaic in La Martorana, Palermo. Mid twelfth century. (Photo Anderson-Giraudon)

ORIENTAL INFLUENCES

303   Pleated, goffered bliauds decorated with embroidery suggest, despite their stylization, the new luxury of silk materials. They are fitted, and held by a double girdle of *lorins* (plaited thongs) round the waist and hips. The long sleeves were sometimes knotted to prevent them from trailing on the ground

304   Saint Giles, wearing a cote, gives the poor man, clad only in draped breeches and bamberges (leggings) his surcoat, opening at the neck in an amigaut (slit), a fashion allegedly brought back from the Crusades

COSTUME IN SICILY

306–7   Roger II wears the costume of Byzantine emperors with the loros and the stemma type of crown with pendants. The cape-type of mantle is in purple embroidered with gold and beads; the cloth came from the royal workshops in Palermo and the decorative motifs, showing a fight between a lion and a camel, are Oriental in inspiration

LONG COSTUME

308–12   Men and women wear the same *cote*, long and flowing, with sleeves that were wide at the top and fitted tightly at the wrist, without embroidery or other ornament. Over this they wore the *surcoat* (plate 310) without sleeves, with armholes whose size varied. The cloak seems to be rectangular: it is the *mantel à parer* or *manteau noble*, sometimes lined or trimmed with fur (plates 308 and 310) fastened with a cord held in place by hand (plates 308–9, 312).
The curled fringe worn by men (plates 308, 310–11) is the *dorelot*. Women's and men's hair is hidden by the coif, sometimes accompanied by a circlet in finely worked precious metal (plates 308, 312). Reliquaries are worn at the neck (plate 311). The knight (plate 308) wears a circlet round his neck and falconry gauntlets, he wears *solers* on his feet

VARIOUS FORMS OF LONG COSTUME

313–4, 316–7   The costume remains long and loose, with a low girdle which might be hidden by the pouching of the gown. The open surcoat leaves the arms free (plate 313). Hair is still curled or massed behind the head, hidden by the coif (plate 314) or held by a circlet (plates 313, 316). The gathered coif of Margaret of Cobham (plate 318), known as a nebulated head-dress, was still to be seen in the fifteenth century. Men's cloaks are *garde-corps*.
English gowns (plate 316) are decorated with armorial bearings and Italian women's gowns (plate 317) are in richer material than French garments of the same period. The décolleté neckline of gowns becomes more pronounced

ACADEMIC COSTUME (LONG GOWN)

315   The doctor wears a surcoat (perhaps a *cotehardie*) with a fur-lined hood; open in front, with short, elbow-slit sleeves through which we can see the tight sleeves of the cote, fastened with *noiels* (buttons). The surcoat is slit with *fichets* at the side, for the hands to pass through. The patient wears a similar costume, but with long slit sleeves. The shoes are *poulaines* or *crackows*.

Count Henri de Champagne a magnificent tunic and turban which the Count duly wore at Acre: 'You know', wrote the Count, 'that your gowns and turbans are far from despised here: I shall certainly wear your gifts.' The Emperor Baudoin I had already set them an example by entering into Jerusalem in 1100 wearing a 'burnous woven with gold'.[3]

Nor were 'Frankish' women settled in the East slow to adopt *barbaresque* styles: long gowns with flaring sleeves, muslins (then cloths of silk and gold from Mosul), locally produced gauzes and crepes, Indian crepes and foulard silks of Chinese origin.

It was probably through them that the luxurious textiles of Asia Minor were introduced into the West, at least among the upper classes: before the Crusades, they had only been imported into Europe by pilgrims, in the form of rare, precious specimens still preserved today in cathedral treasuries. Chroniclers and preachers, our best sources in this connection, convey well the taste for luxury and softness that several generations had already carried back with them, but bear witness particularly to the immense vogue for the textiles popularized by the Crusaders: yarn or cotton stuffs like fustian, woollens like the camlets of Cyprus, Syria and Asia Minor, precious silks from Persia, Syria, Cyprus or Egypt, siglaton, damask, marramask, samite, cendal... not to mention the rich Almerian cloths known as *ispahanis*, which were the first Oriental textiles to be manufactured in the West.

EASTERN INFLUENCES TRANSMITTED BY SICILY AND SPAIN

Sicily and Spain, the first points of political and spiritual contact between Christian Europe and the Moslem world, also introduced, well before the eleventh century, Eastern textiles into Western countries.

The conquest of Sicily by Norman knights had begun by 1060, with the support of the Italian fleets; the last resistance of the Saracens was overcome in 1091 after just over thirty years of fighting. Norman pilgrims returning from Syria in 1016 were originally seduced, after expelling the Moslems from

307 Coronation cloak of Roger II. 1133
Vienna, Kunsthistorisches Museum. (Museum photo)

309 Statue on the tomb of Adelaide of Champagne, Joigny. Thirteenth century. (Photo Archives Photographiques)

310 Tomb slab of Ulric of Regensburg *c.* 1290. Zürich, Schweizerisches Landesmuseum. (Museum photo)

308 Drawing by Villard de Honnecourt. Thirteenth century. Paris, Bib. Nat. ms fr. 19093 f. 27. (Photo Flammarion)

311–2 Statues of Count Eckhart and Countess Uta, Naumberg Cathedral. Thirteenth century. (Photos Giraudon)

313 The Tale of Meliacin. Late thirteenth to mid fourteenth century. Paris, Bib. Nat. ms fr. 1633 f. 4. (Photo Bibliothèque Nationale)

314 Tomb of Kuno von Falkenstein and his wife, Lich, 1333. (Photo Bildarchiv Marburg)

315 GUY OF PAVIA: *Anatomy*. Early fourteenth century. Chantilly, Musée Condé. (Photo Giraudon)

Salerno, according to the chronicler Aimé of Monte Cassino, by the gifts they received from the citizens of the town, particularly by mantles of purple. When, after Robert Guiscard, the Duchy of Normandy had been transformed into the Kingdom of the Two Sicilies, Roger II was to have himself represented in a Byzantine dalmatic in the paintings and mosaics of La Martorana in Palermo.

The Saracens had established their textiles as firmly as their costume, by setting up factories in Sicily. 'Christian ladies', says Ibn-Jobaïr, 'completely follow the fashions of Moslem women in the way they veil themselves and wear their mantles. For the feast of Christmas, they go out clad in gold-coloured silk gowns; wrapped in elegant mantles, covered with coloured veils, with gilded brodequins on their feet, they flaunt them-selves in church in perfectly Moslem toilettes.'[4] Here we see the same assimilation that took place in the Holy Land.

We know the importance acquired by the royal textile workshop in Palermo, installed in the Tiraz Palace where, apparently, the magnificent royal cape in the Vienna Treasury was made for the same Roger II, who died in 1154. The Sicilians also supplied textiles to the Crusaders, making them cloth suited to the tastes for Oriental luxury they had acquired in Asia.

The striking colours, the lightness and the rich, novel ornamentation of these Arab textiles won them growing favour in the West at the expense of the heavy Byzantine cloths. The similarity of the motifs of animals, horsemen, etc., often set in roundels, used in Saracen textiles from Sicily and Spain often makes it difficult to distinguish between the two groups. With considerable changes, these motifs are found later in certain medieval textiles. Later, the Sicilian textile industry went into a rapid decline and the weavers from the old workshops of Palermo emigrated to Lucca, where Byzantine-Saracen ornament became mingled with elements of the Gothic style which had already been introduced into Italy from the north-east.

However, Oriental influence continued to penetrate through Sicily as far as Central Europe when Frederick II of Hohenstaufen, after his defeat at Bouvines (1214) and his coronation as emperor (1220) once and for all turned from his German Empire towards the Mediterranean. He made his capital in Palermo, where his court took on a cosmopolitan aspect, half Christian and half Moslem, and adopted Oriental ways.

In Spain, the celebrated pilgrimage to the shrine of Saint James at Compostela had created a continous movement from France to Galicia from the middle of the eighth century. French expeditions designed to protect this route began in 1018, followed by more than thirty others over the next two centuries. The first attempt at the deliverance of Spain, by the Aquitanian Gui Geoffroi in 1063, placed in his hands a quantity of wealth whose splendour is recorded in the *Chansons de Geste*. There again, as in the Holy Land, the French barons easily adopted Moorish customs, as in the case of the Aquitanian lord who, after the capture of Barbastro in 1064, settled, according to Ibn-Haiyân, in the house of the former Moslem governor, wearing his clothes and slippers. From this time on, exchanges of textiles were very frequent between Spain and Italy.

ECONOMIC AND SOCIAL CONDITIONS

One thing that can certainly be said for the Crusades is that they brought about the emergence of new conditions, aiding the development of international communications, the revival of economic exchanges, the strengthening of royal power and, in trading and industrial cities, the appearance of a system of compulsory corporations, and the emergence of a new social class composed of merchants and craftsmen. In the evolution of costume during this period the economic factors are of considerable importance.

The expansion of international exchanges resulting from the Crusades, the formation of important industries in Flanders, the south of France and the north of Italy contributed to the birth of a new capitalism, which provided a source of luxury in clothing and led to the consitution of organizations for the trades involved. Moreover, the Mediterranean had regained its mastery of trade, which it had lost with the Arab invasions in the eighth century. With maritime contact between East and West completely re-established, Byzantium, thus deprived of its sea-power, lost its supremacy, the route from the Baltic by

316 PIETRO LORENZETTI: *Good Government* (detail).
Fourteenth century. Siena, Palazzo Communale. (Photo Scala)

317 Luttrell Psalter, *c.* 1340, London, British museum. Ms f. 202 v.
(Museum photo. Courtesy of the Trustees)

way of the Dniepr was given up and the Russian markets were gradually abandoned in favour of London and Bruges.

Thus, from the end of the eleventh century, two particularly important basic materials of costume, wool and silk, gained a degree of availability which was to increase from century to century, in the case of wool by means of technical improvements and commercial organization, and in the case of silk because of political and military events which led to new international relationships.

During the twelfth and thirteenth centuries, costumes benefited from social changes: a courtly nobility, qualified by administrative functions or military services, gathered round the sovereign, and a rich, powerful middle class, born of the increase in trade, took shape. Quite naturally rich burghers tried to imitate the nobles, and both profited from the economic prosperity that was added to the intellectual and artistic renewal of the whole of Europe. Chroniclers have mentioned this general increase in the richness and luxury of costume, particularly in France: at the rejoicings that marked the victory of Bouvines (1214) and the coronation of Louis VIII (1223) everyone wore samite, scarlet stuff and fine linen, and all classes of society decked themselves in brightly coloured materials embroidered with gold.

Furthermore, literary culture and 'courtly' customs gave added strength to the taste for elegance among this nobility and middle class.

Women looked to romances for ideas as to what shoes to wear, how to buy embroidered belts or caps with carved rosettes, how to accentuate their slim waists by holding back a panel of the mantle, how to show off their graceful feet by tucking up their skirts, or how to cultivate a swaying walk. The fashion for swinging the hips began about 1240 and became general about 1300.

Writers obligingly accorded these excesses greater attention than they deserved: when the *Roman de la Rose* (*c.* 1225) recommended women to wear false hair in rolls and horns, to leave their gowns open a good half foot in front and down the back, it recorded only the caprices of a minority.[5] This must be borne in mind when we are considering these modes.

THE EFFECTS OF LUXURY

An elegance that had until then been reserved exclusively for a traditionally privileged sector of society now came within the reach of new social categories.

This competition in splendid costume eventually led the nobility to demand – and obtain – at the end of the thirteenth century certain sumptuary regulations: they hoped in this way to use costume to maintain social distinction threatened by the rise of a new capitalism. The civil authorities followed the example of earlier councils, such as the Council of Le Mans, held in 1188, but with other motives than Christian charity and humility.

Certain colours and styles, certain ornaments were forbidden to the middle classes. In Germany, for example, sable and ermine were reserved for noble ladies. In France the Consuls of Montauban promulgated in 1274 and 1291 interdicts against

318 Tomb brass of Lady Margaret of Cobham. 1315.
(Photo Flammarion)

179

319 Cap and aljuba belonging to Ferdinando de la Cerda, who died aged twenty, 1211

320–21 Tunic and pellotes of Leonora of Aragon. 1244. Monastery of Las Huelgas, near Burgos. (Photos Dominguez Ramos)

the wearing of certain furs, silk or purple garments or luxury ornaments in the street.

The better to stifle this rivalry, attempts were made to limit spending on costume in proportion to the resources of the wearer. The royal ordinance of 1294 repeats earlier edicts: no man or woman of the middle classes might wear *vair*, squirrel or ermine, gold or precious stones, crowns of gold or silver; but in particular, it makes several new points: dukes, counts, barons, knights and squires might buy only a certain number of new gowns each year. This applied equally to their wives, according to a decreasing scale of incomes from 6000 to 200 livres annually; moreover, the ordinance fixed the average price of the materials to be used.

In the event, these regulations never had any appreciable effect: the *Tournament of the Ladies of Paris* (c. 1290) shows middle class women of the Grand Pont, the Grève and the Courroierie districts displaying the excesses of their costume without apparent care for the sumptuary restrictions then officially in force.

Costume in Western and Central Europe

Numerous representations (miniatures, wall paintings, bas-reliefs and sculptures) permit us to observe the uniformity of costume throughout Western Europe in the thirteenth century. The work by Matthew Paris, *Les Vies des Offas*, and the *Livre de Santé* (late thirteenth century), and the Trinity College *Apocalypse* present the same types of costume to be seen in France during the same period: cote, doublet, cotehardie, surcoat with amigaut, cape or tippet for both sexes; breeches for men and the *sorquanie* for women. We find similar garments in Italy in the paintings decorating San Benedetto at Subiaco and

Santa Croce in Florence, except that the surcoats worn by men were made with more cloth, and women's gowns had longer trains.

In Spain, the costumes of the Spanish royal family found in tombs at the monastery of Las Huelgas, near Burgos, are identical with those worn by the princes of the French branch of the Valois family: the same cotes fastened with side lacing, and surcoats with wide arm-openings. Certain miniatures such as those in the *Book of Chess* of the Castilian King, Alfonso X the Wise (1221–1284) represent women with moderately decorated costumes and tall, narrow head-dresses, a style that may have been specifically Spanish.

Lastly, the same stylistic traits are found in Germany, in the costumes of the Rhineland, Franconia and Bavaria, as they appear in the cathedral sculptures of Cologne, Mainz, Strasbourg or Bamberg. We can compare the corresponding French sculptures at Saint Trophime in Arles, and the cathedrals of Chartres and Bourges.

However, names in *langue d'oïl* replaced the old Latin terms: old words disappeared (for instance, 'tunique' was replaced by 'bliaud'), and new terms were invented – *doublet*, *peliçon*, *gippon*, *guimple*, *amigaut* – whose appearance is difficult to date either from texts or from carved or other representations. Nor is it easy to follow the career of any one part of costume and trace its development across these changes in nomenclature: many authors limit themselves to enumerating the terms without specifying to which elements of clothing they referred, and a whole study could be devoted to this question, aiming at throwing a little light on the confusion which reigns and establishing exact correspondences between medieval costume and its vocabulary.

We must stress that the wearing of long costume affected only the upper, wealthier classes; the costume of poor people and workers was hardly to change until the end of the Middle Ages.

CIVILIAN COSTUME

The sovereigns, who wore the ordinary costume of the wealthy classes in everyday life, retained in ceremonial costume a dal-

322 Bas-relief on the door of Saint Mary of the Capitol, Cologne. *c.* 1065. (Photo Hugo Schmölz)

323–4 Sculptures from the tympanum of the basilica, Vézelay. Twelfth century. (Photos Collection Vogade and Archives Photographiques)

SPANISH COSTUME

319–21 The costumes found in the tombs of Ferdinando de la Cerda (died 1211) and Leonora of Aragon (died 1244) are the only European garments of this period to have survived. They are simple in cut, similar for both sexes, with seams slanting to give fullness at the foot.

The *aljuba* (Arabic word, from which the Western *gippon* and the French *jupe* derive) is in Castilian cloth with a heraldic design, lined with crimson taffeta and worn with breeches fastened at the waist. The *pellotes* (open surcoat) of the same cloth is longer than the aljuba and breeches.

The tunic of Leonora of Aragon, which is badly damaged, shows the side lacing; her pellotes in Arabian brocade is very long and must have trailed on the ground.

The armorial bearings are to be seen again, embroidered in coloured beads, on the cap, which is further decorated with gold and precious stones

ORDINARY PEOPLE'S COSTUME (TENTH TO TWELFTH CENTURIES)

322–6 The costume worn by ordinary people always included the short gown or *cottelle*, and breeches (plate 326) tucked into the brodequins. The costume was completed by a hood; when it was attached to the gown it was known as the *sayon* (plate 323), the ancestor of the caped hood. The cape with hood is a survival of the bardocucullus (plate 323); in the South it was known as the *balandras*

matic, slit at the sides and initially shorter than the cote, with long sleeves which stopped at the elbow in the reign of King Louis, then lengthened at the beginning of the fifteenth century. The royal cloak or *soccus*, which had kept the form of the Classical pallium, was still pinned on the right shoulder.

The whole set of pieces then took on the name *robe*,[6] which did not, as it does in modern French, refer to a single garment, but to all the clothes worn by one person: a *robe* could be formed of three, four, five or six *garnements* according to the number of pieces, which were not necessarily worn simultaneously. Only in the middle of the twelfth century do we find the term *robe* applied solely to the undergarment.

The *bliaud* which, contrary to the affirmation of Enlart[7] is not mentioned before the *Chanson de Roland*, disappeared at the beginning of the fourteenth century and was replaced by the *cote*, a long tunic fitted on the upper part of the body and flaring out from the waist. The surcoat was a sleeveless over-

325 Shepherds, on the royal portal, Chartres Cathedral. *c.* 1150. (Photo Giraudon)

326 Carolingian Gospel Book. Ninth to eleventh centuries. Paris, Bib. Nat. ms lat. 8851 f. 12. (Photo Bibliothèque Nationale)

328 Tapestry of Queen Matilda ('Bayeux Tapestry'). Late eleventh century. (Photo Giraudon)

329 The Apocalypse of Saint Sever. Eleventh century. Paris, Bib. Nat. ms lat. 8878 f. 193. (Photo Bibliothèque Nationale)

ORDINARY PEOPLE'S COSTUME (THIRTEENTH TO FOURTEENTH CENTURIES)
327, 330–31 The short smock or *cotteron* is still the main item of ordinary costume. For harvesting, people wore wide hats over skull-caps or hoods (plate 327)

MILITARY COSTUME, TENTH, ELEVENTH AND TWELFTH CENTURIES
328–9, 333 The type of equipment does not vary: a *broigne* whose sleeves are hidden by the bliaud or hauberk of mail slit back and front for horseback (plate 328). The conical helm with nasal is worn above a collar of mail whose front part, protecting the chin, is movable. The multicoloured hose (plate 333) reach up over long, plain-coloured braies. The shield with a central umbo is convex

327 Martyrology of Usuard *c.* 1270. Paris, Bibl. Nat. ms lat. 12834 f. 59 v. (Photo Bibliothèque Nationale)

330 *The Charivari*, Romance of Fauvel. Late thirteenth century. Paris, Bib. Nat. ms fr. 146 f. 34. (Photo Bibliothèque Nationale)

tunic. The surcoat worn by women was very long and trailed on the ground, and was later to have very wide openings, often edged with fur, under the arms, becoming the open surcoat, a fashion which was to prove long-lasting.

The cut of outer garments at that time was very varied and carefully executed, but it is not easy to identify the different models: it seems that the *sorquenie* worn by women was a cote with a particularly close-fitting bust, while the cotehardie worn by both sexes was a fitted, full-skirted surcoat, short or long. In addition, the *garde-corps* and the *corset*, which could be worn over the former garments or replace them according to the season, seem to have been the first outer garments and were sometimes confused. The variety of sleeve styles: tight or loose, with or without hanging panels at the elbows, flaring wing sleeves or sleeves left open under the arms, may not always have entailed changes in the name of the garment, but they modify the general shape sufficiently to render identification difficult.

Outer garments and cloaks can be divided into two categories. Firstly, there is the open mantle, open down the front or at one side, also seen in the preceding period, which was a rain-cape called *balandran* in the south of France, or a *mantel à parer* or *mantel noble*, less full and generally fastened in front with a cord whose length could be controlled by holding it in the hand. Secondly, there is the *slip-on* or poncho-type *cloak*, slipped over the head and slit under the arm, which was known as *housse*, *hérigaut* or *garnache*, forms which are difficult to tell apart. While several authors agree that the garnache had two tabs crossed in front over the chest, it is nevertheless always for housses that we find mentions in account-books of the fur used for the tabs. In the fourteenth century the housse and the garnache formed part of the *robe à six garnements*.

The intermediary garments already worn in the preceding period (doublet, pelicon, gippon or jupe) had not been modified; however, they had been joined, for men, by the *cotte gamboisée* (gambeson) padded with wadding, and the *hoqueton*, a waistcoat, also padded, which were both worn under the armour and were assimilated into civilian costume at the end of the fourteenth century. All these quilted and padded garments

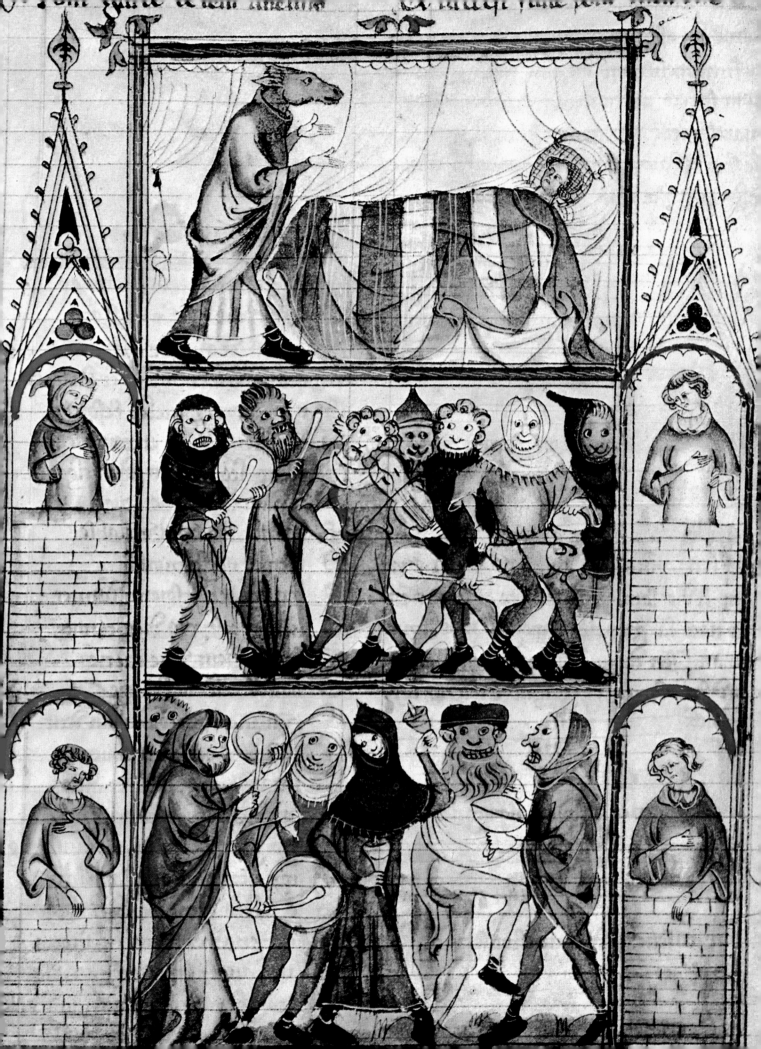

MILITARY COSTUME, THIRTEENTH CENTURY

332, 337 The hauberk is continued by a collet and coif, sleeves and wrist-pieces, and mail hose fastened up the back of the leg. A coat of arms camouflages the shiny armour. The length of the coats of arms (plate 334 and the use of a flat-topped helm without mobile visor, pierced with a sight-slit and holes, distinguish these knights from the preceding types

LITURGICAL COSTUME

335–6, 338 Episcopal costume consists of an alb with embroidered decoration, the amict round the neck, the wide-sleeved dalmatic and the chasuble (plate 335). We also see the manipule over the left arm and the ends of the stole, the episcopal gloves embroidered with a cross, the mitre (plate 338) worn by Saint Martin and the early form of tiara worn by Saint Gregory (plate 336). The pallium is of white wool embroidered with red crosses

331 Fresco. c. 1305.
Zürich, Schweizerisches
Landesmuseum.
(Museum photo)

332 Drawing by Villard de Honnecourt.
Mid thirteenth century.
Paris, Bib. Nat. ms fr. 19093.
(Photo Flammarion)

333 BOETIUS; *De consolatione philosophiae*. Eleventh century.
Paris, Bib. Nat. ms lat. 6401 f. 13, originally from Saint-Omer.

were to develop into the pourpoint of the following century.

The chemise of fine linen or even silk had taken the place of the *chainse*. Chausses, or hose, always made of tailored cloth, fitted very closely to the legs and became increasingly higher, particularly for men.

Men's breeches were worn draped at first, then took on the form of short pants; they were held up by a belt known as a *braiel*, to which the hose were also attached.

As for women's costume, while the sleeves of outer garments were often flaring or full, those of cotes were so tight that they had to be resewn at the wrist whenever they were put on, which gave rise to all manner of caprices in colour and in the use of contrasting cloths. But they were also easily unpicked and young women took scissors in their purses when they went to play in the woods 'with unsewn sleeves'; this fashion explains the habit of knights who in tournaments fixed a sleeve given by their lady to their helmet or shield.

Under Charles V these sleeves were to flare so widely from the elbow that they trailed on the ground.

The outer garment was sometimes so close-fitting that a belt was no longer needed; the neck became progressively more open and trimmings of embroidery and fur multiplied.

HAIR AND HEAD-DRESSES

Until the thirteenth century it seems that the only head-dresses worn by men and women alike were *circlets*, also called *tressoirs* or *frontals*, made of precious metals, braid or flowers, recalling the Classical band holding back the hair.

From the thirteenth century, men began to wear the *cale*, a fine linen cap, fastened under the chin, which was worn under a cap or a hat, and was called a *coiffe* when it had no chinstrap. They also wore the *calotte*, or skull-cap, a flat cap which could be hemispherical or take various forms, and lastly, *barrettes*, soft caps whose forms were probably very varied, whose name was later to pass to a cap built over a rigid framework with three or four panels, which was to become the head-dress of ecclesiastics and doctors in the sixteenth century.

334 Victory of Humility over Pride. Twelfth-century ms from Trier. Hanover, Kestner Museum. (Museum photo)

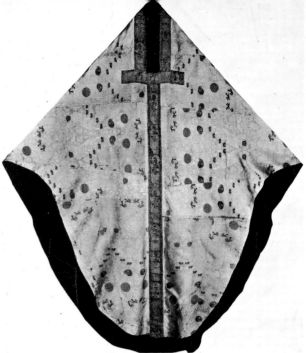

335 Chasuble in silk decorated with orfrays. Twelfth century. Berne, Historical Museum. (Museum photo)

The *aumusse* was a sort of very simple hood, a rectangle of folded, sewn cloth. The ecclesiastical aumusse was lengthened with bands that fell down the neck. The royal aumusse was only a skull-cap worn under the crown.

The term *couvre-chef* (coverchief) was applied to head-dresses in general but more particularly to a sort of linen or velvet turban worn at night, and also to a light type of cloth with which women covered their hair in various ways. Around 1280 it passed over the head to be fastened under the chin, and was crowned with a sort of standing starched band which some authors call *touret*: it is difficult to accept this as a precise term, for the same word is used in the fifteenth and sixteenth centuries for veils covering the brow or even the face, or bandeaux of gold or gems.

Towards the end of the twelfth century, the cape hood had been detached to form an independent head-dress, composed of a hood attached to a sort of closed *camail*, although women wore it open, hanging free on the shoulders. This head-dress was to play an important role in the costume of the following century and its transformations deserve detailed study.

FOOTWEAR

The shoes and boots of the preceding period survive: a type of light, short boot called *estivaux* seems to have been very popular. However, towards the middle of the fourteenth century, people often wore soled hose which did away with the need for shoes. Pattens and galoshes protected fine shoes.

UNIVERSITY COSTUME

In the twelfth century some social categories adopted a style of dress close to that of the clergy, in order to command respect and denote authority. Those people who wore long, austere costumes, sometimes with various special features, were to be called *gens de robe longue* in France, after the appearance of short costume.[8]

336 Saints Martin, Gregory and Jerome. South portal, Chartres Cathedral. *c.* 1250. (Photo Flammarion)

337 Psalter of Saint Louis. Thirteenth century. Paris, Bib. Nat. ms lat. 10525, f. 52. (Photo Bibliothèque Nationale.

338 Episcopal mitre with embroidery in gold thread and silk. Late fourteenth century. Paris, Musée de Cluny. (Photo Flammarion)

From the thirteenth century the *mires*, or physicians, wore long gowns, and are described by the chronicler Jean de Jeandun as 'walking through the streets of Paris in their bright costumes and doctoral caps'. Surgeons, on the other hand, wore the short gown; they were not entitled to wear long gowns or caps because they were considered to be more 'surgical workmen' working under the direction of the physicians.

On their emergence in the thirteenth century, the Universities obtained from Rome the right to fix their own costume, which was influenced by the religious habit since they were Church institutions. At the University of Paris, the rules took care to specify, for both masters and students, suitable, though not uniform clothing, which showed both the influence of the century's styles and considerations of discipline in dress.[9]

From 1215 to 1274, it was therefore prescribed that masters should wear a full, round, black *talaris* cape (cloak), similar to the pluvial but slit to allow the arms to reach through, and they were forbidden to wear pointed, laced or open-work shoes, or outer tunics (surcoats) slit down the sides. The mitre was reserved for indoor wear. In 1252 English students and in 1274 those of the Collège de Sorbonne were forbidden to wear capes without hoods in the same cloth, or the buttoned chaperon; those at the Sorbonne were also obliged to wear closed outer gowns and to eschew any *vair* or *petit gris* fur or red or green cendal in their costumes. All leanings towards elegance were thus rigorously discouraged.

In the Middle Ages this costume is to be found in substantially similar forms in the various universities of Christendom. Bachelors, on beginning to teach, wore the full, sleeveless, entirely closed cape, as did all graduates. Over this, the chaperon appears as a hooded cape, which was to be preserved in Spain and Portugal, or as a hood, which was to survive only in England.

This university costume was to undergo few changes in the sixteenth century, and throughout Western Europe it was to retain a certain uniformity, setting apart its wearers all the more strikingly as changes in fashion became more frequent and more radical.[10]

WORKING AND PEASANT COSTUME

The extreme poverty of the villein (workman or peasant) and the many burdens and restraints that weighed on his class kept this sector of society in a very simple costume until its liberation from serfdom. Men wore braies, a coarse blouse, coarse linen hose, heavy tied shoes and sometimes a shirt; for women, a chemise, a gown or cote, and hose. The hooded *sayon* or the frieze cape completed for both sexes the costume often represented in miniatures or cathedral sculptures (plates 323–5, 330–31) in cycles of the labours of the months.

This situation was modified as a result of the serf's gradual release from his lord's excessive fiscal demands, and under the influence of the Crusades which contributed to a social levelling. The increased trade in textiles produced by fairs – which spread rapidly after the twelfth century – and the prosperity 'unknown in Roman times' were no less important in bettering

339–40 Troparium originally from Saint Martial, Limoges. Mid eleventh century. Paris, Bib. Nat. ms lat. 1118 f. 112 v, 111. (Photos Bibliothèque Nationale)

341 Gothic fibula of gold and precious stones. Fourteenth century. Stockholm, National Museum of Antiquities

the serfs' lot, and it has been noted that at the beginning of the fourteenth century workmen and peasants wore 'body linen, woollen garments and shoes'.

RELIGIOUS COSTUME

Liturgical costume, whose forms were fixed definitively in the twelfth century, presented only modifications of detail (slits, neck openings) and of orfrey decorations during this period. Only the two-horned mitre was completely transformed at the end of the twelfth century to take on its present form, with the horns at back and front (plate 338).[11]

The regular orders that were multiplying were distinguished from one another only by the colour of their garments, the forms being those of ordinary civilian costume: for the Dominicans and later for the Celestines, a white gown and black caps; for the Franciscans, a brown hooded cote and a girdle of rope; for the so-called 'striped' Carmelites, a gown in alternating brown and white bands; for the Sachet brethren, simple linen peasants' smocks, and white gowns for the Carthusians and Premonstratensians.

In women's orders, the cowl was replaced by the coverchief or head-rail and the widow's head-rail covering the hair, ears and neck. In the daytime, a veil was added.

Pilgrims' dress was more or less closely related to religious costume – the pilgrims of Saint James at Compostela all wore a sort of uniform, and in 1096 Pope Urbanus II commanded the first Crusaders to wear a woollen cross on their clothes, at once a religions emblem and a rallying sign.

The three great Military and Hospital orders, half soldiers, half monks, were the Hospitalers or Knights of Saint John of Jerusalem, founded in the mid-eleventh century, the Templars, created in 1128 and the Teutonic Order, founded in 1198. All three adopted uniform clothing which assimilated them to religious communities: their long gowns, white for knights and black for brothers, were distinguished by the colour of the cross: white for the first order, red for the second and black for the third.[12] However, the activities of these orders were very different from those of monks, and their equipment developed according to the circumstances and the period; they had special costumes for war and in time lost their medieval character. Today such of those orders as have survived, for instance the Knights of Malta and those of the Holy Sepulchre, retain only the external insignia, cloak, hat and sword, worn on ceremonial occasions.

MILITARY AND KNIGHTLY COSTUME

The new element in military life under the feudal system at the end of the eleventh century was the knight, recruited from the nobility and recognizable by his special costume,[13] completed by distinctive signs after about the middle of the twelfth century (plates 332, 334, 337).

Over the bliaud of civilian costume, the knight wore a *broigne*, a jerkin of strong leather or linen, strengthened with a framework of metal or horn, which was already to be seen under the Carolingians, or a *hauberk* or coat of mail, already worn by the Assyrians in the seventh century BC and by the Romans, formed of rivetted rings and scales. The unarmed broigne was called a *gambeson* and was worn under the hauberk; it was slit at back and front to facilitate the mounting of horses and its two panels, laced or buckled over the thighs, formed a protective skirt. A baldrick supporting the sword was worn over the bliaud.

The hauberk formed a coif protecting the head and neck and leaving the upper part of the face exposed. An iron cap was added, and the large combat helmet, whose form varied, with a nasal and later a visor, was worn over it. The hauberk, which we find as early as 1100, was improved during the Crusades, made lighter with the use of fine Oriental mailed cloth made in Damascus, and completed with mailed hose and gauntlets lined with cloth or leather. Its currency corresponds exactly to the period when long costume was becoming general wear, from the mid-twelfth century to the mid-fourteenth. Rigid pieces or plates strengthened the coat of mail at the end of the thirteenth century.

187

Over the hauberk, the knight wore the coat of arms, a sleeveless or short-sleeved surcoat in cloth; his feet were shod in leather shoes.

The noble squires who accompanied and served knights formed a light cavalry on their own, under the name of 'horse serjeants', with less complete protective clothing. Infantry troops wore the broigne or the gambeson, the former particularly at the end of the twelfth century, when knights had abandoned it after improvements in the hauberk, and a woollen, leather or metal cap.

The Crusades added the flowing Arab gown, and the *kuffish* of samite or brocade wrapped round the helmet to this battle costume; the leather panel of the helmet was transformed into a light, flowing drapery. Horses, which until then had carried nothing under the high-pommelled saddles, were protected against arrows by long, flowing coats. In the *Roman de Galeran* the hero, after being installed as a knight, puts on a gown of gold and silk lined with ermine, one of those 'made in the land of the Moors'.[14]

The most curious practice borrowed by Crusaders from the East was that of having their arms painted on their shields, originally to rally round their men in the battle, then later as a fashion, perpetuated by tournaments.

The use of this decoration attached the art of heraldry, which remains closely linked to the history of European knighthood, to Oriental blazonry: indeed, the emirs had borne coats of arms before the eleventh century. Raymond de Saint-Gilles, Count of Toulouse, seems to have been the first of the Crusaders to wear a blazon, choosing the cross of Constantine 'voided and pommelled.'

The knight's arms figured on his shield, his helmet and his surcoat. The designs and colours, originally painted on the leather of the shield, became the pieces and enamels of the fully fledged armorial devices we see on the enamelled funerary effigy of Geoffroi Plantagenet (*c.* 1152) and in the monument to Pietro d'Eboli (1196).

According to some authors, armorial bearings have their origins in garments: the terms of heraldry are borrowed from the vocabulary of clothing: 'couped (cut), divided, split, hatched, fillet, band (or bend), chevron' etc.[15]

Romances of chivalry tell of the sumptuous coats of arms worn by knights in tournaments: 'in green samite sewn with golden eagles', with black lion-cubs and leopards. Philip the Bold followed the fashion for these coats in which prodigal use was made of gold and silver. In Saint Denis in Paris, a stained glass window represents the Holy Father handing his banner of 'glowing red samite' to a donor.

In combat, knights often decorated the crown of their helmets with a crest, a sort of identifying panache made of feathers or aigrettes, which might be a heraldic ornament or simply a decoration. At Bouvines in 1214, Renaud Count of Boulogne crowned his helmet with a double panache of whalebones; in the *Châtelain de Coucy*, a knight carries off to the Holy Land the plaits of his lady, and the Saracens call him 'he who wears tresses on his helm.'[16]

The vogue for emblems was so widespread that by the middle of the twelfth century even the costume of the nobility was to include suits of arms entirely made in the colours of the blazon, or of the 'lady' and decorated with motifs from the blazon appliquéd, or directly embroidered.

This fashion gave rise, at the beginning of the fourteenth century, to the 'parti-coloured dress', whose vertically divided halves were in different colours. Suits of livery and those worn by royal officers were often made in the colours of the overlord or the town during the next two centuries.

THEATRICAL COSTUME

From the thirteenth century, two clearly differentiated genres can be identified in the theatre.[17]

The liturgical drama of the Romanesque period was followed by the semi-liturgical drama, which was no longer played in the church itself but on a stage built in front of the main door.

The most important roles were played by specially chosen clerics. As women could not appear on stage, their parts were taken by young men whose long, flowing costume scarcely differed from that worn by women.

The brotherhoods continued to put on their plays, with some gradual modifications, until the sixteenth century. We know the Gréban (*c.* 1420–71), version of the Passion as well as the costumes worn by the participants. God the Father was dressed as a Pope or bishop, and Jesus wore a long, white robe; angels and seraphim wore choirboys' costume, and the prophets wore the garments of kings; Abel, Cain, Joseph, Lazarus and many others were clad like ordinary citizens of the time, with hoods, short pourpoints or long, loose gowns.

Towards the end of the thirteenth century we see the appearance of comic theatre, played by the 'joyful' brethren. This sometimes consisted of satirical revue, but more often *soties* or fanciful pieces mingled with jokes, singing and dancing. In farces such as the *Farce de Maistre Pathelin* or the *Mestier et Marchandises*, the actors wore everyday costumes. When angels or devils intervened the former simply added wings to their costumes, the latter, masks and tails. Finally, in the representations mounted by the *Basoche*, important characters often wore brilliantly coloured costumes. It is curious to note that much later, in 1529, one of the Basoche companies had adopted women's costume.

Fools and stupid characters wore a traditional costume of a scalloped or tooth-edged pourpoint with yellow and green striped hose, to make them easily recognizable by the audience.

We know that in the fifteenth century the chapel of the Dukes of Burgundy had its Feast of Fools: they formed a brotherhood whose members seem to have worn wide toothed collars and hats decorated with long ears. We also know the costumes worn in the *montrées* which included Mother Fool.

It seems that in the various theatrical genres before the Renaissance no considerations of historical accuracy troubled the actors of mystery plays or farces, and that the majority of the participants wore contemporary costumes, regardless of the setting of the action.

MISCELLANEOUS COSTUMES

After the twelfth century certain new varieties of costume appear, some springing from fanciful modes, others imposed by rules corresponding to new social needs.

Although originally *jongleurs* (plates 339–40, 342–3) had plain, simple costumes, by the twelfth century they drew attention to themselves by the strangeness of their accoutrement and brightly coloured stuffs. Among examples mentioned, some wore gowns of red silk and red cloaks with yellow cowls, or parti-coloured costumes. These costumes began a fashion, and were condemned by preachers for their frivolity.[18]

In the thirteenth century, in several Western European countries, edicts were issued to impose or forbid certain costumes or accessories to particular classes of persons, such as Jews, Saracens and people condemned for offences connected with religion. We know the dispositions of the Fourth General Lateran Council, obliging Jews to wear a special sign, the wheel or rowel in yellow or green, and pointed hats; similar examples are mentioned by texts in Germany and Strasbourg. Saracens and Moors were likewise constrained. Heretics, Waldensians and people convicted of witchcraft were obliged to wear special signs and cut their hair in specified ways.

These edicts were most often issued by religious authorities, but they could also emanate from royal authority, as in Portugal and France, or from local authorities.[19]

It has rarely been stressed that the Arabs imposed similar measures: in 1300 (700 after the Hegira) they imposed white turbans on Christians, yellow on Jews and red on Samaritans.[20]

When, in the middle of the fourteenth century, this period of two and a half centuries in the history of costume comes to an end, we can observe that while its development was influenced by a renewal of maritime trade and the rise of towns; it also benefited from the major role played by French civilization in Europe.

Indeed, French culture made a capital contribution. The first Crusade had made French an international language, which had then spread from the religious to the commercial sphere with the fairs of Champagne, which propagated it throughout Europe. The revival of courtliness, of the chivalrous spirit and the idealization of love and women left their mark on clothing, which was adapted to a new conception of life.

To this twofold search for intellectual and physical elegance was added in the thirteenth century an increasing taste for liveliness and realism in art. This new tendency is apparent if we compare the statue of the Queen of Sheba in Rheims cathedral, (c. 1250) with the slightly later statue of one of the Foolish Virgins on the west façade of Strasbourg cathedral, represented in an ungirdled surcoat, with affected gestures and swaying posture.

In the early fifteenth century, European costume still appears to be dictated by the nobility, though less so than before. After the slow disappearance of the powerful Imperial rulers and their courts, costume tended to organize itself around the great royal or princely administrations of the newly emerging countries. In the reconstitution of political and religious power that accompanied the economic reorganization of Europe and its artistic and moral reawakening, it acquired a new characteristic: that of unity, even of universality; it was not then apparent whether this would persist as a visible constant in a changing world.

342–3 Troparium originally from Saint Martial, Limoges. Mid eleventh century. Paris, Bib. Nat. ms lat. 1118 f. 109 v. 114. (Photos Bibliothèque Nationale)

Notes

1 Rey, *passim.*; Cohen, *passim.*
2 Mazaheri, *passim.*
3 Michel, *passim.*
4 Ibn Jobaïr, p. 49.
5 Langlois, p. 252.
6 *Roman de la Rose*, line 2, 153; Harmand, p. 146.
7 Enlart, p. 18; *Chanson de Roland*, strophe 190, line 2, 172.
8 Dauvilliers, *Actes*, p. 254.
9 Denifle and Chatelain, vol. I, pp. 79, 218, 230, 506.
10 Dauvilliers, p. 254.
11 Braun, *passim;* Enlart, pp. 328 ff.; Linas, *passim.*
12 Enlart, pp. 310–317.
13 *Ibid.*, pp. 447 ff.
14 Langlois, p. 26.
15 *Ibid.*, p. 26; Enlart, p. 474.
16 Langlois, p. 556.
17 Cohen, *passim.*
18 Faral, *Jongleurs*, p. 64, note 7.
19 Sequeira, in *Actes du I*[er] *Congrès International d'Histoire du Costume*, p. 64.
20 Mayer, pp. 65 ff.

Bibliography

ETIENNE REY: *Les Colonies franques en Syrie*. 1883.

CLAUDE COHEN: *La Syrie du nord à l'époque des Croisades*. 1940.

ALI MAZAHERI: *La Vie quotidienne des Musulmans au Moyen Age*. 1951.

FRANCISQUE MICHEL: *Recherches sur le commerce, la fabrication et l'usage des étoffes de soie, d'or et d'argent*. 1852.

IBN JOBAIR: *Voyages en Sicile*. 1846.

C. V. LANGLOIS: *La Vie en France au Moyen Age d'après les Romains mondains*. 1908.

E. FARAL: *Au temps de Saint Louis*.

A. HARMAND: *Jeanne d'Arc, son costume, son armure*. 1929.

J. DAUVILLIERS: 'Les Costumes des anciennes Universités françaises' in *Actes du Ier CongrèsInternational d'Hist. du Cost.*, 1952. Venice, 1955.

DENIFLE and CHATELAIN: *Chartularium Universitatis parisiensis*. 1894.

LINAS: *Anciens vêtements sacerdotaux*. 1862.

GUSTAVE COHEN: *Histoire de la mise en scène dans le théâtre religieux au Moyen Age*. 1926.

E. FARAL: *Les Jongleurs en France au Moyen Age*. 1910.

G. DE MATOS SEQUEIRA: 'Le Costume défendu' in *Actes du Ier Cong. International d'Hist. du Cost.*, 1952. Venice, 1955.

L. A. MAYER: *Mameluck Costume*. Geneva, 1952.

E. RATHBONE GODDARD: *Women's Costume in French Texts of the Eleventh and Twelfth Centuries*. Paris-Baltimore. 1927.

189

Chapter VII

Costume in Europe from the Four-teenth to the Early Sixteenth Century

The Appearance of Short Costume and its Development until about 1520

CAUSES AND CONDITIONS

The great innovation in the development of costume in Europe after the mid-fourteenth century is the abandonment of the long flowing costume common to both sexes; costume then became short for men and long for women, fitted and generally partly or wholly slit, and buttoned or laced. This development led to the disappearance from everyday wear, except for a few special social categories, of ancient forms inherited over several thousand years; it also represented a first step towards modern costume.

Around 1340–1350, this change was general in the West: it is mentioned in Italy, in England and in Germany as well as in France, though its original starting point cannot be established with certainty. Some attribute it to Spain (particularly to Catalonia), others to Italy, who herself attributed it to France.[1] This geographical area of expansion corresponded to that of long costume, which had previously been worn within the region influenced by the French-inspired international art of the twelfth and thirteenth centuries.

THE NEW SPIRIT

We cannot neglect the importance for costume of the appearance of a new spirit, already perceptible at the end of the thirteenth century, and confirmed and developed at the beginning of the fourteenth century, initially in Italy. The first symptoms of Humanism were a leaning towards secular art, an ideal of man at once more independent and more avid for action, an interest no longer applied to the universal, but to the individual and particular.

At the same time we can see considerable social changes: the feudal system was coming to an end, and the seigneurial class was moving towards its future, more limited role in court society, while the trades were organizing themselves into economic groups supported by an already powerful capitalism.

Another factor, more subtle but not less important for that, was the development of the concept of ideal beauty which took precise shape in the visual arts and literature in the thirteenth century in France and, most of all, in Italy where the theme inspired all poets and artists from Dante to Giotto, from Petrarch to Pisanello, from Boccaccio to Raphael.[2] Greater importance was attached to the perfection of the female body, and indeed, to outward appearance in general. In all the Italian states men and women translated this search after formal beauty into costume, thus satisfying their taste for elegance, their passion for colour harmony and their aspirations towards a greater distinction.

It was then that the fashion designer made his appearance, in Italy: artists of the calibre of Pisanello (plate 345), Pollaiuolo and Jacopo Bellini created costume models and designed textile patterns.[3]

BURGHERS' COSTUME

344 The man wears a *huque* in velvet lined with fur, over a black pourpoint with the cuffs embroidered in gold, and a hat of shaved felt, in the shape of an inverted truncated cone. Beside him are his wooden pattens with wide straps and two heels. His wife wears a cloth gown trimmed with fur; her wide, open sleeves are decorated with shell-shaped cut work. The fine linen *huve* rests on two *truffeaux* held inside a gilded hairnet. The high belt accentuates the prominent abdomen, which it was then fashionable to stress

344 JAN VAN EYCK: *Jan Arnolfini and his Wife*, 1435. London, National Gallery, (Photo Thames and Hudson Archives)

ECONOMIC CONDITIONS

Despite the disruptions caused by wars, the transformation of costume benefited not only from a new psychological and artistic climate, but also from exceptionally favourable economic conditions.

It has justly been remarked that at the beginning of the fourteenth century European trade became stabilized and, instead of noticeably extending its sphere of activity, concentrated on expanding traffic along existing routes. Faced with the insecurity caused by the Hundred Years' War and the occupation of the Eastern Mediterranean by the Turks, traders gradually replaced the great land route from Italy to Flanders with the sea route from the Mediterranean to the North Sea via the Atlantic. But in each country the state of trade depended on the policies of the government.

In the West there followed the beginnings of a move towards developing commercial centres, among them Venice, Genoa, Marseille and Barcelona. In the North the great international ports of Bruges and Antwerp were established, in liaison with the Teutonic Hansa towns which controlled traffic from Novgorod. We shall probably never know how the fashions brought to France at the time of Charles the Bold came to be in Greenland in the same period, as we know to have been the case from excavations on the sites of old Norman colonies.

At the same time in the Netherlands, in Milan and Florence, and other places besides, industries were set up which were supported by merchant capitalism and profited from technical progress in weaving and dyeing.

This general improvement was demonstrated by the revival of gold coinage in all the states of Europe; the taste for luxury and the increase of buying power were, as always, to have repercussions on costume.

THE INFLUENCE OF MILITARY COSTUME

At this time we see the appearance of short plate armour, which increasingly replaced the old, half-length coat of mail (hauberk) obviously as a consequence of the recent introduction of more powerful cross-bows and of the first firearms, bombards or swivel-guns. The last years of the thirteenth century saw the appearance of the *brigandine* (plate 346),[4] which reached to the upper thighs, and was formed of small plates rivetted together to cover an outer garment of cloth or leather, shaped like the civilian pourpoint or the fitted *jaque*.[5] It is difficult to say which, of civilian and military costume, influenced the other; we must, however, note their parallel tendency to become shorter.

THE BIRTH OF FASHION

While the development of fashion is a capital change, and of far greater significance than a mere passing change of style, it is nevertheless possible to regard the appearance of the short tunic as the first manifestation of fashion. And indeed, from the fourteenth century onwards we find the appearance in costume of new elements that owe less to function than to caprice. Although costume was still influenced, often gradually, by political, economic and even ethnic factors, its variations became less general, and more directly dictated by the occasion. Styles came to correspond to smaller, more specifically

'national' zones, and to employ more regional products. New influences were more frequent, less lasting, their effects more spectacular.

NATIONAL FEATURES

The development of short costume did, indeed, conform to geographical divisions, and those which expressed new, national distinctions. While spreading gradually across the greater part of Europe, it met with fresh conditions and was modified according to what were already 'national' characteristics. Unlike the more or less uniform long costume, short costume was never exactly the same in France, Germany, England and Italy.

During this period, European costume sometimes bore the impress of Italy, whose role as a precursor is of vital importance, at other times reflected the influence of France and Burgundy. From north and south it gained a splendour and opulence previously unknown, perhaps more noticeable in men's than in women's costume. But these two poles of influence were markedly different in their nature.

In Italy, divided into a dozen independent states, it was the feeling for form and the creative imagination that transformed costume. And it was the development of silk weaving and the continuous improvement in commercial organization that made possible its spread through the adjacent countries: thus, economic factors played a major part.

In more closely knit France and Burgundy, the dominant influences were the courts. Despite the difficult conditions created by the Hundred Years' War, clothing was sumptuously rich, matching the ambition of the Dukes of Burgundy and their royal power, which the recent vicissitudes had not profoundly affected. The enrichment of the States of Burgundy and the prosperity of Flanders were only accessory factors. Here politics were the mainspring of development in costume.

The transformation of costume in the fourteenth and fifteenth centuries thus appears as the expression less of a general, common culture, than of groups of nations with equal, but different, development. From being universal, uniform and impersonal, costume was to become particular, personal and national.

Costume in Western Europe

THE INFLUENCE OF COURTS AND TOWNS

During the second half of the fourteenth century and the fifteenth century, throughout Europe political power became more concentrated. The privileged classes lost their old feudal power and status, and social and economic emancipation were widespread.

The constitution of national powers brought with it, despite wars, a burgeoning of luxury in royal and princely courts which remains one of the most remarkable phenomena of this period: these courts were grouped round the king in France, England and Spain, and elsewhere, in the Holy Roman Empire and in Italy, they were adapted to the local system of principalities and dukedoms. The growth of towns and the enrichment of the

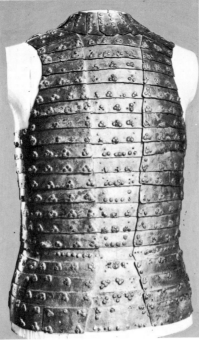

345 PISANELLO: *Designs for Court Costumes.*
Early fifteenth century.
Chantilly, Musée Condé. (Photo Giraudon)

346 Brigandine worn by Philippe le Bel.
Late thirteenth–early fourteenth century.
Chartres, Museum. (Photo Flammarion)

347 Archer, miniature from a Burgundian manuscript. Mid-fifteenth
century. Paris, Bibliothèque
Nationale. (Photo Flammarion)

ITALIAN FASHION DESIGN

345 Although these costumes were probably never worn, this drawing
shows the new spirit of individualistic invention at the end of the fifteenth
century. The long *gamurra* worn by the woman, her voluminous head-
dress, the decorations of feathers and complicated shapes of the male
costume deserve the epithet of *costumes déguisés* then applied to garments
that departed from conventional forms

THE BRIGANDINE

346-7 The brigandine, a sleeveless waistcoat made of metal plates
rivetted to a rigid lining, and plate armour made of articulated metal
plates combined with a hauberk of mail, are two types of fourteenth-
century fitted armour. They led to the fashion for short garments for
men

COURTLY LUXURY IN THE FIFTEENTH CENTURY

348 Jean de Berry wears a black garde-corps brocaded in gold and fur-
lined, a link collar and pendant, and a hat with a cut brim. The pink
houppelande lined with white worn by the herald has scalloped edges and
a high collar known as a carcaille; his orange head-dress is arranged in a
cockade

mercantile classes led to the emergence everywhere of a rich
bourgeoisie which aspired to the privileges of the nobility.
Costume thus became a means for one class to demonstrate its
rise, and for another to emphasize its jealously guarded pre-
eminence.

In France, after the wise, thrifty reign of Charles V, the
government of the princes during the minority, and then the
illness, of Charles VI, was marked by princely ambition
and taste for luxury. Louis d'Anjou, Jean de Berry, Philip,
Duke of Burgundy, Louis, Duke of Orléans who married
Valentina Visconti, all lived lavishly on the royal treasury. We
shall see the competition in dress set up in Flanders and Dijon
by the Dukes of Burgundy.

In England, however, where the ambitious House of Lancaster was slowly rising in spite of the rival Yorkists, while the
war with France alternated victories and defeats, the court
never achieved a luxury equivalent to that of its continental
rivals, yet the young contemporaries of Chaucer gathered
round Richard III (1377–1399) wore brightly coloured capes,
parti-coloured hose, jewels and precious stuffs, much as did
their wives.

348 POL DE LIMBOURG: *The Duc de Berry setting out on a journey.*
Before 1415. *Grandes Heures du Duc de Berry.*
Paris, Bib. Nat. ms lat. 18014, f. 288 v.
(Photo Bibliothèque Nationale)

349 The Three Magi, altar front from Espinol. Late 13th century. Vich, Episcopal Museum. (Photo Mas)

350 Draped hose, Album of Villard de Honnecourt. Thirteenth century. Paris, Bibliothèque Nationale ms fr. 19093 f. 6 and 28.

In divided Germany, where several states were taking shape amid internal struggles, an almost permanent civil war and the threat of Turkish invasion restrained the luxury of the scattered courts. In this purely dynastic empire, without political, social or economic centralization, there could clearly be no national costume.

After the autonomous policies followed by Aragon and Castile, Spain only latterly regained its unity with the marriage of Ferdinand and Isabella the Catholic, followed by the end of the Moslem Kingdom of Granada in the late fifteenth century. Not only did the nobility maintain its power and wealth for longer there than elsewhere, but the circumstances were favourable for the monarchy, and for the predominance of the court with its sartorial luxury.

In Italy, unlike Germany, the development of luxury was not hindered by the constant political disorder and a system of dukedoms. From the middle of the fourteenth to the end of the fifteenth century the general economic prosperity, the ennoblement of rich citizens and the domination of a few families, such as the Viscontis in Milan and the Medicis in Florence, and the extension of the power of Venice, created in these Italian city-states a studied pursuit of elegance and a taste for lavish, sumptuous costume in which even the Papal court participated.

The appearance and development of courts and large urban centres, both generating luxury, goes hand in hand with the formation of the concept of nationality in Europe; the adoption of the short costume marks the beginning of this particularism in European costume.

Costume in France

Although France 'of the fleur-de-lys' was geographically so close to the Duchy of Burgundy, the costume of each area was subject to different influences.

Perhaps the fashion for short clothing may have been introduced to France from Italy: at first the new costume's forms, ornamental details and textiles were Italian.

However, this influence weakened after 1350, whether because Italian style had been assimilated by French taste, or because it had been supplanted by the Burgundian influence, due to the political power of the Duchy and to the occupation of Paris by the English.

Despite political and military vicissitudes, there was a second period of great luxury in costume in France between 1380 and 1420, followed by the difficult times of the reign of Charles VIII and the reconquest of the territory occupied by the English.

Around the reign of Charles VII a third period of luxury followed, perhaps under the influence of Agnès Sorel, who was the King's mistress between 1444 and 1450 and was severely judged by the chronicler Georges Chatelain: 'She wore trains one third longer than ever princesses of this realm wore, headdresses half as high again, more costly gowns, and day and night thought only of vanities.' But after her, women adopted equally costly modes no less quickly. Towards 1467 trains were no more to be seen: gowns were edged with fur.

Curtailed under Louis XI, this taste for luxury in costume spread again after the first French expeditions into Italy.

It was owing to the intermediate position of Burgundy that certain details of German fashion, particularly cut-work, were introduced into France. This has been attributed to the influence of Isabelle of Bavaria, but it seems unlikely that this queen, who was tastelessly dressed and prematurely fat on her arrival in France, could have played the part of an arbiter of elegance. However, spendthrift and dissolute as she was, she must certainly have led her maids of honour to wear sumptuous garments such as those seen in the *Très riches heures du Duc de Berry*, whose fanciful nature and elegance inspired the chronicler Jacques Legrand to remark, 'Venus has taken up her abode at the court of France.'

MEN'S COSTUME

From about 1340, in spite of scandalized opposition, the surcoat was replaced everywhere – or almost everywhere – by

194

351 JEAN FOUQUET: *The Hours of Etienne Chevalier.*
Chantilly, Musée Condé.
(Photo Giraudon)

UNDERGARMENTS
349–50 This form of pre-fourteenth century breeches continued with the appearance of long costumes; chausses reaching to mid-thigh are rolled down at the top. Under their gowns the Magi wear multicoloured chausses, short on the thigh, where tabs at the sides attach them to a hidden belt (the remains of a similar system were found in the Las Huelgas tombs).
351–2 The hose reach to the top of the thighs, where points fasten them to the gippon. Leather soles were sometimes sewn to them

THE MALE HOUPPELANDE
353–5 The loose, often fur-lined houppelande, which was sometimes decorated with german-style cut-work, had a standing collar known as a carcaille (plates 354–5). The gippon sleeve which covers the hand is a *moufle* sleeve; the houppelande sleeve is stuffed out. The two figures on the right (plate 353) wear *robes à plis gironnés* and hoods worn as hats. One of them wears the Order of the Genêt at his throat; the figure on the left has a pudding-basin haircut

short garments, gippons or pourpoints. Long costume survived at court and in ecclesiastical and academic circles. These new modes led to great changes in costume as a whole.

The short garment, exposing the leg, demanded hose that was tighter and better supported; therefore they were generally made to measure, 'after the fashion of the Court'. We find fur-lined hose, special hose for riding, and soled hose which replaced shoes.

The 'round hose' of the preceding period were replaced by much longer hose or *chausses à queue*, which could be fastened to the gippon not only in front but also at the back and sides. Towards 1371, to meet the criticisms of immodesty levelled against the new clothing, someone had the idea of sewing the two parts of the hose together: this gave the *chausses à plain fond* ('full-bottomed hose'), with a small triangle added between the two front parts, the *braye*, covering the opening of the breeches. This piece, which was removable and fastened with eyelets when the hose reached waist-height at the end of the fifteenth century, was to become the *braguette* or codpiece.

Braies, which were then no more than undergarments worn 'for cleanliness', according to the chroniclers, were always made of linen, and became increasingly shorter.

In the middle of the fifteenth century the upper part of the hose was covered by a sort of roll of padded cloth called a *lodier*; this *boulevard*, a primitive form of upper stocks, became generally worn only at the end of the century.

Around 1360, perhaps to satisfy tailors who were threatened with ruin as a result of the disappearance of the surcoat, a new garment, the *houppelande*, appeared (plates 353–5). This was a very wide, generally long gown, with full, flaring sleeves, caught in tightly at the waist by a belt underneath which the material formed regular, pipe-like folds or *plis gironnés*. It is probable that these folds were fixed inside, as the fullness of the front and its opening down to the waist made it possible to slip the garment on easily. It was finished at the neck with a tall standing collar. A short form of the garment was the *haincelin*. The style lasted until about 1425.

From this date, the term *robe* in French lost the meaning it had formerly had, the whole set of garments, and was used to refer

352 PISANELLO: *Drawings of a hanged man.* Early fifteenth century. Formerly Oppenheimer collection. (Photo Giraudon)

353 Pierre Salmon and Charles VI. Late fourteenth –early fifteenth century. Paris, Bib. Nat. ms fr. 23279, f. 5. (Photo Bibliothèque Nationale)

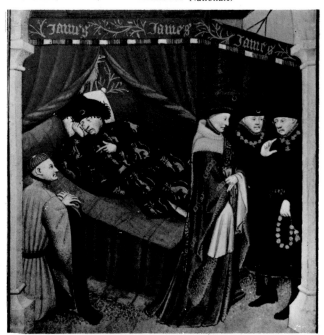
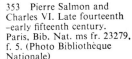

354–5 *Le Roman de la Rose*. Late fourteenth–early fifteenth century.
Paris, Bib. Nat. ms fr. 12595 f. 1 and 2.
(Photos Bibliothèque Nationale)

356 Italian Breviary. *c*. 1380. Paris,
Bib. Nat. ms lat. 757, f. 109.
(Photo Bibliothèque Nationale)

THE JACK

356–7 The short, close-fitting *jack* is made of expensive, often fur-lined materials. Its form follows the chest padding of the pourpoint whose tight sleeves (plate 356) or 'small bombarde sleeves' (plate 357) show under the jack sleeves. The hood, slipped back and worn round the neck (plate 356) has a long, thin point known as a *liripipe*, also found in Italy and France

THE SKIRTED POURPOINT

358–9 This is a unique example of a fourteenth-century pourpoint worn without other outer garment. It is in silk brocaded with gold; its wide-sleeved cut required a pattern of 32 pieces. It is fastened with 32 buttons, 15 of which are convex and the others flat

361–2 These manuscripts show the jack moulding the body, with rich belts round the hips, pointed-toed poulaine hose and hoods with liripipes (plate 361), details typical of the years 1370–1410

only to the short, wide outer garment; the term *robe longue* (long gown) was always used to designate the long garment worn by dignitaries or by old men who, in the fifteenth and even the sixteenth centuries, refused to give up their old costume.

In the fifteenth century the 'gown of the common and ancient type' was the style generally worn, contrasting with the 'disguised gown' which was a fanciful garment worn by the nobility in feasts, tourneys and assemblies. During the whole of the Middle Ages, the cut of gowns remained more or less uniform, only the quality of the cloth used distinguishing between the various classes of society, damask, velvet and satin being reserved for nobles, and broadcloth mainly for burghers.

With the progressive disappearance of the surcoat, the doublet, which until then had been the garment worn directly over the shirt, was assimilated to the *gippon*, already mentioned in the preceding century, to become the *pourpoint*, an outer garment fitting the chest and waist, with tight sleeves which always buttoned down the forearm. Its name was derived from the fact that it was generally made of lined, quilted, rich stuff (plates 358–9). The hose were attached to this garment either by cords (*estaches*) sewn to the lining, or by points, metal-

tipped laces passing through eyelets. This type of fastening may have appeared only after the pourpoint had been worn for some time; this would explain how, later, Rabelais, describing the costume of Gargantua which must have incorporated some ancient features, wrote this phrase which commentators have quoted as a joke: 'Then people began to fasten their hose to their pourpoints and not their pourpoints to their hose, for the latter is against nature...' However, we find representations of points from the first third of the fifteenth century.

It is impossible to embark here on a detailed description of all the forms of the pourpoint. At the end of the fourteenth century the cut generally adopted, *à grandes assiettes*, full-skirted, has carefully calculated arm-holes that fit closely to the shoulder, while in the fifteenth century the pourpoint was cut 'in four quarters', like a very tight waistcoat with a seam down the back, while the lower panels, which were no less fitted, were attached to the garment at the waist.

Towards the end of the fourteenth century in France and England, the pourpoint began to be fitted with a standing collar which, initially of moderate height, rose to ear level at the beginning of the fifteenth century, when it was known as a *carcaille*.

Towards the same date the pourpoint became an outer garment, and it is very rare to find it as a ceremonial garment before 1520; it was then worn under the houppelande or gown.

The vogue for wide sleeves grew everywhere in Europe, first for houppelandes, then for the gowns that replaced them or for short mantles, rather than for pourpoints or the other short garments. They were often sack-shaped or balloon-shaped, and lent themselves to curious exaggerations, particularly in Germany and Italy. 'Closed sleeves' (narrow at the wrist) or 'open (flaring) sleeves' coexisted at first, but soon the closed type was universally adopted until about 1450. During all the fifteenth century and even at the beginning of the sixteenth, there were also sleeves gathered in both at the shoulder and at the wrist and slit vertically on the inside of the wrist (*manches pertuisées*) which were worn particularly east of the Rhine.

At the end of the thirteenth century, but especially in the fourteenth and fifteenth centuries, the *jack* (*jaque*), a sort of

196

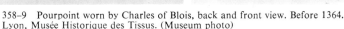

358–9   Pourpoint worn by Charles of Blois, back and front view. Before 1364. Lyon, Musée Historique des Tissus. (Museum photo)

360   Book of the Tournaments of King René. *c.* 1450. Paris, Bib. Nat. ms fr. 2693, f. 38. (Photo Bibliothèque Nationale)

fitted, heavily padded pourpoint (plates 361–2), ending in a short skirt over the hips, had appeared in military costume. The *jacket* (*jaquette*) which must have derived from this was, in the middle of the fifteenth century, a civilian garment similar in general shape but less fitted, worn mainly by peasants, who thus gained themselves the nickname Jacques. In any case, peasants always dressed in the short tunics of previous periods: *colobia* and *coterons*.

The tabard (plates 360, 363–4), a parade garment, was generally short and full, with very short, often open sleeves. In tournaments, it might be worn straight by heralds or covering one shoulder by poursuivants.

The *huque*, a short outer garment, slit at the sides and often also at back and front, appears at the beginning of the fifteenth century as a coat·worn over armour. It rapidly passed into civilian costume, varying in length, and often with cut and fur-trimmed edges, sometimes also belted.

The draped mantles of the preceding periods seem to have disappeared with the arrival of the houppelande. However, some models survived for ceremonial wear, such as the *socq* or *soccus*, a full cloak derived from the chlamys, slit in front or at the sides, pinned at the shoulder and worn with an ermine neck-piece: this was worn by the king and dignitaries for coronation and other ceremonies. In France it was worn, with modifications in detail, until the time of Charles X. Another model, the full-bottomed, bucket or bell cloak, derived from the chasuble, was worn for travelling, as was the shorter riding cloak.

From 1440 on, garments whose origin it is quite difficult to pin down herald by their forms the clothing of the sixteenth century: the *paletot*, an outer garment of the same length as the pourpoint, with *manches pertuisées* or, alternatively, long, fitted sleeves, generally decorated with gold and gems; the *journade*, formed of two flowing panels front and back, which appears to have been inspired by the Italian *giornea*; the *manteline*, similar in form, but shorter. These various garments are sometimes confused with one another and with the huque which they succeeded as a ceremonial garment.

Finally, we must make particular mention of a garment which appeared in the last years of the fourteenth century, the

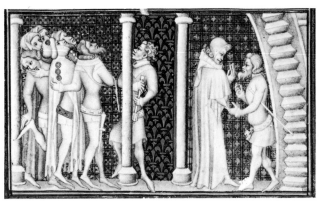

361   Great Chronicles of France *c.* 1380. Paris, Bib. Nat. ms fr. 2813 f. 3 v. (Photo Bibliothèque Nationale)

362   Poems by Guillaume de Machault. *c.* 1370. Paris, Bib. Nat. ms. fr. 1584. (Photo Bibliothèque Nationale)

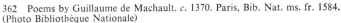

caban, an open, crossed outer garment, with long sleeves, a hood and often a belt. All historians of costume have mentioned its appearance, but without emphasizing its importance; yet this was the first European garment with a fitted back, and it was clearly derived from the Oriental *caftan* introduced to Europe through Venice and Italy, where crossed garments appeared towards the thirteenth century.

This garment is still worn today and is the basis of everything that since then has been called 'coat' in the sense we give the word today.

MEN'S HAIR AND HEAD-DRESSES

At the beginning of the fifteenth century a hairstyle as bizarre as it was unbecoming came into fashion: hair cut high and straight all round in a pudding-basin shape, exposing the neck and ears and covering the top of the head in a small cap of cropped hair. This fashion, perhaps due to the carcaille which fitted closely all the way up the neck, remained in fashion until about 1450, when portraits once more show hair falling to the neck. It was also adopted in England and Spain: the one country where it seems never to have penetrated was Germany. Contrary to a whole body of fanciful iconography, this was the style worn by Joan of Arc, and the fact was held against her at her trial.

The characteristic head-dress of the period was the *chaperon*; a piece which deserves a more detailed examination than would be appropriate here.

The hood had become separated from the cloak by the end of the twelfth century, and was worn with a short neck-cape as an independent head-dress. In the fourteenth century a long band (*cornet* or *liripipe*) was added, hanging down the back or one side (plate 356); the part of the hood that closed round the neck was the *guleron* or *patte* and the opening framing the face was the *visagière*. Worn up in this usual way, the hood was said to be *enformé*; when it was pulled back to uncover the head, it was described as *en gorge*, and when worn pulled forward to hide the face, it was *embronché*. This latter practice was forbidden in 1399 because of the opportunities it gave to armed attackers, and remained in use only for funerals (plate 370a), up until the funeral of Louis XIV.

About 1408, people acquired the habit of rolling the edge of the *visagière* and of putting on the hood by this opening: the *guleron* then spread over the head and the *cornet* could be wound round like a turban (plate 372a), in arrangements which varied widely, particularly with the fashion for cut-work and pinking.

In the fifteenth century, to avoid having to redrape the hood for each wearing, the rolled opening was fixed over a padded ring, and the cornet and guleron were arranged in different ways; this was to all intents and purposes a hat, known as a 'fashioned hood' or a *bourrelet* (roll), made with light wicker hoops or even without an inner roll. Hoods trimmed with pinking were described as 'in the German style'.

Besides the hood, fifteenth-century men wore hats: felt and beaver, smooth or long-haired, peaked, round-crowned, balloon-shaped, high-crowned, like inverted cones, with flat brims, rolled, upturned or cutaway. The variety was so wide it is impossible to describe every form in detail. The hat could sometimes be worn over a round cap or a simple hood. Around 1460 gentlemen of fashion took to wearing *cramignolles* or toques with pinked edges.

FOOTWEAR

Shoes were related to a very ancient type, generally high and laced outside or fastened with buttons or buckles on top of the foot. The sole might be single or double but was always hidden by the upper. Soled hose and pattens were still worn.

The big innovation was the appearance, in the reign of Charles V, of *poulaine* or *Crackow shoes*, which were said to have come from Poland; in vogue for almost a century, they were a revival in exaggerated form of the *pigaches* which had had a short period of popularity in the twelfth century. However general it may have been, this mode does not seem to have aroused as much enthusiasm in France as it did in the second third of the fifteenth century in the court of Burgundy (plates 374–6). It penetrated into France shortly after its introduction in Milan, in 1340; in Montauban poulaines were forbidden by an ordinance of 1367. The points became so exaggerated, measuring more than two feet long, that they were sometimes supported with whalebones. The same elongated shape was adopted for pattens, which were worn with all footwear that did not have thick soles. The fashion for poulaines reached its zenith towards 1460–70; it was succeeded abruptly by the vogue for wide shoes with thick, puffed feet, known as 'duck's bill shoes', which became general wear under François I.

Heuze, which were soft, generally quite high boots in varying shapes, were sometimes worn over light, low-cut or short-legged brodequins.

WOMEN'S COSTUME

A very clear distinction was established between men's and women's garments after the appearance of short costume for men.

On the whole, women's costume fitted tightly to the upper part of the body, while the train lengthened the overall line, concentrating on showing off the sinuous outline, the curve of the hips and the fullness of the thighs and bust. It was very tight, and so the cote was slit and laced at the back, the corset in front. The fashion for protuberant stomachs, which were achieved with small bags of padding under the costume, affected all aspects of the plastic arts in the fifteenth century. Welted seams slimmed the waist. Gradually, low-cut necklines, elaborate hairstyles and the vogue for details such as elbow-sleeves and pinking and slashing gained in importance and broke up the original line.

The low-cut neckline was an innovation that was to arouse strong clerical disapproval. It was thought to have Cypriot origins because of the influence exercised in Europe by the elegant Lusignan court. The fitted bust and wide décolletage underlined the wearer's new concentration on her individuality.

As undergarments women wore chemises of fine linen or silk, with sleeves and low-cut necks, and the *blanchet* which in the preceding period had often been confused with the doublet: it remained a long, outer garment, sometimes lined and fur-trimmed, and occasionally made of linen, since it is mentioned as having been worn for bathing. It also served as a dressing-gown.

The *corset* replaced the cote and differed from it only slightly; it was generally low-cut, with short sleeves showing the chemise, or open and laced. It was worn over or instead of the gown.

363 Tabard of heralds of Burgundy. Mid-fifteenth century. Vienna, Kunsthistorisches Museum. (Museum photo)

364 Italian tabard in cut velvet. Sixteenth century. Lyons, Musée Historique des Tissus. (Museum photo)

The open surcoat was one of the most elegant inventions of the Middle Ages, and its vogue lasted almost two centuries. This was a garment whose bodice was open from the arm-hole to the hips, showing the cote. The front formed a sort of waistcoat, most often covered with ermine, as were the edges of the arm-holes; a row of finely worked hooks or decorative buttons ran down the middle to the skirt. The skirt itself was very full and trailed on the ground; for certain ceremonies it could be '*partie*' or decorated with heraldic motifs, as in the preceding period. The round, fairly low-cut neckline became triangular in the fifteenth century, when the waistcoat part was reduced to two narrow bands of ermine outlining the arm-holes and joining the full, often fur-lined back. This surcoat was worn ungirdled, but the rich girdle worn with the cote showed on the hips.

At the beginning of the century, women wore the long houppelande also seen in men's costume (plates 379–80, 382–3); it always buttoned down the front and had voluminous sleeves, flaring or closed.

There has often been confusion between the gown and the cotehardie. The terms 'gown' or 'robe' remained widely used, although 'woman's coat' was preferred. This was a long garment, slipped over the head like a chemise and held up for walking, either by hand, or fastened with a pin called a *troussoir*.

The pointed décolletage gradually reached down the front to waist level, and less far down behind; the *tassel* (plates 394–7) was a band of cloth, generally black, which modified the décolletage and produced a square neckline. A gauze fichu known variously as *gorgias*, *gorgerette* or *touret de col* covered the edges. A fairly wide belt (*bandier*) was worn just below the breasts.

At the end of the century, under Charles VIII and Louis XII, the gown had replaced all other garments except for the open surcoat, which still appeared for ceremonial wear. The general line of the gown remained unmodified, except for the flat bodice with a square neckline, inspired by Italian styles, framed between *parements* of coloured embroidery; sleeves were straight and full and had deep revers. This type of sleeve was *à la française*, contrasting with the Italian sleeve, which was in two parts (*mancheron* and *brassard*) linked together with

365 Harvesting barley. Late fourteenth century. Paris, Bib. Nat. ms 1673 f. 47 v. (Photo Bibliothèque Nationale)

366-7 *The Labours of the Months*. From the *Très Riches Heures du Duc de Berry*. Chantilly, Musée Condé. (Photos Giraudon)

pins at the elbow, with the chemise sleeve puffing out between them.

The cape and *mantel* seem to have been worn during the whole of the century: some authors mention surtouts known as *beluques* and *brancs*, but we have no documents from which we can describe them.

In women's clothing the silver chain worn at the girdle, with all sorts of useful everyday objects hung from it, went by the name of *demi-ceint*. This fashion was worn from the fourteenth century to the mid-seventeenth century, lasting longest among ordinary people.

WOMEN'S HAIR AND HEAD-DRESSES

Hair was piled up in rolls over the temples or plaited into templets coiled round metal frames over the ears. At first it was covered with a light kerchief over which another piece of linen, the *barbet* or towel, was pinned to mask the neck and chin. When these two pieces were joined together they formed the guimp or wimple, which was later to remain the head-dress of widows and of nuns, many of whom still wear it.

At the end of the fourteenth century, the mass of hair was generally held in a silk coif or beaded net, often wrongly referred to as the *escoffion*.[6] On top of this erection a linen veil was worn, the *huve*, often decorated with ruching or fine pleats and held in position with long pins, forming a sort of canopy jutting out from the head. The volume of these rolls rapidly grew to surprising proportions.

At the beginning of the fifteenth century hair had been crowned with a slim roll, which did not enlarge the head, but gradually its volume grew, as did the temple rolls and the coif, and became the tall head-dress whose double lobed or butterfly shapes are the most typical of a range of variants too wide to enumerate.

These were the 'horned head-dresses', about which Juvénal des Ursins wrote in 1417: '... horns marvellously tall and broad... with long ears on either side...' and which, from that moment on, attracted the fiery condemnation of preachers outraged by these rolls 'stuffed with the hair of dead women who may well be in hell...' The Bishop of Paris promised indulgences to anyone who insulted women wearing these styles, by shouting after them '*hurte, belin!*' (roughly: Nanny-goat, use your horns!) and in 1418 a certain Carmelite monk called Thomas Couecte made the same promises to children if they shouted '*au hennin*'. This last term, which is still unexplained, was the source of a double error concerning these head-dresses.

In 1556 the *Annales de Bourgogne*, relating these facts taken from the *Chronique* of Monstrelet (died 1453) commented on them by saying that the monk used the term *hennins* for these head-dresses 'tall as steeples', a good ell high, 'with long veils hanging from them like standards'. Now, the tall, pointed head-dresses, fitting closely to the head and hiding the hair except for one small lock on the brow, were virtually unknown before 1440. Thus it was not this model, but the horned head-dresses with their evocation of the devil, which deserved anathema; moreover, this 'preacher' did not actually call them hennins, but suggested the term as an insult to be hurled at them. The tall 'sugar-loaf' head-dress was perhaps ridiculous, but is was so innocuous that it could be adopted by religious orders, among them the Order of the Hospice at Beaune, whose members still wear them, though their height is now more discreet.

We have therefore every reason to believe that the term *hennin*, whose real meaning remains obscure, which does not figure in any contemporary text or dictionary and cannot be translated directly in any language, can only have been a satirical, insulting term applied to horned head-dresses without ever designating headgear in the fifteenth century.[7]

The banner head-dress, often adorned with a long veil hanging from the point or held on brass wires to form butterfly or *beaupré* head-dresses, was worn mainly in Northern France, Burgundy and the Low Countries. It was never current in England, Italy or Spain.

It is possible that Eastern influences – the visit to Europe of the King of Cyprus, the capture of Alexandria – may have contributed to the invention of these extravagant head-dresses which do, indeed, recall certain mitres worn by Syrian women.

368 *Comedies of Terence.* Fifteenth century. Paris, Bib. Nat. ms lat. 7907, f. 12 v. (Photo Bibliothèque Nationale)

But the inspiration could have come from still farther afield, for these models have also been compared with Chinese head-dresses in the Hu style, from statuettes of the Wei and T'ang periods.[8]

All these head-dresses, huves, horned head-dresses and varied head ornaments, shared the favour of elegant women until about 1480. The chaperon worn during the preceding period had, like the male model, been transformed into the fashioned hood then, towards the end of the century, having lost its original form, it became a sort of capulet, in velvet for noblewomen and broadcloth for burghers' wives, worn over a linen coif that framed the face simply, but often had embroidered edges.

During the fifteenth century we also see women's hats made of felt, with peaks or with brims turned up in front, apparently worn only for travelling or pilgrimages.

FOOTWEAR

In the fourteenth century women wore laced ankle-boots, generally lined with fur in winter. However, it seems that the term *botte* was used then in a very different sense from its present meaning: the frequent use of the expression *bottes à relever la nuit* (boots to wear getting up at night) indicates this clearly.

In the fifteenth century women also wore poulaines, and pattens still protected their tight shoes.

THE LONG GOWN

Long costume did not disappear completely with the arrival of short garments. As we have seen, middle-aged wearers remained faithful to their long garments for some time.[9] Thus the long gown with elbow-sleeves and a tooth-edged hood similar to that worn by women existed side by side in male costume with the short, low-waisted surcoat.

The long garment also became the garb of a new class that formed around kings and princes in the fourteenth century.

369 NICOLAS FROMENT: Detail of the Altarpiece of the Burning Bush: *King René of Anjou.* Aix, Museum. (Photo Giraudon)

370 Classic hood, from *The Book of King Modus and Queen Ratio.* 1379. Paris, Bib. Nat. ms fr. 12399 f. 26. (Photo Bibliothèque Nationale)

372 Hood with vertical cornet. Weeper from the tomb of the Duke of Burgundy. 1405–11. Dijon. (Photo Giraudon)

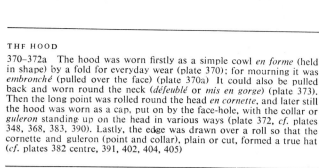

THE HOOD

370–372a The hood was worn firstly as a simple cowl *en forme* (held in shape) by a fold for everyday wear (plate 370); for mourning it was *embronché* (pulled over the face) (plate 370a) It could also be pulled back and worn round the neck (*défeublé* or *mis en gorge*) (plate 373). Then the long point was rolled round the head *en cornette*, and later still the hood was worn as a cap, put on by the face-hole, with the collar or *guleron* standing up on the head in various ways (plate 372, *cf.* plates 348, 368, 383, 390). Lastly, the edge was drawn over a roll so that the cornette and guleron (point and collar), plain or cut, formed a true hat (*cf.* plates 382 centre, 391, 402, 404, 405)

370a Hood. Weeper from the tomb of Jean Sans Peur and Margaret of Bavaria, 1390–1411. Dijon. (Photo Giraudon)

371 Hood. *c.* 1410. Paris, Bib. Nat. ms fr. 23729 f. 119 v. (Photo Bibliothèque Nationale)

372a Closed hood with cornet swathed in turban style. *Boccaccio* of Jean Sans Peur. *c.* 1410. Paris, Bibliothèque de l'Arsenal, ms 5193 f. 159. (Photo Flammarion)

Formerly a small body of councillors had worn the livery of their master, but then bodies of administrators were constituted to look after law enforcement and tax collection; drawn from the rich middle classes or from the Universities, these high officials of modest origins tried to use costume to distinguish themselves from the middle classes and nobility. Thus a *state costume* emerged. Similarly, the magistrates of the Paris parliament held session in talaris gowns, which gave them their name, '*gens de longue robe*', later extended to judges, advocates and procurators: at the end of the century they wore the long gown with the housse, the tabard and the mantle.

A further special characteristic was added to this costume by the attribution of distinctive colours to given occupations: black, red and violet were often reserved for magistrates, judges and officials. These colours might change according to the province: the magistrates of Charles of Burgundy wore black gowns, the colour of their master Charles the Bold. Violet seems to have been adopted for advocates' gowns in some provinces. The regulations of the Paris and Toulouse parliaments specify that their members should wear gowns, mantles and chaperons in red lined with ermine: members of parliament in Burgundy and in the Low Countries, under the Dukes, also wore red: but it is not impossible that Philip the Good, who himself dressed in black, may have imposed his own colour.

The Universities retained the costume that had been theirs since their foundation in the thirteenth century: cape with chaperon. Apparently it was in the fifteenth century that the epitoga, a type of housse, was added.

Burgundian Costume

The court of Burgundy surpassed all others in the richness of its costume, sumptuous textiles, varied embroidery, and an incessant renewal of garments, even more among men than among women.

The marriage of Philip the Brave and Marguerite of Flanders, daughter and heiress of the powerful count Louis de

Mâle, added to the duke's important patrimony the enormous resources of the largest, richest country of all Christendom, with the prosperous towns of Ypres, Bruges and Ghent, a flourishing cloth and silk industry, a Stock Exchange and the Antwerp Fair which had become a centre of international trade. Between Flanders and the Low Countries and Burgundy exchanges developed as the result of an improved financial system, in an economic structure incomparably stronger than that of the Kingdom of France.

In their ambition to equal the kings surrounding them, the dukes spent their considerable crown revenues on personal luxury, particularly on costume. Their conscientious striving neared the point of obsession. Philip the Brave was irresistibly attracted to finery; for example, for the entrance into Paris of Queen Isabeau, he wore in succession four gowns of velvet decorated with flowers in gold and precious stones, a scarlet jaquette with forty lambs and swans picked out in pearls and a green gown whose sleeves were embroidered with hawthorn branches and sheep in pearls. Jean Sans Peur bought his textiles and gold-threaded '*baudequins*' (brodequins) mainly from the Italian merchants of Lucca.

The dukes' account books enlighten us not only about their own garments, but also about those of their households, and inform us of their suppliers. We know the liveries of their pages, their squires and their matrons of honour, comprising mantles, hoods and chaperons in Malines cloth, often lined with fur, decorated with flowers and emblems. Buttons, pompoms and plumes of feathers decorated caps; summer hats of straw, with ribbons and other ornaments, came from Italy, while winter chaperons in felt or velvet were made in Germany, at Regensburg. The silk hat crowned with rare feathers, flowers and gold paillettes, ordered by Philip the Good in 1420, must have been an expensive caprice... In the booty taken by the Swiss at Grandson, we find a hat belonging to Charles the Bold, made of yellow velvet and trimmed with a circlet of gold and rubies, pearls and sapphires.

Philip the Good distinguished himself from his predecessors and court by his garments of black, dark blue or violet, which set off his jewels. Charles the Bold inaugurated a revival of

373 Pierre Salmon and Charles VI. Late fourteenth–early fifteenth century. Paris, Bib. Nat. ms. fr. 23279 f. 119 v. (Photo Bibliothèque Nationale)

Shoes with pointed toes (*poulaines*): 374 Musée Bally, Shoenenwerd, Switzerland. 375 Victoria and Albert Museum, London. 376 Deutsches Leder Museum. Offenbach-am-Main. (Museum photos)

luxury in dress, whether on his marriage with Margaret of York, herself magnificently dressed in a gold damasked gown, or when he met his rival, the Emperor Frederick III at Trier, a meeting whose failure was perhaps due to the rivalry in costume between the two heads of state and their partisans, for the Burgundians made mockery of their awkward Teutonic adversaries.

The taste for richness, the use of luxurious, often foreign, cloths and silks, and the exaggerated head-dresses show a tendency, more accentuated in Burgundy than in France, towards a broken, asymmetrical line, already governed by a powerful Baroque spirit. As a result of the diversity of its provinces and the complex diplomacy of the dukes, Burgundian costume underwent very varied influences: Isabella, the third wife of Philip the Good, brought in new fashions,[10] while Italy, Spain and Germany sent their rare textiles, pleated linen and pinked gowns respectively. The fashion for the latter can be explained by the marriage of Jean Sans Peur and Margaret of Bavaria in 1404.

The broad shoulders of the pourpoint, which were accentuated in Italy and Spain, and later in France, in the sixteenth century, may have come from the *maheutres* (wings) which appeared in the Burgundian court towards 1450. On the whole, Burgundian styles absorbed outside elements to recreate a costume of unparalleled individualism.

The lavishness and splendour in costume, soon to be inherited by the House of Hapsburg, gave the court an unrivalled brilliance; in Burgundy costume was indeed the dukes' ally.

Costume in Italy and Spain

In Italy as elsewhere, the transformation of costume results as much from economic and social factors as from the appearance of a new spirit. However, it was through Italy that the East supplied the great innovation, the open-fronted costume, which was to become one of the characteristics of modern dress throughout Europe.

377 *Boccaccio* of the Duc de Berry. *c.* 1410. Paris, Bib. Nat. ms fr. 598 f. 49 v. (Photo Bibliothèque Nationale)

378　Italian breviary. c. 1380.
Paris, Bib. Nat. ms lat. 577, f. 380.
(Photo Bibliothèque Nationale)

379–81　*Valiant Ladies*. Late fourteenth century. Frescos in the castle, Mantua Piedmont.,
(Photo Alinari-Giraudon)

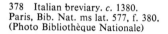

382　Women's costumes, drawing. Early fifteenth century.
Paris, Louvre. (Photo Giraudon)

THE TIGHT-FITTING, LOW-NECKED FEMALE GOWN

377–81　The two gowns worn one on top of the other by women in France and Italy fit tightly to the body; the *gamurra* or *gonella* over the cote, the *cote* under the *cotehardie* (plate 378). The head-dresses give the impression of a tiny head; Italian women wore the *balzo* (plate 381), while Frenchwomen wore *templettes* (plates 382, 386). The man (plate 377) whose houppelande is half off, showing the lining, wears a gippon underneath, and has pointed poulaine hose

FEMALE HOUPPELANDES

379–80, 382–3　Like men, women wore wide houppelandes, with or without belts, with wide, hanging open sleeves (plate 379) or closed sleeves (plate 382 centre), fashioned chaperons with german cut-work or *huves* (plates 379–80) and chaplets of flowers (plate 380 right). In the tapestry the woman wears a sinister or falconry gauntlet, and the man a garde-corps and a chaperon with its point tucked into the face-band

THE CORSET OR BODICE

384　The tight-fitting corset or bodice is laced in front, which distinguishes it from the cote; tight sleeves reach over the wrists

It would be wrong to believe that short costume was adopted in Italy without opposition: the contrary is proved by the sumptuary laws of 1430 in Florence, designed to halt the shortening of pourpoints. But if, in spite of these laws – or because of them – short garments spread quite fast through the various Italian states, it was because the courts of the lords, centres of luxury, provided the most favourable climate for this type of innovation.

Certain characteristics soon appeared in the art of the Italian Trecento. We see low-cut gowns (possibly a style from Cyprus), fitted to the body, complicated head-dresses of tiered rolls and sleeves slit to show the chemise; men wear short, fitted garments, tight hose, breeches and slim, pointed hats.

From the mid-fourteenth to the mid-fifteenth century, male costume changed little. A short mantle, often fur-lined, covered the shoulders and was worn over the fitted garments already mentioned. During the second half of the fifteenth century the tight pourpoint, with a triangular opening in front, had puffed sleeves gathered at the elbow and fitting tightly over the forearms, where they were buttoned or laced. It was only at the beginning of the sixteenth century that slashing appeared on sleeves, upper hose and mantlets, and various shapes, decorations, even colours, gave Italian fashions a sometimes exaggerated character.

In the second half of the fifteenth century the Italian mantlet[11] reached to the knees, with a low belt, large folds and a scalloped lower edge. The sleeves, sewn with gold braid and embroidered with arabesques and flowers, showed great imagination. Drawings by Pisanello show that the same motifs were used indiscriminately for the costume of both sexes. In Venice, fashion dictated sack-shaped sleeves, wide at the shoulder and tight at the wrists, with a side-slit for the forearm. They were decorated, particularly the right sleeve, with all manner of insignia, emblems, arms, names and mottoes. These hanging sleeves, attached at the shoulder or elbow with ribbons or laces, were all the more popular among elegant men because they stressed the idleness of their way of life. In contrast the *abito alla dogalina* (coat in the style of the Doges) with its wide sleeves gathered on the shoulder, enhanced the dignity of the wearer.

The same desire for originality was shown in the hose, where one leg might be plain and the other striped or decorated with some pattern. This was, however, less often an individual caprice than the distinctive sign of one of the societies that were so numerous in Italy. The 'Compagnia della Calza', in Venice at the beginning of the fifteenth century, scattered precious stones on one leg of their striped hose.

Painted and sculpted portraits show the variety of head-dresses: draped or high-crowned toques, and the Florentine *cappuccio* whose originality astonished the rest of Italy, but which was basically a variant of the chaperon.

Italian women never wore the pointed head-dresses erroneously called hennins (see above), but showed a preference for complicated hairstyles of tiered rolls.

The trousseau which Valentine Visconti brought to France in 1389 revealed the very great luxury of Italian courts and, in particular, their taste for textiles embroidered with pearls or with birds, flowers, fruit and various emblems: roses, bunches of grapes, fig-leaves. While great ladies vied in luxury with the princesses, contemporary inventories show that even women of modest condition wore gowns with similar decoration.

Italian costume, like others, was subject to strong foreign influences. French styles (after the expedition of Charles VIII) and later, flowing Spanish cloaks with wide, fur-trimmed sleeves or without sleeves, both left their mark.

In Spain, the fashions which were to prevail throughout the whole of Europe first began to appear around 1460.

Here too, the characteristics of women's costume at the beginning of the fifteenth century were a fitted outline with accentuated waist and hips, and wide, trailing sleeves. Then Burgundian influence introduced fur edgings, regular folds and pointed neck openings. However, the short cloak made of three widths of cloth, a typically Spanish style, survived. Horned head-dresses bore witness to the influence of French kerchiefs. But Spanish costume showed its national character with the *verdugo*.

The *verdugo* first appeared towards 1470 in the court of Castile. It was to become the French *vertugade* and the English farthingale. Queen Juana of Portugal, married to the invalid Enrique V, invented a system of rigid hoops to support her skirts so as to disguise a pregnancy that could not be attributed to her husband. This fashion spread rapidly through Castile and Aragon and lasted until about 1490, then became rarer for a time. Meanwhile, in about 1498 it penetrated into Italy, where it did not fail to create a scandal, being banned in several towns, and shortly after, it was abandoned. From France, where it was introduced about 1500, it was to spread through the whole of Europe.

For men in Italy as elsewhere, the new short costume transformed their clothing and gave them a sharp, sinuous outline. Tight garments, new hairstyles and the first peaked hats showed a clear military influence; then, towards 1400, short jaquettes and houppelandes were introduced from France through the court at Pamplona. Exaggeration showed principally in the excessively tight, padded chest, low waist and gathered sleeves.

Towards 1470, Burgundian styles disappeared to give way to Italian modes.

In general, Spanish costume, which provided original creations in women's dress, showed the influence of Burgundian and, up to a point, Italian fashions. It used textiles edged with ornament in the Moorish style, and even Moorish garments like the *quixotes* or the *marlotte*, which were loose and sometimes reached to the ankles.

383 Offering the Heart, tapestry. First half of the fifteenth century. Paris, Musée de Cluny. (Photo Flammarion)

384 JEAN FOUQUET: *Virgin and Child*, also known as *Agnes Sorel*. *c.* 1480. Antwerp, Museum for Fine Arts. (Museum photo)

386 Jeanne de Bourbon and Jeanne d'Armagnac (or Isabeau of Bavaria). *c.* 1388.
Poitiers, Palais de Justice. (Photo Flammarion)

Costume in Germany and England

We have already mentioned the special German fashion for cut-work or foliate rag-edges 'in the German style'; this technique was used to decorate gown hems, the necks of chaperons and the ends of cornets. This cut-work, the fashion for which reached France around 1430, varied considerably and was adopted mainly for *robes déguisées* or liveries.

Belts were worn low and, towards the mid-fifteenth century, folds were all gathered to the front.

Closed sleeves in the shape of a bouffant sack, which were introduced to Venice and France at the beginning of the fifteenth century, also seem to be of Germanic origin.

In England, German cut-work and closed sleeves were part of elegant costume.

The Regulation of Luxury in Clothing

All over Europe exaggerated luxury provoked numerous sumptuary ordinances aimed at halting abuses or caprices. In Italy, where the first edicts had been issued in Florence (1330, 1334, 1344, 1355) they multiplied in all the larger towns, in Bologna (1400, 1433), Milan (1396, 1512, 1520) and Venice (1453, 1504, 1514) forbidding poulaine shoes, trains and low-cut necklines. Sometimes they limited the number of velvet or silk garments that any individual might own, and those garments that were authorized had to be marked with a seal. In Rome, in 1464 Pope Paul II even published vestimentary laws for cardinals. In France, similar regulations were promulgated in 1350, 1387, 1400 and 1485. In Spain, a series of laws, the first of which dated from 1234, was directed mainly against the misuse of silk stuffs in costume; these were reserved in 1348 for the sons of King Alfonso XI of Castile, but in 1395 silk garments were authorised for owners of horses; in 1490 Queen Isabella forbade the wearing of all silk or gold textiles.

The vogue for short costume also had curious repercussions in the clothing trades.

In France, it provoked conflicts between the corporations of tailors, who specialized in the *robe à garnements,* and the doublet-makers, when the tailors claimed the right to make doublets: they were authorized to do so only in 1598.

The immense popularity of fur at the end of the Middle Ages led to excesses which a multiplicity of rules attempted to halt. We know of French ordinances of 1350, 1367 and 1380 which do not seem to have been observed. After the middle of the fifteenth century, however, when textiles had become much less expensive and had gradually supplanted fur, sumptuary edicts controlling its use in the various countries of Europe became rarer and were scarcely ever applied.

387 Jean Chousat.
1433.
Poligny Church,
Jura. (Photo Hurault)

THE OPEN SURCOAT

385–6 A ceremonial garment, the open surcoat, trimmed with fur on the plastron and at the arm-holes or fastened with buttons of precious metals, reveals the fine gold girdle; it is rarer in Italy than in France, where it was still worn in the early sixteenth century

AUMONIÈRES

387–9 As garments had no pockets, purses or pouches were attached to the belt. Jean Chousat (plate 387) wears, over his riding robe, a *charnière* containing his falcon's food; his cloak is buttoned on the shoulder; his belt is a low-slung girdle with elaborate metal ornaments and hanging tassels

388   *Escarcelle* of cut velvet with ornate iron clasp.
Fifteenth century.
New York, Metropolitan Museum. (Museum photo)

389   *Escarcelle* of leather with ornate iron clasp.
Late Middle Ages.
New York, Metropolitan Museum. (Museum photo)

390   Dutch count in a *haincelin* (short houppelande) with wide, open sleeves edged with cut work, a hood fashioned in the shape of an open hood, worn like a cap, with a long slit point

391   Dutch count in a long houppelande with organ-pipe folds, wide, open sleeves with toothed cut-work edges and a rolled hat

392   Woman in a houppelande with cut sack sleeves; outer mantle held in place by a strap; chaperon in cut shell form, over templet hairstyle

393   Woman in surcoat with short sleeves over a bodice with elbow length hanging sleeves, horned head-dress known as a 'split loaf' over a crepine or woman's coif

390–93   Elegant costumes. Statuettes from the Dam chimney-piece, Amsterdam. (Photos Giraudon)

394–5 *Roman de la Violette.* Mid-fifteenth century. Paris, Bib. Nat. ms fr. 24376 f. 5,8. (Photo Bibliothèque Nationale)

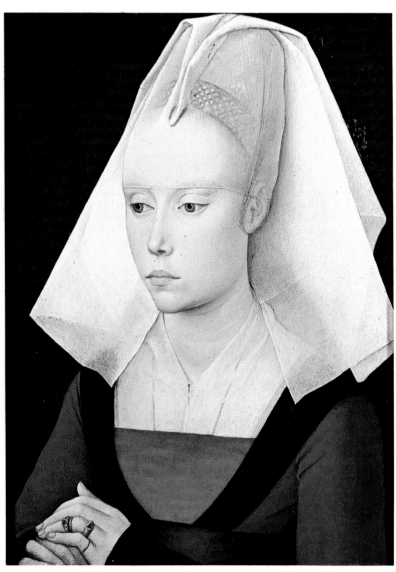

396 ROGER VAN DER WEYDEN: *Portrait of a Woman.* 1433.
London, National Gallery. (Photo Freeman)

397 PETRUS CHRISTUS: *Portrait of a Girl.* Mid-fifteenth century.
Berlin, Staatliche Museen, Gemäldegalerie. (Museum photo)

398 Jacket worn by Charles the Bold. *c.* 1477. Berne, Historical Museum. (Museum photo)

We must remember that these numerous regulations were aimed principally against the excessive use of luxury textiles rather than at exaggerated forms. However, there was a link between the many caprices of short costume and the increased output of costly textiles in the fourteenth and fifteenth centuries; to dissociate them would be to minimize the advantages they brought each other.

Costume in Eastern Europe and Asiatic Influences

In Eastern Europe costume was marked by the changes that had taken place in Asia, and the break-up of the Byzantine Empire.

Before the twelfth century, three zones of the vast Asiatic land-mass – southern China, Indochina with Insulindia, and the central and southern states of India – enjoyed a high degree of prosperity, civilization and culture, developed with the aid of continual trade links and a common maritime economy, having escaped the population movements and wars that had affected the rest of the continent.

The advanced, dynamic civilization of Southern Asia contrasted with the primitive, static cultural conditions of the Northern Asiatic nomads, the three branches – Turkish, Mongol and Unguz – of the Altaic race, composed of steppe shepherds and forest huntsmen, that had covered the immense northern part of Asia.

At the beginning of the thirteenth century, from one of the Mongol tribes to the west of Lake Baikal, Genghis Khan suddenly arose, took 150,000 horsemen and swooped down on North China, then pressed on into Central Asia, advanced as far as the Crimea and reached the mouth of the Danube. At the price of terrible massacres, he imposed the Mongolian Empire over this whole vast area, which during the thirteenth century was to take in all southern China, Russia as far as Cracow and the Middle East from Damascus to Baghdad (1255). Then, however, the rivalry between Islamic, Mongolian and Christian influences reversed this situation: the Mongolian Empire abandoned Russia and Central Asia, which returned to Islam under a Turkish feudal system.

In Europe, Turkish invasions gradually dominated all the eastern regions, finally coming up against the line of greater resistence formed by the Christian nations: on one side, Poland and Hungary, and on the other, Serbia and Bulgaria, which eventually succumbed (1483) as had the Eastern Empire, to the invasion of the Ottomans, who had been converted to Islam since the end of the thirteenth century.

The Mongolian and later Turkish waves which thus covered all Asia and the whole of Eastern Europe for two centuries naturally brought their civilization, and Asiatic elements appeared at different periods in the costume of the Slavs, the Hungarians, the Greeks and the Latins, who finally fell under Ottoman domination in the fifteenth century.

The preponderant type of costume introduced was the Asiatic *caftan*, a long, long-sleeved garment generously crossed in front. Varying in its details, it left durable traces in European costume.

The Golden Horde had gradually mastered the whole of European Russia. Then, abandoning the Byzantine tunic for the costume of the invaders, the Boyars wore a shirt and, over it, a caftan with a straight or slanting open collar and, on top, a second, long caftan with full sleeves tightly fastened at the wrist, or slit and hanging loosely. They kept this costume even after Ivan III had reconquered the country.

One wonders if the Poles borrowed the caftan from their Russian neighbours or from the Tartar Khans of Crimea and the Turks, copying the ceremonial caftans captured in battle. From the thirteenth century to the fifteenth, they wore the outer caftan or *zupan*, buttoned to the neck and trimmed with frogged braid.

Hungary, where German and Rumanian groups were juxtaposed with the Uralic race of Hungarians proper, had no distinctive civilization of its own, and the first Angevin kings

399 ANON: *The Marriage of Boccaccio Adimari.* Mid-fifteenth century.
Florence, Galleria dell'Accademia.
(Photo Sovrintendenza alle Belle Arti)

400 The art of the Netherlands: Brooch in gold, enamel
and pearls representing a bridal couple. *c.* 1450.
Vienna, Kunsthistorisches Museum

FLORENTINE COSTUME

399–401 Absalom (plate 401) and some of the wedding guests (plate
399) wear very short huques; the short garment with cape sleeves is the
giornea, which in France was to become the *journade*. The balloon-crown-
ed hats are specifically Italian, as is the chaperon with the very long
point. The sleeveless giornea worn by women is slipped over the tight-
sleeved *gamurra*; the *cioppa* is the closed gown with open sleeves. The
woman on the right of plate 399 wears a small padded head-dress, the
second right a 'peacock hat'. Several of the men wear quartered hose

ROBES DÉGUISÉES

402 This painting illustrates a feast held in *robes déguisées*, that is,
gowns departing from the ordinary. It must date from about 1442, as
the Limburg lions in the coat of arms were only added at that date to the
arms of the Dukes of Burgundy. However, for the most part the costumes
correspond to earlier dates and the uniform adoption of white suggests
that the colour had been laid down as the motif of the feast. All the men,
including the servants, wear short gowns *à plis gironnés*, enriched with
embroidery for gentlemen. Head-dresses vary enormously in shape. The
Duke sitting by the table has a *têtière proéminente* (projecting headpiece);
another wears his chaperon as a turban with a falling point in German
foliate cut-work, a detail which reappears in several of the women's
head-dresses. The same motif is to be seen for example in the cut gown
worn by the figure mounting a horse in the foreground. The men seen
from the rear near the Duke wear cloaks inspired by Italian fashions. In
the centre foreground a young man wears a close-fitting gippon with
hanging bobbles; another near by is wearing a huque and like yet another,
carries his hat in his hand so as to show his pudding-basin haircut
In the centre, the duchess is enveloped in a cloak lined with ermine; like
several other women, her hair is dressed in a beaded net *crépine*. Only
one woman, near the Duke, has a padded hairstyle; the others wear
fashioned chaperons over *crépines*. The young woman in the centre foreground wears beneath this a conventional hood fastened in front with
a pin. Several of the men wear soled hose and some of them, including
the Duke, have poulaine pattens. Only falconers wear laced ankle-boots.
Note also the embroidery of the gowns, the long gold or coral necklaces,
the cut-work *déchiquetures* of sleeves and camails, the flat-brimmed hats
decorated with feathers and sometimes with gold and jewelled bands
round the crown, the red gloves of the young woman to the left of the
middle ground, her standing collar and that of the woman centre foreground (very rare at that time) and the gold and jewelled girdles worn
very high by most of the women

400, 403 Gold, enamelled over relief and mingled with precious stones,
was widely worked in Burgundy and the Low Countries. The bridal
couple wear garments with round folds, and the young woman has a
padded head-dress over which the veil still stands in horns. The necklace
(plate 403) is an excellent example from the sixteenth century of the
potence worn by the Herald at Arms of the Order of the Golden Fleece
founded in 1429 by Philip the Good. It is formed of the coat of arms of
the fifty knights, divided between twenty-four small panels, the twenty-
fifth in the centre bearing the device and arms of Charles V. The border
is composed of Burgundian heraldic bosses alternating with knotted
crosses

401 PESELLINO: *The Death of Absalom:* Mid-fifteenth century.
Le Mans, Museum. (Photo Bertlène)

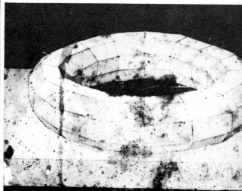

403 Grand collar or *potence* of the Herald at Arms of the Order of the Golden Fleece. Sixteenth century. Vienna, Kunsthistorisches Museum. (Museum photo)

405 PAOLO UCCELLO: *Support for the cappuccio worn as a turban,* drawing. *c.* 1450. Paris, Louvre. (Photo Flammarion)

recognized by the Diet in 1309 had tried to introduce Oriental civilization, at the same time extending their own power along the Danube, round the Black Sea and in Dalmatia.

Finally, in the old Eastern Empire, we notice that imperial costume was worn less and less frequently at and around court during the period of the Empire's ruin, from its restoration in 1261 to the fall of Byzantium in 1453. Among the peasant and merchant classes, we observe only the retention of the earlier type of costume of the primitive type worn in Asia Minor, increasingly influenced by the proximity of the Ottoman Turks. Immediately after his victory, Mahomet II installed a court in Byzantium, which rapidly became a centre of luxury.

While Asiatic costume was introduced along the immense front of Eastern Europe in the fourteenth and fifteenth centuries, to some extent by trade, but most of all by force of arms, it was purely as a result of international exchanges that it penetrated the west and centre.

The traffic by the long sea-route that, since the Crusades, had brought Oriental produce to Europe had remained active in spite of the clash between Christian and Moslem civilizations.

Textiles passed along this series of ports, and so did Oriental traders: Carpaccio and Bellini painted them in Venice, while European traders visited the nearer centres of Asia. Bertrandont de la Broquelière, councillor to the Duke of Burgundy, met Jacques Cœur in Damascus. We see Oriental influences on many occasions. The Comte de Nevers, taken prisoner at Andrinople and Gallipoli, sent a Turkish garment to the young Philip the Good; Manuel Paleologue, Emperor of Byzantium, made his entry into Paris in 1400 in a suit of white silk and wore Oriental costume at the wedding of the Comte de Clermont with the elder daughter of the Duc de Berri. 'Mysteries' everywhere were peopled with Turks and Moors; sculpture and painting reproduced picturesque silhouettes representing Saint Mary Magdalene or the Holy Women at the Tomb.

In this way, Oriental materials, decoration and forms were introduced into Europe. They were to be found again later, transformed and imitated, under the influence of political, economic and artistic relationships that differ little from those

that had first established them in the fourteenth and fifteenth centuries.

Costume Materials

TEXTILES AND THEIR DECORATION

Even before the first symptoms of costume change appeared towards 1340, their beginnings were contained in the sumptuous nature of the costume textiles introduced into Western Europe or manufactured in certain regions of Spain and Italy, notably in Lombardy, from Genoa to Venice.

Silk weaving had expanded considerably in Lucca, where it had originally been brought by Jews in the tenth century. At the beginning of the fourteenth century, internal party struggles forced several Tuscan silk-weavers and merchants into exile, and they settled with their looms and employees in northern Italy. In Venice, where the first corporation of weavers had obtained its statutes in 1265, the Grand Council was quick to accord refugees special privileges and a district near the Rialto, while imposing strict controls on manufacture and sales. It is incontestable that it was the arrival of the Lucca weavers that made the Most Serene Republic an important silk producer from the fourteenth century to the sixteenth.

From the year 1000, Venice had poised herself skilfully between East and West, entrusting the services of her fleet to the highest bidder and opening her port to the produce of the West as well as to the Levant, so that the city became the most important supplier of the international market. She had also secured important privileges. We must not forget the Venetian Niccolò Polo who, half a century later, in 1260, travelled from Kazan through Bokhara to China, and whose son Marco, the author of the famous *Book of Marvels*, accomplished his own renowned expedition. In all her transactions Venice gave priority

406 BENOZZO GOZZOLI: *The Procession of the Magi*. 1468–9. Florence, Palazzo Ricardi. (Photo Alinari)

407 A. DÜRER: *Venetian Woman*, c. 1495–1510. Vienna, Albertina. (Museum photo)

408 DOMENICO GHIRLANDAIO: Frescos of Santa Maria Novella, Florence (detail). Late fifteenth century. (Photo Alinari-Giraudon)

to the importing of silk and precious textiles from the East, as well as spices and fine gems; Western products she exported included woollen stuffs and linen, with other, unworked materials.

In Spain, in the fourteenth and fifteenth centuries, silk was used all the more widely because it had from olden times conferred on its wearers a particular distinction that appealed to the Spanish temperament. The silk mills set up by the Moors survived the end of the Moslem domination.

At that time the industrial capacity of a town was matched by its pride in clothing its inhabitants in its own products: when Venice sent ambassadors to the marriage of the Duke of Ferrara and Lucrezia Borgia in 1502, they made a public appearance in the great Hall of State wearing ceremonial costumes, so that the whole town could admire them, as well as the two fur-trimmed crimson cloaks brought as gifts for the young couple.

This considerable spread of silk, maintained by regular trade with foreign markets, was also facilitated by the fairs of Champagne, Bruges and Paris. We know the details of how much silk was bought and sold, mainly in Genoa, how it was worked and transformed in the Italian weaving and export centres: the technique of Italian traders showed its superiority in every way.

The enormous Italian output of satins, velvets, taffetas and other silk textiles satisfied the taste for luxury in costume of a considerable class, composed at first of patrician and feudal noble society, then of all the wealthy throughout Europe. Tales of travel, descriptions of towns, account-books of royal houses, inventories of lords and private individuals show that silk occupied a place of honour in all official and private ceremonies.

The general evolution of costume also benefited from other circumstances.

The use of silks and other costly stuffs gave clothing more variety than it had had while wool and linen had been in favour. There was a vast range of new tints provided by dyeing and the mixture of different coloured threads. Silk's softness, brilliance and smooth texture were better fitted to stress the lines of the body, which lost their medieval verticality.

ITALIAN COSTUME

404–5 The short houppelandes with wide flaring sleeves are made in patterned, brocaded velvet. The turban *cappuccio* (plate 404) is built up on a cork base (plate 405)

ITALIAN COSTUME IN THE SECOND HALF OF THE FIFTEENTH CENTURY

406–9 Certain new fashion details appear. Women's gowns, which are still made of patterned silk, have the high girdle; the head-dress reveals the curled hair which is decked with jewels and light veils (plates 407–8); for both men and women, the *finestrella* sleeves allow the flowing sleeves of the chemise to pass through: these are the first occurrences of slashing (plates 407–9). The small caps are in bright colours. The King (plate 406) appears to be wearing a caftan buttoned down the front, with a full skirt, the first example of this garment, which was brought by the Greeks expelled from Constantinople

VENETIAN COSTUME AT THE END OF THE FIFTEENTH CENTURY

407, 409, 414 Women wear gowns with wide, low necklines and slashed sleeves; blonde hair, the fashionable colour, was dressed in a chignon on top of the head (plates 407, 414). Men also adopted the fashion for slashing. Hose were still tight-fitting and vari-coloured. Fitted pourpoints opened in front to show the shirt. A short, open garment of the garbardine type (plate 409 right) was also worn. Caps had ostrich and peacock feathers. Members of the Council wore the long simarra with ducal sleeves, a traditional costume, which remained in use until the eighteenth century

409 CARPACCIO: *The Miracle of the Holy Cross at the Rialto* (detail). Late fifteenth century. Venice, Accademia. (Photo Anderson-Giraudon)

410 FERRARESE SCHOOL: *The Betrothal.* 1470. Berlin, Staatliche Museen, Gemäldegalerie. (Museum photo)

411 Ralph Neville, Earl of Westmorland and his children. *c.* 1410–30. Paris, Bib. Nat. ms lat. 1158 f. 27 v. (Photo Bibliothèque Nationale)

412 SWABIAN SCHOOL: *The Lover* *c.* 1470. The Cleveland Museum of Art, Delia and L. E. Holden Funds. (Museum photo)

Another important change was this: colours no longer had the symbolic meaning that had until then been attached to them, so that particular colours ceased to be imposed on different classes. As early as the thirteenth century chroniclers such as Villani and Sansovino noted how men and women wore purple or hyacinth-coloured cloaks. An immense variety of armorial motifs was used in silk textiles: stripes, checkerboards or figures. Never before had textiles in Europe placed so much brilliance, richness and charm at the disposal of costume.

To escape from the ordinances aimed at limiting the manufacture of the most expensive cloths, particularly those with gold threads, Florentine producers manufactured mixtures of silk and linen or silk waste: in this way they created *brocatelle* and *filaticcio.*

However, in spite of its enormous popularity, silk did not supplant linen cloth, whose manufacturers in Flanders had supplied Europe since the early Middle Ages; linen seems to have represented two thirds of the textiles used, silk one third.

Spain, which produced woollens, as did Flanders and some regions of France, set up an important cloth industry in the fifteenth century, as a consequence of the marriage of Enrique III of Castile and Catherine of Lancaster, who is said to have brought a flock of sheep in her dowry. Segovia became a very flourishing centre.

In the fourteenth and fifteenth centuries, certain woollen cloths copied the fine Oriental materials like *camlet.* These inferior imitations and the manufacture of more common qualities led to a noticeable lowering of prices from the middle of the fifteenth century.

Unlike silken cloths, woollen cloths were made in single colours (plain broadcloth). Ordinary and ceremonial costumes were adorned with embroidery and appliqués forming *devices,* figures of objects, plants or animals chosen as personal emblems: the broom for Charles VI, the bear and the bleeding swan for the Duc de Berry. Some pieces of everyday costume might also be decorated: the dark green broadcloth *huque* and gown given to Joan of Arc by order of the Duke of Orleans in 1429 were decorated with nettle leaves in a paler green, another device from the Duke's arms.[12]

214

FUR

Fur continued to play an important role: it was now that its favour among the various classes of society reached its highest point. It remained a sign of luxury and all elegant, costly garments were trimmed with it as edging or lining. Paintings and sculptures provide innumerable examples, even in the Mediterranean area. The cape and pourpoint worn by Lorenzo the Magnificent in his portrait by Benozzo Gozzoli are trimmed with fur, as are those of the elegant young men in the *Marriage of Boccaccio Adimari* (plate 399).

The furs most commonly worn were the back-fur of the grey squirrel, fox, marten, beaver and lettice, which was white and imitated ermine. Marten, *gris, vair* (see below) and ermine were generally reserved for princely or court garments, while beaver, otter, hare and fox were worn among the lesser nobility and the middle classes, and lambskin, wolf, goat and sheepskin were left for the common people.

Vair, which was widely used during the Middle Ages, referred to the skin of the northern squirrel: the back (*petit gris*) and the white belly, arranged in a checkerboard pattern, gave *menu vair; gros vair* was marked by coarser quality. The consumption of *vair* was enormous: in eighteen months Charles VI used 20,000 bellies and Isabeau of Bavaria 15,000 for the linings of their garments.

The activity and extent of fur-trading show the highly developed organization of the corporations of furriers throughout Europe. The two main centres were the Hanseatic League, founded in the middle of the thirteenth century with trading posts in Russia, and Bruges, which was admirably placed between the northern producers and the Mediterranean buyers.

ORIENTAL INFLUENCES

Despite the activity of European textile centres, Oriental cloths exercized a continued attraction for Western countries. They were used for luxury garments, and also for the costumes of participants in the ceremonial entries of princes or sovereigns.

411 English residents in France wore costume similar to French costume: fur-lined houppelandes of all lengths, with closed sleeves or wide, hanging sleeves; pudding-basin haircuts. Women also wore horned head-dresses arranged over pads

COSTUME IN GERMANY IN THE FIFTEENTH CENTURY

412, 416 The young girl (plate 412) has a jewelled circlet on her unbound hair, similar to the necklace with central pendant and bracelet she wears. Her left sleeve is in different stuff from the rest of her gown. The young man also wears a costume parti-coloured from top to bottom, poulaine shoes on his feet, and a *iembelet* (jewelled garter) on his left leg. In plate 416 the young man has long pointed poulaines, as does the young girl, who wears pattens over hers

SPANISH COSTUME IN THE SECOND HALF OF THE FIFTEENTH CENTURY

413, 417, 421 Some French influence survives in the form of the gowns and of the fur-edged surcoats and the rolled and padded women's head-dresses.
The rich materials and men's silk caps are inspired by Italy (plate 413). But around 1474 (plate 417) we see the appearance of the gown supported by *verdugos*, the first form of the *vertugadin* (farthingale)

413 CATALAN SCHOOL:
Banquet of Herod.
Mid-fifteenth century.
New York, Metropolitan Museum.
(Photo Cummer Gallery of Art, Jacksonville)

414 CARPACCIO: *Two Venetian Women.* Late fifteenth century. Venice, Museo Correr.
(Photo André Held)

415 *Tapestry of the Unicorn Hunt.* New York, Metropolitan Museum, Cloisters Collection, gift of John D. Rockefeller.
(Museum photo)

Silk and gold muslin from Mosul; damaskeen with woven ornaments from Damascus and Persia; *baldacchino* silks decorated with small figures, which are to be found as far away as England; cloths from Antioch with gold or blue birds on a red or black ground; *camocas* brought from China through Persia and Cyprus, where *maramoto*, damask and fine gold cords were made; Egyptian *dabiki* with gilt flowers: even this brief list shows that all the great centres of the East provided Europe with textiles.

Oriental cloths were highly prized because of their decoration as well as their technical perfection. They found favour not only in courtly circles, where they were used for garments and standards, but also among the clergy who used them for altar cloths and bishops' mitres. While before the middle of the thirteenth century the favourite decoration was Classical with fantastic creatures whose origins go back to the Sassanian workshops, later we see a tendency towards abstract decoration.

This was the repertory of ornament adopted by Italian centres and others, farther afield. In the mid-thirteenth century the mills of Regensburg and Cologne demonstrated the penetration of certain Oriental prototypes, whose motifs were gradually adapted to European tastes. Italy broke free from Eastern tutelage quite early, in the fourteenth century, and gave increasing importance to stylized floral decoration, leading to the virtually complete elimination of animal themes and architectonic divisions; the fashion for these scattered flowers became general and developed particularly in Genoa and Florence.

The curvilinear patterns formed by stylized flowers and tendrils also derived from an Oriental principle: in the fifteenth century Italy was to exploit this device widely and textiles of this type were worn by the figures painted by Andrea Orcagna and his school.

From the fifteenth century Italian weavers, though retaining traces of Oriental influence in their decorative repertory, enlarged their own floral motifs to unusual dimensions, decorating their embossed velvets with large pomegranates or thistles set between wide, wavy lines (plates 394–5).

416 SOUTH GERMAN SCHOOL: Drawing. 1470–80. Erlangen, University. (Photo Erlangen University Library)

417 CATALAN SCHOOL: *The Banquet of Herod. c.* 1470. Barcelona, Collection Muntadas. (Photo Mas)

418 Letter of Ovid. Late fifteenth century. Paris, Bib. Nat. ms fr. 874 f. (Photo Flammarion)

FRENCH COSTUME IN THE LATE FIFTEENTH AND EARLY SIXTEENTH CENTURIES

415, 418–20, 425 The form of garment differs little from that of the preceding period: round folds, long hose, pourpoints, but there are numerous new details: tunics for hunting are of white linen (plate 425); there are square bear's foot shoes with slashing (plate 418). Ostrich feather plumes decorate men's caps, which have turned back and slashed brims called *cramignoles* (plate 425). There is separation of the close-fitting nether hose and the upper hose, called *boulevarts*, with visible codpiece. Women wear gowns cut at the waist and velvet or linen chaperons worn over *tourets*, headbands edged with gold and jewels (plate 423)

WOMEN'S ROBE A LA FRANCAISE AT THE BEGINNING OF THE SIXTEENTH CENTURY

422–3 The overgown is opened in front over an underskirt in a different colour, supported even then, in Spain, on *verdugos* (farthingales); the wide, square neckline reveals a chemise or gorgerette of linen with coloured decorations that appear again at the foot of the wide sleeves, which may have increasingly thick fur edgings (plate 422). The velvet chaperon is worn over a touret. The general line is simple and smooth. Marguerite d'Angoulême is in mourning and wears a widow's mantle (plate 422)

SURVIVALS OF LONG COSTUME

424 The long costume remained as traditional clothing for certain posts, such as the Squires of Paris, who have the hood hanging free over the shoulders. Serjeants wore the short gown with the city arms embroidered on the left arm

Notes

1 Bernis, *Indumenteria medieval española, passim.*
2 Renier and Houdoy, *passim.*
3 Cf. also Pisanello drawings in the Louvre and Ashmolean Museum, Oxford.
4 Enlart, pp. 475–482.
5 At Benevento in February 1266, Charles of Anjou, attacking Manfred, King of the Two Sicilies, had to face German horsemen clad in plate armour, which was then unknown in France.
6 The term *escoffion*, from the Italian *scuffia*, appears only in the sixteenth century.
7 The Dutch *toppenhoed*, the German *Zuckerhut* and the English *steeple head-dress* refer only to pointed head-dresses. Philologists have provided varying explanations for this term, without reaching a conclusive version.
8 Baltrusaitis, p. 177, fig. 85.
9 Cf. Christine de Pisan on the resistance to new fashions of Charles V and Jeanne of Bourbon.

10 She received Burgundian envoys dressed in a slit gown and a sort of turban.
11 Italians also wore a type of huque which showed all the pourpoint sleeves.
12 Harmand, pp. 311, 317, 318.

Bibliography

GENERAL

P. POST: 'La Naissance du costume masculin moderne au XIVe s.' in *Actes Ier Cong. Int. d'Hist. du Cost.*, 1951. Venice 1955.
FRANÇOIS BOUCHER: 'Les Conditions de l'apparition du costume court en France vers le millieu du XIVe s.' in *Recueil des travaux offerts à M. Clovis Brunel.* 1955.
EVA RODHE LUNDQUIST: *La Mode et son vocabulaire.* Göteborg 1950.
RODOLFO RENIER: *Il Tipo estetico della donna.* Ancona 1889.
RODOCANACHI: *La Femme italienne.* 1907.
J. HOUDOY: *La Beauté des femmes dans la littérature et dans l'art.* 1876.

COSTUME

MICHÈLE BEAULIEU and JEANNE BAYLÉ: *Le Costume en Bourgogne de Philippe le Hardi à Charles le Téméraire.* 1956.
HENRI DAVID: *Philippe le Hardi, le train somptuaire d'un grand Valois.* Dijon 1947.
O. CASTELLIERI: *La Cour des ducs de Bourgogne.* 1946.
A. HARMAND: *Jeanne d'Arc, son costume, son armure.* 1929.
C. COUDERC: 'Les Comptes d'un grand couturier parisien du XVe s.' in *Bull. Soc. Hist. Paris*, 1911.
CARMEN BERNIS MADRAZO: *Indumenteria Medieval Española.* Madrid 1956.
MANUEL GOMEZ MORENO: *El Panteón de las Huelgas de Burgos.* Madrid 1946.

TEXTILES

F. PODREIDER: *Storia dei tessuti d'arte in Italia.* Bergamo 1928.
FRANCISQUE MICHEL: *Recherches sur le commerce, la fabrication et l'usage des étoffes de soie, d'or et d'argent.* 1852.
JEAN H. PRAT: *Fourrures et pelleteries à travers les âges.* Paris, n.d.
G. BIGWOOD: 'La Politique de la laine en France sous les règnes de Philippe le Bel et de ses fils', in *Revue Belge Philologie et Histoire*, 1937.

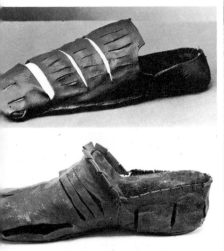

419 Eschapin. Fifteenth century. London, Victoria and Albert Museum. (Museum photo)

420 Escolleter (cutaway) shoe found in the château at Issogne. Fifteenth century. Musée Bally, Schoenenwerd, Switzerland. (Museum photo)

421 MARCUELLOS: *Devotiones de la reyna doña Juanà.* (Ferdinand V, Isabella the Catholic and their daughter Juana.) 1488. Chantilly, Musée Condé. (Photo Flammarion)

422 Marguerite d'Angoulème offering the '*Coche d'Amour*' to the Duchesse d'Etampes. 1540. Chantilly, Musée Condé, ms fr. 978. (Photo Flammarion)

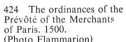

Far left:
423 THE MASTER OF THE LEGEND OF ST MADELEINE: *Jeanne la Folle.* Formerly Wilkinson Collection. (Photo Giraudon)

424 The ordinances of the Prévôté of the Merchants of Paris. 1500. (Photo Flammarion)

425 The Unicorn Hunt. Late fifteenth century. (cf. plate 415)

427 PARMIGIANINO: *Turkish Slave Girl.* c. 1530. Parma, National Gallery. (Photo Vaghi)

426 F. DE LLANO: *The Infanta Isabella Clara Eugenia.* 1584. Madrid, Prado. (Photo D. Manso)

428 Tapestry of courtly life. Late fifteenth century. Paris, Musée de Cluny. (Photo Flammarion)

Chapter VIII

The Sixteenth Century

Until the end of the fifteenth century, population groups were comparatively isolated from one another. Europe knew nothing of America and little of Africa and Asia; in the sixteenth century, these civilizations discovered one another and developed closer relations.

In the Old World, particularly in Western and Southern Europe, important changes were to take place in a context of monarchies and principalities; elsewhere the continent remained under the domination of feudal lords.

The general political reorganization, often assisted by princely marriages, brought about the disappearance of some medieval states, such as the Duchy of Burgundy, 1493, and the Duchy of Brittany, 1532, and the emergence of new political entities, such as Aragon and Castile in Spain. The European courts, each with its own particular styles of clothing, gave way to fewer, more homogeneous states, and costume tended to express their 'national' character.

In Italy the situation remained unchanged and Venice maintained her independence. To the east were Russia and Lithuania and the kingdom of Poland, to the north the three Scandinavian kingdoms, to the west the kingdom of England. Europe was divided between the kingdoms of Spain, France, Naples and Sardinia on one hand, and on the other, the Holy Roman Empire of Charles V and the Ottoman Empire of Suleiman the Magnificent.

In the Western world, therefore, the accepted political and artistic divisions no longer coincided with those of costume.

The renaissance of literature and the visual arts was still taking place: it was at the beginning of the sixteenth century that art completed the slow transformation which led to the idealization of the human body. To endow it with the power and dignity of which Renaissance man dreamed, artists set themselves to create costumes, combining line and colour to produce elegance and harmony.

This pride in physical beauty, this refinement of the art of pleasing, accentuated by clothing, were sustained by the sixteenth century's luxurious materials – rich, heavy stuffs, thick embroideries, sumptuous jewels and fragile lace. No other period, not even the *Grand Siècle*, was to give men more precious adornments to attain the perfection of human beauty.

Luxury and the Economy

In 1492 Christopher Columbus arrived in the West Indies; in 1498 the Portuguese navigator Vasco da Gama sailed round

219

429 Attributed to G. DA CARPI: *Portrait of a Lady*, c. 1530. Frankfurt, Städelsches Kunstinstitut. (Photo Bruckmann-Giraudon)

430 A. DÜRER: *Man in Festive Costume*, 1515. Vienna, Albertina. (Museum photo)

431 HOLBEIN: *Woman from Basle*, c. 1520. (Photo Giraudon-Haufstaengl)

432–3 SOUTH GERMAN: *Princely Couple*, c. 1535. Lucerne, Collection Igo Levi. (Photo Germanisches Nationalmuseum, Nuremberg)

WOMEN'S COSTUME IN ITALY IN THE FIRST HALF OF THE SIXTEENTH CENTURY

427, 429 The short bodice has a wide, square cut neckline over the light chemise or guimp. The voluminous sleeves and flowing skirt accentuate the full-blown outline (plate 429). The *balzo* (roll of gilt openwork) is the usual head-dress. The feather fan (plate 427) is a flywhisk

THE ROBE À L'ITALIENNE DURING THE RENAISSANCE

428 The square-cut neckline is an Italian fashion

COSTUME IN THE GERMANIC COUNTRIES

430–33 Survivals from the Middle Ages (muslin guimps and veils, fur linings) combine with the new taste and with slashing (plate 431) The male outline was broadened by the *schaub* (*chamarre*), a garment which may have originated in Germany, but was perhaps originally Oriental (plate 433)

SPANISH COSTUME AND ITS INFLUENCE

426, 438, 440, 443 These portraits illustrate the passage from an Italian style (low-cut gowns, wide sleeves, cf. plate 429) to the severe style of Spanish costume (plates 438, 440). The Infanta wears a light coloured *vaquero* with flowing false sleeves below padded epaulettes scalloped with *piccadils* (plate 438). Hair is dressed in a pyramid, and the toque is already tall (plate 426). Ann of Austria (plate 440) wears a basquine fastened with *puntas* (points) over a farthingale. The gown clearly shows the horizontal pleat designed to hide the feet of the wearer when seated (plates 426, 440).
The handkerchief (*pañuelo*) is trimmed with Italian lace or Spanish embroidery (plate 438)

WOMEN'S COSTUME IN SPAIN IN THE EARLY SEVENTEENTH CENTURY

434–5 While the general shape and line of the garment does not change, there are modifications of detail: the high flaring collar tends to replace the ruff; there is increasing use of Italian lace, and the head-dress becomes lower and laden with jewels

THE FRENCH ROLL FARTHINGALE

436–7 The caricature shows the roll being fitted below the waist between the undercoat and the overgown. The cloth of the gown is gathered at the waist and spreads over the roll, emphasizing the slimness of the waist, which is confined in a high boned bodice *à l'espagnole*, ending in a ruff at the throat. Plate 436 shows the effect of these farthingales in profile

434 SANCHEZ COELLO: *Portrait of a Spanish Princess*, c. 1615. New York, Collection Mercer. (Photo Frick Art Reference Library)

435   PANTOJA DE LA CRUZ: *Portrait of a Lady*. c. 1620. Madrid, Prado. (Photo Anderson-Giraudon)

436   Funerary statuette of Antoinette de Fontette, c. 1580. Dijon, Museum. (Photo Rémy)

437   I. DE VOS and GALLE: Engraving satirizing rolls, 1595. (Photo Flammarion)

Africa by the Cape of Good Hope and reached India at Calcutta. For some time Seville and Lisbon held the monopoly of trade between Europe and the Americas and Asia, at the expense of the trade of Venice, whose galleys came back empty from Alexandria in 1504.

Many of the basic materials of European costume became involved in a commercial redistribution which neither the Portuguese nor the Spanish could organize unaided. Thus merchants from Germany, Flanders and France brought goods to Lisbon and Seville to barter for the produce of exotic countries, carrying home with them Egyptian cotton, Persian, Iraqui and Syrian silks, Indian cotton stuffs. In this way the new centres of Lyons, which became the principal financial centre of Europe, and Antwerp, to which the Emperor Maximilian had transferred the privileges of Bruges in 1488, rose to prominence.

Faced with this situation, Italian towns soon reacted: Venetians, Milanese, Florentines and Genoese hastened to develop their banking organizations and luxury industries, particularly the silk industry and the new lace-making industry, derived from cut-stitch work, whose artistic qualities were to make it one of the most highly prized elements of dress. On their side, France, England and the Low Countries supported their own woollen industries. Centres of wealth were thus formed by the large and developing trading towns of Europe: Genoa, Venice, Florence, Lyons and Paris. The populations of London, Augsburg and Munich were estimated at 40,000, 50,000, even 100,000 inhabitants, and they became great centres of consumption, exchange and distribution.

Further, in order to supply a clientèle whose higher standard of living brought with it a taste for luxurious costume, merchants introduced into country regions not only the essential raw materials, but also manufacturing equipment formerly prohibited by the corporation rules of the old cloth-making towns: fulling mills and, from 1589 on, William Lee's knitting machine.

As the resources of craft industries remained insufficient, important manufacturing centres were set up in an effort to compete with the light English textiles then in use. Industrialists settled in Ypres, Honschoot, Armentières, Rouen and Languedoc, as well as in Lancashire. Under Henri IV, the Volf factory

438   Attributed to SANCHEZ COELLO: *The Infanta Isabella Clara Eugenia*, 1579. Madrid, Prado. (Museum photo)

439   *Three Princesses of the House of Lorraine*, c. 1595. Madrid, Prado. (Photo Anderson-Giraudon)

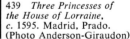

at Saint-Sever, Rouen, which produced fine stuffs, had three hundred and fifty looms and between five and six hundred workers.

Changes in rural life followed: in England, landowners turned their arable land into pasture in order to produce more wool; elsewhere, they planted mulberry trees and woad for dyestuffs, or even built fulling mills.

The production of textiles had a stimulating effect on the importation of dyestuffs: scarlet and cochineal from Armenia, madder from Arabia, woods from Brazil, the Indies or Ceylon, indigo from Baghdad, Coromandel or Bengal, saffron from India and the Levant, and henna from Arabia.

Political changes, industrial and commercial development, and a sudden flow of precious metals from America, all led to a general increase in wealth and an increasing taste for personal elegance during the first half of the sixteenth century. While there were fewer courts than before, the luxury in costume remained unabated in those that had survived. The nobility gathered there, surrounded by swarms of servants. For a single ball the court might wear 'a whole flock on its shoulders' in costumes.

Castiglione, in his treatise on manners, *Il Cortegiano* (first published in 1528 and translated into all the European languages), gave a code of behaviour for the new social phenomenon we know as the 'gentleman'. But a new atmosphere favoured the fusion of the courtly élite with the upper middle classes and the more important administrative officials.

Luxury blossomed in the costume of courtiers and bourgeoisie all over Europe. Charles VIII, Louis XII and François I (plate 442), entering Italy with their armies, discovered new social pleasures. Mythological entertainments, tourneys, balls, processions and masquerades provided opportunities for new costumes: the Platonic Academy of Florence celebrated the beauty of the human body and of all things reflecting the beauty of the Creator. The French were captivated by the revelation of such elegance and brought back to France not only painters and architects, but also tailors.

Large numbers of Italian workers then settled in Lyons, Paris and Tours, and their workshops supplied the French court. But Italian fashions influenced French styles more in materials and ornament than in form.

In England, Henry VIII came one day upon his Chancellor, Cardinal Wolsey, at table with twelve lords disguised as shepherds dressed in cloth of gold or crimson satin: Holbein recorded the sumptuous doublets and diamond-studded bodices worn at court.

There was, however, another side to this brilliant picture: the financial crisis of 1557-9 brought about a general rise in prices. Ruined aristocratic families could ally themselves with the bourgeoisie, whose members sometimes gained important places at court, but the standard of living of workers, craftsmen and peasants declined. The religious wars contributed to their distress. This poverty of the lower classes was expressed by extremely poor clothing: however, this is rarely represented in the arts, for at this time painters were still concentrating on the rich garments worn in court and urban circles. The sixteenth century lacked the Callots and Le Nains who were to record humble life in the following century.

Italian Costume

Italian influence in fashion, which had dominated Europe since the end of the thirteenth century, had become gradually weaker after the mid-fifteenth century, at a time when the peninsula's medieval divisions exposed it to the ambitions of Western monarchies attracted by its wealth. In contrast, the second half of the fifteenth century saw national unification of France, Spain and the Low Countries, with a consequent improvement in their economic development.

At the end of the fifteenth century, Italian costume became influenced by foreign fashions, sometimes French and German, but above all Spanish. In 1494 mantles in Ferrara were 'in Spanish style', and, for ceremonial occasions, women generally preferred Spanish costumes because of their magnificence. Lucrezia Borgia, herself of Spanish extraction, set the example. In 1491, at the marriage of Beatrice d'Este and Ludovico il Moro, all the women wore Spanish toilettes. The influence of German modes was more limited, although in 1504 Venice had been obliged to prohibit garments 'in the German fashion'.

French fashions, which were widely followed in Piedmont, were less successful in the rest of Italy before the arrival of the French; in 1494, only hats and shoes were mentioned as being 'in the French style'. But the Naples expedition turned the tide in favour of France, for, knowing the Italian weakness for elegance and display, Charles VIII shrewdly deployed a magnificence which won him the whole of Italy. While he himself was being captivated by Italian fashions, French styles were being adopted all over Italy and adapted to the national taste: in Venice and throughout northern Italy, wide French cloaks were worn. When the ambassador Calco went to France to negotiate the alliance of the Sforza family with Charles VIII, Beatrice d'Este, who was, as we have seen, won over to Spanish fashions, charged his secretary to bring her back detailed descriptions of the costumes worn by Anne of Britanny, and Ludovico il Moro asked for drawings – evidently the enthusiasm was mutual.

In this period of adjustments, the eccentricities of the preceding century gradually grew less marked. The campaign against them continued: restrictions against low-cut necklines were imposed in Genoa and Milan in 1512 and in Rome in 1520; in 1514 Venice laid down sumptuary laws and set up a special controlling office. Perhaps we should interpret these prohibitions as the delayed effects of the already distant campaign of Savonarola, who had been burned in Florence in 1498, but whose ardent fight against the Medici and profane art in general had not been without results.

A sixteenth-century Florentine historian, B. Varchi, wrote:[1] 'There can be no doubt that since 1512 the manner of dress for men and women has acquired much elegance and grace; people no longer wear... those loose saies with short front and long sleeves, nor those caps with brims turned right up... nor those little shoes with riduculous heels. Mantles... are normally black...' The *Dialogue between Rafaella and Margherita*, written in 1538 by Alessandro Piccolomini,[2] assumed a 'rich and pleasant' fashion, and stated that the best thing for a woman was 'to imagine fashions for herself'.

Not only taste, but the physical type itself was transformed, a phenomenon of adaptation which fashion was to repeat often in later times. The Italians showed increasing appreciation of women 'full in flesh' and, according to Montaigne, 'fashion

439–441   The Spanish style of bell farthingale was little worn in France; La Belle Corisande (plate 441) wears Spanish Court costume because her husband was governor of Bayonne: this costume comprizes a *saya* with a girdle of precious stones; the child wears the same costume, but with open sleeves. Note the rings worn on thumb and index finger.

The arched neckline of the Valois court (plate 439, centre) is worn over a guimp with a small ruff. The three-strand necklace is a *cottoire*; the hair is swept up over *arcelets* and covered with an *attiffet*. The figure on the left wears a mourning mantle and gloves cut in piccadils. Two of the princesses carry closed fans, a new style

MALE COSTUME IN THE TIME OF FRANÇOIS I

442   The doublet with a wide-cut neck over the shirt is a fashion shared by Italy and France. The doublet worn by François I has slashings and is worn under a *dogaline* with wide, turned-back sleeves fastened up to the shoulder. A flat hat is trimmed with a white feather and studded with gems and an ensign; the shirt with coloured embroidery is a Spanish fashion

440   SANCHEZ COELLO: *Anne of Austria, Queen of Spain*, 1571. Vienna, Kunsthistorisches Museum. (Photo Meyer Erwin)

441   *Diane, comtesse de Guiche,* known as *La Belle Corisande, with her daughter c.* 1580. Collection Duc de Grammont. (Photo Duteurtre)

442   Attributed to F. CLOUET: *François I, c.* 1525. Paris Louvre. (Photo Flammarion)

443   TITIAN: *Isabella of Portugal, Wife of Charles V, c.* 1535. Madrid, Prado. (Museum photo)

444 ANTONIO MORO: *Marguerite of Parma, c.* 1570. Philadelphia Museum, John B. Johnson Collection. (Museum photo)

445 PANTOJA DE LA CRUZ: *The Infanta Isabella Clara Eugenia,* 1584. Château de Villandry, Indre-et-Loire. (Photo Giraudon)

446 H. KRELL: *Anne of Saxony,* 1551. Dresden, Gemäldegalerie. (Photo Bruckmann-Giraudon)

447 VAN DEN MAST: *Port... a Woman,* 1587. Amsterda... Rijksmuseum. (Museum ph...

THE SPANISH ROPA

444–5, 452 The *ropa* was perhaps Oriental in origin, not cut at the waist, worn open down the front with padded rolls at the top of the sleeves

EUROPEAN IMITATIONS OF THE ROPA

446–7, 451 All over Europe women wore gowns inspired by the ropa: the *simarra* (plate 444) in Italy, the *marlotte* (plate 451) in France and the *vlieger* (plate 447) in Holland.
Ann of Saxony (plate 446) wears one, open over an apron, a specifically German style. The winged Dutch head-dress (plate 447) is very similar to the French *attiffet* (plate 451)

PADDED HOSE

448–9, 453, 460–61 Puffed, padded upper hose with stiff bands, or *panes,* which let a soft lining show through were known in France as *grègues,* then as *trousses.* Here they are almost spherical and are worn with doublets with standing collars

448 Male costume: doublet, upper hose, red velvet cape, leather hat, gloves. 1575. The London Museum (Museum photo)

224

them large and stout'. Muralti[3] compared them with wine-barrels. This was the type represented by Palma Vecchio and Bernadini, and it became current under the brushes of Titian, Bronzino, Sodoma and Palma Giovane. Garments were overloaded with ornament, scarlet brocades and stiffly folded velvets set off magnificent *parures,* girdles of precious stones, chains, gold rings, pearl necklaces, ruby and emerald pendants. Other artists added some luxury object in their sitters' hands, a jewel, fan or fur, emphasizing their rank and wealth. Costume gradually imposed itself on the Italian Renaissance artist, and we see it come to dominate formal portraits at the end of the century, an indication of the important place clothes occupied in society.

SPANISH FASHIONS IN ITALY

In 1525, when the battle of Pavia decided matters in favour of Charles V, Spanish predominance reappeared, if not in the details of costume, at least in its general spirit of stiff magnificence. The court costume of Charles V gave Italy the system of supporting frameworks round the chest and waist and the inflexible arrangement of formal folds, and Italy adapted its rich textiles to these styles.

Men wore this Spanish costume with melon-shaped upper stocks and dark-coloured doublets. They took to heart Rafaella's maxim, 'Costume is poor when cloth is coarse', and looked above all for quality and beauty in the materials used. Silk doublets, velvet mantles trimmed with fur, and velvet hats usually decorated with carved or enamelled emblems were worn; as contemporary authors said, men were covered in silk from head to foot, even more than women, and were so elegant that towards the end of the century, courtesans and even middle-class women dressed in men's fashions.

Spain also imposed the fashion for black, which dominated male costume, as we see from the portraits of Titian. Women willingly wore green, azure or dark purple costumes, but Lucrezia Borgia showed a marked preference for the harmony of black and gold; a letter from Laura Bentivoglia to Isabella d'Este (after 1502) described her lying on her bed in a black

450 Buff jerkin, late sixteenth century. The London Museum, London. (Museum photo)

449 ANTONIO MORO: *Alessandro Farnese. c.* 1550. Parma, Galleria Nazionale. (Photo Vaghi)

451 CLOUET (School of): *Portrait of a Young Girl, c.* 1560. Lille, Museum. (Photo Gerondal)

silk gown with a jabot and narrow sleeves that showed the cuffs of her chemise. Baldassare Castiglione, in *Il Cortegiano*, considered that black, more than any other colour, gave grace to a garment and that failing this, a dark colour should be used. 'For the rest, I should like costume to show the gravity so strongly maintained by the Spanish nation,' he added, though at the same time complaining of 'the invading foreigners' then imposing their fashions in Italy.

Until the end of the century Spanish influences continued to become increasingly marked. No man or woman fails to flaunt them in the magnificent portraits by Salviati, Bronzino (plate 466), Moroni (plate 462) or Barrocchio. Almost invariably women's costume was composed of an outer gown, the *gamurra* (simarra), related to the surcoat and the old houppelande, and an undergown or *sottana*, which was longer, both made of costly stuff heavily decorated with embroidery. The train was often long and caught up; sleeves were sometimes loosely puffed, or might be tightly fitting, with epaulettes. This costume was completed with a veil: the straw hat was to appear only in the middle of the century.

Following her Spanish sisters, the Italian woman stiffened her silhouette with the cone of her farthingale and the height of her pattens. These were the tangible signs of the Spanish tutelage under which Italy had fallen, thus losing, with the exception of Venice, her old role as the most active centre in Europe. Placed as she was, after the abdication of Charles V, between the effective domination of the Spanish dynasty and the influence of the Hapsburg Holy Roman Empire, her costume was from then on to express the decline of her economic and social autonomy.

Spanish Costume

The astonishing spread of Spanish costume in Europe from the end of the fifteenth century came firstly from the prestige the

452 ANTONIO MORO: *Catherine of Austria, Queen of Portugal, c.* 1552. Madrid, Prado. (Museum photo)

453 ANTONIO MORO: *Portrait of a Man. c.* 1560. Washington D.C., National Gallery of Art, Mellon Collection. (Museum photo)

454 H. KRELL: *Augustus of Saxe*, 1551. Dresden, Gemälde-galerie. (Photo Bruckmann-Giraudon)

455 NICOLAS DE NEUFCHATEL: *Jerome Köhler, c.* 1560. Kassel, Staatliche Kunstsammlungen. (Museum photo)

GERMAN COSTUME UNDER SPANISH INFLUENCES

454–5 Padded hose were often worn in Germany and Switzerland with the lining prominently shown. Jerome Köhler wears a *saie* with short basques over a slashed doublet with speckled sleeves, a dagger, probably Swiss made, and an almoner at his belt

LONG GOWNS

456 This Doctor of Law wears the long academic gown, similar to the robes of the medieval church, a red *muceta* or hood, and a fringed biretta

MALE COSTUME IN FRANCE UNDER SPANISH INFLUENCES

457–8, 464 Spanish taste shows itself in padded hose *à la Garguesque* with visible codpiece, pourpoints with standing collars, over which there lies a soft linen collar in Italian style (plate 464), or a small ruff (plate 458). Shoes (*escaffignons* or *escarpins*) are no longer square, but are slashed on the upper (plate 464). The toque is worn tilted to the left, contrary to Spanish custom. The black garment worn by Henri II (plate 464) is decorated with gold tracery. Charles IX (plate 458) wears a sleeveless *sayon* over a white doublet. The cape was the usual mantle

Spaniards gained from the discoveries of Christopher Columbus who, although he did not immediately find a new sea route for silk, at least established the immense flow of precious metals from the Americas to Spain. This was the source of luxury in the Renaissance period.[4]

But Spanish costume also benefited from the political prestige gained after the expulsion of the Moors from Andalusia, consolidated with the unification of the Iberian peninsula and, after the defeat of François I at Pavia, linked with the political predominance of Charles V on the chess-board of Europe.

In 1516 the Hapsburg and Aragon-Castile territories had been united in the hands of Charles V; after 1519, the conquest of Mexico was followed by that of Central and North America and the Pacific coast. The marriages of Charles V with Isabella of Portugal and of her sister with King John III brought the Portuguese crown, Brazil and the colonized Indies. It is difficult to overstate the importance of these events and the wealth they brought to Spain.

This dazzling political supremacy inevitably included luxury among its manifestations: it may not have been of primary importance, but as far as Hispanic prestige was concerned it was by no means the least consideration.[5]

In fact Spanish costume itself had undergone various influences. Philip le Beau had already introduced the splendours of Burgundian court costume and probably some Flemish details to Spain. German styles had been brought to Madrid in 1517 by the Teutonic knights.[6] These interpenetrations continued throughout the entire century and in his *Comentarios* (1552) Luis de Peraza mentioned *picados a la flamenca* and *cortados a la alemana*, and said that Spanish ladies wore skirts in French or Flemish style and coifs in Portuguese style. Strict codes of etiquette laid down by the Hapsburg monarchs brought about the unification of these diverse elements at court.

The prestige of the Spanish court was more apparent in the west of Europe, with its urban, monarchical organization, than in Central Europe, more agricultural and feudal. It benefited from the interdynastic marriages which Charles V tried to arrange through his embassies and by his own travels through all the Catholic countries. Such circumstances as the captivity

456 ZURBARÁN: *A Salamanca Doctor*, c. 1525. Boston, I. S. Gardner Museum. (Museum photo)

457 CLOUET (School of): *François de Guise*, 1550–70. Paris, Bib. Nat. Cab. des Estampes, Rés Oa 17 f. 24. (Photo Bibliothèque Nationale)

458 FRANÇOIS CLOUET: *Charles IX*, c. 1565. Vienna, Kunsthistorisches Museum. (Photo Giraudon)

in Madrid of François I and, later, of his children, must also be taken into account.

The dominant feature of Spanish costume was its sobriety and austere elegance. Though rich, the stuffs used were always in dark tones: even the buffoons of the Escurial did not wear garish colours. This fashion for black spread, as we have seen, through Italy, and through the courts of Henri II and his sons in France. Mary Stuart ordered for her mourning clothes a black satin bodice 'in Spanish style' like those worn by the ladies of honour for the entry into Paris of Eleanor of Austria in 1530.

The solemn, heavy effect produced by these stiff garments did not exclude luxury: the kings of Spain and Portugal even had to multiply sumptuary laws curtailing excesses; but when silver and gold embroideries were prohibited (four times, in 1515, 1520, 1523, 1534), embroiderers replaced them with braid and passementeries.

According to an eighteenth-century Spanish author, 'This series of laws presents a phenomenon worthy of our reflexion: the most rich and powerful nation in the universe, the land which added new immensities to the vast territories acquired in Europe, the nation with the finest craftsmen and manufacturers of all in gold, silver and silk... this nation limits or forbids her subjects the greater part of these materials.'

Furthermore, Spanish costume stylized the lines of the body.

In women's costume, the great transformation was the discarding of softness in favour of straight, stiff forms. This has been interpreted as a mixture of Spanish and Italian styles; be that as it may, these new forms were referred to by Spanish names.

Two elements of costume were characteristic: the bodice and the farthingale. A stiff, high bodice ending with a point at the waist, lined with stiff canvas and edged with wire, the *corps* imposed a virtually geometrical form on the bust and lengthened the waist, compressing the breasts until they almost disappeared. The *farthingale* was a stiff, bell-shaped underskirt to which were sewn hoops made of supple switches of wood (*verdugo*) to hold out the skirt, which was not gathered at the waist, thus accentuating the slimness of the body. Under this farthingale

women often wore a black skirt called a *basquina*, also sometimes stretched over hoops; later this was confused with the farthingale itself.

Thus the general outline from head to foot was a stiff cone, expressing in its rigidity the moral preoccupations of the Counter-Reformation and the ascetic ideology of the Spanish clergy. Except when out in the street where, perched on their high cork chopines, they walked with a slight swing of the skirt, women appeared to be made in a single piece, moving on casters. A long pleat inset above the hem of the skirts made it possible to sit down without exposing one's feet – the height of impropriety.

It would not be necessary to point out that the French word for farthingale, *vertugadin*, has nothing to do with *vertu* (virtue) which must be *gardée* (preserved), were it not for the fact that histories of fashion continue to perpetuate this mistake.

The farthingale spread at first in court circles in Madrid, and remained in fashion for ceremonial occasions until about the middle of the seventeenth century; it was never worn by the common people.

To complete this geometrical outline, the *fraise* (ruff) made its appearance towards 1555.[7] Originally a narrow, ruched band finishing the high collar of the bodice, it soon grew to large proportions (plates 438, 426) and towards the end of the century it was supported by a wire framework (*rebato*) which held it high round the neck. There was a degree of concordance between the exaggerations of the ruff and farthingale; the latter was to survive longer, as the former was condemned by a sumptuary law of 1623.

Another women's garment became very widespread in Europe – the *ropa*, which may, however, have been Portuguese in origin; it was a sort of loose-waisted mantle open in front, in which some authors have seen the continuation of the fifteenth-century surcoat. It often had double funnel sleeves, one part of which could be worn hanging (plate 434), in accordance with a purely Spanish tradition. This ropa was transmitted mainly to the costume of the Low Countries, which borrowed from Spain; there it developed into the *vlieger*.

It is impossible to enter into a detailed description of all the current Spanish women's garments here: the *saya*, in two parts;

227

459 TITIAN.
Charles V, *c.* 1530.
Madrid, Prado.
(Museum photo)

SPANISH MALE COSTUME

459, 461 It is easy to distinguish here between the *barrel breeches* and the *nether hose* which reach just above the knees. The shirt collar shows over the collar of the basqued saie, worn over a doublet whose banded sleeves with tiers of puffs emerge from the huge puff sleeves of the fur-lined *chamarre*; the flat hat studded with gems can be seen again in the portraits of François I and Henry VIII (plate 492). Codpieces are prominent; the dagger is often decorated with an enormous tassel. Round the neck of Maximilian II (plate 461) we can see the chain of the Order of the Golden Fleece

ITALIAN COSTUME UNDER SPANISH INFLUENCE

462–3, 465–8, 475–6 The rich brocade of the gown worn by Eleanor of Toledo corresponds to the Spanish chasuble back preserved in Lyons (plates 463, 465). Spanish influence shows in the elongation of the bodice, constructed over a rigid framework. Laudonia de' Medicis (plate 466) wears a black gown embroidered with pearls and carries a short fur stole with a jewelled metal animal's head. However, Spanish influence was to be more noticeable at the very end of the century and in the early seventeenth century. The garment in plate 466 is clearly related to the *ropa*; the open neck shows how the ruff was orginally worn. Pace Spini (plate 476) carries a feather fan then known as a *plumail*. The black costume of Bernardo Spini (plate 462) has all the austerity of Spanish tradition; only his tall toque is very Italian

the *vaquero*, which derived from the primitive combination of a fitted bodice with removable sleeves (*cuerpo baxo*) and a bell skirt. The very wide sleeves were worn over tight sleeves which cannot always be assigned decisively to the gown or to a *jubon* (pourpoint) worn underneath (plate 426).

Lastly, the black mantilla, a reduced version of the old *manto* or cape, was worn indoors and out, recalling Oriental styles.

Although men's costume often borrowed elements from abroad, it often modified them: for example, the slashings which spread from Swiss uniforms throughout Germany, France and England, were smaller and more sparingly used in Spain. The Valladolid Cortès even forbade these *acuchillados* in 1548; simple, straight slits were then adopted, and were very widespread after 1550.

Slashed and puffed upper stocks were highly fashionable in Spain before they reached France. In every country except Italy, upper stocks retained until about 1580 a prominent codpiece, exaggerating the wearer's endowments: it is possible that this may originally have derived from the mail gusset filling in the crotch of military costume, rendered indispensable by the coming of plate armour.[8]

From the middle of the century the Spanish doublet accentuated the slimness of the waist and the reduction of the basques; it had a row of buttons in front, and was generally slashed and worn over a sleeved *jubon* whose long slashings were held together by transversal cords along the arm (plate 461). This gave the torso the general aspect of a cuirass. The silhouette was enlarged with padding (cotton wadding, whalebone) and this militarization of costume even extended to women's clothes. A lightly padded, projecting form of pourpoint presaged the humped 'peascod belly'. Courtiers added padded crescents round the top of the sleeves, which became exaggeratedly wide in the *ropillas* of the end of the century, with their hanging sleeves.

While the traditional wide cape, the *capa*, an inheritance from the Middle Ages, was decreasingly worn from 1550 on, Spain rapidly adopted the shaped coat, perhaps borrowed from Germany or Central Europe; full or half-length, this *ropon* was less cumbersome and better suited to long Spanish or Italian

460 SEISENEGGER: *Archduke Ferdinand of Tyrol*, 1542.
Vienna, Kunsthistorisches Museum. (Photo Meyer Erwin)

461 Antonio Moro: *Maximilian II*, 1550. Madrid, Prado. (Museum photo)

462 Gianbattista Moroni: *Bernardo Spini*, c. 1570. Bergamo, Accademia Carrara. (Museum photo)

463 Spanish brocaded velvet. Mid-sixteenth century. Lyons, Musée Historique des Tissus. (Museum photo)

swords, and its form varied little despite the wide range of names it acquired: *ferreruolo*, *boemio*, *balandran*, *fieltro* and *capa*, the last fitted with the hood which was to be the distinctive feature of this cape worn in Spain and elsewhere during a part of the seventeenth century.

As in the rest of Europe, the satin used for shoes at the beginning of the century was replaced, from about 1570, by leather for all classes of society. The high boots rising to meet the upper stocks seem to have been specifically Spanish in origin.

Men's hats, which were flat until 1580, then adapted to the high-crowned Italian fashions: they were often stiff, and decorated, generally on the left, with aigrettes (which French fashion placed on the right). However, the soft hat worn throughout Europe at the end of the first quarter of the seventeenth century certainly seems derived from the *sombrero* mentioned by Vecellio in 1590 in Galicia and Portugal.

During the first half of the century the low neckline of the fifteenth century – at first square cut, and becoming a 'boat' neckline towards 1515 – was preserved; then the neck gradually became enclosed to give a high, tightly fastened collar with a purely Spanish, rather prudish character. In the portrait of Charles V by Titian (plate 459) we find one of the first examples of this high collar, and of tight upper stocks. The portrait of Henry VIII (plate 492) and that of François I by Titian (Louvre) show its rapid spread through England and France. By the middle of the century it had replaced the low-cut necks of Holbein and Cranach portraits.

The ruched edging of the collar was to develop into the ruff, whose origins and evolution will be dealt with in the section on French costume.

Though sixteenth-century Spanish costume was highly individual, it nonetheless borrowed certain details from foreign styles. Towards the end of the century, Spain ordered haberdashery from Venice and Germany, gems and combs from France, fine linen from Flanders, velvets or Milanese gold thread from Italy.

Spain's influence on European costume was to decline in the seventeenth century, while Dutch and French costume

464 Attributed to François Clouet: *Henri II*, c. 1550. Paris, Louvre. (Photo Flammarion)

467 Venetian chopine. Sixteenth century. Schoenenwerd, Musée Bally. (Museum photo)

465 A. Bronzino: *Eleonora of Toledo and her son Ferdinand*, c. 1550. Florence, Uffizi. (Photo Alinari)

466 A. Bronzino: *Laudonia de' Medici*, c. 1560–65. Florence, Galleria Antica e Moderna. (Photo Anderson-Giraudon)

468 Venetian shoe with two heels. Sixteenth century. Schoenenwerd, Musée Bally. (Museum photo)

469 FRANÇOIS QUESNEL: *Portrait of a woman*, c. 1570. Oslo, Kunstindustrimuseet. (Photo Teigen)

reached its zenith. Against the economic preponderance of the Netherlands and the military force of France, Spain suffered a general decline which was reflected in the country's fashions.

Costume in France

THE PERIOD OF ITALIAN FASHIONS

During the first quarter of the century, as we have seen, French costume continued its earlier style, though with greater richness in material and decoration, reciprocally influenced by Italian fashions.

It is enough to recall that under Louis XII male outer costume consisted of three essential pieces. First, the low-cut doublet, showing the shirt, often made in two different stuffs, rich for the front and sleeves, and coarser for the back, with sleeves slit from shoulder to elbow or cut off at the elbow to form elbow-sleeves.

Second, the stocks, which after this period finally became separated from the nether hose to become true short breeches, with the first signs of a projecting pouch, the codpiece, in front. And thirdly the cloak, whose form varied considerably. The *robe* or *gown* was now worn only by old people or as the sign of some special function.

Women's gowns kept their late-fifteenth-century cut; they were worn over a chemise, hose and a cote or laced corset. Women also wore a velvet or silk *touret*, a type of veil often embroidered or set with precious stones, which was later to be fixed to a circlet adorned with gems or enamels, before becoming the veil that fell from the heart-shaped chaperon. This touret, a head-dress inherited from preceding centuries, must not be confused with the *touret de nez*, which was the old barbet covering the lower part of the face, hiding the nose and mouth, before masks came into fashion.

470 *The Courtier and the Maiden*, c. 1580. Paris, Bib. Nat., Cab. des Estampes. (Photo Flammarion)

471 After ANTOINE CARON: *Festivity at Fontainebleau*. Tapestry, c. 1580–85. Florence, Uffizi. (Photo Alinari)

Both sexes still wore fur, whether as edging, as revers or as linings.

Such elements as had survived from the Middle Ages were to undergo important modifications under the influence of Italian fashions, which penetrated to the court after the expedition of Charles VIII and, above all, under the aegis of François I (plate 442), who made a study of triumphal splendour and princely magnificence. The words originally spoken about the French Renaissance: 'It was the work of the Prince', are apt here. François I used his prestige to support the vogue for the fashions of Genoa, Florence, Venice and Milan, for woven silk stockings and, most of all, for the marvellous silks and velvets imported from Italy. He had asked Isabella d'Este to send him a doll dressed in Mantuan styles, and when the Marchesa, who then passed as the 'source and origin of all fine ways of dressing', came to Paris in 1517, she showed herself a most effective ambassadress for the fashions of her country.

Men wore two closely related outer garments, loose and fairly short: the *chamarre*, which was open in front, lined with fur or contrasting silk, and with sleeve openings circled with puffed wings, often decorated with coloured braid or passementerie (plates 449, 454), and the *casaque*, an unbelted overcoat slit at the sides and fastened with bows, barely reaching to the knees, with short, wide sleeves slit to expose the forearm. The casaque seems to have been a close relation of the sayon, which had long sleeves and a flat collar.

The soft doublet had a boat neckline which showed the tucked edge of the shirt, embroidered in colours *à la sarrazine*, and its slashings showed the shirt or a rich lining, in accordance with a brand new fashion (plate 442). A basque lengthened it at the waist. In 1518 a member of the Guise family already wore a slashed doublet and upper stocks, like those of a lansquenet.

The hose, which were also slashed, were often parti-coloured, that is, each leg was a different colour or differently decorated. 'Venetians' or *chausses en tonnelet* fitted closely to the thigh down to the knees (plate 459), but in the course of the century they were to develop very varied forms and names, the most current of which were *martingale breeches*, an early form of

COSTUME IN FRANCE AFTER 1570: THE RUFF
469, 470–71, 474 The closed ruff worn with the high Spanish style of bodice was normally in plain linen in France, and more modestly proportioned than in the rest of Europe. Plate 472 shows how the starched tubular folds were dressed. The hair is swept up over an arcelet and covered with an attiffet.
At the same time the whaleboned bodice became longer, moulding the bust; sleeves were decorated with a roll recalling the *maheutres* worn in the fifteenth century, then became exaggeratedly swollen, giving a heavy silhouette (plates 472, 474).
The King (plate 471) wears a pourpoint with a 'peascod belly' and excessively short trunk hose known as *culots*. The Lansquenets have doublets and hose with long slashings and *lodiers*. The gentleman seen from the back wears Venetian style breeches. The Queen's fan is a plumail

FROM THE RUFF TO THE MEDICIS COLLAR
471–4 The collar standing above the guimp, which from the time of Henri II on covered the deep, square-cut neckline of gowns, took on larger dimensions under Henri III and framed the head in a fan shape. It began to flare further still at the end of the century and was much later to be known as a Medici collar, because it figures in portraits of Marie de Medicis, but it dates from twenty years before her reign

472 Caricature of the wearing of ruffs, c. 1595. (Photo Flammarion)

473 *Ball for the wedding of the Duc de Joyeuse, c.* 1581–2.
Paris, Louvre. (Photo Flammarion)

476 GIANBATTISTA MORONI: *Portrait of Pace Rivola Spini, c.* 1570
Bergamo, Accademia Carrara. (Museum photo)

475 A. BRONZINO: *Lucrezia Panciatichi, c.* 1550–60.
Florence, Uffizi. (Photo Scala)

474 *Evening ball for the wedding of the Duc de Joyeuse, c. 1581–2.*
Paris, Louvre. (Photo P. J. Oxenaar)

joined upper stocks. The codpiece became increasingly prominent (plates 455, 457, 459, 460, 464). Codpiece and slashings were Germanic in origin, while the chamarre recalled Italian short capes.

The broad duck's bill shoes of the early years of the century were replaced by slimmer shapes, first the low-cut *escaffignons*, wide and puffed at the toes, then the heelless *eschapins* which covered the foot and were slashed on top (plates 419–20, 464).

Beards were fashionable after 1515, while hair was worn shorter, following the example of the King who, after an accident in 1521, had his head shaved. The most currently worn headgear came from Italy: this was the Florentine toque, with upturned brim, decorated with an emblem. The shallow-crowned felt hat, edged with a long plume falling down one side, was the model favoured by elegants; round and flat *ballets* in felt, cloth or velvet, or summer hats of *estrain* (straw) or lime bark were also worn. Peacock or ostrich feathers or woollen imitations were often adorned with paillettes and pendants.

An innovation: the sword was worn as part of civilian costume, a borrowing from military costume which modified masculine behaviour. Until 1789 it was to remain a distinctive attribute of social rank, particularly at court.

Finally, the Italian example gave male costume in general an extraordinary richness – precious stuffs, an abundance of braid, gold and silver embroidery; the sumptuary laws of 1532 and 1554 failed to check this luxury. The law of 1554 forbade scholars to wear cut hose and obliged professors and masters to wear long gowns without cut sleeves and with hooded caps worn on the shoulders. From the sixteenth century on, this hood shrank until it became a sort of emblem, and under the names of *chausse*, *épomine* or *epitoge* it still figures on French academic robes.

From the beginning of the century, women's clothing underwent noticeable changes. The gown was slit in front to show the cote through a triangular opening, the neckline kept its square shape with a curved line that may have been due to the boning of the bodice. Towards the middle of the century, this neckline was to be filled in with a light modesty vest, often richly decorated with bead embroidery (plate 443), which was to harmonize with the standing collar edged with a more or less voluminous ruche that was later to develop into the Medici collar.

However, it was only at the end of the reign of François I that, perhaps under the influence of Eleanor of Austria, the general form of women's gowns was transformed with the appearance of the Spanish farthingale. Full-length portraits of this period are unfortunately too rare to allow us to give an exact account of the changes in women's fashions between 1525 and 1545; it seems that the neckline varied little, but that for a fairly short time sleeves borrowed the slashings, tiered puffs and tight wrists of men's pourpoints; but we have too few dated examples to be able to say whether this fashion was widespread.

The chaperon placed over a linen coif, worn by Anne of Brittany, was followed in the reign of François I by a beaded net or snood (*escoffion*) which enveloped the hair in various ways: it was worn at the same time as the bonnet-chaperon, a light head-dress held in place by one or two circlets of pearls or metalwork, worn either flat or raised over a stiff framework

477 Tennis (*courte paume*) player, *c.* 1580.
Paris, Bib. Nat., Cabinet des Estampes.
(Photo Flammarion)

478 CLOUET (School of): *Saint-Mégrin, c.* 1581–2.
(Photo Flammarion)

COURT COSTUME AT THE TIME OF HENRI III

473–4, 477–9 Men wore the long padded doublet with a prominent point, or 'peascod belly,' with the long, tight upper hose which Henri III brought back from his travels, and which were therefore called *Polack* or *Venetian* breeches (plate 477), or extremely short breeches (plates 478–9) known as *culots*. In plate 479 the man on the left seems to be wearing Pisan-style *pianelle*; the short capes were known as *clysteriques*; the small hats or 'Polack caps' were worn by men and women alike.
The ruff and the turned-down collar (plate 479) were both worn at the same time. Sleeves of women's gowns puff out heavily, but the basic form of the gown has not varied, with the flat farthingale that succeeded the roll attached below the waist. The open, flowing sleeve (plate 474) is still Spanish-influenced

479 CAULERY: *Ball at the Valois Court, c.* 1582.
Rennes, Museum. (Photo Guillaume)

233

480 HOLBEIN: *Male costume*, 1525–50, London, British Museum. (Museum photo. Courtesy the Trustees)

481 HOLBEIN: *English Noblewoman*, c. 1535. London, British Museum. (Museum photo. Courtesy the Trustees)

482 FLEMISH SCHOOL: *Portrait of a young woman dressed in English style*, 1525–40. New York, Metropolitan Museum. (Museum photo)

483 HOLBEIN: *English Burg* *Wife*, c. 1540. Oxford, Ashm Museum. (Museum photo)

484 ANON: *Sir Edward Hoby*, 1577. Ipswich, Museum. (Museum photo)

485 NICHOLAS HILLIARD: *Portrait of a Young Man. c.* 1588. London, Victoria and Albert Museum. (Museum photo)

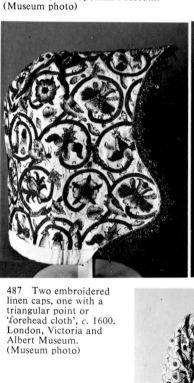

487 Two embroidered linen caps, one with a triangular point or 'forehead cloth', c. 1600. London, Victoria and Albert Museum. (Museum photo)

488 Woman's jacket in embroidered linen. Late sixteenth century. London, Victoria and Albert Museum. (Museum photo)

486 NICHOLAS HILLIARD: *Young Woman*, 1583. London, Victoria and Albert Museum. (Museum photo)

489 HEADBORN: *Margaret Laton of Rawdon*, 1620.
Collection Viscount Rothermere.
(Photo Victoria and Albert Museum)

490 ANON: *Sir William Playters*,
1615. Ipswich, Museum.
(Museum photo)

491 ANON: *Pocahontas*, 1616. Washington D.C.,
National Gallery of Art, Mellon Collection.
(Museum photo)

that held it away from the head, with the panels falling over the shoulders (plate 469). This head-dress is known to us through the portraits of Diane de Poitiers, the *Grande Sénéchale*.

THE PERIOD OF SPANISH FASHIONS

After 1525 Spanish modes had a progressively simplifying effect on dress: this tendency, which was sharply defined at the end of the reign of François I, manifested itself abundantly under Henri II. Henri (plate 464) had a predilection for dark stuffs lightly overtraced with gold, and his court also adopted this style. Doublets fitting closely to the body, high collars, longer basques and narrower sleeves all followed Spanish costume.

Thus, from 1540 to 1575, male costume underwent a slow transformation, borrowing details from Flemish and Spanish fashions, while Italian influence decreased. Trunk hose in varying forms were distinguished by an innovation, built-in pockets, in which the fashionable watches made in Nuremberg were carried. The chamarre was replaced by the Spanish cape. Beards were cut to a point. Hose, which generally became longer, were fastened to the trunk hose (upper stocks) and made of knitted silk instead of tailored cloth.

This new tendency towards a more sober general line did not, however, preclude exaggerations which in 1561 provoked yet another sumptuary law, ineffectual since in any case it did not apply to princes or the court.

After a period of sumptuous stuffs and embroidery in the fashions of the court of François I, women's costume also took on a note of austerity.

The boned bodice, low-cut and often laced, showed the chemise sleeves, as did the male doublet; and the skirt, which was always slit to show the cote, was supported over a farthingale. Spanish influence increased under Henri II, producing a high-cut, closed gown with a more or less voluminous collar and sleeves tightly fastened at the wrist. The increasing slenderness of the waist was accentuated under Charles IX with the stiff *corps piqué*, while the farthingale continually increased in size, though undergoing changes.

COSTUME IN ENGLAND
480, 492 The broader line of costume at the beginning of the sixteenth century is noticeable in these figures where, as in France, we find the long-basqued *sayon* (plate 492), the *dogaline* (plate 480), the fur-lined *chamarre*, slashings, prominent cod-pieces and square-toed shoes (plate 492), flat hats (plate 492) and the pointed hat (plate 480) which was rarer in France. The man in plate 480 wears an Orientally inspired buttoned caftan with *gamaches* or gaiters

WOMEN'S COSTUME IN THE TIME OF HENRY VIII
481–3, 493, 495 The most outstanding characteristic of this costume, which otherwise resembles French court costume quite closely, is the Tudor head-dress, the Tudor or gable coif, formed of a frame of gold cloth round the face, to which the cornet was attached; this was often black, and could hang down or be worn up (plate 495). A rigid framework seems to have supported the wide, square-cut neckline; undersleeves are slashed (plate 495). The guimp (plate 482) recalls the Moorish-style Spanish chemises for which the fashion may have been introduced to England by Catherine of Aragon, although the fashion for black embroidery seems to date from before her arrival in England. A starched veil (plate 483) recalls the head-dresses of the preceding century; the overgown is held in place by a complex system of fastenings (plate 483)

MEN'S COSTUME UNDER ELIZABETH I
484–5, 494 At the beginning of the century, Spanish influence can be seen in the stiff doublet with standing collar, and the piccadils (plate 494); on the other hand, plate 485 shows short trunk hose or galligaskins and the padded peascod belly doublet; the ruff has grown in size and may be plain or embroidered

WOMEN'S COSTUME UNDER ELIZABETH I
486, 497–8 Spanish influence can be seen in the *verdingale* or farthingale, the boned bodice and ruff, the feather fan (plate 486); and French influence shows in the hair, dressed over *arcelets*, and the *attiffet*. The ribbon bows on the skirt (plate 486) probably fasten a removable panel. The other illustrations show the fashion for the French style of farthingale, the roll farthingale (plate 497), or the tray farthingale (plate 498). Mary Stuart wears a curious ruff pleated on only one side, and a flowing veil of transparent gauze which underlines the English taste for these light trimmings, probably imported from Italy; this is shown again by the *conque* worn by Queen Elizabeth (plate 498). Elizabeth wears a very rich, gem-incrusted gown with balloon sleeves covered with false sleeves of the Spanish type; in her hand she holds a folded fan, a new fashion

ELIZABETHAN EMBROIDERY
487–9 The invention of steel needles and increased imports of coloured silks in the sixteenth century gave a new impetus to English embroidery, which had been renowned since the Middle Ages. Techniques vary, silk is mixed with metallic threads, decorations of stylized flowers, sometimes interspersed with small animals and arranged in an overall ornamental pattern of tendrils, are used for both men's and women's clothing

235

492 HANS EWORTH (after Holbein): *Henry VIII*, c. 1539. Chatsworth Collection. (Reproduced by permission of the Trustees of the Chatsworth Settlement)

493 HOLBEIN: *English Lady, perhaps Margaret Roper*, c. 1535. London, British Museum. (Museum photo. Courtesy the Trustees)

494 FLEMISH SCHOOL: *Robert Dudley*, c. 1560. London, The Wallace Collection. (By permission of the Trustees)

495 HOLBEIN: *Jane Seymour*, 1536. Vienna, Kunsthistorisches Museum.

The Spanish hooped skirt gave way to a circular roll which spread the fullness of the gathered overskirt evenly round the body. This French form of the farthingale, for which special high chairs known as 'farthingale chairs' were made, was never worn by Spanish women. It was still worn at the end of the century; a Dutch caricature dating from 1595 (plate 437) shows the manner of wearing these padded rolls, presented as artifices of the devil:

> See here the shop of sprites by Eros crazed
> Sells vanities, for pride and pleasure raised,
> With them some dames adorn their stinking flesh
> And reach Gehenna's fires in Satan's mesh.
> Come, fine young maidens with your skimpy thighs,
> Soon we shall make them round as Paris' prize.
> Like all the rest I'll wear a gown
> To wrap and hide a pregnant womb.

This type of farthingale drew the irony of Montaigne: 'Why do women cover themselves with so many barricades over the parts on which our admiration principally lingers? And what is the use of these heavy bastions with which women have now begun to adorn their flanks, but to ensnare our appetites and attract us to them, the while keeping us at a distance?'

The increasingly rigid whalebone bodice which tightly compressed the breasts (plate 498) is described by contemporaries as a veritable instrument of torture. Once more Montaigne notes: '... to have a fine Hispanized body, what Gehennas do women not suffer?'

It is probably on a late, misunderstood interpretation of the Spanish term *cuerpo baxo* that French historians of the last hundred years have confused the *corps rigide* or stiff bodice with the *basquine* or *vasquine*, which in any case was little worn in France. Seventeenth century authors define it as a sort of gown 'very wide, worn open and stretched over hoops,' and the inventories of Mary Stuart refer to 'fine basquines of cloth of gold with bodices (*corps*)', thus clearly signifying that *corps* and *basquine* were two separate parts of costume. This is what we have already seen in our study of Spanish costume.

496 ISAAC OLIVER: *The Three Brothers Brown*, 1598. Collection Lord Exeter, Burlington House. (Photo Courtauld Institute of Art)

497 ANON: *Mary, Queen of Scots*. Before 1575. Glasgow, Art Gallery and Museum. (Museum photo)

498 ANON: *Queen Elizabeth I*, c. 1593. London, National Portrait Gallery

While we still find representations of the conical Spanish farthingale after 1580 in the portrait of Diane de Grammont, known as *La Belle Corisande*, the celebrated favourite of Henri IV, this was explained by the fact that as her husband was then governor of Languedoc, she wore Spanish costume with the dark *ropa* adorned with embroidery covering the seams.

On the other hand, at the end of the sixteenth century France saw a third type of farthingale in the form of a wheel or flat drum, over which the gown spread out (plate 498); it was generally covered with a gathered flounce. According to Taillemant des Réaux, whose stories are however a little suspect, Queen Margot kept the hearts of her lovers underneath.

Inspired by the Spanish ropa, the *marlotte*, a half-length coat with sleeves padded at the shoulder, open down the front, must have appeared by 1530, for Rabelais mentioned it among the clothing envisaged for the women members of the Abbey of Thélème in 1530; it also figures in inventories as a garment of Southern origin, but no text describes it precisely.

The origin and form of the *berne*, in the same period, are still less clear; at first it seems to have been a large rectangular mantle imported from Andalusia under the name *berne à la mauresque*; according to some it was worn on the head, while others claim it was draped 'in Apostolic style', passed under one arm and knotted on the other shoulder. This garment, described and engraved by Vecellio,[9] is the Italian *sbernia*, a name which is alleged to have come from Ireland (Hibernia). A coarse cloth used for military cloaks of the same shape and name was indeed imported from Ireland.

It is difficult to explain why costume historians have applied the name 'berne' to a woman's garment of the marlotte type, full-backed and corresponding quite closely to the Italian simarra; a very fine example is preserved in the Victoria and Albert Museum, London.

We find excellent specimens of the *sbernia* in the light, elegant, draped cloaks in English portraits of the first years of the seventeenth century (plates 505–7).

After its successive crazes for Italian and Spanish styles, towards the middle of the century France seems to have participated in the effort made by Henri II to introduce a simpler

499 ANON: *Sir Walter Raleigh and his Son*, c. 1590 London, National Portrait Gallery

500 Blue leather hat slashed over pink lining. Late sixteenth century. London, British Museum. (Museum photo. Courtesy the Trustees)

501 Black carved velvet hat trimmed with passementerie. Late sixteenth century. London, British Museum. (Museum photo. Courtesy the Trustees)

502 White leather hat in Spanish style, c. 1580. Offenbach, Deutsches Leder Museum. (Museum photo)

503 Suit in slashed white satin, doublet and slops with cannons, 1610–15. London, Victoria and Albert Museum. (Museum photo)

504 Jacket in white brocade with motifs in gold, silver and blue, pink and green silk, c. 1620. Nottingham, Collection Lord Middleton. (Photo W. Spencer)

general style, stripped of the excessive Italian ornament and retaining only the essential elements of the Spanish contribution.

THE SEARCH FOR A NEW STYLE

While we cannot yet speak of a French style, we can still note certain details due to the industrial development of the times, of which we can only indicate the general outlines here.

The organization of work was modernized: certain producers or merchants grouped craftsmen round them. The clothiers and cloth traders dominated the weavers and fullers and sold their manufactures in Toulon; the merchants who provided silk for the spinners, weavers and dyers undertook the sale of the cloths produced.[10]

Some industries expanded considerably. The progress of the hatmaking and dyeing industries were particularly noticeable in Paris, where 'Saint-Marcel' caps and the scarlets of the Canaye and Gobelins families were highly valued. The mills serving these cap producers were at Essonnes.

The weaving of silk kept 8,000 looms occupied in Tours in 1546, and employed 12,000 people in Lyons, at about the same time. At the end of the century velvets and satins were made at Nîmes and Montpellier, silk stockings at Dourdan and silken cloths at Orléans. The production of cotton fustian employed 5,000 workers in Lyons.

To protect these new industries, the State established a system of restrictions on imported dress materials. By an ordinance of 18 July 1540, foreign cloths of gold and silver and silk could enter France only through certain towns and were then sent to Lyons for the levying of import taxes. Another ordinance, in 1572, forbade the unauthorized export of textile raw material, and at the same time prohibited the import of broadcloths, linens, velvets, taffetas etc.

Against this background of economic progress, the Renaissance spirit remained dominant. This period of discoveries on land and sea encouraged a taste for exotic or merely foreign costumes. After the alliance which François I contracted with Suleiman the Magnificent (plate 530), the fabulous East, whose

languages were taught in the Collège de France by men like Guillaume Postel, was revealed to Paris in 1552 in the person of an ambassador from the 'King of Argos'. The Parisians admired his gown in cloth of gold 'figured in Turkish style', and his attendants clad in scarlet. As a result we see in the Louvre court ladies and Knights of Malta disguised 'à la turque' for an evening fête, or a masquerade in which dancers are dressed as 'kings and queens of Mauretania', or even as savages, in plumes of various colours. A royal carnival given in the rue Saint-Antoine by Henri III one night in January 1558 followed the theme of a battle between Turks and Moors. The imagination was satisfied by the luxury of these costumes as it had been by the fabulous descriptions in the romances of chivalry: every page in a romance like *Amadis de Gaule* describes dazzling garments of crimson satin patterned with gold, azure or green, nodding with plumes and sparkling with precious stones, and royal receptions attempted to revive this fairy-tale spectacle.[11]

These displays of wealth continued throughout the century, although Spanish religious austerity and Protestant restraint both sought to limit the luxurious follies which ruined all classes of society: 'the great man over-reaching himself, the common man would imitate him...'

Henri III, with his rather effeminate tastes, constant pursuit of fashion and preoccupation with detail and refinement, certainly exercized a marked influence on French costume. The costume worn at Henri's court (plates 473–4, 477–9) presages the eccentricities of the Directoire period. This development, which had already shown itself under Charles IX (plate 458), can be explained in part by a general relaxation of morals and the freedom enjoyed by the homosexual favourites surrounding the King; it also expresses the uncertainties of a period troubled by civil wars and persecutions, and marks the falling off of a taste which had searched from the time of Henri II for a severe, original art, and now lapsed into heavy vulgarity. Costume at this time was marked by an outdated Italianism and ostentatious extravagance.

All sorts of borrowings from foreign fashions distinguish costume, particularly men's clothes, during the quarter century from 1570 to 1595. Robert Estienne notes in his *Dialogue du*

MEN'S COSTUME AROUND THE END OF THE ELIZABETHAN PERIOD
490–91, 496, 499, 510 The most typical feature of this period is the
invention of *canons* (plates 496, 499) covering the thighs down to the
knees. After this longer hose were worn (plates 490, 510). Shoes open
at the sides, with movable tongues, are a novelty; they were later to have
heels and be trimmed with rosettes in gold lace (plate 510). The ruff was
replaced by the standing collar decorated with drawn thread work and
punte in aria (the serrated lace edging, plates 490, 510). Hose were richly
embroidered (plate 510). A long-stranded woven tassel hangs from the
left ear of Sir William Playters (plate 490). Emblematic embroidery decorates the hose of the Earl or Dorset (plate 510). The metal gorget
worn with civilian costume was a privilege granted to soldiers (plates
490, 501).

SURVIVING MALE COSTUMES
500–504 Sixteenth- and seventeenth-century garments are extremely
rare; England shares with some Nordic countries the distinction of
having preserved a certain number

COSTUME IN THE LOW COUNTRIES IN THE EARLY SEVENTEENTH
CENTURY
509 While Spanish influence still shows in some details, flowing sleeves,
tight bodices, a new tendency from Germany, more relaxed and bourgeois, begins to appear at the beginning of the century

505 ANON: *Elizabeth, Countess of Suffolk.*
c. 1610–15. Collection Dowager Countess
of Suffolk.
(Photo National Portrait Gallery)

506 Attributed to MYTENS:
Lady Isabella Rich.
Early seventeenth century.
(Photo National Portrait Gallery)

507 PAUL VAN SOMER: *Mary, Countess of Pembroke, c.* 1605–10.
Collection Sir Felix Cassel.
(Photo National Portrait Gallery)

508 MARCUS GHEERAEDTS: *Portrait presumed to be of Mary Herbert,*
Countess of Pembroke, 1614.
London, National Portrait Gallery. (Museum photo)

509 H. AERTS: *Festivity in a Palace*, 1602. Amsterdam, Rijksmuseum. (Museum photo)

510 ISAAC OLIVER: *Richard Sackville, Earl of Dorset*, 1616. London, Victoria and Albert Museum. (Photo Thames and Hudson Archives)

langage françois italianisé that gentlemen dressed in Spanish, Germanic, Flemish, Hungarian or Polish styles. At the carrousel in 1584, Henri III galloped through the streets of Paris with thirty gentlemen on horseback 'dressed like himself in pantaloons of various colours', a reminiscence of the visit of the Italian Comedy in 1577, or of the time the King had spent in Venice on his return from Poland. From his brief occupation of the throne of Poland he brought back the fashion for the Polish style of toque, with narrow brims edged with piping, decorated with gems and trimmed with an aigrette. Hose, in wool or silk, were worn very tight; the doublet, with widely padded sleeves, was reinforced in front with a busk and presented a projecting, padded plastron known as a 'peascod belly' (plates 478–9).

It is impossible to follow all the various forms of trunk hose: the *Grègues* with slashed, puffed legs were highly fashionable in Spain (plate 461), then in France (plate 464), but as they were wide enough to hide weapons, an edict of Henri II limited their volume in 1553. They were to remain in fashion until the time of Henri IV, and survived very late in the costume worn by pages. They must not be confused with cannons, tube-like breeches fitting skin-tight over the thighs, from the bottom of the short trunk hose to the knee, and often made in contrasting cloth.

Certain trunk hose, culots, were so short that they barely showed below the shortened basques of the doublet: others covered the thigh to the knee and were covered by a roll (*lodier*) at the waist. The short cape was fastened on the left shoulder. Shoes, which took the form of light slippers, were the Italian *pianelle*, often worn with pattens originally from Turkey and transmitted through Venice. The beard was reduced to a small point. With the disappearance of the codpiece, the overall costume showed a tendency towards the feminization inspired by Henri III, accentuated by the small muffs carried and the earrings worn. The painting of the *Ball for the Wedding of the Duc de Joyeuse* in 1581 (plate 473) gives the most complete idea of this world.

One of the most characteristic of these excesses was the ruff. Its origins[12] went back to the straight pourpoint collar which showed the ruched edging of the shirt or guimp; the ruche developed slowly after 1550 and became the large independent ruff only after 1575.

The very origins of the ruff are a subject of controversy. It is implausible to see the ruff as an innovation brought by Catherine de' Medici, for Italian fashion favoured a wide, low-cut neckline at the time of her marriage in 1532, and the large ruff appeared during the reign of her son, Henri III, when the widowed Catherine had been in deep mourning for over twenty years, which was scarcely compatible with innovation or extravagance on her part. As some historians have observed, Europeans returning from India and Ceylon at the beginning of the century may have been struck by the wide collars starched with rice water (the use of which was already mentioned in the *Livre des Lois de Manou*) which, in these countries, protected clothes against the contact of long, oiled hair. This manner of starching seems to have been brought to France from the Low Countries, whence it passed to England – where it was already in use in 1564 – and, naturally, to Spain.

Possibly Henri III, always on the look-out for new fashions, was attracted by the sheer extravagance of this accessory. In any case, in 1578 he appeared in a starched ruff made of fifteen ells of muslin half a foot wide; this provoked the comments of the Parisians, who compared it with the platter bearing the head of John the Baptist and shouted, 'You can tell the calf's head by the ruff' at courtiers who ventured out thus adorned.

WOMEN'S COSTUME FROM 1580 TO 1630

505–8 The rigid lines of the Elizabethan gown become more relaxed: an original element is the Moorish *sbernia* (plates 505–7), a garment imported from Italy, worn draped over one shoulder, often made of light material. The 'shadow coif' shading the face (plates 505, 508), made of lace, gave way to hairstyles decorated with precious gems. Vast necklines were edged with lace, with fan-shaped collarettes (plate 507) or standing collars (plate 506). Embroidery continued to be very fashionable (plates 505–8); the Spanish *ropa* was still worn (plate 508)

WOMEN'S COSTUME IN GERMANY AND ITS INFLUENCE ABROAD

511–3, 526 Swedish costume is very similar to German costume; a fine guimp with a standing collar, innumerable jewels, a wide felt or velvet hat trimmed with ostrich feathers and gold tassels, worn over hair bound into a bead-embroidered net. Elegant hats were not to be worn again in Europe until the eighteenth century. German modes keep a certain medieval character

COSTUME IN GERMANY UNDER SPANISH INFLUENCE

514 The high bodice with ruff, the skirt worn over a Spanish-style bell farthingale, show the persistence of Spanish influence. Embroidery, gold chains and pleated aprons which played a role similar to that of the contrasting underskirt, but were more economical of material, are typically German details

511 L. CRANACH: *Portrait of a Woman, c.* 1525. Chicago, Blair Collection. (Photo Giraudon)

512 ANON: *Marguerite Wasa,* 1528 Stockholm, Nordiska Museet. (Museum photo)

513 L. CRANACH: *Woman with a Hat, c.* 1525. Frankfurt, Städelsches Kunstinstitut. (Photo André Held)

DVPVER ALVEOLO FVRATVR IP ELLA CV
FVRANTI DIGITV CVSPITE EIXIT A
SIC ETIA NOBIS BREVIS ETPERITVR
QVA PETIMVS TRISTI MIXTA DOLORI

241

517 ANON: *Gustavus I, c.* 1560. Gripsholm Castle, Sweden. (Photo National Museum, Stockholm)

514 ANTON HOLLER: *Portrait of a Woman.* Late sixteenth century. Cologne, Collection Neuerburg.

515 ANON: *A Queen of Denmark and Norway c.* 1600. Oslo, Kunstindustrimuseet. (Photo Teigen)

516 Tombstone in the Church of Inkoo, Finland, 1631. (Photo Finlands National Museum)

Each country was to have its own typical form of ruff: it was tall and closed in Flanders; almost always trimmed with lace and often higher at the back than in front in England (plate 485) and Spain; in France it was usually plain, with a single row of pleats, sometimes open in front and tending to width rather than to height until the appearance, at the end of the century, of the ruff made of several layers of unstarched material, called a 'falling ruff' or, in French, *fraise à la confusion*, and of the lace-edged standing collar or *collet monté*.

Men and women alike wore their hair *en raquette*, brushed up all round the face; women's hair was supported on light metal hoops. The same little toque, trimmed with an aigrette, adorned male and female heads, but women also wore a chaperon in the shape of a heart with the point in the centre of the forehead while the sides curved over the puffs of hair (plate 469); this is the model which took the name *attifet*, which until then had been used for all head ornaments since the end of the fifteenth century.

Towards the end of the reign, toques were to disappear and women scarcely wore hats for almost two centuries (until the last quarter of the eighteenth century); it was to be only out of caprice – as at the time of the Fronde – or in special circumstances, as for hunting, that women wore hats, which in any case were taken from men's fashions. Only chaperons, coifs and cornets survived, in various forms and under varying names.

A curious mode which appeared at this time was the *conch* or butterfly head-dress, made of light, gauzy veils mounted on a large metal frame, on which they stood up behind the head and sometimes even enveloped the back (plate 483). In France they were adopted particularly for widows' costume, but it is not certain that they were worn exclusively for mourning.

It is probable that the unceasingly changing character of French costume served the reputation of France in Europe; from the sumptuous display of the Field of the Cloth of Gold to the lavish reception of the Polish ambassadors, the vivacity of the French spirit, even more than simple creative activity, radiated over all the Western countries. Compared with the austerity of Spain, a Protestant Germany, a divided Italy and an intransigent England, she presented seductive variations of elegance despite violence and internal troubles.

Without imposing forms and line like Spain, masses and complicated details like Germany, proud attitudes like England, French costume nonetheless, paradoxically, introduced to other countries a spirit of changeability that generated new styles: under the Renaissance this vocation of adaptation and recasting was pursued and took precise form, a vocation that could be felt as early as the Middle Ages, which was to become the art of nuances proper to the French taste in costume.

Costume in England

From the beginning of the sixteenth century the evolution from medieval to modern costume began to take place in England, as in all Western Europe.[13]

Under Henry VII (1485–1509), the first Tudor king, the medieval forms were retained in their original simplicity, but even then were penetrated by some foreign characteristics: for women, low head-dresses, low-waisted gowns and square necklines and long, tight sleeves, and for men, very short doublets, open-necked shirts, tight, often parti-coloured trunk hose, which later were puffed and slashed. All these features show German, French or Italian influences.

Under Henry VIII (1509–1547) the transformation became more apparent. At the beginning of his reign, peace and prosperity allowed a degree of luxury equal to that at the court of his rival François I. In the display of magnificence at the Field of the Cloth of Gold, both sovereigns made use of Italian textiles. In the last years of the reign of Henry VIII we can detect the Puritan influence of the Reforming party. Beside the extravagance of puffed, detachable sleeves, the sumptuousness of embroidered plastrons and long, long-basqued, slashed doublets, new signs appeared: the reduction in size of women's head-

519 Costume worn by Maurice of Saxe-Laurenburg, in red fashioned velvet, perhaps Spanish. Late sixteenth-early seventeenth centuries. Hanover. Landesgalerie. (Museum photo)

518 ANON: *Portrait of a Young Man.*
Before 1610. Rijnge, Sweden.
(Photo Finlands National Museum)

520 Parade armour simulating knightly costume, worn by Charles V at fourteen, 1512–13. Vienna, Kunsthistorisches Museum. (Museum photo)

521 HANS ASPER: *Portrait of Colonel W. Frölich of Zürich-Riesbach*, 1549. Zürich, Schweizerisches Landesmuseum. (Museum photo)

WOMEN'S COSTUME IN THE NORTH

514–6, 527 Plate 527 shows a gown of Spanish inspiration, with false sleeves, while the ruff is similar to Dutch models; the imported gloves with embroidered gauntlets were a great luxury in Sweden, and the kerchief recalls Spanish *panuelos*. The Queen (plate 515) wears a flaring collar of Venetian lace; her jewel-studded hairstyle seems to show French influence, which appears again in the drum farthingale (plate 516) covered with a pleated flounce

MEN'S COSTUME IN THE NORTH

517–8, 524 The costume of Gustavus I (plate 517) is thoroughly Spanish, although the hanging lining of the breeches evokes German styles, as do the visible codpiece and the *lodier* (lined overgarment). The soft, flat-soled boots or *saapas* are of Russian or German manufacture. Charles IX (plate 524) wears a doublet with a turned-down collar, of lace like his cuffs; his breeches have *canons*. The young man's suit (plate 518) is similar, but the breeches are panelled by embroidery, a fashion seen in France during the Henri II period

SURVIVING GERMAN GARMENTS

519, 522 These well-preserved garments can be compared with those seen in German, and even Dutch paintings (plate 509)

MILITARY COSTUME

520–21, 523 Metal is ornamented as if it were cloth. The armour of Charles V (plate 520) represents a full-skirted jerkin; the jerkin of metal scales (plate 523) recalls antique cuirasses. The cavalry officer's armour has a 'peascod belly', which was to be a feature of civilian costume twenty years later (plate 521). Footwear is in the broad *gueule de vache* shape of the time (plates 520–21)

522 Velvet beret decorated with plumes and pendants, worn by Christoph von Kress, 1530.
Nuremberg, Germanisches Nationalmuseum. (Museum photo)

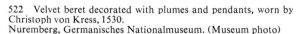

523 Jaseran worn by Francisco Maria della Rovere I, Duke of Urbino, *c.* 1532. Vienna, Kunsthistorisches Museum. (Museum photo)

dresses presaged the small cap, colours became more sober, puffings and slashings appeared less frequently and women adopted a large, stiff open collar.

Towards 1540–45 English costume, moving away from German models, which incidentally were then disappearing almost completely throughout Europe, became influenced by Spanish styles. Over and above one particular reason for this – that in 1554 Queen Mary had married a Spaniard, Philip II – the Spanish movement was general. The prestige of Spain had then reached its highest point and continued until almost the end of the century. Even the hostility felt towards Spain in England, even the defeat of the Armada in 1588 could not weaken the influence of Spanish fashions, and the tendency to stiffness and solemnity symbolized by the ruff and farthingale had its origins at the court of Philip II.[14]

Under Elizabeth I, 1558–1603 (plate 498) and James I, 1603–1625, extremely luxurious, richly decorated garments still remained under this Hispanic influence, which gave them a stiff, artificial appearance. Women wore very tight bodices with tight sleeves and excessively wide skirts, and men a tight-fitting doublet with puffed trunk hose. English costume historians judge that towards 1570–80 women's costume, more elaborately worked and tending to be made in fresh spring colours, may reflect, at least in part, the Queen's efforts to recapture her fading charms.[15] Men dressed extravagantly with plumed toques, very high collars and wide sleeves; yet the elegance of a young man painted by Nicholas Hilliard (plate 485) makes us accept the exaggerations of his doublet and ruff.

But towards the end of the reign of Elizabeth, a reaction against excessive elaboration began to take place: men preferred the falling collar to the ruff (plate 496) and wore a simpler doublet; women transformed their bell-shaped gowns into a drum-shape, with still tighter bodices. Under James I (1603–1625) the farthingale was reduced to a piece of padding and the ruff replaced by a lace-trimmed collar or neckline, while the male doublet became fuller and longer.

The ruff, which balanced the padded trunk hose, had appeared initially, as in other countries, as a ruche edging the collar. An edict of 1562 limited its width to four inches on either side of the face; it then increased rapidly, reaching its maximum size towards 1585. The use of starch paste dated from 1564 in England, where it had been introduced by a Dutchman: Queen Elizabeth engaged a Fleming to prepare her ruffs. Elegant men later replaced the ruff with a wide falling collar decorated with rich lace, often dyed saffron yellow. Women's costume at the beginning of the seventeenth century combined embroidered ornament with gauze and lace.

It should be noted that the variety of types of ruff was much greater in England than in other countries; for instance, instead of having one single layer of cloth with more or less deep folds, English ruffs often had several tiers, often of different types of fold. Corresponding to the English taste for thickly packed, florid ornament, the ruff of very fine lace was much more frequently worn than in France. Furthermore, Englishwomen showed a particular affection for starched conch headdresses, of a volume unheard of elsewhere (plate 505), and also for a kind of transparent mantle.

When Spanish influence declined in elegant society, fashion turned towards other foreign modes, even the most costly, as Philip Stubbes remarks in his *Anatomie of Abuses*. And Portia in *The Merchant of Venice* says of her English suitor: 'I think he bought his doublet in Italy, his round hose in France, his bonnet in Germany, and his behaviour everywhere.' Among all

these modes, French fashion seems to have been the most widely followed at court and among the upper classes.

However, these borrowings from abroad and imports must not make us forget the clothing produced by England herself. Indeed, we should stress the important development of the woollen industry and cloth trade in England during the Renaissance. The increase in sheep-farming facilitated by the enclosure of common grazing ground led to a considerable extension of clothing production, rather than to an increase in the export of raw wool. As in Flanders, looms were brought to the countryside, creating a system of cottage industry. The volume of the domestic market was then much greater than foreign trade: England imported only luxury textiles intended for the wealthy classes, while ordinary people dressed in local products. Scottish woad, madder and saffron supplied the dyers.[16]

Mercantile expansion was aided by the great overseas trading companies: the Muscovy Company (1554), the Eastland Company (1579), the Levant Company (1581) and the Maritime Company (1585) imported Nordic, Slav, Oriental or American produce. In 1591 an early expedition led by John Lancaster went to India by the Cape and brought back silks and cotton stuffs. This led to the foundation in 1600 of the East India Company, which rang the death-knell of the Portuguese trade monopoly.

During the first quarter of the seventeenth century, the decrease in size of the farthingale, the predilection for subdued colours, the increasing use of lace, the higher position of the waist and, in general, a less rigid outline, presaged the development of costume towards new types, in England as elsewhere.

The Evolution of Costume in Northern and Eastern Europe

The factors that affected the evolution of clothing in Eastern and Northern Europe during the sixteenth century were not the same as those which influenced Western and Southern Europe.

The United Provinces, Germany under the Holy Roman Empire and the Nordic States had much in common economically. The struggle of the Low Countries against Spain and the Dutch maritime supremacy in the Baltic, the feudal chaos of Germany followed by the continental policies of the Hapsburgs, the ruin of the Hanseatic League and the orientation of the Baltic countries towards the sea led to close relations between these neighbouring lands, all of them coastal. These relations were strengthened by the introduction of the Reformed Church.

In the context of clothing, we may note tendencies which, if not actually common, were at least fairly similar, in these various countries. Indeed, a type of costume took shape which retained some parts of Spanish clothing while assimilating other – particularly Dutch and Hanseatic – elements.[17]

Among the countries that were dominant at this period – Italy, Spain and France – the first played virtually no role in the clothing of the Northern countries. Even when the Low Countries were attracted towards the Italianized French School of Fontainebleau, 'this courtly art, imported from abroad,

524 ANON: *Charles IX, King of Sweden.* Early seventeenth century. Gripsholm Castle, Sweden. (Photo Nationalmuseum, Stockholm)

525 MAITRE DES MOULINS: *The Dauphin Charles Orland,* 1495 Paris, Louvre. (Photo Flammarion)

526 L. CRANACH: *Portrait of Sybilla of Cleves.* Weimar, Staatliche Kunstsammlungen. (Photo Klaus G. Beyer)

527 ANON: *Portrait presumed to be of Elizabeth, daughter of Gustavus I.* c. 1590. Gripsholm Castle Sweden. (Photo Nationalmuseum, Stockholm).

528 GENTILE BELLINI: *Turkish painter*, 1501. Boston, Isabella Stewart Gardner Museum. (Museum photo)

529 A. DÜRER: *Turks*, 1514. London, British Museum. (Museum photo. Courtesy the Trustees)

530 NIGARI: *Suleiman The Magnificent*, 1560. Constantinople, Topkapi Saray Museum. (Museum photo)

clearly in contradiction with local tradition and the temperament of the people', did not extend to costume, which until the end of the century showed no Italian traits but remained basically Spanish.

Spanish costume did in fact leave the deepest impression on clothing during the second and third quarters of the century. But from 1581, when the Low Countries were split in two, only their southern provinces maintained any dependence on the Spanish and then the Austrian Hapsburgs. Those to the north passed to Protestantism when they won their independence.[18] So the disappearance of Spanish influence in Dutch costume was brought about the Reformation.

Beyond the Low Countries, the complex influence of Spanish modes weakened progressively the farther away they went.

In Germany, the Italian Renaissance had a particular influence on the south,[19] in Nuremberg and Augsburg which were centres of the new art; the costumes of the Northern regions were permeated by Hanseatic traditions, which in their turn were influenced by the styles of the Dutch Netherlands. The women's costumes painted by Cranach around 1525–30 (plates 511, 526) show heavy embroidery and complicated head-dresses and ornaments, a late continuation of the Flemish and German styles worn at the Court of Burgundy in the fifteenth century. Some Spanish influences were also added after 1550 in the wealthy circles of the court and the mercantile and manufacturing middle classes.

The middle classes were at that time enjoying a period of considerable prosperity: in South Germany, the Schetz family in Leipzig and the Fuggers in Augsburg controlled the basic industries. In the north in Lübeck, Bremen and Hamburg, sartorial luxury developed among the great families of shipbuilders and traders. As a result of its trade with Lübeck from the thirteenth century on, Danzig became an extremely important centre, the intermediary between East and West for many of the basic materials of costume: cloth from England and Flanders, silks from Asia sent through the Italian colonies on the Black Sea and furs from Russia or the Nordic countries.

In the countries round the Baltic, we see a combination of Spanish, Dutch and Hanseatic influences. It is difficult to define the chronological order of these contributions and the zones of their respective influences, in the absence of specialist studies of costume in these countries. However, while costume in Denmark retained a more specifically Dutch character, the artistic primacy of Lübeck contributed to the spread of Germano-Hanseatic costume as far as Sweden and Finland,[20] where French art had disappeared in the eleventh century. We find the presence there of traders and artisans from Antwerp and even from London, and of some French embroiderers; but the tailors empolyed by the Vasa court came mainly from Germany, imposing their styles by a special system of circulating patterns and costumes.

Sailors and businessmen from Friesland, Holland and Zeeland, regions in direct contact with the North Sea, introduced Dutch costumes into Denmark, Sweden, Norway and even Finland and the shores of Germany, by way of the sea routes and, initially, through the Hanseatic League.

During the last third of the century, although certain Spanish modes brought a southern luxury of textiles, Germano-Hanseatic costume dominated in the middle and lower classes, leaving the preceding styles to courtly and aristocratic circles. The few costumes preserved in the Royal Armoury in Stockholm were ordered in Hamburg at the beginning of the seventeenth century.

Poland, however, presented a special case.[21] The artistic influence of Germany, which had supplanted French influence after the fourteenth century, gave way to that of the Italian Renaissance. But though Italianism spread through architecture, it did not affect clothing, which presented the same complex character as that to be seen in Northern Europe. And although Henri d'Anjou, the future King Henri III of France, occupied the Polish throne in 1573, his reign was too short for French fashions to become established in Poland.

In Central Europe, where the danger of the Turks was ever-present, the Austrian monarchy took shape, under the double crown of Bohemia and Hungary worn by Ferdinand I, who was first King, then Emperor in 1554. With Prague as its imperial residence, this Austrian monarchy became to all intents and purposes German, and clothing became Germanized. The

531–4 NICHOLAS DE NICOLAI: *Costume engravings made during travels in the East,* 1587. Paris, Bib. Nat. Cab. des Estampes (Photo Flammarion)

535 Portuguese Soldier, Benin bronze plaque. Sixteenth century. Neuchâtel Museum

536 CLOUET: *The Duc d'Alençon, c.* 1556. Chantilly, Musée Condé. (Photo Flammarion)

ORIENTAL COSTUME AND ITS INFLUENCE IN EUROPE

528–34 Turkish merchants traded in Venice, and Gentile Bellini went to Constantinople (plate 528), thus we have perfect images of Oriental costume, with several *caftans* of different lengths worn one on top of the other, a style later to be imitated in Europe.

Turkish sources complete our information (plates 530, 537). The caftan of Suleiman the Magnificent is flaring, with short sleeves showing the longer sleeves of the *zupan* worn underneath, buttoned up to the neck and made of luxurious materials.

The Turkish costumes sketched by the traveller (plates 331–4) show that men and women wore the same outer caftan in rich stuffs, with hanging false sleeves. The braid that was sometimes used for decoration was copied in Germany, and later worn in France in the seventeenth century, under the name of *Brandenburgs*

PORTUGUESE COSTUME AS SEEN BY AFRICA

535 The African sculptor has given a faithful representation of European costume; we can recognize the buff-jerkin worn over a tight-fitting doublet

CHILDREN'S COSTUME

525, 536, 538 Children's costume in the sixteenth century was still largely practical: flannel gowns, linen bibs, caps with turned-up flaps worn over *béguins* (plate 525). In the course of the century they began to be dressed like miniature adults. The infant Duc d'Alençon (plate 536) has a guimp with a ruched standing collar, *slashed sleeves* of silk and a plumed cap over his *béguin*. Henri IV, Prince de Nevers, wears a costume exactly similar to that of adults of the period

POPULAR COSTUME AT THE BEGINNING OF THE CENTURY

540 A short jacket replaced the fifteenth-century smock. Hats were made of straw or lime-bark. Stirrup-hose (with no feet, but instep straps) are the new elements in ordinary people's costume

POPULAR COSTUME IN FLANDERS IN THE MID-SIXTEENTH CENTURY

539, 41 Ordinary people's costume is basically similar to that of the more prosperous classes, but the materials are simpler. Breughel (plate 541) shows hose with exposed codpieces, and sheepskin waistcoats fastened with points

ORDINARY PEOPLE'S COSTUME TOWARDS THE END OF THE SIXTEENTH CENTURY

542 The woman wears a gathered skirt, a short-basqued jacket prefiguring the *hongreline* of the following century, which was to become a standard piece of everyday costume, worn until 1944 by the Sisters of Saint Vincent de Paul. The linen head-dress is folded into a *bavolet* over the nape of the neck

537 Caftan worn by Fatih Mehmet II. Late fifteenth–early sixteenth centuries. Istanbul, Topkapi Sarayi Museum

538 FRANÇOIS BUNEL (Attrib.): *Retrospective portrait of Henri IV as a child,* c. 1563. Versailles, Museum

539 PETER BREUGHEL THE ELDER: *Two Peasants.* Mid-sixteenth century. Cleveland Museum of Art, J. H. Wade Collection. (Museum photo)

luxury, feasts and lavish spending of the German nobility contrasted with the wretched poverty of the Czech peasantry.

In the sixteenth century German influence thus dominated the costume of the upper classes from Warsaw to Budapest, to the exclusion of the other – particularly Italian – tendencies that appear in the arts. Here again fashion was determined by economic and political factors.

Military Costume and the Appearance of Military Uniform

After the sixteenth century, some soldiers wore uniforms; for example, in Nuremberg the troops enlisted by the city for the Imperial army wore red coats; in England in 1547 the Duke of Norfolk gave the men placed under his command suits of blue piped with red; in Denmark, in 1562 we find troops equipped with black hats and coats and red trousers. This uniformity in clothing was an innovation, doubtless inspired by considerations of economy and for greater ease in obtaining supplies. These first uniforms were modelled on civilian costume.[22]

From the end of the fifteenth century, towards 1480, Swiss mercenaries wore short doublets and fairly tight breeches with slashings and puffings, wide plumed hats and very broad shoes, as represented by Albrecht Dürer in 1524 and Niklaus Manuel Deutsch about 1520. This clothing, made in bright colours, was more often than not parti-coloured, i.e. with one stocking striped and the other plain. Germany took not only weapons and tactics from the Swiss, but also their costume, and we see these characteristics in all the foreign armies that employed mercenaries from the Federated Cantons, after the defeat of Marignan which in 1515 marked the decline of Swiss political influence.

The use of long breeches and cloaks was then spread by German lansquenets. Towards the middle of the century, military clothing everywhere underwent the influence of French and Spanish modes. And to meet the improvements in firearms, around 1550 half and three-quarter armour was adopted for infantrymen.

This armour followed the same variations of style as civilian costume, though with less pronounced changes. The waist became slimmer.

The decoration of the rich stuffs used for clothing was often reproduced on the metal of this armour,[23] by engraving rather than by damasquine or repoussé techniques. Designs from silks, braid and passementerie motifs and even interlacing embroidery were imitated (plate 520–21, 523).

Furthermore, several specific traits of military costume could also be found in civilian clothes: the shell shape of the codpiece and perhaps the broadening of duck bill shoes, known as *solerets*. The central ridge of the cuirass, intended to deflect bullets, was imitated in the peascod belly doublet. The slits cut in military costume had originated in the tears received in combat; the thick padding of the sleeves and the chest, originally intended to deaden the impact of blows, became transformed into a fashion and from then on slashings served to show off the lining. This type of sleeve was ultimately reproduced in armour.

It is difficult to decide which, of military and civilian costume, inspired the other in the sixteenth century.

Theatrical Costume

Theatrical costume in the sixteenth century brought no great innovations. As in the Middle Ages, the religious brotherhoods contrived to rent ecclesiastical vestments from chapterhouses, for the traditional form of these garments was well suited to the repertory of Mystery plays. Sometimes, as at Bourges for a performance of the *Acts of the Apostles* in 1536, the participants themselves bore the expense of their costumes, often very rich, which were also those worn in everyday life. But a celebrated edict of 17 November 1548 prohibited the playing of 'any sacred mystery', thus marking the end of the medieval religious theatre; the evolution of public taste had already led the *Confréries* (the religious brotherhoods) to make their peace with the *Enfants Sans-Souci* ('Carefree Children') who played all types of comic pieces.

Perhaps the newest element in theatrical costume during the Renaissance appeared with the feasts and masquerades given in France at the courts of Henri II and his successors, for which Francesco Primaticcio, who occupied a position of great importance in Paris after the death of Rosso in 1540, executed a series of costume designs, now in the National Museum in Stockholm. Others, attributed to Niccolò dell' Abbate or to unknown artists, show Italian influence in the spirit of these performances as well as in their costumes.[24]

The First Historical Engravings of Costumes

A new source of documentation on costume and costume accessories appeared in the sixteenth century in the form of collections of engravings, the first of which date from 1520.[25] Forty or so were published before 1540, and their number later grew, particularly in the great publishing centres of Venice and Paris and, in lesser numbers, in Antwerp and Frankfurt. Only one is to be found in England, in 1585, and this is only a reissue of a collection from Lyons. There are none in Spain where, however, we find the appearance of the first manual for tailors, written by Juan de Alceya and published in Madrid in 1589.

These collections, which responded to the period's desire for knowledge, were veritable fashion books and for the first time gathered together models of costume ornament and jewellery, then new decorative motifs, such as embroideries, for the 'art of clothing', and latterly representations of the garments of all countries.

The authors and artists who published these works, such as F. Desprez, N. Nicolaï d'Arfeuille, Jost Amman, P. Bertelli, A. de Bruyn, J. J. Boissard and C. Vecellio were forerunners. This type of publication received a new, greater impetus in the following century.

540 Threshing wheat.
Early sixteenth century. Paris,
Musée des Arts Décoratifs.
(Photo Flammarion)

541 PETER BREUGHEL THE ELDER: *The Proverb of the Bird-Nester*, 1568.
Vienna, Kunsthistorisches Museum. (Photo Erwin Meyer)

542 *The Nurse.*
Late sixteenth century.
Paris, Musée des Arts
Décoratifs. (Photo Flammarion)

Notes

1 B. Varchi (1502–1565), vol. IX, pp. 45–61.
2 Piccolomini, cf. Rodocanachi, p. 148.
3 Rodocanachi, p. 168 no. 3.
4 In this chapter we have drawn largely on the excellent studies by Brian Reade and Don Manuel Rocamora.
5 Cf. the extremely complete study by Carmen Bernis Madrazo.
6 Cf. Stella M. Pearce, *passim*.
7 Sloman, pp. 95–6.
8 Enlart, pp. 403, 582.
9 Vecellio, plates 184, 343.
10 Sée, *passim*.
11 Cimber and Danjou, III, p. 453.
12 Sloman, pp. 95–6.
13 For details of clothing in this period, cf. Kelly and Schwob and London Museum catalogue, *passim*; Laver, pp. 3–4; Cunnington, *passim*.
14 Laver, p. 10.
15 Reynolds, p. 135.
16 Trevelyan, pp. 126, 138, 143.
17 Van Thienen, pp. 250, 269 ff., plates 57–8.
18 Réau, pp. 8–12.
19 Post, *passim*.
20 Pylkkanen, *passim*.
21 Irena Turnau, *passim*.
22 Schneider, *passim*.
23 Thomas, *passim*.
24 A. Beijer: 'Sixteenth–Seventeenth Century Theatrical Design', in *Gazette des Beaux-Arts*, 1945.
25 Tuffal, pp. 262–9.

Bibliography

GENERAL

JEAN ALAZARD: *Le Portrait florentin*, 1924.
V. SLOMAN: *Bizarre Designs in Silk*, Copenhagen, 1953.
H. SÉE: *L'Evolution commerciale et industrielle de la France sous l'ancien régime*, 1925.
C. M. TREVELYAN: *A Social History of England*, 1945.
ROBERT ESTIENNE: *Dialogue du langage françois italianisé*, 1578.

COSTUME

ANDRÉ BLUM: 'The Last Valois'. *Costume of the Western World*, 1951.
ANDRÉ BLUM: 'Early Bourbon'. *Costume of the Western World*, 1951.
B. VARCHI: *Storia fiorentina*, vol IX.
A. PICCOLOMINI: *Dialogo dove si ragiona delle belle creanze delle donne*, 1539.
E. RODOCANACHI: *La Femme italienne*, 1907.
BRIAN READE: 'The Dominance of Spain'. *Costume of the Western World*, 1951.
DON MANUEL ROCAMORA: 'La Mode en Espagne au XVIe S.' in *Actes Ier Cong. Int. Hist. Cost.* 1952.

CARMEN BERNIS MADRAZO: 'Les Modes espagnoles du Moyen Age dans la Renaissance européenne', in *Waffen und Kostümkunde*, 1959.
LONDON MUSEUM, *Catalogue* (No. 5): *Costume*, (2nd ed.) 1946.
JAMES LAVER: 'Early Tudor'. *Costume of The Western World*, 1951.
GRAHAM REYNOLDS: 'Elizabethan and Jacobean'. *Costume of the Western World*, 1951.
FRITHJOF VAN THIENEN: 'The Great Age of Holland'. *Costume of the Western World*, 1951.
H. K. MORSE: *Elizabethan Pageantry* (*Costume* 1560–1620), London, 1934.
C. WILLET and PHYLLIS CUNNINGTON: *Handbook of English Costumes in the Sixteenth Century*, London, 1954.
RITTA PYLKKANEN: *Renessanssin Puka Suomessa*, Helsinki, 1956.
PAUL POST: 'Das Kostüm der deutschen Renaissance, 1480–1550', in *Anzeiger des Germanishen National Museum*, 1954–9.
BRUNO THOMAS: 'L'Esthétique de l'armure', in *Actes Ier Cong. Int. Hist. Cost.*, 1952.
HUGO SCHNEIDER: 'Le Costume militaire suisse du XVIe s.', *Ibid.*
JACQUELINE TUFFAL: 'Les Recueils de costumes gravés du XVIe s.', *Ibid.*

TEXTILES

L. A. BOSSEBOEUF: *La Fabrication des soieries de Tours*, Tours, 1904.
AUGUSTE BLETON: *L'Ancienne Fabrique des Soieries*, Lyons, 1897.

543 BONNART: *M. Le Noble in a Dressing-Gown*, 1695.
Paris, Bib. Nat., Cabinet des Estampes, Oa 49 f. 125.
(Photo Flammarion)

THE FASHION FOR INDIAN COTTONS

543, 545 The fashion for Indian cotton stuffs mentioned in texts produced few representations, since the trade was prohibited. However, plate 543 recalls the vogue

FRENCH COSTUME IN THE TIME OF HENRI IV

544 The drum farthingale is worn very close to the waist and gives the skirt its characteristic shape; it is often covered by a flounce in the same material as the gown

SPANISH INFLUENCES IN ITALIAN COSTUME

546-51 Spanish influence completely dominated Italian costume during the first quarter of the seventeenth century. For women, there was the bell fárthingale (plates 546, 547), the voluminous ruff edged with serrated lace *punte in aria*, supported by a *rebato* trimmed with passementerie; a very tall hairstyle with a toque worn straight on the head; double funnel sleeves (plate 547) or full cape sleeves (plates 549, 550). For men: *chausses en bourse*, ruffs, Spanish capes over garments similar to the *ropilla* (plate 548). Claudia de Medicis (plate 550) wears a high standing collar and turned-back sleeves that announce a new mode

544 Attributed to L. DE CAULERY: *Court Ball*, 1611.
Rennes, Museum. (Museum photo)

545 Almanach recalling Colbert's edicts concerning Indian cotonnades, 1681. Paris, Bib. Nat., Cabinet des Estampes. (Photo Flammarion)

547 POURBUS: *Young Princess*. Florence, Uffizi.
(Photo Brogi-Giraudon)

546 FRANKEN and POURBUS: *Ball at the Court of Isabella Clara Eugenia*, 1611. The Hague, Mauritshuis. (Photo A. Dingjan)

Chapter IX

The Seventeenth Century

From 1590 to 1715, while Europe was passing through a period of almost continual wars, political divisions and religious strife, costume continued its evolution, more influenced by currents in art and thought than by other factors. Never before, perhaps, had so great an effect been produced on costume, which, in the span of 125 years, became even more refined, elegant and modern.

The further the Middle Ages were left behind, the more numerous were the influences on costume and, without neglecting the various economic pressures, the struggle for power among the nations of Europe, or the social changes within each country, by the seventeenth century we must devote increasing attention to the formation of a new esthetic and a different conception of life.

For economic and political reasons Italy and, more particularly, Spain lost their former supremacy in the course of the century. France, on the other hand, in successive phases of recovery, authority and absolutism, and the newly independent Holland which was entering on its 'Golden Century' of dazzling prosperity, imposed their dominance on Europe. England was concentrating all her efforts on ruling the waves and gaining economic power.

France and Holland were thus gradually to exert their superiority as the two dominant influences on the evolution of costume.

THE PREPONDERANCE OF FRENCH AND DUTCH STYLES

These two countries exercised an almost absolute domination over European clothing. Where France was concerned the influence was extensive but sometimes superficial, while Dutch influence was limited to the Reformed countries: England and the Nordic states, North Germany and, shortly after, America.

Why was influence divided between only these two countries, while England was hardly to figure at all as an initiator in costume during the rest of the century? To this question we can only reply that nothing in England corresponded to the balanced prosperity and taste that France and Holland managed to acquire during the first quarter of the century.

ARTISTIC DOCTRINES AND COSTUME

The influence on costume of art, which had been noticeable particularly since the fourteenth century, became more profound in the seventeenth century (in France the *Grand Siècle*),

under the effect of new doctrines codified by the recently founded Academies. The influence of the Baroque and Classicism on costume in Europe was not equally apparent at all times, but it was nonetheless a determining factor.

Between 1625 and 1670 a correspondence was indisputably established between costume and the Baroque taste, in terms of the recourse of both to imagination and virtuosity.

The essential characteristics of Baroque – disdain for restraint and an accentuated taste for liberty, a search for oppositions and movement, abundant details – are to be found in clothing, which abandoned its former symmetry and balance and, escaping to a greater or lesser degree from Reformation and Counter-Reformation coldness, was attracted by experiment, singularities and exaggerations which went as far as the preciosity of cannons and petticoat breeches.

From its native land of Italy, this movement spread over the whole of Europe. Its repercussions on costume, as on all the arts, differed according to the country: less accentuated in some (the Low Countries, England, North Germany, Scandinavia), and more noticeable in others (France, Flanders, Spain and Central Europe), it also varied according to the spiritual climate, more rational in Paris, austere in Madrid, prone to excess in Rome and realistic in Brussels.

After yielding to the vogue of this international Baroque style for almost fifty years, from 1670 costume reflected the influence of the French variety of Classicism. The reaction against 'the anarchy of Baroque' aimed at clarity and dignity, and corresponded to the establishment of authoritarian regimes.

In the last years of the *Grand Siècle*, costume was affected by the repercussions of the conflict between the followers of Rubens and the disciples of Poussin which, after it broke out in France in 1688, gradually turned to the advantage of the former. When, at the very beginning of the eighteenth century, the arts attempted to express aspects of life and individuals through light and colour, costume participated in this general development, interpreted with genius by Watteau, and became imbued with lightness and fancy, adapting itself not only to the practical needs of the moment but also to the sensibility of a new society.

During the whole century, the strengthening of France's international position was matched by the growing spread of the country's fashions through Europe. From the negotiation of the Treaties of Westphalia, where great ambassadors vied with one another in the splendour of their liveries, to the princely marriages of the end of the century, fashion throughout Europe was a vain but brilliant reflection of French prestige.

France's political triumph owed much to a group of high-ranking officials who were the architects of her industrial and commercial recovery. To the country's artistic and literary revival they added a prosperity encouraged by royal authority. The great merchants, more particularly the mercers, such as the cloth-merchant Claude Parfaict and the muslin-trader Nicolas Colbert, father of the famous minister, amassed considerable capital, and at the same time, from the reign of Louis XIII, would become magistrates; to this privilege Louis XIV added that of becoming royal secretaries, a path to ennoblement. Such men were prominent in the privileged trading companies and manufactories.

The predominance of French costume, marked under Henri IV and more pronounced during the reign of Louis XIII, became dazzling under the *Roi Soleil*. Most noticeably of all, changes in fashion became more and more frequent.

548 SANTE PERANDA: *Unknown Young Man,*
c. 1600. Mantua, Museum. (Photo Calzolari)

549 VAN DYCK: *Duchess Doria,* 1625.
Paris, Louvre. (Photo Flammarion)

550 J. SUSTERMANS: *Claudia de Medicis,*
Countess of Tyrol, c. 1640.
Florence, Palazzo Pitti. (Photo Alinari)

Costume in France

FASHIONS FROM 1590 TO 1625

The influence of Spanish fashions reappeared after the death
of Henri III, as if their gravity counterbalanced the eccentricities
of the last of the Valois. Most of the elements of Renaissance
costume survived in an ensemble which was not clearly defined
and as yet did not show signs of a really new style.

Women's costume retained slashing on the bodice and the
sleeves, which were still voluminous. The farthingale was transformed, and the roll of preceding years gave way to a sort of
tray worn on the hips, over which the skirt, tightly gathered
at the waist, was spread so as to give the feminine silhouette
the general line of a drum softened by a gathered flounce.

Men wore doublets with rounded or slightly pointed waists,
trimmed with epaulettes and wings at the shoulders, with short
or long slashings and standing collars. Ruffs could be round,
as in the preceding period, or soft and falling (plate 561), or
alternatively a stiff collar (*collet monté*) supported by a frame
could be worn. Trunk hose had to compete with *chausses en
bourse* (slops), and with longer breeches, known as *leg-of-mutton
breeches* or *Venetians.*

FASHIONS FROM 1625/30 TO 1645/50

The court of the Béarnais (Henri IV) was not at first outstand-
ingly elegant; however, as the result of the rapid improvement
he initiated, the author of the *Chasse au vieil grognart de l'antiquité* could note in 1622 that in the morning one might meet
tradesmen at the Pont-au-Change dressed so becomingly that
they could not be recognized for what they were; and the *Almanach pour le temps passé* observed that there had never been
more 'superfluities' in clothing, 'as can be seen right down to
the points on the shoes and pattens worn by the ladies'. A petition from the city to the Etats-Généraux of 1614 had vainly

551 P.-P. RUBENS: *The Proxy Marriage of Marie de Medicis,* 1600.
Paris, Louvre. (Photo Giraudon)

552 CORNELIS DE VOS: *The Painter and his Family,* 1621.
Brussels, Museum

553–4 ABRAHAM BOSSE: *Woman following the edict*, and *Philandre following the relaxation of the edict*, 1633. Paris, Bib. Nat., Cabinet des Estampes. (Photo Flammarion)

555 ABRAHAM BOSSE: *The Costume Ball*, *c.* 1635. Paris, Bib. Nat., Cabinet des Estampes. (Photo Flammarion)

called for the strict observance of rules governing the wearing of jewels and silk clothes, and the prohibition of velvet and other rich materials for farmers and people of humble condition. It was recalled that burghers might not keep more than one lackey and that gentlemen were limited to two, clad in brown frieze and not in dyed broadcloth. A character in Sorel's novel *Le Berger extravagant* (1628) explodes: 'How I hate the sumptuous splendour of our town! Lackeys parade about covered in silk and I doubt not that luxury will soon be so great that our cobblers will wear aprons of scented leather...'

This Parisian society, whose whole aim in dressing was to display itself, naturally paid no more attention to these sumptuary edicts than to those of January 1629 and November 1633 forbidding lace, embroideries, etc., whether made in France or abroad,[1] or to that of April 1634 prescribing the cloths and trimmings that might be used, or those issued by Mazarin in 1644, forbidding the use of gold and silver in costume. An ordinance from the Civil Lieutenant of the Châtelet noted that nobody had taken any notice of the royal prescriptions.

Well before this century, any fashion set by the nobility was certain to catch on, but gradually the burghers began to wear the stuffs reserved for nobles, forcing them to change constantly. Formerly it had been possible to tell a person's social rank from his costume and the cloth it was made of: a man clad in silk ranked higher than one in camlet, who took precedence over a man in serge; but under Louis XIII this was no longer. The different ranks were equally well dressed and everyone aspired to carry a sword. A contemporary observed that the Parisians no longer seemed able to live without ribbons or laces or a mirror.

The anxiety to maintain his prestige increasingly imposed on every self-respecting nobleman the obligation to change clothes and ornaments every day. Thus young men of good birth, the 'muguets' (lilies-of-the-valley) threw themselves into the pursuit of elegance: satin suits, cloaks of silk panne, beaver hats, scented suede collars known as *collars of flowers*. Even when the nobility were impoverished by devaluation (as happened in 1615) and were forced for economy's sake to take to wearing boots and cloth boot-hose, since they could no longer afford

to wear delicate, costly silk stockings, these were soon imitated. The luxury of the town and country bourgeoisie was disapproved of by the common people and by the minor country gentry, whose daughters married working men. The women of Alençon revolted on hearing the rumour that they might have to pay 'six deniers for each white chemise'.,

For men, the *Courtisan à la mode* (1625) affirmed that clothes, bearing and beards were still 'in Spanish style'; yet 'Spanish fashions' had virtually disappeared from France after 1635, except in literature.

This nobility, which Richelieu had deprived of all political power, Louis XIV was shortly to organize round him as his court at Versailles: thus, from 1635 to 1655 we see it paying increasing attention to matters of fashion, and we also note the appearance of an 'arbiter of elegance', who was often the favourite of the King. Of the two brothers of Charles d'Albert de Luynes, one, the Seigneur of Brantes, gave his name to elongated pearls worn in the ears, while the other, the Sieur de Cadenet, named a new hairstyle; Cinq-Mars became in his turn the oracle of fashion; Balagny changed the way people wore their cloaks; Guiche modified the curve of spurs to avoid damaging women's gowns; Choisy laid down the law about shoes; the Duc de Candale is alleged to have invented straight breeches worn without hooks or points, with ribbons round the hem.

The doublet, which could be plain or have long slashings and basques known as *tassettes*, was buttoned only at the top and opened down the front to show the shirt jabot, of fine linen or lace. Sleeves, which were similarly slashed or slit lengthwise to show the shirt sleeves, were tightly fastened at the wrists. Trunk hose, which were less full than formerly, but longer, stopped above the knees, either fastening closely to the leg or hanging freely as *pantaloons*.

The cape was henceforth a *manteau*; it was sometimes worn over both shoulders, more often over one only, *à la Balagny*. A long-basqued surtout, probably brought from Central Europe through Germany, the *hongreline*, which was often lined with fur, spread through military and civilian costume. The *casaque*, a short, flowing garment, was characterized by open cape sleeves

254

558 Suit worn by Gustavus Adolphus, 1620. Stockholm, Royal Armoury. (Museum photo)

559 ABRAHAM BOSSE: *Male Costume*, 1629. Paris, Bib. Nat., Cabinet des Estampes, Ed 30 rés. (Photo Bibliothèque Nationale)

556-7 CRISPIN DE PASSE: *The Royal Stables of M. de Pluvinel*, 1618. Paris, Bib. Nat., Cabinet des Estampes. (Photo Flammarion)

560 *Charles, Marquis de Rostaing*, 1633. Collection Gaignères. Paris, Bib. Nat., Cabinet des Estampes, oa 18 rés. Photo Bibliothèque Nationale)

which could be closed with buttons or buttoned to the body of the garment. The *rochet* or *roquet*, a short mantle with short, hanging sleeves and no collar, seems to have been mainly a ceremonial garment. The fifteenth-century *caban* was still worn, with some changes in the cut, for travelling or country wear.

Silk stockings of all colours were worn, and were displayed by cut-outs *à la Pompignan* in the shoes. For winter or for hunting they were made of wool. *Boot hose* in cloth were worn over the stockings; they could be full-footed or fitted only with instep straps, flaring out at the top into wide funnels trimmed with lace which spread over the boot tops.

Elegant men vied with women in inventing new fashions.

Once more, women's clothes were much more restrained than those of men. The silhouette took on a completely new appearance, with broad shoulders and high waists. The boned bodice or *corps de jupe* was characterized by a stiff plastron whose point overlapped on to the skirt or *bas de jupe*; it was often covered with a *busquière* in some rich material. Sleeves, slashed and bouffant, were supported by cushions stuffed with rushes. Clothes in general were always in light, figured stuff: over this, the black robe with slit half-sleeves knotted at the elbow to the bodice sleeves opened from top to foot over the skirt or *cote*: the latter was sometimes caught up to show the underskirt. These three superimposed underskirts were picturesquely named *la modeste*, *la friponne* and *la secrète* (modest, frivolous, secret).

These three essential pieces were completed by the *hongreline* (see above), shorter than that worn by men, a sort of unboned basqued bodice, and the justaucorps *à la Christine*, in imitation of the Queen of Sweden.

Beneath, with the chemise whose form scarcely varied, women wore the sixteenth-century drawers, fitted with pockets and trimmed with passementerie, to which the stockings were fastened.

Lastly, for riding, women often wore skirt fronts in the form of large aprons, known as *devantières*; at home they wore long aprons known as *laisse-tout-faire*.

Women led fashion, and they also dictated the adoption of less coarse manners and a more delicate language, reigning in

THE SUMPTUARY LAWS OF 1633

553, 534 The woman wears a dress of plain stuff, with cuffs and a linen cape collar without lace.
A black coif is worn over hair dressed in a fringe and puffs. The man demonstrates the excesses the sumptuary laws sought to curb. Men also gave up lace and ribbon bows. They wore wide collars of plain or embroidered linen, simple bows and hose tied with a single ribbon. The edicts were not observed for long.
Beards are *à la royale*; a lock of hair (*moustache*) hangs down over the collar, tied with a ribbon. A rosette decorates the shoe

SOCIETY LIFE

555 This engraving evokes the elegant worldliness that was to have a lasting influence on fashion of the period. The line of the garments is simple, but decoration is very varied: linen collars for men and women, long Venetian or pantaloon breeches, soft bucket-top boots, shoes trimmed with rosettes. The man on the right wears a short coat called a *rochet* over his shoulder. Men's fashions were seldom as elegant as these

SPANISH INFLUENCES ON THE COSTUME OF THE SPANISH NETHERLANDS

546, 552, 564 Spanish influence is still very strong in Flemish costume: the ruff is still very deep, up to six inches (plate 552). The *ropa* worn by Isabella Clara Eugenia (plate 546) can be compared with the *vlieger* (plate 552). Men's breeches are cut wide *en bourse* (plate 551). Women's bodices are low-cut, with high flaring collars for those who do not wear ruffs. Isabella Brandt (plate 564) wears a tall felt hat, rare for the period, over her diadem coif, and her gown opens over a stomacher in rich material; she wears a Spanish ruff, whereas the wife of Cornelis de Vos (plate 552) wears a Flemish ruff and the child a soft ruff or *fraise à la confusion*

561 Soft ruff. Early seventeenth century. Basle, Historisches Museum, (Museum photo)

562 VAN DYCK: *Lord Denbigh in Pyjamas*, 1633.
London, The National Gallery.
(Photo Freeman)

563 P.-P. RUBENS: *Nicolas de Respaigne*, c. 1620. Kassel, Museum.
(Museum photo)

564 P.-P. RUBENS: *Rubens and his wife Isabella Brandt*, 1610.
Munich, Museum. (Photo Giraudon)

the new salons of the *Précieuses*, forcing men to politer behaviour.

In the Hôtel de Rambouillet Voiture gave a dissertation in refined, elegant language on the new spurs invented by the Duc de Guiche, or upon the merits of the wig, the first of which had been worn solemnly by the Duc de Montausier.[2] Between a madrigal and a sonnet in the house of Mlle de Scudéry, the witty wives of the Marais did not scorn to work on the costumes of two dolls, *la Grande Pandore* and her little sister, which were to spread French fashions through the whole of Europe.

The mode of life had changed since the wars of the beginning of the century. During the regency of Marie de' Medici and the reign of Louis XIII, numerous feasts for princely and royal marriages, ballets and carrousels marked the resumption of social life; the worldly influence of the court was accentuated by its closer relations with the town. This worldliness and new luxury intensified the pursuit of elegance.

Indeed, the line of costume had been progressively simplified during this quarter century. Width had decreased for men and women alike; superfluous ornaments had disappeared, and even hairstyles had become more restrained. It may perhaps be an exaggeration to see in this the influence of the emergent Jansenism, whose doctrines penetrated to some extent even into aristocratic and intellectual circles. What is certain is that at the death of Louis XIII fashion had reached a sobriety and elegance that was not to be recaptured for many years.

FASHIONS FROM 1645 TO 1675

It is astonishing to observe that from 1650 costume abandoned this line, at once noble and studied, in favour of the extravagant *rhinegraves* or *petticoat breeches* (plates 569–70, 577–8), garments whose fashion was only to dwindle towards 1675 and which remain by far the most curious part of men's costume in this period.

These were short trousers, extremely wide (one and a half ells for each leg), with such full, generous folds that they presented the appearance of a skirt, showing no sign that the legs were divided.

Some examples of petticoat breeches are known in England, in particular the specimen dating from 1660 in the Victoria and Albert Museum – the only one quoted by historians[3] – and in the Scandinavian countries. In France, where they had been worn since about 1652, they were represented particularly in Lebrun's tapestries of the History of Louis XIV (plate 569); Molière mocked them in *L'Ecole des maris* ('ces cotillons appelés hauts de chausses' – 'these coat-skirts called breeches') and in *Le Festin de Pierre* in 1665. On these wide, floppy legs, trimmings of lace or tiered ribbon loops gave bulk to the silhouette, which the deep linen flounces attached to the cannons further distorted.[4]

This garment has sometimes been confused with the *bas de saie* which also resembled a short skirt, but without the fullness or length of the petticoat breeches: it was probably a ceremonial garment, and figures in engravings representing ceremonial occasions. It has also been confused with some types of full, soft breeches, caught in at the knee by the cannons to give the effect of a skirt, but these were only another type of upper stocks, perhaps worn under the petticoat breeches, becoming visible when the dimensions of the outer breeches decreased; they then replaced them below the justaucorps.

565 Attributed to Mathieu Le Nain: *Tric-trac players*, c. 1650.
Paris, Louvre. (Photo Flammarion)

SPANISH INFLUENCES ON FRENCH COSTUME IN THE TIME
OF LOUIS XIII

556–561 Plates 556 and 557 still show *grègesque* breeches (short spherical puffs) derived from the Spanish *gregas;* they were also known as
trunk hose and remained part of pages' costume. The fitted doublet with
hanging sleeves (plate 557) recalls the *ropilla.* Falling ruffs of which the
one in the Basle Museum (plate 561) is one of the rare examples to have
survived, were worn by most people, although some wore standing collars. The suit preserved in Stockholm (plate 558) has a doublet along
the same lines, but with *chausses pleines* (full breeches)

THE DEVELOPMENT OF MEN'S COSTUME IN THE TIME OF LOUIS XIII

559–60, 565–6 Men's costume was stripped of the ornament that had
loaded it at the beginning of the reign: plate 566 shows the long-slashed
doublet with trapezoidal skirts over which we see the points fastening
the breeches. These breeches are leg-of-mutton shaped and decorated
with small medallions. The cuffed boots are trimmed with boot hose
decorated with lace matching the falling collar. On the feet, the quatre-
foil-shaped instep-piece is held in place by a *soulette* that passes under
the heel. The gorget is of leather.
Plate 560 shows a noble's costume: the doublet sleeves open over the
shirt; the breeches are shorter and less tightly fitted, and the rosettes on
the *drawbridge shoes* worn over *socques* are more discreet. Plate 565
illustrates more bourgeois costume: lace and bows have disappeared;
collars are smaller, and shorter doublets open over the stomach so that
the shirt jabot shows; breeches are cut straight, *à la marinière.* The valet's
casaque (on the right) is a sort of *roupille* recalling peasant dress. The
high-crowned felt hats had fox-tail plumes; the outer garment is still
the cape, worn *à la Balagny* over one shoulder. The soft cuffed boots are
ladrines

EASTERN INFLUENCE IN EUROPE

562–3 Lord Denbigh (plate 562) wears the first example known in
Europe of a garment borrowed from India: the pyjama suit in pink
Indian cotton, made of soft trousers (Moghul breeches) and a long, loose
jacket. Nicolas de Respaigne (plate 563) wears Near-Eastern costume:
two superimposed caftans, a rich scarf knotted as a belt, and a small
turban

566 F. Elle: *Henri II of Lorraine*, 1631. Rheims, Museum.
(Photo Dumont et Babinot)

567 JACQUES CALLOT:
Noble Lady, c. 1625.
Paris, B. N., Cab. des Est.
Ed 25 rés. (Photo
Bibliothèque Nationale)

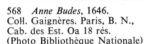

568 *Anne Budes*, 1646.
Coll. Gaignères. Paris, B. N.,
Cab. des Est. Oa 18 rés.
(Photo Bibliothèque Nationale)

569 LEBRUN: *Meeting of Louis XIV and Philip II*, 1669.
Engraving after the tapestry of the *History of the King*.
Paris, Bib. Nat., Cabinet des Estampes. (Photo Flammarion)

570 *A Ball in the French Style*, 1682. Paris, Bibliothèque Nationale (Photo Flammarion)

Several theories have been put forward to account for the origins of petticoat breeches. As their alternative name, rhinegraves, indicates, they were German, and their invention was at first attributed to Charles, Count Palatine, the brother of the Princess Palatine, the second wife of Monsieur (the brother of Louis XIV); they were then attributed to the Rhinegrave of Maastricht, who had been to Paris on a mission about 1655. But these two hypotheses seem implausible: the former came to Paris only in 1671, when petticoat breeches had already been worn for over fifteen years; the second seems to have been a serious man, entirely occupied with his diplomatic mission and, despite his high-ranking post, hardly an obvious leader of fashion. There is, however, a third candidate, who does not seem to have occured to anyone: the Count Palatine Edward, son of the Count Palatine Frederick V, the 'Winter King', renowned for his eccentricities, married to Ann of Gonzaga and Nevers, lady in waiting to the Queen Regent (widow of Louis XIII) and known as the Princess Palatine. Though no text permits us to assign the inspiration of petticoat breeches to this Count Edward, the supposition could explain the initial error through the confusion of the two Princesses Palatine.

The doublet worn with these astonishing breeches was now only a sort of bolero, open in front and short enough for the full shirt, following a mode which some authors name *Candale*, to show between the jacket and breeches. The very short doublet sleeves showed the shirt sleeves below. The entire costume was heavily loaded with small bows of ribbon, or *petite oie* ornament. The extreme complication of this type of costume seems to have reached its maximum in France, Germany and England; Spain does not seem to have known it and other countries wore it in less exaggerated forms.

At the same time a type of overcoat or surtout, already worn in military costume, began to take its place in civilian clothing. This was the *justaucorps*, which had short sleeves and was long and slightly flared at the bottom, and was perhaps derived from the hongreline. It was worn for a few years over full, floppy breeches, then, after 1680, over short breeches that gradually lost their fullness until, in the last years of the century, they became skin-tight.

The old doublet then became an inner garment, under the name of *veste*. The front and sleeves were always made of rich material and the back of lining cloth.

In 1662, according to Bussy-Rabutin, Louis XIV granted first a dozen, then about forty of his familiars permission to wear clothes similar to his own – a blue justaucorps lined with red ornaments, and a red veste or jacket – when staying at Saint-Germain or Versailles. These coats were embroidered with gold and a little silver 'according to a magnificent design special to this garment'. The happy few admitted to this favour received letters patent entitling them to wear this coat even during periods of private mourning (though not during deep, general mourning) and even when gold and silver embroideries were prohibited. The *justaucorps à brevets* ('patent justaucorps') were thus the first example of a codified form of Court costume. We must wait for Napoleon I before we see another similar regulation of Court costume. It seems that the last recipient of this privilege was the Duc de Chevreuse in 1743, but by that time the favour was too widespread to have kept much value.

When, after 1665, restrictions were placed on the use of gold embroidery, this was replaced, among the unprivileged population, by such a quantity of braids, buttons and fringes that for a short time at least, the justaucorps became overloaded with trimmings.

The use of precious stones, on the other hand, increased for both men's and women's costume, reaching its maximum for princely marriages.

In 1644 a merchant in the Temple district of Paris had discovered a process for colouring crystal and imitating precious stones; these were 'Temple diamonds' which spread as rapidly as did paste jewels, invented at the end of the century by a Strasburgher who gave the stones their French name, *strass*.

Women's costume underwent fewer changes than did men's clothes in the same period. Gowns still had oval necklines and the tiers of skirts fell in soft folds. The one innovation, at the beginning of the reign, was the broad collar of guipure lace, placed at the neckline of the gown instead of round the neck.

From 1680 on, ornaments and trimmings became more numerous: skirts and bodice fronts were covered with passemen-

571 Suit with petticoat breeches worn by Sir Henry Verney. in reseda brocaded silk, trimmed with varicoloured ribbons known as *petite oie*, 1660. London, Victoria and Albert Museum. (Museum photo)

572 Suit with petticoat breeches in cloth of silver trimmed with silk and silver ribbons and silver lace, *c.* 1665. Edinburgh, Royal Scottish Museum

573 G. SOEST: *John, Second Marquis of Tweeddale, c.* 1665. Edinburgh, National Galleries of Scotland. (Photo Ideal Studio)

574 G. GHISLANDI: *Count Girolamo Secco Suardo*, 1721. Bergamo, Accademia Carrara. (Museum photo)

DEVELOPMENT OF WOMEN'S COSTUME IN THE TIME OF LOUIS XIII

567–8 Women's costume also became simplified; the farthingale disappeared; a soft collar replaced the ruff and standing collar; the paned padded sleeves of the undergown are tied at elbow height; the black gown skirt opens over the light-coloured underskirt, called the *friponne* (plate 567). Plate 568 shows a still simpler fashion, with a wide, closed cape collar, three-quarter sleeves with turned-back cuffs, and hair dressed in ringlets; the folded fan has replaced the feather flywhisk

COSTUME IN THE TIME OF LOUIS XIV. THE DEVELOPMENT OF PETTICOAT BREECHES

569–70, 577–8 The baroque, heavily-laden effect that characterized costume at the beginning of the reign of Louis XIV is reflected in the fashion for *rhinegraves* or *petticoat breeches*, whose very wide legs formed a sort of skirt shape, and which became progressively wider. They were worn over loose, puffed upper hose, which were to remain as a last survival of petticoat breeches after their disappearance, when they were replaced by the *justaucorps* (plate 570). Butterfly bows replaced shoe-roses (plate 569)

SURVIVING PETTICOAT BREECHES

571–2 These precious specimens enable us to appreciate the width of petticoat breeches, trimmed with ribbons known as *gallants* or *brandons;* the very short doublet *en brassière* allowed the shirt to puff out; the shirt sleeves also showed beyond the short jacket sleeves; the jacket and breeches were trimmed with the same ribbons

PETTICOAT BREECHES IN EUROPE

573–5, 579–80 In these portraits we can see the extravagance of the *petites oies*, the enormous lace *canons* round the legs, baldricks or fringed scarves (plates 573, 574), and enormous wigs, which in England were fluffy (plate 573)

FASHION AT THE BEGINNING OF THE REIGN OF LOUIS XIV

576 The simple character of fashions is worth emphasizing: women wore plain gowns trimmed with embroidery, with a fairly wide lace collar over the shoulders and moderately wide three-quarter sleeves; there was no special bridal costume.

Men wear petticoat breeches, military cloaks, high-crowned hats trimmed with hat-ribbon (*bourdalou*) and draped stockings. Barrel-topped ladrines are worn with matching boot hose. Women wore hanging feathers known as *guirlandes* on their heads

575 J. VAN NOORDT: *Young Lord*, 1665. Lyons, Museum. (Photo Bulloz)

576 TENIERS: *The Painter's Marriage*, 1651.
Collection E. Ivens. (Photo Swaebe)

577 ANON: *Louis XIV Visiting the Grotto of Thetis*, c. 1675.
Versailles, Museum. (Photo Flammarion)

terie and embroidery and were dotted with ribbon bows known as *galans*. The overgown, in rich stuff, became the *manteau*; it was held up on either side in front by large bows of ribbon and was finished behind by a train whose length indicated the rank of the wearer.

The *boned bodice* was stiff, tight-fitting and lengthened in front into a point; the short, full sleeves showed the chemise sleeves, which were likewise full and finished with lace flounces.

As in the preceding period, women of the middle and lower classes still wore their skirts caught up over an underskirt.

We know little of women's cloaks during this period: it seems that the type principally worn was a short, scarf-shaped tippet with a detachable hood. In winter, women wore gowns lined with a material called *panne* and carried muffs. The fur tie appeared in 1676 when the Princess Palatine 'thought, during the cold weather, of wearing an old sable to keep her throat warm, and now everyone is wearing furs like it.' (Letter dated 12 December, 1676)

In 1672 the *Mercure Galant* noted that Perdrigeon, the famous merchant who supplied the court, launched the fashion for Chinese silk stockings 'whose patterns were the most charming in the world'. A similar vogue for things Turkish led the manufacturers of Rouen, Lyons and Sedan to seek inspiration in Ottoman costumes for the decoration of their materials.

FASHIONS FROM 1675 TO 1705

The strict ceremonial patiently built up by Louis XIV limited the extent of individual caprice in dress and influenced fashion in general. The disappearance of petticoat breeches towards 1678 marked the end of a period of splendour and pleasures: order, majesty and solemnity were thenceforth to reign.

After the King's marriage to Madame de Maintenon, a note of gravity was to be added, and La Bruyère noted its effects in 1682: 'Formerly a courtier had his own hair, wore doublet and breeches and wide cannons and was a libertine. This is no longer in favour: now he has a wig, a tight suit and plain stockings and he is fervently religious.' Gone were light colours, masses of ribbons, plumes and points; now long, severe, buttoned justaucorps, tight breeches and dark stockings were worn; gone was lace, except on the cravat and sleeves; gone were plumes, except for hats and, rarely, as edgings; at the end of the century the cravat itself had given place to a simple neck ribbon, the *chaconne*.

In this climate of rigid dignity the justaucorps found a propitious climate for its development and spread. It was generally made of French broadcloth – in 1687 striped stuff from Sedan, imposed by the King – or of brocade or velvet for ceremonial occasions.

The change in pockets which, originally vertical, now became horizontal, is difficult to date: the year most generally mentioned is 1684, although pages' costume had had horizontal pockets since 1674, and even at the end of the century we still see long, vertical pockets.

While the form of women's gowns had changed little, their decoration tended to become heavy at the beginning of the last third of the century, lightening once more shortly after. In a stiff, affected style, their neckline was always rectilinear, and an unusual trimming then came suddenly into fashion: *prétintailles*, motifs cut out of different coloured materials and appliquéd to the fronts of gowns; this fashion seems to have been exclusively French. The overgown was caught up higher

578 VAN DER MEULEN: *Louis XIV receiving Swiss Ambassadors*, 1663. Versailles, Museum. (Photo Flammarion)

579 M. WRIGHT: *John Granville, Earl of Bath, c.* 1663. Collection The Duke of Sutherland. (Photo Ideal Studio)

than before, thus changing the silhouette, which was loaded with deep flounces or *falbalas*.

But softer gowns were already making their appearance, known variously as *Innocentes*, *battantes*, *déshabillées*, *négligées* or *robes de chambre*. They are supposed to have been invented by Madame de Montespan to hide her pregnancies; they were adopted by many women and were admitted to Court, and we can see them in the drawings and engravings of Bernard Picart (plate 610). They presage the lighter styles of the following century,[5] although they were still very different in form, for the transformation of women's costume, which took place later than the change in men's costume, only showed after 1705. The main characteristic of these new gowns was their fitted back; they covered the shoulders, accentuating a square neckline highlighted by the lace or linen flounce of the chemise, and had flat sleeves with a turn-back on the inside of the forearm from which the lace or lawn *engageante* fell loosely. Oval necklines and very short sleeves were – and were to remain so during part of the eighteenth century – the prerogative of Court costume.

The vogue these new fashions enjoyed clearly shows the nature of a society that already lived on the fringe of Versailles, composed of a younger generation from new *milieux*, from the worlds of finance or commerce, with freer ways, less encumbered with court obligations, intent more on finding their own pleasure than on submitting to the sovereign's authority. This development of French costume at the beginning of the eighteenth century reflects a social revolution, in which the Court was giving place to 'Society'.

It is in this change of spirit and taste that we must seek for the causes of changes in costume, and of the new fashions that were to typify the eighteenth century.

Costume Accessories

In the seventeenth century the accessory details of costume took on an importance and diversity which make it necessary to study them separately.

580 GERARD TER BORCH: *Man in Black, c.* 1673. Paris, Louvre. (Photo Flammarion)

581–3 BONNART: Male costumes, 1693–5. Paris, Bib. Nat., Cabinet des Estampes. (Photos Flammarion)

584 *The Princesse de Conti*, c. 1682. Paris, Bibliothèque Nationale. (Photo Flammarion)

585 J. D. DE SAINT-JEAN: *Woman walking in the Country*, c. 1675. Paris, Bib. Nat., Cabinet des Estampes. (Photo Flammarion)

HEAD-DRESSES

At the end of the sixteenth century the Renaissance cap, in its varied forms, remained in fashion for men, as did the Spanish hat with its high, round crown pinched in at one side. The plumed Albanian hat popularized by Henri IV was followed under Louis XIII by soft, low-crowned, broad-brimmed hats since known as Musketeer hats. Crowns were round and changed shape when pulled on the oval of the head, to give the characteristic wavy, upturned brim. These hats were trimmed with long, standing or flat ostrich plumes. There were also simpler styles, with the crown edged with twisted braid called *bourdalou*. A sort of two-visored cap known in France as a *boukinkan* (a corruption of *Buckingham*) was English in origin and worn mainly by soldiers.

After the Thirty Years' War, a broad, soft hat worn aslant with plumes tossing in the wind was adopted by the greater part of the armies of Europe: this was the grey felt hat worn by peasants during the Renaissance, later prohibited for farmers. After passing into military costume, it returned to civilian dress.

In Germany this so-called Swedish hat took on extraordinary forms, while Holland adopted a simpler model, retaining the black colour of Spain. In England, Cromwellian Puritans, hoping to re-establish the austerity of the Reformed Church, rejected flowing locks and wavy hats in favour of the stiffer, cylindrical black felt. This Puritan hat was taken to America by the Mayflower emigrants and in time came to be considered typically American. In the following century, with the War of Independence, it won a new lease of life in Europe and became to some extent a symbol of liberty.

Under Louis XIV the wearing of wigs made hats useless accessories; gentlemen wore them rarely, but were obliged by polite custom to carry them under their arms: thus the crown became lower and the wide brims were raised back and front. This led to the bicorne or tricorne hat in 'grey-white' or 'matt black' beaver, trimmed with a flat plume and a broad, embroidered ribbon, as we still see in the drawings and paintings of Watteau.

HAIRSTYLES

At the beginning of the seventeenth century women still wore a tiny chaperon or a silk coif; widows remained faithful to the chaperon with a point in the centre of the forehead and a smaller conch than that worn in the preceding period. However, the hair was flatter: a fringe, the *garcette*, hung over the forehead, with two crimped puffs or *bouffons* over the ears and the rest of the hair plaited and rolled into a chignon at the back. Towards the end of the reign of Louis XIV the hair, arranged in a crimped roll or *rond*,[1] formed a bowed hoop; sometimes a lock known as a *moustache* was allowed to escape, tied with a ribbon. Then hair again became flat and the puffs were replaced by long locks or *serpentaux*.

Varyingly crimped serpentaux and puffs continued until about 1670. Then a new hairstyle, the *hurlupée* or *hurluberlu* ('scatterbrain') was all the rage for several years: this was a simple mass of hair. 'It gives you a head like a cabbage,' wrote Madame de Sévigné.

Finally, towards 1678, the *Fontanges* hairstyle appeared. Originally a simple bow lifting the curled hair to the top of the head, it was transformed into a complex scaffolding of locks completed with a cap that crowned the head in a veritable architecture of muslin, lace and ribbons mounted on brass wire. This fashion lasted for thirty years despite criticism and even royal disfavour.[8]

During the reign of Henri IV, no doubt in reaction against the crimped hairstyles adopted under Henri III, men wore their hair loose; it was only with Louis XIII that elegant men's hair, parted in the centre, was to fall in curls to the shoulders; one lock, the *moustache*, was combed forward and took the name *cadenette* when the brother of the Duc de Luynes, the Marquis de Cadenet, had the idea of tying it with a ribbon bow decorated with a gem.

But when the King lost all his hair as the result of an illness, about 1633, a new accessory appeared, the *wig*, initially limited to switches mingled with the wearer's own hair, then complete. In fact it was then worn only in cases of necessity, and old men wore the *tour*, a round skull-cap to which hair was sewn. Nat-

586 *Lady at the Harpsichord*, c. 1688. Paris, Bib. Nat., Cabinet des Estampes. (Photo Flammarion)

587 BONNART: *Lady and Gentleman Walking*, c. 1693. Paris, Bib. Nat., Cabinet des Estampes. (Photo Flammarion)

588 Gown of blue and silver wool, of English origin, c. 1690. New York, Metropolitan Museum. (Museum photo)

589 GOHERT: *The Duchesse de Bourgogne*, c. 1709. Versailles, Museum. (Museum photo)

THE DEVELOPMENT OF MEN'S COSTUME AT THE END OF THE SEVENTEENTH CENTURY

581–3 The justaucorps is generally worn over a vest (plate 582). The *habit d'agrément* (informal suit) is worn without waistcoat (plate 581). The *Steinkerck cravat* is negligently knotted and passed through a buttonhole (plate 582). The increasingly large cuffs are buttoned to the sleeves. The wig, initially left to fall freely at the back (plate 581), is brought forward over the shoulders to become an *in-folio* wig (plate 582). The justaucorps with full-length buttoned revers is *à la tékéli* (plate 583). The fur muff is attached to a ribbon called a *passacaglia*. Stockings have embroidered clocks; Brandenburg trimmings appear after 1674 (plate 582). Pockets, slit vertically until 1690, were soon horizontal, with flaps (plates 582, 583). The shoes with straps fastened by buckles are *à la cavalière*, and the flat-crowned hats with upturned brims are trimmed with feathers round the edge

THE DEVELOPMENT OF WOMEN'S COSTUME

584–8 The general line of women's costume was not to change during the reign of Louis XIV: a cote bodice over a stiff boned bodice that reached below the waist, a wide neckline showing the lace of the chemise whose sleeves can also be seen below the gown sleeves; the front piece may be decorated with a jewel known as a *boute-en-train* or *'tâtez-y'* (lit.: 'touch here'). The skirt visible below the caught-up overgown, could be decorated with *prétintailles* (plate 587), adorned with fringes and passementerie. The gown in striped *Siamoise* (plate 585), the mask carried at the belt, the parasol, a new invention (plate 585), the small ladies' cuff decorated with ribbons, the *mouche*, *assassine* or *passionnée* (patch) at the corner of the eye (plate 587), worn by women and men alike, were all elegant accoutrements

HUNTING COSTUME

589 For hunting, women wore a costume copied from male dress; a braided justaucorps open over a brocade waistcoat, a cravat with a ribbon bow and a tricorne hat

WOMEN'S HEAD-DRESSES

590–601 After the puffed hairstyle (cf. plate 553), then ringlets (plate 568) came the *hurluberlu* (scatterbrain) or *hurlupée* hairstyle (plate 590). Towards 1682–3 we begin to see the ribbon bow *à la Fontanges* on the top of the head, also known as the *duchesse*, soon to be replaced by the *sultana* style (plate 591), c. 1685–6, with the scarf of *crapaudaille* or striped Siamese stuff (plate 586). Ribbon bows multiply among the lace flounces on the top of the head: c. 1688 they form the *culebutte*. The Fontanges cap takes on different forms: when it reveals the ears, (plate 598) it is *effrontée* (shameless), while the kiss-curls on the brow are *fripons* or *guigne-galants*. Towards 1695 the construction is tall and narrow, fairly light, with long *cornets* flowing over the nape of the neck (plates 595, 596) and *guêpes* and *papillons* (lit.: wasps and butterflies) in precious stones set in the hair (plates 599, 601). At the end of the century the Fontanges style took on the *palissade* form (plate 600), wide and forward-tilted. However, it is difficult to follow the development of a fashion which included innumerable variants and whose vocabulary differs from author to author. Patches emphasize the whiteness of the face, which is also excessively painted

590–601 Engravings by BONNART, TROUVAIN and J. D. DE SAINT-JEAN (details). Paris, Bib. Nat., Cabinet des Estampes. (Photos Flammarion)

ural and curled hairstyles remained in vogue, and, though a *hair wig* figured in the Cing-Mars inventory, the manufacture of wigs for purposes of fashion became general only towards 1655. For a long time Louis XIV, who had fine curly hair, refused to sacrifice it and at first accepted only wigs through which he could pass his own hair. However, in 1672 he resigned himself to wearing a *natural hair wig*, for which he had to shave his head.

After 1680 the wig took on monumental proportions, which decreased only towards the end of the century. Generally made *in-folio* or *full-bottomed* (originally *à crinière*) with tiers of curls falling over the shoulders and back, it later stood up in two points in the Fontanges style; later, divided into three tufts with one on either side, it was known as the *binette*, after its inventor, the Sieur Binet. Wigs were made in a wide range of colours, particularly among courtiers; they were dusted with starch or Cyprus powder.

The professions adopted the wig, which compensated for their lack of the sword prescribed for everyone who entered the Royal household except magistrates and the clergy.

Colbert, worried by the quantity of hair bought from abroad, thought of prohibiting wigs, but France sold wigs in so great a quantity to the whole of Europe that exports amply made up for import expenditure. From 1703 to 1715 they were subject to taxation. The art of wigmakers became truly creative, and in 1678 the *Mercure de France* presented two models designed by Bérain and made by a certain Evain, half crimped and half curled, and admirably light.

We know that wigs appeared in Venice in 1665,[9] and that they were forbidden by an edict of the Council of Ten in 1668, but reappeared later. The women of the Roman Ghetto had already worn wigs for a long time.

NECKWEAR

The ruff survived for a little while after the death of Henri IV, in the form of the soft, falling ruff, together with the *carcan*, a semi-circular standing collar mounted on a metal frame.

606 FRANS HALS: *Aletta Hanemans*, 1625. The Hague, Mauritshuis. (Museum photo)

607 VAN DER MAES: *Standard-Bearer of the Civil Guard*, 1615. The Hague, Gemeentemuseum. (Museum photo)

608 DIRK HALS: *Meeting in an Inn, c.* 1630 (detail). Collection H. Leroux. (Photo Flammarion)

In the Louis XIII period it was replaced by the falling collar, a flat collar decorated with lace and following the line of the neck by means of graded tucks; this collar was worn narrow by ecclesiastics, from which came the nickname *petit collet*, which stuck to them and which bears no relation to the cloak collar, as some authors seem to have believed.

After the beginning of the reign of Louis XIV this flat collar which, like all costume, had been simplified over the preceding twenty-five years where size and trimmings were concerned, once more expanded and changed its shape, becoming shorter at the sides and longer in front. It was tied under the chin by two or four cords ending in tassels, generally visible through the front opening.

Linen cuffs or *rebras* matching the collar were folded back over the edge of the sleeves.

The appearance of the cravat more or less coincided with that of the justaucorps; it was already worn by soldiers, simply knotted and hanging loosely. Civilian costume gave it greater variety and imagination, with panels of rich lace and a fairly full butterfly bow of ribbon under the chin. Cravats were made ready-tied, mounted on a ribbon which was fastened at the back of the neck. According to tradition, on the day of the Battle of Steenkerck in 1692, the officers were surprised by the enemy attack, and had no time to tie their cravats. So they hurriedly wound them round their necks, pushing the ends through the sixth buttonhole of their coats. Whether the story is true or false, the fashion lasted until the very end of the century and was even adopted by women for hunting costume.

At the beginning of the century, tall starched collars spreading out in a fan shape round the head were worn by women; this fashion lasted as long as the vogue for the farthingale. Towards 1640 this style was followed by a flat collar that increasingly bared the breasts, sometimes accompanied by a light guimp; otherwise it was itself covered by a knotted kerchief. In 1645 the starched collar disappeared and the linen closely followed the line of the shoulders: at first it formed a large kerchief folded diagonally and tightly tied in front, then, towards 1650, a flat flounce which, with variations, lasted until the end of the century, edging the deep décolletage associated for the first

COSTUME AT THE END OF THE REIGN OF LOUIS XIV

602–5 While forms changed little, new details appeared: coat revers were sometimes partly covered by waistcoat revers. Wigs had Fontanges fronts, and shoes had red heels: coats were trimmed with Brandenburg braid, frogged in a new style. The cravat was still tied in Steinkerck style, ending in tassels that could be passed through the buttonhole (plate 605, right). The young Duc de Bretagne is still in long clothes and his governess, Mme de Ventadour, holds him on leading-strings; she wears a black gown with fastenings and bracelets of precious stones; her black lace Fontanges head-dress is less tall than those worn previously

LACE IN FRANCE

603–4, 614–5 The taste for lace, particularly for Venetian lace, had become widespread in France since the end of the sixteenth century. Sumptuary edicts had not succeeded in limiting the resultant expenditure. In 1666 Colbert opened the first lace factories, and the masterpieces they produced soon competed with the products of other countries

SPANISH INFLUENCE ON WOMEN'S COSTUME

606, 617, 621 Spanish influence can be recognized in the dark colour of the *vlieger*, derived from the Spanish *ropa* (plate 606). A richly decorated stomacher adorns the front of the gown, as in the Spanish Netherlands (plates 552, 564); the skirt is supported by the *fardegalijn* or farthingale (plate 617). The *millstone ruff* was never as thick as in Flanders; it could be decorated with lace, as were the cuffs and the head-hugging cap (plates 606, 621). The shoulder rolls trimmed with passementerie were *bragoonen*

SPANISH INFLUENCE ON MEN'S COSTUME

607 Costume gradually breaks free from Spanish influence: it adopts loose, full breeches, fringed, ribboned garters, rosettes on shoes and round collars: the broad military sash ends in long fringes

COSTUME IN HOLLAND TOWARDS 1630

608, 618–9 Surviving garments can be compared with those shown in paintings: the cavalier's casaque and leather waistcoats known as buff jerkins, soft hats with fox-tail plumes, soft breeches buttoned down the side, trimmed with ribbons, doublets with deep skirts, cut with long sashes as in France, and falling collars and soft ruffs

COURT COSTUME

609 The justaucorps in rich material is sometimes braided down the seams. Chamillart (seen from the back) wears the plain grey costume of Secretary of State. Wigs are for the most part *in-folio* or *mane wigs*; several of the cravats are Steinkerck style, passed through buttonholes; hats have plumes and shoes are *à la cavalière*

265

609 TROUVAIN: *The Apartments at Versailles.*
Late seventeenth century.
Paris, Bib. Nat., Cabinet des Estampes. (Photo Giraudon)

610 BERNARD PICART: *Couple*, 1708.
Oxford, Ashmolean Museum.
(Museum photo)

611-2 Lyons silks: dress brocades with polychrome brocaded
decoration. Late seventeenth century.
Lyons, Musée Historique des Tissus. (Museum photos)

613 TROUVAIN: *Mme de Soissons
in 'robe de chambre'*, 1685. Paris,
Bibliothèque Nationale, Cabinet des
Estampes. (Photo Flammarion)

time with day gowns. Sometimes the neckline was highlighted
only by the narrow flounce edging the chemise.

FOOTWEAR

With Henri IV, *eschappins* and *pianelles* disappeared and shoes
developed more solid forms, which were to stay in fashion without major change for most of the century: they were fastened
on the instep with a bow, then with a buckle and finally, under
Louis XIII, with ribbon or gauze roses. Their toes were first
rounded, then long and pointed; they were raised on heels,
probably inspired by Venetian chopines, which won them the
name *draw-bridge shoes.*

At the beginning of the century fashion still favoured boots,
Henri IV sent a skilful tanner to Hungary to study the special
way leather was prepared in Central Europe and bring back
the secret, which had been lost in France in the preceding century. The industry of *hongroyeurs* revived and the production
of soft boots met with such success that boots were even admitted in salons and ballrooms in 1608. A leather flap, the *surpied*, covered the instep, held in place by the *soulette*, a strap
fastened under the foot, which also held the spur in position.
These boots were high: the funnel top covered the knee
for riding and could be turned down for town wear. Under
Louis XIII a shorter, lighter model of boot was known as the
ladrine.

At the beginning of the reign of Louis XIII, boots were only
acceptable for riding. A Gascon shoemaker by the name of
Lestage won himself a universal reputation by making the first
seamless boot in 1663.

Towards 1652 fashion turned towards pointed shoes. Twenty
years later, they became square-toed again, and heels became
higher, probably because Louis XIV wanted to increase his own
height. In the early years of his reign he had the heels of his
shoes covered in red leather and courtiers hastened to imitate
him; in England red heels and welts had been worn since the
beginning of the seventeenth century. Between 1670 and 1680
buckles replaced bows on the instep.

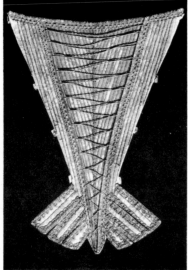

616 Stomacher in pink taffeta with decoration in silver cord forming a gourgandine. Late seventeenth century. Collection Fulgence. (Photo Flammarion)

619 Dalmatic worn by Casimir of Nassau, c. 1630. Amsterdam, Rijksmuseum. (Museum photo)

615 French lace (*point de France*). Late seventeenth century. New York, Cooper Union Museum for the Arts of Decoration. (Museum photo)

617 DIRK HALS: *Flemish Lady*, c. 1620. Manchester, University, Whitworth Art Gallery. (Photo Norris)

618 Doublet and breeches worn by Gustavus Adolphus, 1627. Stockholm, Royal Armoury. (Museum photo)

THE APPEARANCE OF A SOFT GOWN FOR WOMEN

610, 613 The origin of the soft, flowing gown which was to be fashionable under the Régence should probably be sought in the indoor gown or gowns *à l'Innocente* which were not déshabillés, but simply unstiffened gowns. The style becomes simpler: the laced bodice or *gourgandine* has no longer the rigidity of the old corps; skirts and mantles are still richly decorated (plate 613) but were later to be simplified (plate 610). The inspiration of these gowns is attributed to Madame de Maintenon, who wore them to conceal her condition when she was pregnant

LYONS SILKS IN THE SEVENTEENTH CENTURY

611-2 The technical quality of the Lyons silk-weaving shows in these materials with rich, complex floral motifs; the background is often cream and the decoration multicoloured; at the end of the seventeenth century lighter designs were adopted. Their average width is 20 to 23 inches

EMBROIDERY IN THE SEVENTEENTH CENTURY

613 Embroidery was less widely practised in France than in England; brocaded materials did not lend themselves to this type of ornament; however corded embroidery and gold and silver thread enrich plain silks and velvets

THE CORPS PIQUÉ

620 The *corps piqué* was a strongly boned outer bodice, normally lined with strong linen, which showed through the front opening of the gown.

---

621 SALOMON MESDACH: *Anna Bouden Courten*, 1619. Amsterdam, Rijksmuseum. (Museum photo)

620 Boned bodice in mauve silk with appliquéd white ribbon and multi-coloured fringe trimming on the sleeves. Late seventeenth or early eighteenth centuries. Honfleur, Museum, Collection Louveau. (Museum photo)

622　HONTHORST (School of): *William II of Orange and his wife Mary Stuart, c.* 1650. The Hague, Gemeentemuseum. (Museum photo)

623　DANIEL MYTENS: *First Duke of Hamilton,* 1629. Collection The Duke of Hamilton. (Photo Tom Scott)

624　VAN DYCK: *Henrietta of Lorraine,* 1634. (By permission of the Trustees of the Iveagh Bequest, Kenwood, London)

625　G. NETSCHER: *Young Girl, c.* 1660. Collection H. Leroux. (Photo Flammarion)

PETTICOAT BREECHES IN HOLLAND

622, 633　As in France, the width of petticoat breeches decorated with ribbon fringes increased (plate 622). They were worn with a short doublet, with draped stockings and linen boot hose or vast canons ending the breeches

MEN'S COSTUME IN BRITAIN AT THE BEGINNING OF THE SEVENTEENTH CENTURY

623, 626　The remains of the Elizabethan fashions are eliminated from male costume of the Charles I period, which was very close to contemporary French styles: long-slashed doublet, breeches fastened with points tied at the waist; falling collars (plate 623). The long, soft tight-fitting boots are an English style, as are the long-gauntleted gloves, whose overlong fingers were padded (plate 626)

WOMEN'S COSTUME IN HOLLAND

625　As in France, young women wore medium width three-quarter sleeves, dark gowns caught up over light underskirts. The linen guimp is more typically Dutch

626　DANIEL MYTENS (School of): *Henry Rich, First Earl of Holland,* 1640. London, National Portrait Gallery. (Photo Freeman)

Women's shoes were inspired by men's styles, but with much higher heels, originally straight; they were often made of brocaded silk or velvet. Some leather shoes were decorated with silk embroidery; we know of others in silver-embroidered velvet, even for men, under Louis XIV.

GLOVES, BELTS, ETC.

The luxury of gloves, which was already noticeable in the sixteenth century, became even greater under Louis XIII. They were generally imported from Spain, made of soft skins with deep, flaring gauntlets covered with embroidery, known as

Henry Rich Earl of
H........l

627 D. SANTVOORT: *Burgomeister Dirk Bas Jacobs and his Family*, 1635. Amsterdam, Rijksmuseum. (Museum photo)

628 Broadcloth suit: long breeches and loose jacket with applied silver trimming, 1635. Copenhagen, Rosenborg Castle. (Museum photo)

crispins, and were often scented. Their varied names corresponded to the perfumes with which they were impregnated. Common people wore mittens or mitts (*moufles*), gloves in which only the thumbs were separated.

Another luxury was the embroidered, pierced, braided or fringed baldrick, which replaced the sword-belt worn at the beginning of the century; the sword was fastened with four buckles. However the baldrick suffered eclipses in the course of the century: seldom worn at the time of petticoat breeches, it reappeared with the justaucorps, and towards 1675–1680 reached large dimensions accentuated by heavy decoration; towards 1684 it once more gave way to the sword-belt.

Men showed studied negligence in knotting scarves in *point d'Espagne*, embroidered net, then fringed silk over their justaucorps, with the ends falling over the hip. At the time of the last baldricks, the richness and variety of these scarves had reached its peak, and their vogue lasted until the end of the reign of Louis XIV.

Costume was completed, for gentlemen, with walking-sticks and swords, originally hung obliquely from the baldrick, then fastened to the sash under the justaucorps. In winter, all elegant people adopted the plush or fur muff, fastened to the waist by the *passacaille*. Women wore – often to excess – patches, the names of which varied according to their shape and their position on the face. The mask, which was held in place by a button gripped between the teeth or by a thin handle pushed into the hair, protected the complexion or preserved the wearer's incognito.

Fashion Trades and Publications

The tailor's trade had been carried on in seventeenth-century France in conditions that had changed little since the Middle Ages. The rich, powerful corporations were still subject to severe prescriptions, strictly limiting individual initiative and excluding any worker who did not belong to their ranks. They stood as guarantors for the craftsmen, at the same time developing their own corporate powers.

Over the centuries, however, they lost part of their power. The authorities saw them only as a source of revenue: in 1690, tailors were forced to accept foreigners among their number or buy back their posts at high prices.

Only in 1655 were 'suit tailors and master doubleteers and hosiery merchants' united in one corporation, each category producing one part of clothing. Their continual rivalry led men's tailors to separate from women's tailors, who were from then on entitled only to make women's clothes. Female workers in the tailoring trade were not authorized to form their own corporation until 1667, and then only because of the support of influential women customers: their work was limited to undergarments and clothes for boys under eight years of age. Not until a century later were they to have the right to make all parts of women's clothing.

Numerous collections of fashion engravings were published between 1600 and 1670, devoted mainly to the ancient and modern costumes of Europe, but also showing clothing from various other parts of the world; they followed the great work of Vecellio printed in Venice in 1590.

In 1671 the only technical treatise devoted to the cut and sewing of costumes appeared in France: this was Benoît Boullay's *Le Tailleur Sincère*, whose authority remained considerable even in the following century. In 1678 the *Mercure Galant* by Donneau and Vizé began the periodic publication of fashion articles and engravings.[11]

During the last quarter of the century, a group of print-sellers in Paris published fashion engravings often grouped together in spurious series; most of them were portraits of prominent figures at Court and in Parisian society, while others were genuine fashion plates. They are all of considerable value for the study of French costume under Louis XIV, and it is indispensable to consult them in the corpus of engravings by Saint-Jean (plate 585), Arnoult, Picart, among others, and above all by the Bonnart family (plates 543, 581–3, 587).[12]

629 Suit worn by Prince Christian of Denmark, brocaded cloth; long breeches and loose jacket, c. 1634. Copenhagen, Rosenborg Castle. (Museum photo)

630 Circular cape in brocaded cloth, 1630-35. Copenhagen, Rosenborg Castle. (Museum photo)

631 Suit worn by Gustavus X, embroidered in gold, 1650. Stockholm, Royal Armoury. (Museum photo)

632 GERARD TER BORCH: *Portrait of the Artist's Brother Moses Ter Borch, c.* 1665-6. New York, Historical Society

Costume in Holland and England

The extraordinary rise of Dutch trade had begun with the exodus of merchants fleeing from the Spanish invasion of the Southern Netherlands in the last years of the sixteenth century; Flemish capital flowed out of Antwerp and was placed in Amsterdam. Oriented towards the Levant and Guinea and Indonesia, and even towards America, Dutch traders organized themselves into powerful companies and reaped immense profits, enriching a matter-of-fact bourgeoisie that surrounded itself with opulence and luxury. In this class, which held the administration and fortunes of the country in its hands, a new style of costume took shape.[13]

At the beginning of the century some features of Spanish Renaissance women's costume – straight bodice and farthingale – were preserved more strikingly in Holland than in France: the *ropa* became the *vlieger*, a full, open-fronted garment. The front part of the bodice, which was richly decorated and embroidered, formed a bowed curve in front, highly fashionable from 1620 to 1635. The gown opened down the front and was sometimes caught up to show the petticoat: it tended to broaden the general outline. The traditional local head-dress was often supported on a metal hoop. Men still wore Spanish doublets, short trunk hose and later long, loose breeches, and wide-brimmed or cylindrical hats.

As in France, Dutch men's costume showed a very noticeable change between 1620 and 1635, and this gradually spread over the rest of Europe: doublets became shorter and tighter and short breeches supplanted the old *trousses* and trunk hose. These breeches progressively lengthened to give the silhouette a long, vertical line finished off by moderately flaring boots. The cloak was still worn, but as a cape.

About the same time women's costume became more slim and elegant. It discarded the last details of Spanish costume that had been preserved during the first quarter of the century: the ruff, the straight, stiff bodice, the farthingale (in Dutch, *fardegalijn*) and the bell skirt, adopting instead the plain standing or falling collar which still covered the throat, the full,

FRENCH INFLUENCE ON DUTCH AND NORTHERN COSTUME

627-30 In Holland, older people remained faithful to the black costume of the Regents, with plain ruff, *vlieger* and diadem head-dress, while their children wore garments similar to those worn in France, as shown by excellent specimens preserved in Denmark: longer, narrower breeches, full casaques (plates 627-9), long-basqued doublets, and falling collars trimmed with lace, as were the cuffs and boot hose (plate 627). Young women wore high-waisted gowns, with ribbon rosettes and overgown sleeves slashed (plate 627, right) or slit for convenience (plate 627, left). The wearing of several superimposed cape collars is typical of these new fashions; the hairstyles have simple ornaments

633 PIETER DE HOOGH: *Skittle Players,* 1660. St Louis, Missouri, City Art Gallery. (Museum photo)

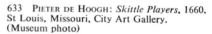

634 ANON: *Margaret Hamilton*, *c*. 1630. Edinburgh, National Portrait Gallery. (Photo Annan)

635 ANON: *Mary, Daughter of Henry Edgar*, 1633. Ipswich, Museum. (Museum photo)

636 JOHN TRADESCANT: *Portrait of the Artist's Wife and Son*, 1645. Oxford, Ashmolean Museum. (Museum photo)

637 HONTHORST: *The Countess of Devonshire and her Children*, 1628. Devonshire Collection, Chatsworth. (Reproduced by permission of the Trustees of the Chatsworth Settlement)

638 DAVID DES GRANGES: *The Saltomsall Family*, *c*. 1640–45. Collection Sir Kenneth Clark

WOMEN'S COSTUME IN BRITAIN AT THE BEGINNING OF THE SEVENTEENTH CENTURY

634, 637 French fashions, with some traces of Elizabethan styles, can be seen in the sprays of precious stones in the hair (plate 637), and some typically English features, such as the style of wearing collars caught by a bow in the middle of the bodice: the ribbon that catches in the gown sleeves is known as a *virago*

COSTUME UNDER ITALIAN INFLUENCE

635–6, 638 Before Cromwell seized power, the Puritan spirit shows in costume in the use of dark-coloured broadcloth, and fichus over women's shoulders. Women still wear ruffs, but they are elliptically shaped (plate 635). However, lace had not yet disappeared. The broad-brimmed hats which women wear over their coifs (plate 636) were to pass, along with other elements of Puritan costume, to America with the first English colonists. The young woman in bed (plate 638) wears a nightgown; this garment was gaining in popularity. The man wears a suit with a very short, narrow doublet, *innocent*-style, a specifically English fashion

ELEGANT COSTUME AT THE COURT OF CHARLES I

639–43 We note, in young women's costume, specifically English details: the fichu open over the low-cut bodice, and the short hooded cape for winter wear, the embroidered *secrete* (inner petticoat), with over it the spotted caught-up *friponne*, and the *modeste* carried over the arm.
The mask is typical of the period, as was the sable muff, an indispensable accessory in winter, and the fur cravat, which does not seem to have been worn in France at this time.
The Earl of Pembroke (plate 643) is dressed in French style. His square-collared cloak is, however, a late fashion, unless it is part of the robes of an Order of Chivalry

272

639–42 HOLLAR: *The Four Seasons*, 1643. Paris, Bibliothèque Nationale, Cabinet des Estampes. (Photos Flammarion)

643 *Philip Herbert, Earl of Pembroke, c. 1650.* Paris, Bibliothèque Nationale, Cabinet des Estampes. (Photo Flammarion)

short, high-waisted bodice, three-quarter sleeves and the looser, softer open gown. Several types of cloak were added. One type of Dutch garment never worn in France was the *huik*, a large black veil enveloping the wearer from head to foot, which in Spain became the typical garment of the duenna.

It may be that the main influence of the Netherlands on European costume depended less on basic lines than on the very unusual Dutch linen trimmings. After the toothed edgings that appeared towards the middle of the sixteenth century, *passements dentelés* (toothed braids) were produced in the southern, Flemish provinces, which provided the necessary fine thread and, above all, an astonishingly skilled labour force: after 1585 this industry showed extraordinary activity, permitting the addition of openwork floral or geometrical decoration to the austerity of pure white linen.

The reputation of the Flemish *point en l'air* was already widespread enough at the beginning of the century for Vecellio to show specimens of *punti flammenghi* in his book of models published in 1617. Women then wore spreading collars that stood up in fan-shapes behind the head, as in France. The woven trimmings used to edge head-dresses and cuffs at this time were in the shape of long, loosely designed, sharply pointed teeth: then, towards 1620–25, they became heavier, with a larger, more vigorous palmette decoration more suited to the new mode for plain collars.

In the middle of the century Dutch costume was affected by the caprices and superfluities that were later to show in French clothes: wider, floppy breeches were decorated with bunches of ribbons and the shirt showed between the breeches and doublet and below the doublet's short sleeves. Towards 1660 petticoat breeches appeared in the form of short trousers which could be puffed, or straight and wide. Lastly, the justaucorps was worn mainly by young bloods. Until the beginning of the eighteenth century, French fashions tended to replace Spanish styles for men and women.

This last development took place, however, with a certain delay and without touching the circle of 'regents' and their wives, who remained faithful to more austere traditions in clothing; thus the distinguished middle classes of Holland, who were generally Protestant, retained their predilection for black, even though this was the colour of the 'Spanish Papists'.

ENGLAND

Elizabethan influence on costume lasted until well after the death of the Queen in 1603. While some forms were inspired by the Continent – tight doublets and knee-length *trousses* for men, drum-farthingales and starched fan collars for women – the volume of the silhouette, the richness and stiffness of materials and the heavily loaded decoration kept the character of sixteenth-century modes.

Until about 1620, women still wore embroidered *jackets* and the wide *shernia*, which was draped over the left shoulder.

On the other hand, after 1625 we find virtually the same costume as in France: slashed doublets, Venetians, falling collars for men, and for women coats of a uniform type with the same detail of the gown half-sleeve fastened to the slashed sleeve of the undergown below the inside elbow.

This situation was to continue until about 1650 when Puritan styles, already worn among the middle classes, were imposed on society at large by the austere government of Cromwell. The relationship between Dutch and English costume in this period was more apparent than real. The costumes of the ordinary middle class offered analogies by virtue of their simple lines and colours; however, the costume of the English aristocracy showed a splendour and richness without any equivalent in Holland or perhaps even in French portraits of the period. We should probably interpret this as the continuation of the Elizabethan taste for heavy materials and closely packed ornament.

Historians have claimed that the introduction of French fashions coincided with the return of Charles II in 1666: it is certain that the widening of the fitted garment for men followed, in Great Britain, the French vogue for wider coat-tails permitting greater ease in movement, which were transformed into fan pleats towards 1700. Similarly, women's clothing assimilated a large number of French fashions, particularly in décolletage, after 1660.[14]

Some definite facts allow us to follow the penetration of French fashions into England. After 1630, Queen Marie-Henriette of France wrote to her friend Madame de Saint-George to arrange for Pin the tailor to come to Great Britain to make her bodices and underskirts; then Charles II bought suits in Paris, made by a certain Claude Sourceau, although he already had a tailor, John Allen, in London. The new Queen, Catherine of Braganza, Infanta of Portugal, found that the clothes worn by herself and her retinue were mocked when she arrived in England, where French fashions had become solidly implanted. It is certain that the marriage of Charles II's sister with Monsieur, the brother of the King of France, brought him into closer contact with the French Court and tempted him to imitate its splendour. Moreover, a reaction against Puritan forms set in, bringing an almost excessive penchant for trimmings, accessories and ribbon. The exquisites cultivated a studied negligence; women covered their faces with the patches that were then the rage. All this explains why England was much less receptive than Holland to the influence of the Huguenot manufacturers who settled there after 1685; they did not find the same austere climate in England.

The industrial development then beginning in Western Europe aroused a curious rivalry between England and certain continental countries, which led to the use of surprisingly cynical tactics.

In England, industries devoted to costume materials were established at the beginning of the century, while the new trading companies demonstrated British Maritime supremacy.

Indeed, English traders exported to the Levant, as outgoing freight, materials that were greatly sought after in the East: the rupture between England and the United Provinces was partly due to this competition. Under Cromwell and later under William of Orange, they introduced fine broadcloths to France, where Colbert had them imitated in the new State factories, meanwhile doubling the import tax on English products; English production nonetheless remained cheaper because it was not subject to the strict regulations imposed by Colbert to obtain impeccable products. Cloths known as *londrins*, fine and middle-weight, were copied at Lodève and Carcassonne: 'Ascot style' serge, known as *escot* in France, was made in inferior qualities in Flanders, and plush, panne, taffeta and moire from England were also copied by the textile industries of Picardy and Normandy.

The English government in its turn attracted foreign weavers: in 1685 Flemish refugees were making cottons in Lancashire. In 1690, a French refugee set up a factory for making '*toiles peintes*' in Norwich, which by the beginning of the eighteenth century had acquired a virtual monopoly of spinning and weaving wool. With the development of the cotton industry, a trade in calico, muslins and perses was shortly to appear.

In 1662 Parliament had forbidden the importing of Flemish lace and English merchants tried to attract Flemish weavers to work in England, but the attempt failed as English flax did not provide a suitable quality of thread. To provide the Court with the lace it demanded, merchants smuggled in Flemish lace, which they sold as *point d'Angleterre*. Once we realize that a boat inspected in 1678 provided almost 800,000 ells of lace, not including all the pieces of linen trimmed with *point de Bruxelles*, we see how such a traffic could win a lasting reputation for a *point d'Angleterre* which in reality was no such thing.

The knitting machine, invented by the Rev. William Lee, had been refused by Elizabeth and tried out unsuccessfully in France by Henri IV; Lee died in poverty in Paris in 1610. How-

ever, this industry began to develop in the Midlands, aided by the import of cotton from the East Indies.

It was in order to support English industry that, towards 1666, as Evelyn notes in his *Diary*, Charles II agreed to abandon the over-luxurious French fashions in favour of a new, purely national style of clothing; a sort of tunic, worn with a 'Persian'-inspired jacket, as it was called at first. But this attempt failed: so many changes were made to the original model that almost all its English character had disappeared a few years later, under the influence of the victorious French fashions.[15]

Costume in the Rest of Europe

CENTRAL AND NORTHERN EUROPE

Between 1590 and 1620, from the North Sea to the Vistula, from Stockholm to Budapest, the costume of the wealthier classes retained elements of Spanish clothing: the farthingale, the stiff bodice and the ruff. The curious portrait of the Countess of Neuburg painted by Hans Werl in about 1613 (plate 656) shows the prolongation of this influence due to the support of the Imperial court and Hispano-Austrian marriages. On the other hand, the second quarter of the century saw the rise of the influence of French and Dutch costume among the richer classes; the lower classes in town and country kept the main features of sixteenth-century costume, with regional characteristics that were more marked towards the East.

The fashion engravings of Wenzel Hollar (plates 639–42) in Germany, the Low Countries and England, the prints of the Dutch de Hoogh and the paintings of Kneller in England and Gaspar Netscher in Germany (plate 625) showed that in all these countries costumes differed little: for women the main garment was the plain, shimmering satin gown, loose and high-

644 ANON: *The Empress Marie of Hungary*, c. 1613. New York, Hispanic Society of America

645 LUCRINA FETTI: *The Empress Eleonora Gonzaga*, 1622.
Mantua, Palazzo Ducale. (Photo Calzolari)

646 ANON: *Sophie de la Gardie*, 1643. Stockholm, Nordiska Museet.
(Museum photo)

647 M. C. HIERT: *Margareth Bromsen*, 1641. Lübeck, Saint Anne Museum. (Photo Castelli)

648 ANON: *Princess Magdalena Sybilla*, c. 1635. Copenhagen, Rosenborg Castle. (Museum photo)

Right: 654 Man's suit in slashed grey si[l]
doublet with deep basques, short breech[es]
and cape. Early seventeenth centur[y]
London, Victoria and Albert Museu[m]

649 L. SCHUNEMAN: *John Leslie, First Duke of Rothes*, 1667. Edinburgh, National Portrait Gallery

650 Jacket (short doublet), silk-embroidered linen, *c*. 1610–35. Nottingham, Collection Lord Middleton. (Photo Victoria and Albert Museum)

651 Wide double collar of white linen, embroidered with pineapple motifs and edged with tatted lace, *c*. 1600–25. Nottingham, Collection Lord Middleton

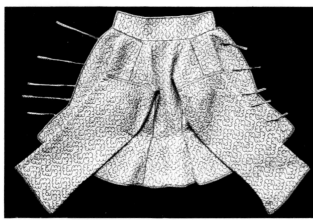

652 High-collared quilted jacket, *c*. 1615. Nottingham, Collection Lord Middleton. (Photo Victoria and Albert Museum)

653 Man's waistcoat, knitted green silk, Italian make. First half seventeenth century. Collection Lord Middleton. (Photo Victoria and Albert Museum)

waisted, with a wide collar in the shape of a truncated cone; and for men, the shortened doublet, wider, longer trousers, a more visible white shirt and high, conical, broad-brimmed hats. The ruff disappeared everywhere after 1650.

The wealthier circles of society followed the modes of France, with a time-lag depending on their distance from Paris, and with unimportant modifications due either to the lesser skill of local tailors, the character of each people, its way of life and its Catholic or Reformed religious beliefs.

French influence dominated in Court costume, particularly after 1660, but the persistence of Spanish influence led to the use of neutral or dark colours, and some austerely stiff elements hark back to Holland. We find only a very little of the fanciful nature of Paris fashions, which were nonetheless available in French fashion prints, pirated and circulated throughout Europe with the captions changed. The wealthy middle classes most often substituted fine broadcloth for silk, and women had themselves portrayed in indoor clothes, while men wore the uniform of some corporate body, an innovation characteristic of the association spirit that was highly developed in the Northern countries, from Flanders to the Hanseatic coasts.

In politically unsettled provinces, from the Tyrol to Seeland and Scania, regional costume took on individual forms, which had first appeared in the sixteenth century. Hollar represented curious garments from Franconia, Swabia and Alsace; we know that in Holland, Denmark, Sweden and Switzerland the same phenomenon appeared. Broad-brimmed hats or fur caps, long tunics or justaucorps, laced doublets and bodices confirm this everywhere.[16]

Germany, still recovering from the effects of the Thirty Years' War, submitted to constant imitation of foreign, particularly French, styles. 'Nowadays,' wrote the author of a pamphlet published in 1689, 'everything must be French.' Paris fashions benefited from this enthusiasm, as did literature and the visual arts. The Grand Elector of Brandenburg, Frederick III, crowned King of Prussia at Königsberg in January 1707, displayed all possible sartorial luxury on that occasion, which marked the fulfilment of his ambitions: a scarlet suit enriched with gold and precious stones and a purple cloak decorated with diamond[s]

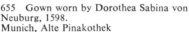
655   Gown worn by Dorothea Sabina von Neuburg, 1598.
Munich, Alte Pinakothek

656   HANS WERL: Countess Madeleine von Neuburg, c. 1613. Munich, Alte Pinakothek

buttons; the Queen, the beautiful, witty Sophia Charlotte of Hanover, was as superbly dressed. This, however, was no reason against levying heavy taxes on all costumes and dresses so as to increase tax revenue.

Although fashion came from France, clothing industries were national, thanks to the Huguenots. In his *Mémoires pour servir à l'histoire de Brandebourg*, Frederick II wrote: 'They have helped to repeople our empty town and created the manufactories that we lacked... The few cloth factories that existed were of little importance... they were almost ruined by English competition. When Frederick-William I mounted the throne (1713) there was not a stocking, not a cap that was not made by the French. They made all sorts of broadcloth, knitted caps and stockings, worked felts and all types of dyeing...'

In the Nordic and Baltic countries, the influence of Dutch costume remained dominant. The royal garments (plate 631) from the Royal Armoury in Stockholm[17] resemble those in portraits of Holland's Golden Age and the rare specimens preserved in Dutch museums, such as the dalmatic worn by Ernest Casimir of Nassau (plate 619) in the Amsterdam Rijkmuseum. Doublets and breeches worn by Gustavus Adolphus between 1620 and 1627 (plate 618), a costume belonging to Gustavus X, embroidered with gold (plate 631), and to Charles XI (plate 669) come extremely close to Dutch types, even when they have an abundance of braids and frogging. A small child's dress in pink with gold ornaments nevertheless seems to be of Parisian origin. For some Swedish royal garments of the 1630–60 period, the materials were ordered from Paris. For the costumes worn by Christina of Sweden, the descriptions left by Mlle de Montpensier in her memoirs suggest that they were in the Dutch style, but it is impossible to be certain.

A very few specimens of costumes of the same type have been discovered in Sweden, and in the tombs of Turku Cathedral (Finland). They show that lace imported from abroad was used in seventeenth-century Finland[18]: the identical appearance of the ceremonial garments used for burial with those found in Germany until the end of the century allows us to believe in the wide spread of German styles, which were gradually substituted for Spanish modes in northern Europe.

FRENCH INFLUENCE ON MEN'S COSTUME
649   After accepting the extravagance of petticoat breeches, the British adopted the justaucorps, whose decoration was more elaborate than in France at the same period; here it is worn with an open-sleeved surtout: the curled wig is a purely British style

SEVENTEENTH-CENTURY GARMENTS PRESERVED IN ENGLAND
650-54   These admirable pieces preserved in England illustrate the rather heavy richness of seventeenth-century technique

WOMEN'S COSTUME IN SPAIN
658-9, 661, 680   Towards the middle of the seventeenth century women's costume in Spain was transformed; the farthingale gave way to the *guard-infanta*, also known as *sacristan* or *tontillo*, which spread the fullness of the skirt evenly over the hips. The bodice is much shorter than before, leaving the shoulders bare; the hair, plaited with plumes and jewels, falls over the shoulders (plate 659); ear-rings are large (plate 658); sleeves swell out in thick padded rolls (plate 658) and the general outline from the front is broadened. Children are dressed like adults

MEN'S COSTUME IN SPAIN IN THE SEVENTEENTH CENTURY
660, 662, 681-2   Male costume was to keep its austere character throughout the whole of the seventeenth century. The young Philip V (plate 682) adopted on his arrival in Spain the starched *golilla* which fitted tightly round the neck, the *ropilla* with bouffant sleeves, and straight-cut breeches in Spanish style, derived from late sixteenth-century *venetians;* this model was to spread through Europe. The small 'Imperial' beard, the cloak (*ferreruolo*), the plumeless hat and the absence of wigs (plate 660) are all styles reaching back to the preceding century

657   Baptismal procession. German engraving. Mid-seventeenth century. Paris, Bibliothèque Nationale, Cabinet des Estampes, Ob 63 a. (Photo Flammarion)

658 ANON: *The Duchess del Infantado, c.* 1665.
New York, Hispanic Society of America

659 VELAZQUEZ: *The Infanta Maria Teresa, c.* 1659–60.
Madrid, Prado. (Photo André Held)

In Denmark, whose frontiers abutted on Holland, Dutch influences were naturally preponderant: the very important collection of costumes from the Danish Royal House (plates 628–30) preserved in Rosenborg Castle proves this.[19] For the 1625–1700 period, some Spanish elements can be seen (casaques and capes), and English embroidery, with unusually long, indeterminately shaped doublets and breeches of Dutch cut. A costume from the coronation of King Christian V, reputedly in 'Danish style' consists of a fairly short doublet and moderately bouffant breeches edged with gold lace (plate 670); this style was to be maintained in coronation costume for over a century. Only in 1695 do we see, in this astonishing royal wardrobe, a long coat with a doublet and breeches (plate 671), clearly inspired by French fashions.

Sweden and Denmark, along with England, have the rare privilege of having preserved many men's suits with petticoat breeches from the 1655–65 period; these are precious evidence for the study of this piece of clothing, which until recently was almost unknown in France.

SOUTHERN AND EASTERN EUROPE

In Spain, stiffness remained a characteristic of costume until about 1620; then, as had happened some time before in other countries, a reaction set in, moving towards greater softness and ease.

More often than not, passementeries and braid were used to make good the lack of decorated textiles. The disorganization of the textile industry after the expulsion of the Moors, decreed by Philip III in 1609, and the prohibition of the use of brocades amply proved the important repercussions political and economic measures may have on costume.

For women, the bodice left the shoulder more exposed after 1640–50; skirts kept their former bell shape, and the old cape (*manto*) shrank, becoming the black mantilla.

Men's cloaks grew to three-quarter length, and breeches were sometimes bouffant, sometimes tight. At the beginning of the century the French style of suit, more precisely the *costume à la française*, had been introduced to Spain by Flemish lords. At the end of his life Charles III (d. 1700) abandoned Spanish costume, and it seems that his widow would have sent the young Duc d'Anjou a suit *à la wallonne*, covered in precious stones, but for the opposition of the Junta; for the solemn entry of Philip V, the whole court dressed in French style,[20] with the exception of the King, who wore Spanish costume. Soon the restricting garments of the past were to survive only in the starched *golilla*, the last form taken by the ruff, which fitted tightly round the throat and was soon to be left to the legal profession. The Iberian *sombrero* was at the origin of the soft plumed hats that had been worn in Europe since 1625–30.

Towards 1640–48 noblewomen and court ladies replaced their bell farthingales with a very broad type of skirt support, worn on the hips; this was the *tontillo*, also called *sacristan* or *garde-infant*. It is described by Mme de Motteville at the time of the Spanish marriage of Louis XIV: 'Their garde-infant was a circular machine, and a monstrous one, for it was like several barrel-hoops sewn into the skirt, except that hoops are round, and their garde-infant was a little flattened at the front and behind, and spread out at the sides. When they walked, this machine bobbed up and down...' In 1705 Mme d'Aulnoy, visiting the Spanish court, gave a similar description.

Despite their ungraceful appearance, not only did these accessories remain in vogue at the Spanish court, but royal marriages with the Hapsburgs were to lead to their adoption in Vienna and the courts of Germany.

The ruff, the fashion for which had persisted in Spain, disappeared suddenly towards 1630, simultaneously with the pyramidal hairstyles, giving way to a fashion for low-cut necklines and hair flowing freely over the shoulders. These two features were to remain without imitators, except perhaps in Austria. Even the Spanish Netherlands had worn a costume very close to the Dutch style, owing nothing to Spain, since 1630.

The hieratic appearance of Spanish women in the seventeenth century was perhaps due to their excessive use of cosmetics and their unduly heavy jewellery, which added to an already formidable outline.

In the urban and rural lower classes, costume kept the main features of the sixteenth century and the very simple type that can be seen in the paintings of the Le Nain brothers.

While Spanish influence on European costume was declining, the reputation of Spanish tailors for high quality of workmanship remained, and people still spoke of 'Spanish cut'. It is legitimate to see in this one form of expression of the Spanish character, which inclined towards fantasy despite the rigid Catholicism manifested by Spanish ladies, vowing themselves to some saint or other in the absence of their husbands and wearing grey or blue gowns with rope or leather girdles. The influence of the Counter-Reformation was certainly responsible for this deliberate austerity, designed to modify – if not actually to hide – the female form.

Nothing better marks the contrast between the two countries than the costumes worn by the French and Spanish courts for the marriage of Louis XIV with Maria Teresa of Austria in 1660. On the French side, petticoat breeches were worn, with generous bunches of ribbons, 'windmill' shoe-bows, wigs and gloves embroidered with gold lace; women's long-trained mantles revealed the skirt, and their half-length sleeves and puffed trimmings were held here and there with pearls or bows. The Spaniards, on the other hand, wore the Infanta's enormous *garde-infant*, her flesh-coloured satin gown embroidered with gold and silver and her Spanish head-dress. When on the evening of her arrival at Saint-Jean-de-Luz she tried on French style garments with a *corps de jupe*, she at first found them uncongenial; Spanish Grandees wore very tight breeches and clothes that were less lavishly embroidered than those of the French, but with many precious stones.

In Lisbon the Queen of Portugal imposed the gown *à la française* on her ladies-in-waiting.

In Italy[21] costume was determined by many foreign or national influences. Venice was independent, the Papal States lived in luxury and splendour, Milan and its surrounding country and the south of Italy had become part of the Holy Roman Empire: this distribution of power maintained an extreme

661 Velázquez: *Woman in a Mantilla, c.* 1625–30. Devonshire Collection, Chatsworth. (Reproduced by permission of the Trustees of the Chatsworth Settlement)

660 J. Carreño de Miranda: *Barnabé de Ochoa de Chinchetru y Fernandez de Zuniga, c.* 1660. New York, Hispanic Society of America

662 Velázquez: *Philip IV, c.* 1625–30. National Gallery, London. (Reproduced by courtesy of the Trustees. Photo Freeman)

663–5 Mid-seventeenth century engravings, showing, left to right: *Two townswomen going to Mass. Catholic couple in wedding dress. Protestant couple in wedding dress.* Paris, Bibliothèque Nationale, Cabinet des Estampes, Ob 64. (Photos Flammarion)

666 *A Group of Citizens.* Mid-seventeenth century. Private collection. (Photo Flammarion)

variety of costumes. Thus we see the women of Genoa wearing Polish cloaks, Turkish hairstyles and Spanish trains all at almost the same time. But in Messina, after the withdrawal of the French occupying troops in 1678, the inhabitants refused to give up their clothes 'in the style of Paris', and, even though Spanish modes had still been followed at the beginning of the century, Priuli could later write: 'The Italians detest the French, and dress like them.' The farthingale had disappeared after the plague of 1657.

Luxury was still extremely pronounced in women's headdresses, provoking not only rigorous ordinances from the Vatican, in the Papal States, but also repeated edicts in the most extravagant city of Italy, Venice. In fifty years, the Council of Ten published more than ten prohibitions, levelled against sleeves, gown trains, wigs, etc. Naples was probably one of the few towns in the Peninsula which did not then have its sumptuary laws.

Costume Materials

From the earliest years of the century, the costume market made the most of the general increase in prices that took place throughout Europe during the entire Renaissance period and was halted only towards 1625–30. This situation favoured the already long-standing prosperity of manufacturing merchants. In France drapers, mercers and furriers found themselves able to buy themselves administrative posts, and were often ennobled. The same happened in England where the textile industry, more advanced than on the Continent, was to develop very rapidly, particularly in Lancashire and Yorkshire, the central countries which, with London, remained the richest parts of the country. In Holland the considerable expansion of overseas trade and its European function as a clearing-house began to bring increased prosperity to the middle classes.

667 MAGALOTTI: *Wedding Procession in Sweden,* 1674. Stockholm, Nordiska Museet. (Museum photo)

668 Page's suit (perhaps French) in yellow and black, the colours of the Wasa Family, c. 1620. Stockholm, Royal Armoury. (Museum photo)

669 Suit with very long justaucorps worn by Charles XI, c. 1670–80. Stockholm, Royal Armoury. (Museum photo)

670 Suit worn by Christian V for his coronation, 1671. Copenhagen, Rosenborg Castle. (Museum photo)

TEXTILES AND DYESTUFFS

The application of the mercantile system, particularly of the protection granted to locally manufactured goods, had a great influence on trade in dress materials in the seventeenth century.

Though hardly any specimens have survived, the everyday garments worn by all classes were apparently made of broadcloth; this is borne out by the number of mills producing this cloth in the principal countries of Europe. As the quality of wool sometimes left much to be desired, England and the Low Countries tried to corner the woollen output of Europe; the main wool market was at Medina del Campo in Spain, and the *lonja* in Seville was the principal clearing house. This attempt at monopoly aimed at supplanting French stuffs, the production of which was being increased by Colbert, who granted privileges to numerous industrialists. These three countries fought for the Middle-Eastern market as an outlet for their fine cloths, which Levantines used for their full-pleated undergarments and long turbans.

Wool's main competitor was silk, supplied mainly by Italy, which exported costume materials, and Spain: Murcian silk was generally used for passementerie. Levantine and Chinese silk also catered for the large European demand.

Certainly silk was the stuff most widely used in rich costume. However, it soon had to face the dangerous competition presented by printed cotton.

Towards 1630–40 printed cottons were introduced to Europe from Asia Minor, probably by Portuguese traders: their bright colours and variety of motifs immediately won them a popularity which grew constantly during the ensuing half century in elegant society, particularly in France and England. Ladies used these stuffs for aprons and men adopted them for their dressing-gowns (plates 543–4).[22]

In France these materials went by several names: *indiennes*, *chites*, *surates* or *patnas*, according to whether they came from Chittagong (Bengal), Surah (North of Bombay) or Patna on the Ganges; it appears that materials which were imported through Marseille were known as *perse* or *toile du Levant*,

672 Mule with lace appliqué decoration, probably French. Second half of the seventeenth century. Musée Bally, Schoenenwerd. (Museum photo)

673–4 Felt hat and gloves with embroidered gauntlets worn by Frederick III, 1650. Copenhagen, Rosenborg Castle. (Museum photo)

675 G. FORABOSCO: *Portrait of a Lady*, c. 1635. Vienna, Kunsthistorisches Museum

676 P. F. CITTADINI: *Woman and Child*, c. 1665–70. Bologna, Museo Civico. (Photo Fast)

677 PHILIPPE DE CHAMPAIGNE: *Little Girl with Falcon*, 1628. Paris, Louvre. (Photo Flammarion)

678 J. SUSTERMANS: *Anne-Marie-Louise de Medicis*, c. 1670. Florence, Palazzo Vecchio. (Photo Alinari)

while *toiles d'Inde* or *indiennes* were brought in the ships of the *Compagnie des Indes*. These varied names are difficult to assign to textiles surviving today.[23]

One thing that is certain is that the term *indienne* referred to a dressing-gown for men or women;[24] Monsieur Jourdan in *Le Bourgeois Gentilhomme* (1670) confirms this: 'I had this *Indienne* made... My tailor tells me that people of quality dress like this in the morning.' In 1672 the *Mercure de France* mentions the craze for indoor gowns and casaques: 'Ladies... have dressing-gowns that cost almost as much as gowns in cloth of gold or silver,' and the *Mercure Galant* tells us that 'Psyche skirts are still in fashion, but less so than gowns in Indian stuffs.' At the same time Mme de Sévigné brought her daughter a length of *indienne*.

The favour enjoyed by these painted stuffs increased on the occasion of the visits of Eastern ambassadors, and their relative rarity favoured their vogue and increased their price, which was almost beyond the means of middle-class women. Therefore shrewd industrialists tried to produce similar, cheaper cloth, discarding the Indian painting process as too complicated, and using printing instead. When the spread of European factories had led to a decline in their fashion, a French Royal edict in 1686 prohibited both the import and the production of these cotton materials.

This Draconian prohibition, which dealt a severe blow to a young industry, clearly met a four-fold need: the reduction of spending abroad, the protection of the 'old' silk and wool manufactures, the prohibition of poor quality merchandise and the reservation for established industries of the existing labour force, depleted by the exile of Huguenot workers after the revocation of the Edict of Nantes. However, the *Compagnie des Indes*, founded by Colbert in 1664, and traders established in the kingdom, were still permitted to sell the painted cloths – *pintados* or *chints* – they already had in stock.

Naturally this prohibition revived the fashion for *indiennes*: it became a matter of personal prestige to defy the regulations and to wear these and other painted stuffs in public, even in the King's presence. The police confiscated these stuffs in Paris, where they were sold at the Fair of Saint-Germain, and had hundreds of garments burned, tracking down ladies who had

675–6, 678, 686 Spanish influence still shows in the broader outline (plate 675), with the black mantle worn over a light-coloured gown and the Italian needle-point collar. French influence was next to be seen with simpler, more relaxed styles (plate 676), which became heavier with more direct inspiration from Louis XIV styles

CHILDREN'S STYLES

677–9, 686, 688–91 In the seventeenth century, apart from details, children were dressed exactly like adults (plate 678). The little girl with the falcon (plate 677) wears a gown with slit sleeves *à la commodité*, an apron of silk edged with lace matching the collar and cuffs. The little English boy (plate 688) wears the same doublet, with wide skirts and sleeves in panes, as can be seen on adults of the period; but he wears this garment above a skirt, although he is five years old. The son of Mlle de Lavalière (plate 679), about the same age, wears a jacket, a sort of blouse which small boys wore over their breeches; his shoes are of white doeskin, a style reserved for children. The Stuart children (plate 691), who were of course in exile in France, wear absolutely French costumes: a justaucorps with wide, flaring folds from the end of the seventeenth century, and shoes *à la cavalière* for the young prince, while Princess Louisa wears a Fontanges head-dress and has a lace apron over her gown. Dutch children's costume (plate 689) seems to have undergone different influences: while some details, like the wide-brimmed hat and the doublet with long skirts worn by the boy are in the tradition of Dutch portraits, as is the traditional pleated collar, the girl and the baby are dressed in a style closer to that of Frenchwomen, and the chain on the girl's shoulder, linking the ribbon rosette on the shoulder and the brooch fastening her collar, are scarcely found outside English portraits, like the geometrical shoe-rosettes

679 MIGNARD: *Mlle de Lavallière and her Children*, c. 1672. Versailles, Museum. (Photo Flammarion)

been imprudent enough to show themselves at their windows wearing négligées in *toile peinte*. In some provincial towns, the police even went so far as to tear the offending garments from their wearers' backs. Only 'privileged quarters' like the Temple or Arsenal neighbourhoods of Paris, where the police could not enter without special authorization, escaped these measures. Between 1686 and 1716, over thirty arrests were made on these grounds in France.

Similarly in England, sheep-farmers and weavers protested to Parliament about the considerable imports of cotton made by the East India Company; in 1697, their wives forced their way into the House of Commons to make their point of view heard. Finally, in 1700 Parliament forbade the import of all Indian stuffs, except for plain white.

In the following century the 'cotton war' was to unleash violent polemics between French economists and the Press. Then, after 1750, these rigorous measures were no longer applied, and ultimately, after protracted hesitation, the government issued a general authorization for the production of printed stuffs, the result, in reality, of the suppression of certain privileges by the inspector Etienne de Silhouette.

Naturally imports of white cotton increased on both sides of the Channel; in France, where they were not free, contraband was big business and smugglers did not scruple to forge the lead seals used to identify authorized imports.

The spread of cotton stuffs brought with it some costumes of Asiatic origin: Portuguese in India always slept in *calsons*; and *pyjamas* (in Hindustani: *epai-jama*) or 'Moghul breeches' were often worn as night or informal dress in England towards 1625 (plate 562).

At this time experiments in dyeing presented a special interest, not only for their technical achievements, but also because of the variety fashion drew from them.

In France, in place of imported dyestuffs, Colbert stimulated the use of national products, pastel from Languedoc and woad from Normandy, Indian indigo being admitted when mixed with pastel; detailed regulations were completed in 1671 by a set of *General Instructions for Dyeing Wools in All Colours and for the Cultivation of the Drugs and Ingredients Used Therein.*

Continuing the work of Henri IV at Gobelins, in 1662 Colbert acquired the old workshops founded in the fifteenth century by the dyers of that name.

According to statutes granted to dyers in 1668, they had to observe the conditions of *grand teint* and *petit teint* strictly; the producers of each category were entitled to use a certain number of colours, while some products were denied them.

Indigo, which in the sixteenth century had been prohibited in many countries, including France, once more came into use, at first in limited quantities but on a larger scale later: this led to the wider use of blue materials, particularly in the French Army, which discarded its russet colour to be 'clad in blue'.

At the end of the century England and Holland could draw on imported dyes of excellent quality. In London, Burghley sent for a sample of Oriental dyes so as to incite British dyers to do better 'for the honour of their native England and for the universal profit of the kingdom.' But France, with its taste for more subtle colour combinations, now occupied the front rank in experiment in this field. This work was to lead to a considerable improvement in the quality of dyestuffs and the use of delicate shades, examples of which are to be found in portrait-paintings of the period.[25]

LACE

After embroidering on linen, then drawing out threads and embroidering over the open-work thus produced, and later cutting the cloth and embroidering in the holes, Italian craftswomen were inspired, in the sixteenth century, to fix loose threads round the edge of the piece of cloth and embroider on them. This was the beginning of *punto in aria*. It became immediately successful everywhere in Europe. We cannot go into the detailed history of lace or lace-making techniques: needles and bobbins were used to create incomparable masterpieces.

In the seventeenth century there was an immense vogue for lace. Sully, followed by Richelieu, tried in vain to prohibit it, with a view to limiting French imports from the two great lace-making countries, Italy and Flanders.

680 *The Infanta Margarita Teresa,*
c. 1655. Vienna, Kunsthistorisches
Museum. (Photo Flammarion)

681 VELAZQUEZ: *Philip IV,* 1644. Dulwich
College Picture Gallery

682 RIGAUD: *Philip V, c.* 1701. Paris,
Louvre. (Photo Giraudon)

683 Woman's gown in three-pile velvet,
richly embroidered in gold thread and
braid. Seventeenth century. Barcelona,
Museo de Arte, Collection Don Rocamo

685 ANON: *Portrait of a Lady.* Mid-seventeenth century.
Oslo, Kunstindustrimuseet. (Photo Teigen)

686 J. SUSTERMANS: *Vittoria della Rovere, c.* 1645.
Turin, Pinacoteca. (Photo Brogi-Giraudon)

684 Man's shoe in carmine three-pile velvet, relief embroidery in silver
thread. Late seventeenth century. Barcelona, Museo de Arte, Collection
Don Rocamora. (Museum photo)

687 BONNART: *Royal Swiss Guard.*
Second half of the seventeenth century.
Paris, Bibliothèque Nationale, Cabinet
des Estampes. (Photo Flammarion)

688 ANON: *Portrait of a
Child,* 1630.
Ipswich, Museum

689 JACOB GERRITSZ CUYP: *Three Children in a Park, c.* 1640.
Rotterdam, Boymans-Van Beuningen Museum. (Photo Frequin)

Colbert was the first to understand France's interest in producing her own lace; he brought thirty lace-makers from Venice, who were instructed to train French craftswomen, and in a few years the centres of Normandy and Burgundy could hold their own against foreign competition. At the same time, he supported bobbin-made lace, which was less highly regarded but widely produced. Valenciennes gained a reputation that has survived the centuries, but it was *point d'Alençon* and *point de France*, the latter inspired by *point de Venise*, that made the new French industry's reputation.

Miscellaneous Costumes

FESTIVE AND THEATRICAL COSTUME

In the first half of the century the atmosphere created by the Wars of Religion and the economic difficulties and hardships brought by the Thirty Years' War were scarcely favourable for the revival of feasts and entertainments in Renaissance style. However, theatrical shows, popular celebrations and spectacles in which lavish use of crowds was made, royal or ambassadorial entrances, funerals, etc., and princely entertainments in general were gradually resumed, providing increasing scope for inventiveness in costume.

Reviving the exoticism of the preceding century, Louis XIII gradually inaugurated Court ballets and danced carrousels, which show a purely French style: the ballet of the *Four Quarters of the Earth* given in the Louvre in 1625 brought together costumes of Indians, Moors, Negroes and Asiatics.

After 1650, the young Louis XIV gave a new stimulus to originality. Thus, at the Carrousel of 1662, Monsieur, the King's brother, was dressed as a Shah of Persia, the Prince de Condé as a Turk, the Duc d'Enghien as a rajah and the Duc de Guise

as a 'savage chief', while the 1685 Carrousel had as its theme the legendary struggle between the Abencerages and the Zegri, for which the costumes were designed by Bérain; at Marly in 1702, the onlookers saw a Chinese emperor carried in a palanquin by thirty Chinamen.

Contemporary accounts boast of the brilliance and richness of these feasts and of the ceremonies that centred round the King: the marriages of the Dauphin (1680) and the Duc de Chartres (1692) and the masked ball given by the Dauphin in 1705, when the Duchess of Alba astonished the guests by wearing a Spanish court costume the like of which they had never seen before. Chroniclers describe the gorgeous costumes of gold brocade covered with lace, diamonds and emeralds, pale pink ribbons shot with gold, gowns in cloth of gold or silver, brilliants stuck into the ribbon shells of head-dresses, and immense trains which ranged from three ells for duchesses to up to eleven for the Queen.[26]

In this way Le Roi Soleil maintained the brilliance of his reign despite the difficulties of its last years.

As for Henri III's ballets, artists were commissioned to create costumes for this type of princely entertainment: Daniel Rabel worked under Louis XIII and Henri de Gissey during the youth of Louis XIV, followed by Jean Bérain, whose fertile imagination could cope with machinery as well as illuminations and décor, and who designed a number of costumes for operas, ballets and carrousels. One type of long, tight sleeve, buttoned at the wrist, designed to cover the unsightly arms of an Opera actress, was adopted by fashion under the name *Amadis sleeve*.

'The French', wrote a foreign observer in 1702 ,'surpass the Italians in opera by their costumes: these are of a richness, a magnificence and taste that outstrip anything one can see elsewhere.' This reputation quickly spread beyond the boundaries of France.

In the Louis XIV period, opera costumes followed an almost uniform type: for women, a tight bodice with flaring basques, a skirt with train and a head-dress with tiara; men wore justaucorps fitting tightly to the chest, a sort of short kilt and high boots; both sexes wore flowing capes fastened to the shoulders. However, monotony was avoided by the variety of colours, inventiveness in embroidery, a wide range of combinations of tones, trimmings of ribbons, fringes, slashings and puffs. Alongside 'Classical' costume, 'character' costumes survived into the eighteenth century, with attributes personifying Bacchantes, Genii and the Four Elements. All were aimed at the general taste for the marvellous, other interpretations of which were given in art and literature.

In his instructions written for the Dauphin, Louis XIV showed that he appreciated the usefulness of 'representation'. The 'people... take pleasure in spectacles... By their means we can hold their spirits and their hearts.' Luxury and the pursuit of the rare and spectacular expressed the desire to dazzle. Festive costumes came close to theatrical clothes; there was scarcely any difference between Louis XIV dressed as a Roman emperor and Ulysses dying on the boards in cuirass and kilt. After all, Jean Bérain *père* who directed so many festivities and was 'Designer to the Chamber and Cabinet' also produced the models for 'extraordinary' costumes worn by the King and the Royal Family for princely marriages.

The costumes worn in the ballets and entertainments in vogue at Versailles added their influence to that exercized by the rest of French costume. The allegorical symbolism and 'heroic' atmosphere that appealed to Louis XIV in his entertainments harmonized with the rather stiff solemnity and love of spendour that Court costume created around him; both were necessary for his lustre.

MOURNING CLOTHES

In all times mourning had been marked by the adoption of sober-coloured, unadorned garments, but it does not seem that strict rules of etiquette were established before the sixteenth and, more particularly, the seventeenth century. Until then, while black, white, blue-grey and violet were considered suitable colours for mourning, they were often modified as the result of individual initiative. In the Middle Ages queens wore white to mourn the death of the king; Anne of Brittany was the first to wear black, for the death of Charles VIII, and after her death Louis XII also wore black, though the traditional mourning colour for monarchs was violet.

At the end of the century a new custom appeared: widows wore bandeaux of white linen, a survival of the chaperon, and skirts of black frieze known as 'nages'. Mourning for close relations was shown by wearing the chaperon, a sort of long, tight cloak topped with a soft, narrow hood.

In the seventeenth century mourning customs became codified: at court funeral ceremonies, princes appeared in black gowns covered with a domino, and over this, long-trained black mourning cloaks, and long crape bands round their hats. Mourning visits were paid in full, long-trained black cloaks and, for princesses, in *mantes*, long single pieces of crape attached to the head-dress, the arms and the belt, trailing generously behind.

When not taking part in ceremonies, mourners wore black garments with deep cuffs of plain white, also known as *weepers* (*pleureuses*), whose size was reduced for half mourning. White or coloured stockings, lace and powdered or beribboned wigs were forbidden at court for mourning or mourning visits.

CHILDREN'S CLOTHING

In the seventeenth century, children's clothes were more than ever small-scale versions of their parents'. Boys wore doublets and breeches, while little girls were dressed in long gowns with lace collars and aprons, and caps trimmed with plumes and aigrettes.

Very small boys who were not yet old enough to wear breeches wore a garment called the *jaquette*,[27] a dress that was shorter than that worn by girls, and probably less closely fitted. Leading strings, which nurses familiarly called *tatas*, were long bands of cloth sewn to the shoulders, so that the child could be held when he began to walk; these bands can also be seen in portraits of little girls too old to need them (plate 691); in England, recalling the flowing sleeves of the preceding period, they remained visible in portraits of young girls until the mid-eighteenth century.

Children's shoes were made from a type of woollen velvet known as *tripe blanche*, which does not seem to have been put to any other use.

MILITARY UNIFORM

The seventeenth century saw the final abandonment of armour and the appearance of the first regular uniforms.

Without being condemned officially, the cuirass, which was too heavy and hindered the wearer's movements, was increasingly replaced by the *buff-jerkin*, the leather waistcoat and the hongreline, which afforded better protection against bad weather. The puffs and padding of earlier periods disappeared and ornaments were more sparingly used. Turn-down boots replaced the shoes of the sixteenth century; belts and bandoliers were more solid, better fitted to the weapons used, which were becoming heavier.

Insignia appeared in the form of sashes in the national colours, worn round the waist or over one shoulder by officers. During the Thirty Years' War, these colours were red for Germany, white for France, blue for Sweden, orange for Holland and red and yellow for Denmark. However, sashes of different colours could be worn by units belonging to the same nation. During the English Civil War, the Royalist and Parliamentary troops wore red and white sashes respectively.

Conscripts also found their own distinctive emblems: Germans tied white ribbons round their hats, while the Swedes wore a handful of straw and the Danish white paper leaves. Long after, the Austrians would be wearing leaves in their hats and the Swedes straw cockades.

The introduction of regular military uniform dates from the second half of the seventeenth century.

In France in 1660, troops wore a full, tunic-shaped coat over a long, sleeved waistcoat, along the lines of civilian costume; shortly before 1670 this coat, which had already been worn for some time, became tighter, which won it the name of justaucorps, which was also adopted for the civilian garment.

In 1670, at the instigation of Louvois, this model was extended to the entire French army by Louis and each unit had its own colour. A complete uniform was rapidly adopted throughout Europe: justaucorps, coat (or waistcoat), breeches, cravat, boots and tricorn hat. The justaucorps worn by the infantry was pale grey, while the artillery wore royal blue; cavalry uniform was brighter and more varied with the revers in contrasting colours. At the end of the reign of Louis XIV the army still wore the old style of heavy boot, which otherwise was then worn only for hunting; *houseaux*, light leather leggings covering the boot, appeared among the light cavalry.

These modifications in military costume served two purposes: they met the need for tighter garments because of the new weapons, musket, bayonet and cartridges, and aided Colbert's new regulation of the woollen industry in 1665. The adoption of uniform entailed a vast consumption of cloth, which strengthened the industry's position. Lodève, for instance, which was famous for its pale grey cloth, disposed of almost half its output as military supplies.

This development in military costume, beginning in France, affected all the countries of Europe. Like weapons and equipment, clothing became standardized everywhere. Its civilian appearance is one example of the continual mutual reaction between civilian and military costume.

ORDINARY PEOPLE'S COSTUME

The very simple forms of costume worn by the lower classes continued those of the preceding period. Women wore a skirt, tucked up for work, with a tight bodice, linen head-dress and enveloping cloak. Men wore a buttoned jacket with calf-length or short breeches and wide-brimmed felt hats. In general, costume was less stable among town workmen than among peas-

690, 692–3 Ordinary people's costume reflects the styles worn by the more prosperous classes, but the fashions were followed with some delay, preserving at the same time traditions later to be perpetuated in regional costume. The farmer (plate 693) wears a surtout under which one can see his petticoat breeches, resembling the simple model worn in the Low Countries; his collar, tied with a narrow ribbon, seems to be a later fashion, as do the horizontally slit pockets of his surtout.

The woman (plate 692) wears a rigid bodice recalling those of the sixteenth century, and her head-dress draped down the back is a survival of the chaperon cornette; it is worn here over a stitched *calipette*.

One of the card-players (plate 690) seems to be wearing a casaque with buttoned sleeves, and the other a buff-jerkin with cloth sleeves, a compromise between peasant and military costume

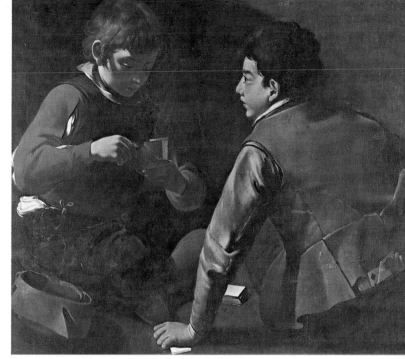

690   CARAVAGGIO: *Card-players*, c. 1590–95. Courtesy of the Fogg Art Museum, Harvard University, Cambridge, Mass.

691   LARGILLIÈRE: *James Stuart and his Sister*, 1695. London, National Portrait Gallery

ants, where some rich costumes, such as wedding gowns, were handed down from mother to daughter.

Both sexes wore fairly coarse woollen stuffs: broadcloth, drugget, panne, serge or rateen, fine woollen cloth being the prerogative of more prosperous craftsmen. The shirt was often of unbleached linen for men, even of hempen cloth in country districts. Only craftsmen and women employed in luxury industries increasingly imitated the middle classes, sometimes dressing in velvet and, more rarely, silk, for special occasions.

The costume of the people was made in dark or dull colours, greys or browns. Black predominated for women's clothes, while the grey colour of the garments worn by girls produced their French nickname of *grisettes*.

Silver buttons, velvet bands, taffeta scarves and even muffs brought touches of luxury into these drab costumes. The craftsman's serge differed widely from the silks and velvets of the nobility or upper middle classes: one had the essentials, the other excess. Only at the end of the century did industrial progress bring a wider variety of cloths and colours within the reach of the working classes in Europe.

EUROPEAN COSTUME IN THE WORLD

It has not been pointed out often enough that the seventeenth century gave European costume a fresh field for expansion which was gradually to assume considerable proportions: the New World of the Americas, North America for French and, above all, Anglo-Dutch costume, and South and Central America for Spanish and Portuguese styles.

In 1626 Manhattan Island had been bought by a Dutch merchant for the fur trading which was to spread rapidly northwards towards Canada and Hudson's Bay. This trade became organized with the *Compagnie des Cent Associés* in France, with the West India Company, which obtained a monopoly in 1663, and the Hudson's Bay Company, founded in 1672 by the Frenchmen Radison and Des Groseillers. Thus the entire northern part of the American continent provided an immense harvest of furs and a new market for European costume, and we can see the importance of the entry of America into the raw-materials commerce of the Old World.

While in the Southern countries furs were worn only by the middle classes and the provincial aristocracy, having been supplanted by luxury cloths in courts, they kept their vogue in the colder climates of Europe as the necessary adjunct to princely formal cloaks, military capes and ecclesiastical robes. American furs competed with those provided until then by the Slav and Nordic countries.

To counterbalance this Atlantic maritime movement, Russian traders in search of hides had to push deeper and deeper into Asia: in 1643 they reached the Pacific and in 1696 they settled in Kamchatka, from where they crossed to America.

The European costume introduced to the New World was at first that of the traders and soldiers who took possession, later that of immigrants: there were nearly 15,000 of these in New England in 1640. Swedes had settled in Delaware from 1638 on, and in 1683 Germans began to move in to Pennsylvania. Naturally, the costumes introduced were those in everyday wear in the various European countries, and luxury garments, particularly those worn by women, appeared only very late. We find little except working clothes and short skirts, worn with Indian mocassins.[28]

In Spanish America, the imported costume was at first that of the conquerors, then that brought by immigrants: 6,000 came from Spain in 1601. To protect their own trades, the Spaniards prohibited cloth and silk weaving; this favoured the industries set up in Toledo, Seville and Segovia to feed the American market. Later, the war with Holland led to the decline of these exports. A few mills which had escaped the ban in Mexico and Peru used Indian labour, treated with the utmost brutality. Set over the wretched, depressed Indian population, the idle, uncultivated Creole aristocracy kept the costume of its native country, adopting the light stuffs appropriate to the climate.

At the same time, the ceremonial costumes of the Old World were becoming Americanized. Although the Indian ambassadors of Maranhão appeared before Louis XIV in courtiers' suits and beaver hats, the ballets at Saint-Germain-en-Laye in 1629 and the Louvre in 1662 were danced in fanciful native and pseudo-American costumes. From time to time a sensational boatload of 'savages' came to revive the taste for the exotic: the Topinambus brought back from Maragnon Island by the Baron de Razilly in 1630 made women's hair bristle with plumes. On the other hand, Baron Le Hontan, in his attempts to convert a newly arrived savage to French fashions met with the reply: 'How could I ever get used to spending two hours dressing and preening myself, wearing a blue coat, red stockings, a black hat, a white feather and green ribbons...?'

These relations with faraway lands naturally left their mark on textile decoration and led to the adoption of new materials. Colonization became a new influence on fashion everywhere.

Although fashion was not to be influenced by the bison skins and plumed head-dresses brought back by the conquerors, exotic elements were drawn from a wider sphere: India, Siam, China and Turkey provided not only rare woods, coffee, tobacco and sugar, but also new motifs and colours that designers interpreted in terms of European taste. The spread of European costume took place in the countries receiving immigrants – America and the Cape – reather than in those where only commercial exchanges took place; it had no effect at all in more distant but, what is more important, more highly-cilivized countries such as India and China.

Notes

1 Abraham Bosse's engraving, *Le Courtisan suivant l'édit*, which appeared shortly after, indicates only that the publication of the edict was followed by a short period of austerity.
2 Cf. E. Magne: *Voiture et l'Hôtel de Rambouillet*.
3 Cf. M. Leloir, *passim*, who mentions only the London specimen (1935), as with Toudouze (1945). Mme Charles Müller's study of the Rosenborg costumes dates from 1940 (cf. particularly figs. 23, 25, 26, plates XXVI, XXIX, XXX). No petticoat breeches have been found in France.
4 Cf. Nevinson, *The Mercury Gallant*.
5 Cf. Mlle Duportal, 'B. Picart', in *Peintres Français du XVIIIe s.*, vol. II, and Mlle H. de Vallée, 'Ch. Simpol', in *Prométhée*, April 1930.
6 Cf. *Cahiers Ciba*, no. 54, 'Le Chapeau'.
7 Furetière, *Dictionnaire*, 1690.
8 Laran, *passim*.
9 Rodocanachi, pp. 181–2.
10 Such as those by Glen, Hollar, Saint-Igny, C. de Passe, Quast and A. Bosse (plates 553–5, 559).
11 Cf. Nevinson, *L'Origine de la gravure de modes*.
12 Cf. Maumené, 'Petits graveurs de portraits de la cour de Louis XIV', in *Amateur d'Estampes*, 1923–4.

13 Van Thienen, *passim.*
14 London Museum: *Costume.*
15 Evelyn, *passim.*
16 F. Lipp, *passim.*
17 T. Lenk, *passim.*
18 R. Pylkkanen, *passim.*
19 S. C. Müller, *passim.*
20 Saint-Simon, *Mémoires*, vol. VIII, pp 184, 191, 671 (notes)
21 Rodocanachi, *passim.*
22 Depitre, *passim*; Baker, *id.*; d'Allemagne, *id.*; Trévoux, *Diction-naire*, 1704; Sloman, *passim.*
23 Savary, *Dictionnaire du commerce* (1723) vol. II, p. 240.
24 A. Franklin, *Dictionnaire historique*, p. 398.
25 Cf. H. Winsher, 'Les Grands maîtres dans l'art de la teinture' in *Cahiers Ciba*, no. 2.
26 A. Weigert, *Jean Ier Bérain*, vol. I, pp. 65, 59.
27 *Dictionnaire de l'Académie*, 1716.
28 cf. Maclellan, *passim*; Earle, *id.*

Bibliography

GENERAL

G. Martin: *La Grande industrie sous le règne de Louis XIV*, 1896.
Paul Masson: *Histoire du commerce français dans le Levant au XVIIe s.*, 1896.
A. Babeau: *Les Artisans et les domestiques d'autrefois*, 1889.
Rodocanachi: *La Femme italienne*, 1907.
H. Sée: *Histoire commerciale et industrielle de la France*, 1925.
E. Levasseur: *Histoire des classes ouvrières et de l'industrie*, 1900–1901.

COSTUME

James Laver: *Early Tudor.* (*Costume of the Western World*), 1951.
Benoit Boullay: *Le Tailleur sincère*, 1671.
John Evelyn: *Tyrannus or the Mode*, ed. Nevinson, 1952.
J. H. Kinderen-Besier: *Spelevaart der Mode* (*XVIIIe s.*), Amsterdam, 1950.
F. M. Kelly and R. Schwabe: *A Short History of Costume and Armour*, 1066–1800.
Ritta Pylkkanen: 'Vêtements mortuaires du XVIIe s.' in *Actes Ier Cong. Int. Hist. Cost.*, 1952.
Torsten Lenk: 'La Garde-robe royale du Cabinet Royal des Armes de Stockholm', *ibid.*
Franz Lipp: *Osterreichische Volkskunde*, Vienna, 1952.
Jean Laran: 'La Coiffure des femmes à la fin du règne de Louis XIV', in *Bull. Sté. Hist. du Costume*, 1919.
M. Braun-Ronsdorf: *Reallexicon zur Deutschen Kunstgeschichte*, *passim*, Canons.
S. Christensen-Muller: *De Danske Kongedragterne...* 2 vols, 1940.
J. L. Nevinson: 'The Mercury Gallant or European Fashions in the 1670's', in *Apollo*, 1934.
R. A. Weigert: *Jean Ier Bérain*, 1937.
J. L. Nevinson: 'L'Origine de la gravure de modes', in *Actes Ier Cong. Int. Hist. Cost.*, 1952.
Frithjof van Thienen: *The Great Age of Holland.* (*Costume of the Western World*), 1951. (1600–1660), Berlin, 1930.
Elisabeth Maclellan: *Historic Dress in America*, 1937.
Alice Earle: *Two Centuries of Costume in America*, 1903.

TEXTILES

George Baker: *Calico Painting and Printing in the East Indies in the Seventeenth and Nineteenth Centuries*, London, 1921.
Edgard Depitre: *La Toile peinte en France au XVIIe et au XVIIIe s.*, 1912.
Juan de Alcega: *Libro de geometria pratica y traca*, 1589.
Henri d'Allemagne: *La Toile imprimée et les indiennes de traite*, 1942.
M. Paraf: *La Dentelle et la broderie*, 1927.
—: 'La Dentelle', in *Cahiers Ciba*, no. 33.

692   J. D. de Saint-Jean: *Peasant woman from the Paris region.* Late seventeenth century. Paris, Bibliothèque Nationale, Cabinet des Estampes. (Photo Flammarion)

693   J. D. de Saint-Jean: *Peasant from the Paris region*, c. 1660. Paris, Bibliothèque Nationale, Cabinet des Estampes. (Photo Flammarion)

694–5 Fashioned brocaded silks with polychrome silk decoration, Louis XV-XVI periods.
Lyons, Musée Historique des Tissus. (Museum photos)

LYONS SILKS

694–5 The richness and variety of techniques in the Lyons silk mills provide a wide range of decoration for dress silks; taste changes with the times, from the full-bodied naturalistic style of the beginning of the reign, to a lighter type of ornament in which floral elements combine with decorative scrolls. Eastern-inspired stylization can also be seen. Under Louis XVI, the style becomes plainer, with a marked preference for vertical lines. The cut of gowns, *à la francaise*, allowed these motifs to be shown off properly. Colours are clear and bright

RIBBONS

696, 698–700 Political and literary events are reflected in the patterns of ribbons

MEN'S CAPS

697 The fashion for wearing wigs obliged men to shave their heads and, consequently, to wear caps or swathed scarves at home

701 Stiff bodices imprisoned the bust and also served to support paniers and petticoats

697 Men's caps in brocaded silk. Eighteenth century.
New York, Cooper Union Museum for the Arts of Decoration. (Museum photo)

696 Ribbon with a cockerel motif (*à la coque*) commemorating the appearance of a book on Marguerite-Marie Alacoque, 1730

698–9 Harlequin and Pulchinello ribbons, created for the return of the Italian comedy, 1718

700 Ribbon in honour of the election of Stanislas Leczinski to the Polish throne, *c.* 1733. Richelieu Collection. Paris, Bibliothèque Nationale, Cabinet des Estampes. (Photos Flammarion)

701 Woman's bodice pink faille decorated with flowers, edged with white skin and stiffened with rush.
Eighteenth century.
Collection Fulgence.
(Photo Flammarion)

Chapter X

The Eighteenth Century

Costume in Europe

THE POLITICAL AND SOCIAL SETTING

Between the Treaties of Utrecht and Rastadt, which in 1713 put an end to the War of the Spanish Succession, and the first partition of Poland in 1772, the balance of power in Europe underwent profound transformation. France retained the cultural side of her seventeenth-century hegemony, but with the loss of her colonial empire she also had to bid farewell to her sea power and her role in international affairs. England, which had benefited at first from her rivalry with France, was weakened by the emancipation of her American colonies, but began nonetheless to orient herself towards world sea supremacy. While Sweden, Spain and Holland gradually retreated to become powers of secondary importance, Prussia, Austria and Russia, who had shared Poland between them, moved the centre of gravity towards the east of Europe, to their own advantage.

At the same time, there was a general change in European civilization.

In the countries to the west of the Elbe, which were moving towards liberalism, a free, active middle class was consolidating its old position in trade and taking part in the more recently founded industries. To the east of the Elbe, on the other hand, the authority still wielded by feudal overlords limited social progress in the middle and lower classes, which were kept enmeshed in a situation unfavourable to economic change.

At that time there was no such thing as 'European civilization', but rather a 'Western' one, which took shape around the great sea powers. In the eastern area this was assimilated only by small élites who lived surrounded by uncultured masses. Consequently international exchanges were made principally through intellectual movements, and costume, as the expression of taste and refinement, was to become one means towards the penetration of this civilization from land to land. To the west of the Elbe, the Christian and intellectual frontier of western thought, costume spread its new seductions everywhere, no longer through courts and noble courtiers, but through what people were coming to call 'Society'; and it was indeed a 'Society' rather than a 'class' that produced the new freedom and inventiveness, the devotion to pleasure which polished taste and refined costume.

Therefore it is hardly surprising that in this context, in this atmosphere, a transformation took place, affecting women's costume most of all. Whereas in the preceding periods men had been as splendidly dressed as women – and often more so – in the eighteenth century women not only became men's equals by virtue of their increasingly important role in society, but surpassed them in rich clothing.

THE NEW ECONOMY

The considerable development of industry and trade made such great contributions to costume that they might almost seem to have taken place solely with costume in view.[1]

In England, the weaving industries were rapidly and completely transformed, as a result of the new market opened up with the Spanish colonies, and abundant imports of Indian cotton and the extension of the silk mills founded at the end of the previous century by exiled French Huguenots.

The production of broadcloth still remained the backbone of British activity, but cotton, which entered the country in large quantities in spite of the prohibition engineered by English woollen manufacturers, opened a new field for British industry, further extended by the Treaty of Paris, which ceded India to Britain at the end of the Seven Years' War.

Moreover, new inventions considerably increased the output of all types of textiles: the new flying shuttle invented by John Kay in 1733, James Hargreaves' 'spinning Jenny' in 1765, Richard Arkwright's cotton-spinning loom in 1767, Josiah Crane's chain loom in 1768, perfected by Samuel Crompton in 1775 to give the 'mule', then Edmund Cartwright's weaving loom in 1785, while Jephediah Strutt was perfecting Lee's old invention which made it possible to knit the ribbed edgings known as 'Derby Ribs'. In 1750, 14,000 knitting machines were in operation, and by 1780 their number had increased to 20,000. In 1768, Hammond had begun to make tulle on stocking looms in Nottingham, where the Duc de Liancourt came to study the process in 1774. A steam engine, invented by James Watt, was installed in a cotton mill for the first time by the Robinsons at Papplewick, in 1785.

Immediately the industrial, spinning and weaving centres grew considerably, Manchester producing cotton, Norwich wool and Coventry silk. The appearance of mechanization led to a fall in prices, and the cheapness of English textiles won them a world market.

The use of cotton had a completely unexpected side effect: the slave trade. The Liverpool 'Slavers' transported cotton cloth to Africa, where the cargoes were bartered for Negroes, who were then taken across the Atlantic, after which the boats returned loaded with raw cotton from the new American states, where cotton had been grown since the seventeenth century, spreading rapidly through Virginia, South Carolina and Louisiana. The first cotton from Carolina reached London in 1763, three years after Horace Walpole had admitted that 45,000 Negro slaves were sold each year to the English plantations of the New World.

Thus the extraordinary cotton circuit took shape towards the middle of the century: leaving the Indies or America, it reached British industry by way of Africa... When East Indian or American planters bought Manchester cottons to dress their slaves, they were clothing the very Africans whose presence enabled them to send raw materials to the great industries of Lancashire.

Transformed into light, white materials, cotton brought about a revolution in European clothing as rapid and complete as that provoked in the Middle Ages by the discovery of Oriental

702 Woman's shoe of green damask with metal thread embroidery and high red heel, c. 1730.
Musée Bally, Schoenenwerd. (Museum photo)

WOMEN'S SHOES
702-3 Women's shoes are often made of silk; the increasingly high heel remains balanced because of its position under the arch of the foot, whether for closed shoes or for mules

EMBROIDERY
704 Waistcoats of this type, still long and with striking embroidery in seventeenth-century style, nonetheless announce the lighter forms of the eighteenth century

INDIAN COTTONS
705-6 The vogue throughout Europe for painted cottons imported from India was to lead to the establishment in Europe of textile industries imitating Eastern products. There was a great fashion for these materials for simple types of garment

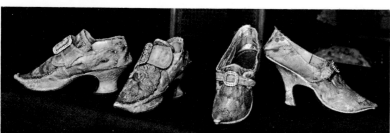

703 Silk high-heeled shoes with buttoned straps. Eighteenth century. Collection Fulgence. (Photo Flammarion)

silks. The use of *indiennes*, lawns and batistes also showed a taste for simplicity in harmony with the new ideals of 'democracy'.

In eighteenth-century France the progress of trade outstripped that of industry, as a result of the political difficulties of the first years of the century. Indeed, the War of the Spanish Succession had caused the sea blockade of France by England, and consequently a serious industrial crisis which particularly affected textiles: the silk and cloth industries were ruined in even the most prosperous centres, such as Nîmes, Lyons or Rheims.

However, the treaties of 1713 restored France's freedom at sea, and gave new life to the country's industries, in particular to the small producers whose prosperity considerably surpassed that of larger industries towards 1723.

Despite the violent shock that follow Law's crash, the Scots economist's 'system' had had favourable consequences for the French economy, by setting up a free capitalism and reviving sea trade. The textile centres of the North, Lyons and Rouen gained in importance, while Provence and Languedoc exported light cloths, cottons and cheap silks to the Levant and even silk stockings to Peru.

Naturally France's foreign trade was affected by wars and treaties in the course of the century. For instance, in 1778 Spain closed its markets to French clothing materials. After 1763 the clothing trades progressed rapidly, but this situation changed in 1786 when England, thanks to an unreciprocated exemption from customs duty, could flood the French markets with its textiles, at the precise moment when a Council decree of 1784 had opened trade with the French colonies to foreign merchants. Despite all this, the prosperity of several great French ports was partly founded on textiles: Nantes, where the trade with the 'American islands' gave birth to factories producing *indiennes*, and Rouen, where imported cotton led to the installation of factories in the region of the lower Seine.

As in the seventeenth century, the State continued to support the foundation of certain factories, by granting privileges, for instance the one granted to a Swiss for his cotton mill at Le Puy in 1736, or to a Lyonnais for his silk velvet factory; subsidies, particularly to the cotton industry; and monopolies, as for

the manufacture of stockings in Paris, Caen, Rouen, Nantes, Nîmes, Lyons, Poitiers, Bourges, Amiens and Rheims.

It was above all between 1730 and 1750 that industrial progress could be traced in the French textile industry, for these were years of peace, expenditure and luxury. The manufacture of silks spread beyond Lyons; in Paris Jean Simonet produced gold and silver cloths, and cottons expanded considerably in the East and in Normandy.

While France had no need of foreign inventions for silk-weaving, her cotton industry depended on English machines: the Holkers and later the Milnes spread them through Picardy, then to Lyons and Orleans.

The commercial treaty between England and France in 1786 led to equally severe crises in industry and trade, aggravated by the revival of competing industries in Italy, Spain and Germany. Thousands of workers were thrown out of work in Lyons, Troyes and Sedan.

PRINTED COTTONS

The 'cotton war' which had begun in the seventeenth century continued through part of the eighteenth; only in 1759 did the Council and the *Bureau de Commerce* authorize printing on cotton, by invoking the usefulness of an industry that could provide cheap clothing for the poor.

In the middle of the century factories producing printed cloths had already been set up, particularly by Swiss émigrés settled in France: Girtanner from Saint-Gall began in 1729 at Montbéliard, R. J. Wetter came to Marseilles in 1774, and A. Frey opened near Rouen in 1750. Later Wetter founded an important industry in Orange, which gave its name to '*toile d'Orange*', designating all products of this type.[2]

Another Swiss, Christophe Philippe Oberkampf, who had Franconian ancestry, set out to replace the blotting-out technique used until then, by the direct printing of blue. He managed to set up a modest factory at Jouy-en-Josas, on the banks of the Bièvre, in 1760, and won world-wide renown for the French printed cloth known as *toile de Jouy*. As a result of developments in physics and chemistry he perfected his tools and dyeing techniques and produced fast dyes. Ennobled by Louis XIV and supported by the Revolutionary and Empire governments, Oberkampf was defeated by the international trade blockade, and his successors failed to revive the firm, which closed down in 1843.

In 1746 the industry of 'Indian' cottons was introduced to Mulhouse by Koechlin and Dollfus, and launched cotton spinning and weaving in Alsace. There were other centres of production in Provence and Normandy: attractive dress material

292

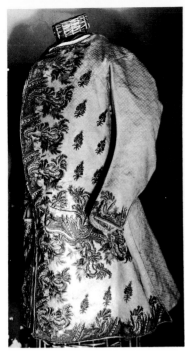  

704 Man's jacket, white, embroidered with silk and metal thread. Early eighteenth century. Collection Fulgence. (Photo Flammarion)

705 Pierrot jacket and skirt in hand-painted linen, trimmed with multi-coloured silk fringe. Louis XVI period. Union Française des Arts du Costume. (Photo Flammarion)

706 'Linen polonaise', 1776. Engraving by LEROY after SEBASTIEN LE CLERC, *Galerie des Modes et Costumes Français*. Paris, Bibliothèque Nationale, Cabinet des Estampes. (Photo Flammarion)

designs have been preserved from a factory in Orleans founded by Jacques de Mainville.[3]

The vogue for Indian cottons, white garments in plain cloth or cotonnade, accessories in lawn, muslin or gauze, dealt the Lyons silk industry as heavy a blow as the 1786 commercial treaty: the number of looms dropped by a quarter and the industry was not to revive until the nineteenth century.

COLOURS AND DYES

Increasingly active scientific research made noteworthy progress possible in the eighteenth century.

In his *Treatise on Optics*, translated into French in 1720, Sir Isaac Newton (1642–1727) had been the first to isolate the principal colours of the spectrum: red, yellow and blue, of which the other tones are only mixtures. Johann Tobias Mayer, of Göttingen University, established the principle of these mixtures, obtaining ninety-one principal shades and 9,381 that could be distinguished by the human eye. These findings provided the basis on which to search for the way to produce these tones and tints. The new possibilities of composite tones, half-tones and shadings provided textile manufacturers with numerous combinations of colours, more subtle under Louis XV, brighter and more garish under Louis XVI. The taste for these new stuffs grew with the increased production that placed them within the reach of anyone with a desire for elegance, regardless of his or her social position.

Throughout the century works were published from which dyers could gain practical information, not only about colorants, but also about bleaches, for in 1791 Berthollet had discovered the process of bleaching by using chlorine.

Costume gained from these developments a wider variety of colours, a more extensive choice of textiles, a greater range of invention in contrasts and harmonies. Decoration became more ornate and rich, plain and pale tones were more refined. In half a century costume was transformed; the bright colours of the earlier years gave way to muted shades or, under Marie-Antoinette, to strong tints.

COSTUME OUTSIDE FRANCE

The same transformations in industry and trade touched the other countries of Europe in varying degrees, especially in the second half of the century.

In Spain, production increased as the result of the rapid rise in exports to America after ports were opened to free trading in 1778. Cloth came from Biscay and Andalusia, silk from Valencia and Seville, while Catalonia, with Barcelona at its centre, became the great industrial region of the peninsula. As a result Spanish costume spread through the whole of Latin America.

In Holland, wars diminished the importance of the country's industries, until the foundation of sugar plantations in Java, and the crisis of trade halted the expansion of its fashions.

On the other hand, Belgium expanded its cloth mills. Privileged factories, linen and cotton mills producing *indiennes* were founded at Tournai by Clémen. Similarly, in the Rhinelands, Crefeld became a centre of the production of silks and velvets, and woollen weaving spread in Saxony. Further South, Switzerland enjoyed considerable industrial prosperity, and employed a large labour force on the production of cotton, silks or ribbons.

By contrast, Italy remained on the margin of this revival, and Florence, which was absorbed into the possessions of the Habsburgs in 1738, ceased to be a powerful weaving town. In Bavaria and Austria, agriculture was the dominant activity.

This unequal distribution through Europe of industrial development and its attendant prosperity explains the currents of influence we can trace in fashion.

Costume and Fashions in France

At the beginning of the eighteenth century, the impetus of the *Grand Siècle* continued for some time, despite financial crises and an unsettled situation in home and foreign politics. Shortly

707 SEBASTIEN LE CLERC: *Fashion figure*. Late seventeenth century. Paris, Bibliothèque Nationale, Cabinet des Estampes. (Photo Flammarion)

708 Engraving after WATTEAU: *Figures of Different Characters, c.* 1715. Paris, Bibliothèque Nationale, Cabinet des Estampes. (Photo Flammarion)

709–10 Sack gown of green damask brocaded with multi-coloured flowers, *c.* 1730. Union Française des Arts du Costume. (Photos Flammarion)

after the death of Louis XIV, however, we can see the first signs of changes which were to become more pronounced, and extend the field of French influence in elegance.

CUSTOMS, IDEAS AND SOCIETY

The foremost of these changes were in social customs, rapid, profound transformations which have been studied so widely elsewhere that there can be no point in covering the ground again here. From the last years of Louis XIV, the rigidity of the social hierarchies became modified and an aristocracy of wealth supplanted the hereditary nobility; at the same time the link, formerly so firm and close, binding prince and courtier began to weaken.

The young Louis XV's return to Paris permitted a whole society, weary of the etiquette and ceremonial of Versailles, to come back to the capital and savour an almost forgotten independence. Aristocratic society mingled there with the circles of high finance and the merchant middle classes, who had long dreamed of equalling the Court, and now seized the opportunity of outshining it.

In a feverish burst of emancipation and an immense redistribution of wealth, a whole society set out to enjoy the charms of luxury, organizing an elegant way of life that flowed easily as if in one vast drawing room, where display and taste were paramount, where wealth poured forth in cascades, and the luxury and inventiveness of costume brought the classes closer.

This tendency can be seen clearly from Dangeau's report of a meeting held in the Duchesse de Berry's house in July 1715, for which the hostess had summoned 'the most skilful tailors and renowned tailoresses, and Bertin, the Opera designer, to change the fashion.' On 1 August, the Duchesse d'Orleans and the young Prince de Conti went to Marly to present these novelties to the King. 'The King told them that they might dress as they pleased… it was all one to him.' He had only a month to live, it must be remembered. Dangeau adds: 'Many ladies disapprove of these new styles, which leads one to believe that they will not last.'

This new fashion, which some court ladies had tried to bring about in the last days of the *Grand Siècle*, was to blossom forth under the Regency and the century of the Enlightenment – the '*Siècle des Lumières*'.

Women's Costume

THE SACK GOWN

The more noticeable innovations in women's clothing – the *sack gown* and *paniers* – appeared successively but nonetheless constitute two very close stages in one and the same line of development.

Towards 1705–15 we see the rapid spread of the soft, flowing dresses that have often been classed together too readily under the title of 'Watteau gowns', though it is certain that Watteau played no part in their creation.

They have often been interpreted as forms inspired by the theatre, no doubt because of the vogue for Terence's *Andriana* in which Mme Dancourt, playing the role of 'Glycera rising from childbed' wore a shapeless gown which won the name *andrienne* and which spread under the name, slightly corrupted abroad, of *adrienne*.

The types of gown in this period, as we know from paintings and drawings by many artists, are very varied and did not all appear at the same time.

As early as the end of the seventeenth century, we find a toilette composed of a pointed boned bodice and a wide *manteau* (overgown), which might be plain or decorated with gathered panels, with a train that might be caught up in a sort of bustle behind. The underskirt was also sometimes trimmed with one or more flounces. This costume was generally worn with a Fontanges head-dress or a cap. It appears to have been discarded towards 1715.

Another model, definitely later than 1715, comprising a very

709–10, 712–4   The sack-back gown (*robe volante* or *ballante*), derived from the *andrienne* and the *robe de chambre* of the end of Louis XIV's reign, is the gown most typical of the French Regency period, and was to be worn for a long time as a simple gown. It seems to hang straight from the shoulders, flowing loosely round the body, without any passe-menterie decoration. The fullness of the back, gathered or pleated at the neckband, spreads out over a more or less circular panier, and the elbow-length *pagoda sleeves* are finished with cuffs gathered on the inside sleeve and above the chemise sleeve or with a linen or lace ruffle known as an *engageante*. The small flat cap makes the head seem small

PANIERS IN FRANCE

711, 713   The panier was initially a stiff underskirt fitted with more or less circular (or dome- or cupola-shaped) boned hoops, worn under the *robe volante* (plate 713). It was then divided and took the form of oblong paniers, spreading the fullness of court gowns on either side of the hips (711)

711   MOREAU LE JEUNE: *Les Adieux*, 1777. *Monument du Costume*. Paris, Bibliothèque Nationale, Cabinet des Estampes. (Photo Flammarion)

712   J. F. DE TROY: *Reading Molière*, 1727. Collection Marchioness Cholmondeley. (Photo Giraudon)

713   *Paniers*, engraving from the *Recueil Hérissot*, 1729. Paris, Bibliothèque Nationale, Cabinet des Estampes. (Photo Flammarion)

wide gown open all or half-way down the front, was characterized by a gathered or pleated piece attached at the shoulders flaring out towards the ground. The term 'sack gown' must certainly be reserved for this type of garment; it was generally worn over a circular panier and combined with a light head-dress, generally without a cap.

The terms 'Watteau gown' or 'Watteau pleats' do not seem to have any valid justification, for the drawings by Watteau known as *figures de modes* almost all represent gowns of the first type, and his Gersaint shop-sign, though showing a sack gown, dates from 1720, when the fashion had been widespread for some time. The sleeve of this model is particularly interesting, as it has vertical folds falling from the shoulder and its horizontally pleated cuff ornament is fastened with a loop to a button sewn directly to the sleeve.

Some of these gowns seem to have been made in one piece, without a shoulder seam, but it is always difficult to use a work of art to establish precisely a detail of cut.

Very often the fullness of this overgown was caught up into slits specially placed in the underskirt, to give access to the pockets placed under the paniers. This was called a *robe retroussée dans les poches* (gown turned up into the pockets). This fashion lasted as long as the pleated gown, mostly among towns-women and domestics.

These full gowns were worn for a long time, for in 1729 the *Mercure de France* noted that they were 'universally worn... one scarcely sees any other clothes'; and the paintings of elegant life by de Troy (plate 714) show them even after 1730, still put together with folds at the back and *pagoda sleeves*, flaring out and finished with a stiff, horizontally pleated cuff that fills out *en raquette* over the elbow.

PANIERS

The origin of paniers is still a subject of controversy. Whether the fashion came from England, where it was known as the *hoop petticoat*, towards 1714, or whether it originated from theatrical costume in Paris towards 1715, or even if it was invented in Germany, paniers were probably derived from *criardes*,[4] which were petticoats so called because of the noise they made.

These calf-length underskirts in gum-starched cloth were worn by actresses to fill out their outer costumes and make their waists appear slim.[5] This form shortly after became a petticoat with three tiers of whalebones.

This first type of paniers is mentioned in Paris about 1718–19. In about 1725, it was more rounded at the top and stiffened by five circles of steel strips, the top circle being known as the *traquenard* ('ambush'). From 1725–30, the paniers took on the shape of an oval bell, with a circumference of more than three ells (about eleven feet), supported by bones or light metal strips.

There were all sorts of paniers: funnel-shaped paniers *à guéridon*, dome-shaped paniers *à coupole*, paniers *à bourrelets* flaring out at the foot of the gown, paniers *à gondoles* which made women resemble 'water-carriers', and *elbow paniers*, on which the wearer could rest her elbows, and which the 1729 *Mercure* describes as being more comfortable than paniers *à guéridon*. There were also 'Jansenist' and 'Molinist' paniers; the former, also called '*considérations*', were simply short quilted petticoats lined with horse-hair; the more free-flowing Molinist paniers were better for tall women, as they slimmed the fat and filled out the thin.

Despite their inconvenience and discomfort, paniers enjoyed a persistent vogue during the reign of Louis XV. However, the form of the skirt was modified after 1730, when its front was flattened by a system of cords inside. Then, after about 1750, it was split into two parts: made of strong canvas over semi-circles of bone or rush, fastened to the waist by ribbons and held apart by other ribbons; this double panier could be lifted up under the arms. It may have existed earlier, for in a comedy of 1744 entitled *Les Paniers de la vieille Précieuse*, Harlequin sold them, calling out: 'I have solid ones which can be raised, for prudes, folding ones for gallant ladies and half-and-half models for members of the Third Estate...' Paniers were dignified by inclusion in the *Encyclopédie*, but only to record their fall from favour in 1765. They remained in wear until the reign of Louis XVI, for court costume with its long closed bodice, in which young women were forced to stifle during their presentation.

THE GOWN A LA FRANCAISE

Towards 1720 the sack gown was transformed into a pleated gown later known as the gown *à la française*. The pleats, arranged in two layers, fell from the centre of the neckline and hung loosely at the back. In front, the fitted bodice was fastened on either side of the *stomacher*, a triangle of richly decorated stuff which masked the bodice opening. This piece was often replaced by a ladder of bows decreasing in size towards the foot, and later this in turn gave way to two small facings fastened on either side of the bodice, known as *compères*. The overgown opened widely over the petticoat, which could be heavily or lightly decorated. A flat *parement*, which could be puffed or decorated with passementerie, edged the front, running round the neck and down to the foot of the hem. The flat sleeve stopped at the elbow, ending in pagoda style with one or more flounces cut with three notches to show the *engageante*, a cuff made of two or three graded flounces of lace, shallow inside the arm and deep outside, slightly different from the type worn

in the previous century. This type of gown was worn by all women, with variations only in the richness and material of the cloth used; this was often painted or printed silk or stuff, known as *indiennes*, which were produced in increasing quantities.

The gown *à la piémontaise*, which was worn at Lyons in 1755 by the Princess of Piedmont, was a variant of the gown *à la française*; the back pleats were independent, fastened to the bodice neck and spreading out to form a sort of court mantle, the fullness of which was held in the hands on either side.

COURT COSTUME

Eighteenth-century court costume or *grand habit* was only the continuation of court costume under Louis XIV: it retained the traits of the seventeenth-century gown until the early years of the reign of Louis XV, and when it was modified, the general line changed very little.

It comprised a stiff bodice with horizontal epaulettes, leaving the shoulders bare, ending in a pronounced point at the waist. The skirt had a train which could be picked up and carried. The epaulette covered the top of a lace sleeve which clothed the upper arm and was decorated with two symmetrical pleats known as *petits bonshommes*. Gown and bodice were made of the same material and embroidery on the bodice imitated the triangle of the stomacher. For presentation bodices, overgown and petticoats had to be black, with cuffs and trimmings in white lace, with a black bracelet formed of a series of pompoms. After the day of presentation, everything that had been black was changed for gold-coloured material. If the lady could not bear the stiff *corps*, she was allowed to wear an ordinary *corset* covered with a mantilla.

In court costume paniers reached such extravagant widths that in 1728 those worn by princesses of the royal blood, who flanked the Queen in accordance with protocol, hid her from the public in theatres; the prime minister, Cardinal Fleury, ordered that one seat should be left empty on either side of the Sovereign; to calm the princesses' protests, orders were given to leave empty seats between them and their neighbours also, so as to dispose of the paniers worn by the two duchesses who followed; however, these duchesses, supported by their husbands, rose up in protest against such measures, which diminished their rank.[6]

ENGLISH STYLES

More practical considerations dictated the introduction in France of the gown *à l'anglaise*, in a very different style.

We must go back to the very last years of the reign of Louis XIV to see the first signs of Anglomania and its influence on costume in France and in other countries. It showed initially in men's costume, then quickly spread to women's clothing, but did not develop fully until after 1775.

A first wave reached France with sport and riding, and the craze gradually spread for all simple, comfortable English garments, which were practical in wear and showed off the waist. Towards 1765 the boned bodice, which was even imposed on children (plate 743), began to become softer and its cuirass developed into an easier funnel-shape; bodices *à l'anglaise* had side seams that curved inwards to follow the lines of the waist. They were 'closed for five inches from the waist, then opened

714   J. F. DE TROY: *The Declaration of Love*, 1731. Berlin, Staatliche Schlösser und Gärten. (Museum photo)

715   FRANCOIS BOUCHER: *The Marquise de Pompadour*, 1759. London, The Wallace Collection. (Reproduced by permission of the Trustees)

716   F. H. DROUAIS: *The Marquise d'Aiguirandes*, 1759. The Cleveland Museum of Arts, John Peverance Bequest (1936). (Museum photo)

717 MENGS: *Portrait of the Queen of Spain, Maria Luisa of Parma, c.* 1765. New York, Metropolitan Museum. (Museum photo)

718 FRANÇOIS BOUCHER: *Mme de Pompadour, c.* 1745–50. Collection Maurice de Rothschild. (Photo Bulloz)

719 MME LAVILLE-GUIARD: *Mme Adélaide,* 1786. Versailles, Museum. (Photo Flammarion)

720 Coronation gown worn by Queen Louisa Ulrica, 1741. Stockholm, Royal Armoury

721 Formal *grande parure* gown in white silk brocaded in polychrome silk and gold and silver thread, *c.* 1780. Amsterdam, Rijksmuseum. (Museum photo)

THE ROBE À LA FRANÇAISE

715–6, 718–9, 722 The *robe à la française* derives from the sack gown, but double pleats on either side of the centre back seam spread the fullness at the back. The bodice is fitted in front and more often than not opens to reveal the *stiff bodice*, trimmed in front with a *stomacher*, triangular and richly decorated, or with a ladder of ribbons. In the case of the *grande robe* (plates 718, 722), the overgown opens over an underskirt of the same material, with the same trimmings of flowers and various types of ornament; collarettes and collars of lace or ribbon decorate the neck. The chemise flounce often fills the décolletage of this gown, which was elegant wear during the reigns of Louis XV and XVI. The cut does not vary; the linen or lace *engageantes* (ruffles), generally with three flounces, follow the cut frill that finishes the flat sleeve, and replace the gathered cuff *en raquette*

PANIERS OUTSIDE FRANCE

717, 720–21 Details of decoration, but also the form of the paniers show that the gowns are not French: the extreme width and almost right-angled outline of the paniers, clearly separated on either hip, have an ungraceful, exaggeratedly artificial style which was to last until the end of the century in court costume in the Northern countries

COURT COSTUME

711, 723–5 Court costume (plates 711, 723) differs only in the paniers from the costume worn at the court of Louis XIV; it is formed of a stiff bodice with adjustable shoulder-straps, back-laced, and a richly trimmed skirt half covered by the train of the gown, which was fastened at the waist and could be removed. The sleeves are decorated with lace ruching, arranged symmetrically and known as *petits bonshommes;* the head-dress or hairstyle is dictated by the fashion of the moment. With slight variants adapted to the customs of each country, similar court costume was worn throughout Europe.

Plates 724–5 are designs for a national court costume inspired by styles of the time of Henri IV; these costumes, executed by Sarrazin, the court tailor, were worn only at formal balls from 1774 to 1776

slightly towards the top, and were laced with a cord to within an inch of the top.'[7]

In 1768 the *Courrier de la Mode* recommended, even for balls, 'English gowns with tight sleeves and collars trimmed with gauze,' worn with small, flower-trimmed hats.

After 1750, fashion turned towards England inspired by the interest in the novels of Richardson, the first horse-races in Paris and English landscape gardening. 'An English lady,' said Parisians, 'almost always wears déshabillées at home, harmo-

722 *Robe à la française* in white silk brocaded with flowers, 1750–70. Union Française des Arts du Costume. (Photo Flammarion)

723 MOREAU LE JEUNE: *The Queen's Lady-in-Waiting*, 1776. Paris, Bibliothèque Nationale, Cabinet des Estampes. (Photo Flammarion)

724–5 DESRAIS: *Costume of Court Lady under Louis XVI* and LE CLERC: *Suit Imitated from the Time of Henri IV*, 1774–6. Paris, Bibliothèque Nationale, Cabinet des Estampes. (Photos Flammarion)

nizing with the interior of her house; if she shows herself in St James's Park in the morning, she wears a little dress, a big white apron and a fairly flat hat.'

The introduction of English fashions must be laid to the credit of a charming minor talent, an engraver and, most of all, a book-illustrator, Gravelot (plates 766, 774), the son of a Parisian tailor. On returning from a stay of almost twenty years in England he published, in 1744, studies of men and women drawn after three lay figures made in England with wardrobes that covered every occasion, from town wear to the theatre. He introduced France to the taste for innocent-looking straw hats, plain gowns and white stuffs.

The gown *à la française* was reserved for ceremonies, while the English style was worn in everyday life.[8] The back of the bodice, boned at the seams, formed a long point at the waist, which was fitted. The skirt had a short train, and was gathered from the hips, supported only by a padded bustle. In front, the bodice was laced, often with a plunging neckline filled with a fine linen fichu, and the skirt opened wide over the underskirt. This marked the disappearance of the boned bodice and the evolution towards the one-piece gown.

Still inspired by English styles, the *coat-dress* (*robe-redingote*) was to appear shortly after; it also had a fitted bodice, buttoning in front or crossed like the male greatcoat, with pointed lapels and the skirt either closed or opened widely over the underskirt; the large oval buttons were made of English steel.

As fashion made no claims to logic, people saw nothing strange in wearing a gown *à l'Insurgente*, out of sympathy with the Americans; this was nothing more than a gown *à l'anglaise* with the front turned up to show revers in a contrasting colour. Franklin's mission to Paris, the Franco-American alliance and the expeditions of Lafayette and Rochambeau gave names to all manner of fashions, but these were applied only to details of trimmings and brought no important innovation.

The most decisive import from England was the fashion for hats. As we know, women in the Nordic countries had worn hats in the sixteenth and seventeenth centuries, but Frenchwomen had gone hatless, apart from the brief appearance of toques in the sixteenth century, and hats taken from men's

styles for riding or in exceptional circumstances, as during the Fronde.

In England, hats were currently worn in all classes of society from the middle of the eighteenth century. This fashion spread to France with the taste for pastoral life, but only for very elegant women, whose hats were designed as part of their hairstyle. The wave of Anglomania in the years from 1775 to 1780 brought large hats in the English style which were worn outdoors, a habit which has persisted since: the *Marlborough* had a bunch of ostrich feathers, while the *Devonshire* had fourteen plumes mixed with aigrettes, and the *Charlotte* was a large muslin cloche launched by the Queen of England and worn for over a century. The inventiveness of French creators made the most of this enthusiasm and all current events were translated into concoctions of plumes and ribbons. Women wore them with *cadogans*, a male hairstyle that owed its name to Lord Cadogan and was also known as the *English queue*.

EASTERN AND ORIENTAL INFLUENCES

The early years of the reign of Louis XVI saw the appearance of a series of fashions inspired by the countries of eastern Europe and the Orient, if not always in form, at least in name.

The marriage of Marie Leczinska and Louis XV in 1725 had already stimulated a Polish fashion for ribbons woven to simulate fur. In 1717 Peter the Great had brought his out-of-date brown suit, wig and fur cap, an ensemble that was adopted by artists such as Aved, or writers, such as Jean-Jacques Rousseau. The Franco-Russian alliance accentuated this Russophilia further in 1750, and it was counterbalanced by the Russian nobility's craze for French fashions. Catherine II wrote to Grimm, her Paris correspondent, in 1780: 'At present you in Paris wear Russian hats and ribbons: the French have gone head-over-heels for me, as if I were a feather for their hats.' And the *Cabinet des modes* in 1788 mentions a gown *à la Tzarina*.

Fashion had always drawn inspiration from the East; in 1755 Mme de Pompadour commissioned Carle van Loo to do a series of portraits of her as a sultana for her château at Belle-

299

726 ELIZABETH VIGÉE-LEBRUN: *Madame Molé Raymond*,
1787. Paris, Louvre. (Photo Flammarion)

727 FRANÇOIS BOUCHER: *Breakfast*, 1739. Paris, Louvre.
(Photo Flammarion)

728 CHARDIN: Morning Toilette, 1741. Stockholm, Nationalmuseum.
(Museum photo)

vue. In 1773 Mme du Barry asked Amedeo van Loo to paint her in the same costume.

But after 1775, fashions followed one another in an almost uninterrupted succession – *à la polonaise* (plate 740), *à la circassienne*, then *à la lévite*, *à la levantine*, *à la turque* and *à la sultane* (plate 761) – due to a wide variety of causes: the success of portraits in Turkish style painted by the Chevalier de Favray, Aved and Liotard, or the travels of ambassadresses who wore Oriental costumes on their return to France. Mme Geoffrin's triumphal visit to her 'son', Stanislas Augustus Poniatowski in Warsaw may even have been a powerful propagandizing element.

The earliest in date of these innovations was the gown *à la polonaise* (plate 740), which appeared towards 1772–4, coinciding with the partitioning of Augustus III's former kingdom. It is enough to mention this style's essential features without going into detail about the innumerable variants; it was fastened high on the chest and opened wide over the underskirt, with the overskirt drawn up over the hips by two drawstrings, forming three rounded swags, short on either side (the 'wings') and long at the back (the 'train'), or vice versa. The flat sleeves covered the elbows with a sort of cuff of gauze or cloth, in the so-called *sabot* shape. This gown was fitted at the back, and produced a lively, shortened outline, soon replacing the gown *à la française* for normal wear.

It seems that this gown *à la polonaise* was never worn in Poland, and in view of the eighteenth-century taste for symbolic translation, we may well wonder if the three swags represented the partition of Poland, which was a live issue in France in 1772; however there are no texts to confirm this.

Gowns with Oriental names were strongly influenced by the theatre; the first inspiration for the gown *à la lévite* came from productions of *Athalie* at the Théâtre Français, when Jewish priestly costume was worn. This straight gown, with its shawl collar and back pleats, was held at the waist by a loose scarf; Marie-Antoinette contributed to its popularization by wearing it during her first pregnancy in 1778.

There were many other 'Oriental' gowns: the *circassienne* had 'an undergown with long, very tight sleeves with an over-

729 ROSLIN: *The Martineau de Fleuriau Family*, 1785.
Collection The Marquis and Marquise de Gontaut.
(Photo Flammarion)

730 TRINQUESSE: Young Woman in gown *à l'anglaise*, 1782. Collection Cailleux. (Photo Routhier)

731 *Robe à l'anglaise*, white satin striped with pink. Union Française des Arts du Costume. (Photo Flammarion)

732 Redingote in lemon yellow cloth striped with apple green, slit marinière sleeves and bonnet hat, 1776–7. Engraving by DUHAMEL after DESRAIS. Paris, Bibliothèque Nationale. (Photo Flammarion)

733 Half redingote in lemon yellow taffeta, hat *à la Tarare*, 1786–7. Engraving by DUHAMEL after DEFRAINE, *Cabinet des Modes* 1786. Paris, Bibliothèque Nationale, Cabinet des Estampes, Oa 85 d. fo. (Photo Flammarion)

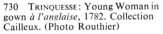

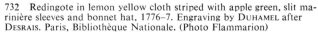

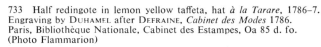

MIDDLE-CLASS COSTUME

728 Gowns are shorter, revealing the feet; the overgown is tucked up into the pockets, revealing the underskirt; a Coqueluchon covers the shoulders; caps are of the *dormeuse* type; the little girl's muff is in velvet edged with fur

THE ROBE À L'ANGLAISE

729–31 The *robe à l'anglaise*, which appeared towards 1778, opens in front over a waistcoat formed of two *compères* (panels); the closely-fitting boned bodice ends in a point at the back; the flat sleeves do not have *engageantes*, but are sometimes flounced on the elbow; the fullness of the skirt is brought back over a 'false bottom'; this gown is not worn over paniers

WOMEN'S REDINGOTES

726, 732–3 Redingotes were flat-collared gowns buttoned up the front (plate 732), imitated from English-inspired male costume; their vogue is attested by very precise engravings from the *Galerie des Modes;* however, there were to be numerous variants of this style, including the half-redingote with a more open skirt (plates 726, 733). Broad-brimmed hats, which had recently come into fashion, are often inspired by plays, as was the bonnet hat (fig. 732) worn over a cap and baptised 'upturned boat' or *à la Théodore* (from the opera *Le Roi Théodore à Venise*). Similarly the hat *à la Tarare* (plate 733) owes its name to a play by Beaumarchais

WOMEN'S HATS

734–9 England was the source of the vogue for large hats; contemporary events gave their names to various extravagant models

THE ROBE À LA POLONAISE

740, 746 The Polonaise was fastened at the neckline beneath the bow, called 'perfect contentment'; at the waist it divided to show a waistcoat; draw-strings enabled the wearer to drape the gown in panels of varying lengths; it had *sabot sleeves*, fitting tightly as far as the elbow, trimmed with symmetrically arranged gauze ruffles known as *petits bonshommes*. The neckline of elegant Polonaises could be edged with a standing collarette called an *archduchess* (plate 740)

---

734 Hat *à l'anglaise*, 1785   735 Montgolfier Hat, 1785

736 Newmarket Hat, 1785   737 Globe of Paphos Hat, 1785

738 Cherubino Hat, 1785   739 Cherubino Hat, 1785

Paris, Bibliothèque Nationale. (Photos Flammarion)

gown tucked up all round and short sleeves cut straight across'; the *levantine* consisted of a sort of pelisse edged with ermine, opening over an undergown and petticoat; the sultana gown, which was short-sleeved and completely open in front, stood out mainly because of the use of contrasting colours for the different parts of the gown, as was the case for the *circassienne*.

The East was also probably responsible for the new taste for pelisses lined and edged with fur, which appeared after 1770 – the first type of an outer garment that was neither a voluminous scarf, as in the preceding century, nor a *mante* recalling the old cape, as worn around 1730.

Where Oriental head-dresses – *levantine*, *sultana* or *crescent* caps, *poufs à l'asiatique*, crowned with plumes and lilac blossoms, with tiger-skin centre-pieces, and turbans trimmed with aigrettes – are concerned, their names suffice to indicate the source that inspired them. In 1776 Lallemand, 'attitled wigmaker to the King of Prussia and correspondent to the Grand Turk', published an *Essai sur la coiffure*, translated from the Persian.

SIMPLE GOWNS

Towards 1778–9 the already time-honoured vogue for Indian cotton gowns was succeeded by the fashion for gowns *en chemise* or *à la créole* (plates 747, 749), whose simple, soft shapes were very much alike.

Mentioned in Jaubert's dictionary (1778), the chemise gown could be stepped into or slipped over the head, and was a 'false gown without a train'. It was launched by Mme Vigée-Lebrun's portrait, exhibited at the 1783 Salon, in which the Queen (plate 747) 'wore a straw hat and a gown of white muslin'. Critics made violent attacks on Marie-Antoinette, but she and her entourage had already worn this type of garment for some time, if we are to believe Mme Vigée-Lebrun, who mentions meeting her in 'a white gown' at Marly about 1775.

Gowns *à la créole*, were chemise-shaped, with wide sashes and allegedly reproduced the gowns worn by 'French ladies in America'. They are said to have been launched by a Creole ballet in a travelling theatre troupe. These gowns were worn under a *caraco* (also called *pet en l'air*), recalling the peasant jacket (plate 750); this was the upper part of a gown *à la française* cut off at pocket level, said to have been worn by the women of Nantes when the Duc d'Aiguillon passed through their town.[9]

Like the preceding types of gown, the *fourreau* or sheath marks a reaction against the tyranny of the boned bodice; this was a gown cut in one piece, with a lightly boned, back-lacing bodice and a closed skirt. This model had already been worn by children since the middle of the century; its ease and comfort together with the new ideas on hygiene that were beginning to spread led to its adoption by women and it became fashionable towards 1781. Mme Vigée-Lebrun shows Mme Dugazon in *Nina ou la Folle par Amour* in this gown (plate 765), and in 1786 the Marquise de la Tour du Pin ordered a sheath gown in white gauze with one broad blue ribbon, from England; this seems to indicate that the fashion had crossed the Channel earlier, and been brought back by the craze for things English.

The enthusiasm for simple forms and white gowns, though frivolous, nonetheless reflect influences that did not depend on pure caprice. Under the influence of Jean-Jacques Rousseau's philosophy people's heads and hearts were filled with ideas of

740   Young élégante in Polonaise dress in painted linen, 1786. *Galerie des Modes et Costumes français*. Paris   Bibliothèque Nationale, Cabinet des Estampes, Oa 81. (Photo Flammarion)

motherhood, education, sensibility and humanity; the *Nouvelle Héloïse*, the love of the countryside and the rediscovery of nature gave rise to the simple white gowns worn in the Trianon Village. At that time every woman aspired to ingenuous candour; elegant women and city housewives chose their gowns to express the peasant simplicity hymned in the exalted pages of Bernardin de Saint-Pierre or Gessner.

The theatrical character of this nature cult was a European phenomenon. In the English landscaped gardens of the royal castle of Drottningholm in Sweden, sheep grazed under the watchful eyes of shepherds and shepherdesses dressed by the castle's theatrical designer.

Moreover, allusions to Classical times – the great literary success of the time was the *Voyage du jeune Anacharsis*, by Barthélémy – spurred elegant women to turn to pseudo-Greek or Roman styles: this was to be the craze of the next period, under the Revolution and the Empire.

'NÉGLIGÉES'

A history of eighteenth-century fashions cannot be complete without mentioning, as well as the great gowns that characterized the period, the multitude of small, light feminine garments brought into vogue by comfort or coquetterie throughout the century.

As early as the Regency period we see *casaquins*, short, hip-length jackets, which were fairly fitted in front and loose at the back: these were 'pleated gowns' cut off at pocket level. Some historians have also tried to assign this name to riding jackets and bodices; however these were special riding garments, with their varied forms, tight cut and with short basques, just as in the preceding century women's hongrelines and justaucorps had been adapted for riding. In fact the casaquin was an 'informal garment'.

It became less current towards the middle of the century, then reappeared towards 1768 under the name of *caraco*: it was then a gown *à la française* or *à la polonaise* cut off at hiplevel. A less clearly defined form was known as a *pierrot*, and also

741 ELIZABETH VIGÉE-LEBRUN (attr.): *The Dauphin* (future Louis XVII) playing with a yo-yo, wearing a sailor suit, *c.* 1790. Auxerre, Museum. (Photo Philippot)

742 L. BOILLY: *Ce qui allume l'amour l'éteint* ('What kindles love extinguishes it'), 1790. Saint-Omer, Museum. (Photo Giraudon)

CHILDREN'S COSTUME

741–3 It was only gradually, probably under English influence, that children's costume stopped resembling adult styles; little boys wore sailor suits with long trousers and a soft belt, while girls wore straight sheath dresses with the soft fichu worn by young women

EASTERN INFLUENCE

744, 761 The Orient left its mark on silk patterns, and there was a predilection for Oriental styles of dress throughout the eighteenth century

743 F. H. DROUAIS: *Charles de France and his sister Marie-Adélaïde,* 1763. Paris, Louvre. (Photo Flammarion)

seems to have been the ensemble formed by a caraco and skirt.

A very tight-fitting jacket with a full basque at the back was known as the *juste*; formerly the term had referred to a man's garment and become confused with the justaucorps. Next it had been applied to a tight peasant bodice, barely distinguishable from the hongreline; it was certainly by analogy that the name was given to the short, almost mannish jacket best known as the *juste à la Figaro* or *à la Suzanne* worn in the fifth act of *The Marriage of Figaro* in 1785.

ACCESSORIES

We should mention, among the numerous accessories that completed women's clothing in the eighteenth century, the *apron*, a functional garment for the working classes but also a luxury object, made of embroidered silk, for elegant women, the *mantilla*, introduced from Spain in 1721 by the ladies-in-waiting accompanying the Infanta, the *mantelet à coqueluchon*, which replaced the scarf after 1730, and *nightgowns*, already worn in the preceding century under varying names, but then increasing in variety and elegance.

Where underclothes were concerned, the chemise was scarcely changed; it probably lost its trimmings and sleeves, which were no longer visible in the new styles, but its neck frill still fell out over the gown. Drawers, which had gone out of fashion, had been obligatory wear in the theatre since 1760 and were also to be found in ordinary costume.[10] Fine linen petticoats were indispensable with paniers, but do not seem to have been particularly ornate.

The fine linen fichu appeared with the white or pale cotton gown towards 1778; later it became larger and latterly framed the face, under the name *fichu menteur*. It was often lengthened, crossed and tied behind the back. Until the Revolution it was to remain the perfect accessory for Creole or country gowns of silk or printed cotton.

744 LIOTARD: *Simon Luttrell of Luttrelstown, c.* 1755. Berne, Kunstmuseum. (Museum photo)

745 MOREAU LE JEUNE: *Leaving the Opera*, 1781. *Le Monument du Costume*. Paris, Bibliothèque Nationale, Cabinet des Estampes. (Photo Giraudon)

746 WILLE: *Two Young Women, c.* 1785. Private Collection. (Photo Flammarion)

747 ELIZABETH VIGÉE-LEBRUN: *Marie-Antoinette wearing a gaulle*, 1783. Collection H. R. H. The Prince of Hesse and Rhine. (Photo Versailles Museum)

HAIRSTYLES

During the eighteenth century the arrangement of women's hair went through some surprising extremes. Under the Regency and Louis XV, short, crimped hair was dressed in a small chignon. According to the *Mercure de France*, after 1730 women began to use false hair which enabled them to dress their hair with as little trouble as a man putting on a wig. Then came the fashion for hair swept up above the forehead and temples for everyday occasions, although false switches were retained in court costume for the long ringlets that fell to the shoulders.

748 WILLE: *Little Vauxhall*, 1775. Paris, Musée Carnavalet. (Photo Flammarion)

749 *Costume à la Créole* 'imitated from that worn by our French ladies in America...' 1787

750 *Young woman in caraco, gauze trimmed like the skirt, with cap in the new peasant style*, 1786. *Galerie des Modes et Costumes français.* (Photos Flammarion)

In his *Art de la coiffure des dames*, which ran through several editions and supplements between 1765 and 1768, the celebrated court hairdresser Legros gave numerous models of the hairstyles, using real or false hair, that he had created; in 1769 he even founded an *Académie de Coiffure*. The success of Legros and his many colleagues led them into a lawsuit with the corporation of barbers, who obtained an ordinance in August 1777, stipulating that the six hundred women's hairdressers should join their corporation.

After the disappearance of the Fontanges style, women wore caps, except with court and ceremonial costume, during the whole of the eighteenth century. These were minute under the Regency period, barely covering the top of the head, later becoming larger to form a fairly pronounced point in the centre of the forehead (the *bonnet à bec*). Towards the middle of the century they multiplied into variants that are often difficult to identify: *papillons* (plate 758), *dormeuses* (plate 756), *baigneuses*, *battant l'oeil* and *cornettes* were worn according to the time of day or the wearer's social rank and occupations. The *Bagnolette*, a sort of hood gathered at the back of the head, and the *Thérèse*, a vast head-dress mounted on a metal framework, were worn particularly out of doors.

Little by little the most extravagant caprices began to dominate the vogue for caps. Anything could be taken as a pretext for changing their shapes and trimmings; current affairs and events, notorious lawsuits or successful plays were transformed into pleats, ruchings and puffs which, after 1772, were

751 *Casakeens*, 1729. Engraving from the *Recueil Hérissot*. Paris, Bib. Nat., Cabinet des Estampes. (Photo Bibliothèque Nationale)

752 *Young woman in jacket and skirt of zebra striped cloth, with marinière sleeves and hat à la Tarare*, 1788. Engraving by DUHAMEL, *Cabinet des Modes*. Paris, Bibliothèque Nationale, Cabinet des Estampes Oa 85 d. (Photo Flammarion)

753 JANINET: *Mademoiselle Contat in the role of Suzanne in The Marriage of Figaro*, 1784. Paris, Bib. Nat., Cabinet des Estampes Rés E f 106 f t. IV. (Photo Bibliothèque Nationale)

754 *Young woman wearing a baigneuse and a fur-lined satin pelisse*, 1778. Galerie des Modes et Costumes français. (Photo Flammarion)

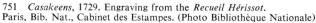

THE CIRCASSIAN GOWN

745, 748 The Circassian gown is a variant of the Polonaise, from which it differs only by its short sleeves revealing the sleeve of the underbodice or *soubreveste*. The flower-girl (plate 745) wears a short cloak known as a *parlement*, and the woman in Circassian gown (plate 748) a *helmet à la bellona*

THE CHEMISE DRESS

747, 749 The chemise dress, also called *gaulle* or baby dress, or *à la Créole*, was worn without a bodice; tied with a sash below the breasts it was generally in muslin or light gauze, opening over an equally light underskirt. It was one of the fashions imported from America, and the hat (plate 749) trimmed with grenadine flowers with a grenadine on the bow commemorates the capture of Grenada by the French

CASAKEENS AND CARACOS

750–52 Throughout the century women wore short garments like the usual dresses, but cut off at hip-level; the truncated sack gown, or *casakeen*, the shortened *robe à la française* or *caraco*, the abbreviated redingote or *veste*. However, the names are sometimes imprecise and some caracos are called *pierrots*, although it is not possible to seen any appreciable difference between them (cf. plate 705). The young woman wearing a caraco (plate 750) is wearing a head-dress 'à la physionomie élevée'; the cap exposes the *temperament* (Pompadour above the forehead) and the side-curl falls in front of the ear

---

755 JEAURAT: *The Thrifty Wife*, 1754. Cap with scalloped barbs worn over the head. (Photo Flammarion)

756 MOREAU LE JEUNE: *Announcing Pregnancy*, 1776. Night-cap. *Monument du Costume* (detail). (Photo Flammarion)

757 MOREAU LE JEUNE: *'It's a son, sir'*, 1776. *Cauchoise* cap. (Photo Flammarion)

758 MOREAU LE JEUNE: *'I accept the happy omen'*, 1776. Butterfly cap. (Photo Flammarion)

759–60 Caleche and cap with marmotte. c. 1780. *Galerie des Modes et Costumes francais.* (Photo Flammarion)

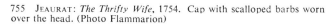

married to the enormous hairstyles to give a new combination each day, with plumes and flowers and miscellaneous objects: *poufs au sentiment*, assembling cherished objects on the wearer's head, coiffures *à la grand-mère*, with springs that made it possible to lower them, coiffures *à la loge d'Opéra* (1772) or *à la Comète* (1773), or even *à la Belle-Poule*, which included a fully-rigged frigate (1778); the *coiffure à l'Insurgent* (1780) included a snake so convincingly imitated that the style had to be forbidden, to spare ladies' nerves. Heads carried tiers of cypresses, horns of plenty, whole menageries and landscape gardens; later, fresh flowers in vials of water tucked into the hair were considered the height of simplicity. The mixtures of hats and hairstyles were characteristic of the whole pre-Revolutionary period; these were the joint creations of hairdressers and milliners whose imagination proved inexhaustibly fertile; the Comtesse de Matignon made a bargain with the famous Baulard who, for 24,000 livres a year, was to provide her with a new headdress every day.[11]

These overblown monuments inspired caricaturists: a hairdresser balanced on top of a ladder to put the finishing touches to one of his creations, and a wigmaker using scaffolding to move round his client's head without disarranging her hair. This did not stop elegant women throughout Europe wearing these styles until the eve of the French Revolution, even in England where women preferred immense hats and bonnets to high hairstyles.

Women's and men's hair was powdered with starch, and consequently to avoid going through the dusting operation every day women went to bed in taffeta caps covering the hair. For powdering, or *accommodage*, the client wrapped herself in a peignoir and covered his or her face with a paper cone.

FOOTWEAR

From the Regency to the Revolution women's shoes changed little. Until 1770 they were long and pointed, slightly upturned at the tip; then they became shorter and round-toed. Generally there were crossed straps over the instep, with buckles; then the quarter was fastened to the upper at the side.

Fashionable shoes (plates 702–3) had high, forward-tilted heels under Louis XV, lower heels set further back after 1775. Mules, shaped like shoes, had lower heels.

White or coloured leather was most often used for everyday wear, with silk matching the gown for elegant occasions. The upper was also embroidered. The heels, made of hard wood, were covered with red leather.

Buckles varied considerably, being round or square, made of silver, steel or diamanté; under Louis XVI they were replaced by pleated ribbons or by a shoe-lace covered by two padded shells.

The shoes woven from very small beads, also known as *sablés*, which had been worn at the beginning of the century, were scarcely to be seen in the last years; however, it seems that this type of work was still used for mules.

There was a characteristic sign of prosperity: in the eight or ten years before the Revolution, shoemakers kept increasingly large shops and Sébastien Mercier noted that 'with their black coats and well-powdered wigs you would take them for solicitors'.

Men's Costume

Throughout western Europe, including France, men's costume did not undergo any important transformation. However, its general line gradually became simplified so that the male silhouette of 1789 had virtually nothing in common with that of 1710.

MISCELLANEOUS GARMENTS AND COURT COSTUME

At the beginning of the century men's costume already included the essential elements of modern costume: an outer garment (justaucorps), another undergarment (the jacket), and a garment covering the legs to the knee (breeches). The combination of these three pieces was the *habit* or suit, worn by all social classes, with differences in cloth or ornament which could make it a simple or a ceremonial garment. Gradually the term *habit* (coat) became used for only the justaucorps, whose old name disappeared from current usage; tailors were alone in keeping to the old term until about 1770.

The justaucorps, which had had a flaring shape at the end of the reign of Louis XIV, initially tended to become simpler; after 1720 a fan of flat pleats was sewn to the hip seam to 'imitate a panier', supported by panels of horsehair. The front edges were straight, with buttons and buttonholes all the way down; sleeves were finished with deep, broad facings, and pockets had straight or cut revers. Towards 1740 the size of pleats and facings decreased, and the fronts slanted to the waist, departing from the old straight line. After 1760 they opened to form a triangle below the last button, and the sides lost their fullness.

The jacket always had its back made in ordinary material, with very rich stuff for the front and the sleeve ends. It was generally fastened only at the waist, to show the jabot and lace of the shirt. The line of the front underwent the same change as the justaucorps, and the length of the basques decreased. At the end of the reign of Louis XV this under-jacket barely reached beyond the waist, and had lost its sleeves after the narrowing of the justaucorps sleeves. It then took the name of *gilet*, which appears in the 1762 *Dictionnaire de l'Académie*, or *waistcoat*. Lamé or brocaded cloth was replaced by cloth embroidered in many colours. The two short points of the front spread apart to form a triangle, but towards 1785 waistcoats appeared cut straight across at the waist, often with military-type revers.

Breeches did not change much in shape during the century. They were closed with buttons before 1730 and, after then, by a panel of varying size: they were then known as *culottes à la bavaroise*, almost like the breeches worn today by mountain-dwellers. They always reached below the knee, fastened with a buckled garter or a ribbon. As the jacket became shorter, the breeches had to reach higher and it became necessary to hold them up with braces, which were originally two ribbons passing over the shoulders; they were not to be crossed over the back until the end of the century.

One of the century's great innovations was the *greatcoat* or *redingote*. This full, broadcloth garment was fairly long, with buttoned cuffs and two collars, the lower of which, the *rotonne*, covered the shoulders. Its appearance was mentioned in Barbier's *Journal*, where the author mentions that when the court

761 AVED: *The Marquise de Saint-Maur dressed as a Sultana*, 1743.
Collection Wildenstein. (Photo Flammarion)

762 NATTIER: *The Comtesse de Tillières*, 1750.
London, The Wallace Collection.
(Reproduced by permission of the Trustees, Photo Freeman)

763 MAUZAISE (after GIROUST): *Princess Adélaïde d'Orléans taking a harp lesson with Mme de Genlis*, c. 1789.
Versailles, Museum. (Photo Flammarion)

764 GAINSBOROUGH: *Lady Gertrude Alston*, 1750.
Paris, Louvre. (Photo Flammarion)

765 JANINET: *Madame Dugazon in the role of 'Nina or The Woman Crazed with Love'*, 1786. Paris, Bib. Nat., Cabinet des Estampes, Rés E f 106 f t. IV. (Photo Bibliothèque Nationale)

767 MOREAU LE JEUNE: *The Precautions*, 1776. *Monument du Costume.* (Photo Flammarion)

766 GRAVELOT: *English Gentleman*, 1730. Paris, Bib. Nat. (Photo Bibliothèque Nationale)

768 Frock-coat with red panne coqueluchon over a waistcoat of knitted chiné, Swiss cocked hat. 1786–7. *Galerie des Modes et Costumes français*

THE JUSTE À LA SUZANNE

753 The *juste* is a garment fitting tightly to the bust, trimmed behind with a short gathered basque, first worn by Mlle Contat to play in the *Marriage of Figaro;* it is often dark-coloured, worn over a light skirt, and its open neck is filled by a bouffant fichu called a *fichu menteur*

PELISSES

754, 762 Throughout the century these fur-lined or fur garments were worn either shorter (plate 762) or longer (plate 754), both indoors and out. They are characterized by the fur-trimmed slits for the arms

CAPS

755–60 There are numberless variants of caps; only illustrations can give even a partial idea

THE SHEATH DRESS

763, 765 The sheath, borrowed from little girls' costume, has a back-laced bodice; a brightly-coloured ribbon sash is tied over it; it was greatly in fashion at the beginning of the Revolutionary period, because of its simplicity. It has no bust bodice and no paniers. Its novelty was that it was a *closed* gown, and it was called a 'false gown', the term 'gown' meaning a dress that opened over an underskirt

COSTUME IN ENGLAND

764, 774, 776–8 English fashion keeps fairly close to the general lines of French costume.
Typical features are the use of quilted underskirts (plates 764, 778), which were relatively rare in France at that time. Black lace mantillas worn over the shoulders (plate 764) were seen with kerchiefs folded as fichus or tucked through a ribbon bow decorated with a jewel, a detail which passed into American fashions (plate 775).
Hair is unpowdered, and women wear caps under straw hats known as mushroom or shepherdess hats (plates 776–8), whereas this fashion was unknown in France. The man (plate 777) wears a cocked hat known as a *kevenhuller*

THE FRAQUE OR FROCK-COAT

768–72 The *fraque* is imitated from English fashion, and is always less formal than the French *habit* (plate 768). It is always plain and without pockets, with a flat collar; two watches hang at the belt (plate 771) of Dandies, who also carry large muffs (plate 769). The Swiss hat (plate 768) is one version of the tricorne; the jockey (plate 769) was one of the simpler styles that originated in England
Fancy stockings (plate 772) are widely worn; shoe buckles are broad *à la d'Artois* (plates 768, 770)

769 Frock-coat *à la polonaise*, trimmed with gold acorns; jockey hat, 1779. *Galerie des Modes et Costumes français*. (Photo Flammarion)

770 Top coat *à la Lévite*, with three-tiered collars; bavaroise waistcoat with revers, coal-man hat, 1786. *Galerie des Modes et Costumes francais*. (Photo Flammarion)

771 Young man in 'cocoon' morning dress, 1786–9. Engraving by DUHAMEL. (Photo Flammarion)

772 Young man in striped coat, waistcoat and stockings, androsman hat, 1786–7. Engraving by DUHAMEL. *Cabinet des Modes*. (Photo Flammarion)

773 Gown with muslin apron and
hat, 1730. English fashion plate.
Paris, Bib. Nat., Cabinet des Estampes.
(Photo Bibliothèque Nationale)

774 GRAVELOT: *Woman in coat
draped at the back, with long barbs*.
1730. (Photo Flammarion)

DEVELOPMENT OF MEN'S COSTUME

766–7 During the first third of the century the *justaucorps* or long coat broadened with the addition of pleats arranged in a fan shape over the hips. The waistcoat was long, and the wig, less voluminous than during the preceding reign, was dressed in *pigeon wings* over the temples (plate 766) and sometimes was mingled with natural hair.

At the end of the reign of Louis XV, the narrower coat without pleats but with flaring panels in front opened over a waistcoat which was also shorter. The *coiffure en bourse* was lengthened into a cadogan (plate 767); sleeves are tight-fitting, with shallow cuffs. A small neckpiece of pleated muslin replaces knotted cravats and the shirt jabot is seen through the waistcoat opening (plate 767).

Tight-fitting *breeches à la Bavaroise* are fastened with garters at the knees (plate 767) whereas formerly breech bottoms had been loose (plate 766). The tricorne hat is carried under the arm more often than it is worn; it may be edged with gold braid or with a narrow *plumet* (feather edging). Men begin to wear two chatelaines at their belt, with clinking ornaments; this was high fashion

TOPCOATS OR REDINGOTES

770 Though these garments were never called 'riding-coats' they always took the derived name *redingote* in France. A topcoat with tiered collars, it originated in England and spread throughout France. Its length and fullness followed fashionable trends; in its original form, the first collar could be turned up to protect the lower part of the face, as it was essentially a travelling garment. The second collar, worn flat over the shoulders, was known in France as the *rotonne*

FASHION AT THE END OF THE REIGN OF LOUIS XIV

771–2 To wear informal morning dress was – in 1760 – to be *en chenille* ('like a cocoon', before turning into a butterfly later in the day); the frock-coat was made of ratteen or twill, hair was plaited, hats had steel buckles, waistcoats and stockings were striped, while the indispensable baubles hung over the breeches 'which might be replaced with upper stocks known as pantoloons or trousers'. Just before the Revolution, coats are cut in the English style: the collar is often high and often *cut*, i.e. in a colour contrasting with the rest of the coat (plate 772); waistcoats are square-cut at the foot; sleeves have no cuffs and are buttoned in English style; garters are tied with tabs instead of buckled. The *androsmane* hat, a tricorne whose third point is only a fold in the front brim, prefigures, with its tall shape, the hats of the very end of the century

ENGLISH FASHIONS

775–7 The 'Van Dyck' style, which was very widespread in English fashion at the end of the eighteenth century, is characterized by soft stuffs and the cut of sleeves, necklines and cuffs

went to meet the new Queen in September 1725, the Duc de Gesvres, who thought himself in disgrace and was preparing to take leave of the King, wore a *redingote*, 'a garment taken from the English... very commonly worn at present for cold or rainy weather and especially for riding.' This new garment made the King laugh and brought down mockery on those who wore it, but twenty years later it was irresistibly fashionable. The Duc de Caylus noted that the English had formerly taken the style from France, where coachmen and lackeys had worn it fifty years before, under the name *hongreline*.

Little by little, with the increase in Anglomania, the redingote, in a slightly lighter form, became a day-time garment, no longer confined to travel or sport.

In the course of the century, desire for simplicity and convenience led to the introduction of increasingly relaxed forms of garment: first of all the *surtout*, a sort of country justaucorps, with a flat collar and buttons only to pocket level; then, towards 1766–7, the *frac* or *frock-coat*, a light justaucorps without pockets or pleats, flaring widely at the bottom.

For bad weather, the garments worn on top of the coat were still, as before, the *roquelaure*, which was bell-shaped and covered the shoulders, or the *balandran*, a garment for rainy weather fairly similar to the roquelaure but with two slits for the arms, or the period's one innovation, the *volant*, a sort of pocketless justaucorps crossed at the back,[12] without buttons or buttonholes on the sleeves, and with a one-buttoned collar.

For indoor wear the dressing gown, similar to that worn in the preceding century, could be short or long, with frog and loop brandenburgs or shawl collars, with fitted or chemise sleeves, the latter consisting of straight bands continuing either side of the body, without arm-holes.

After the beginning of the century, when the Steinkerck was replaced for some time by the lace-edged ribbon or *Cremona*, the decorated cravat was discarded from men's costume. A neckpiece of three folds of plain muslin filled in the shirt neck, with the jabot, finely pleated or lace-trimmed, showing through the jacket opening. The black bow of the *solitaire*, the ribbon which tied the purse-string wig, became broader on the throat

777 GAINSBOROUGH: *Conversation in a Park*, c. 1750.
Paris, Louvre. (Photo Flammarion)

778 REYNOLDS: *Nelly O'Brien*, 1763. London, The Wallace Collection.
(Reproduced by permission of the Trustees)

towards 1750, but for a cravat clothing the neck in a completely new form, we must wait for the end of the century.

Men still wore full-dress court costume, just as women still kept their court gowns. Even more than private evening dress, it formed a sumptuous architecture over the body, weighted down with decorative embroideries. According to contemporary painters, it was often worn with a cloak.

As Barbier says, authors have often cited the splendid suits worn by courtiers at royal and princely baptismal and marriage ceremonies, for which the Duc de Chartres and the Duc de Penthièvre displayed buttonholes embroidered with diamonds and the other guests wore clothes in cloth of gold and silver or richly embroidered and lined velvet. Some of these habits are alleged to have cost 15,000 livres, and each person had to have three of them, one for each of the days the festivities lasted; but to avoid such expense which 'incommoded people of the court' the wearers could hire them from tailors. The embroidery, of paillettes, gold or silver threads, etc., was astonishingly rich and varied; their execution was work reserved for male embroiderers.

The sumptuous tradition introduced by Louis XIV in his ceremonial and festive costumes continued under Louis XV and Louis XVI. In 1721 the ambassador of the Sultan Mehmet-Effendi could admire three suits worn by the young King: one trimmed with pearls and rubies, another with pearls and diamonds and the third with very fine diamonds alone. To receive him, Louis XV wore a flame-coloured velvet coat, adorned with precious stones estimated at more than 25 millions and weighing between 35 and 40 pounds. The Regent wore a justaucorps of blue velvet covered with gold embroideries.

Fifty years later, the coronation of Louis XVI occasioned another display of magnificent toilettes, shown in a collection of engravings by Patas: all the suits worn by the King, the princes, high dignitaries and crown officers and other noblemen taking part in this ceremony had been designed by Louis-René Boquet, painter and inspector of the '*Menus Plaisirs*', and executed by Delaistre, the royal tailor.

The court costume inspired by 'Henri IV' costume and designed by Sarrazin was only worn in a few court balls from 1774 to 1776.

We must make particular mention of the innovation of a tailor by the name of Dartigalongue, who in 1770 announced that customers could obtain 'ready made' garments in all sizes, which could be sent to the provinces and abroad.[13] This was the first time anyone had conceived the modern ready-to-wear system, which developed rapidly.

ACCESSORIES

The voluminous seventeenth-century wig shrank, returning to a more natural style; in any case, many men now wore their own hair, sweeping it up in front and crimping it into a *toupet*; the hair over the temples was arranged into crimped and curled tufts known as *cadenettes*, which had nothing in common with those worn under Louis XIII. Others, preferring wigs but anxious to conceal the fact, wore their wigs slightly back on the head and covered the front with their own hair. Cosmetics and powder masked the distinction between real and false hair.

The great vogue was for light wigs, either *club-wigs* or *queues*. Club-wigs had wide queues, filled out with horse-hair and tied with a large ribbon rosette. Queues differed in shape, and the arrangement of curls round the front and sides of the wig also varied constantly. Square, long or full-bottomed wigs were worn only for mourning, or, in a shorter form, by some magistrates.

Evidently wigs were taken off at night, when cotton nightcaps were worn.

After 1700 the tricorne hat remained the universal headgear; it shrank in proportion to the hairstyle. Towards 1730 it was fairly wide, with wavy brims and an upturned peak, then it became smaller and was often inspired by foreign modes; it could have three peaks, with straight folds. Otherwise, hats were round, with rolled brims in moleskin felt, or with wide brims in *Quaker style* in 1776. Finally the tricorne hat *à la suisse*[14] won the field and was worn until the Revolution.

Hats were almost always carried under the arm, to avoid raising clouds of hair-powder; this gave rise to the custom of standing bare-headed in company. In 1726 the *Mercure de France* noted: 'Hats are of a reasonable size; they are carried under the arm and hardly ever worn on the head.' Hatters even produced some almost completely flat models, made exclusively to be carried under the arm, which explains their name of *chapeaux-bras*.

The importation of skins from Canada had revived the fashion for beaver hats from the seventeenth century on; then their high price had led to the invention of 'half-beaver', produced by sticking beaver hair on to woollen felt; the fabric was at first prohibited by law, then authorized after 1734. This industrial transformation of a millinery accessory which had become scarce and dear into an ordinary, cheap article marked the beginnings of a development that was to lower quality.

Children's Costume

During a large part of the century, children's costume remained, as before, a miniature version of the clothes worn by adults.

Little girls wore stiff bodices and panier skirts, while little boys had more or less full-skirted justaucorps and tricorne hats. The *bourrelets* or pudding-rolls worn round the head for protection and the long leading strings attached to the shoulders were the only special features.

Men's costume became considerably simplified during the century, and consequently young boys' silhouette lost its fitted appearance, although the costume was no more adapted to its wearer's age for that. And even this held good only for middle-class costume, as shown in the paintings of Chardin, for instance (plate 728); the portraits of young princes show costumes every bit as laden with ornament as before. A portrait of the young Comte d'Artois towards 1763 shows him wearing a suit *à la hongroise* in moiré heavily decorated with passementerie, with deep basques supported on horse-hair panels, the whole completed with little, side-lacing boots.

After 1775, we find portraits of little boys in sailor costume: long, soft trousers buttoned under short, loose jackets (plate 741). Until then even boys had worn boned jackets which differed from the girls' model only in that it was rounded and without basques; there was even a special model for 'boys in their first breeches', that is, for small boys who had just outgrown the *jaquette* worn in the preceding century.

779 GAINSBOROUGH: *The Blue Boy*, 1779.
Henry E. Huntingdon Art Gallery, San Marino. (Museum photo)

780 REYNOLDS: *Henry Fane and his Gamekeepers*, 1766. New York, Metropolitan Museum. (Museum photo)

781 Boy's light grey frock coat with silver buttons and braid, 1780. London, Collection Mrs Doris Langley Moore. (Photo M. Winslade)

782 REYNOLDS: *Lady Skipwith*, 1787. New York, Frick Collection. (Photo copyright Collection)

Although middle-class girls were not hindered by paniers, they still had to wear long skirts. It is only towards 1740 that we see little girls wearing *fourreaux*, fitted but unboned gowns.

It was English influence which, after 1780, really delivered children from the strait-jackets worn until then (plates 787–90). At last royal portraits show little girls in lawn and muslin frocks with hair hanging loose, and boys without uniforms or ceremonial garments.

Theatrical Costume

Under Louis XV theatrical costume struck a curious compromise between traditional seventeenth-century forms and the caprices of fashion: the public was not shocked to see Brutus in a waved wig and doublet or Phaedra in a panier gown. Boquet, the chief designer at the Opéra, continued these models until 1760, but towards the middle of the century there was a reaction, introducing more simplicity and historical accuracy into Opera costumes.[15]

In France, after efforts by Adrienne Lecouvreur and Mlle Dangeville around 1727, Mlle Clairon undertook this reform of theatrical costume before she left the Théâtre Français in 1766. Not content with getting rid of paniers, she urged her colleagues, in her *Réflexions sur l'art dramatique*, to avoid fashions 'of the moment', particularly where hairstyles were concerned; she condemned as absurd the tradition which dictated that Electra must be played in pink court costume trimmed with jet, and taught that designers should seek inspiration in the shapes of Greek and Roman costumes, though without copying them exactly. The great actor Lekain, who died in 1778, is said to have designed his own costumes to ensure their historical accuracy. In 1773, Mme du Barry gave him a 'Greek' and a 'Roman suit' which cost her 4,800 livres.

The director of ballet at the Opéra, Noverre, who shared the famous Mlle Salé's ideas about the use of soft, light stuffs, also tried to suppress the traditional plumes, masks and wigs. His efforts did not meet with success, but a few years later Mme Saint-Huberty insisted on a gown exactly copied from classical models to sing Dido in Spontini's work.

The same reforming movement affected the Italian Comedy. For her role as Bastienne in 1753, Mme Favart dressed as a peasant woman, with a woollen gown, clogs and a flat hairstyle. At the Opéra Comique Mmes Dugazon and Clairval rejected the satin jackets and frilled silk skirts previously worn by Annettes and Lubins.

This movement spread to other countries: the Royal Armoury in Stockholm contains a Roman senator's costume inspired by Lekain's reforms; it was worn by Prince Charles, the younger brother of King Gustavus III. The curious theatre of the Royal Palace at Drottningholm still possesses eighteenth-century ballet costumes inspired by those which Vestris created at the Paris Opéra.

These experiments extended to cover exotic themes; in 1755 Lekain and Mlle Clairon arranged the production of *L'Orphelin de la Chine*, in which the women were dressed in Chinese costumes 'without paniers and bare-armed', and the men as Tartars and Chinamen. In 1767 Mme Favart appeared in *Soliman*, 'dressed in a genuine Turkish costume' made in Constantinople.

However, none of these more or less bold and lasting attempts at reform completely destroyed the prejudices of the time. Even the artists who paid them lip-service remained convinced that theatrical costume – particularly for tragedy – should always produce a particular effect, and that it should not mould the body or show parts of it uncovered. Consequently Lekain's Greek costume included an undergarment of speckled satin, a cap trimmed with ostrich feathers and circled with a diadem, and a gilded bow and quiver. Talma provoked a scandal in 1789 by appearing in *Brutus* in 'all the severity of Antique costume'.

The theatre, which aroused a great passion in the society of the century, in turn provided inspiration in decoration and colour, particularly in women's costume. Theatrical and court costumes shared an excessive use of gauze, embroidery and aigrettes; the gown *à la polonaise* corresponded to the stage

783 Brocade jacket, perhaps French, worn under Peer's robes for the coronation of George III, c. 1760. Nottingham, Collection Lord Middleton. (Photo W. Spencer)

784 R. WAITT: *Lord Duffus*, 1734. Edinburgh, National Galleries of Scotland. (Photo Annan)

785 RAEBURN: *Sir John Sinclair*, c. 1794. Collection Viscount Thurso. (Photo Annan)

MEN'S COSTUME IN ENGLAND

780 Men's costume is simpler than in France; the collared frockcoat without cuffs, slit *à la Marinière*, the jacket lined with cloth matching the waistcoat and embroidered down the front and at the wrists, constitute a typically English fashion. The boots, like those worn by gamekeepers, are soft and tight-fitting, with boot-garters fastened with buckles

SURVIVING ENGLISH COSTUMES

781, 783 The brocade jacket (plate 783) embroidered with sequins and trimmed with silver lace forms part of a ceremonial suit, which probably explains its richness and cut, and recalls the elegance of the beginning of the century. The deep sleeve-cuffs had not been worn in France for a long time. On the other hand, the young man's costume (plate 781) is simple in line and material, and already corresponding to the restrained taste which was spreading throughout Europe

SCOTTISH DRESS

784-6, 789 The outstanding feature of Scottish costume is the tartan woven in the colours of the clan, originally worn in one piece swathed round the body, then divided into two pieces: the kilt, and the plaid worn round the body. It was worn with a short or long doublet according to the period, and matching hose

furs and brandenburgs. While Mlle Clairon pioneered historical exactitude in a way that won her the esteem of Diderot and Marmontel, she still appeared virtually in court costume when she played Athalie at Marie-Antoinette's wedding celebrations; and in J. B. Rousseau's *Pygmalion*, Mlle Raucourt still played Galatea in a panier gown. The reciprocal borrowings between theatre and court can be explained by the fact that under Louis XIV Boquet worked not only for the Opéra but also for the 'Menus Plaisirs', meaning the court, while under Louis XVI Sarrazin, who was both 'costumier to their Highnesses the Princes and Director of the Salon du Colisée', designed the new models.

786 ANON: *Major Frizell of Castle Leather*, c. 1750. By permission of Inverness Town Council. (Photo Whyte's Studio)

787 ZOFFANY: *Lord Willoughby and his Family*, c. 1775.
Collection Lord Willoughby de Broke.
(Photo Archives Presses Artistiques)

CHILDREN'S COSTUME

787–8, 790 The disappearance of the rigid bodice and the powdered wig and the adoption of fine linen frocks with ribbon sashes for girls, and simply cut, fitted suits for boys were happy innovations which were soon to be adopted in France

ELEGANT COSTUME IN THE GERMANIC COUNTRIES

791–2, 795–6 French fashions were followed everywhere, but with a certain simplicity. The man's coat (plate 795), with its folded collar, is inspired by the English frock-coat, and is decorated with rather heavy braid galloons

788 GAINSBOROUGH: *Miss Haverfield*, c. 1780.
London, The Wallace Collection.
(Reproduced by permission of the Trustees)

789 MICHAEL WRIGHT: *Unknown Scottish Chieftain*, c. 1660.
Edinburgh, National Portrait Gallery. (Photo Tom Scott)

790   ZOFFANY: *The Bradshaw Family*, c. 1770–75. London, The Tate Gallery. (Reproduced by courtesy of the Trustees)

791   J. V. TISCHBEIN: *Count Giech*, 1756.
Nuremberg, Germanisches Nationalmuseum. (Museum photo)

792   A. PESNE: *Countess Sophia Maria de Voss*, 1745.
Berlin Staatliche Schlösser und Gärten. (Photo W. Steinkopf)

317

793 LARGILLIÈRE: *La Belle Strasbourgeoise*, 1703. Strasbourg, Musée des Beaux-Arts. (Photo Giraudon)

794 CHODOWIECKI: *The Quantin Sisters*, 1758. Paris, Bibliothèque Nationale, Cabinet des Estampes, Ec 18 f 9. (Photo Flammarion)

795-6 J. G. ZIESSENIS: *Prince and Princess von Schaumburg-Li c.* 1760. Collection Schaumburg-Lippe. (Photos Marburg)

The Spread of French Fashions

To the dynastic alliances contracted by the Bourbons, the dispersal of Huguenot artisans, the brilliant personalities of diplomats on missions and the increasing superiority of the French silk industry, we must now add the surviving prestige of Versailles, the formation of a salon society, a courtly spirit at large receptive to French taste and art, and lastly the adoption of the French language by all cultured circles in western and eastern Europe.

From this range of causes followed the pre-eminence of French civilization and the popularity of French gowns.

The spread of French fashions was not in the least diminished by the two currents of outside influence, British and Oriental.

This 'universality' of French costume in the eighteenth century was largely the work of women. In France they controlled everything, King and country, the royal will and public opinion. But most of all, they were increasingly mistresses in their own homes. In all the capitals of Europe they waited impatiently for the arrival of the 'doll from the rue Saint-Honoré'. Women were the architects of France's uncontested supremacy.

Need we recall the role played by Mme de Pompadour at the Versailles court? She was clever enough to receive friends only when she was at her toilette; she flattered a small group of favourites with the 'uniform of the small châteaux', green with gold braid; to open Bellevue she thought up an 'ordered costume' in purple worn over a grey satin jacket worked with a flocked design in purple and edged with gold embroidery.

Around 1750 everything was *Pompadour style*: cloth, ribbons, négligées. Textile designers created chinoiseries and eastern curiosities specially for her; she has been credited with the vogue for négligées inspired by Turkish jackets. After her death there were found nine trunks crammed with gowns, casaquins and surtouts, in bazeen or Indian taffetas, in pekin or perse, and even full or half-mourning toilettes in 'black and white *indiennes*'.

Private receptions, festivities, the theatre were all opportunities for wearing '*grande et petite toilette*' and disguises, which multiplied incessantly in accordance with the caprice of fashion.

Creators and Fashion Publications

The statutes of the clothing corporations still limited individual initiative. In 1776, the minister Turgot tried to change the situation of artisans and merchants by inducing the King to sign an edict abolishing corporations: each individual was to be free to exercise his trade, to open a workshop and choose his employees; but reaction against this was so strong that the edict was revoked shortly after.

Only tailors had the privilege of making outer garments, full gowns and corsets; but we should remember that under Louis XIV tailoresses had become independent.

Towards 1776 a new category of artisans obtained the right to form an independent corporation, that of '*marchands et marchandes de modes*', drawn from the great corporation of mercers. 'Creating head-dresses and trimming gowns are what women consider as their talent,' wrote F. A. Gersault in the capital work of the period, *L'Art du tailleur*. From then on *marchandes de mode* or haberdashers could legally work and sell all the accessories applied to clothing, including head-dresses; indeed, they became veritable creative artists in fashion, trimming the garments provided by tailors and tailoresses according to their imaginations and completing them with caps, flounces and, later, hoods and mantillas. At the end of the Ancien Régime they even made the ornaments of Court costume.

Going beyond the limits of their trade, haberdashers soon exercised an absolute power, explained by the infinite number of different types of embellishment mentioned in contemporary sources: one hundred and fifty different dress trimmings, two hundred forms of head-dress... In his *Tableau de Paris*, Sebastien Mercier recognized that the inventor's talent was the source of glory: 'Who can tell from what women's head we shall have the fertile idea that will change all the bonnets of Europe?' The *Magasin des Modes nouvelles* declared in 1787 that a 'frivoliste' – a fashionable haberdasher – could provide a living for 10,000 people.

Without forgetting their forerunners in the previous century, we should place the appearance of these creators of fash-

793-4 Ordinary people's costume follows the general lines of elegant costume, but retains certain sixteenth-century elements, for instance the big hats worn by the beauties of Strasbourg (plate 793), whose costume otherwise showed great attention to fashionable detail

797 GOYA: *Queen Maria Luisa of Parma in Maja's Costume*, 1798. Madrid, Prado. (Photo Anderson-Giraudon)

ion in the middle of the eighteenth century. From then on – doubtless as a result of changes that had taken place in corporations – we learn the names of tailors (Sarrazin, Pamard) and tailoresses (Mlle Motte, Mme Eloffe, Mme Pompée, Mme Alexandre) and haberdashers (Mlle Bertin, Baulard, Mlle Drouin). The most famous of all was Rose Bertin:[16] after beginning as an errand-girl, she attracted customers such as the Duchesse de Chartres or the Princesse de Lamballe, who introduced her to the Queen in about 1772. She must take much of the blame for the excessive passion of Marie-Antoinette for fashions and her considerable spending, whereas as the young Dauphine she had been noted for her extreme simplicity. There was a famous rivalry between Baulard, the sometimes extravagant creator of mechanical hairstyles, and Rose Bertin, jealous and proud, but with imagination and talent which won her fame throughout Europe.

While we know only a few textile designers' names before the time of Jean Bérain *père*, from the first years of the century we find a whole school of 'silk illustrators' in Lyons. Profiting from technical and industrial progress which placed new processes at their disposal, (brocaded warp, moiré effects,[17] certain designers invented ornamental models whose novelty and taste guaranteed the dazzling success of the *Grande Fabrique Lyonnaise*. Jean Pillement, the author of the *Fleurs idéales*, created charming floral stylizations and chinoiseries, and also, though unsuccessfully, proposed to M. de Marigny, in 1763, that he should direct a factory producing 'silk painted in the Indian taste' invented by him. Peyrotte, Ranson and J. F. Bony belonged to this phalanx of artists who worked mainly for Lyons, while the Tours factory called on such lesser known, but still talented figures as Barrot, Riffe, La Chèze and Villey.

The eighteenth century produced exceptional conditions for embroidery. Money was plentiful and fed a taste for luxury and inventiveness in men's and women's costume, and the formation of a worldly society and the ritual of court life opened a vast field to this type of decoration. The most varied textiles, taffeta, satin, velvet, etc., lent themselves to needlework, which scattered flowers, birds and figures over court gowns and men's coats and waistcoats. Silk mingled its colours with gold, and silver metal threads, paillettes and chenille, with cut-out insets of lace, feathers, etc. The fragment of a gown belonging to Marie-Antoinette preserved in Denmark is still today one of the most precious specimens of this art.[18]

At the head of these specialized creators we find Jean-François Bony, who continued to invent models until the First Empire. He treated floral decoration with a consummate art perfectly adapted to the needs of costume. Ranson published models for 'coats and waistcoats in fashion', imitating the great ornamentalists and decorators of the period, such as Delafosse, Cauvet, etc., while in 1770 Germain de Saint-Aubin composed the *Art du Brodeur*.

While the *Mercure Galant* had been alone in mentioning new fashions in the Louis XIV period, from 1760 there was a general blossoming of small fashion journals, antecedents of the specialist press of the present day.[19] These publications appeared almost simultaneously in France and England, and soon after in Germany, Holland and Italy. From the appearance of the *Journal du Goût* in Paris in 1768 and *The Lady's Magazine* in London in 1770, to 1790, almost fifteen periodicals were published in these countries, and half of them continued during the French Revolution.

In France the *Cabinet des Modes* – the first to present engravings in colour – the *Magasin des Modes nouvelles françaises et anglaises*, the *Journal de la Mode et du Goût*, and numerous almanacks, handouts and pamphlets, were devoted to all the aspects of fashion, not neglecting its extravagances. The plates were engraved after specialists such as Le Clerc, Desrais, Simonet, Schenau or Watteau de Lille. The *Galerie des Modes et Costumes français* (1778–87) collected about five hundred plates drawn by Desrais, Le Clerc, Augustin de Saint-Aubin, Watteau de Lille and J. B. Martin.

Besides these informative reviews, the eighteenth century also saw the appearance of a swarm of illustrators and engravers who provided costume illustrations of a quality hitherto unknown, for the better publications. Artists like Gravelot, Moreau le Jeune, Dupin, A. de Saint-Aubin and Trinquesse remain the best historians of the costume of their time.

A special mention must be made of the various *Suites d'Estampes pour servir à l'Histoire des Moeurs et du Costume dans le dix-huitième siècle* (Series of Prints to serve for the History of Costume in the Eighteenth Century) published in 1775, 1777, and 1778, and again in 1789 under the title *Monument du Costume physique et moral de la fin du XVIIIe siècle*, with text by Restif de la Bretonne and engravings from drawings by Freudeberg and Moreau le Jeune.

CURRENT AFFAIRS IN COSTUME

A new caprice made its appearance: the exploitation of current affairs in costume. This was a passing craze – the word then used was *fureur* (furore) – perhaps a satire, expressed through a hat or a ribbon.

319

798 GOYA: *The Parasol*, 1777. Madrid, Prado. (Museum photo)

799 MENGS: *Maria Luisa of Parma, then Princess of Asturias*, 1765. Paris, Louvre. (Photo Flammarion)

320

The names given to new styles were no longer inspired by their native countries (*à l'allemande*, *à la portugaise*), nor by the people, generally male, who originally launched them (*à la Balagny*, *à la Guiche*). After the Regency, they borrowed names from all the events of the day: from the theatre (*Harlequin*, *à la Figaro*), songs (*à la Marlborough*), from inventions and discoveries (*à la Montgolfière*, *à l'Innoculation*, *à la Harpie*),[20] from the latest literary work (ribbons *à la coque* in 1730, with the appearance of the biography of Marguerite-Marie Alacoque), and most of all, from political events (tight suits *à la Silhouette*, from the name of the inspector-general; hat *à la d'Estaing*, cap *à la Caisse d'Escompte*, which was a bonnet *sans fond*; and even *au Collier de la Reine* and *au Cardinal sur la Paille*).

Current events were also used to give names to fashionable colours and clothing materials; the best-known example was the *cheveux de la Reine* (Queen's hair) shade, which, chosen by the Comte de Provence during the reign of Louis XVI, was an immediate success with courtiers: discarding the dreary puce then in vogue they swooped down on merchants to buy stuffs in this new colour, so that their price quickly rose from forty to eighty-six livres the ell.

This enthusiasm for the events of the day in clothing became more intense as the century progressed, signifying both the competition between designers and the results of publicity. The rapid succession of 'creations' served to catch the moment of topical interest and profit from it.

Costume in England

English costume evolved under the influence of customs, ideas and industrial and trading conditions that reflected an advanced economic development. Its reputation for quality and innovation considerably helped its spread, particularly for men's costume.[21]

CUSTOMS AND THE INDUSTRIAL REVOLUTION

In England and France, as in all western Europe, the spirit of the century made a powerful contribution to modifying the style of costume. But England added to the desire for convenience that could be seen everywhere a certain Puritan sobriety, and innovations connected with sport. The taste for the countryside, the passion for hunting and shooting and the general practice of outdoor games were more widespread there than in other countries. This explains the most noteworthy English innovations: the vogue for informal garments, white or printed cottons and certain particular types of clothing.

The habits of country life led to the introduction of a certain *laisser-aller* in men's and women's costume, also stimulated by the Romanticism that was then prevalent. As early as 1731 newspapers criticized the 'rustic mode' of women who, according to them, 'desired to insinuate the idea of innocence and rusticity'.[22] Gentlemen did their best to resemble servants and coachmen. Later, we see even Charles James Fox launch casual clothes in political circles, and foreign visitors gained the impression of 'informal dress' at the House of Commons.[23]

WOMEN'S COSTUME IN SPAIN

797–9, 802–3 Court costume alone was inspired by French fashion, but, from about 1780 on, we can see a strong reaction against this among elegant women, who moved towards the costume of the *maja* (plate 797). Hair was unpowdered and dresses had no paniers; light stuffs, white or black were used, trimmed with reds and pinks; lace mantillas were worn, and short skirts revealed the wearer's feet; waists were accentuated. This was costume which was to be worn only in Spain

SURVIVING SPANISH GOWNS

800 This rare model has a pleat at the back, as in the *robe à la française*, but added after the rest of the gown was finished, like a train attached at the neck; apparently this was worn for the first time in 1785; however the style is already mentioned in 1769

ORDINARY PEOPLE'S COSTUME IN SPAIN

801 In Spain as in many other countries, popular costume retained the characteristics of seventeenth-century clothes (cf. plate 690)

800 Gown of the 'Piedmontese' type: Bridal gown in ivory satin, sabot-sleeved, embroidered with silver, c. 1765–75. Barcelona, Museo de Arte, Collection Don Rocamora

801 *A Spanish shepherd who led merino sheep to Rambouillet.* Eighteenth century. Paris, Bibliothèque Nationale, Cabinet des Estampes. (Photo Flammarion)

802 GOYA: *The Marquesa de la Solana*, c. 1792. Paris, Louvre. (Photo Flammarion)

803 GOYA: *Doña Tadea Arias de Enriquez*, 1793–4. Madrid, Prado. (Museum photo)

804 VENETIAN SCHOOL: *The Billet-doux, c.* 1750. Collection F. Lugt. (Photo A. C. Cooper)

805 Man's jacket in white silk embroidered with multi-coloured silks. Early eighteenth century. New York, Cooper Union Museum for the Arts of Decoration. (Museum photo)

806 A. LONGHI: *A Venetian Gentleman, c.* 1765. Private Collection

British women's clothing profited from the progress made in the nation's cotton mills, whose material was provided by the East Indian colonies; it took its inspiration from exotic gowns brought back by 'Creoles' from the West Indies as well as by 'nabobs' from Calcutta and Ceylon: we must therefore remember the role played by overseas colonies in its evolution.

MEN'S COSTUME

During the first quarter of the century, French influence, which dated from 1660, continued to leave its mark on English costume. As in France, the old justaucorps, worn with a waistcoat, became looser to allow greater ease of movement. After 1770 the panels intended to give the impression of fan-pleats were at least partially cut back. But the excessive weight of these exaggerated panels led to a reaction: towards 1750 the coat with basques disappeared. Then the form of the coat followed the same development as in France: the panels separated, the sleeves became longer and the ornaments shrank, then towards 1776 lace ruffles disappeared.

However some differences in detail from French costume can be traced from the very beginning. In the first place, the three pieces of male costume were made in the same cloth, which was less often the case in France. The waistcoat became shorter and finally was buttoned all the way up, with deep lapels; the collar tended towards height. Breeches, which were sometimes of suede or buckskin, did not stop above the knee but reached below, and fitted tightly over the thighs; the *élégants* of the 1770's – the 'macaronis' – wore breeches 'in Dutch style'. Lastly, towards 1780, the waist became higher, the civilian coat was faced with long square panels and the waistcoat was cut square at the waist. Neither coat nor waistcoat were embroidered.

The elegant Englishman wore, as well as the dressing-gown, a curious soft garment, the *banyan*, which reached to the knees and was generally light-coloured or in a floral pattern. It was Indian in origin and was essentially an indoor garment, but could be worn out of doors in the morning.

The British *frock* worn in the first half of the century, as we see in 1745, seems to be related to the French *volant*. Later it ceased to be a garment for wearing over the coat, and seems to have become the frock-coat as we know it, an outer garment without pockets, replacing the coat and adopted for riding and sport because of its comfort.

Towards 1740 we also find a *great-coat* or surtout, a sporting and travel coat also worn over the coat, and another heavy overcoat known as the *wrap-rascal*, with a double flat collar and wide, deep-cuffed sleeves. The British taste for open-air living and the damp climate required a greater variety of more comfortable overcoats than in France. These garments were almost always adaptations of forms worn among the working classes, which were elevated to the rank of elegant garments because of their practicality. These simple garments were so universally admitted that at the end of the century broadcloth had supplanted velvet and silk, even at court.

Where head-dresses are concerned, the *Spectator* of 1711, commenting on how behind the fashion country districts were, mentioned that out-of-date wigs were worn within a few miles of London. But towards 1728 hair was drawn back and tied into a bag, as in France, or else plaited and tied into a *pig-tail*, a specifically English mode.

Towards 1760 the macaronis, as fashionable young men were called, still wore very tall wigs, with curls twined round the ears; but except with full dress, people were beginning to wear their own hair, with less and less powder.

Almost the chief male headgear in eighteenth-century England was the tricorne, whose proportions and trimmings could vary, as in France, though it was edged with braid and generally trimmed with short feathers. After 1770 it was often very small and was worn tilted on top of the wig. Less fashionable people were content to wear round, flat-brimmed hats, known as Quaker hats which, towards 1776, began to replace the tricorne.

From the earliest years of the century, no elegant Londoner could dispense with a long cane, which he hung from a ribbon wound round his third coat-button, any more than he could walk on heels in any colour other than red; he also cultivated an 'interesting' paleness, heralding the Romantic dandy.

322

807 MENGS: *Maria Carolina, Queen of Naples,*
c. 1766.
Madrid, Prado. (Photo Anderson-Giraudon)

808 A. TRIPPEL: *Aunt Trippel.* Before 1745.
Schaffhausen, Museum zu Allerheiligen.
(Museum photo)

809 PETER ALS: *Portrait of a Lady,*
c. 1750. Oslo, Kunstindustrimuseet.
(Photo Teigen)

WOMEN'S COSTUME

Even if England may be credited with the introduction of paniers to France, their history in British women's fashions can only be explained in terms of a return to the seventeenth-century. Possibly the vogue for paniers may have come from the minor courts of Germany, if we remember that these little communities still kept, albeit in new forms, the old Spanish farthingales. We have seen that the latter were worn less in France during the seventeenth century than in Spain, where they survived late enough for the Austro-Spanish marriages to introduce them into Austria, then Germany, in the late seventeenth and early eighteenth centuries. It is curious to note that the arrival of George of Hanover on the British throne corresponds with the period when paniers were worn in Britain.

While following French fashions, elegant English women interpreted them in a very particular way.

The loose gown with pleats in the back was known as the *sack* in England, where it was less fashionable than in France. The back soon became more fitted; some models were crossed in front and the wide sleeve was cut from the same piece as the bodice. When the gown was open, the decoration generally stopped at the waist; it was unusual to see it continue on the coat facings. The so-called *riding-coat* which appeared towards 1785 was buttoned in front but could open over a white skirt; the fitted bodice had a double cape collar which opened out in large pointed lapels, like men's coats. Lastly, the use of quilted and padded stuffs for skirts was far more widespread than in France; this was a more particularly provincial mode.

Caps remained far more reasonable and uniform than in France during the first half of the century, and hats, simple at first but later extremely elegant and laden with trimmings, became general wear thirty years before their appearance in France.

The spread of English costume styles was most marked in Europe at the end of the century. It slowly reached the American colonies, where clothing remained under the influence of a half-Dutch, half-British style for a long period; a provincial time-lag. Only the cloth was truly English.

On the whole, eighteenth-century English costume presents a clearly national character, reflecting a climate of opinion which refused to admit French superiority in any field, even in fashion. A correspondent to the *London Magazine* in 1738 protested vehemently against the 'ridiculous imitation of the French', and the members of the Antigallican Society, founded by London merchants in 1745, undertook never more to wear French lace or wigs.

As a detailed description of English costume was given above in discussing its introduction into France, it is needless to repeat it here.

Scottish Costume

In the eighteenth century traditional Scottish costume possessed its two essential elements, the *plaid* and the *kilt*. The large portrait painted by John Michael Wright, probably about 1660 (plate 789) shows the point to which it had evolved from the mere piece of cloth wrapped round the waist with the end flung over the shoulder which it had been in more primitive times.

The only difference between male and female costume was the length of the skirt or kilt.

An Englishman by the name of Rawlinson, the director of a foundry at Glengarry, is said to have conceived the idea about 1720 of separating the lower part of the plaid, which was wrapped round the body and fastened with a pin, so as to give his workmen greater freedom of movement. The upper part was thus transformed into an independant scarf. It appears that the upper classes wore very short trousers – *trews* – under the plaid. After the defeat of Culloden in 1746, when the Jacobites were beaten by the Duke of Cumberland, the wearing of Scottish costume was forbidden for thirty-five years; then the Highland regiments wore it as military uniform, and it gradually came to be regarded as the typical Scottish costume and was worn by those who had never been Highlanders.

810 P. LONGHI: *The Perfume Seller*, 1757.
Venice, Museo Correr. (Photo André Held)

811 P. LONGHI: *The Dancing Lesson*, c. 1760.
Venice, Accademia. (Photo Giraudon)

812 G. D. TIEPOLO: *The Sicisbeo*, c. 1785.
Venice, Ca' Rezzonico. (Photo Ferruzzi)

WOMEN'S COSTUME IN ITALY

804, 810–12, 815 As in France, the elegant gown (plate 804) is the *andrienne* worn over a *sottana* (short underskirt) and the corset bodice. For outdoor wear there was a short cape, the *tabarrino*, and the *bauta*, a white half-mask (plates 804, 815) continued in a flounce of black lace and worn by men and women during the long Carnival season. The round black mask is the *moreta*

MEN'S COSTUME IN ITALY

805–6, 827 Count Valetti (plate 827) wears a dressing-gown in gold brocade with multicoloured flowers, and under this a long jacket or *camisole* in red and gold brocade. All three pieces of the grey suit worn in plate 806 are of the same material, which was not the custom in France

COURT COSTUME

807 Court costume is international. It is worn over very wide paniers

COSTUME IN SWITZERLAND

808 Although the details of this bust indicate an elegant costume, by comparison with French costumes it has a markedly provincial air

WOMEN'S COSTUME IN SWEDEN

809, 825 Women's costume closely followed French fashions. Court costume has rigid bodices and sleeves decorated with *petits bonshommes*, while butterfly caps and patches, ribbon or lace collars are purely French in inspiration

Costume in the Rest of Europe

Western and Central Europe

Except in France and England, west of the Elbe the eighteenth century brought few changes in the costume of the working classes; they made do with simple, rough garments, the line and materials of which kept some medieval and Renaissance characteristics almost unchanged. These garments were fairly similar to those painted in the preceding century by the Le Nain brothers in France, Jan Steen in the Low Countries, David Rijckaert in Flanders and Murillo in Spain.

In contrast, the rich aristocratic and middle classes continued to follow French modes, then, still following Paris, adopted English styles. For them Paris alone could set the tone. In all the great and small courts of the West luxurious clothing was still the distinctive mark of a rank in the social hierarchy, but it also became the reflection of the culture and manners of a refined society, the prototype of which was French.

THE HOLY ROMAN EMPIRE

In the weakened Holy Roman Empire, the Viennese court of the Austria of Leopold I and Joseph I maintained rigorous observance of Spanish etiquette.

Costume at the Court followed both France and Spain, although the hold of Spain still remained the more influential. While the Emperor adopted the Louis XIV wig, his courtiers wore the plain costume and short cloak of Spanish lords. The accession in 1746 of Francis I, prince of the House of Lorraine, and the marriage of his daughter Marie-Antoinette with the French Dauphin in 1770 favoured the expansion of French

813–4 Male and female national costumes designed by Gustavus III, 1778. Stockholm, Nordiska Museet. (Museum photos)

815 P. LONGHI: *Masked Conversation*, c. 1760.
Venice, Museo Correr. (Photo Ferruzzi)

styles in Austria; but the royal pleasure controlled some modes right down to the last detail. Maria Theresa herself instituted a compulsory costume for her guests in Laxenburg Castle: a red cloth frock-coat over a gold-embroidered waistcoat for men, and a red gown woven with gold and silver and trimmed with lace for women.

Curiously enough, the Austrian court also extended Imperial control in matters of costume to the nation at large. A regulation divided secular society into five, later three, classes and laid down the garments to be worn by each, inviting tailors to denounce anyone attempting to violate these rules.

In almost all the minor courts of Germany we find this mixture of rigid Spanish etiquette and attention to the latest lead from France. The latter influence was favoured by the atmosphere of the numerous princely castles and palaces built in imitation of Versailles.

We see the Dresden court impose scarlet and gold for men, blue and gold for women; Hesse created a special costume for each of the royal residences; in Munich the Elector Max-Joseph III not only stipulated that his guests at Nymphenburg must wear a green uniform piped with white round the lapels, but specified every detail of the costume to be worn by his courtiers during the thirty-three gala days each year.

The one discordant note in this concert of elegance and luxury came from Prussia. Frederick-William I (1713–1740), far from having the same tastes as his father Frederick I, despised splendour and clothing; his son, Frederick II the Great, had the same attitude even more strongly, and while expanding Prussia's essential industries, importing sheep from Spain, improving cloth and cotton-dyeing mills, introducing silkworms, and planting mulberry trees, he threatened corporal punishment for anyone he saw wearing foreign silk or lace, threw the muff carried by one of his father's courtiers into the fire, and forbade the wearing of cottons and *indiennes*, the import of which was suspended until 1750 in the Leipzig market.

As always in such situations, the commands of an authoritarian sovereign did not prevent French fashions from dominating an elegant society. Paris provided the models that were copied by German fashion periodicals, the first of which appeared between 1782 and 1787; French tailors travelled the length and breadth of Germany to propagate them. France also provided the voluminous paniers German women loved so much that the Berlin Court had to impose regulations on the wearing of them. High-ranking ladies allowed their companions only small paniers, and townswomen had to be content with simple drapes known as *commodes*. But they all vied with one another to achieve the smallest waist, and the Countess Elia de Bernsdorf recounts that many ladies, invited for an evening party, began to lace their bodices in the morning.

The imitation of French modes led to absurdities and extravagances. In a memorandum to the Berlin Academy[24] Eberhard noted: 'German women buy "good taste" with its weight in gold, being convinced that there is nothing good or beautiful in dress, equipages or furnishings outside what comes from Paris... Any poor rag of fashion no longer in favour there is good enough for Germany, provided it be extravagant and new.' Consequently we see Count Brühl, the arbiter of elegance in Dresden, boasting of possessing five hundred suits, twelve muffs, forty-seven furs and one thousand five hundred wigs: 'rather a lot', remarked Frederick II, 'to cover an empty head.'

SPAIN, PORTUGAL AND ITALY

In High Society in these three countries, French fashions were generally followed, but against a certain degree of resistance, and national characteristics added particular details.

In Spain the elegant women painted by Goya wore clothes inspired by Paris models, but their gowns were shorter and lighter (plates 802–3). They wore dazzlingly coloured shawls and black or white mantillas hanging from tortoiseshell combs, with sometimes a flower over one temple, and carried fans or sheltered under pretty parasols.

For men the difference consisted mainly in the belt that held the breeches tightly at the waist, wide cravats and increasingly short, tight garments.

Spanish costumes had no reciprocal influence in France during this century, in spite of the popularity of the novels of Lesage. Spanish modes do not appear in the Don Quixote tapestries designed by Coypel. There was, it is true, the picturesque episode of the flock of sheep brought from Spain with its own shepherds at vast expense in 1786, by order of the Duc d'Angivilliers, to introduce Spanish qualities of wool into France; only a few animals finally arrived at Rambouillet (plate 801).

In Portugal, where French art found favour at the Lisbon court, 'Paris fashions' were also imitated.

Italy regretted her old supremacy in Europe, and her national self-esteem tolerated rather than sought for French costume. As always, French influence was introduced through the large towns – Venice, Milan, Rome and Naples – with luxury models interpreted in bright colours and light textiles suitable to a Mediterranean country. Elsewhere, provincial costume with its regional variants had scarcely changed since the sixteenth century.

The Président des Brosses notes in his travel journal in 1739 that noblewomen's costume in Florence and Genoa was dominated by black, and that noblemen's costume in Venice had 'breeches in Indian cotton, a jacket or pourpoint in the same stuff and a wide black pleated cloak'. He did not explain that the ell of coloured cloth everyone wore on one shoulder was the vestige of a very enduring piece, the fifteenth-century hood.

THE LOW COUNTRIES, SWITZERLAND AND THE SCANDINAVIAN COUNTRIES

In the Low Countries, a rich, mercantile, uncourtly society adopted French fashions as well as learning the language, and its bourgeois way of life did not preclude elegance. Women adopted the wide straw hat with strings of ribbon. Everyday clothing followed regional tradition.

The same is true of Switzerland, where the difficulty of communication between valleys favoured the survival of simple local types of costumes: only in towns like Geneva were Parisian styles introduced, slightly modified. There too, French refugees from the Revocation of the Edict of Nantes, with increasing numbers of travellers, imported and sustained the taste for French costume. We must not forget that it was a Bernese, Freudeberg, who began the illustrations in the *Monument du costume*, which were to be continued by Moreau le Jeune.

Although they were far enough removed from France, both Denmark and Sweden, where French artists had worked since the middle of the *Grand Siècle*, were as enthusiastic about French costume as about French art. An important collection

816 LEVITSKI: *Catherine Nelidov*, 1766. Leningrad, Museum. (Photo Archives Photographiques)

817 LEVITSKI: *Alexander Kokarinov*, c. 1765. Leningrad, Museum. (Photo Archives Photographiques)

818–9 NORBLIN DE LA GOURDAINE: *Ancient costumes worn by the Polish Nobility*, 1810. Paris, Bibliothèque Nationale, Cabinet des Estampes. (Photos Flammarion)

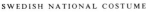

SWEDISH NATIONAL COSTUME

813–4, 822, 839 Gustavus III's attempt to creat a Swedish national costume, simpler than the foreign styles from which it is remotely derived, came to nothing. However, plates 822 and 829 show that an improved version of this costume was worn at court, with clear sixteenth-century reminiscences (slashed sleeves and standing collars); it can be compared with the contemporary attempt in France to create a similarly inspired court costume (plates 724, 725)

COSTUME IN EASTERN EUROPE

816, 828 The young pupils of the Russian Imperial college wore dresses in French style, with stiff bodices

MEN'S COSTUME

817 Over the Western-style coat and jacket is worn a fur-lined caftan decorated with passementerie

POLISH COSTUME

818–9 Over the *zupan*, a very tight-fitting under-caftan, the nobleman wears a *kontush* with hanging sleeves. Belts are reserved for the nobility after the time of Jan Sobieski. Boots are red, with upturned toes. The woman also wears a kontush

ORDINARY PEOPLE'S COSTUME

820–21 The permanent features of steppe costume can be seen here: boots, which are sometimes laced; felt Phrygian caps (plate 820); a crossed caftan with a *turlup* or sash tied at the front (plate 821). The woman's diadem head-dress is a *kakofnitch* (plate 820). All these costumes were made in bright colours further decorated with embroidery

820–21 LE PRINCE: *Costumes worn by the Russian people and a Samoyed Woman*, 1810. Paris, Bibliotheque Nationale, Cabinet des Estampes, Dc 12 fol. (Photos Flammarion)

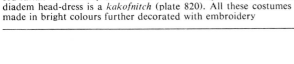

822 PER HILLESTROM: *Conversation at Drottningholm*, c. 1778. Drottningholm, Royal Castle. (Photo Nationalmuseum Stockholm)

823 PER HILLESTRÖM: *Interior*, c. 1780. Stockholm, Nationalmuseum. (Museum photo)

824 *The Ridiculed Husband*, c. 1735. The Hague, Mauritshuis. (Museum photo)

825 C. G. PILO: *Queen Sophia Magdalena*, 1765. Stockholm, Nationalmuseum. (Museum photo)

826 LORENZ PASCH: *Children Dancing*, 1760. Stockholm, Nationalmuseum. (Museum photo)

COSTUME IN HOLLAND

824 The woman's gown without passementerie and the man's justau-corps with sleeves slit *à la marinière* are more British than French in inspiration

CELEBRATION COSTUMES IN SWEDEN

826 The style of festive costume is international, in the spirit of the costumes of Italian opera

SWEDISH COSTUME AT THE END OF THE EIGHTEENTH CENTURY

823, 830–31 The general softening of fashionable styles is seen in dresses without paniers, knotted scarves and broad hats worn over loose curls. The drawings of Elias Martin are witty caricatures of the voluminous *calèches* worn by women

827 GHISLANDI: *Count Valetti*, 1710. Venice, Accademia. (Photo V. Rossi)

828 LEVITSKI: *Theodore Rierzki and Princess Davidov*, 1766. Leningrad, Museum. (Photo Archives Photographiques)

829 PER HILLESTRÖM: *The Game of Cards.* Late eighteenth century. Stockholm, Nationalmuseum. (Museum photo)

of costumes from royal wardrobes shows the persistence in court costume of gowns with very wide paniers, following a model closer to Spanish style, to judge from G. Pilo's royal portraits. Men's suits were often ordered from Paris.

In Sweden we also find the last official reform in costume attempted during the century, when in 1778 Gustavus III tried to impose a 'Swedish national costume' on all classes of society. In the preceding century, in a Denmark that was then still part of Norway, King Christian IV had also dreamed of a national costume, a sort of uniform reserved for the lower classes. Neither of these projects was successful.[25]

Sweden was the only example of a country in which political factions took their names from pieces of costume: from 1731 to 1772 the 'Hat' party and the 'Cap' party fought each other for power.

In Denmark, despite a very strong German influence, particularly at the court of Christian VI, French fashions met with the same enthusiasm among the upper classes as in neighbouring countries.

Eastern Europe

East of the Elbe and the Danube, the influence of French styles diminished with the increase in distance from Paris. While French styles were the adornment of a large, brilliant society in Warsaw, Prague and Vienna, they reached only a privileged few in St Petersburg and Moscow.

RUSSIA

Peter the Great had set out to Europeanize Russia. His daughter, the Empress Elizabeth, was the first to introduce French modes. As coquettish as she was religious, she was more interested in Paris gowns than in the works of French painters engaged by the court. She had toilettes and silk stockings sent from Paris. She never wore the same gown twice, and it is said that on her death more than fifteen thousand gowns were found in her cupboards, together with thousands of shoes and mules.[26]

Outside the extravagant aristocracy, the ordinary classes of Russian society continued to wear a costume dominated by ancestral Asiatic features: for men, the fur overcoat, caftan and cap, and for women, long, wide gowns belted at the waist, and a sort of diadem on the head with a veil attached to it. A French artist, Le Prince, drew several examples of these clothes during his stay in Russia.

POLAND

During the reign of the last King of Poland, Stanislas-Augustus Poniatowski (1764–1795), while the country was still feudal, French styles were predominant and increasingly widespread, as we learn from Mme Geoffin and other contemporary travellers to Warsaw. They had been popularized by the wife of Jan Sobieski, Queen Marie-Casimir of Arquiem, who came to Poland as lady-in-waiting to the preceding queen, Marie-Louise de Gonzaga, herself of French stock.

Provincial nobility, however, remained more attached to the so-called *Sarmatian* costume, Hungarian in origin. The middle and lower classes still wore the traditional costume which had been strongly marked with Oriental features by the proximity of Muscovites, Turks and Tartars. The outer garment was a gown known as a *zupan* with, over this, a *kontush* with slit sleeves; the latter name was later inexplicably to be applied to the gown *à la française* in Germany and further east. Caps were generally worn.

As in Austria, this costume was controlled by the Diet in 1776, which imposed zupans and kontushes and standardized the colours and trimmings for each province: crimson, purple, garnet-red, sky blue, sapphire, dark and light green.

Thus French costume had been imposed in different degrees throughout Europe, and was welcomed everywhere: 'One saw only powdered wigs, short breeches, buckled shoes and panier gowns'. The small courts tried to imitate the ceremony and

329

majesty of Versailles, and French clothes were copied for all the fêtes and 'inventions' got up by princes and their circles.

The spread of French fashions was also aided, in most foreign countries, by the large number of French artists travelling abroad, and artists of other countries coming to work in France; both proved themselves excellent ambassadors.

Information about the styles of the other European countries is less easy to come by, for documents and studies are relatively few. Some modes have been glimpsed, at least, through their vogue in France. The study of the national costume of Europe is for the most part still to be written: French costume may have dominated them, but it certainly did not eclipse them completely.

Military Uniform

At the beginning of the eighteenth century, the essential elements of European military costume were those worn in France at the end of the preceding century, namely, justaucorps, jacket or waistcoat, breeches, leggings for infantry and boots for cavalry. It was only in 1698 that French officers had to dress in the colours of their regiments.

This situation continued until the general adoption of Prussian manoeuvres, which necessitated the suppression of anything hindering rifle movements and contributed to the lightening of military costume. Gradually the old justaucorps became shorter and lengthened its basques, then folded them back, ultimately cutting them away; the coat became skimpier in cut, ornaments were reduced and pockets only simulated.

These successive modifications must be compared with the influence exercised on civilian costume by the riding garment worn in England, the 'riding coat'.

In 1799 French uniform adopted a form that was to last almost sixty years. It became a coat and jacket of broadcloth with knitted, linen-lined breeches; it had wide lapels to distinguish it from civilian costume and was cut off above the stomach; the belt, worn over the justaucorps since 1690, was replaced by the bandolier; the tricorne felt hat was also modified, the front point being turned up.

The already time-honoured use of grey or white for military uniforms, which continued at the beginning of the century, resulted from the use of undyed natural wools. After 1779, colours were fixed for the different sections of the French army. The seventy-nine French infantry regiments wore white coat, jacket and breeches; artillery and engineers were in blue; cavalry of the line generally wore French blue, with a chamois-coloured waistcoat, while dragoons had adopted green coats with leather cassocks in the 1764 reforms.

When the 1793 National Convention suppressed all distinctions between French regiments of the line and national volunteers, the uniform became the same for everyone, in the national colours: blue coat and white waistcoat. The shako, which was introduced in 1804, was made compulsory in 1806.

In 1806 the beige broadcloth overcoat was added to infantry uniform, but for a short time there was a return to the white cloth coat, as worn before 1793, with series of distinctive colours for every eight regiments. Six years later, in 1812, the form of the coat was changed: its facings were cut straight and its basques were shortened. This produced a coat-jacket on more modern lines, in dark colours, which developed into the modern formal morning coat. Breeches were replaced by trousers in white knit worn inside gaiters which reached to below the knee. In 1829 the cloth trousers were madder red.

In 1845 the coat disappeared once and for all, to be replaced by the tunic, a consequence of the substitution of percussion firearms for flint-fired weapons.

Consequently during the whole eighteenth and almost half the nineteenth centuries military uniform and men's civilian costume present certain common points, granting discrepancies in dates, in the form of the coat, the replacement of breeches by trousers, the hat by the shako or tall hat. Depending on the period, the influence of one or the other predominates. These alternating phases can be seen in all the armies of Europe.

The Evolution of Eighteenth-Century Costume

Some special characteristics of the development of costume can be seen clearly in the eighteenth century.

Changes in fashion accelerated once the first specialized journals appeared. Which had more influence, the creators who were making their mark or the gazeteers who installed them in power? It is often difficult to decide. Fashion changes became more frequent with the increasing domination of milliners, dressmakers, hairdressers, textile manufacturers, etc., particularly in the last decades before 1789.

This excessive changeability was a sign of the wordly boredom which was one of the century's ills. The unbridled *engouement* for anything touching costume seems to denote a certain moral unease, a lassitude, a scepticism which was increasingly seeping through society. There was even boredom with change itself, as we can see from Marie-Antoinette's declaration in February 1785 that she would soon be thirty years old, and did not want anything more to do with 'fashions that suit only extreme youth: pierrots, chemises, redingotes, polonaises, lévites, turques or circassiennes.' People must go back to serious pleated gowns; the princesses had already been invited to proscribe all else for ceremonial visits.

This continual pursuit of new forms doubtless also expressed a general movement in women's costume towards greater comfort, softness and ease. This gradual transformation, slow but uninterrupted, is what emerges most clearly from these three-quarters of a century of evolution. The vogue for paniers or the immense head-dresses à la Belle Poule are merely sports, occasional spectacular modes against a steady background movement.

Moreover, we notice a profound transformation in the social function of costume. The substitution of the prestige of a whole society for the authority of a class or court, the prominence achieved by women, the luxury sustained by money and a life of salons, balls and pleasure, a spiritual discipline directed towards ideal simplicity and liberty, all combined to modify the role of costume and to produce a trend towards a universal type of clothing, no longer subject to rigid social demarcations.

Throughout the century it is possible to note an increasing degree of egalitarianism in costume, although this varied in different countries and took long to make itself felt. The classes,

830 ELIAS MARTIN: *The Artist's Brother and Wife*, c. 1780.
Stockholm, Nationalmuseum. (Museum photo)

831 ELIAS MARTIN: *Young Woman*, 1788.
Stockholm, Nationalmuseum. (Museum photo)

except for the poor, began to dress more and more in the same way. This inevitably meant that the old value of quality had passed its zenith and was beginning to be replaced by quantity; and this progressive substitution was to form the succeeding stage of the development of costume.

Notes

1 Pirenne, vol. III, *passim*; *Histoire du Commerce*, vol. IV, *passim*; Sée, *passim*.
2 Roy, *passim*.
3 Clouzot, *passim* and plates III and XIII.
4 The word seems to appear for the first time in a dictionary in 1721 (*Dictionnaire de Trévoux*).
5 Blum, p. 36; Goncourt, II, p. 52; Leloir, X, p. 36; Franklin, p. 538; Cunnington, pp. 88 ff.
6 Cf. *Mercure de France*, March-May 1728.
7 Garsault, *passim*.
8 Cf. *Galerie des Modes et Costumes français*, cahier 13 (1777), 27 (1779) and 28.
9 *Ibid.*, cahier 27; Nolhac, p. 60.
10 Leloir, XI, p. 65.
11 Nouvion and Liez, *passim*.
12 Garsault, *passim*.
13 Franklin, p. 194.
14 Cf. *Cahier des Modes françaises pour les coiffures depuis 1776*.
15 Julien; Fischer; Bernadin, *passim*.
16 Langlade, Nouvion and Liez, *passim*.
17 Algoud, d'Hennezel, Leroudier, *passim*.
18 Exposition Marie-Antoinette (Versailles, 1955), no. 518.
19 Nevinson, *The Connoisseur*, 1934, 1937, 1939 – *Mercure de France* resumed publishing fashion articles in 1729 and 1730.
20 The hat and costume *à la Harpie* were launched in 1783–1784 when an alleged monster, thought to be a Harpy, was discovered in Chile.
21 Malcolm, *Anecdotes of London*.
22 Cunnington, *passim*.
23 Mortitz, *Travels*, p. 53.
24 *Des Sources de l'expansion de la langue française en Europe.*
25 Lenk, pp. 185-187; Müller, *passim*.
26 Cf. Y. Maliszewski, *The Last of the Romanoffs*.

Bibliography

GENERAL

HENRI SÉE: *L'Evolution commerciale et industrielle sous l'Ancien Régime*, 1925.
PAUL MANTOUX: *La Révolution industrielle au XVIIe s.*, 1906.
G. M. TREVELYAN: *A Social History of England.*
E. and J. DE GONCOURT: *La Femme au XVIIIe s.*, 1892.
LOUIS-SEBASTIEN MERCIER: *Tableau de Paris*, 1781.
MALCOLM: *Anecdotes of London*, 1811.
Y. MALISZEWSKI: *The Last of the Romanoffs.*
BARONNE D'OBERKIRCH: *Mémoires*, ed. 1853.

COSTUME

F. A. GARSAULT: *L'Art du Tailleur*, 1769.
Galerie des Modes et Costumes français, 1778–1788.
MAURICE LELOIR: *Histoire du costume*, vols. XI and XII, 1938.
P. NOUVION and E. LIEZ: *Mlle Bertin, marchande de modes de la Reine*, 1911.
E. LANGLADE: *La Marchande de modes de Marie-Antoinette, Rose Bertin*, 1911.
COMTE DE REISET: *Livre-Journal de Mme Eloffe*, 1885.
ANDRÉ BLUM: *Les Modes au XVIIe et au XVIIIe s.*, 1928.
C. W. and PHYLLIS CUNNINGTON: *Handbook of English Costume in the Eighteenth Century*, London, 1957.
TORSTEN LENK: *Nationella Dräkten*, Stockholm, 1951.
ADOLPHE JULLIEN: *Le Costume au théâtre au XVIIIe s.*, 1880.
R. M. BERNADIN: *La Comédie italienne en France*, 1902.

TEXTILES

B. ROY: *Une capitale de l'indiennage*, Nantes, 1948.
H. CLOUZOT: *Histoire de la Manufacture de Jouy et de la Toile imprimée en France*, 1928.
— *Les Toiles peintes de l'Inde*, 1920.
E. LEROUDIER: *Les Dessinateurs de la fabrique lyonnaise au XVIIIe s.*
H. ALGOUD: *Le Décor des soieries françaises*, 1931.
— *Grammaire des arts de la soie*, 1912.
H. D'ALLEMAGNE: *La Toile imprimée et les indiennes de traite*, 1942.

833 NAIGEON: *Family Portrait*, 1793.
Collection R. W. (Photo Flammarion)

834 FRANÇOIS SABLET: *Family Portrait*, c. 1794.
Lausanne, Musée Cantonal des Beaux-Arts. (Photo André Held)

Chapter XI

From the French Revolution to the Early Twentieth Century

The Revolutionary Period from 1789 to 1815

832 P. P. PRUD'HON: *The Schimmelpenninck Family*, 1801.
Amsterdam, Rijksmuseum. (Museum photo)

Costume in Europe

On the eve of the outbreak of the French Revolution, English and French modes were still preponderant, but were more dependent on political events.

For the quarter-of-a-century which followed, the French Revolution created a new situation both within Europe, and between Europe and the rest of the world. Constitutional changes were brought about by wars and invasions, economic circumstances were altered by new conditions of production and exchange. All those changes naturally precipitated new developments in European costume.

THE POLITICAL SITUATION

During the three successive phases of the French Revolution – monarchical, republican and imperial – France's progressive conquests ensured a wider, readier distribution of her styles through the continental countries she occupied. England, who escaped this occupation, spread her own modes to the rest of the world with the aid of her sea power.

French styles in continental countries benefited in turn from the new regimes set up by the Revolution, as well as from the new economic links and the propaganda for France. Even England and the Scandinavian and south-eastern countries were more or less affected by this French expansion so that the evolution of European costume does not, as we might expect, reflect the division of Europe into two opposing camps.

ECONOMIC TRANSFORMATION

The increased prosperity of Europe was general, but not everywhere equal. It was considerable in the Rhinelands and northern Italy, and very great in Belgium, where the economy was oriented towards the rest of the continent; Verviers became a major cloth-making centre, and Ghent ranked behind only

833-5   While France was adopting styles inspired by Classical Antiquity, the rest of Europe remained faithful to chemise dresses (plate 835) and sheaths (plate 834). Round gowns were made of striped muslin or French calico; the crimped, high-crowned cap with a large rosette (plate 833) is a typically Revolutionary model. The standing girl is probably wearing an *Iphigeneia* garland of flowers. Men wear tight costumes, with square-cut waistcoats; long muslin cravats appear, and the vogue for top hats increases (plate 834). The English fashion for high-waisted dresses is closer to French fashion than is the Swiss style

COSTUME IN FRANCE IN 1790

836-9   Tricolor rosettes and the use of the national colours add a contemporary touch to fashion; paniers have totally disappeared and only a 'false rump' supports the fullness of the gown at the back. Men's coats, open high to the waist, are typical of the new cut

835   Formal toilette in muslin, *toupée* head-dress, 1797. Gallery of Fashion. Paris, Bibliothèque Nationale, Cabinet des Estampes. (Photo Flammarion)

836   'Young man in *demi-converti* coat in scarlet over black casimir breeches; one of the watch-straps is black,' 1790

Lyons and Rouen in the production of cottons and prints. In Flanders the lace-making industry, whose main customer was Paris, provided employment for 12,000 women. On the other hand, the continental blockade was a disaster for Holland, for it closed her ports to the important colonial and overseas trade.

England was the country which benefited most from the situation created by the French Revolution between 1789 and 1815.[1]

Mechanization was applied particularly to clothing textiles, with a continual increase in the output of Indian cotton, then of silk, and more slowly, of linen. The difficulty of importing wool held back the woollen cloth industry, and consequently – as in France and the rest of Europe – cotton was chiefly used for women's dress, and the white toilettes inspired by French models remained popular.

After the crisis of 1808, English trade, supported by important capital reserves, expanded rapidly to make London the most powerful economic centre in the world. There was regular trade with Canada and America, the Mediterranean and the Baltic, the Cape and the Indies, the Far East, and even Australia, where sheep-breeding provided wool for the home country. British clothing spread in all these corners of the globe.

The great systems of international trade routes developed: on the Continent there was a network of roads and canals, with new ports in Antwerp and Venice; by sea, trade routes served Africa, the Far East, North America and the West Indies and even crossed Central America through Honduras. European textile materials and colorants were the first commodities to benefit.

France expanded her trading empire by creating the Batavian, Helvetic, Cisalpine and Ligurian republics. European exports resumed under the Consulate, while the prohibition of goods bought directly or indirectly from England was extended. From June 1803 until 21 November 1806 and the Berlin Decree establishing the blockade of the British Isles, there was an incessant series of taxes and levies on thread and cotton cloth, prohibitions of nankeens, muslins, etc., which were widely used for clothing. Nevertheless, a fairly active trade finally developed with the United States, particularly in silk, linen and millinery.

There were, of course, loopholes on both sides of this blockade, some covered by import licences, other depending purely on smuggling, and these were never completely closed by repressive measures. Dyes and even cotton stuffs thus continued to pass between the two opposing blocs.

While costume generally benefited from this major economic boom, currency restrictions affected the quantity and even the quality of raw materials available. In a world increasingly mechanized, costume came to depend increasingly on economic factors.

THE CHARACTERISTICS OF EUROPEAN COSTUME

The unification of almost the whole of western Europe under French institutions did not lead to an unimpeded propagation of new French fashions. For one thing, French émigrés maintained eighteenth-century styles abroad, all the more influentially because they were regarded as representatives of traditional French taste, and often made important family alliances. On the other hand, French soldiers and officials brought with them liberal, revolutionary ideas, automatically considered subversive by the new country, and this had its influence on the country's styles. English travellers' visits to Paris at the time of the Peace of Amiens, and its occupation by allied armies in 1814-15 did more to get French modes accepted than had all the efforts of the Consulate and the Empire.

As was amply proved by British tourists in France in 1802, England was open to French women's fashions as soon as they interpreted Classical styles. The practical, comfortable styles which had won success for English gowns on the Continent at the end of the Ancien Régime were discarded by London ladies in favour of French models. English men's costume, on the other hand, kept to its purely national inspiration and gained wide acceptance. From then on France lost any claim to supremacy in this particular field.

837 'Woman dressed in Constitution style in very fine Indian cotton in the national colours,' 1790

838 'Woman in royal blue *coureur* with red facings piped in white, waistcoat of white bazeen, black hat with *cocarde* and band in the colours of the Nation,' 1790

839 'Nankeen-coloured skirt and *coureur* jacket, crown-shaped toque with heron feathers.' Engravings by DUHAMEL, *Cabinet des Modes*. Paris, Bibliothèque Nationale, Cabinet des Estampes, Oa 85 d. (Photos Flammarion)

Elsewhere in Europe fashion began to apply more exclusively to women's clothes. Men's costume, which had been so rich and varied before the Revolution, now became less interesting. This development accompanied a mechanization in which men played an increasing part. But it may equally have been an effect of the wars which took countless men from their homes and families to serve under the colours, depriving them of their interest in civilian clothes.

During the Empire, the spread of French fashions was helped considerably by the establishment of members of the Bonaparte family on the thrones of allied countries, and by marriages between members of this new aristocracy and foreign nobility. In the towns and cities the ruling classes aided the spread of French modes, but these styles did not penetrate deeply in country districts. Indeed, regional costume became more pronounced among the lower classes, and even the provincial lower-middle classes. While peasant costume seems to have been fairly uniform until the end of the eighteenth century, after the Revolution we see the first local variations. The first collections of provincial costumes were made during the First Empire.

Costume in France

FACTORS AFFECTING DEVELOPMENT

From the end of the eighteenth century it is possible to detect the first signs of the great changes to come. After 1789, a general democratization and social and economic progress put an end to the regulations of the Ancien Régime, these being superseded by utilitarianism and individualism. Later, economic circumstances forced the Republic and, in its turn, the Empire to abandon some of the early principles of the Revolution.

The initial burst of idealism, and the accommodations which followed, produced modifications in costume rather than the complete transformations we might expect. In fact, the trend of French costume had already begun before the Revolution and there was continuity during the entire Revolutionary period, as witness the persistence of taste for white gowns.

The liberty of the Republic and the authority of the Empire helped fashion to become free from the dictates of centralized power.

THE DEVELOPMENT OF POLITICAL REGIMES AND COSTUME

In France the end of the monarchy and the disappearance of court life entailed the suppression of all 'court costume', although it was later to be reintroduced under Napoleon.

Elsewhere, however, from London to Naples and from Lisbon to Moscow, this costume persisted and came through this difficult quarter-of-a-century intact in essentials, though not unchanged.

'Society life' in France was superseded by political assemblies. The Third Estate wore black clothing for the 1789 *Etats-Généraux* – legal costume consisting of short black cloak, black breeches and an unbraided, buttonless toque. This aroused public protest, nobody appears to have noticed the fact that this costume, prescribed by royal decree, was an effort to distinguish a body that was representative. Faced with the Third Estate's costume, whose simplicity and austerity had political overtones, the nobility appeared in a dazzling display of gold-embroidered cloaks and white-plumed hats. When the minister Roland went to the King's Cabinet in 1792 wearing shoes without buckles, flat hair with little powder and a worn suit, he seemed to be committing a revolutionary act.

Here again, the phenomenon was exclusively French: nowhere else in Europe do we see any traces of a particular costume reserved for one category of citizens or dictated by their political functions, as was to be the case of Senators during the Consulate.

Under the Empire, Napoleonic politics produced a revival of sumptuous court costume, modelled on that worn under the

335

840 P. P. PRUD'HON: *Madame Coppia*, 1790. Collection Vicomtesse de Noailles. (Photo Flammarion)

841 L. BOILLY: *The Actor Chenard as a Sans-Culotte*, 1792. Paris, Musée Carnavalet. (Photo Flammarion)

842 ANON: *Portrait of Robespierre, c.* 1792. Paris, Musée Carnavalet. (Photo Flammarion)

843 L. BOILLY: *The Optics Lesson, c.* 1796. Private Collection. (Photo Flammarion)

monarchy. The triumph of the Imperial armies, efficient administration at home and the embellishment of Paris all produced a triumphal, luxurious way of life in the capital, with brilliant official receptions that naturally enough benefited costume. Napoleon's coronation was the first of these great occasions, with special costumes designed and made by the Imperial suppliers Isabey and Percier, and a profusion of uniforms and court gowns and trains.

This magnificence was to last until the abdication, though it became less brilliant after Napoleon's marriage to Marie-Louise, when court spending was strictly controlled and great ladies patronised their suppliers less frequently.

IDEOLOGY AND CHANGE

Frequent changes in public sentiment accompanied the political events of the period. After a ferment of idealism in the early years, the republican Revolution passed through twelve years marked by constant innovation directed towards completing the break with the past. In this time of unrest, this heady access of liberty, the individual who suddenly found himself promoted to the rank of citizen found in clothing both a relaxation and an opportunity for self-expression.

After 1789, vices of the eighteenth century which, with the dominant role played by women, had contributed to luxury in costume – idleness, dissipation of effort, scepticism and destructive hedonism – had all but disappeared. There yet remained the tendency to do today the opposite of yesterday. As the Comte de Ségur put it, there were still 'laughing rebels against old modes and serious etiquette...'

The repercussions of this social upheaval on costume were extensive and profound, particularly in the first years of Revolutionary activity in France.

The 'Belle Monde' of the preceding period began to disappear during the monarchic phase of the Revolution: the nobility abandoned its charges and pensions, the clergy lost its benefits and income, financiers left their great houses and ostentatious way of life, and magistrates and the rich bourgeoisie were

844 DELAFONTAINE: *Bertrand Andrieu*, 1798.
Paris, Musée de la Monnaie. (Photo Flammarion)

845 L. BOILLY: *Point of Convention, c.* 1801.
Collection Alain de Rothschild. (Photo Flammarion)

thrown back among the middle classes. All these groups omitted costume from their budgets, where they were not actually forced to pawn their wardrobes or sell them to rag-men.

It was mainly after 1791 that the disappearance of privileges and immunities rapidly eliminated the former élites, and, with them, luxury in costume. Styles reflected the new democratic spirit and the idea of 'citizen' which replaced that of 'individual', besides the new dominant role played by the urban masses in political events. A fashion journal mentioned a gown necessary for 'every nun newly returned to society…'

Even before 1780, costume had begun to be less closely linked than before to social class; later, with the return of a degree of political stability under the Consulate and the Empire, the successors of the nobility remained parvenus ignorant in matters of dress.

The end of the Reign of Terror created an atmosphere dominated by the need to forget and the desire to enjoy life. In the parvenu society of the Directoire period women found new opportunities; fashion journals reappeared[2] and pleasure resorts opened once more: Tivoli, Frascati, and the *Jardin d'Italie*. The public once again developed a taste for incessant novelty. The 'proletarian' garments of the beginning of the Revolution already set their wearers apart, and were out of favour, but the opponents of the Revolution on the other hand, wore black or '*demi-converti*' (half-converted) costume, and even accentuated their peculiarity with black collars (*collets noirs*) for royalists, as against red collars (*collets rouges*) for republicans.

On the whole, men's costume was elegant and restrained, far removed from the eccentricities, which were exceptional anyway, of some of the very young: the *Incroyables* never really represented the costume of their time.

The main trend to make its appearance in this atmosphere of reaction was, for women, the 'passion for things Antique' which began in limited circles, but soon became general. Only the emigrées, who were gradually returning to France, kept to costumes in English style.

This Classically-inspired feminine costume was in perfect harmony with the prevailing moral freedom. It revealed as

COSTUME DURING THE REVOLUTION

840, 843   During the years of the French Revolution, women's busts were no longer supported by stiff bodices, and the waist moved to just below the breasts; the *coureur* (plate 838) is followed by the spencer with very small basques or no basques at all (plate 843). Unpowdered hair is worn loose over the shoulders; the hat *à la Paméla* (plate 840) was to remain in fashion for a long time

SANS-CULOTTE COSTUME

841   Workmen's costume (trousers and a short jacket called a *carmagnole*) was never worn by other classes of society

MEN'S COSTUME FROM 1791 TO 1801

842, 844–7   The waistcoat is square-cut with lapels (plate 844); the coat is plain, with a high, turned-down collar, often lined in another colour; breeches *à l'anglaise* reach to below the knee; shoes and boots have pointed toes; full cravats wound several times round the neck are called *écrouelliques* (plate 845), and 'dog-ear' hairstyles (plate 845) are part of the eccentricities of elegant men of the Directoire period, corresponding to the transparent tunics and laced *cothurnes* and Grecian hairstyles of women (plate 845). Plate 847 records these exaggerations to the point of caricature. Hats (plates 844–5) are *en bateau*

COSTUME DESIGNED BY DAVID

848–9   This costume, vaguely inspired by Classical reminiscences, was never worn, but women adopted styles that were straightforward transpositions of the neo-classical paintings of David and his school

OFFICIAL DIRECTOIRE COSTUME

850–52   These costumes, designed by David, were actually worn by the members of the government, but disappeared after the *coup d'état* of 18 Brumaire; the only element to have survived to our times is the tricolor sash worn by French municipal functionaries

846 P. P. PRUD'HON: *The Younger de Gassicourt*, 1791. Paris, Musée Jacquemart-André. (Photo Bulloz)

847 LA MÉSANGÈRE: *Young Man's Dress*, An 8, 1800. Paris, Bibliothèque Nationale, Cabinet des Estampes, Oa 87 4°. (Photo Flammarion)

848 JACQUES-LOUIS DAVID: *Indoor Dress of a French Citizen*, 1793

849 JACQUES-LOUIS DAVID: *Civilian Dress of a French Citizen*, 1794. Paris Bibliothèque Nationale, Cabinet des Estampes, Oa 288. (Photos Flammari

much as possible of the form, did not hamper women's movements and thus increased the pleasures of dancing, the sovereign amusement of the Directoire period, along with spectacles, which had gradually reappeared after 18 Brumaire. The Opera Ball was revived in February 1800, Mi-Carême was re-established the following March, and in 1801 the local authorities authorized Carnival disguises in the streets, and in 1802, masks.

While the splendours of the Empire set out to revive the past, they still touched only part of Parisian society – that part which gravitated round the Emperor. The reserve, if not the opposition, shown by other classes kept them apart from the Tuileries court and the worldly life led there. The Parisian bourgeoisie, who were temperamentally and consciously conservative, saw in the constant wars only a threat to their peaceful tastes. They were jealous of the presence of military and courtly elements, and moved away from the Emperor after his divorce. Similarly, when the mercantile class was affected by the 1806 continental blockade, it split away from political circles. The salons of the old aristocracy in the Boulevard Saint-Germain were still mostly closed; there were no more great evening parties, but only small gatherings where proverbs were acted. The Empire nobility gathered round the Duchesse de Montbello, and the world of finance flocked to Madame de Récamier, the queen and model of elegance until 1808 when, after the death of her husband, she retired to the Abbaye au Bois, where she led a simple life.

Some classes thus found their sartorial expression curtailed. During the whole of the Imperial period, only a privileged few – financiers, or dukes and counts created by Napoleon – could provide their wives with really ample means to spend on clothes.

The constant adaptation of costume to social changes during the First Empire yet continued a fashion originating from before 1789, one which was to take its inspiration, during almost a third of a century, from a single source: Classical antiquity.

From 1789 to 1815, then, there was no true 'costume revolution' in France: the only change attempted was already complete by the 18 Brumaire.

THE ECONOMIC SITUATION

The effects of the revolutionary period on the costume industry and trades were swift and drastic.

At first their craftsmen and employees were reduced to working on the roads for thirty *sols* a day, or else had to sign on at the Montmartre charity workshop. A long slack season was beginning for an industry which only shortly before supplied all Europe with silks from Lyons, lawns and batistes from Valenciennes and Saint-Quentin, chamois from Grenoble and millinery from Paris. A contemporary caricature shows a skinny craftsman wearing a garment worn transparent, with the bitter caption: 'I'm free!'

The trades had been disorganized everywhere by the abolition of internal customs in 1790 and of mastership and guildmastery in March 1791. Marat himself wrote in *L'Ami du Peuple*: 'I may be wrong, but I should not be surprised if in twenty years we cannot find a single workman in Paris capable of making a hat or a pair of shoes.'

After this there was a slight improvement: in 1792 French industry exported its silks 'with a favour long forgotten', wrote Roederer, the Minister of the Interior.

During the Directoire period, towards the end of 1797, complete chaos reigned, with unemployment and low wages; in 1795 the overall production of broadcloth and woollens had declined by two thirds.

To revive the textile industries, the Directoire spent four millions, and concentrated on improving techniques by using English machinery. The result was economic regeneration. All materials for the costumes of public officials had to be 'grown in the territory of the Republic or be produced nationally.'

The progress of the woollen and cotton industries was forwarded again under the Consulate; a law from the month of Germinal, An XI, imposed strict regulations on factories and workshops and organized the protection of particular marks stamped on manufactured goods.[3]

The quality of woollens changed. In 1789 there was either coarse common cloth, stiff, heavy and badly finished, available in few varieties but at fairly uniform prices, or light, soft,

heavily filled, often flimsy stuffs. After the Consulate period the use of British Douglas machines allowed the production of fine broadcloths which outclassed the old products. Under the Directoire, Ternaux began to make light stuffs known as *mérinos* and shawls as fine as those from Cashmere, and he continued their production with increasing success until the Restoration.

On becoming Consul, Bonaparte set himself to revive industry and trade, at the same time restoring social and financial stability. Gradually the situation improved in Flanders, Normandy, Alsace and the Vosges. The cotton industry was established and made rapid progress, thanks to the use of the 'flying shuttle'.[4] Textile printing was mechanized: in 1802 Oberkampf's factory at Jouy began to use copper cylinders to apply the dyes.

Under the First Empire, however, this general recovery was complicated by difficulties arising from events outside France; the continental blockade imposed restrictions and slowed down exports. Thus the industry showed a recession in comparison with the developments of the mid-eighteenth century. Textiles, the basic material of costume, raised the most complex questions of supply and manufacture.

It seems paradoxical that the Imperial wars placed French cotton in a privileged position; in fact, sheltered from British competition, French spinning centres caught up on their British rivals and managed to equal them in most yarns, apart from fine cotton *filés*, which were still imported from Great Britain, often smuggled through Holland. Bauwens, Richard and Lenoir perfected cotton weaving, for which there were two hundred and fifty specialized spinning mills in 1806.

The difficulties in finding supplies of this material favoured Levantine cotton, which reached France by land, up the Danube Valley or through Trieste. After 1810, however, there was a marked rise in prices, and imports dwindled to the point of crisis in the cotton industry. This state of affairs lasted until 1814 and was aggravated by the sale of English cottons on the French market.

The silk-weavers of Lyons had been ruined by the Revolution, and above all by the siege of Lyons in 1793. In 1810 a petition was presented to the Emperor by a number of traders, including a son of Charles Dutillieu, one of the men who had renewed the arts of silk weaving in the eighteenth century. The crisis was then so serious that half of the fourteen thousand looms in Lyons had had to be dismantled. Two years later the situation improved, with ten thousand looms in production, and silk weaving made considerable progress with the inventions of the Jacquards.

This revival of textile industries and the improved quality of materials woven had a noticeable effect on costume. Women's costume made increasing use of white or pale cottons or silks, and the growth of trains consumed more metres of cloth per gown. Both sexes wore more heavy stuffs, velvets or dark silks, which were imposed by Napoleon for ceremonial dress. The best proof of the close links between clothing and the general economy is to be found after 1812, when the end of exports and absence of great occasions were to provoke another unemployment crisis in the textile industry.

MEN'S AND WOMEN'S COSTUME FROM 1789 TO 1792: THE MONARCHY

At the beginning of the Revolution it was fashionable to affect simplicity and pay homage to Liberty in costume as in other things. Everything became free: 'Nowadays,' remarked a contemporary,' every movement can be seen under a long gown or a caraco.' Marquises and Counts, who no longer wore swords, jabots, cuffs or purses, dressed 'like jockeys'.

However, the general type of costume remained linked to the way of life of the Ancien Régime: older people merely tempered their costumes with a judicious sobriety.

Since the beginning of the century men's costume had remained more or less unchanged; its transformations were thenceforth to affect points of detail.

The tight, buttoned, long-basqued, high-collared coat, and the frock-coat, of a similar but looser cut, shared men's favour. Both were cut over the stomach; the tight breeches were worn without braces; the short waistcoat was cut square across and

854 C. G. SCHICK: *Frau von Cotta*, 1802.
Stuttgart, Staatsgalerie. (Museum photo)

855 BERJON: *Mlle Bailly*, 1799.
Lyons, Museum. (Photo Camponogara)

856 GÉRARD: *Mme Barbier-Walbonne*, 1796. Paris, Louvre. (Photo Flammarion)

was often embroidered. The long, narrow redingote was worn over the coat. It was smart to wear one's heart almost literally on one's sleeve; the coat in black broadcloth was *à la Revolution*; firm aristocrats 'wore only black, mourning for despotism'; young men wore the costume called *demi-converti* (plate 836) with a scarlet coat, black waistcoat, breeches and stockings, and one of the two watch-strings in black. Patriots happily concocted royal-blue suits trimmed with red and white, and wore waistcoats decorated with emblems and coat-buttons with patriotic devices.

Clothes in bright colours were also worn: violet was one such colour, and might be combined with orange breeches and waistcoats. High collars were generally *cut*, that is, in a colour contrasting with the coat. Plain or striped stockings were also in colours contrasting with the rest of the clothing, and shoes were adorned with ribbon rosettes. Hair was normally plaited *à la Panurge*, and high-crowned hats *en bateau* replaced the tricorne.

Naturally young people ostentatiously exaggerated these badges of up-to-date citizenry; in the Luxembourg, the Tuileries and the '*Jardin-Egalité*' (formerly the Palais-Royal), *petits-maîtres* and the ladies of the Town wore the national colours in cockades or large ribbon bows in their hats, or in their tricolor-striped frock-coats and caracos.

Women rejected paniers and still wore either gowns *à l'anglaise* worn over a small pad or *cul*, or the half-redingote over a short-cut waistcoat, or else, more simply, very loose-waisted gowns. The general effect was informal; there was no more powder, but, low *ingénue* hairstyles, flat-heeled shoes *à la Jeannette* and full fichus crossed on the chest. Hats with tall, narrow crowns were trimmed with a cockade or *follette* feathers; they were often worn over *colinettes*, which were caps of fine pleated lawn with the edge falling over the nape of the neck.

Naturally women made greater borrowings from the ideas and events of the day, but in names and details rather than in forms: the redingote was *nationale*, the cap *à la Bastille* and the gown *à la Camille française*. There was no elegant woman who could not combine a fine royal blue worsted *coureur* with a standing collar in scarlet edged with white. Women who wished

857 J. F. A. Tischbein: *Gräfin Theresa Frees*, 1801. Hamburg, Kunsthalle. (Photo Kleinhempel)

858 La Mésangère: *Hair in Titus style, scarf fastened at the shoulder, mantle over the arm*, An 6, 1798

859 *Ball accessories, 'Etruscan' costume, spencer, c. 1798*

860 La Mésangère: *Pink organdie bonnet, fichu apron*, An 7, 1799. Paris, Bibliothèque Nationale, Cabinet des Estampes. (Photos Flammarion)

to be noticed and appear 'free citizens' affected details inspired by men's costume: men's shirt-collars, flat hairstyles, black felt hats and laced boots.[5]

Alternatively, with naive enthusiasm, they might take inspiration from the uniform of the new Paris militia, wearing military-looking redingotes and even fashioning their hats in helmet shapes. But it was rare for these 'national' styles to appear in the fashion journals.

One particular feature of this period was the rapidity with which fashions changed. The *Cabinet des Modes* mentioned this in 1790, indicating that as garments were now the same for every class, frequent changes were the only way in which the old aristocracy could distinguish itself from the rest. Textiles were renewed: silk and velvet gave way to broadcloth for men and, for women, light stuffs with wide sashes at the waist.

Children benefited from these developments; already they had ceased to resemble the miniature adults painted by F. H. Drouais (plate 743), and under the joint influence of English fashions and the new ideas of liberty they were dressed in simple, practical garments. Boys wore jackets and waistcoats *à la marinière* with straw hats, and girls a muslin sheath over a taffeta underskirt with a sash and a coloured ribbon in unpowdered hair.

FROM 1792 TO 1795: THE REPUBLIC

The year 1792, with the fall of the monarchy and the establishment of a People's Commune, marked a decisive date in the evolution of costume, particularly for men.

The revolutionary ideology was then expressed by the spread of a proletarian costume, that worn by the *Sans-Culotte*, reserved for street demonstrators rather than for the 'pure' frequenters of clubs. This costume comprised wide trousers with front flaps, of coarse wool, with the compulsory accessory, braces, a short jacket known as a *carmagnole*, a red cap and sabots. This costume was first worn by the actor Chenard, as standard-bearer at a civic celebration on 14 October 1792 (plate 841), and was adopted mainly by the members of the

WOMEN'S COSTUME UNDER THE DIRECTOIRE

853, 855-6 The white tunic in light material, with short sleeves and a high waist, was a general fashion. The laced sandals, *caracalla* (crimped curls) or *titus* (with the neck shaved) hairstyles are Classically inspired. As light gowns made no provision for pockets, bags became indispensable and the *balantine*, (plate 853) was one type that appeared. The *cornet* hat and *bavadere* (striped) scarf were also in vogue (plate 855)

CLASSICAL STYLES IN EUROPE

832, 854, 857 The flowing, transparent gown with a soft Grecian neckline (plate 832) is worn, after a short time, throughout the countries under French influence. The *Infanta* hairstyle and striped shoes (plate 854) are inspired by Directoire extravagances

OUTER GARMENTS

858-9 Long scarves and short spencers went well with Classical gowns, compensating for their lightness

APRON SKIRTS

860 With tunic-dresses, aprons, differing from the skirt, were to be worn for a long time. This engraving shows their clever cut and also the appearance of the first poke bonnets

EXTRAVAGANCES OF CLASSICAL FASHIONS

861 These caricatures emphasize the ridiculous side of skirts draped up, and the masculine fashions adopted by women: wide lapels and *écrouellique* cravats, and the slave earrings worn by both sexes

861 After Desrais: *Today's Heroines, c.* 1799. Paris, Bibliothèque Nationale, Cabinet des Estampes, Oa 20. (Photo Flammarion)

862 DAVID: *Comtesse Daru*, 1810. New York, Frick Collection. (Copyright the Collection)

863 Court gown with train over panier, 1800. *Gallery* of *Fashion*. Paris, Bibliothèque Nationale, Cabinet des Estampes, Ob 106. (Photo Flammarion)

864 GROS: *Duroc, Grand Court Marshal*, 1805 Versailles, Museum. (Museum photo)

General Council of the Commune. It was designed by the painter Sergent,[6] and transposed 'the everyday clothes of town and country', but was also that worn by seamen, and the red cap for the authorities recalled the caps worn by convicts.

This popular formula coexisted with the classic garment, which was still worn by almost all important men;[7] nobody was more careful about his clothes than Robespierre (plate 842), who appeared at the feast of the Supreme Being, on 8 June 1794, poured into a cornflower-blue coat over a nankeen waistcoat, with a wide silk sash in the national colours and a hat decorated with a tricolour plume. This was no more than men's fashion in 1792, represented by Debucourt in the famous engraving *La Promenade Publique*.

An effort was made in 1793 to create a typically revolutionary costume, but despite the enthusiasm of certain artists this remained a political fancy. What the innovators were trying to do was to introduce a new style, promoted by the State, in order to express its reforming zeal.

The guiding idea came from a group of artists proposing to 'work for universal regeneration by regenerating costume'. In the month of Germinal, An II, the *Société Républicaine des Arts* devoted several sessions to the question. The painter Lesueur put forward the principle that the costume then worn was unworthy of free men and should be entirely redesigned. Sergent contended that, in the name of Equality, there should be only one type of clothing, while the sculptor Espercieux, supported by a *citoyenne*, suggested the Greek helmet and chlamys, and a 'friend of nature' argued more prosaically for the prohibition of the boned bodice.

It was not the intention of the innovators to impose a compulsory garment, but simply to propose one type and recommend its adoption. The Committee of Public Safety issued a bulletin on Floreal 25, An II (May 1794), inviting the painter David to present his projects for improvements to the national costume, so as to make it more appropriate to republican ways and the character of the Revolution. The National Convention would transmit the verdict of public opinion.

The costume designed by David (plate 849) – tunic, tight trousers, short boots, a round cap with aigrette, wide belt and cloak flowing from the shoulders – was only worn by some of the painter's young pupils. The ideas of the *Société Républicaine des Arts* and of David himself succeeded only in wrapping the pupils of the *École de Mars* in an archaic costume.

These determined innovators then declared that it was 'among the fair sex that costume must be regenerated'; however, men's clothing was subject to their efforts. They never attempted to impose a Republican style on women. Indeed the women had forestalled them: their clothes were already expressing the rage for the Antique, the symbol of the new times.

This development had begun in 1789 with the loose hairstyles painted by Mme Vigée-Lebrun in 1790 in her famous portrait of Mme Grand, the future Mme Talleyrand. It had been followed by the prohibition of the boned bodice and heeled shoes. After 1792 it continued with the abandonment of fichus and with the straight falling line of the gown, and after 1793 with the adoption of small hats.

A curious letter written from the Hague by the Princess of Orange, Frederica of Prussia, the wife of William, comments on Paris gowns in 1793: 'the gown is a sort of chemise, but cut lower than the ones worn before and without lacing. Just below the breasts one wears a kerchief as a belt, fastened behind with a bow between the shoulders; from this the garment falls straight to the floor, like a sack, without marking the waist. It is horrible on ugly, ill-made or old people, and excessively indecent on the young...'

This chemise-dress which so shocked the Princess of Orange had come from England before the Revolution; it had then spread through a Europe conquered by the ideas – and weapons – of the Revolution, and had been adopted in other countries, presenting the double attraction of coming from London and being worn in Paris, where it had become even more revealing, with a higher waist.

FROM 1795 TO 1799: THE DIRECTOIRE PERIOD

During the four years of the Directoire period, costume continued and accentuated the trends of the preceding period. The

865 GÉRARD: *Maria Carolina, Queen of Naples*, 1808. Versailles, Museum. (Museum photo)

866 Court gown in white silk covered with an olive green silk tunic embroidered with metallic thread. Late eighteenth century. Barcelona, Museo de Arte, Collection Don Rocamora. (Museum photo)

867 Court gown in white tulle embroidered with sequins and brilliants, worn at a reception given by Louis Bonaparte at Amsterdam, *c.* 1808. Amsterdam, Rijksmuseum. (Museum photo)

excesses we find are only the exceptional result of the permissive moral climate or the efforts of a few young men and women to attract attention to themselves. The reaction of 9 Thermidor had at least led to the disappearance of Sans-Culotte costume, and even tricolour cockades.

On the whole, men's costume became lighter and more definite in shape. The crossed redingote had deep lapels and two rows of buttons, cravats were high and waistcoats tight, with lapels. Above all, trousers became tight. Hair was cut short *à la Brutus* or worn long *en oreilles de chien*. Boots were very soft, with turned down tops, and bicornes or hats *en bateau* were worn.

The very young men who had expressed their opposition to the revolutionary regime during the Terror by particular details of dress, now emphasized them still further, wearing coats with square skirts, very low-cut shoes, hair hanging on either side of the face and caught up behind over a comb, locks of hair known as *faces*, and carrying cudgels or short, weighted sticks. After being called *les fats* (fools), in 1794 they were called *muscadins*,[8] according to Amaury Duval, who mocked their bobbing gait, their puffily knotted cravats and shoes which barely covered their toes.

A curious blossoming of administrative uniforms resulted from law embodied in the Constitution in 1795. The Five Hundred, the *Anciens, Directeurs* and their secretaries, numerous officials in various services and even Government agents in the colonies all had new costumes, enhancing their prestige. This attachment to uniform even reached the artists living in the French School in Rome: in 1798 they asked the Minister of the Interior for an official costume like that worn by State students from other countries, composed of a coat in 'French national blue' with velvet lapels and silver embroideries or piping, waistcoat and trousers in 'kingfisher cashmere' with hussard buttonholes and a sky-blue cord, boots with a small tassel in front and a round hat with a band.[9]

For women, the modes announced by fashion journals were often exactly interpreted by contemporary artists such as Boilly (plate 843), Sergent-Marceau, Garneray, Danloux (plate 874) or David (plate 862).

ELEGANT COSTUME DURING THE FIRST EMPIRE

862, 869–71 Women's costume remains faithful to the high-waisted dress, with deep square-cut necklines and short sleeves known as *bretelles* (shoulder-straps) because they replaced the shoulder-straps of the dress. Towards 1808–9, fashions began to make use of heavy materials, satins and velvets; hair was dressed in chignons and curls with considerable imagination. The Cashmere shawl, generally longer than it was wide, was the indispensable complement to any elegant toilette. Women also wore the *palatine scarf* of swansdown (plate 869). Madame de Senonnes (plate 870) wears Spanish sleeves, slashed and buttoned here and there

COURT COSTUME

863–8, 872 Though the English court kept paniers longer than did others (plate 863) the rest of Europe, including Sweden and Spain (plates 868, 872), was quick to adopt the high-waisted, richly-embroidered gown worn at the court of Napoleon I. Rich, heavy ornament is the distinctive feature of these gowns. Men's court costume is inspired by the costume of the Order of the Holy Spirit during the Ancien Régime (plate 864)

868 Coronation gown worn by Queen Désirée (Clary), 1819. Stockholm, Royal Armoury. (Museum photo)

869 GÉRARD: *Portrait of a Lady*, 1806. Nancy, Museum. (Photo C. André)

870 INGRES: *Mme de Senonnes*, 1806. Nantes, Museum. (Photo Viaud)

871 RIESENER: *The Artist's Wife and Sister*, 1088 Orléans, Museum. (Photo Giraudon)

872 LOPEZ Y PORTANA: *Queen Maria Cristina*, 1830. Madrid, Prado. (Museum photo)

All elegant women wore long gowns of lawn or muslin, gathered and deeply décolleté, with a shawl or *spencer*, a novelty which appeared in 1789; a narrow ribbon tied at the back marked the waist under the armpits: this was the girdle *à la victime*. Some other innovations were the tunic *à la romaine*, draped over the shoulder, and aprons, which were a sort of double skirt open behind, the fashion for which spread in the following years.

Women wore wigs *à la grecque*, particularly towards 1794–5, made in all colours, and over these placed helmets or *casques*, with round crowns and long visors, trimmed with a falling plume. At the end of the Directoire period they were to prefer caps, bonnets or turbans in light colours. The fashion then favoured bonnets with wide, rounded brims; the rivalry between falling plumes and standing aigrettes (*esprits*) which alternated in fashion for some years, ended only in 1799. Coquettes carried a small bag called a *balantine* or *réticule*, soon renamed *ridicule*.

There were, inevitably, excesses. None of these pretty, elegant women, Mme Récamier, Mme Tallien, Mme Hamelin, Mlle Georges, Mlle Lange or *La Générale* Bonaparte would have refused to become one of the *Merveilleuses* who were soon to be the talk of Paris, by showing themselves in gowns of tulle so light, over muslins so transparent that onlookers could tell the colour of their garters. In October 1798 two women dared to walk down the Champs-Elysées almost naked in gauze sheaths. Shortly after, a critic wrote that 'the garment that best suits a woman is nudity'. During the winter season 1799–1800, during a formal performance given at the Opéra in the presence of Bonaparte, Mme Tallien and two of her friends appeared as nymph-huntresses, clad in tunics that reached barely to the knees, with bare feet adorned with rings in light sandals with purple straps. This was the costume suggested by Amaury Duval, chief of the Arts and Sciences Bureau of the Ministry of the Interior and occasional critic; but the next day Josephine de Beauharnais influenced the First Consul to inform the three nymphs that 'the time of fable was over and the reign of History had begun'.

873 ROBERT LEFÈVRE: *Comtesse Walther*, 1811.
Versailles, Museum. (Museum photo)

873–5 Mameluck sleeves (in tiered rolls) and fine linen trimmings, sometimes profuse, decorated white gowns (plate 874). The Pamela bonnet remained in fashion (plate 875)

874 DANLOUX: *Delille Dictating his Works*, c. 1801.
Versailles, Museum. (Photo Flammarion)

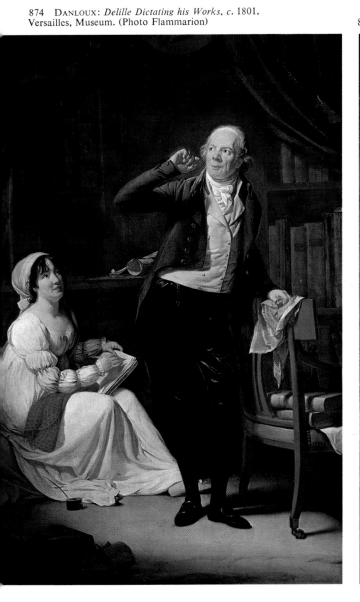

875 ROUGET: *Mlles Mollien*, 1811. Paris, Louvre. (Photo Flammarion)

345

876 LA MÉSANGÈRE: *Le grand négligé*, informal Parisian costume, 1808. Paris, Bibliothèque Nationale, Cabinet des Estampes, (Photo Flammarion)

877 SULZER: *Three Wintherthur Girls*, 1822. Wintherthur, Museum. (Photo Flammarion)

878 SUHR: *Hamburg Fashions: the Serving-Girl and the Seamstress*, 1808. Paris, Bibliothèque Nationale, Cabinet des Estampes, Ob 63. (Photo Flammarion)

FROM 1799 TO 1815: CONSULATE AND EMPIRE

With the Consulate, Paris regained her role as the leader of fashion.

The relations which had been resumed with Great Britain, and perhaps also the remains of the old Anglomania, gave unprecedented vogue to certain elements brought from England at the end of the Directoire period: the spencer, which has already been mentioned, was a short jacket with or without lapels, which stopped at the waist, that is, just below the armpits, and was generally in a dark colour contrasting with the white gowns. It was fitted, and had long sleeves which almost covered the hands. The shawl was another importation. It had been mentioned in 1790 by the *Journal de la Mode et du Goût*, but its adoption was stimulated by the Egyptian Campaign. While cashmere was the material most generally employed, shawls were also made of muslin, percale and gauze, embroidered or woven with patterns, floral shawls being more highly prized than the commoner checked variety.

But innovations from England were really of little importance compared with the creations of French fashion, which was following its development towards Classical styles.

The essential of women's costume, which was no longer made only in light stuffs, was a very high-waisted sheath, generally with a square, low-cut neckline covering the shoulders, girdled below the bust with a narrow belt. It fell in straight folds to the knees for the tunic, to the feet for the skirt, which kept its train during the first years of the Empire. Gowns without trains appeared in 1804 and spread to become general wear in 1808, apart from court gowns. Gown sleeves, which were initially very short and puffed or draped, or elbow-length and buttoned *à l'anglaise*, could also be very long and gathered *à la mameluck*, with several cuffs.

At the end of the Consulate, pleated, starched collerettes rose round the neck; these could be very high, *à la Gabrielle*, almost hiding the head, or flat and fixed to the neckline *à la Cyrus*, a name corrupted into *chérusse*, then *chérusque*.[10]

A new accessory appeared in 1801, the *canezou*, a sort of guimp or short bodice, or even a tippet with long ends that were always caught in the belt, made only in light stuff, with or without sleeves. Its fashion lasted through a large part of the century, but its form was subject to so many variations that it is impossible to define it precisely.

Tunics *à la mameluck* or *à la Juive*, inspired again by the Egyptian campaign, were very successful in 1802–3, but after 1804 they were supplanted by the *apron-gown*, which had appeared in the Directoire period and was to last for several years. The skirt was always to keep its character of a large panel of light stuff, open at the back and flowing freely, but the bodice took on the most varied forms. The *Mathilde* appeared in 1804; this was an embroidered band reaching from the centre of the neckline to the foot of the gown, inspired by the Bayeux Tapestry which had been exhibited in Paris. The following year, this band was joined to another similar band round the foot of the gown, spoken of as 'embroidery in an inverted T or Y'; this fashion became the rage, then disappeared in 1806, so that the Duchesse d'Abrantès could call it an 'antique, altogether forgotten mode' in 1807.

During all this period the fashion was mainly for light, white gowns, which necessarily entailed thicker outer garments. This is the period when we first see women's coats in the sense we give the term today. The collared redingote was no longer a gown, but became a worsted garment, as did the *douillette* ('cosy'), similar in shape but without the folds at the back. We also hear of *capotes*, but La Mésangère says that this was only a new name for the redingote. The *witchoura*, of Polish origin, which appeared in 1808, at the zenith of white gowns, was a wider, fur-lined coat, sometimes with a hood, which was initially worn with the sleeves hanging down behind.

After 1808, velvet caught up on lawns and muslins, as a result of the efforts made by the Emperor to revive the industry of Lyons. Sleeves, which were sewn in with rolls or slashed, reveal Spanish influence. Bodices were cut higher and a shallow ruff surrounded the throat. The fashionable colours were black, poppy-red, purple, marigold yellow and bright green. In summer, finely pleated percale came into its own again, and indeed, the taste for white and pale shades was to outlast the Classical styles.

879 BOROVIKOVSKI: *Princess Catherine Lapoukhin*, c. 1800. Leningrad, Museum. (Photo Archives Photographiques)

880 P. BRULOW: *Princess Wolkonski*, c. 1825. Leningrad, Museum. (Photo Archives Photographiques)

881 Woman's hat in white silk trimmed with striped ribbons, c. 1789. Zürich, Schweizerisches Landesmuseum. (Photo H. P. Herdeg)

The *corset* reappeared in 1804, lightened and shortened, without any resemblance to the old *corps*. Initially it was a sort of small, elastic, linen bodice, which covered only the bust, from the shoulders to the high waist. After 1806 it was boned and fitted with a busk, and in 1808 some were designed to flatten the stomach and hips, *en forme de Médicis*. The corset can sometimes be seen in the opening of low-cut gowns. Most women still laced themselves so tightly that Napoleon said to Corvisart: 'The corset is the murderer of the human race.' A specialist, A. Bretel, in 1808 created the corset *à la Ninon*, without bones, with only one busk to give it the indispensable rigidity.

The undergarments which had disappeared with Directoire fashions became more important again. Chemises and petticoats reappeared towards 1809, and were finely worked, which was a great innovation. In the same year, women began to wear long-legged linen pantalettes, imported from England where they were worn only by young girls for gymnastics. These showed a little beneath the gown at ankle level, and, although they were barely visible, women found them embarrassing and this mode did not spread.

Braces met with unexpected success. Initially, at the end of the Consulate, they were ribbons passed over the shoulders or crossed over the back. Towards 1811, 'elastic' braces appeared, a recent invention. These were knitted with a special stitch and enabled women to support their petticoats; the convenience of this material led to its use not only for garters, but also for bracelets holding on gloves, bandeaux for the hair and even *sautoirs* worn as bandoliers. Before coming into fashion, these braces had been considered more dangerous for men than the *corps rigide* had been for women! Rubber was not to be introduced into these accessories for thirty years.[11]

Footwear was generally, throughout the period, limited to flat, light, low-cut pumps sometimes fastened by a lace round the ankle or by thin bands over the instep.

The fashion for hair cut short *à la Titus*, which had appeared in the Revolutionary period, was followed by most women at the end of the Directoire period and during the Consulate. It has been attributed to various causes: the influence of Antiquity through paintings and the theatre, a reaction against the

MEN'S COSTUME UNDER THE EMPIRE

876, 884 While civilian costume was still sober and restrained, military uniforms were covered with embroidery; coats were still close-fitting and trousers tight; boots had turn-down tops and waistcoats were worn one on top of the other. The spencer was worn under the coat and the boat-brimmed hat was still in vogue (plate 876)

COSTUME IN EUROPE DURING THE FIRST EMPIRE

877–80, 882, 894 The high-waisted costume is worn throughout Europe, with Cashmere shawl, laced cothurnes and cornet hats (fig. 882) or *capotes* (plate 878). We also see deep necklines and *bretelle* sleeves (plate 877, cf. plate 870); certain hairstyles, such as those in plates 877 and 880, have no equivalent in France. Popular costume (plate 878) as always shows older influences

347

complicated hairstyles of the preceding period, an allusion to the hair sacrificed during the Terror... After An VI, hair cut *en porc-épic* and *à la Titus* is constantly mentioned in fashion journals, as was the style *à la Caracella*. A story, which may be nothing more than a legend, published by Sophie Gay in *Les Modes Parisiennes* in 1851, attributes this fashion to Mme Tallien who, during the Terror, is said to have cut off her hair, strand by strand, to pass notes to her husband through the window of her prison cell. When she was set free on 9 Thermidor, she had her hair cut equally short all over *à l'antique*, and all fashionable women hastened to imitate her. In any case, the fashion became so widespread that special ribbons were made for bonnets; these were indispensable 'since the shrinking of heads'.

Short hair led to the wearing of all types of bonnets fitting closely to the head, and turbans covering shaven crowns: the turban *à la turque* had been launched for the visit of the Turkish Embassy in 1802. The use of wigs and, towards 1807, of *cache-folies*, which were false switches in varying forms, allowed women to wear small hats that were less enveloping than bonnets *à l'invisible* or hats *à la Pamela* (plate 875).

The Empire brought some innovations to men's costume. There was the *carrick*, a full coat reaching to the ankles with tiered cape collars, worn by young men for driving the light, open carriages of the same name.[12] The stove-pipe hat with wide brims was also introduced then, as was the coat in restrained tones, open or closed, full above the waist, with loose basques. This was worn either with breeches or trousers worn inside half-boots.

After the Consulate, the greatest inventiveness was shown in men's waistcoats, whether in their cut – shawl-collars, lapels, crossed, etc. – or in their material. They could be made from the most varied materials, though embroidery was no longer as sumptuous as in the preceding period. Towards 1804 fashion favoured several waistcoats, as many as four being worn at once.

The last years of the eighteenth century revived the fashion for the muslin cravat, but in a very different form from the cravats worn under Louis XVI. This was a large square folded diagonally then rolled round the neck, tied only with a small knot without rosettes. During the Directoire it grew to an exaggerated depth. In the morning, men wore cravats in madras or foulard silk which was often striped; this was the height of fashion, for these stuffs were very rare as the result of the war with England. With the high-pointed collars that appeared towards 1804, the *col-cravate*, at the very beginning of the Empire, was a more practical form of embellishment, doing away with the bother and costly upkeep of the untied cravat; it was mounted on a fixed collar which was fastened by a button or a spring-pin, and made in the most varied stuffs, either with a ready-made bow or with loose ends.

For his coronation, Napoleon resurrected the royal cravat with a small, lace trimmed collar and cascades of Alençon lace; senators wore this without the collar, while officials wore cravats in muslin without visible collars or points. In civilian costume the cravat was often tied *en chou*.

During the First Empire and the Restoration, cravats were white and could be long or short, with complicated knots and subtle ways of tying, which partly gave rise to the fame of Beau Brummell. Brummell made cravat-tying one of the main preoccupations of Dandies, who turned all their attention to accessories when distinction in the actual clothes consisted merely of an impeccable cut.

EMBROIDERY AND LACE

Most changes in costume affected details during this quarter century, and were initiated by elegant individuals or interested professionals. Some changes, however, show more general influences.

This was the case of embroidery, which returned to particular favour under the Empire. It had been used continuously during the Revolution, but was then kept for decorating waistcoats, belts, the foot of gowns, etc., with patriotic motifs. Under the Consulate and the Empire, its old vogue was revived by the renewal of administrative costume and the reappearance of court costume.

The predominantly male labour force employed for embroidery before the Revolution was still large enough to satisfy this public demand after 1800. Specialists such as Dechazelle and Bony devised models which were reproduced in silk, precious metals or pinchbeck paillettes, with paste jewels, lace appliqués, feathers or kid; the embroideries on ceremonial costumes were often executed in platinum to avoid tarnishing. Men once again wore embroidered waistcoats and women decorated the foot of their muslin, cotton or jaconet gowns with a variety of embroidery, or paillettes which had the advantage of weighting the light stuffs so that they fell straight and smooth to the ground.

The use of lace stemmed from the same causes: it became compulsory for court costume during the Empire, to the advantage of workshops in Alençon, Brussels, Chantilly and Arras.

FRENCH COSTUME FROM THE REVOLUTION TO THE LATE EMPIRE

When the extravagances of the Directoire period are thought of as the eccentricities of a few individualists eager for publicity, we see that general lines of costume did not change radically from the Consulate to the Restoration. Costume was both the reflection of a society allegedly working its own transformation, and the achievement of a military authority that prized order in costume as well as in the State.

This latter influence is perhaps particularly noticeable in women's fashions, yet in the form it reached under the Empire, after unimportant modifications produced by a few passing audacities, this costume remained the continuation of the innovations at the end of the Ancien Régime, under the influence of English and semi-Classical styles. Women's costume threw off the former influence, and followed only the latter, which provided the same degree of comfort, purified by a pseudo-revolutionary ideology. What resulted at first from a wave of curiosity about Classical art and times, became the expression of a political regime which took its name and its power structures from Antiquity. Costume before 1789 was oriented towards a Classicism based on archaeology and imagination, but finally was diverted into a Roman academism more suited to the official aspirations of the new Empire.

However, in this period the evolution of French costume did not follow purely national lines, as formerly, but for ideological reasons set out to break with the immediate past; paradoxically, this break led to the adoption of the styles of an archaic, foreign past.

The influence of military costume showed in men's clothing with the bicorne, which replaced that all hat, or the cravat

882 F. MASSOT: *Isaline Fé, c.* 1810.
Geneva, Musée d'Art et d'Histoire. (Photo J. Arlaud)

883 L. DAVID: *Mme Morel de Tangry and her Daughters.* After 1816.
Paris, Louvre. (Photo Flammarion)

884 L. GIRODET: *Murat, c.* 1810.
Private Collection. (Photo Giraudon)

885 B. VAN DER KOOI: *The Billet-doux*, 1808.
Leeuwarden, Fries Museum. (Photo Frans Popken)

Fashion engravings:
886 *Plush hat, gown in merino*, 1817

887 *Italian straw hat, gown in percale*, 1818

888 *Crêpe hat, muslin gown*, 1821

knotted round the throat. In women's costume, embroideries and epaulettes on the costume of elegant women of the Empire period owed much to the braid and lace of marshals' costumes. The same thing happened in England – an interesting resemblance.

From the Consulate on we can see an affirmation of power. Costume was subjected to 'the force of reason', aided by the programme of official art initiated by Napoleon and realized by the incontested masters of the official style, Percier and Fontaine: 'the imitation of the Antique in its spirit, its principles and maxims, which belong to all times'. This neo-classicism in the decorative as well as the major arts and the new, rigid academicism affected costume with its rather cold atmosphere. The luxury of the ornaments of precious stones worn for official ceremonies, the heavy materials worn at court, the tendency towards darker, more solemn colours, matched the vogue for gilded bronzes, massive ormulu and opulent stuffs in furnishing. But Empire costume was not, unfortunately, designed by Prud'hon.

The development of court costume, which has received little detailed study, was not the same in France and in the rest of Europe.

The disappearance of the court at Versailles broke the tradition of costume there for over ten years. In the other courts special costumes survived, though progressively adapting themselves to French civilian styles, particularly for women; in a painting by Goya of the Spanish royal family in 1800, the gowns worn by Queen Maria Luisa and the princesses are still close to those worn in Directoire Paris. While the tradition of European court costume was not interrupted, it nonetheless remained under the influence of French inspiration.

On the other hand, when French court costume reappeared under the Empire, after its complete eclipse, it was still a straightforward extension of full-dress military uniform, though created by Percier and Fontaine for Napoleon I and intended to be an absolutely new type. It was imposed as an innovation, although it was only a suit *à la française* with some new features, and the cape worn by dignitaries was exactly the same as that worn in the eighteenth century by the knights of the

Saint-Esprit, a distant reminiscence of the fashions of the Henri III period.

Women's court costume, first worn by Josephine for the coronation ceremonies, with the straight, low-necked gown framed with a *chérusque* and a train, both with full and half-dress, did, however, represent an entirely new conception.

Costume in England

Two factors dominated changes in English costume. One was the French influence on women's fashions, which presented few national characteristics. The other was the increased prestige of British tailors, which resulted in a progressively more restrained style of men's clothing.

WOMEN'S COSTUME

Simplicity in cut remained the general trend, facilitated by the absence of the corset and the vogue for light, white stuffs. All the fullness of the gowns was at the back, and bodices, which fastened behind, were gathered to fit more closely. However, there was one type of gown that was specifically British and was worn only in the Anglo-Saxon countries: this was a closed gown with a falling front. The bodice opened in front, and the front panel of the skirt was ruffled on a ribbon which fitted to the bodice, passing through two loops placed under the arms to prevent it from slipping. When the neckline was low-cut, this panel had a bib front which was buttoned or pinned to the bodice so as to form a square neckline.

The redingote, which had been widely current at the end of the eighteenth century, became less popular.

Towards 1810 we see the influence of Romantic literature which brought Walter Scott's Middle Ages and Renaissance

889 *Muslin gown, scarf in barèges*, 1822

890 *Hat in material known as 'paille de riz' (rice straw), blouse-dress in muslin*, 1823

891 *Muslin gown with flat-pleated sleeves*, 1829. *Costumes Parisiens*

892 *Advertisement for the drawstring corset with continuous lace*, 1840. Paris, Bibliothèque Nationale, Cabinet des Estampes, Md 43. (Photos Flammarion)

into fashion, twenty years before there was any similar movement in France.

The eccentricities of the Parisian *Merveilleuses* were followed little in London, and by 1808, contemporaries such as Malcolm, in his *Anecdotes of London*, mentioned their complete disappearance. Furthermore, French styles entailed the use of stuffs that were unsuited to the British climate: silk or light pelisses were not enough protection against bad weather.

When, towards 1809, we see the fashion for coloured spencers worn with white gowns under very varied mantles, women's costume on the hole shows a confusion of styles, shapes and colours that is also to be seen in head-dresses and hairstyles.

After 1810, when the corset reappeared, the skirt acquired flounces and began to shorten; the waist became more pronounced in 1816, while the Oldenbourg bonnet, the precursor of the Quaker hat, was introduced, along with the reticule.

MEN'S COSTUME

The English Dandies, grouped round the Prince Regent, the future George IV, and George Brummell, gradually imposed the new style of men's clothing, typified by studied correctness and impeccable fitting, which led English tailors to perfect cut as well as to give attention to the smallest details. Coats with falling skirts, restrained colours, button waistcoats, buckskin breeches and short boots, very tight, ankle-buttoned trousers, and low, square beaver hats, were adopted by all elegant men.

At the very moment when the Dandies were making their contribution to the transformation of men's costume, it is curious to note that periodicals lost almost all interest in this field, reserving their rapidly increasing space for things connected with women's toilettes.

THE DEVELOPMENT OF WOMEN'S SILHOUETTE DURING THE FRENCH RESTORATION

886–91 Skirts gradually became wider; it was not until 1823 that their fullness, formerly swept to the back, was spread in gathers round the waistband; the waist gradually came back to its natural place; the shoulder line widened and reached its maximum breadth with leg-of-mutton sleeves and jockey sleeves. Similarly, hat brims no longer frame the face closely and hat ribbons need not be tied under the chin. Skirts become shorter, revealing feet shod in heel-less slippers; dresses are still white and large scarves are still in fashion

893 DEVERIA: *The Stockings*, 1831. Paris, Bibliothèque Nationale, Cabinet des Estampes, Oa 20. (Photo Flammarion)

351

894 GATINE (after LANTÉ): *The Bonnet-maker*, 1824. Paris, Bibliothèque Nationale, Cabinet des Estampes, Oa 136. (Photo Flammarion)

895 *Formal morning dress*, 1830. *La Mode*. (Photo Flammarion)

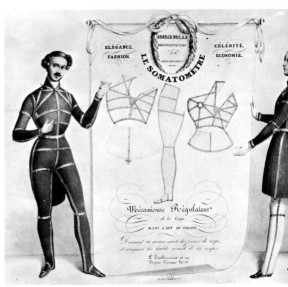

896 The *Somatomètre*, 1839. Paris, Bibliothèque Nationale, Cabinet des Estampes. Oa 19. (Photo Flammarion)

897 *Percale gown*, 1816. *Costume Parisien*. Collection Union Française des Arts du Costume. (Photo Flammarion)

898 Bridal gown in ivory faille, 1832. Collection Union Française des Arts du Costume. (Photo Flammarion)

TECHNIQUES

894 The little draw-string bonnet is the characteristic head-dress of the French Restoration period

TRANSFORMATION OF CUT

895, 897–8 The details of these costumes show the new refinements introduced into the fashioning of dresses during this period, in the cut and variety of sleeves and in the richness of embroidery; the abolition of the stiff bodice allows the bust and shoulders more importance

PUBLICITY

896 While fashion journals give more and more credit to the creators of the models they reproduce, a special branch of publicity develops for fashion accessories, foreshadowing modern procedure. The apparatus for taking measurements shows the care taken to perfect fitting

DANDIES

899 The imitation of English fashion, introduced into France by Dandies such as the Comte d'Orsay, led to the wearing of pantaloons, light-coloured for riding and dark for evening wear, progressively more tight-fitting and generally fitted with instep-straps. White or black cravats are as voluminous as those worn by the Incroyables of the Directoire period and hold the shirt collar in a funnel-shape round the neck; the roll-brimmed top-hat is a Bolivar

THE INFLUENCE OF THE ALLIED OCCUPATION OF 1815

900 The high-crowned hats of the 1815–1830 period were decorated with plumes of cock or ostrich feathers which accentuated their military aspect; dress sleeves had mitten cuffs falling over the hand; the vogue for starched collarettes, recalling sixteenth-century ruffs, increased

WOMEN'S FASHIONS DURING THE RESTORATION PERIOD

883, 901–3 The waist remains high and the vogue for Cashmere shawls, soon to undergo a temporary eclipse, still remained established. Turbans were still worn, though they had not reached the size they were to have in 1830. A family tradition has it that Ingres placed Mme Destouches' high-crowned hat back to front; perhaps he only turned up its brim (plate 903)

899 INGRES: *The Florentine Cavalier*, 1823. Courtesy of the Fogg Art Museum, Harvard University, Winthrop Bequest, Cambridge, Mass. (Museum photo)

900 CARLE VERNET: *A Russian's Farewell to a Parisienne*, 1816. *Le Bon Genre.* (Photo Flammarion)

901 ANON: *The Duchesse de Duras, c.* 1823. Private Collection. (Photo Giraudon)

902 INGRES: *Lady with a Parasol*, 1823. Courtesy of the Fogg Art Museum, Harvard University, Winthrop Bequest, Cambridge, Mass. (Museum photo)

903 INGRES: *Madame Destouches*, 1816. Paris, Louvre. (Photo Bulloz)

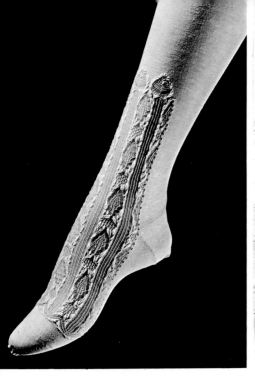

904 White lisle stockings with openwork insets. Romantic Period. Collection Union Française des Arts du Costume. (Photo Flammarion)

905 Devéria: *The New Taste: Morning gown*, 1830. Paris, Bibliothèque Nationale, Cabinet des Estampes. (Photo Flammarion)

906 Devéria: *Evening gown*, 1830. (*Ibid.*)

WOMEN'S UNDERGARMENTS

893, 904, 907 Undergarments lose the simplicity they had during the eighteenth century; stockings, which showed beneath the shorter skirts, had openwork inserts (plate 904). The corset, very different from the eighteenth-century bodice, no longer compresses the bust into a rigid cone; it slimmed the waist and supported the breasts (plate 893)

WOMEN'S FASHION FROM 1830 TO 1835

905–6, 908–9, 913 The full-blown, well-balanced silhouette of the years 1830 to 1835 is characterized by the varieties of the leg-of-mutton sleeve; the beret sleeve (plate 906) with a jockey or sometimes puff sleeve covered by a loose sleeve fastened tightly at the wrist, known as sleeve *à l'imbécile* because of its resemblance to a strait-jacket (plate 913). The deep décolleté is sometimes covered with a *canezou*, a kind of short cape in transparent material (plate 913)

HAIRSTYLES AND ACCESSORIES

910–12, 914–5 Romantic tastes are expressed in the use of Renaissance styles of jewellery, like the *ferronnière* (plates 911, 914, 915), also worn outside France a little later. Dangling earrings and deep belt buckles were also worn. The hairstyle dressed in bands with V-shaped partings is *à l'anglaise*. Hair *en touffes* (in tufts) followed the flaring of hat brims; starched caps *à l'alsacienne* complete them (plate 912)

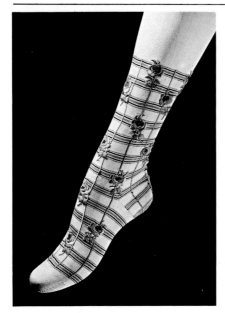

907 Romantic Period: Stockings in golden-yellow silk embroidered with red roses (Milon). Collection Union Francaise des Arts du Costume. (Photo Flammarion)

From 1815 to 1850

At the beginning of the nineteenth century, the essentials of the new costume styles had already been fixed; there were to be changes, but they would be minor ones.

Details, on the other hand, changed more and more rapidly, with endless variations of the trimmings of gowns, sleeves and hats for women, and the coat, breeches or trousers, waistcoats and cravats for men. From then on it is extremely difficult to follow the numerous variants mentioned in specialized journals, which themselves multiplied. The development of costume in this century can only be traced along general lines and in terms of broad periods. In reality, it is less a matter of the history of costume, than the social history of a transformed world, and the role of clothing in it.

Throughout Europe costume showed the first tendencies towards internationalism. England still showed some special features, but in other countries, influenced by French styles, there is no more need for national studies.

Costume in Europe

In Europe, the collapse of the Napoleonic Empire produced an immediate change in the way of dressing. Under the influence of a reaction in France, clothes – particularly women's clothes – took on a slightly more serious tone, with more enclosed forms.

SOCIAL AND ARTISTIC INFLUENCES

After 1815, people tried to forget the events they had lived through since 1789. The lassitude and exhaustion following the revolutionary wars, the need for moral relaxation, the

908 CHAPONNIÈRE: *Young Woman Seated,*
c. 1832. Paris, Musée des Arts Décoratifs.
(Photo Flammarion)

909 GATINE (after LANTÉ): *High Society Fashions,*
c. 1824. Paris, Bibliothèque Nationale, Cabinet des
Estampes, Oa 136. (Photo Flammarion)

910 L. NOËL: *Mademoiselle Déjazet,*
c. 1835. Paris, Bibliothèque Nationale,
Cabinet des Estampes.
(Photo Flammarion)

desire to make use of the profits made on military budgets, all created a fresh outlook, one without grandeur or lavishness, basically hard-headed and individualistic.

In most of Europe taste was no longer directed from above: of the two great influences exercised on clothing before 1789, one, that of the court of Marie-Antoinette and French Society, was revived under the Revolution and the Empire; the other, English influence, survived only in men's clothing. Vienna remained fixed in out-moded etiquette, and the Italian states were under Austrian protection: they, and the states of the archaic Germanic Confederation, fell back into the atmosphere of the Ancien Régime. For forty years, then, no court controlled costume in Europe, so that it could be modified by the influence of other social groups and by economic progress.

The appearance of a middle class whose fortunes and power were to increase, throughout all western Europe, influenced the development of costume in each country. Society was to become generally more bourgeois.

This development took place by stages.

From 1815 to 1822/5 – the period of the French Restoration – costume in western Europe continued to display most of the previous Classical features; it participated in the general return to purely Greek sources, after the over-Romanized ideal of the Empire. This renewed Hellenism, which took clear-cut forms in France with the painting of Ingres and sculpture of Pradier, was particularly noticeable in architecture, with the works of Schinkel in Germany, Nash in England and Hittorf in France. It counteracted the other embryonic movement, which arose from the practical needs of the middle class, but without halting it. The period 1815–25 was one of transition; gradually the straight form took on fullness and women's waists moved downwards, while Dandies dressed their hair *à l'Antinöus.*

From 1825 to about 1850, costume was influenced by the Romantic movement, and by a new generation who preferred dreams to hard cash. While liberal political ideas were emerging, an increasingly lively taste for music, poetry, things spiritual and things past marked these young people, as if to counter-balance the materialism and mediocrity of an excessively bourgeois

class. They were to enliven fashion with fantasy that was often completely wanton, enchanted by the ephemeral. Their own costume innovations were limited. Georges Sand took to wearing trousers mainly as a blow for feminism, and for publicity.

Costume reflected several very different influences, both successively and concurrently. English neo-Gothic or neo-Renaissance styles each found their circles of adherents. Aristocratic circles kept to a more Classical style, particularly in countries like Britain, where they had remained aloof from the consequences of the Revolution, and in the absolute monarchies of the continent. From 1830 to 1850 then, the bourgeoisie chiefly set the fashion throughout the west, imposing its garments: trousers, jacket, frock-coat and tall hat for men, gowns trimmed with embroideries and ribbons, bonnets and muffs, bright colours for women. Men and women of the working classes, whose wages were falling, wore and caps blouses and simple straight skirts respectively.

In western Europe costume translated the new middle classes' ambition to reach positions of power in the State. In central Europe and Russia the 'common man', branded by his costume, was excluded from official posts.

SOCIAL LIFE AND THE ECONOMY

Among the different influences which shortened women's skirts but lengthened men's breeches, which filled out women's skirts and slimmed down men's silhouettes, there was a new factor: the return of women from public life under the Empire to their role as mistresses of their own homes. Women throughout Europe once more became the guiding spirits of homes in which leisure time was parcelled between dancing, reading, perhaps intrigue. No longer shackled by official duties, they stamped the events of the day with their passion for elegance. Great ladies who directed fashion emerged from an upper middle class which was gaining in refinement and from an aristocracy which had newly adapted itself to a new world.

In the middle of the century women had once more finally regained domination of Society.

WOMEN'S RIDING COSTUME
916 The dark broadcloth of women's riding costume gives it a masculine character further accentuated by the white shirt with a plain collar. The impression is softened here by the hat

911 HORACE VERNET: *Madame Eynard*, 1831. Geneva, Musée d'Art et d'Histoire. (Museum photo)

912 DU PAVILLON: *Madame Dobrée*, *c.* 1833. Nantes, Musée Dobrée. (Photo G. Madec)

913 CHAMPMARTIN: *Mme de Mirbel*, 1831. Versailles, Museum. (Photo P. J. Oxenaar)

914 D. Favas: *Portrait of a Young Girl, c.* 1835.
Geneva, Musée d'Art et d'Histoire. (Photo J. Arlaud)

915 Nordgren: *Emilie Högqvist,* 1837.
Stockholm, Nordiska Museet. (Museum photo)

At the same time the development of costume was power-
fully aided by society's liberation from the strait-jacket of political direction by the Empire.

If for the first ten years after the collapse of the Empire these
factors were slow to show their effects, this was because of the
difficult economic situation in Europe.

Despite the peace that followed the Treaty of Vienna, lively
competition developed between the more industrialized nations, particularly in textiles, where increasing imports of
American cotton put them in rivalry with Indian cottons.
Differences in the degree of mechanization of French and
English industries, among others, led them to adopt different
import-export policies, protectionism in France and free trade
in England and the Low Countries.

This soon led, especially between 1816 and 1830, to the reappearance of French textiles on the continental and international
markets, where they benefited from customs regulations sus-
pending charges or granting premiums. The Swiss textile industry on the other hand, was ruined by French protectionism.
Spain was thrown into a major economic crisis after 1824 by
the loss of the South American colonies, but the western and
southern regions of Germany joined in the industrial development of Western Europe, and the northern states tried to com-
pensate for their fragmentation by forming a customs union.

In this way a vast trade network took shape among the
maritime powers of Europe. Exports, particularly of textiles and
costume, played an increasingly important role and conditioned part of domestic trade and prices. This current of exchange became linked increasingly closely to the development
of the United States, where cotton production increased ten-
fold between 1815 and 1830, supplying the vast quantity of
printed cotton cloth which was used for western costume of
the period. To the east of the Elbe, on the other hand, there
was no economic change. ·

During this period there was continued technical progress
in the textile industry. Bauwens' loom revolutionized woollen
production in Flanders, and the Jacquard loom applied to lace-
making made the fortune of Calais. Looms for knitting and
making seamless corsets appeared; the stitching-clapper (*bat-*

916 E. Devéria: *Maria Devéria, c.* 1845.
Pau, Museum. (Photo Montagne)

Fashion engravings:
917 *Redingote in Lyons velvet with shawl collar*, 1833

918 *Flounced dresses. Hat and bonnet*, 1837

919 *Gown over Oudinot underskirt*, 1841

THE DEVELOPMENT OF WOMEN'S SILHOUETTE UNDER LOUIS-PHILIPPE

917–21 The skirt lengthens to the ground, becomes flatter on the hips until about 1845, then regains its width with the wearing of the round crinoline.

Leg-of-mutton sleeves let their fullness slip from the shoulder to the elbow, then give way to a narrow sleeve fitting tightly to the arm, whose line harmonizes with the general trend of the years 1842–47. We see the appearance of flounced skirts, a novelty which was to remain in vogue for a long time. Hats disappeared, replaced by bonnets, whose brim became progressively narrower. The waist, slimmed by its corset, remains more or less at its normal place

SHAWLS

922 The vogue for Cashmere shawls was revived, but they were now worn as outer garments and not as scarves: long or square and very enveloping, they lent themselves to various arrangements

WOMEN'S FASHIONS UNDER LOUIS-PHILIPPE

923–4, 926–7, 933 The fashionable style of the Louis-Philippe period is soft and relaxed; it shows some historical reminiscences: hair dressed in bands with chignons and long ringlets framing the face (plate 933), and flat Bertha collars covering the shoulders (plate 926). These, and the flounced dresses which were becoming more common, are the main features of women's costume

SURVIVING DRESSES

925, 932 Dresses of this period, often in light materials, are characterized by the volume of their sleeves, the oval neckline more or less exposing the shoulders, and when there is embroidered decoration, by its fineness

MEN'S COSTUME UNDER THE FRENCH RESTORATION

928–30 Men's costume, sober in colour, keeps to its tight-fitting line; the cape or 'mantle' is an outer garment for evening wear

tant-brocheur) added lightness and strength to the silks of Lyons. The sewing-machine, invented by a small French tailor, Thimonnier, then perfected by Howe and Singer, was to revolutionize the garment industry.[13] At almost the same time the first sewing-machine for leather appeared in America, destined to facilitate mass production. In 1834 the embroidering machine, invented shortly before by Heilman in Mulhouse, began to compete with handicrafts for producing festoons, openwork and lace.

Progress in industrialization and trade, the development of the railways and fast transport, but also, with the appearance of the cheap press, modern advertising, all produced major changes in the economy and in social life, and contributed to improving the production and industrialization of costume. New categories emerged in the clothing trade: there were firms which specialized in exporting, and, on a lower but still important level, we see the first commercial travellers, who 'placed' costume materials and accessories, sometimes reaching the consumers in their homes. In England the young Cobden travelled in muslin, and in France Balzac penned the typical *Illustre Gaudissart* who was to sell hats and shawls from door to door.

Capital also had an indirect interest in costume. The mechanization of the textile industry and the opening of department stores could not have taken place without capital investment. The first to benefit from this development were the large towns, where the increased populations provoked a concentration of industries by providing a clientèle with continually growing needs. 'The Bank is at the head of the State; it is the fountain of honour for the bourgeoisie which has taken the place of the Faubourg Saint-Germain,' Stendhal wrote.[14] The great banks played an increasingly important part, particularly in providing credit; some combined finance with the business of transporting woollens and cottons.

After 1820, the second-hand dealers in the Marché Saint-Jacques tried to expand their business by setting up branches selling new clothes. Tailors no longer received their materials from their customers, but bought their own supplies, and got rid of any unsold goods by selling them also in the Marché

TROIS CHALES EN UN.

920 *Gown and spencer bodice*, 1839

921 *Gown with three flounces and basqued bodice*, 1852

922 Advertisement for the '*Perfect Patent Shawl or Three Shawls in One*,' *c.* 1845. Paris, Bibliothèque Nationale, Cabinet des Estampes, Oa 20. (Photos Flammarion)

923 WINTERHALTER: *Princesse de Joinville*, 1844 Versailles, Museum. (Museum photo)

924 WINTERHALTER: *Marie-Clémentine d'Orléans, princess of Saxe-Coburg*, 1845. Versailles, Museum. (Museum photo)

925 Gown in white self-striped bazeen with puffed and banded sleeves, c. 1830. Collection Union Française des Arts du Costume. (Photo Galerie Charpentier)

926 CHASSERIAU: *Mademoiselle Cabarrus, c.* 1848. Quimper, Museum. (Photo Le Grand)

Saint-Jacques. The same trend followed the 1825 financial crisis which led to unemployment and poverty among the working classes, when philanthropic societies persuaded clothing manufacturers to sell workers garments at cut prices. Soon, the first ready-to-wear shops were opening in Paris. The *Belle Jardinière* was established in October 1824 by M. Parissot, and was followed, in 1838, by *Le Bonhomme Richard*, owned by a lawyer from the Cher department, Ternaux, the great producer of cashmere shawls.

TECHNOLOGY AND COSTUME

During the first half of the nineteenth century, technical works concerning clothing were mainly published in England, and books devoted to cut and dress became increasingly numerous. In 1829, there was *The Improved Tailor's Art*, by J. Jackson; in 1839, *Science Completed in the Art of Cutting*, by W. Walker; in 1848, *A Practical Guide for the Tailor's Cutting-Room*, by J. Coutts. Meanwhile France produced the *Traité encyclopédique de l'Art du Tailleur*, 1834, by F. Barde, and in 1837 the *Manuel du Tailleur*, by G. Dartmann. In Germany A. Haimsdorf published *Der Praktische Unterricht* in 1832.

Technical training developed slowly. Although as early as 1780 the Duc de La Rochefoucauld had founded a school for tailors and shoemakers in Liancourt, it was not until 1852 that Elisa Le Monnier opened a professional school in Paris, including sewing and the fine linen trades amongst its courses.

THE TREND TOWARDS UNIFORMITY

A whole range of new conditions – the climate of opinion, the progress of industry and commerce, the spate of technical inventions, the concentration of capital and the improvement of exchange facilities – brought about an egalitarian evolution of costume during this half-century. The two main influences, those of France and England, dominated women's and men's costume respectively.

Costume in England during the Romantic period responded to practical considerations: for men, it was more high-cut, with less ornate shirts than those worn in France, where fancy-fronted shirts were sold as 'London' style, though they were no longer worn in London. Was it because England was too busy with trade that she shed Romantic styles sooner than did continental countries? Disraeli's famous remark: 'Look at Manchester' might seem to indicate that an Englishman's income impressed people more than his shirt.

It is clear that foreign fashions did not have the same currency or duration in all the countries of Europe. Each country adapted foreign tendencies to its own national tastes, and this assimilation, which can be seen in all periods, does not seem to have weakened in the nineteenth century, except under the influence of mass production which standardized garment types on a world-wide scale.

927 CHASSERIAU: *The Artist's Sisters*, 1843. Paris, Louvre. (Photo Flammarion)

928 *Velvet-collared topcoat, grey
aver hat, 1818. Costume Parisien.*
ris, Bibliothèque Nationale,
abinet des Estampes, Oa 19.
hoto Flammarion)

929 *Young man in frock-coat
and light trousers, 1823.
Modes Françaises. (Ibid.)*

930 *Velvet-trimmed broadcloth cloak
with cords and tassels in gold over an
evening suit, 1820. Costume Parisien.
(Ibid.)*

931 A. Devéria: *Alexandre Dumas*, 1830
Paris, Musée Victor Hugo.
(Photo Bulloz)

932 *Bridal gown in Indian muslin, c. 1837.*
New York, Metropolitan Museum. (Museum photo)

933 Winterhalter: *The Duchesse d'Aumâle*, 1846.
Versailles, Museum. (Photo Flammarion)

934 E. DELACROIX: *Portrait of the Comte de Mornay and Alexander Demidoff*, 1833. (Photo Archives Photographiques)

935 C. HANSEN: *Meeting of Danish Artists in Rome*, 1837. Copenhagen, Statens Museum for Kunst. (Museum photo)

Costume in France

MIDDLE-CLASS TASTES AND THE ROMANTIC INFLUENCE

The new climate of opinion in France as in the rest of Europe came from a rich, increasingly powerful middle class, the main beneficiary of the post-Revolutionary period, anxious to settle down to a period of general peace and work, renouncing the brilliant display of the Empire period and looking above all for convenience and intimacy, wrapped in a certain Romantic sentimentality.

An austere bourgeoisie[15] was to impose its down-to-earth attitudes on costume as well as art; aesthetic problems were to give place to practical needs. A bourgeois style replaced the centuries-old one of the court, as a wealthy, unadventurous class became acquainted with one of the more accessible forms of luxury.

There were still a few centres of elegance outside this middle-class world. From 1824 to 1830 the Duchesse de Berry exercised some influence over a limited circle; but the former émigrés who had returned to their houses in the Faubourg Saint-Germain kept themselves apart. In the Tuileries neither the court of Louis XVIII nor that of Charles X were of any account where elegance was concerned. Under Louis-Philippe, soirées were considered enough – admittedly they were very brilliant – and Queen Marie-Amélie was not made to lead fashion. Only under the Second Empire was Paris to become the centre of elegant life once again.

A new wave of Anglomania swept over Paris with the Restoration, encouraged by a strong British colony living on the right bank, centered on the Duke of Wellington, and by the popularity of the salons opened by English ladies such as Lady Morgan. The thriving French Romantic movement looked to Byron and Sir Walter Scott for the image of an ideal devoured by 'spleen'; and found in Beau Brummell the supremely elegant, refined creature, the 'Dandy'; the influence of these masters on young people mingled a passion for literature and a love of elegance.

As before 1789, one had to 'be English' to be fashionable. In her book *La France*, Lady Morgan wrote: 'Everything English is now in favour in Paris and is reputed to be Romantic. So we have Romantic tailors, Romantic milliners, Romantic pastrycooks and even Romantic doctors and apothecaries.' The influence of British writers imposed itself in costume as well as in literature; the popularity of Sir Walter Scott is not only to be measured by the number of translations of his works, but also by the amount of tartan worn; children in particular were dressed as tiny Scotsmen.

The perfect figure of fashion then had to be a man in whom spleen and elegance were indissoluble. After all, dandyism was only the Romanticism of fashion, was it not? Chateaubriand said of a fashionable man that in 1822 'he had to appear ill and sad at first glance... he must have something neglected about his person, neither clean-shaven nor fully bearded, but as if his beard had grown without warning during a moment of despair; locks of windblown hair, a piercing gaze, sublime, wandering, fated eyes, lips puckered in disdain for the human species, a bored, Byronic heart, drowned in disgust and the mystery of being...'[16]

'This vogue found its most receptive ground among the elegant, idle Parisian society that flocked to the Odéon to applaud Harriet Smithson, the delightful Shakespearean actress, that enthused over exhibitions of Bonington and Constable, gloated over 'Keepsakes' published in London and enthused over the Franco-English marriages of Lamartine, Berlioz and Alfred de Vigny.

The snobbish attraction of things English far outstripped a certain fashion for Spain, the Romantic country par excellence. Spain was visited by Baron Taylor and the Comte de Laborde, and came to public notice with the triumphal campaign of the Duc d'Angoulême. What can we say about the craze for Greece? Episodes from the Greek War of Independence gave their names to colours and ribbons.

The middle-class attitude to life and these foreign influences were joined by other inspirations drawn from contemporary art and literature. One must, however, beware of establishing too simplified a correspondence between these influences. The

936 *The Sculptor Pradier*, 1830.
Paris, Musée des Arts Décoratifs.
(Museum photo)

937 *Summer dress*, 1835. *Modes de Paris*.
(Photo Flammarion)

938 *Coat in corded silk, trousers in casimir*,
1830. *La Mode*. Paris, Bibliothèque Nationale.
Cabinet des Estampes, Oa 19.
(Photo Flammarion)

Romantic movement began before 1830 and was by no means spent in 1848, and similarly fashion shows Romantic features after 1820, which persisted until after the February Revolution. It has accurately been said that there was also to be a 'Second Empire Romanticism' which was to continue until after 1870. While Romantic and Classical art confronted one another after 1820, fashion also abandoned the reason and discipline of Antique costume, to pursue variety: it looked to the Middle Ages and the East, as these were reflected and heightened in history and novels.

The taste for Sir Walter Scott and the success of Victor Hugo's *Notre-Dame de Paris* – presenting a fairly conventional Middle Ages – were the influences that marked the styles of the time. In his *Causeries sur les artistes de mon temps*, Jean Gignoux wrote: 'People even took to wearing shoes with poulaines'; and the opera made from Victor Hugo's masterpiece produced the 'Esmeralda' shawl in 1836. Casimir Delavigne's *Marino Faliero* (1829) resurrected the costume of medieval Venice, and operas such as *Don Juan de Maraña*, adapted from a play by Dumas, Bellini's *Norma* and Donizetti's *Anna Bolena*, produced in 1836, gave their names to accessories. If the beauties of yesteryear did not always inspire revivals of past fashions, they did at least often give their names to hairstyles, which might be *à l'Isabeau de Bavière*, *à la Marguerite de Bourgogne*. *à l'Agnès Sorel*, or even *à la Marie Stuart* or *à la Sévigné*.

This Romantic elegance was codified after 1830, not only among the rich middle classes but also among the aristocracy, who, despising the Orléans family, lost interest in politics and devoted themselves to cultivating refinements and elegance. Under Louis-Philippe the 'gilded youth' were all young men from the aristocratic neighbourhoods of town, all had slim, curved waists, ideally dressed in *English green* redingotes, wore wide cravats and straw-coloured gloves and toyed with a gold-pommelled cane.

The despairing 'fashionable' of yesterday had become a brilliant Dandy who 'should have a light, insolent, conquering air, take care over his toilette and wear moustaches or a round-cut beard'. He talked only of horses, racing and carriages and scarcely knew of the existence of women.

ROMANTIC COSTUME

931, 934–6 Young Romantic artists and writers might follow the styles of the Dandies or adopt informal garments such as blouses, flowing shirts, and indoor costumes in Oriental style (plate 934)

939 BOURDET: *Une promenade*, 1838.
Paris, Bibliothèque Nationale, Cabinet des Estampes, Oa 38
(Photo Flammarion)

940 Plate from the *Journal des Tailleurs*. Paris, Bibliothèque Nationale, Cabinet des Estampes. (Photo Flammarion)

941 *Percale smock with small tartan fichu, 1810. Costume Parisien.* (Photo Flammarion)

942 *Small boy in 'straw hat, percale frock and pantaloons', 1816. Costume Parisien.* (Photo Flammarion)

943 J. A. D. INGRES: *The Montagu Sisters*, 1815. Collection The Earl of Sandwich. (Photo Giraudon)

With 1848 the favourite haunts of the Parisian Dandy – the boulevards, with their clubs, restaurants and *grisettes* – lost their aristocratic aspect; the 'handmade' era was nearing its last days. The conditions of life were changing under the influence of increasingly numerous new machines and inventions. With the flood of technical innovations, costume lost its elements of fantasy and caprice, which it was only to recover under the Second Empire, in the Court of the Tuileries.

WOMEN'S COSTUME

The proliferation of fashion magazines, and of reviews basically devoted to literature that nevertheless gave considerable space to fashion, provides us with abundant documentation on the changes that took place in women's clothes after 1815.

The Restoration Period

At the beginning of the Restoration period, Leroy, who had served the old Imperial Court, still dressed elegant women in Paris and abroad. He had, however, to adapt his ideas to the tastes of a clientèle which preferred English skirts and low waists. It was aptly remarked that between 1820 and 1830 the entire imagination of dressmakers was concentrated on three points: 'to make the skirt into a bell, the head into a monument and the body into a slim stalk.'[17]

For a time the fashionable Anglomania imposed some English features on women's costume: green gauze squares worn as veils, spencers that showed off the waist, and fitted carricks (capes with overlapping folds). But the witchoura and 'Polish boots' were still the only wear for cold weather. In aristocratic salons, the shortened white gowns were decorated with a band of lilies round the foot of the skirt and had embroidered sleeves, but waists were still high and the overall form rigo-

944　Small girl in 'straw hat, percale frock and pantaloons', 1817. Costume Parisien. (Photo Flammarion)

945　La Promenade sous le berceau, 1820. Le Bon Genre. Paris, Bibliothèque Nationale, Cabinet des Estampes, Oa 94. (Photo Flammarion)

MEN'S COSTUME FROM 1830 TO 1850

937–40　The curved, high-waisted outline and the contrast between the trousers (generally light-coloured) and the darker coat, and the tightness of the trousers, often with instep-straps and sometimes even with feet, characterize Louis-Philippe period men's fashions, the line of which became simplified towards 1850 with the appearance of the jacket and the plastron cravat. The coat worn by the gentlemen on the right of plate 940 is probably the *bucksain*, a recently invented edged short coat, and that on the left, the coat-jacket

CHILDREN'S COSTUME IN THE FRENCH RESTORATION PERIOD

941–6　Children's costume in France retained its English character, with light, washable materials and simple forms. However, it differed only in a few ways from adult costume, which for women affected childish simplicity (plate 945). It is difficult to distinguish between little girls and boys (plates 942, 944) except by their toys. Boys and girls both wore pantalettes to ankle-level

CHILDREN'S COSTUME UNDER LOUIS-PHILIPPE

947–8, 951–2　Children's costume is similar to that worn by adults; it reproduces the same pseudo-historical traits (plate 952). However, it develops along its own lines and often seems almost a fancy dress (plate 951 left). The first communicant's dress is a recent fashion

CHILDREN'S COSTUME IN ENGLAND

949–50　Children's fashions kept their basic simplicity longer in England than elsewhere

946　HERSENT: The Duc de Bordeaux and his Sister, 1821. Versailles, Museum. (Photo Flammarion)

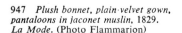

947 *Plush bonnet, plain velvet gown, pantaloons in jaconet muslin,* 1829. *La Mode.* (Photo Flammarion)

948 *Child's frock in velvet,* 1842. *La Mode.* (Photo Flammarion)

949 Child's long-sleeved dress in silk lamé, with spencer, 1816. Collection Mrs Doris Langley Moore. (Photo F. Fonteyn)

950 Child's frock in muslin with mob cap, 1830. Collection Mrs Doris Langley Moore. (Photo F. Fonteyn)

rously straight. This worldly society was susceptible to fashion when this was of its own invention; for instance, when the Vicomte d'Arlincourt's *Ipsiboé* and the Duchesse de Duras' *Ourika, l'Atala des Salons* appeared, all Paris wore hats, gowns and colours bearing the names of these heroines.

Merino cloth and Levantine velvet in winter and percale, muslin, silk and crêpe in summer adorned women's slim, pale distinction. As in furnishing, preference went to light, sentimental colours: lilac, heliotrope and reseda.

During this first phase, we can see a certain military influence, with hats in the shape of helmets and bearskins.

After 1821–2, transformations in costume corresponded to Baroque, Rococo or Neo-Gothic movements in taste, bringing heavier, more expansive and solemn forms, popular particularly among the rich middle classes. This trend reflected improvements in business, a rise in the standard of living and the strengthening influence exercised on costume by literature and history.

In 1819 Ingres painted Francesca da Rimini in the purest 'Troubadour style', the first phase of the medieval styles of the following years; the success of *Der Freischütz* in 1824 produced a *Robin Hood hat*. Toilettes were inspired by reminiscences of the past, with Sévigné sleeves, the Montespan cut. Some elegant women even brought back the *ferronnière*, a fine chain with a pearl on the forehead, as worn during the Renaissance (plates 914–5).

This period was characterized more by this historical movement than by marked innovations. The waist gradually returned to its natural position, skirts became shorter and more flaring, the bodice back, which had been narrow during the Empire, became progressively wider. Decolletages grew, uncovering the throat and the upper part of the chest, accentuating the effect of the sloping shoulders, which were considered essential for beauty; sleeves increased in volume, and the Duchesse de Berry launched the vogue for 'leg-of-mutton sleeves', a modification of the sixteenth century style. The Renaissance also inspired the *jockey*, a sort of round epaulette placed at the top of the sleeves, vaguely reminiscent of the old *maheutre*, or shoulder-piece.

The corset reappeared, alternating periods of fashion and decline. We should also note that this corset was designed exclusively to slim the natural shapes of the body, not to impose an artificial shape, as in the preceding century. As the waist returned to its natural place, the corset became indispensable: soft models *à la paresseuse* were made for wearing with loose morning clothes, but the 1823 Exhibition presented metal models equipped with pulleys so that the wearer could lace or unlace them without help. The fullness of the skirt seems to have resulted from the renewal of the textile industry in France, whose rise was complete by 1830; it was to increase further until 1868.

In head-dresses, Empire influence persisted until about 1822; bonnet brims were always deep and funnel-shaped and closed, without reaching the exaggerations of the old bonnets *à l'invisible*. After 1822 hats began to overtake bonnets, brims were turned up and the hat was worn to one side and, towards 1827, one or two ribbons dangled down behind as far as the waist. Materials were crêpe, satin, straw or velvet, with feathers round the crown and often excessive ornament of bows, flowers and ribbons under the brim. Large or flat berets and turbans loaded with feathers were also in fashion. Only in 1829 were costumes inspired by the Renaissance. After rolled caps and linen cornets covering the ears, the bonnet and hat were worn indiscriminately and took the same names; both were often decorated with multicoloured cockades of feathers (plate 903). Generally two ribbons were tied under the chin. The crown, which was very high in 1815 (plate 900), under the influence of foreign modes introduced by allied officers, later took on more varied forms: fashion then swung to turbans and toques *à la russe* or *à l'espagnole*.

A clear change can be seen after 1824, when wider brims spread out round the face, while the crown still fits closely to the back of the head. In profile, hats resembled broad-brimmed bonnets with ribbons that were not always tied, while from the front it rose up in a halo completely framing the face. The volume thus given to the head balanced the wider skirt.

951 JULES DAVID: *First Communicant's dress,* 1843. *Le Moniteur de la Mode.* Paris, Bibliothèque Nationale, Cabinet des Estampes, Oa 20. (Photo Flammarion)

952 *Child in bonnet of white satin with crimped feather, velvet chatelaine trimmed with ermine, grey braided cashmere dress,* 1848. *Journal des Femmes*

953 *Woman's Opera costume,* 1809. Paris, Bibliothèque Nationale, Cabinet des Estampes, Ob 107

954 *Walking Dress,* 1812. Paris, Bibliothèque Nationale, Cabinet des Estampes, Ob 107. (Photos Flammarion)

The Romantic Period

If it is agreed that the Romantic style in general crystallized in the decorative arts around 1830, the same date also applies to its impact on costume styles. Women seemed to dream of becoming ethereal, of resembling angels or butterflies, lacing themselves more and more tightly and wearing increasingly wide bell skirts and leg-of-mutton sleeves (plates 905, 908, 913). To achieve wasp-waists they increasingly wore corsets; the number of patents increased from two in 1828 to sixty-four twenty years later. Corsets, which were always white and seamless, woven on Jacquard looms, could also be simple belts. Large stores sold cheap models and, as the latest novelty of presentation, their windows displayed wax figures of women wearing then.

The Romantic woman liked to show herself in tight-fitting riding costume (plate 916) with a wide feathered hat, but towards 1830 her silhouette took on a loose elegance that had nothing in common with the swaddled tightness of the Restoration period. Her small head was covered with hair dressed in plaits or curls piled up *à la girafe* or *à la doña Maria,* and with 'Alsatian' caps (plate 912), wide flat berets worn almost vertically, or, for evening wear, a chaperon of feathers or a *petit bord,* a new type of hat allegedly inspired by Renaissance fashions, which was to enjoy a long spell of fashion. The low-cut 'boat' neckline bared the shoulders, and *leg-of-mutton, beret* (plate 906) or *elephant ear* sleeves covered with wide *jockeys* which added width to the shoulders and so accentuated the slimness of the waist, imprisoned in a wide-buckled belt. The skirt was flat at the top, flaring out towards the foot, where its hem could reach a 'quarter ell', with trimming placed above: garlands, fringes, plaited rolls. Skirts stopped a hand's breadth above the ankle, showing the pale stockings (plate 904) and flat shoes or *cothurnes* with criss-cross ribbons in soft leather, plum or bordeaux red, which were so narrow and thin that walking and dancing seemed to be out of the question.

The year 1830 was also the finest hour of the *canezou,* an upper bodice, often of linen, differing greatly from the model that appeared at the beginning of the century, but still keeping one characteristic: whatever its shape, its lower edge was caught into the gown belt (plate 906).

This particularly graceful new silhouette soon became thickly wrapped once more; the fullness of the sleeves was to move down to the elbow and wrists, while a cape hid the bust to waist-level, which in its turn was weighted by the gatherers of a long skirt whose width increased continually. 'A husband might well draw back in horror,' wrote *La Mode* in 1838, 'on hearing our Minettes or Palmyres ordering nineteen ells of taffeta for a morning gown…' Leg-of-mutton sleeves were fortunately replaced in 1837 by the sleeve *à la jardinière*: this was moderately wide, lightening the silhouette, though without restoring the slightly provocative elegance it had had at the end of the Restoration period. Evening gown necklines were decorated with a *Bertha* collar, a flat band of lace, reminiscent of the eighteenth century. Double skirts opened in a triangle in front, recalling the same period, but they were excessively ornamented with flounces.

To support the volume of these gowns, the *crinoline underskirt* appeared in 1842; this garment was to spread and develop until the beginning of the Second Empire.

The *redingote* was a day dress, soberly cut and opening in front.

The large or small, long or square *cashmere shawl,* which had been almost completely discarded for about ten years, returned triumphally to fashion after 1840. Its increasing dimensions gave it the role of a true outer garment. The *visite,* whose form hesitated between the shawl and the tippet, was a small, sleeveless cape with slits for the arms; it appeared towards 1845 and was in and out of fashion until 1885.

The variety of textiles used gave great charm to women's costume: silk, cashmere, crêpe, taffeta, tulle, muslin, gauze, velvet or cotton; striped, checked, brocaded, damasked, plain or printed. Textile designers concocted delightful patterns of flowers or bouquets or reproduced slightly modified versions of Empire or Restoration designs. Evening dress and fine linen were finished with hand embroidery, an expanding trade which kept many workers employed.

955 CARLE VERNET: *Englishman in full dress*, 1817. Paris, Bibliothèque Nationale, Cabinet des Estampes, Ob 107. (Photo Flammarion)

956 *Court gown*, 1825. Paris, Bibliothèque Nationale, Cabinet des Estampes, Ob 107. (Photo Flammarion)

957 *Costume for driving*, 1828. Paris, Bibliothèque Nationale, Cabinet des Estampes, Ob 107. (Photo Flammarion)

958 *Archery costume*, 1833. Paris, Bibliothèque Nationale, Cabinet des Estampes, Ob 100 a. (Photo Flammarion)

959 WHITE: *Florence Nightingale and her Sister Parthenope*, c. 1836. London, National Portrait Gallery. (Photo Freeman)

After 1835 the size of hats decreased, and in 1840 they took the form of the poke bonnet, completely enclosing the face. Between 1840 and 1850 the brim shrank so that it no longer hid the face. Hairstyles became lower, with swathed lines. Bangs *à la Berthe* and knots *à la Mancini* framed the face and softened the severity of bonnets.

MEN'S COSTUME

In Paris, English styles remained in fashion after 1815, even when Brummell, the 'god of the Dandies' fled from his creditors and relinquished his place as the supreme arbiter of British elegance. Young beaux imitated him by wearing either *German boots* inside their trousers, or turn-down boots and buckskin breeches in the morning; in the evening the required wear was a plain, buttoned coat with black trousers reaching to above the ankle, showing the embroidered stocking or the open-work sock worn over a white stocking. Waistcoats were fanciful: piqué waistcoats might be worn over or under silk waistcoats.

The short-waisted bronze or blue suit with long basques *à l'anglaise* or short, flowing basques *à la française* (plate 929) was to remain in favour throughout the reign of Louis XVIII. Belts were *à la russe*, and wide Cossack trousers had instep straps (plate 938). Bolivar hats vied with curved top hats; the high neck was covered with a plain or flowered cravat, in black silk or madras, unless the two pieces merged into a leather collar-cravat.

L'Art de mettre sa cravate enseigné en seize leçons (The Art of Tying a Cravat in Sixteen Lessons) which appeared in Paris in 1827 and was attributed to Honoré de Balzac, had a great success, proving the importance attached to this last vestige of sartorial fantasy. But the carelessly knotted black tie worn by elegant men was soon adopted by Daumier's bureaucrats and Gavarni's Louis-Philippe bourgeoisie, and gave the cravat the *coup de grâce*.

English influence had to compete with the vogue for uniforms. The *militaire* or *demi-solde* was a long, low-waisted re-

ENGLISH COSTUME FROM 1810 TO 1830

953–9 While the general lines of costume are similar in England and in France, historical reminiscences appeared in Britain before they came into fashion in France (plates 953, 956)

GOWNS PRESERVED IN ENGLAND

960–62 As is often the case, dresses that have been preserved appear simpler in form than those represented in fashion plates. The boat neckline and balloon sleeves are very similar to French fashions of the same period

COSTUME IN EUROPE DURING THE RESTORATION PERIOD

963–5 A conservative, bourgeois tone is seen in all the elements of dress: we find collarettes standing round the neck and mameluck sleeves (plate 963), high feathered toques, Cashmere shawls, children's long pantalettes, and the high cravats and costumes without embroidery worn by men (plate 965)

960 White gauze gown decorated with insets of yellow satin, *c.* 1817. Birmingham, City Museum. (Museum photo)

961 White tulle gown embroidered with garlands of oak leaves in gold thread, balloon sleeves, 1825. London, The London Museum. (Courtesy the Trustees. Museum photo)

dingote with one line of buttons (plate 928); this was the coat worn by the old soldiers of the Imperial Armies, disbanded by the Bourbons. The elegant model had an accentuated waist with sleeves *à l'imbécile*, wide at the shoulder and tight at the wrist. This type of garment, which then embarked on a century-long career, certainly benefited from the taste for race-going which brought the old English style back into fashion.

Out of doors, fashionable men draped themselves in wide capes (plate 930). The most widely worn type of coat had a cape collar, but other styles, open at the sides or short, *à l'espagnole*, were worn.

In 1823 the *chapeau claque* or folding *Opera hat* was invented; this mechanical hat was perfected by Gibus the hatmaker, and took his name. The tall hat, in felt or silk, shaped like a flaring stove-pipe, was highly fashionable, and took its names (e.g. Bolivar) from Spain or South America.

There was one important innovation in men's costume: the informal *paletot*, described as 'this outrage to good taste, a surtout from overseas which is at best suited to inspecting one's horses in the stables'. It appeared towards 1835, and 'despite its ugliness' its comfort finally won it general acceptance.

The coat and redingote were worn according to the time of day; from year to year they differed in colour, in the shape of the basques or skirts, the model of their buttons or the trousers and waistcoat worn with them. It is impossible to trace in detail the fluctuating demands of fashion during the century.

CHILDREN'S COSTUME

Under the Empire, children's costume had remained simple and practical, as indeed had adults' clothes. Light, pale stuffs were used with restrained trimmings, and the cut allowed freedom of movement.

But as soon as fashions in general became more elaborate, children's costume followed this development, with exaggerations that brought it to the point of historical fancy dress.

For little girls, pantalettes to the ankle remained in vogue

962 Bridal gown worn by Queen Victoria, white satin trimmed with lace, 1840. London, The London Museum. (Courtesy the Trustees. Museum photo)

963 C. W. ECKERSBERG:
The Nathanson Family, 1818.
Copenhagen, Statens
Museum for Kunst.
(Museum photo)

964 HESS: *The Marchesa Florenzi, c.* 1820.
Munich, Bayerische Staatsgemäldesammlungen. (Photo J. Blauel)

during the whole of this period (plate 945); boys were dressed like girls while they were small, but wore long trousers as soon as they went into masculine costume, and never had shorts.

EXHIBITIONS AND DEPARTMENT STORES

At the end of the Louis-Philippe period, the clothing trade was transformed by the opening of large department stores, and by the national exhibitions organized in Paris, the last of them just before the Second Empire in 1849.[18]

These events, held in the Invalides, in the Champ-de-Mars, in the Champs-Elysees and even in the Palais du Louvre, deserve mention, for in their temporary galleries the public learned to appreciate the continual improvements brought about in clothing techniques.[19]

Department stores were born of the idea, formulated by a number of traders, of gathering several shops together in large, common premises; at first these were just groups of small shops, like the *Galeries du Commerce et de l'Industrie*, opened in 1838 at 30 Boulevard Bonne-Nouvelle. This enterprise was not a true association of common interests, and was doomed to failure, being replaced in 1841 by the *Palais Bonne-Nouvelle*. After some adaptation to meet customers' needs, these stores multiplied so fast that in the middle of the century there were more than four hundred of them in the capital.

From their founding, these shops attracted mainly women customers, and by the choice and range of articles they sold, they exercised an undeniable influence on women's clothing. Moreover, their appearance coincided with new egalitarian ideas, and their founders grasped that social classes whose needs and habits were changing must be offered the means to satisfy new-found tastes for elegance and comfort as cheaply as possible.

The commissioning, making and buying of men's, women's and children's clothes soon became the province of these large stores: this organization of mass-produced ready-to-wear imposed styles, materials, colours and accessories which created a new type of 'middle class' costume.

965   CARL BEGAS: *The Begas Family*, 1821.
Cologne, Wallraf Richartz Museum. (Photo H. Doppelfeld)

966   C. A. JENSEN: *Madam Birgitte Hohlenberg*, 1826.
Copenhagen, Museum of Fine Arts. (Museum photo)

Costume in England

After 1815, English influence on men's clothing increased, but for women's costume it diminished compared with the end of the eighteenth century. This situation resulted not only from the isolation of England during the French Revolution, but also from the attraction that French styles continued to exercise on elegant British women, even from 1789 to 1815, an appeal that was increased by their scarcity.

These opposite tendencies in men's and women's fashions were demonstrated after 1815 in Ackerman's *Repository of Fine Arts*,[20] by an increase in the space devoted to women's clothes and a corresponding decrease in coverage of men's fashions.

MEN'S COSTUME

From this time forward costume followed the lead of London, and the styles that resulted were to spread throughout the Old and New World.

English Dandyism was still embodied after 1815 in the person of George Brummell, who was to remain its incarnation from the day when the Prince of Wales' favour launched him into society, when he was still an Eton boy with curly hair.

His distinguished elegance and 'passionate moderation' in costume made Brummell the arbiter of London elegance for over fifteen years. Hypersensitive to any lapse of taste and shunning eccentricity, he had the inborn sense, according to Lord Byron, 'of a certain exquisite suitability in dress', and unfailingly expended infinite care on the details of his costume. We know of the effect he made by appearing at the races with a white cravat and boots with white-tops. He did not follow fashion: fashion followed him.

The 'Beau' dressed in a blue coat, buckskin waistcoat and tight black trousers buttoned a few inches above the ankles, with laced boots or low slippers; in the morning he wore boots with turned-down tops and buckskin breeches.

967   F. G. WALDMULLER: *Portrait of a Lady*, 1836.
Munich, Bayerische Staatsgemäldesammlungen. (Photo J. Blauel)

968   P. Brulow: *Mr and Mrs Alenine*, 1840.
Leningrad, Museum. (Photo Archives Photographiques)

969   F. G. Waldmuller: *The Painter's Mother*, 1830.
Vienna, Österreichische Galerie. (Museum photo)

His tailor Meyer shared his place of honour as arbiter of Dandyism, while Schweitzer and Davidson dressed the Prince Regent in suits 'without a wrinkle on the body'.

This severity and calculated simplicity was imitated throughout all nineteenth-century men's fashions. We must stress that Brummell and the Dandies gave men's costume its cold, correct style precisely when women began to break free. Fashion then turned away from men's clothes and concentrated almost exclusively on women's styles. It is only within the last few years that a reverse tendency has shown itself, especially in England.

After 1820–21, the Englishman's wardrobe gave a more important place to the frock-coat (*redingote*), in blue or brown, with a roll collar and braided buttonholes. After 1830 it was worn only with trousers, never with breeches. Later the frock-coat underwent the same modifications that affected it in France: a less fitted waist, an increased length after 1820, with narrower skirts, lapels on the collar and the disappearance of the fur from the lower hem. The coat, cut straight at the waist, always fell behind in two wide tails. The opera hat was obligatory for evening wear, and for the morning a low, square beaver hat began to replace it. The overcoat called *surtout* by Dandies, was trimmed with braid and frogging, or, for winter, with fur, which had come into fashion.

WOMEN'S COSTUME

Under French influence, Englishwomen adopted the Classical style at the beginnnig of the nineteenth century, but with a certain delay due to the protests aroused by the exaggerations of the '*Merveilleuses*' (see above, page 344). Pall Mall's elegant ladies waited until these scandals had died down, but in 1802 all England was captivated by the appearance of Mme Récamier in Kensington Gardens.

However, the new style had to surmount a serious obstacle: it was impossible to wear white muslin out of doors in winter; and pale, light stuffs had to be kept fresh, not crushed by heavy mantles. Consequently, elegant women simply added fur boas and muffs to their pelisses.

970 Redingote of blue-grey silk, c. 1820. Amsterdam, Rijksmuseum. (Museum photo)

971 Gown of brown glazed taffeta with fichu of embroidered tulle and straw bonnet, c. 1830. Amsterdam, Rijksmuseum. (Museum photo)

972 Italian straw hat trimmed with flowers, gauze ribbon and blond-lace. Romantic Period. Barcelona, Museo de Arte, Collection Don Rocamora. (Museum photo)

After 1810, numerous fashion engravings show evening toilettes with more sharply defined waists and fuller backs; they fell less straight than did French models, and even had short trains. This change resulted from the reappearance of the corset in 1810. A Bond Street firm attracted a large number of clients by announcing simply that the manageresses, 'who had arrived from Paris' – which was an untruth – made corsets *à la Diane*.

Muslin or lace gowns were worn over satin linings. The mantles of all forms and inspirations, generally foreign, often included fairly heavy, complicated arrangements which detracted from the general effect and were deplored by fashion writers.[21]

There was an exodus of tourists to France in 1814, and once again after the interlude of the Hundred Days. Balancing the new Anglomania which was developing in Paris, French modes met with extraordinary success in London. To this we should add a craze for pelisses, as in France.

The decade after 1815 was marked in England by studied attention to gown trimmings, the continued wearing of the spencer – though it was a difficult garment for any woman to wear – a rather special taste for lace and originality in the shapes of hats. But in spite of British efforts to form a national fashion, France increasingly inspired women's costume. British fashion magazines never ceased to promote Paris models and engaged French correspondents to keep them abreast of the latest innovations in Paris.

So in 1820 we see the waist move downwards, bodices with boned points appear, and the burgeoning of the enormous leg-of-mutton sleeves imported from France in 1829. The latter, supported by a rigid framework, enabled the wearer to display several bracelets at once, but went out of fashion in 1836. Wide sleeves were then *de rigueur* for evening gowns. With wide skirts, small capes and *jockeys* were adopted in England from the moment of their launching in Paris. Then skirts became less full, and women wore redingotes with shorter sleeves and flat capes, still under the same influence.

British taste scarcely underwent any modification until the zenith of the crinoline adopted by Queen Victoria. Taine,

973 Gown in red silk embroidered with floral motifs in white, bodice and apron embroidered in silver, 1850. Barcelona, Museo de Arte, Collection Don Rocamora. (Museum photo)

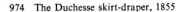

974 The Duchesse skirt-draper, 1855

975 The Parisien, tournure petticoat, 1857   976 Over-petticoat, 1860

977 Crinolines.
Paris, Bibliothèque Nationale, Cabinet des Estampes.
(Photos Flammarion)

during his stay in London, made this rather severe judgment: '... colours are outrageously crude and figures lack grace. Crinolines are too heavily hooped, hats are overloaded and hair is too shiny, the general effect bad, ill-made, ill-arranged and badly worn...'[22]

It was in England that the crinoline met with the most violent opposition in its early days; a curious 'anti-crinolinist' reaction, of Transatlantic origins, joined with an attempt to introduce the rational reform of women's costume by replacing the full skirt with long, full trousers, tightly belted at the waist and made in the same stuff as the bodice. These trousers, known as *bloomers*, took their name from the originator of this reform, the American Mrs Amelia Bloomer who, surrounded by numerous disciples, held meetings with displays of models in London and Dublin in 1851. Women even wore bloomers in the streets.

This initiative caused considerable agitation in England, where it was considered an attack on the sanctity of the home and liable to lead to the emancipation of women and the degradation of men. Mrs Bloomer, with the support of doctors, replied by asking why the English public should be so horrified by the idea of women in long trousers, since it was generally accepted that many men north of the Tweed wore skirts, some of which were ridiculously short. Mrs Bloomer's experiment, which failed in the face of ridicule, was merely premature. It should not be forgotten when we recall the various attempts to 'masculinize' women's costume.

978 'D.D.' petticoat, 1858

979–80 Tavernier underskirt, 1857

981 Patent Medicis underskirt, 1865

THE CRINOLINE

974–85, 987 The crinoline, originally a stiff underskirt of horsehair, more or less circular in shape (plates 974, 975, 978), became a cage of whalebone or metal hoops (plates 979, 982, 983), which did not do away, however, with the wearing of petticoats. To make walking easier, the front remained soft and unboned. Dimensions increased steadily, while the hips were flattened and the fullness was concentrated at the back (plate 985).

This arrangement was to be retained for ball gowns, when the crinoline had been abandoned for day dresses

982 American Thomson cage, 1862

983 Duchâteau underskirt, 1858

984–5 'Magic' underskirt. Pompadour underskirt with train

986 WINTERHALTER: *Queen Maria-Amelia and her Grandchildren*, 1850. Private collection. (Photo Archives Photographiques)

987 *The Fitting*, 1865. (Photo copyright James Laver)

988 Gown in white silk brocaded with blue, 1850–55. Birmingham, City Museum. (Museum photo)

From 1850 to 1868

Costume in Europe

THE POLITICAL AND ECONOMIC SETTING

During this period, which can be considered as an important stage, if not actually a turning point, in the century's history, the wars that were shaking the Continent (in the Crimea, Italy, Schleswig-Holstein, Austria and Prussia, Austria and Italy) and the general European upheaval had little effect on costume, doubtless because the expenses resulting from these wars were borne not out of capital but out of indirect taxation.[23] Costume, which now depended closely on money, was less affected by political events than by general economic trends.

The completion of the main communication routes and the progress in transport – the construction of new roads and canals, and in particular, the development of steamships and the railways – enabled Europe to shop in the whole world for the products she needed, and this international development exercised its influence on costume in indirect ways. The cost of products became highly material, sheep-rearing was relegated to the least valuable lands and the wool-buying policy was thus modified; the cultivation of flax was pushed eastwards.

The growing industrialization which justified the saying that 'the workshops of the world were being built in Europe', forced an increase in imports. Silk imports increased after disease had ravaged European hatcheries, as did those of cotton, which was more widely used each year, and of wool.[24] The Continent then exported the finished products. At the time of the American Civil War in the 'sixties England bought about 70 per cent of the American cotton harvest, processed 60 per cent and re-exported the rest.

Machinery, which was ceaselessly improved, increased the efficiency of all industries. In weaving, the shuttle worked fas-

ter, and in spinning, the number of spindles per loom increased from 400 to 1,200. The Bonnaz sewing and embroidering machine, invented in 1863, could be applied to clothing or furnishing materials. The improved sewing machine dominated the garment industry and was used in glove-making. In shoe-making, machines placed the heel, sewed the upper and attached the upper to the sole; in 1851 Bally began mass production of footwear at Schoenenwerd.

Two other important developments mark this period.

The year 1856 opened a new chapter in the history of dyes; in England Perkins discovered the first synthetic dyestuff, mauvine, which produced violet tones that could not be obtained from natural dyes; at the same time Verguin was perfecting fuchsine in Lyons. Modern synthetic dyes gradually replaced natural dyes.

Furthermore, in 1858 Worth founded the first modern *haute couture* firm in Paris, while mass production was being organized and extended.

These innovations spread rapidly through the whole of Europe.

THE PSYCHOLOGICAL SETTING: THE CREATIVE SPIRIT

To the intense industrial, commercial and capitalist financial development of the period were added social phenomena which were favourable to costume and had been becoming more pronounced since 1815: a general orientation towards democracy, brilliant international events, the development of luxury among the upper classes.

The period therefore reveals two complementary aspects of the history of costume; on one hand, costume was subject to the material factors of national economies in expansion, and the Great Exhibition of 1851 in London provides ample proof of this. On the other hand, the appearance of Couture demonstrates the concern with creativity and taste. While the Great Exhibition showed the supremacy of the English clothing industry by virtue of the cheapness of the materials, French

989   Flounced ball gown, 1854.
Paris, Bibliothèque Nationale, Cabinet des
Estampes, Oa 20. (Photo Flammarion)

990   Flounced gown of pink tarlatan, c. 1855.
Amsterdam, Rijksmuseum. (Museum photo)

991   Flounced gown of pink taffeta, c. 1850.
Collection the Société d'Histoire du Costume.
(Photo Bulloz)

FLOUNCED DRESSES

986, 988–92   The fashion for skirts entirely covered with flounces began towards 1846, but they really came into favour towards 1850–54, when the general line was almost round. The number and disposition of the flounces is extremely variable – from three to sixteen. Sometimes the gown is made of several skirts of different lengths worn one over the other, which gave a similar effect. Manufacturers produced special materials the decoration of which was designed to correspond to the proportions of the flounces and the different parts of the gown (plates 988, 989)

992   *Mlle Rosati*, c. 1850. (Photo Collection Sirot)

993   Ball gown, c. 1868. Paris, Bibliothèque Nationale, Cabinet des Estampes, Oa 95. (Photo Flammarion)

994 DUBUFE: *Princess Mathilde*, 1861.
Versailles, Museum. (Photo Flammarion)

995 Statuette, believed to be of the Comtesse Greffühle, *c.* 1868.
Paris, Musée des Arts Décoratifs. (Museum photo)

COURT COSTUME UNDER NAPOLEON III

994 The court gown retains the deep décolleté of preceding centuries with the very tight bodice and the long velvet court cloak

BALL GOWNS

993, 995–7 Ball gowns are worn over voluminous crinolines and have deeply cut necklines that expose the shoulders. The flat bertha of the preceding period is now a shawl bertha passing over the shoulders and descending in a point at the waist over the bodice. The hair is decorated with flowers, feathers and ribbons; smooth hair (plates 994, 996) is followed by light waves (plates 993, 995). Silks and light stuffs were used simultaneously, and towards 1867 trains were added to lengthen the heavily-trimmed gowns

TOWN DRESS

999 The flounces of 1850 are followed by a simpler gown, circular at first, then progressively lengthening behind; the waist rises; costumes made from different stuffs become more common; hairstyles become more complicated and bonnets alternate with large hoods

CHILDREN'S COSTUME

1000–1002, 1008 Little girls, like their mothers, wear waist-crinolines; little boys begin to wear sailor suits, although this style was no more identical with that actually worn aboard ship than was the eighteenth-century sailor suit; the fashion came from England and was to last for over a century

THE HOUSE OF WORTH

1003–6 Under the Second Empire Worth launched Haute Couture in Paris. His creations, introduced to court by the Princess Metternich, soon became famous, not only in Paris but also in England and the rest of Europe

MEN'S COSTUME

1007 The lines and details of men's costume became progressively simpler during the Second Empire; however, trousers and jacket are rarely in the same colour. The evening suit is black; cravats are still pale; the top hat was the only headgear worn

996 J. A. D. INGRES: *Mme Moitessier*, 1856.
London, The National Gallery.
(Reproduced by courtesy of the Trustees. Photo Freeman)

997 J. A. D. INGRES: *The Baroness Rothschild*, 1848.
Collection Guy de Rothschild. (Photo Flammarion)

378

998 GAVARNI: *Young Bride*, 1855.
Paris, Bibliothèque Nationale,
Cabinet des Estampes, Dc 218.
(Photo Flammarion)

999 Town dress in grey and black, *c.* 1867.
Paris, Bibliothèque Nationale, Cabinet des
Estampes, Oa 95. (Photo Flammarion)

1000 SIMON DENNING: *Princess Victoria*, 1844.
London, Dulwich College Picture Gallery.
(Photo Flammarion)

quality dominated by virtue of its elegance and invention.[25] Léon de Laborde, one of the French Commissioners at the Exhibition, used his famous report to stress the importance of aesthetics as well as economics, the two influences that confronted each other, and foresaw their reconciliation in the future.

Costume in France

THE 'FÊTE IMPÉRIALE'

From the distance of a century the Second Empire still seems a peak of brilliant living and feminine elegance, and one immediately associates this period with the *crinoline*.

Indeed, this crinoline, which revived the great ceremonial gowns of the seventeenth century, though without ever adopting their oval line, undeniably epitomized the splendour of the Imperial regime, and a still essentially monarchical society. Both the Tuileries and the fine private houses built under the Ancien Régime were the setting for display and luxury, ministered to by servants in dazzling liveries.

But this should not lead us to forget that the original *crinoline* (a pad of horsehair – *crin*), much older than the Second Empire, had then not been worn for some years, and had given its name to a voluminous accessory – the *cage* – which was then enormously expanded. Once again in the history of costume, the name of a material was taken over by the object made from it, which kept the name once the material had been discarded.

Although it represents only the final stage in the evolution of a certain type of garment, the crinoline (or cage) may be said to owe its fame to the middle of the Second Empire period, so closely was it identified with the atmosphere of the 'Fête Impériale'. After the lacklustre, bourgeois Louis-Philippe and the 1848 Revolution, women dreamed of luxury, pleasure and clothes, as had their great-grandmothers before the French Regency. A beautiful sovereign with fine shoulders inaugurated

a feverish round of receptions, balls and visits, sumptuously adorned and surrounded by the ten most beautiful women of her court, and set off by brilliant masculine uniforms and decorations. Society had more than enough money to squander, was given over to ostentation and frivolity, dressing for evenings at the Tuileries or 'slumming' at the Bal Mabille, in an intoxicating whirl of spectacles, caprices and *bons mots*. Business was transacted in a spirit of financial rivalry, despite notorious failures. In a gallant *demi-monde* people could win (or lose) houses, carriages, jewels and lovers in a night of pleasure. Foreigners from the Old and New Worlds flocked to Paris to enjoy a princely way of life, then disappeared again one morning, without sound or trace, in ruin or suicide. International exhibitions attracted all the crowned heads of Europe, the capital was embellished with new avenues and monuments, prosperity fed industry, stimulated trade and enhanced the renown of France. From this world the crinoline was born.

It was also the triumph of 'mechanized' dressmaking, which was hallowed by the Universal Exposition of 1855. Seamstresses equipped with the sewing-machine at last had the time to cover vast skirts with a whole range of trimmings, whose development and excess – bias binding, braids, plaits fringes, ruchings, etc. – were to give the *tapissier* style that followed the Second Empire.

WOMEN'S COSTUME

The historical reminiscences that had marked women's clothes after the 1830–35 period became progressively stronger, borrowing forms from one period after another, and ending, ten years later, with a style steeped in heaviness and solemnity. The closed bonnet, crinoline gowns and tippets or shawls were the three typical elements of the feminine silhouette towards 1840–45, giving a pyramid shape recalling the creations of the eighteenth century.

The chief characteristic of women's costume in the mid-nineteenth century is the great width at the base. As neither the use of flounces nor an abundance of pleats nor even boning

the foot of the skirt sufficed, after 1841[26] we see the appearance
of horsehair underskirts which progressively replaced woollen
or cheap cotton petticoats. Over long, lace-trimmed pantalettes, the nether garments of an elegant woman comprized a
very stiff petticoat woven from wool yarn and horse-hair,[27]
three or four yards in circumference, a second petticoat padded
from the knees down and boned above, a third one, white, with
several starched flounces, and finally a muslin underskirt over
which the gown was worn; this became progressively wider
after 1850.

Crinoline cloth[28] was only a makeshift, and was replaced
by hooped petticoats as early as 1850. The hooped cages which
replaced these again took the name *crinoline*, and though they
did not relieve the body of the weight of petticoats, they enjoyed
an unprecedented vogue from 1856 on.

Could it be that the immense network of iron struts Paxton
devised for the Crystal Palace inspired the invention, in 1856,
of this cage of flexible metal strips, patented by Tavernier?
It bore only an imperfect resemblance to the eighteenth-century's panier gowns.

Upheld by *chansonniers*, defended by Theophile Gautier in
his essay *De La Mode* (1858), the crinoline-cage conquered all
women, who were already won over to the 'Pompadour' style,
despite the difficulty they found in walking, going through
doorways or getting into carriages, and also despite the re-
proaches of men who were held at a distance by this contri-
vance and could no longer offer their womenfolk their arms.[29]

After 1860, the stiff, dome-shaped iron cage became softer,
acquiring articulations and following the movements of the
body. Two years later, it was already flattened in front and
was gaining in length behind, reviving the train which had
disappeared during the First Empire. By 1867, the crinoline
was only a petticoat with hoops on its lower part, supporting
the modest fullness of princess gowns, which moulded the
upper body to give the silhouette the form of a slim triangle.

The crinoline has remained so symbolic of the Second Empire that we tend to think of gowns from the years 1856–66 as
a single model under this one title, and similarly to attribute
all full-skirted gowns to this period. Yet, since 1840 at least,

381

1008 MANET: *Henry Bernstein*, 1881. Private collection. (Photo Giraudon)

1009 A. DE DREUX: *Woman on Horseback in a Blue Gown*, c. 1860. Collection Hermes. (Photo Flammarion)

1010 FRITH: *Derby Day*, c. 1855. London, The Tate Gallery. (Reproduced by courtesy of the Trustees. Museum photo)

petticoats of horse-hair or crinoline, or the cage, had only been a support whose form was not invariable, and they were worn under gowns which the imagination of dressmakers changed ceaselessly.

While the plain gowns preferred by the Empress kept a certain vogue, there was also the *tunic*, a skirt that covered the petticoat, but was draped so as to show it. Worth is said to have devised this model after meeting a working woman who had tucked up her skirt at the waist to avoid dirtying it. This mode spread quickly, for it facilitated varied combinations by changing the petticoat, or even only the lower part of the petticoat. The *Journal des Jeunes Personnes*, in 1864, recommended that this petticoat be fitted with buttoned tabs so that the gown could be raised or lowered depending on the circumstances; 'custom', it specifies, 'allows one to wear the skirt up even on visits and in all circumstances in which a woman does not remove her hat.'

The wearing of crinolines and the exaggerated size of skirts influenced the other under-garments. Initially the corset became more flexible and lost its gussets, the bust becoming more free as the lower part of the body was encaged; it was normally made of elastic silk and ribbon and had few bones; it shortened the waist, and was cut high at the front and low at the back.

There was a great increase in lavishly embroidered and lace-trimmed undergarments, from ankle-length pantalettes to peignoirs for wearing at one's toilette. But at that time discretion demanded that one should speak little of them. In May 1850, *Les Modes Parisiennes*,[30] reporting the display of a marriage trousseau, contained this prudent reflexion: 'Have these displays not their danger? Should a mother allow her daughter to see them?'

The Empress had a high conception of her role as sovereign, and in her eyes dress was one of its most important aspects.[31] Accordingly she directed fashion in town dress as well as in court costume. When she became enthusiastic about Marie-Antoinette and employed the architect Lefuel to execute Louis XVI salons in the Tuileries, around 1865, she happily wore, in the image of the unfortunate queen, fichus knotted in a point at the waist. For day wear, she launched shorter skirts and

short, tight, buttoned jackets which, long or shortened, turned into *zouave* or *Garibaldi* jackets or Spanish *boleros*.

Basqued bodices, sometimes cut like men's jackets, often had long sleeves with lace cuffs, but they also had reminiscenses of the sixteenth and eighteenth centuries.

Hats were varied. At the beginning of the Second Empire period, closed hats were worn with flowing hairstyles; they were succeeded by upswept hair and round hats slightly recalling those worn by men or young girls; lastly, after 1865, loose hairstyles were combined with tiny hats poised above the forehead. Bonnets, worn well back on the head with ruchings and long tabs, were followed by small toques tipped forward and trimmed with showers of fine ribbons tumbling over ringlets. The style of hair and hat tended to decrease the size of the head to accentuate the fullness of the bust.

Shoes were influenced by the eighteenth century. For example, there were low-cut shoes with Louis XV or Louis XVI heels for evening wear. For walking in town, women generally wore side-laced boots matching their gowns. The Empress appeared at the Longchamps races in tasselled boots.

The *mantelet* or tippet, already worn under the July Monarchy for evening outings, lasted until the end of the Empire, but more as a day-time town garment. After 1850 it was a great success as the *pardessus*. Its form varied, and it could be short, fitted or semi-fitted, and was often trimmed with a flounce of lace or wool, the novelty of the moment; it is difficult to keep track of its caprices. The Cashmere shawl, which had become a little *déclassé*, nevertheless retained the favour of women in all classes, while elegant women threw a semicircular scarf of wool or muslin over their shoulders, particularly for walking.

Women's adornment reached its highest point during the Second Empire. The fashion for large necklaces (*rivières*) and jewels interspersed with leaf-motifs of silver continued. In the crinoline-gown period, the vogue was for long ear-rings that hung almost to the shoulders. The ancient jewels from the Campana collection in the Louvre were faithfully imitated. Many women wore oval medallions or *lockets* of matt gold, which generally opened, hung from chains or necklaces, and flexible bracelets (*jarretières*) or rigid ones (*porte-bonheur*).

SPORTS COSTUME
1009 The only sport then practised by women in France was riding;
equestrian elegance is always in the English style

THE CRINOLINE OUTSIDE FRANCE
1010–15 The typical features of the costume are the same throughout
Europe: for women, lightly flounced skirts, metal cages and small bonnets, and for men, light trousers for elegant wear, dark coats and top
hats

COSTUMES PRESERVED IN ENGLAND
1016–8 While the forms are fairly close to those of French fashions,
the general line and decoration nonetheless maintain a simpler, more
practical character – perhaps only because the specimens preserved were
more currently worn than those that have survived in France. The gown
with the overskirt caught up over the petticoat (plate 1018) is specially
designed for garden games; this fashion was to spread a few years later
for everyday dresses

1011 CARMIGNANI: *The Orangery, Parma, c.* 1850.
Parma, Museum. (Photo Vaghi)

1012 A. M. HUNÆUS: *Evening Walk, the Evening before 'Prayer Day',* 1862.
Copenhagen, Royal Museum of Fine Art. (Museum photo)

During the fifteen years of the 'fête impériale' there were
very few foreign influences on Paris fashions, except in details
and in some accessories, such as *Spanish jackets*, a discreet
allusion to the origins of the Empress. Names reflect current
affairs: the *Tannhauser* cloak after Wagner's resounding success
at the Opéra in 1861, and, after the Crimean War, the imposing
Malakoff crinolines. 'Bismarck' brown, which was all the rage
in 1866, came from a dream of Worth's, in which the Princess
Metternich suggested that he give that name to a shade she did
not like.

During the last years of the Empire the tendency which,
since 1825, had orientated fashion towards grace and smooth-
ness, towards greater fullness and ease, began to weaken. The
crinoline became the answer for a time (at first crinoline cloth,
then the crinoline-cage), but each year people announced its
imminent disappearance. After 1858 rumours circulated that
Queen Victoria was going to discard it; people also said that
the Empress Eugénie had appeared in a ball gown without a
crinoline;[32] the same intentions were imputed to the Empress
Elizabeth of Austria. Finally, it was in 1866 at Longchamps that
most elegant women replaced it with a simple petticoat-skirt
with a wide ruffle at the foot, 'without artificial support.'[33]

At the same time, the *princess gown*, cut in one piece with
the bodice, completely changed the fashionable line, though
it was not universally adopted at once.

People soon realized that without the support of the cage,
the full gown fell ungracefully. Consequently, from 1869 on,
the skirt was drawn up on to the hips over a padding of flounces and small boned cages – the fullness had already been swept
to the back for several years. This was the beginning of a new
development in women's costume: *style tapissier* (upholsterer
style).

MEN'S COSTUME

Without undergoing major transformations, men's costume
during the Second Empire approached the forms it was to
keep for the rest of the century.

1013 SONCOFF: *The Rainbow* (detail), *c.* 1860.
Leningrad, Museum. (Photo Archives Photographiques)

383

1014 V. Becquer: *Gustavo Becquer and his Family, c.* 1860.
Cadiz, Museo Provincial de Bellas Artes. (Photo Mas)

1015 V. Becquer: *Study of a Carlist Painter, c.* 1850.
Madrid, Museo de Arte Moderna. (Photo Mas)

The coat *à la française* was extremely simplified to give the frock-coat, while the old frock-coat, cut off at the waist, became the tail-coat for evening wear, the English evening-dress, worn with the top hat. The redingote remained a formal garment.

Under English influence a short jacket appeared towards 1850, called *paletot, peel* or *bucksain* depending on its material, and worn with striped or patterned trousers; evidently it was only an informal, indoor garment. Only at the end of the reign do we see the suit (*complet*) – jacket, trousers and waistcoat in the same material – but this ensemble was also to remain, until the last years of the century, an informal costume, only worn in the morning, in the country or for travel.

The brilliance of the regime revived interest in costume, at court as well as in town. Details distinguished the man of the world: velvet collars, longer or shorter basques, silk lapels, narrow ties or wide bows, flaring, stiff, straight, or down-turned wing collars.

Sporting costume was limited to riding clothes, with tight breeches, boots and crop, always worn with top hats.

Only some artists and individualists wore eccentric clothes: Villemessant, the founder and director of the sophisticated *Figaro*, wore a hairy white angora hat, a flame-coloured coat and an astonishing chestnut-brown redingote called a *balayeuse* with skirts in wavy organ-pipe folds. In the years before 1870, these *élégants* were nicknamed *petits crevés* (tired little ones) because they always pretended to be exhausted by the round of soirées and parties and also because they wore skimpily-cut clothes: very short jackets and straight, often checked trousers.

At receptions at the Tuileries men's costume, laid down by the Emperor himself, comprized coat, short breeches and black silk stockings. The costumes of the various court officials were dazzling: chamberlains in red coats, palace prefects in poppy-red, masters of ceremonies in violet, pages in green, ordnance officers in pale blue, all more or less ornamented with embroidery according to rank. Footmen wore green liveries with gold braid, red waistcoats and white breeches and stockings.

Men's costume was codified in the increasing number of clubs and circles. Some were famous for their elegance, for

instance the '*Cercle de la Rue Royale*', founded in 1856 in the Hôtel de Coislin. But none of them produced an undisputed master of elegance; neither the Duc de Gramont nor the Prince de Sagan aspired to the sceptre of a Brummell or a d'Orsay.

The later changes in men's costume affected only details of shape and colour. The use of some parts of this costume was also to be modified, but the essentials were not to be noticeably affected.

Even in England, men's costume did not undergo a transformation in the mid-nineteenth century equivalent to that of women's clothes around 1850. The main garments remained fixed until the First World War, while others are still worn today, after more than a century, though with some modifications.

One of the most important changes after 1850 was the replacement of the coloured coat by black, worn with checked trousers that fitted tightly to the legs. The fashion for instep straps ended in 1855. An attempt to revive wide trousers was made, unsuccessfully, in 1860. It was not judged suitable to wear trousers in the same cloth as the coat in town; evening dress was worn with black waistcoats instead of the old white waistcoats, and with starched shirts and a bow tie instead of a cravat.

Among men's accessories, made-to-measure boots began to face competition from mass production, which began in a factory opened in Blois in 1850.

The cravat, under the names *régate* and *plastron*, was made in discreet tones and occupied a modest place, a pale shadow of its former glory.

CHILDREN'S COSTUME

We must wait for the Second Empire before we find fashion journals that give detailed information about children's clothes. Little boys under the age of five or six were dressed in the same clothes as little girls: a tunic with a small white *pardessus* or nankeen jacket; then a short skirted frock and a bodice, 'without crinoline', the writer specifies, although a girl of three could

1016 Ball gown of Lyons silk with shadow decoration of flowers, trimmed with white lace and green ribbon, *c*. 1850–60. London, The London Museum. (Courtesy the Trustees. Museum photo)

1017 Town dress in mauve flowered brocade, *c*. 1860–65. Birmingham, City Museum. (Museum photo)

1018 Check taffeta gown over striped petticoat, for croquet, *c*. 1864. Collection Mrs Doris Langley Moore. (Photo F. Fonteyn)

have one. When they were a little older boys were put into tartan suits, while girls became scale models of their mothers. Towards 1850 there was a wave of historical nostalgia, so little boys wore *crispin* suits, which were vaguely Louis XIII, with black collars falling over trousers with gaiters, worn with a plumed felt hat: the effect was of fancy dress.

Very young children, who until now had not entered into the picture, were catered for with patterns for small frocks, especially christening gowns with long embroidered aprons which remained classic styles; but it is with some surprise that one reads in the 1862 *Magasin des Demoiselles* that 'for babies of six to ten months, white embroidered piqué is best, though black embroidery is newer...'

THE BEGINNINGS OF COUTURE AND MASS PRODUCTION

The year 1858, marked by the full development of the crinoline-cage, also saw the emergence of *Couture*, in the sense that has since been given to the word.

The dressmakers still held their old sway over women's clothing in 1850. Since the death of the famous Leroy, who had dressed the Empresses Joséphine and Marie-Louise, women had returned to the head of this corporation, and in January 1853, for the marriage of the Emperor with Eugénie de Montijo, two Court dressmakers, Mme Palmyre and Mme Vignon, made the fifty-two pieces of the trousseau and the white velvet gown and train for the ceremony. This exclusive privilege was to be overturned five years later, when the Princess Metternich introduced Charles Frederick Worth to the Tuileries Palace.

This Englishman had left London in 1845 at the age of twenty, to work in Paris, first in a fashion accessories shop, then in the rue de Richelieu, for Gagelin who sold textiles, shawls and gowns. He married one of the shop-girls, and his wife inspired him to create models which gained increasing success. One day he had the completely new idea of preparing a collection in advance and presenting it to his clientèle: a further success. He then revolutionized cut and launched strik-

ing innovations which his wife wore to the races. In 1857, in association with the Swedish Boberg, he set up a business at 7 rue de la Paix, then a neighbourhood alleged to be impossible for fashion.

Thanks to the favour of the Empress Eugénie, Worth soon won a personal renown which also made the reputation of the couturier. From then on – a purely French situation – men, tailors, became the directors of fashion houses, elaborating the seasonal variations of fashion and presenting them to the customers and the foreign buyers who were to spread French supremacy in women's clothing throughout the world.

Worth was the first to stress the liveliness of his creations by employing young girls to wear his models for customers. It has been said that these 'doubles', who were later to be called 'mannequins', were chosen for their resemblance to his principal customers: his models were conceived for particular women and not, as today, for a certain idealized type. A brilliantly lit room was set aside for trying on ball gowns, so as to present them in conditions approaching reality.

We cannot repeat too often that Worth was in no way responsible for the crinoline: not only did he neither create nor launch it, but on the contrary, he did all he could to suppress it because it did not fit in with his conceptions; after all, one day he said, with an emphatic satisfaction that may make us smile: 'The 1870 Revolution is not much in comparison with *my* revolution: I dethroned the crinoline!' In fact, Worth used his subtle flair to exploit a tendency that was seeking expression even before his arrival in Paris, and, imitated by many other couturiers, he used the full form created by the crinoline to make a fanciful, impractical, even *outré* line, but one essentially feminine, which was suited only for a certain degree of luxury and a life of festivities. It was in this respect that he contributed to women's toilettes between 1850 and 1860, and this, far more than the suppression of the crinoline, is where Worth and couture brought about a true revolution in women's fashion.

The name of Worth has become the symbol of 'Couture', also called *Haute Couture* and *Couture-Création*. Yet the normal evolution of costume and the general climate of the 1850

1019 JEAN BERAUD: *The Cycle Hut in the Bois de Boulogne, c.* 1901–10.
Sceaux, Musée de l'Ile de France. (Photo Flammarion)

1020 JAMES TISSOT: *Festivities aboard Ship*, 1874.
London, The Tate Gallery.
(Reproduced by courtesy of the Trustees. Museum photo)

1021 R. DU GARDIER: *Woman in White on a Beach*, 1904.
Limoux, Museum. (Museum photo)

period already contained all the necessary conditions for this creation; Worth's merit was to have concentrated them and oriented them along new lines, lines dictated by his temperament and personality.

Worth added less to the art of cutting, which had been perfected for a quarter of a century, than some present-day couturiers have done. The essential novelty, to which the name of Worth is still attached, is that with him it became a creative undertaking, producing 'models', which he then distributed commercially throughout the world, the presentation of these models remaining the responsibility of the Fashion trades.

The appearance of Couture was stimulated by the recent formation in Paris of the ready-to-wear industry, which grew out of the combination of various elements. After 1848, Paris counted one hundred and nine garment manufacturers with an annual turnover of thirty millions, as against forty-five millions for tailors. Doubtless the ready-made garment was mainly for men, but from the beginning Parissot sold women's working clothes in his store *la Belle Jardinière*. The low price of ready-made clothing and the fact that one could wear it immediately on purchase soon broke the public of its 'made-to-measure' habits, and, moreover, fashion became more generally available in so far as the stores kept their stocks up-to-date by disposing of lines Paris did not buy to the provinces and abroad.

In his turn, Victor Revillon, the founder of a furrier's firm in 1839, began to produce 'ready-made' furs, in conjunction with the new stores, so as to provide a wider public with cheaper furs.

With the impetus that the Second Empire gave to industry and trade, couture and ready-to-wear represent two separate, divergent trends, each with different clientèles.

Indeed, French society was still divided into clearly separated social classes; these inequalities were accepted by custom and translated into clothing. Paris fashions, gradually penetrating to the most distant parts of France, made the costume of the upper classes – the aristocracy, rich bourgeoisie, liberal and administrative professions – virtually uniform among those who could afford it. The peasant and urban working classes wore blue blouses, even in Paris, where workmen also wore the cap which the February Revolution had made the badge of their class.

This social distinction expressed by costume was increased by the difficult circumstances of the working classes and the struggle between workers and employers.

At this time, when the ideas of Saint-Simon and Marx were spreading, the social dichotomy of rich and poor was reflected in the twin systems of capitalist couture and proletarian costume.

The Second Empire marks the turning point after which high fashion was no longer to be the privilege of an exclusive caste, but would be open to the *nouveau riche* and signal the rise of each generation on the social scale.

COSTUME TEXTILES

During the first half of the century, French weaving extended the mechanization begun during the preceding century: the adoption of improved looms, later powered, was slow, for economic reasons. In 1848 France had only 328,000 automatic looms, as against 675,000 in England, but the variety of French costume materials was endless, corresponding to the increased

1022–3 Advertisements for bathing dresses, 1880–89.
Paris, Bibliothèque Nationale, Cabinet des Estampes, Oa 19, Oa 20.
(Photos Flammarion)

1024 ANON: *Bathing*, 1895. Paris, Bibliothèque Nationale, Cabinet des Estampes, Oa 20. (Photo Flammarion)

1025 *For the Automobile*, c. 1900. Collection Sirot.
(Photo Reutlinger)

individualism of women clients. The quality and production of cotton and wool also improved, more than twice as much cotton being used in 1848 than twenty years previously.

The manufacture of all sorts of fancy textiles, brocades, velvets, tulles, silks, etc., expanded considerably and gave costume an extraordinary variety of decoration, particularly in silks.

Under the Restoration and the July Monarchy, fashion had favoured silks brocaded with bouquets and woven edgings, flowered muslins, satins, moirés, striped, checked and printed stuffs.

However, it was principally after 1850, as a result of the Emperor and Empress' efforts to foster luxury in costume and make Paris the international centre of elegance, that the textile industry embarked on its period of great activity.

The old fashion for Italian silks and English lace was followed by a vogue for woollens from Normandy, lace from the North of France and Lyons silks; all French industries lived on fashion, from jewellers to bootmakers and feather-merchants. Lyons silks, among other products, were favoured by court luxury and the rise of couture, while abroad they spread profitably through the English market, which had been opened as a result of Cobden's free-trade doctrine. After the American Civil War the United States in their turn became important customers of Lyons, where towards 1860 the number of looms had reached almost 10,000, mainly grouped in the picturesque workshops of *La Croix-Rousse*, *Saint-Georges* or *Saint Irénée*. These workshops produced Jacquard-woven French silks, but also plain materials for the Paris couture houses. The Empress' marked preference for plain gowns caused all women to wear shiny rustling taffetas which showed off slim waists and were perfectly suited to balloon skirts; alternatives were heavier faille, glazed silk poults or heavy satins, moirés, classic velvets or light barèges. New fabrics were invented almost daily as the result of continual experiment; mixed weaves provided a wide repertory with constantly changing names.

From then on we can trace the current which was to bring reasonably priced luxury within the reach of customers in town and country alike, and not merely the upper classes and the 'cosseted bourgeoisie'.

1026 Advertisement for bathing dresses, 1880–89.
Paris, Bibliothèque Nationale, Cabinet des Estampes, Oa 20.
(Photo Flammarion)

SPORTS CLOTHES

1019–26 Sport begins to take its place among accepted customs; sea-bathing is fashionable, but bathing dresses are designed more for elegance than for use, at least for women; on the beach or aboard ship, toilettes hardly differ from town dress. As for cycling (plate 1019), initially it was used as an excuse for innovations approaching fancy dress, and aroused the wit of caricaturists and the indignation of critics. The early days of motoring (plate 1025) brought dust-coats and long veils

1027 *Farthingale petticoat*, 1868. Paris, Bibliothèque Nationale, Cabinet des Estampes, Oa 20. (Photo Flammarion)

1028 *Petticoats and bustles*, 1880. Paris, Bibliothèque Nationale. (Photo Flammarion)

The organization of couture in Paris had considerable repercussions on the textile industries. All the creative activity of fashion was centred on the capital, where it regulated the succession of styles without regard for the production requirements of the various textile centres, Lyons in particular. The progress by fits and starts which had affected dress materials since the middle of the nineteenth century was, however, balanced by the uninterrupted growth of couture and the considerable extension of the foreign market.

We must recognize the personal contribution of Worth: his taste for soft, flowing lines requiring large quantities of cloth had much to do with the development of French industry under Napoleon III.

The chemical industry played its part with new, important improvements in dyestuffs. Artificial indigo had been prepared by Guimet in 1826, synthetic indigo in 1876, and in Lyons, Verguin had discovered fuchsine in 1856. The poor lasting-quality of some of these dyes caused a more rapid renewal of garments and helped persuade the public to dress 'à la mode'.

The most typical features of the development of costume in Europe from 1850 to 1868 – the appearance of couture, technical improvements, economic expansion and the preponderance of French fashions – were all linked to a common factor, which in turn corresponds to a general characteristic of society: it was the ever-increasing rapidity of change.

From 1868 to 1914

Two facts stand out in the 1868–1914 period. In the first place, the development of European-style costume was similar in the Old and New Worlds, and in Africa and Asia it spread with the commercial and industrial expansion of Europe and the United States. Secondly, despite national differences and a greater or lesser time lag in adaptation, French influence was predominant in this development and gained world-wide accep-

tance. Therefore where this period is concerned, the history of costume is the history of the costume of France.

Before 1914, political events in the Middle and Far East did not impinge on the Western world as, thanks to radio, television and the cinema, they do now. The general stability favoured a settled way of life and the further enrichment of the wealthy classes. And from this came an increase in polite social intercourse, in official functions and 'full-dress' events, and the pursuit – not merely the acceptance – of rigid dress prescriptions for the theatre, the Opera and the races. This life of ease, combined with a relative price stability, gave people confidence in a cloudless future, an outlook which did nothing to lessen the gulf between the social classes.

Elegant life demanded 'style', expensive, artificial, cultivated by the distinguished woman whether aristocratic or middle-class. The tone was set by 'High Society', but was exemplified equally by the great ladies of the *demi-monde*, who inspired the most dazzling creations by the major couturiers: hats loaded with plumes, hobble skirts or skirts cunningly slit to the knee, chinchilla capes costing ten thousand *louis d'or*, which they displayed in the fashionable restaurants, in their boxes at the theatre, or on the flower-decked stands at the races in the company of prominent, self-confident gentlemen wearing tail coats or frock-coats and plastron cravats.

This kind of life undoubtedly preserved costume little changed for forty-five years, with full-blown forms, overloaded ornament and strictly regulated ways of wearing clothes. Of the few attempts at change, some stemmed from the movement for equality between the sexes, which developed between 1848 and 1914, though without moving women's taste far towards choosing clothes primarily for their convenience. The others came, with greater success, from the development of sport. The element of snob-appeal attached to sporting costume was the achievement of a wealthy, often idle class.

The theatre also exerted a noticable influence on fashion. Great artists such as Sarah Bernhardt (plate 1096), Réjane, Duse or Mme Bartet and couturiers like Worth, Doucet or Redfern combined to produce the harmony that must exist between the role and its interpreter's costumes. Dress rehear-

1029 *Young woman in grey, from the back*, 1867. Paris, Bibliothèque Nationale. (Photo Flammarion)

1030 *Gown with bustle and postilion skirt*, 1874. Paris, Bibliothèque Nationale. (Photo Flammarion)

1031 LEDUC: *Beige costume*, 1880. Paris, Bibliothèque Nationale. (Photo Flammarion)

1032 *Fashion plate*, 1887. Paris, Bibliothèque Nationale (Photo Flammarion)

sals and premières were excellent publicity for the couturier as well as for the author; the gowns worn by the star gave the accolade to a new fashion, as when Marthe Regnier appeared in a play at the Vaudeville wearing a gown that did not touch the ground, or when Mlle Cecile Sorel appeared at the Théâtre Français in a simple cloak by Doucet.

Contributions from different countries were favoured by the expansion of commercial relations. The improvements in transport and the appearance of the motor-car, the great exhibitions held in Paris in 1878, 1889 and 1900, and in Vienna, Chicago, Saint Louis and Liège, all intensified artistic and intellectual exchanges, in which couture played its part. Large stores such as Liberty's and Peter Robinson opened in London and made shopping easier for a multitude of women. Alongside the complicated gowns from the great houses, they introduced sober, practical clothes for everyday wear, in which simplicity did not preclude elegance. Customers became so well used to these styles that they began to ask the great couturiers for simpler forms.

The output of raw materials increased throughout the world towards 1914. Cotton production rose 38 per cent compared with a century before, while in 1900, 1,300,000 tons of wool were consumed in the world, as against 10,000 at the beginning of the previous century. Textile production increased with improved spinning machines and weaving looms: the 'self-acting' loom invented by Roberts and Parr Curtis and Madsley's 'continuous loom', the American Northrop's automatic loom, and brocading machinery (which made the fortune of Saint-Gall in Switzerland). This led to a drop in prices and aided the rise of the large stores, which, after the First World War, set themselves to reach an even larger mass market.

During this half century, costume was more influenced by the decorative arts than by major arts such as painting. The abundance and aggressiveness of the new style of furniture were imitated by fashion between 1870 and 1895, while it was not until the twentieth century that clothing looked to the avant-garde art of Manet or Gauguin for new colours or harmonies. It was scarcely likely that the Impressionist movement should influence the forms of garments: its experiments tended

THE DEVELOPMENT OF WOMEN'S UNDERGARMENTS FROM 1868 TO 1884
1027–8 Crinolines and cages disappeared, giving place to *tournures* or bustles which supported increasingly accentuated poufs on the hips

WOMEN'S SILHOUETTE FROM 1868 TO 1887
1029–34, 1037 After the decline of the crinoline, from approximately 1868 to 1887 dresses were short-waisted and the bustle increasingly accentuated. Towards 1880, the bustle had almost disappeared and the general outline was long and slim (plate 1031); then, about 1885, the bustle reappeared, more accentuated than ever, and entered on a new period of vogue (plate 1032) until it finally disappeared towards 1892

BALL GOWNS FROM 1870 TO 1880
1035, 1038 Ball gowns nearly always included, as well as a bustle, a train heavily ornamented with bows, flowers, masses of ruffles in contrasting colours or similar decorations of the 'upholsterer's style'. As in street dresses, the waist became longer

towards the dissolution of form in light. Impressionism used the costume of the time, surrounding in with the vibrations of its palette, yet costume made scarcely any use of the sensibility and colour of Renoir or Monet.

The influence of decorative art is no less noticeable towards 1900, when the sinuous line of the gown harmonized with the twisting *Art Nouveau* tendrils of Majorelle, and the melting tones of curtains were repeated in the satin of gowns.

Possibly costume from 1870 to 1905 was indirectly influenced by the materialism, sensuality and naturalism of contemporary literature in this period of general prosperity, and afterwards, until 1914, by its greater freedom and avidity for delights. Possibly, too, the degree of materialism and conformity that marked literature and the arts in this period helped to sustain the taste for lavish display in Parisian society, to which costume and interior decoration both contributed.

However, from this *dolce vita* of material progress, from the movements in art and literature, one capital element was lacking: the magnetic centre which had been provided by the court before 1870.

The official receptions of the Third Republic never replaced

389

1033 MONET: *Mme Gaudibert*, 1868.
Paris, Musée du Jeu de Paume.
(Photo Flammarion)

1034 ALFRED STEVENS: *Autumn Flowers*, 1869.
Brussels, Musée Royal des Beaux-Arts.
(Photo Splendid Color)

1035 L. BONNAT: *Madame Pasca*, 1875.
Paris, Louvre. (Photo Flammarion)

1036 CLAUDE MONET: *Women in a Garden*, 1866.
Paris, Musée du Jeu de Paume. (Photo Flammarion)

1037 RENOIR: *M. et Mme Sisley*, 1868.
Cologne, Wallraf-Richartz Museum. (Photo H. Doppelfeld)

the Tuileries events, nor did they arouse the same desire for display in people connected with the Elysée, and even less did they stimulate the competition that had once existed between the great creators.

French 'Society' between 1870 and 1914 was thrown back on its own devices to satisfy its taste for elegance. The Ancien Régime and the Imperial aristocracy, the bourgeoisie enriched by the economic revival, and the spendthrift, frivolous *demi-monde* that succeeded to the follies of the Second Empire, all provided an easy prey for the new lords of elegance, the masters of Couture and Fashion.

It is in the light of these factors that we can understand the role of Parisian Haute Couture during this half century.

THE GREAT MASTERS OF FASHION

While under the Second Empire Worth was the incontested master of fashion, so much so that he has remained the symbol of the period's elegance, leaving his mark on the sumptuous toilettes that were worn almost until his death in 1897, a whole constellation of couturiers shared a well-earned renown after the last years of the nineteenth century.

Their names have come down to us for various reasons, but we shall limit ourselves to mentioning the few who transformed costume between 1890 and 1914.

Redfern, an English tailor with shops in London and Paris, deserves the credit for the introduction of the women's 'tailored suit' after 1885; then, in the early years of the twentieth century, of the 'walking suit' whose skirt, reaching just to the ground, was convenient for outdoor pursuits; and lastly, the 'tailored coat', inspired by the austere cut of men's coats. He also successfully designed theatrical costumes for celebrated actresses.

Another magician made his appearance: Jacques Doucet, a neighbour of Worth, in the same house in the rue de la Paix where in 1824 his grandfather had opened a milliner's shop. Doucet was to reveal himself the most feminine of couturiers, with a preference for delicate, airy toilettes, in which lace and pale silk crêpes transposed the palettes of his favourite eighteenth-century painters. He dressed Society women and the *demi-monde* as well as prominent actresses (plate 1105), and for many years he alone dressed Réjane, the famous actress of *Madame Sans-Gêne* and *Zaza*.

In 1907 Doucet's fashion house acquired a young dress designer, Mme Madeleine Vionnet, who was already experimenting with the bias cut which was to have a triumphal success after the First World War. From her very first collection with Doucet she appeared as a revolutionary, presenting mannequins barefoot and 'in their skin', which meant without corsets. She set up her own house in 1912, and made her faithful customers, Lantelme, Lavallière and Cécile Sorel, models whose bias pleats produced an astonishing falling line which revealed the outline of the body in movement. From 1918 to 1939 she was to be one of the great names of Parisian couture, not only for her accomplished techniques and her faultless handling of fabrics, but also because of her inborn sense of how to enhance her client's femininity (plates 1087, 1089), and the harmony and balance of her creations.

In the first years of the century fur finally acquired the importance it has since kept, after serving merely as a trimming. The disappearance of bustles and balloon sleeves made it possible to use fur for jackets and coats (plate 1112), innova-

1038 J. BERAUD: *Evening party given by the Caillebottes*, 1878. Collection Comtesse Balny d'Avricourt. (Photo Flammarion)

1039 JAMES TISSOT: *Portrait of a Lady*, c. 1865. Paris, Louvre. (Photo Flammarion)

1040　JAMES TISSOT: *Portraits in a Park*, 1863. Paris, Musée d'Art Moderne. (Photo Archives Photographiques)

1041　CAROLUS-DURAN: *Lady with Glove*, 1869. Paris, Louvre. (Photo Giraudon)

1042　A. FEUERBACH: *In Spring*, 1868. Berlin, Staatliche Museen. (Photo Druch Oder)

COSTUME IN EUROPE TOWARDS 1870
1036-9, 1043, 1045, 1049　The simplified, almost geometrical style adopted by women's fashion at the moment when the crinoline was replaced by the bustle spread through Europe. Short waists and small hats reflect Paris fashions

'UPHOLSTERER'S STYLE' AND THE FIRST PERIOD OF THE BUSTLE
1044, 1046-8, 1051　The pouf is heavily loaded with trimmings, gowns are sometimes made of two different materials, with tunics (plates 1044, 1051) or polonaises (plate 1046). The 'two-handled' sunshade (plate 1044) was a short-lived fashion at the beginning of the century

1043　SILVESTRE LEGA: *The Pergola*, 1868. Milan, Brera. (Museum photo)

tions introduced by Révillon, which he constantly varied and perfected.

In 1909, in one of the returns to favour which had occurred in each century since the Middle Ages, supported this time by music and dance, the East again invaded the Western World, with Diaghilev's *Ballets Russes*. In Paris one couturier was already bringing colour to the aid of personality in clothing: Paul Poiret, who had begun as a young designer with Worth, had opened a small fashion house in 1904 and embarked on striking experiments. Even before the Ballets Russes with their costumes by Bakst and Benois, he had revolutionized the range of colours used in women's clothing, replacing pale, evanescent tones with deep violet, vibrant red, warm orange and bright greens and blues 'which made everything sing'. Poiret, who denied having absorbed the violent orientalism of the Ballets Russes, not only imagined 'cloths of fire and joy' but also created the *turban à l'orientale*, hobble gowns (plate 1107), or skirts with small hoops, *sultana skirts*, sumptuous tunics, heavy capes covered with fringes and tassels, cockades of multicoloured feathers and shimmering coils of pearls under white fox stoles. His ideas are immortalized in Iribe's album *Les Robes de Paul Poiret*, which appeared in 1908, and in the appealing *Les Choses de Paul Poiret*, produced in 1911 by Georges Lepape who for twenty-five years was to create the covers of *Vogue*. The *Gazette du Bon Ton* was steeped in the spirit and style of Poiret, in the drawings of Georges Barbier and of Martin. He boldly asked the painter Dufy for textile designs, and also invented the first couturier's perfume: *Rosine*.

Beside these names, symbols of a whole period, others brought less publicized, but no less important innovations: the most representative, Mme Paquin who, like Worth, loved sumptuous gowns, was the first to think of sending several mannequins to the races, all presenting the same gown. She was the first French designer to open branches outside France, first in London, then in Buenos Aires and Madrid.

Other energetic ladies, endowed with impeccable taste, earned lasting renown in couture. The Callot Sisters, directed by Mme Gerber, introduced the mode for lamés, and showed great sensitivity in their handling of different types of cloth. Jeanne

1044 *Couple in a Garden*, 1871. Paris, Bibliothèque Nationale, (Photo Flammarion)

1045 MAXWELL ARMFIELD: *Faustina*, c. 1875. Paris, Musée d'Art Moderne. (Photo Archives Photographiques)

1046 JAMES TISSOT: *Young Woman*, c. 1875. Oxford, Ashmolean Museum

1047 GIRAUD: *Godmother's Garden*, 1876. Paris, Bibliothèque Nationale, (Photo Flammarion)

Lanvin abandoned millinery to make dresses for her small daughter, which rapidly led her to Haute Couture, where she showed a very personal style in the luxurious decoration of her creations: brocades, gold and silver textiles, insets and embroideries (plate 1102). She used a new range of colours, very different from Poiret's.

In millinery, Caroline Reboux showed herself the greatest artist in three generations, from the Second Empire to the present. Others, such as Virot (plate 1070) or Lewis, demonstrated endless resources of taste. Unfortunately the hat is an ephemeral creation; very few models have come down to us.

From our distance in time, we can trace two trends in the years before 1914. On the one hand, there was the new orientalism which showed itself in vibrant tones and bold contrasts. It sheathed women's bodies in narrow, soft tubes and crowned lacquered hair with turbans and aigrettes; full-pleated capes wrapped women in the evening. The sinuous silhouette of these elongated creatures seemed to move in a perpetual tango, like the symbol of a moving line.

Other designers used consummate skill to renew the *Art Nouveau* of the 1900 period. Textiles were soft and clinging, adorned with brilliant embroideries and transparent lace. This style remained the favourite of women frightened by boldness, who were happier to accept new fashions when they did not break with the past.

These two tendencies existed side by side, and despite their opposition, for those who knew them they still remain the symbol of the elegance of a lost world.

WOMEN'S COSTUME

During the forty-five years between the end of the Second Empire and the First World War, the development of women's costume went through three stages.

FROM 1868 TO 1885

After 1870, to follow early fluctuation of fashion would entail a year-by-year chronicle, which would be as wearisome as

1048 DEGAS: *Woman in Town Dress*, 1871–2. Courtesy of the Fogg Art Museum, Harvard University, Cambridge, Mass., Collection Meta and Paul Sachs. (Museum photo)

difficult to compile. Certain modes overlapped; the economic conditions resulting from the Franco-Prussian War combined with a new middle class restraint which succeeded the wild years of the Imperial period. Alongside the Haute Couture gowns launched by Worth, ingenious contrivances appeared, designed to enable women to follow new styles with little expense, for it was a costly undertaking to buy a gown that took fourteen yards of cloth and was constructed in so complex a manner that it was only wearable if it came from the hands of a good 'maker'.

The gown swept backwards, which followed the princess gown, was suddenly drawn over a bustle, a boned half-cage which reached its fullest development in the early 1870s and again in 1885 (plate 1058). Almost at the same time we see the reappearance of *polonaises*, a reminiscence of Louis XVI style; the outer gown completely showed the underskirt and formed a longer or shorter train at the back, edged with pleated frills, ruchings or passementeries depending on the time, for this fashion was to last over ten years (plate 1059). Other models consisted of *tunics* draped at the sides and forming bustles behind (plate 1054). *Aprons*, which were also draped, and scarves were added to these already overloaded forms, which echoed the extravagances of furniture upholstery, evoking the conglommeration of fashionable drawing-rooms crammed with full-fringed curtains, buttoned chairs, bibelots and plants.

During fifteen years this accumulation of cloth, pleats, flounces and ruchings weighed down women's silhouettes. Fashion magazines abounded in judicious advice on how to produce a new toilette out of two slightly tired gowns, while respecting the fashions of the day in combining the materials. The underskirt was always plain with striped polonaise or tunic; if both stuffs were plain, the underskirt was darker; if a spencer was worn it matched the tunic trimming, and its sleeves, if there were any, were made in the tunic cloth, and so on.

This over-loaded style corresponded to the taste for the sumptuous inherited from the preceding period, but – it must be recognized – did not completely suit all women, and it suited even less the more active, less opulent life that was the lot of most. Alongside the formal gowns kept for outings and visits, we see the gradual introduction of the *costume* after 1867. This was initially a 'short' skirt, that is, a skirt without a train, then a skirt and polonaise, often made in one piece. This formula, which naturally appeared in varied forms, was admitted for errands and morning visits, but never for afternoon wear or mourning. It was a subject of argument and controversy, but nonetheless gained ground over fifteen years.

We must note the strict regulation of costume according to the circumstances and the time of day: morning clothes, day clothes, clothes for informal or ceremonial visits, private or formal dinners, informal evenings, balls, theatre parties; the choice of gown, its material and neckline, the hat and coat or cloak were all subject to almost ritual prescriptions, from which one could not depart without appearing lacking in education.

Some textiles such as satin, and some trimmings, including fur and lace, and jewels and cashmere shawls were not admitted for young girls.

Finally, after 1871 we see attempts at special costumes for 'touring', a new word: tartan skirts, bodice and chemisette, caps and tartan stockings. In 1888 a 'walking suit' (*trotteur*) was mentioned as a novelty for travel, composed of a skirt and pleated tunic. Praiseworthy attempts at simplifying uncomfortable clothes, but isolated!

394

WOMEN'S FASHION TOWARDS 1880
1050, 1056 The waist becomes lower, the bustle disappears, the foot of the gown is complicated with drapery

FASHION FROM 1886 TO 1890
1052 Overloaded decoration has disappeared from costumes; the hat also is simplified, and feather or fur boas lend a discreet elegance to costume of this period

1049 THEODOR ALT: *Rudolf Hirth in his Studio*, 1870. Berlin, National Gallery. (Photo W. Steinkopf)

1050 GERVEX: *Portrait of Mme Valtesse de la Bigne*, 1889. Paris, Louvre. (Photo Flammarion)

Between 1870 and 1885 we see the appearance of vast numbers of accessories: fichus and Bertha collars were independent trimmings, with infinitely variable forms, enabling women to transform the flat bodice of any gown at little expense.

Belts developed wide ends, knotted low on the hips and replacing bustles, particularly after 1875, when the cage itself progressively disappeared to give a slim silhouette. But double skirts, pleats and flounces had still not disappeared and gave these straight, semi-princess gowns a hobbled line. Bodices moulded the bust; tight draperies were wound round the hips, reaching almost to the knees; a pleated petticoat or *balayeuse* (*sweeper*) tailed on the ground with a rustling sound.

If there were any logic in fashion, we should conclude that gowns would now become lighter, that the heaps of drapery would disappear and permit ease in movement. But in 1883 the bustle reappeared, larger than ever. The reduced cage was fitted with shells of horse-hair and stiffened gauze, holding the skirt out horizontally behind the waist, and the draped poufs gained unprecedented fullness; about a yard of extra material had to be allowed for this erection, which could form the continuation of the bodice back, or be a tunic draped in 'pipe pleats' or 'butterfly wings'. However, the true pouf was independent of the rest of the gown, consisting of a ruffled width of material fixed to the underskirt. If the gown had a polonaise, this was slit at the back to allow the pouf to spread out.

The hats of these last twenty years, the masterpieces of Virot or Reboux, are less easy to characterize than those of the preceding periods; they were minute – *bibis* – or at least narrow; for some years they grew in height, but in general they were perched on top of the head. The closed bonnet had disappeared, but a little hat with ribbons from the back of the neck and knotted under the chin was greatly in vogue until the end of the century (plates 1050, 1053). For married women it was considered as the full-dress hat (*chapeau paré*). This was opposed to the 'round' hat, with fairly wide brim, worn in the morning or in the country, admitted as formal wear for young girls but never for mature women; the latter were even discouraged from wearing them, for fear of catching cold from leaving the face and ears uncovered.

1051 J. B. COROT: *Woman in Blue*, 1874.
Paris, Louvre. (Photo Flammarion)

1052 FANTIN-LATOUR: *Sonia*, 1890.
Washington, D.C., National Gallery of Art, Chester Dale Collection.
(Museum photo)

1053 JULES DAVID: *At the Races*, 1884. Collection F. Boucher. (Photo Flammarion)

1054 Tunic dress, *c.* 1884. (Photo Collection Sirot)

1055 Evening gown, *c.* 1885. (Photo Collection Sirot)

1056 RENOIR: *Dance in the Country*, 1883. Leningrad, Museum. (Photo Flammarion)

1057 SEURAT: *La Grande Jatte*, 1886. Chicago, The Walker Art Gallery. (Photo Giraudon)

THE SECOND PERIOD OF THE BUSTLE

1053–5, 1057–8 The silhouette is still heavy and the exaggerated bustle gives a strange appearance to women's figures. Gowns are always made in two colours of material. The waist, squeezed into corsets, is in its natural place, and sleeves begin to develop into the leg-of-mutton shape

HISTORICAL REMINISCENCES

1059–61 Historical reminiscences appear periodically in fashion: here we find eighteenth-century allusions

WOMEN'S SILHOUETTE BETWEEN 1895 AND 1904

1062–5 The bustle has disappeared, but the corset imposes a sinuous, curved line; the skirt, flat at the waist, spreads out like a bell towards the ground; high standing collars hold the head erect, and hats become constantly bigger. The exaggeration of the leg-of-mutton sleeve, in a different material from the rest of the dress (plates 1062, 1071) did not last; the fullness became less and moved down towards the wrist (plate 1065)

Caps, which were still to be seen as *negligé* head-dresses for morning outings, and were *de rigueur* at home and even for informal evenings, became the prerogative of old people towards 1875, and particularly after 1880.

The colours in vogue for gowns, skirts and tartans were much more vivid than those before 1868: lightning blue, deep red, apple green, lapis lazuli, cardinal's purple, peacock green and mandarine, though there were calmer years in which colours were 'muted, recalling old tapestries'.

High boots with tassels shared the favour of elegant women with short cloth boots with patent toecaps. Manufacturers tried to launch embroidered red or yellow boots. Shoes were worn only at home or for balls. A caprice led to the appearance in 1879 of stockings 'finely striped in peacock blue and golden yellow'.

FROM 1885 TO 1900

Even before the pouf began to lose its volume, the vertically pleated skirt began, in 1885, to compete with the draped skirt. The 'tailored suit', soon known simply as *tailleur* in France, was formed of a very tight jacket-bodice or jacket, with small basques forming a *postillon* at the back, and a double skirt, the upper part of which was slightly caught up. The only trimmings were saddle-stitching in contrasting colours or flat braid: 'in a word, riding costume, but with shorter skirts.'

We may wonder if this was not the first appearance, under the influence of English tailors like Redfern, of the more severely cut tailored suit which was invented in London and was to return to Paris shortly after, to meet with growing popularity (plate 1081).

The variety of outer garments is impossible to pin down. We must not attach too much importance to names: the term *pardessus* often refers to all varieties; at other times, the same forms are lumped together under the title *mantille*. *Visites* came and went with the years; but around 1880 the great vogue was for the cashmere shawl, worn according to circumstances square, pointed, peplum style or as a scarf. Fashion magazines constantly proffered advice on the buying of cashmeres and the types of drapery they permitted.

1058 J. Béraud: *At the Eiffel Tower*, 1889. Paris, Musée des Arts Décoratifs. (Photo Flammarion)

1059 Madrazo: *The Marquesa de Manzanedo*, 1875. Madrid, Prado. (Photo Mas)

1060 C. Giron: *Mlle de Clomesnil*, 1885. Berne, Kunstmuseum. (Museum photo)

1061 John Singer Sargent: *Mrs White*, c. 1883. Washington, Corcoran Gallery of Art. (Photo Archives Photographiques)

After 1891 the silhouette was totally transformed. While the habit of supporting the skirt at the waist on a small cushion or *strapontin* persisted, gowns became much simpler and fullness moved from the skirt to the sleeves. These puffed out progressively and in 1895 were as voluminous as they had been at the beginning of the reign of Louis Philippe (plate 1079). Successively called 'leg-of-mutton', then 'balloon' sleeves, they were often in a different stuff or colour from the rest of the gown. They brought with them the vogue for shoulder-fitting *collets*, types of cape, cut in varying ways, short and full with standing collars, the only garment that could be worn over these exaggerated sleeves. From 1897 on these sleeves were replaced by small bouffant sleeves for evening gowns and long, semi-gigot sleeves in town dress.

We also note the return to older styles, long jackets in 'Directoire style', 'Medicis' standing collars, and even a 'Henri II *collet* with Watteau pleat'.

These fashions continued with innumerable variations until 1898 when the bell skirt, loaded with flounces, lawn ruffles and lace frills and other trimmings, was worn with a 'wasp waist' achieved through wearing boned corsets. Sleeves were tight, with only a slight puff at the top, and bodices had high collars fitting round the throat. Hats grew larger and were covered with feathers, flowers and ribbon rosettes, but women also wore more restrained toques turned up at one side. Shoes were long and pointed; towards 1890 we see the first experiments with coloured leather, for women at first, then for men.

Some coats with three tiered collars revived *pèlerines* from the Romantic period; simpler models with only one cape collar were worn as sporting costume by elegant women who drove their own carriages. Soon these women were to climb aboard the first motor cars, with vast dust coats in neutral tones and hats hiding gigantic goggles, worn under long veils designed as much to hold the hats in place as to protect the face from the wind raised by the new contraptions.

There were efforts to simplify town dress; towards 1886 the first tailored suits, imported from England, brought a strict line that at first displeased women by its austerity; but French couturiers were quick to adapt it to the tastes of a clientèle that

1062 *Fashion figure*, 1895. Paris, Bibliothèque Nationale, Cabinet des Estampes, Oa 20

1063 *Winter styles*, 1896. Collection Union Française des Arts du Costume

1064 *Figure of fashion*, 1899. Paris, Bibliothèque Nationale, Cabinet des Estampes, Oa 20

1065 *Garden-party dress*, 1904. Paris, Bibliothèque Nationale. (Photos Flammarion)

1066 *Sporting Woman* (detail), 1883. Paris, Bibliothèque Nationale, Cabinet des Estampes, Oa 20. (Photo Flammarion)

1067 JULES LEFEBVRE: *Yvonne* (detail), 1901. Paris, Mobilier National. (Photo Archives Photographiques)

1068 E. DUBUFE: *Mesdemoiselles Dubufe* (detail), 1884. Private Collection. (Photo Archives Photographiques)

1069 L. BONNAT: *Mme Pascal* (detail), 1905. Pau, Museum. (Photo Archives Photographiques)

1070 Hat of white lace trimmed with pink ostrich feathers by VIROT for Mlle Cleo de Mérode, 1904. Collection Union Française des Arts du Costume

1071 LIENZO: *Señora* 1895. Madrid, Museo de Arte Moderna. (Photo Mas)

1073 JOHN SINGER SARGENT: *Mme Gautereau*, 1884. New York, Metropolitan Museum. (Museum photo)

1072 L. BONNAT: *Mme Cahen d'Anvers*, 1891. Bayonne, Musee Bonnat. (Photo Archives Photographiques)

1074 Dress in bead-embroidered yellow tulle, worn by Queen Alexandra, 1907. New York, Metropolitan Museum. (Museum photo)

1075 MONET: *In the Conservatory*, 1879.
Berlin, Staatliche Museen.
(Museum photo)

1076 RENOIR: *Woman in Blue*, 1877.
The Reader's Digest, Pleasantville, N.Y.

1077 JOHN SINGER SARGENT: *Mme Edouard Pailleron*, 1879.
Collection Mme Henry Bourget-Pailleron. (Photo Flammarion)

1078 Giovanni Boldini: *Mme Charles Max*, 1896, Paris, Musée d'Art Moderne. (Museum photo)

1079 J. Béraud: *Place de la Concorde*, c. 1895. Paris, Musée Carnavalet. (Photo Bulloz)

1080 R. Casas: *Señorita Burés*, c. 1900. Barcelona, Museo de Arte Moderna. (Photo Mas)

1081 *English tailored suit*, 1892. *The London Album*. Paris, Bibliothèque Nationale, Cabinet des Estampes, Ob 100. (Photo Flammarion)

HATS

1066–70 Hats around 1900 are large and generally laden with flowers and feathers; this was the fashionable period for ostrich feathers, known in France as *amazones*, or as *weepers* when each strand was lengthened by a further strand minutely gummed on

EVENING GOWNS

1071–3 Although ball gowns do not exactly follow the general line of fashion, their silhouette becomes slimmer and décolletés extremely wide and deep; a train normally completes the gown

SURVIVING BALL GOWNS

1074 Bead embroidery is a characteristic trimming of the fashions of the beginning of the twentieth century; it was later to be even more widely used

TOWN DRESS

1075–6, 1079–81 Town dress becomes simpler with the introduction of the tailored suit, mannish in cut, in plain material, with a leather belt. Shirtwaister bodices with high collars are practical garments for women, who are beginning to lead a more active life

MEN'S COSTUME

1082–4 Men's costume took on an austerity which only the cravat or necktie sometimes relieved. The top hat was currently worn

---

appreciated its comfort and convenience. However, skirts remained long, and the coquettish gesture of the Parisienne who held hers up for walking (plate 1078), sometimes revealing the flounces of her petticoat (plate 1095), remained a symbol of this period, in which constraint became elegance.

In fine weather, the ensemble was completed with a feather boa (plate 1079).

Round hats, with all the new shapes to which they lent themselves brought a new accessory, the hat-pin, which was indispensable to hold them on the carefully constructed hairstyles.

Shoes, which varied considerably, still included low-cut pumps for evening wear, lacing shoes for summer and high laced or buttoned boots for walking or winter.

FROM 1900 TO 1914

After 1900 the silhouette became imperceptibly softer and lighter; the waist was progressively less accentuated, and Empire and Directoire styles were launched yet again. The train disappeared, followed by the collar. The skirt, which fitted closely over the hips, spread out at the foot like a flower (plate 1065). The tailored suit (plate 1095) was now universally worn in town dress and, after 1902, the walking suit made its appearance; this last model was a great advance on the timid attempt in the previous period, for the skirt only just reached the ground or even stopped a couple of inches short of it. Bodices had very high collars, and sleeves at first flared out at the wrist, then tightened. Their fullness moved down from the shoulder to the elbow, then to the wrist, where it was caught in. The new line of the body, obtained by corsets of a completely new cut, was vertical in front and very curved behind, a feature which caricaturists promptly satirized with some ferocity.

The high hairstyles still carried large hats which were held up by barrettes masked behind with flowered comb-covers.

The generally restrained town dress became heavily laden with trimmings for more formal occasions: stitching, embroidery, lace, waistcoats with Byzantine decoration, appliquéd velvet flowers and passementeries and ruchings were all used according to the caprice of fashion, which changed with increasing rapidity.

Short or long cloaks were most often made of broadcloth, but fur was gaining ground every year, because it was far better worked than before, and no longer weighed down the silhouette, and also because the use of cheaper furs, including moleskin, Hudson otter and Siberian beaver, enabled modest purses to indulge in the luxury denied them in sable and chinchilla.

Towards 1910 the S-line disappeared, under the influence of couturiers who were bringing about the disappearance of the corset. There was a return to high waists and the straight line inspired by the First Empire (plates 1105, 1108); the foot of the gown might even be caught in by a straight band which barely permitted walking: this was the 'hobble skirt', a godsend for cartoonists, all the more because these thin tube silhouettes

1082 *Fur-lined pelisse.* 1872. Paris, Bibliothèque Nationale, Cabinet des Estampes, Oa 19. (Photo Flammarion)

1083 *Summer suit*, 1875. *Gravures de Modes*. Paris, Bibliothèque Nationale, Cabinet des Estampes, Oa 19. (Photo Flammarion)

1084 MARCEL BASCHET: *Francisque Sarcey with his Daughter, Mme Adolphe Brisson*, 1893. Versailles, Museum. (Museum photo)

were topped with vast flat-brimmed hats, crowned with extravagant ostrich feathers or *amazones*, or *weepers* (*pleureuses*) in which each strand was lengthened by added strands. The weigh-in at Longchamps provided the setting for these walking mushrooms whose elegance nonetheless disarmed critics. Despite the exaggerations of these toilettes, their cut was so admirable, their colours were so carefully studied and their trimmings and accessories so harmonious that one is forced to pay homage to the artists who created them.

Naturally these creations were not for everyday life; simpler garments had discreet slits at the foot of skirts and pleats or gussets at the seams to give women freedom of movement without changing the overall line.

This period also produced the 'kimono' bodices (plate 1109), with sleeves cut in the same piece as the body, which brought the vogue for short sleeves, and, at the same time, the disappearance of high collars which were incompatible with the supple line of these new forms.

In thirty years underwear had changed much less than outer clothing. During the nineteenth century it had become more elegant with the use of finer materials, embroidery and lace, but forms changed only very gradually; only towards 1880 did the undervest lose the traces of its short sleeves; the Second Empire calf-length pantalettes were succeeded by *zouave pantaloons* gathered at the knees, replaced in turn in 1890 by *sabot pantaloons* with wide, rounded legs decorated with deep pleated flounces trimmed with lace. They were even made in pink batiste trimmed with black.

Towards 1900, to avoid bulk under tight-fitting skirts, *combinaisons* (underskirts), chemise-pantaloons or petticoat-pantaloons, known as *jupons cache-corset*, were introduced.

After 1900 progress in dyes produced fast colours so that coloured lingerie could be produced.

Fancy still reigned where petticoats were concerned. After 1890 the skirt no longer needed a *tournure* or *bustle petticoat*, nor the visible petticoat that nowadays we would call a skirt, and the petticoat became a true undergarment. It took two forms: the under-petticoat, which was fairly short, made of wool or matelassé for winter, or of percale or bazeen for summer, and the outer petticoat, of silk or mohair, which could be enlivened with tiers of flounces, pleats, ruchings or ribbons. This outer petticoat was revealed when the overskirt was caught up, and thus emphasized the elegance of the toilette. In 1907 it reached a circumference of six or seven yards and used fifteen or sixteen yards of taffeta. The appearance of the hobble skirt led to its sudden disappearance and its replacement by the linen or crêpe de chine slip.

We should not imagine that during this period of long skirts stockings were little thought of; fashion magazines indicated new trends each year: sometimes the stocking matched the gown, sometimes the shoes, which towards the end of the nineteenth century were made of coloured leather. Sometimes the embroidery of the stocking recalled the colour of the gown, otherwise openwork stockings or stockings with lace inserts were worn, made of Valenciennes or needlepoint. It is impossible to go into the details of the elaborate styles that were then current. Silk stockings were still luxury objects, and, except for evening dress, lisle was most often worn. After 1910 openwork stockings disappeared, giving way to plain stockings, decorated only with 'clocks' at the sides.

Among considerations whose urgency has been dimmed by the passage of time, in a way of life that has become history, with fashion creators whose names fade slowly into the past, costume remained devoted to woman's adornment until the early twentieth century. The claims of functionalism, the masculinization of women's clothes and the full impact of economics were for the morrow.

In 1914, through varying modes and constant experiment, woman's costume – the only costume that counted at the time – had attained a style that can be expressed in one of the new terms of the time: *line*. This one word sums up the renunciation of full volumes and the new freedom, the softening of textiles and the bold colours, and above all, femininity. In the early stages of this adaptation to a new life, which seemed to promise more independence and activity, women could not foresee the changes in store: they still lived in the illusion that they were free, and their toilettes, rich or simple, helped them fulfil their centuries-old role of pleasing.

1085 TOULOUSE-LAUTREC: *A Passing Conquest*, 1896. Toulouse, Musée des Augustins. (Photo J. Dieuzaide)

MEN'S COSTUME

The essentials of men's costume had been fixed since the beginning of the nineteenth century; only the details evolved, and it is not possible to study fluctuations except through pictures. The few new garments that appeared in the course of the century were only the culmination of a general tendency towards the simplification of clothes.

The *jacket* became more frequently worn after 1870 and the *suit* – jacket, waistcoat and trousers in the same material – came into favour after 1875, though it was still not considered correct formal wear; the tail coat and, above all, the frock coat were the only styles admitted for daytime visits or ceremonies. There were rules governing their cut and materials: according to the year, they might be *full dress* or *half full dress* depending on their length. The same held good for overcoats; long, full shapes were correct for travelling and motoring coats, while elegant coats had to be shorter and more fitted, except, of course, for the fur-lined pelisses worn in winter or in evenings (plate 1082).

Apparently it was in 1880, at Monte Carlo, that the *dinner jacket* first appeared, introduced by gamblers who found it tiring to wear tail coats all evening. Until the death of Edward VII (1910) it was not admitted in public, but was worn mainly in the country in gatherings of men. The tail coat was still compulsory wear for evening parties or the theatre.

Under the influence of a more active way of life and English customs, the fashion for sporting clothes developed gradually after 1870, spreading through France with the invention of the bicycle and increasingly after the turn of the century.

During this late Victorian period, country life led to the adoption of tweeds. Tweed trousers were decorated with wide braid down the side seams, while the jacket could be single or double-breasted, and was made of the same cloth as the trousers. The *Norfolk jacket* was popularized by the Prince of Wales, who wore it for shooting in Norfolk.

Until 1914 the *top hat* remained the elegant model, which distinguished a certain class of wearer; the *bowler hat*, which had appeared at the end of the Second Empire, was initially considered informal, then admitted for everyday wear, but never on ceremonial occasions. In 1885, the first soft felts were made, intended for mornings or travel; but they were little worn until the early twentieth century. In summer, straw *boaters*, in varied forms and colours, were worn by almost all men, and at the beginning of the twentieth century, soft straw *Panama hats* were worn for travelling.

The cap, whose shapes varied considerably, became the working class headgear in the second half of the nineteenth century; because of its comfort it was then adopted generally for travel and sporting wear.

While it is impossible to go into all the details of the changes undergone by men's costume at the end of the nineteenth and the beginning of the twentieth century, we should at least mention the importance attached to accessories. For example, in 1894: 'a man away from home should never be separated from his hat, whether on a visit, out to dinner or at a ball. During the dinner, he leaves it on his seat in the drawing-room and, at balls, on his partner's seat during dances.' And: 'During the day he should never wear more than one watch-chain, one ring on the ring finger and cuff-links and shirt-studs that do not attract the attention, similarly with the tie-pin. No pins or chains in the evening.' Men could take their canes into drawing-rooms 'and the Opera' but it was best that they should be

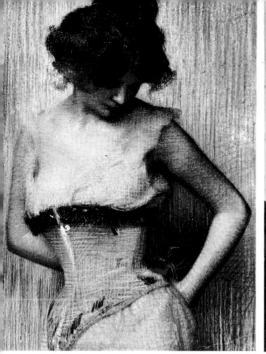

1086 VIDAL: *Young Girl in Corsets*,
c. 1880.
(Photo Archives Photographiques)

1087 Mlle Lantelme in a negligée designed by MADELEINE
VIONNET, 1906.
(Photo Collection Union Française des Arts du Costume)

1088 ABEL FAIVRE: *Woman with a Fan*,
1901. Limoux, Museum.
(Museum photo)

1089 Mlle Lantelme in a peignoir by MADELEINE VIONNET, 1908.
(Photo Collection Union Française des Arts du Costume)

1090 MANET: *Nana*, 1877. Hamburg, Kunsthalle.
(Photo Kleinhempel)

1091 Sailor suit for small girl. 1897. (Photo Collection Union Française des Arts du Costume)

1092 Small boy's tartan suit. Late nineteenth century. London, Collection Mrs Doris Langley Moore. (Photo F. Fonteyn)

'malacca canes with silver or enamelled knobs'. 'For the theatre or small evening parties, pearl grey gloves; for balls, white gloves which dancers must not take off.'

In 1895 we see the new fashion for ironing a crease down each trouser-leg. It was elegant to 'turn up the trouser bottoms, but only in the morning, whether it be rain or shine.' This was a British innovation, and Frenchmen who copied it said 'You turn up your trousers in Paris because it is raining in London.' The pleat at the trouser waist was introduced in 1911–2 by Larsen.

CHILDREN'S CLOTHING

Towards the second third of the nineteenth century we find the first mention of children's styles in fashion magazines. These mainly concern clothes for boys, for whom specialist tailors were beginning to devise models. Until the age of five or six, little boys still wore pleated skirts attached to the bodice; at seven or eight, they went into jackets and semi-tight breeches buttoned at the knee. Then came the fashion for Scottish costume for smaller children (plate 1092), while their elder brothers wore 'well-cut jackets fitting to the waist, with Louis XV breeches'.

Little girls no longer wore scale models of their mothers' clothes. Around 1880, very small girls wore a black gown known in France as an *anglaise*, a sort of sack dress falling over a pleated false skirt; a very wide, low belt cut this almost above the knee, only a couple of inches above the skirt hem. A little later the frock, which was still straight, assumed a bloused-shape at the waist over a narrow belt. This straight shape remained in fashion until the first years of the twentieth century under the name of *robe à l'américaine*.

However, towards 1883–6, at the period of prominent bustles, little girls were for a time loaded with similar contrivances, which gave them a particularly ungraceful silhouette; their poufs and polonaises were at least less exaggerated than those of women's clothes.

Russian blouses and Scottish styles emerged periodically, but the main style was the *sailor suit*, which was to enjoy a long career, increasingly worn by boys and girls alike. It appeared during the Second Empire in a form very close to its twentieth-century style, but it was less typical between 1875 and 1885. It still kept its square collar edged with white braid, opening in a point over a plain or striped plastron, with the straight short trousers or pleated skirts that make it easy to recognize, even when it was at its most fanciful. It was to be interpreted in two main ways: with short or long trousers, in white or blue serge or white or striped duck. A variant before 1900 was the 'quarter-master' in which the blouse was replaced by a jacket opening over a striped front tucked into the shorts or skirt (plate 1091). Its indispensable complement was the French sailor beret, soft-crowned with a red pompom or – more elegant – the English beret with a wider, flat crown.

Few children's fashions enjoyed a longer period of vogue. Apart from this simple, practical costume, before 1914 children were still far from being dressed in the soft, comfortable garments that they were to be given by the fashion for pullovers, but it must be said that the simplification of their clothes was only to follow the increasingly simplified forms of adult costume.

1093 *Outfits for girls and boys*, 1907. Collection Union Française des Arts du Costume. (Photo Flammarion)

1094 PICASSO: *At the Races*, 1901. Private collection. (Photo Galerie Charpentier)

1095 J. BÉRAUD: *Le Trottin*, 1906. Paris, Musée Carnavalet. (Photo Galerie Charpentier)

1096 Carrick style coat worn by Sarah Bernhardt, 1906. (Photo Sirot)

1097 PICASSO: *Woman in Blue*, 1901. Madrid, Museo
Nacional de Arte Contemporaneo. (Photo Giraudon)

1098 J. BÉRAUD: *Jardin de Paris. The Night Beauties, c.* 1905.
Paris, Musée Carnavalet. (Photo Flammarion)

1097–1109 In the first years of the twentieth century, the feminine silhouette, moulded by a foundation garment that understated the hips,
was clad in soft materials: shaped or pleated skirts fell straight, to flare
out at ground level, in what some chroniclers called the 'flower' or 'bell'
skirt (plates 1098, 1104). Hats are immense, trimmed with flowers and
feathers of a size never before approached (plates 1097, 1098)
Then, from year to year, the fullness disappears gradually; the gown
trailing on the ground disappears, first reaching to the ground (plate
1103) then only to the shoe (plate 1102) and constantly becoming narrower round the legs (plates 1107-8). This led to the hobble skirt (plate
1109) whose inconvenience resulted in the progressive shortening of the
skirt.
Elegance made concessions to practical considerations, and later showed
itself mainly in the refinement of details

1099 VUILLARD: *Vallotton and Missia*, 1899.
Collection A. P. Viénot, on loan to the Musée d'Art Moderne, Paris.
(Photo Flammarion)

406

1100 BONNARD: *The Box*, 1908. Collection Bernheim Jeune. (Photo Flammarion)

1101 B. BOUTET DE MONVEL: *Afternoon dress with hoop tunic*, 1914. Collection F. Boucher. (Photo Flammarion)

1102 Afternoon dress, *c.* 1910, in 'Lanvin blue' crêpe de chine trimmed with silver guipure, a LANVIN creation

1103 Afternoon dress of navy and white striped surah with silk fringe and lingerie flounces, created by DRECOLL *c.* 1905

1104 Evening gown of sunray pleated ivory satin inset with bands of guipure lace, designed by AMELIE, 1903.
Collection Union Française des Arts du Costume. (Photos Flammarion)

1105 Evening gown by DOUCET, worn by Mlle Geneviève Vix of the Opéra Comique, 1907–10. Collection Sirot. (Photo Reutlinger)

1106 Princess style afternoon gown, c. 1909. Collection Sirot. (Photo Félix)

1107 Dress by POIRET, worn by Mme Paul Poiret, 1913. Collection Union Française des Arts du Costume. (Photo Flammarion)

1108 Hobble skirted evening gown, with assymetrically draped beaded and embroidered tulle forming a train on the right, 1912–3. Collection Sirot. (Photo Henri Manuel)

To sum up: at a distance of half a century, French fashion of the pre-1914 period appears as a collection of individual creations, created by a synthesis of the personal tastes of the couturier and his customers. Attention was lavished on detail and finish, on the beauty of materials and ornamentation. The 'line' changed only slowly from one season to the next, and the newness of a gown showed as much in its material as in new lace and embroidery trimmings. The couturier conceived and created for each individual woman.

We can see today how far the First World War left a profound mark on the century, and at the same time corresponded to a new development in clothing: the process which gave the costume of today.

The 1914–18 war left women mistresses of their own fashions for four years by freeing them from their dependence on couturiers, only some of whom would reopen their doors after the Armistice. Thus they were liberated from their enslavement to the demands of couture at exactly the time when new needs spurred them to look for more convenience and comfort in clothing. The recruitment of women for war work in factories deprived the middle and upper classes of a proportion of their domestic staff, and nursing and charitable work was carried on by many Society and middle-class women, who also replaced their absent husbands and relatives in trade and even industry: all reasons for women to change their costume and, more important, to change their notions of what costume should express. From the economic point of view, decreased domestic production and currency restrictions contributed towards the same trend. Finally, the suspension of all Society life and the mourning for the war dead inhibited any preoccupation with personal elegance.

The new role of women in society was accompanied initially by the decline of the upper and middle classes. The 'middle class' influence that had so deeply marked the nineteenth century now became weaker; between the capitalist oligarchy and the proletariat, the middle classes were to be increasingly affected, all the more so because their savings were soon to be diminished by successive currency devaluations.

In all classes, though in different manners in each, costume reflected this transformation in women's life. Their role in society at large increased, even though 'Society life' became more limited. Women discarded elaborate, ornate toilettes for simpler styles. Unity of line was soon to be broken by the shortening of town skirts. This led to the adoption of silk stockings, symbols of luxury, and low-cut shoes in place of high boots. Lingerie, too, became simpler and more restrained. In milieux in which women had regular jobs, their clothes tended to become uniform.

Men's costume, which had been stabilized since the beginning of the nineteenth century, received only practical improvements of details. However, its cut became increasingly important, for it had to keep its perfection while its wearer led a more active life than formerly.

For men and women alike, costumes became fewer and less varied. New textiles, on the other hand, became more numerous, and the traditional textiles, which had had the market to themselves until 1914, soon met with redoubtable competition from artificial and synthetic fibres. Moreover, garment production became easier with the use of specialized machines, thought these did not produce the level of 'finish' of hand tailoring. A certain uniformity was from then on to replace the variety and refinement of former years.

The year 1914 remains the watershed after which changes in the way of life brought about changes in costume, and the new developments which have succeeded it make the Edwardian period more emphatically a bygone age with every day that passes.

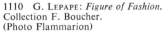

1109 Summer dress of striped muslin and guipure with satin kimono jacket trimmed with black lace, and sunshade matching the jacket, 1913–4. Collection Sirot. (Photo Félix)

1110 G. LEPAPE: *Figure of Fashion*. Collection F. Boucher. (Photo Flammarion)

1111 DRESA: *Fashion plate*, 1912–3. Collection F. Boucher. (Photo Flammarion)

Notes

1 Between 1807 and 1812 English cotton boll imports rose by 40 per cent.
2 The famous *Journal des Dames et des Modes* was first published in Paris in An VI (1796); in 1800 it was revived and directed by the famous La Mésangère, a former professor of philosophy and belles-lettres, who attracted the most famous draftsmen and engravers.
3 The *Société d'Encouragement pour l'Industrie Nationale* was founded in 1801.
4 A model weaving factory was established in Passy by the government to spread the use of the flying shuttle.
5 Cf. *Magasin des Modes nouvelles françaises et anglaises*, 1789.
6 According to Sergent-Marceau (1751–1847).
7 It is said that David still worked in his studio in velvet coat and lace cuffs.
8 In 1747 this word already meant, in a play, a stupid, scented little fop.
9 Villa Medici Archives. Rome.
10 *Journal des Dames et des Modes*, an 13, no. 21.
11 They were also made of tiny metal springs wrapped in cloth.
12 *Ibid. Journal des Dames et des Modes*.
13 It is very important, in order to determine the dates of a costume of this period, to know that the first version of the sewing machine dated from 1825; it was taken up in the United States in 1834, then improved by firms in both Europe and America, and finally perfected by Singer, who took out the patent in 1851.
14 The increase of about 40 per cent in world population between 1800 and 1840 indicates the size of the new market opened to clothing.
15 In 1838 Mlle Dosne, the daughter of a Paris exchange agent, received a trousseau worth 20,000 francs on her marriage with M. Thiers.
16 Chateaubriand: *Mémoires d'Outre-Tombe*, vol. iv, pp. 245–246.
17 Henri Bouchot: *La Mode sous la Restauration*, 1898.
18 Between 1795 and 1849 eleven national exhibitions were held in Paris, with increasing success.
19 Cf. Raymond Isay: *Panorama des Expositions Universelles*, Paris, 1937.
20 Cf. Ackerman; *Repository of Fine Arts*, March 1809.
21 Cf. Ackerman: *Arbiter elegantiarum*, wonders if 'any notion of harmony has entered into the head of a fashionable dressmaker.'
22 Cf. Taine: *Notes sur l'Angleterre*.
23 Cf. R. Schnerb: *Le XIXe siècle* (vol. VI, *Histoire Générale des civilisations*), p. 36.

1112 Chinchilla coat worn by Mlle de Marsy, 1908–10. Collection Union Française des Arts du Costume. (Photo H. Manuel)

24 Twenty-nine sheep were unloaded in Australia in 1788 and had multiplied to 20,000,000 in 1860; the first bales of wool were shipped to England in 1821.

25 The economist Adolphe Blanqui wrote: 'Everywhere we find the immortal flame of the French genius, which has the same significance for us as foundries and coal-mines for England.'

26 *La Mode*, 1814, *passim.*

27 The textile had been invented by Oudinot for collar-cravats for soldiers; it was also used to obtain the bouffant leg-of-mutton sleeves; one variety was the *crinolaine*, used in winter.

28 Less in vogue after 1851: 'Who wears crinolines today?' (*Les Modes Parisiennes*, 15 February 1851).

29 The best-known model, the *Thomson American cage-skirt*, was made in a factory at Saint-Denis; the front part, free of hoops, folded down like a drawbridge and the wearer stepped in through this opening.

30 *Les Modes Parisiennes*, 10 May 1851.

31 In 1869, when she went to the opening of the Suez Canal, she is said to have taken five hundred outfits, which she referred to as her '*diplomatic wardrobe.*'

32 It seems that in these rumours there was often confusion between the *crinoline petticoat*, which was still worn, but less frequently, and the *crinoline-cage*, which was widely worn.

33 Cf. the report from the *Illustrated London News* fashion correspondent in Paris (21 June 1866).

Bibliography

GENERAL

MAURICE DREYFOUS: *Les Arts et les artistes pendant la période révolutionnaire*, n.d.

RAYMONDE SÉE: *Le Costume de la Révolution à nos jours*, 1929.

V. HUSARSKI: *Le Style romantique*, 1931.

HENRIETTE VANIER: *La Mode et ses métiers: frivolités et luttes de classes, 1830–1870*, 1960.

RENÉ KONIG and PETER W. SCHUPISSER: *Die Mode in der Menschlichen Gesellschaft*, Zürich, 1958; Paris, 1960.

EDITH SAUNDERS: *The Age of Worth*, London, 1954.

J. P. WORTH: *A Century of Fashion*, Boston, 1928.

M. BRAUN-RONSDORF: *Modische Eleganz von 1789 bis 1929*. Munich, 1963.

COSTUME

FRÉDÉRIC MASSON: *Le Livre du Sacre de l'empereur Napoléon*, 1908.

HENRI BOUCHOT: *Le Luxe français: la Restauration*, 1898.

Exposition Universelle internationale de 1900: *Musée rétrospectif des classes 85 et 86 – Le Costume et ses accessoires – Notices, rapports.* n.d.

PAUL IRIBE: *Les Robes de Paul Poiret*, 1908.

GEORGES LEPAPE: *Les Choses de Paul Poiret*, 1911.

1113–4 Dress in black velvet, figured in gold and silver (design by MARIANO FORTUNY) with wide black silk chiffon sleeves, designed by PAUL POIRET, *c.* 1920. Collection Union Française des Arts du Costume and Centre de Documentation du Costume. (Photos Flammarion)

Chapter XII

Fashion: 1920–1964

New Conditions

A profound transformation took place in costume after the First World War. Initially it was linked to the various consequences of the war, but it continued and became more marked with further changes in people's way of life, with new attitudes of mind and new modes of production.

Whereas before 1914 economic evolution had produced a trend toward internationalism, the war forced the various countries towards economic centralization for their war efforts. State direction of industry not only accelerated centralization – which had already begun in any case – but also helped to transform the social scene. Women contributed to the industrial war effort, and after the war took on an ever widening range of work, gained civil and economic rights, and played a greater role outside their homes. Between 1920–25 costume adapted to suit this new fact of life. What had begun as mere acceptance of wartime conditions became the preferred style, one stripped of all 'Belle Epoque' reminiscences.

For a woman leading a freer life, trained to work, enjoying sports and dancing, fashion had to be functional. It ignored the waist and breasts, abbreviated the skirt, abolished the corset in favour of the suspender belt, introduced pyjamas for night wear and cropped the hair. This was the transformation awaiting men returning from the war to their wives and sweethearts; clear-cut, consciously young forms, surprising but no less attractive for that, foreshadowing the boyish look of the next decade.

This revolution was not immediately accepted by haute couture, which lost its hold over most of its customers. In a few years, houses such as Doucet, Poiret, Doeuillet and Drecoll were to close, while others reopened and new ones were founded. Among the names that brought back elegance to Paris, in the interwar years, there were a large number of women. This indeed was one of the characteristics of the period: beside Mme Gerber, Mme Paquin and Jeanne Lanvin, Madeleine Vionnet and Chanel were to occupy star positions for twenty years, later joined by Mme Grès, Mme Schiaparelli, Mlle Carven and a dozen others.

1920-1939

As often happens during periods of experiment and uncertainty, we see hints in haute couture of reminiscences of former periods – Renaissance, eighteenth century or Second Empire – which were all attempts to resist this new current. Private balls were given on historical themes, but fashion discarded the Oriental inspiration of lavish receptions of the pre-1914 period for more modern subjects: 'Proust', '1900' and 'Tomorrow's Fashion'. Efforts to put back the clock were resisted. Women preferred their short hair, and enjoyed modern dances and sports.

A characteristic of the period was the appearance of special clothes for tennis or golf, for motoring, for the beach, or for winter sports. These costumes were basically dictated by the need for freedom of movement, lightness and comfort, sometimes to the exclusion of elegance. Then, gradually, sports clothes were no longer left to special outfitters following classic models; fashion entered ready-made knitwear, bathing suits and travel clothes, introducing grace and imagination where it had seemed utilitarianism would prevail. Today there is hardly a great couturier who does not present models for the resorts, and not just for the beach or the casino, but for swimming and skiing as well.

1115 MATISSE: *The Three Sisters*, 1920. Private Collection. (Photo Flammarion)

1116 *Ensemble:* straight skirt and double-breasted jacket with wide revers by PARRY-PATOU. Drawing by V. LHUER, 1912. Collection Union Française des Arts du Costume and Centre de Documentation du Costume. (Photo Flammarion)

1117 VAN DONGEN: *Garden Party at the Poirets',* *c.* 1922. Collection Roudinesco. (Photo Galerie Charpentier)

1118 *Afternoon dress,* 1926. Collection Union Française des Arts du Costume and Centre de Documentation du Costume. (Photo Flammarion)

1115, 1117–9, 1121, 1126, 1130–31, 1133 The line of dresses remains straight; the waist drops imperceptibly and towards 1925 settles round the hips, with a very short skirt that transforms the silhouette.
The reduced area of dresses leaves little scope for complicated fashioning; beads and paillettes cover the material and form very stylized designs brought into fashion by decorative artists and popularized by the Exposition des Arts Décoratifs in 1925. The very low-cut back is a new style that was to be accentuated in later years, even when gowns became longer and fuller. The very simple hats fit closely to the head, with hair cut short in an Eton crop

1119 ETCHEVERRY: *Lady in Pink,* 1922. (Photo Archives Photographiques)

1120 SOULIE: *Short evening dress*, 1928.
Collection Union Française des Arts du Costume and
Centre de Documentation du Costume. (Photo Flammarion)

1121 Suit by CHANEL in large plaid checks, 1928.
Collection Union Française des Arts du Costume and
Centre de Documentation du Costume. (Photo Flammarion)

In 1925, skirts became shorter than ever, and the waist was low and unstressed. Women's clothes were characterized by a sort of tunic, open at the neck and arms and with the hem above the knees. Hair was straight under deep cloche hats pulled over the eyes, and shoes were very low-cut. Chanel, followed by Patou and Lelong created the most typical models of this 'garçonne' line, the boyishness accentuated by the white silk shirt and man's tie worn with the still-fashionable tailored suit. Women borrowed the straight coat and the waterproof from men's wardrobes. Lace was no longer popular, and embroidery became simpler; hat trimmings dwindled, and flowers and feathers disappeared. Evening gowns were short and open, covered with beads or paillettes; they were slipped on over the head, and were unshaped, without décolletage.

While in general costume ornament lost its richness, there were technical experiments in textiles; alongside a vogue for matt or shiny satin we see the appearance of new materials: kashas, metal-brocaded muslins and many more. Black and white were most popular, but the continued influence of the pre-war period is to be seen in the taste for rich stuffs and strong colours for evening dresses, and for handkerchiefs, foulards and scarves. Paul Poiret's creations kept their exuberance of bright, 'solid' (as Poiret said) colours, launched fifteen years before in the Ballets Russes of Diaghilev: Poiret gathered artists like Paul Iribe and Raoul Dufy around him and influenced them in this direction. At the same time, Worth was weaving fishes that Dunand scattered over lacquer screens; Mme Vionnet produced the heavy crêpes which suited her style and her efforts to clothe the body in textiles rather than construct a costume.

In lingerie, the nightgown came into vogue, along with silk for underclothes and stockings. The zip fastener appeared. The 'cloche' style, of high fashion, which remained austere even when Dunand decided to adorn it with his lacquers, and its drab felt progressively retreated before new styles which even used ostrich feathers.

Various countries contributed elements to fashion, providing new clothing or hairstyles and providing the Oriental names of dress materials. The fashionable dances – Black Bottom and Charleston – brought short skirts to the dance floor. The eccentric costumes worn by the inhabitants of Montparnasse popularized Texan shirts, Rumanian embroideries and Indian mocassins.

The *Exposition des Arts Décoratifs* held in Paris in 1925 was influential, providing the Parisian luxury industries with an opportunity for display and enhancing French prestige abroad. If it did not actually create a new costume style, it crystallized the visual setting of a period.

The advent of the music-hall and cinema set new fashions in dress, make-up and behaviour; there was Josephine Baker with her *Revue Nègre*, Greta Garbo, the Dolly Sisters with their widely-imitated short hair and long fringes.

The year 1927 marks the beginning of a very noticeable reaction, led by Mme Vionnet, Mme Lanvin and Mlle Chanel. Mme Vionnet was famous for the excellence of her technique of bias cutting and her success in moulding the gown to the body (plate 1134), Mme Lanvin for her use of embroidery on formal gowns, and Mme Chanel for her understated, easy clothes (plate 1121), using softly-clinging jersey, costume jewellery and a lot of black.

In their different ways these three achieved a return to femininity, often by means of Classically-inspired drapery and subdued colours in contrast with Poiret's bright ones. We see the reappearance in their collections of long evening dresses, at first still short in front but falling to the heels in a point behind – a prelude to the long dresses that appeared, with long hair, at the end of 1929. The Wall Street Crash then hit American customers and affected French couture and Parisian exports.

The 1931 Paris colonial exhibition revived the exotic appeal of the East, influencing colour and popularizing the simple shoulder line worn by the Balinese dancers.

At the same time there were influences from the cinema with Marlene Dietrich and Mae West, and from the theatre with the Pitöeff family, Dullin, Jouvet or Baty. Couturiers made Baty's costumes, but they no longer used the theatre to launch their creations, which were held in reserve for the seasonal collections.

1122   Three evening gowns by MADAME SCHIAPARELLI, 1938. Watercolour by CHRISTIAN BÉRARD for *Vogue*. (Courtesy *Vogue*. Photo Flammarion)

1123   Three-piece suit by NINA RICCI, 1938. Collection Union Française des Arts du Costume and Centre de Documentation du Costume (Photo Flammarion)

1124   Short evening dress of white tulle embroidered with opalescent beads and paillettes, *c*. 1925. Collection Union Française des Arts du Costume and Centre de Documentation du Costume. (Photo Flammarion)

1125   VAN DONGEN: *Madame Jasmy Alvin*, 1925. Paris, Musée d'Art Moderne. (Photo Flammarion)

1126   Shot taffeta dress designed by JEANNE LANVIN, 1920. Collection Lanvin. (Photo Flammarion)

1127 Two-piece dress and contrasting jacket by
MOLYNEUX, 1938–9. Drawing by KOUDINE.
Collection Union Française des Arts du Costume
and Centre de Documentation du Costume

1128 Winter coat with collar and
pockets of fox, 1938–9.
Drawing by KOUDINE

1129 Evening dress, 1938–9. Drawing by
KOUDINE

1130 VUILLARD: *The Comtesse de Polignac*, 1932.
Paris, Musée d'Art Moderne. (Photo Flammarion)

Among the number of new couture houses to make a name
for themselves in Paris in the years before 1939, Mme Schiaparelli was the first to produce bizarre models corresponding to
the extravagances of Surrealism. Balenciaga, who re-established
the waist and stressed curves, revived a feeling of richness, at
once classical and very modern.

1939-1947

The outbreak of the Second World War and the occupation
of France left Paris haute couture cut off for some years from
all contacts abroad. However, it carried on as best it might,
pitting its creative spirit against shortages of materials and
restrictions. This was the time of substitute materials, of shoes
with hinged wooden soles or cork wedges, but also of hats
whipped up from nothing (plate 1147), from a crumpled
newspaper, a ribbon or a wisp of tulle.

Then, after the Liberation, as had happened twenty-five
years before, the new post-war period saw the gradual revival
of the clothing industries and a renaissance of elegance. International contacts were re-established, and proved more important than before; fashion houses everywhere were searching
for models to satisfy a still hesitant and new clientèle. As between the wars, women's way of life was constantly changing,
and the couturier was obliged to strike a balance between
elegance and practicality for day dress, reserving luxury for
evening gowns.

After 1944 the development of 'Boutiques' showed the
efforts made by couturiers to put their creations within reach
of a wider public.

The *Théâtre de la Mode*, presented in 1945 in the Musée des
Arts Décoratifs, stimulated women's desire for beautiful clothes
and allowed the couturiers to show their new models, first in
Paris, then in the United States.

Besides wearing the short, full cocktail dresses which could be made low-cut simply by taking off a short bolero, women 'dressed' once again for important Society gatherings, for balls and the theatre.

It was only a matter of a few years before French prestige in fashion had recovered. Skirts remained straight and shoulders wide, as before the war, until the surprise of the 'New Look' lauched by Christian Dior in 1947. The skirt was lengthened and stiffened with lining, the silhouette once again became waisted and feminine. We can only marvel at the subsequent range of creations by Dior. During his ten years at the head of his house, he kept a unity in costume through his handling of accessories, and this despite the vast yardages and unlimited embroideries which his enormous capital backing put at his disposal.

In general, the trend was towards a 'young' line, and another couturier, Jacques Fath, who had exceptional organizing ability and profound feeling for modern woman, was to develop this further.

COUTURE AND INDUSTRY

During the 1939 period the clothing industry was reorganized on a new basis, in accordance with the rise of new techniques.

Couture, depending on craftsmanship, was dominated by hand tailoring and the client's individual measurements. The clothing industry, which was mechanized, had already existed for years as 'ready-to-wear' and 'mass-production couture'.

Besides the purveyors of Haute Couture (*Couture-Création*) and Haute Mode, the great lingerie houses and the members of *Corset-Création*, for men there were the *Maîtres-Tailleurs* (master-tailors), and *Chemisiers-Créateurs* (creative shirt-makers). The shoemakers worked for both men's and women's fashion.

The couturier (who works in the field of women's fashions) produces original models, then a fairly limited number of copies, some for his exclusive clientèle, and some for clothing manufacturers to be copied in quantity. The handling of silks and soft stuffs (*flou*) and woollens and heavy stuffs (*tailleur*) is divided between employees who specialize in the appropriate techniques.

When preparing a model, the couturier conceives the line and elaborates it with the help of a *modéliste* and a designer, the former translating the couturier's sketch into a rough model, and the latter making the final drawings. The models which result are presented in the seasonal collections.

Alongside the great couture houses, the craftsmanly side is represented by numerous houses which work along the same lines of hand execution and fitting, but with less lavish overheads and materials. The models are evolved in consultation with the clients, and fashion trends are followed through fashion magazines and specialist publications. This type of dressmaking work lays most stress on the customer's taste and personality, and she can often provide her own materials. We find the same type of organization in *Mode-Création* (creative millinery).

Ready-to-wear, of course, is produced to standard measurements and by machine. Particularly in women's clothing, however, finishing may be done by hand.

The menswear industry is divided into bespoke tailoring and ready-to-wear in standardized sizes. Its different branches correspond to the materials used: woollen cloth, linen or waterproof. Some firms also specialize in sports clothes or uniforms.

1125, 1127–9, 1134 The evening dress became longer than before. Day dress, remaining short, kept a straight line accentuated by the squareness of the shoulders but relieved by details (plate 1128) or by fanciful colour contrast (plate 1127)

THE 'NEW LOOK'
1131 A skirt both longer and fuller than those of war-time fashions, a tight-waisted jacket and wide hat gave the feminine silhouette a softness and elegance that had been lost during the war years

1132 The elegance of the evening gown, returning with more prosperous times, contrasts pleasingly with the informality of day dress

1131 CHRISTIAN DIOR'S 'New Look', 1947.
(Photo Collection Union Française des Arts du Costume)

1132 Dress by JACQUES FATH, of white silk chiffon, 1956.
Collection Union Française des Arts du Costume

In the women's clothing industry, the division is in terms of 'quality'. 'Mass-produced couture' aims at reconciling industrial techniques with the artistic creation associated with Haute Couture; it initiates women's 'ready-to-wear' styles by preparing special models which are then mass-produced.

Unfortunately for elegance, since the war we have been witnessing the virtual disappearance of the hat. The reasons are probably the general trend towards a relaxed, sporting look, the wish of working women (and nowadays most young women at least are engaged in some kind of occupation) to be unburdened by headgear, and lastly, the economic factor, for a hat can be very expensive in terms of its wearing life.

Hairstyles have to a large extent usurped the place of hats in fashion, some of them, like the now obsolete 'bee-hive', strangely elaborate. Within recent years, however, there has been a swing to simplicity in line with the general tendency of fashion to revert to the styles of the mid-twenties.

Women's lingerie has been reduced to a few garments generally made of nylon, shadows of the undergarments that were the pride of our grandmothers. We can only mourn the passing of the poetry of the laces and embroidery of the last century, which machine sewing can never equal.

DRESS MATERIALS

The raw materials of costume have been increasingly influential over the last twenty-five years because of the appearance of synthetic textile fibres, which compete with traditional materials. However, the rapid spread of synthetic fibres has not brought, as was predicted, an 'unparalleled revolution' in the textile industry and costume.

We have already seen similar phenomena; the development of silk from the twelfth century on and, most of all, cotton in the nineteenth century; this continued with such impetus that in 1951 world cotton production had almost trebled since 1890. Artificial textiles, for which we have exact figures for the last twenty-five years, have increased more than fourfold. During the same period, wool production has increased by half.

1133 Short evening dress of green shaded tulle embroidered with silk flower motifs, designed by MADELEINE VIONNET, 1929–30. Collection Union Française des Arts du Costume. (Photo Flammarion)

1134 Long evening dress of oatmeal silk chiffon; bodice covered with shaded patches and sewn with steel beads, by MADELEINE VIONNET, 1931–2. Collection Union Française des Arts du Costume. (Photo Flammarion)

1135 Lace-covered high-heeled shoes, by ROGER VIVIER, Paris. 1952–3. (Photo A. Ostier)

1136 High-heeled satin shoe with harlequin embroidery, by ROGER VIVIER, Paris, 1958. (Photo A. Ostier)

1137 Cross-strapped shoe in panama, by ROGER VIVIER, Paris, 1958. (Photo A. Ostier)

1139 Shoe with copper and topaz embroideries on tulle, by ROGER VIVIER, Paris, 1961–2. (Photo A. Ostier)

1138 Straw-coloured shoe with organza bow, stiletto heel, by ROGER VIVIER, Paris, 1961–2 (Photo A. Ostier)

At present cotton represents 55 per cent of world fibre production, wool 9 per cent and artificial and synthetic fibres 15 per cent; natural textiles are produced in the least economically developed countries, artificial and synthetic fibres coming from the highly industrialized countries.

In costume textiles, there have been interesting innovations: cloth woven with metal threads became light and flexible. Printed stuffs have been growing in popularity ever since 1925. In 1930 we first note the appearance of mixed artificial fibres of differing elasticity in *'peau d'ange'*, and in 1932 mixtures of albene and wool, under the names *flamenga* and *lorganza*.

For the last twenty years, each year has brought new discoveries in textile materials, named for their composition as well as for publicity purposes.

1947-1964

Not even the most vigilant historian can follow every twist of fashion. With the increasingly rapid rhythm of change, it is possible only to sum up the general lines of a development over the last fifteen years, which seem to be linked to twentieth-century speed and the shrinking of distances.

An accurate assessment of fashion over this period of time requires the kind of sifting-out process that only hindsight can bring.

Those looking back on this period will probably be struck on the one hand by the astonishing variety of forms and materials, and on the other by the swift ascendancy of forces that had begun to emerge as far back as 1940: the movies and their dazzling stars, automobiles, sports, and the growing influence of a younger generation intent on "dressing its age." The result has been a tendency to "dress down" in a casual, even careless way, as seen in loose-fitting pullovers, blue jeans, and those clinging slacks favored by girls and middle-aged women alike.

COSTUME AND TRENDS IN MODERN ART

Has there been any detectable correlation these past few years between certain trends in art and the evolution of costume, particularly in France, still the trendsetter in fashion worldwide?

As we consider the range of colors various schools of modern painting have favored over the past century, can we legitimately postulate that painters have been a contributing factor in women's clothing? Or is it the other way around? Weren't those painters whose palettes were most attuned to the women of their day really the ones who best expressed the interaction between women and what they wear? Once again, we are too close to these issues to put them in proper perspective. Only now, for example, are we in a position to speculate about the influence of Gauguin at the turn of the century and whether his incredibly intense violets, crimsons, cobalts, and emerald greens had as much of an impact on the emergence of new colors in costume as did the Ballets Russes. Wasn't the "Poiret look" the reflection of a decorative artist steeped more in the sumptuous, exuberant hues of exoticism than in the sprightly palette of Impressionism?

If indeed there is a carry-over from current trends in painting, we see it far less in the color of clothing than in its design, balance, and line. True, colors nowadays are considerably brighter than they were twenty-five years ago, especially in sportswear and outdoor wear (knits, raincoats, overcoats, felt hats, children's apparel). However, with a few exceptions, subdued and even dark colors are still the rule for dresses, tailored suits, and evening clothes. Moreover, these basics of indoor and formal attire are, as they have always been, still subject to every woman's overriding concern: that her clothes match her physical type as closely as possible. It is highly unlikely that, especially when it comes to color, a woman (with her couturier) would not bother to consider what suits her and what does not.

Over the last fifty years, clothing has not manifested the same dramatic shifts that have characterized the styles of painting—from objective and concrete to Fauvist and Cubist to Sur-

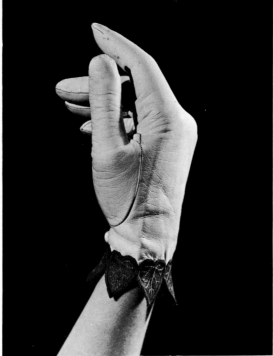

1140 Embroidered glove by HERMÈS, Paris, 1925–40. (Photo Flammarion)

1141 Glove by HERMÈS, Paris, 1925–40. (Photo Flammarion)

1142 Long embroidered glove by HERMÈS, Paris, 1925–40. (Photo Flammarion)

realist and abstract. Unlike the painter, the couturier cannot escape the imperative of working, so to speak, in the round; yet sculpture, independent though it was from painting, did not determine the course of fashion, either.

But one can see over the last twenty years the emergence of certain parallels between women's clothing and movements in painting. After one has untangled the conflicting forces at work in painting and reduced the pivotal ones to their essence, there can be no denying the dominance of a trend that not only pits the intellectual against the sensual, but gives preference to the former, a trend that has by no means repudiated fundamental, timeless forms, but feels free to indulge in bold stylization and provocative asymmetry.

Today's fashion is deeply indebted to this prevailing current for comparable shifts in form and line that are moving feminine attire a long way from the "femininity" of yesteryear. More and more we sense an accommodation to interior design and its growing emphasis on spare, geometrically oriented compositions. Is today's couturier joining the ranks of those for whom truth lies solely in line? Is fashion on the verge of becoming, like modern art, "an art of intolerance and fanaticism," a doctrinaire art that triggers one response after another, resulting in a host of independent creations?

Of course, it is difficult to assess the relative importance of each and every factor now shaping new fashions. Masculinity, materialism in daily life, and abstractionist tendencies in art all play a part; the extent to which each influences the others is still not clear. It is safe to say, however, that the evolution of costume today seems far more complicated than in the past because of the often antagonistic forces at work within it. Stylized designs (modified by the personal taste of individual women) have made their presence felt, but on the whole fashion pays more homage to abstraction in word than in deed. Now more than ever, isn't the evening dress, with its full, sumptuous, graceful, decorative look aimed at pleasing, at odds with a line that is often contrived, arbitrary, and so deliberately spare as to become imperceptible?

Posterity, probably better than we, will see this as symptomatic of the uncertainty of our times, but also of that quest for balance that is the stuff of art.

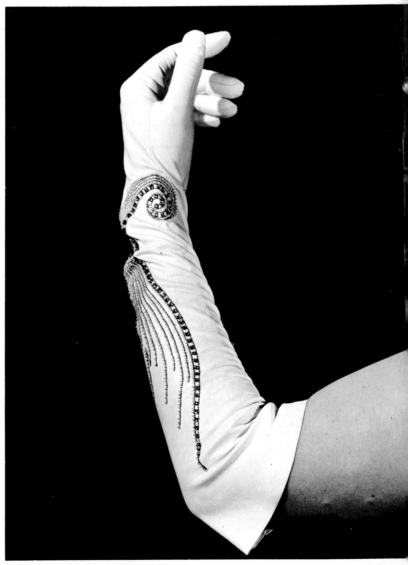

1143 Long embroidered glove by HERMÈS, Paris, 1925–40. (Photo A. Ostier)

1144 'Le Jeu des omnibus et des Dames blanches'. The first scarf produced by HERMÈS, 1935. (Photo Flammarion)

1135–45 The taste for accessories complementing dresses spread, and jewellers worked with fashion designers to create harmonious ensembles

1145 Brooches: left, gilded leaves, flowers in emeralds and pearls; right, oval leaf in sapphire and brilliants. Both by F. WINTER, 1960. (Photo Flammarion)

1146 Hats, 1938–59. FROM LEFT TO RIGHT: toque in red grosgrain (ROSE VALOIS, 1950); cloche in white paillasson (JEAN BARTHET, 1959); head-hugging toque in buff straw (JANETTE, 1958); small pillbox hat in black tulle (ALBOUY, 1938)

Bibliography

P. P. WORTH: *A Century of Fashion*, Boston, 1928.
PAUL POIRET: *En habillant l'époque*, 1930.
NICOLE VEDRES: *Un Siècle d'élégance*, Paris, 1948.
MARCEL ROCHAS: *Vingt-cinq ans d'élégance à Paris*, 1951.
JAMES LAVER: *Taste and Fashion*, London, 1945.
EDITH SAUNDERS: *The Age of Worth*, London, 1954.
CECIL BEATON: *The Glass of Fashion*, London, 1954.
CHRISTIAN DIOR: *Christian Dior et moi*, Paris, 1956.
CÉLIA BERTIN: *Paris à la Mode*, London, 1956.
RENÉ KONIG and PETER W. SCHUPISSER: *Die Mode in der Menschlichen Gesellschaft*, Zürich, 1958; Paris, 1960.
J. PINSET and YVONNE DESLANDRES: *Histoire des soins de beauté*, Paris (*Que-sais-je?*), 1960.
FRITHJOF VAN THIENEN: *Huit siècles de costumes*. Verviers, 1961.
ANNIE LATOUR: *Les Magiciens de la mode*, Paris, 1961.
LUÇIEN FRANÇOIS: *Comment un nom devient une griffe*, Paris, 1961.
Nouvelle encyclopédie, vol XIV, Paris, 1955. Ch. II: JEAN MONSEMPES: 'Les Industries de l'habillement'; Ch. III: PAUL CALDAGUES and DANIEL GORIN: *L'Habillement et la vie sociale*.'

Collection Union Française des Arts du Costume and Centre de Documentation du Costume. (Photo Flammarion)

1147 Hat of wood-shavings, by AGNÈS, 1941. Collection Union Française des Arts du Costume. (Photo Flammarion)

1148 Bead embroidery decorations for dresses and evening bag, by RÉBÉ, 1960–62. (Photo Flammarion)

1149 1950–60: Brooch of grey beads and brilliants. Necklace of turquoises and frosted brilliants. Collar necklace in clear and burnt topazes. All by F. WINTER. (Photo Flammarion)

1150 'Arlequins', bead embroidery by RÉBÉ, 1962. (Photo Flammarion)

Chapter XIII

Fashion: 1960–1983

The New Social Conditions

The profound transformation of the fashion world that became apparent in the 1960s had begun at the end of World War II, but not until the Western world had been reconstructed did fashion's revolution flourish. "At the start of the seventh decade of this century," writes Bruno du Roselle, "it was impossible to imagine the topsy-turvy era to come, an era of unparalleled change in the history of fashion."

1151 Cape and minidress in brown Shetland wool with sulfur-yellow grosgrain trim, CATHERINE CHAILLET for BENJAMIN DAVY, 1967. (Photo IWS)

1152 Couple in pants. Drawing by PIERRE SIMON, 1980.

The high birthrate between 1945 and 1965 almost doubled the prewar number of children throughout the world. By 1965, when five to ten percent of the world population was under twenty years old, a new clientele of young people had emerged whose financial resources were by and large superior to those of their parents at the same age. The young were staying in school longer, and the number of students with access to free education had greatly increased. For the first time, "the kids," as they were called with a hint of apprehension, were being considered a separate group, with their own activities, tastes, and modes of dress. Until then, fashion had been designed for adults; now, the young were demanding a wardrobe of their own to suit their style of life.

The youth movement was born in the United States, a country of abundance where children had not known the miseries of the war years. They scorned the consumer society in which they were submerged and showed their disgust with bourgeois comforts by adopting the appearance of poorer classes: blue jeans, shirts without ties, and leather jackets. This became the costume worn by American college students of both sexes, practically the combat uniform of the "beat generation."

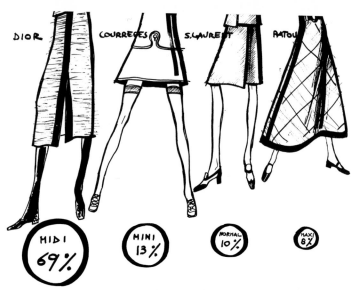

1153   Various dress lengths worn in 1969. Sketch from the International Wool Secretariat.

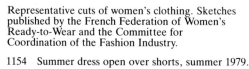

Representative cuts of women's clothing. Sketches published by the French Federation of Women's Ready-to-Wear and the Committee for Coordination of the Fashion Industry.

1154   Summer dress open over shorts, summer 1979.

1155   Broad-shouldered coat over narrow skirt, winter 1981.

1156   Fitted suit with slit skirt, winter 1981.

1157   Dress and vest worn over pants, summer 1979.

During the same period, women began to claim their social and sexual emancipation. As they took a greater part in exercising their role in society, active young women insisted on controlling their own bodies, no longer submitting to the whims of men. Women began to wear pants at all hours of the day. Trying to keep current in fashion, women of all ages discovered, with some surprise, the comfort and convenience of pants; this garment not only suited all temperaments but soon lost its rebellious connotations. An ironic consequence of this trend, seemingly irreversible today, was that it triggered a renewal in men's wear, a realm of fashion that had been stagnant for over a century.

The disappearance of traditional costumes in remote and poor nations increased with the development of Western-style clothes manufacturing all over the globe. Ancient dress was replaced by the standardized, inexpensive clothes worn throughout the world. The clothing industry enjoyed a new field of expansion.

But at the same time, traditional costumes, many of which had never been seen outside their native regions, became sought after and adopted in the West, initially by the young, who wanted to demonstrate their solidarity with cultures uncontaminated by mass industry. The most ardent proponents of such folk costumes were the hippies, who first appeared

In Europe young people dressed like beatniks less to antagonize society than to show an alliance with their age group. They rode motorcycles and covered their jackets and helmets with both innocent and provocative decorations. A little later, T-shirts displayed pictures of favorite celebrities or emblems of the latest craze. This way of dressing, at first limited to a select few, spread to every social class. The effect was clear in the youth demonstrations of 1968, when it was impossible to determine the social origins of the participants, so similar was their dress.

1158 Pink-and-white checked dress of Vichy linen, trimmed in English lace, designed by JACQUES ESTEREL for Brigitte Bardot, on the occasion of her 1958 marriage to Jacques Charrier. UFAC Collection. (Photo J. Davies)

around 1966 in the United States. Pacifists and amateur musicians, these adolescents rejected their origins, expressing their rebellion by wearing a collection of assorted clothing from different periods and countries. They wore long, flowing hair as well, another throwback to an earlier century.

The rejection of sexual taboos was conveyed by the hippies' refusal to wear bras, considered an artifice akin to Grandmother's corset. Women wore see-through garments and sported not bikinis (a term popularized by the Reard Company to describe the effect of the tiny two-piece bathing suit as analogous to that of the atom bomb tested on Bikini Island), but panties alone; this was picturesquely called a "monokini."

These types of clothes became known everywhere, thanks to the prodigious development of the communications industry. Magazines with abundant color photographs, movies, and, above all, television helped disseminate the latest looks, often worn by the most important celebrities. Fashion ceased to be an inaccessible domain reserved for the rich elite. And because the standard of living for most people had become higher, almost everyone could afford to buy clothes in greater quantity.

Mass production meant that clothing of all kinds could be purchased at moderate prices. Retail costs were greatly diminished by the development of more and more sophisticated factory machinery. At the same time, patterns began to be designed especially for industrial production; these became known as "ready-to-wear" designs. Ready-to-wear fashion caught on quickly, as it ceased to represent the bland conformity usually associated with mass-produced wares. Indeed, ready-to-wear collections were now being made by a new breed of creators—the designers.

Haute couture, a prisoner of its special image, could not take advantage of this new mass clientele. To maintain its status, haute couture would continue to serve a small international group of women whose lives were in the public eye. In 1958, however, the famous Brigitte Bardot wore a pink-and-white checked dress of Vichy linen trimmed in lace, designed by Jacques Esterel; he went on to sell the same dress by the millions as a ready-to-wear design. Haute couture was no longer the sole source of women's fashion in the Western world, a role it had played for over a century. Yet it was André Courrèges, a member of the small and envied group of haute couturiers, who in 1965 set off the miniskirt revolution.

1159 Red wool minidress trimmed in white, COURRÈGES, 1967. (Photo Miralda—SCOOP)

1160 White wool ribbed knit bodysuits, COURRÈGES, winter 1969. UFAC Collection. (Photo Gunnar Larsen)

1161 White wool minidress, navy blue-and-white striped wool jacket, white gloves and boots, COURRÈGES, summer 1965. UFAC Collection. (Photo Courrèges)

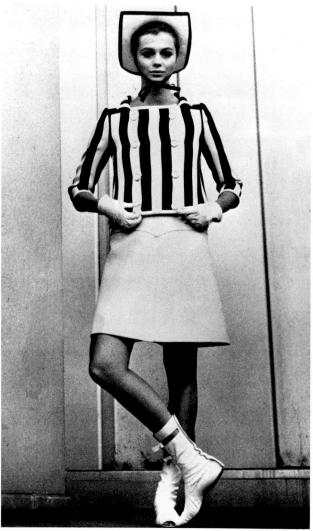

The Designers

The first designers appeared on the scene around 1960, encouraged by the debuts of design houses such as Mafia and Promostyl. They made their mark by offering models that could be produced in large numbers to sell at ready-to-wear prices. Their designs were destined for the young clientele who were refusing the sophisticated look of haute-couture fashion. Whether they owned their own businesses or worked for other companies on one or more collections, these designers began the unprecedented practice of signing their creations. Notable pioneers included Daniel Hechter, whose "Babette" line was inspired by Brigitte Bardot in the film *Babette s'en va-t'en guerre;* Jean Cacharel, who revived the market for blouses by using madras fabric; and Michèle Rozier, who created a sportswear line under the V. of V. label. Also part of this first generation were Emmanuelle Khanh, Gérard Pipart, and Christiane Bailly.

While the new designers' names started to become familiar, haute-couture houses began to launch their own ready-to-wear lines, with clothes of high quality and of a style close to those of couture collections, but not made to order. Pierre Cardin, Saint Laurent, and Saint Laurent-Rive Gauche were the first to follow this road, which had in fact already been paved by the prewar couturier Lucien Lelong. Courrèges went so far as to create three separate parallel collections: Prototype, as haute couture; Hyperbole, as top-of-the-line ready-to-wear; and Couture Future, as inexpensive ready-to-wear. All three lines were established with the same care and vigor used for the couture collections since, contrary to popular belief, a garment that will be sold by the thousands requires no less fine-tuning than a unique made-to-order one.

The gap between the diverse branches of the fashion industry began to close, and the most prominent designers began to group together, at least partly to attain the prestige that accompanied the creations of haute couture. With this in mind, an association called Mode et Création was founded in 1973, in the wake of the founding of the Paris fashion industry's trade union. Mode et Création brought the designers in vogue together with the fashion houses that carried ready-to-wear lines. Today the members of this group of internationally acclaimed designers come together to present their collections for each season. Journalists and buyers from around the world flock to see these prestigious fashion shows. In the same tents, erected in public places in Paris, the Federation of Women's Ready-to-Wear presents its lines. For the last few seasons, with the Ministry of Culture's permission, the presentations have been held in tents in the halls of the Louvre.

The leaders of the fashion industry today are a small group of designers from around the globe who show their collections in Paris, New York, Milan, and Tokyo and sell them, either

1162 "Arthur" flannel coatdress in a pattern of yellow and white rectangles, DANIEL HECHTER, spring 1966.

directly or through licensed distributors, in any country where they are appreciated.

With designers showing two new collections per year, the rhythm of change in fashion has never been so rapid. Today, however, unlike in the past, a "new" style will not necessarily devalue an old one. The offerings of designers are so varied that they are bound to please a diverse public. The most seemingly divergent styles cohabit peacefully.

The choice of clothes depends essentially on the image one wishes to project. In these times of liberalism in life style and morals, people can opt for the "look" that will best express their personalities.

In surveying the evolution of fashion between 1960 and 1980, one's first impression is of impoverishment. Formal dress became less and less common; black suits worn with starched white shirts were rarely seen except at important ceremonies. Women's hats, despite designers' efforts to keep them in fashion, were relegated to weddings and solemn functions. Gloves worn for anything but sports and cold weather all but disappeared. Ties became the symbol of constraining office wear and were increasingly abandoned in leisure hours. Men's hats gave way to berets, caps, and motorcycle helmets.

In terms of the overall line of clothes, the tight-fitting curvaceous silhouette disappeared in the sixties. Although it failed to catch on, the "bag dress" introduced by couturiers in 1959 did serve to accustom the eye to clothes that hung loosely on the body. Balenciaga was undoubtedly the initiator of this relaxed spirit in fashion.

1163 Black silk muslin evening dress in a large red-and-purple floral print, with long flared sleeves bordered in multicolored ostrich-feather fringe, PIERRE BALMAIN, 1979. (Photo Flammarion)

1164 Black Moroccan crêpe day dress in a floral print, with short sleeves, BALENCIAGA, 1964; black straw hat by JEAN BARTHER. (Photo Flammarion)

1165 Black pleated wool muslin skirt in a floral print, with fitted shirt, CACHAREL, summer 1973. (Photo IWS)

THE RISE OF PANTS FOR WOMEN

The newest element in the fashion of the day was the appearance of pants in most women's wardrobes. Western society alone viewed pants as specifically masculine; in the Far East, pants had long been worn by women and men. The practical aspect of pants had been ignored in the Western world, so strong was their association with male authority. But pants quickly caught on, and women began to wear them at all hours of the day. They were worn with tailored or casual jackets, shawls, or tunics. Pant legs could be wide, narrow, gathered below the knee like knickers or above the ankle like harem pants. Around 1969, pants cut at mid-thigh—shorts for city wear—were seen for the first time. More and more pants for women were being manufactured and sold. Numerous studies have shown that the surge in pantswear for women corresponded to the more or less conscious desire on the part of most women to affirm their equality with men by dressing like them. The popularity of pants greatly diminished that of traditional dresses. Even the minidress, which made quite a splash, lasted only for a short time.

The motto of our era could be "anything goes," in every facet of contemporary culture, including fashion. Yet designers continue to give their creations an unmistakable style; it is also a mark of our times that so many talented people have been given the chance to express themselves.

1965-1970

The name André Courrèges already holds historical importance in the evolution of fashion. Like Paul Poiret at the turn of the century, Courrèges knew how to dress women of the time in clothes that were adapted to their diverse aspirations, without reference to the past, clothes in which modern women could feel at ease in their active lives. For the now famous collection of 1965, he designed clothes with an extremely refined cut; he gave his dresses, which were structured without darts and hemmed a hand's length above the knee (a length that had not been seen since prehistoric days), an extraordinary form. Short white socks tucked into little square-toed boots, short white gloves, and plastic glasses completed Courrèges' image of the young, active, and uncomplicated woman. In the same collection he presented tight-legged hip-hugger pants to be worn under tunics or square-cut boleros for day or evening. Stitching was sparse and doubled to form piping. Materials included fabrics in striking colors or white, detailed in navy grosgrain. For evening wear the same models were rendered in organdy or woven ribbon. These styles, created in the image of the rising generation of youth, were displayed in a spectacular style and were met with immediate success.

THE MINISKIRT

Miniskirts were first adopted in England, coming out of London's Carnaby Street boutiques, and aroused an enthusiasm that exaggerated their effect. No longer were dresses tailored for a certain length, and for that length only. Instead, any and all dress cuts were adapted to a hem that fell just below the buttocks. At the same time came the appearance of bodysuits, one-piece garments that combined top and tights and were previously worn only by dancers. Often in brightly colored opaques, they were worn with coordinating overgarments. The garter belt became no more than an erotic accessory.

Boots at this time were the rage. They were made in all colors, with or without heels, short or high, and sometimes adorned with a flap that reached above the knee to the hemline of a skirt. Boots have remained in vogue to this day. Wooden-soled clogs were also popular, with large, often wedged heels.

The innovative styles of Courrèges inspired the haute-couture world. Each house now designed its own short dress: Balenciaga (where Courrèges learned his craft) offered a savvy cut, Balmain a special wrapped effect, and Saint Laurent a geometric patterning borrowed from the painter Mondrian. Pierre Cardin's line was the most original. In 1967, he made flared coats and surcoat dresses with geometric cutouts, complemented by space helmets in honor of the first man to walk on the moon. Ready-to-wear manufacturers were flourishing, taking advantage of the general interest in design for a young public, who were the most likely to change their wardrobes according to the latest looks.

1166 Wool minidress in "Mondrian" design, SAINT LAURENT, 1965. (Photo Peter Knapp—SCOOP)

Pants styles for women:

1167 Pantsuit with vest, SAINT LAURENT, 1967. (Photo IWS)

1168 Unisex uniforms for the French team at the Olympic games in Grenoble: dark blue tight stretch pants, white tunic with two-toned blue trim, RUBEN TORRES, 1968. (Photo Prouvost Masurel)

1169 Knickers jumpsuit in beige poplin, SAINT LAURENT-RIVE GAUCHE, spring–summer 1971. (Photo Giancarlo Botti—Saint Laurent)

1170 "Tania" trousers with long tunic, CHARLES MAUDRET, winter 1966.

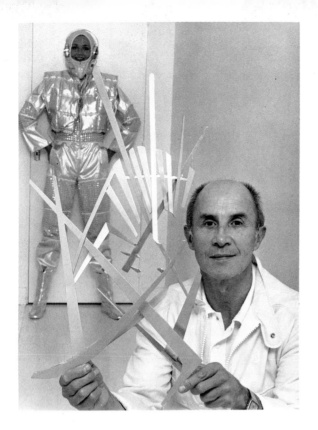

liant idea to design a stable wardrobe of constants that would survive the seasonal caprices of the fashion world. Chanel's tailored suits were made of Scotch tweed, of white or navy wool, or of jersey or shantung, depending on whether they were for evening or day wear. Jackets were mostly short and with cinched waists, ornamented with pockets in varying numbers, closed with gold buttons, and discreetly bordered in two-toned piping or braiding. The designer styled shirts of the same fabric as her jacket linings. Her skirts, narrow or wide, were always cut to cover the knee and were easy to walk in. Worn with playful jewelry, most often gold chains, the new Chanel look became, from 1960 onward, a staple in many women's wardrobes since it gave to all women who wore it the confidence that their clothes would not go out of style the next season. Miss Chanel was not concerned that her clothes were copied to sell at lower prices. She knew that her workroom alone produced perfectly designed and cut Chanel fashions. Women throughout the world donned the eternal Chanel look.

The future of pants, in all their forms, was assured. In 1966, ready-to-wear designers such as Charles Maudret and couturiers such as Saint Laurent introduced the pantsuit. Modeled after jumpsuits, these outfits consisted of a tailored jacket with lapels, worn over a shirt and vest, and straight slacks. At the 1968 Winter Olympics, the French team wore a unisex uniform of pants and a two-toned tunic designed by Ruben Torres. Although the trousers really only suited very thin women, the tunics, cut above or below the thighs, allowed all women to wear them.

To reconcile two extremes, designers created short pants cut to the length of a minidress, mid-thigh or higher. These shorts looked spectacular beneath the floor-length "maxi"-coats that came into vogue in 1969. Jacqueline Jacobson of Dorothée Bis was among the pioneers of this new look. Meanwhile, Pierre Cardin cut slits up the front of his ankle-length flared skirts that hung over very short shorts.

Haute-couture houses were undergoing numerous changes. Balenciaga closed in 1968; Marc Bohan became responsible for the collections of Dior, Jules-François Crahay for those of Lanvin, and Gérard Pipart for those of Nina Ricci. New houses appeared as well, including those of Louis Féraud, Emmanuel Ungaro, and Jean-Louis Scherrer. Courrèges continued to be prolific, creating more and more innovative styles. He considers his most futuristic design to be a white wool bodysuit worn with a short skirt or a little apron. His evening dresses were characterized by clean lines, luxurious materials, and bold details. It is impossible to forget his multicolored silk wigs, created by Alexandre, his both fanciful and more conservative outfits, and his sheer pullovers. In 1981, at an international competition in Los Angeles, Courrèges' adventurous image of women in the year 2000 was triumphant. The prize-winning design was a shiny suit meant for the future city of the sun envisioned by Courrèges, who was becoming increasingly interested in the environment.

Against the modernist current stood Miss Chanel, who had closed her house in 1939. This pioneer of fashion for the liberated women of the twenties returned to the design world in 1954. After a few uncertain seasons, she came up with the bril-

1171 ANDRÉ COURRÈGES in front of his model of the fashion of the future. This outfit in metallic jersey and spangled muslin, giving concrete form to his vision of tomorrow's woman, won the 1981 gold medal for fashion design. (Photo Courrèges)

1172 White wool suit, lined and trimmed in navy blue, CHANEL, 1967. (Photo Chanel)

The Present Structure of the Fashion Industry

The manufacture and sale of clothes figure today as one of the world's most important industries. The structure of the fashion industry has changed as it has expanded and diversified.

Little has changed, though, with regards to the creative aspects of fashion design. The head of a collection is surrounded by a team of designers and dressmakers. He is responsible for choosing the season's line and fabrics and selecting which models will be made on the premises in his workroom. Finally, he chooses the establishment's models, on whom the collection will be presented to the public.

There are two collections a year, one for the spring–summer season, which is shown to buyers and the press in late January, and one for the winter, which is shown in late July. Each collection includes between fifty—the required minimum—and a hundred and fifty pieces. Sales of garments made to order for a specific client, with at least two fittings, are now very rare. Instead, the industry survives by selling working patterns that can be reproduced in simpler versions and less expensive materials by manufacturers. The sale of designer accessories has also been increasing.

The process of industrial manufacturing is a good deal more complex than that of design; in many cases the design house plays a big part. The industry's companies vary: some are private, some financed by professional federations or sectors of the textile industry. These companies serve as liaisons between the various elements of production, including choosing colors and materials, producing a design catalogue, assembling collections meant for firms without a design team of their own, and organizing promotional publicity aimed at department stores and, above all, the mail-order houses that handle a vast amount of the clothing market. If the more daring creations of the great designers prove unacceptable to the general public, they will often consent to design a more modest collection that will sell more widely. The prestige of the label remains, even with clothes that sell for much less than those in the high-fashion line.

The schedule for production is much longer than that for design, which remains an essentially artisanal craft. Colors and fabrics are fixed, in general, two years before the sale of a collection. Materials are chosen between February and April, a line is chosen in May, and then a small number of samples are

1173 Minidress of hammered-aluminum plates with long sleeves tapered into bracelets at the wrist, PACO RABANNE, 1967 UFAC Collection. (Photo Flammarion)

1174 Collar and helmet of plastic and steel, PACO RABANNE, winter 1981–82. (Photo Michel Bechet— Paco Rabanne)

Sketches of couturiers' designs:

1175 Wrap dress, PIERRE BALMAIN, summer 1970.

1176 Knit dress gathered below the knee, PIERRE CARDIN, winter 1976.

1177 Dress and jacket with scalloped lapels, PIERRE CARDIN, summer 1980.

made for sales representatives to test on clients. This process allows manufacturers to adjust their production needs according to the best-received models.

These pieces are presented to buyers in October for the following summer's season, while winter models are shown in April. Clothes are manufactured according to demand. The summer line is ready to be delivered in April, the winter line in October.

The complex operation of the fashion industry requires exacting organization and depends on the perfect synchronization of the suppliers and manufacturers. The stakes are high enough to make clothes manufacturing an extremely rigorous industry. In an effort to avoid the arduous demands of the system, "pirate" companies have sprung up that obtain the most engaging models from the salons and copy them, often using illegal labor. Their clothes are then sold to boutiques that have not managed to secure rights with the original designer.

The fashion industry enjoyed a spectacular rate of development until 1974. Then, due to the worldwide energy crisis that caused prices for raw materials and thus retail goods to soar, the industry slowed considerably until 1980. A number of companies closed during this period. The crisis now seems to be over, and once again the fashion industry is expanding.

TEXTILES AND MATERIALS IN THE FASHION INDUSTRY

In the near future, when the production of natural fabrics will not suffice to clothe a rapidly growing population, synthetic and artificial materials will become a necessity. Though greater discoveries were made in the field of textiles twenty or thirty years ago, researchers today are learning better ways to use new materials, including mixing synthetics among themselves or with wool or cotton. The most popular synthetics remain Tergal and its derivatives, Nylon and Rilsan, which brought new life to the manufacturing of undergarments and stockings and were a particularly welcome development when tights came into vogue.

As for designers, they continue to prefer traditional textiles. It is also interesting to note the designers' use of textiles intended for uses other than fashion: Castelbajac used Pyrenean wool blankets and mattress ticking, while several others used terrycloth in their designs.

The hosiery trade during this period was booming. Hosiery, long seen as unfashionable articles of clothing to be hidden under other garments, were now being produced in mesh fabrics with printed or woven patterns for men and women. Manufactured much more quickly, and thus more cheaply, than woven fabrics, the new mesh fabrics also had the advantage of being more wrinkle-resistant.

The base of "fake fur" was made of mesh material. Designers had long tried to imitate real fur with synthetic materials. With the surge of ecologists' campaigns to protect endangered species, the trend toward fake furs rose. But many designers, Emmanuelle Khahn and Paco Rabanne among them, also fabricated whimsical variations on the real thing—fake animal skins that were cheaper than the original.

Paco Rabanne was the greatest innovator of the day with regards to the use of materials. He made a name for himself in 1966, when he created armored dresses made of chains or hammered-metal plates, decorated with crystal beads, cellophane patches, pebbles, buttons, ostrich feathers, and pieces of plastic and celluloid. Among his inventions were knit fur, molded raincoats, and dresses whose torsos were covered with an African-inspired mask. His dresses made of "normal" fabrics were often adorned with metallic embroidery or large collars that became part of the bodice. Paco Rabanne continues to use the most unusual and varied materials in his embroidered work.

Others followed in Rabanne's path. Issey Miyake created molded-plastic bodices, as well as varnished-wicker collar pieces and headgear. Pierre Cardin made dresses out of "Cardine," a wrinkleproof crinkled fabric. Thierry Mugler designed golden metal armor plates to be worn with crêpe skirts.

This era also witnessed a heightened appreciation for both real and imitation leather, which had the advantage of existing in larger pieces than natural leather. Dull or shiny, leather was very much in fashion, used in pants, jackets, and motorcycle suits, but also in women's coats. The specialists in leather clothes have been Claude Montana, Azzedine Alaïa, and, more recently, Hubert de Givenchy.

Finally, one must mention the new unwoven fabrics that were produced through a process analogous to that of paper manufacturing and were meant for only one wearing. They were used to make surgical uniforms, jackets for airplane passengers, and uniforms for mechanics. When crimped, these fabrics could be used for beach dresses, bathing suits, and underwear. Because the fibers of the material were held together by resin, new self-adhesive facings were obtained that were applied with a hot iron, thus replacing the more expensive traditional methods of lining.

BLUE JEANS

From 1965 to 1975, young people wore jeans more than any other type of pants. Jeans were the indestructible pants originally worn by American workers and cowboys in the West, during the gold rush. Levi Strauss first made these pants out of brown tent fabric and later used blue denim, a fabric whose name derives from Nîmes, the town in France where it originated. Manufactured and patented by Oscar Levi-Strauss, the jeans were finished with noticeable double stitching, a label boldly applied on the rear of the belt band, and pockets attached with rivets; they were extremely solid and inexpensive. Soon it became fashionable to wear washed-out jeans until they were threadbare, and for girls, to choose jeans that were a full size too small. At first blue jeans represented youthful rebellion, but they quickly became the mass-produced mainstay of just about everyone's leisure wardrobe. Contests were organized to encourage young people to "personalize" their jeans and jean jackets with patchwork and embroidery. Jeans became highly coveted in Eastern European countries, where they were not manufactured. In Western Europe, designers have imitated the jean cut using different materials, such as jersey, velour, and, most recently, a stretchy blue material that fits better than denim.

MEN'S WEAR

Over the last thirty years, men's wear has hardly changed at all. When women began to adopt men's styles, certain designers felt it was an opportune time to revamp their men's collections. The public, however, did not readily accept their new inventions. Pierre Cardin's men's line, developed with Paul Bril in 1965, only gradually worked its way into men's daily attire. Little by little, though, men came to appreciate the fitted pants, the long jackets with great zippered closures, and the ornate sweaters of this collection.

At the same time, Michel Schreiber, originally with Hollington, abandoned the cut of traditional jackets, with collars and lapels, for a straight Indian-style tunic with no collar; it was closed from top to bottom and had pockets sewn onto the outside. Made of fabrics of all colors that were softer than those of traditional jackets, these "Nehru jackets" were light, comfortable, and unlined. Few men took to this look, although its adoption by artists and intellectuals paved the way to a simpler, more relaxed spirit in men's fashion in general. Outside of work, for instance, men began to wear colored shirts; today, fifty-three percent of men prefer colored shirts to the traditional white.

As inside jacket pockets disappeared, men began to carry small bags akin to women's handbags. Ties also began to show variations on the old-fashioned styles: some men wore a simple

1179   Red Eural jersey suit with fine white stripes, straight jacket with knight's collar, SCHREIBER-HOLLINGTON for WEIL, 1971.

cord, some a square of printed silk tied nonchalantly around the neck. It is important to note the transformation of the men's underwear trade. Today men's undergarments, which come in all colors, figure prominently in graphic publicity campaigns.

The future alone will tell if the innovations in men's wear will last. According to a 1982 report, eighty-five percent of the men questioned, as opposed to forty-eight percent of the women, considered themselves well dressed.

As for women's pants, styles remained adventurous. Safari jackets took over where pantsuits left off. Fitted pants were cut to many lengths, and the variety of styles available allowed all women to find a suitable pair. But while women's styles borrowed heavily from the male wardrobe—jackets, pants, shirts, and sweaters were manufactured in all sizes to fit the tiniest woman or the largest man—men's wear took nothing from the female wardrobe, thus forgetting that all men wore dresses until the fifteenth century and that Islamic men still do. Jacques Esterel, in 1970, came close to adopting some feminine touches for men with his "unisex" line, for which he created not only pantsuits but shirtdresses. Although his efforts did not inspire the public, his vision was perhaps prophetic.

An unprecedented transformation of the fashion industry and a proliferation of new styles occurred from 1960 to 1970. For the first time in Western culture, people of every social and economic class could choose their wardrobes, following the trends of fashion. By 1970 the multiplication of styles created an impression of total anarchy, undoubtedly corresponding to the explosion of a generation who refused to relate to the habits of their parents.

Men's-wear revival:

1180 Unisex dresses by JACQUES ESTEREL, 1970. (Photo Esterel)

1181 Couple wearing jeans: jean jacket, safari jacket, and pants in denim, LEE COOPER, spring 1982. (Photo Bettina Rheims)

1182 Fitted pants with long jacket belted at the waist; surcoat minidress and boots, PIERRE CARDIN, 1967. (Photo Cardin)

1183 Plastic bodice, ISSEY MIYAKE, 1980. (Photo Daniel Jouanneau)

Photographs 1163, 1173, and 1185 were taken at the Museum of Decorative Arts and the World Exposition, June 1983.

1184 Leather suit with black lace bodice, CLAUDE MONTANA, 1982. (Photo Peter Knapp—Jardin des Modes)

1185 Ivory georgette crêpe evening wear, detailed with lace and embroidered with beads; tunic, pants, and bodice, KARL LAGERFELD for CHLOÉ, 1981. (Photo Flammarion)

1186 Khaki gabardine jumpsuit with officer's collar and raglan sleeves, THIERRY MUGLER. This model was lauded at the Fashion Forum at Galeries Lafayette, October 1980. UFAC Collection. (Photo Flammarion)

1970-1983

In the history of fashion, the years between 1970 and 1983 constituted a period of reorganization and regrouping after a decade of tumultuous experiences. The young, always the most sensitive and dynamic facet of society, refused the commercialization of their particular style by creating what was mistakenly seen as an anti-style. Rather, it was a hyper-stylization that largely called upon the personal tastes of its followers. The designers, whose original customers had grown older, became the most significant force in the fashion world.

The magical atmosphere of the haute-couture collections of days past was now applied to a vaster, more varied fashion industry, which addressed itself to an increasingly diversified clientele. Designers' presentations were eagerly awaited each season, for it was from their collections that the "in" clothes would be chosen, allowing the initiated to set themselves apart before the styles were mass-produced and sold at less expensive prices. Remember that haute-couture clothes are generally ten times more expensive than even the best ready-to-wear styles.

It was around 1970 that certain designers who had apprenticed in couture houses made their mark by establishing, for a brief time, a group of "industrial creators" in the Saint-Honoré district of Paris. The first fashion-design district was in Paris's sixth *arrondissement*, in the neighborhood of Saint-Germain-des-Prés. There, in 1965, the Dorothée Bis boutique, run by Elie and Jacqueline Jacobson, which constituted a center of talent in the sixties, showed its first collection designed entirely by Jacqueline. The collection was characterized by a mix of styles, including supple, shimmering knits, multicolored underskirts, and very short shorts. Later, she created a deservedly acclaimed line of knit "landscape" coats. Sonia Rykiel, another designer from the sixth *arrondissement*, began her career designing dresses for pregnant women and went on to create a line of casual layered knit and crocheted separates that were reversible.

Among the newcomers of the Saint-Honoré market, Jean-Charles de Castelbajac made his name with outfits of ample cut and unusual materials, such as brightly colored jute and Velpeau bands. Bernard Carasso, of the Maison Bleue, created linen pieces with large proportions, generally in black and white. The Japanese designer Issey Miyake adapted the traditional dress of his native country to modern Western society, using pressed cotton and jersey delicately shadowed in stripes for his free-flowing and liberally cut coats and jackets with square arms. Kenzo, another Japanese designer, opened his first boutique in the district of the Place des Victoires. There he offered a collection that melded reassuring classicism and provocative eccentricity. The German Karl Lagerfeld, after having worked in haute couture, chose a different approach altogether. He became the top designer for Chloé, where his refined style bridged the gap between the elegant traditions of old-world Europe and the most recent trends. Nothing is improvised in the designs of Lagerfeld, whose inspiration is exceptional. Since 1983, Lagerfeld has been at the helm of Chanel haute couture.

These new names altered the image of fashion. The press, avidly interested in novelty, began consulting various designers and heartily supporting their efforts. For the general public, designers were no longer the poor relatives of the couturiers, but admired partners in the game of fashion.

Young people of both sexes, rebelling against conformity, began to set themselves apart by choosing clothes that were not mass-produced. They bought second-hand clothes at flea markets, from old American army jackets to turn-of-the-century lingerie. These diverse elements were worn together to create a nonconformist look that some deemed "kitsch" but was really simply retrospective. The "retro" look, because it represented the taste of the times, came to inspire an entire style of dress, the primary proponent of which was the British designer Laura Ashley, who created a line of products loosely derived from Kate Greenaway.

Between 1973 and 1983, new faces appeared in the world of

1187 "Escalier" coat of thick multicolored wool, JACQUELINE JACOBSON for DOROTHÉE BIS, 1973. UFAC Collection. (Photo Flammarion)

1188 Hand-painted silk dress, JEAN-CHARLES BLAIS for JEAN-CHARLES DE CASTELBAJAC, spring–summer 1983. (Photo Castelbajac)

design. From 1974 on, Anne-Marie Beretta showed collections of great daring and originality. She masterfully rendered great wool coats in natural tones, squarely cut clothes with leather piping, prints inspired by contemporary painting, and white dresses that fell with a noble simplicity. Each season, this indefatigable designer seems to push herself beyond the limits of her last collection.

Claude Montana signed his first collection in 1977 and immediately proved himself to be one of the most gifted designers of his generation, combining a technical assurance with an exceptional intuition regarding color and form. His favorite material is leather, which he dares to combine, for example, with lace. Even his most eccentric designs possess an undeniably aesthetic quality.

Thierry Mugler opened his own establishment only after having spent years working for others. He has not lost his taste for scandal, which has made each of his shows into a minor battle, but his well-constructed forms, his excellent choice of fabrics that perfectly express his ideas, and his flair for the spectacular have made him one of today's rising stars.

As for Jean-Paul Gaultier, he came to design through an abiding passion. Since his first show in 1979, he has stunned the public with an assortment of novelties that represent the best and the worst of design. He also presents clothes with a reassuring classicism, but always countered by a provocative edge that seems to be used for its shock value.

It is not yet possible to ascertain the evolution of modern fashion, since it is only with a certain distance that we can clearly determine the dominant trends. The press has the habit of signaling trends that are not always in accordance with what people are actually wearing. Unless the world suffers an economic disaster, it is unlikely we will return to the days when one single style dominated fashion. For now, Western culture seems interested in clothes inspired by the traditional dress of Asia, clothes that hang loosely on the body and can take on various appearances when worn with belts or pins. We will only know later whether this look is merely a passing whim.

For women who desire one-of-a-kind clothes, but cannot make them themselves, there still exist a few artisans who create pieces that, if not unique, are produced in very limited series and will never become factory-made.

This tendency has had only one notorious representative in Paris since 1950, Lola Prusac. A specialist of hand-woven and knit clothes with embroidery executed according to her directives, Prusac created completely original and highly varied models for over thirty years, during a period when craftsmanship was out of vogue. The Prusac firm closed in 1981, but there still exists in France a certain number of artisans who work in textiles and create clothing of all sorts. Monique Maetz, for instance, creates more or less figurative embroidered patchwork designs; Geneviève and Reinhart Sevin Doering make clothes shaped from one piece of cloth that is dyed in shadowy colors, creating an effect similar to that of batik. Caroline Gomez, Dominika, Galliane, and Lena Rahoult all specialize in jackets, coats, and dresses enhanced with embroidery and braided trim.

While haute couture has almost disappeared in Europe, the craft is now being reborn in the United States, where small firms that create one-of-a-kind or limited-series clothes are multiplying. Billie Boy, for example, executes a line of very refined unique pieces.

No designer can forget the golden rule that guided haute couture until World War I: create models that are unique. This preoccupation is evident in designers as different as Paco Rabanne, whose every design is extraordinary, and Jean-Charles de Castelbajac, who, along with his manufactured clothes, makes hand-painted unique dresses and jackets woven with rare materials, creations that remain the prized possession of a single client.

This brief summary of current movements in the world of fashion aims to portray the rich variety in design. Human beings cannot refuse to clothe themselves without losing their identities, and it thus seems impossible that fashion will disappear in the near future. Fashion may soon benefit from innumerable variations with the help of computer technology. There remain in this world many people who have never had access to fashion, and a vast and open terrain exists for designers of the future.

BIBLIOGRAPHY

MARYLÈNE DELBOURG-DELPHIS, *Le Chic et le Look*, Paris, Hachette, 1981.
———, *La Mode pour la vie*, Paris, Autrement, 1983.
YVONNE DESLANDRES, *Le Costume image de l'homme*, Paris, Albin-Michel, 1976.
PRUDENCE GYLNN and MADELEINE GINSBURG, *In Fashion, Dress in the Twentieth Century*, London, George Allen, 1978.
FRANCES KENNETT, *Fashion, the Collector's Book of Twentieth Century*, London, Granada Publishing, 1983.
ISSEY MIYAKE, *East meets West*, Tokyo, Heibonsha Ltd., 1978.
———, *Body Works*, Tokyo, Shogakulan Publishing, 1983.
BRUNO DU ROSELLE, *La Crise de la mode, la révolution des jeunes et la mode*, Paris, Fayard, 1973.
———, *La Mode*, Paris, Imprimerie nationale, 1980.

Conclusion

From the crude garments of prehistory to the studied harmony of ancient costumes, from the solemn dress of the Middle Ages to the fanciful and refined garb of modern times, human beings over the millennia have had at their disposal every possible form, color, and fabric—every possible resource, natural and man-made.

In the vast historical panorama available for study, three major periods of fashion emerge: in the first, clothing was impersonal and generic; in the second, personal and national; and in the third, impersonal and international. Each period, however, reveals contradictory elements and complex and intermittent trends, all resulting from a variety of conditions. The forms of fashion have been at times stable, at others evolving, at times pure and impermeable, at others a stylistic mélange.

While fashion has undergone change all over the globe, there has been a certain continuity in the development of European design. This continuity is surely due to Western society's particular facility at assimilating diverse cultural influences. Gradually, the styles of dress of the Western world have come to suit a wide range of peoples. We must, then, investigate the effects of this "superior civilization," one of many that have dominated the history of humanity. By the beginning of the nineteenth century, the standards of Western dress had been definitively formed; even the nomenclature was fixed by then, except for a few peculiarities.

In an extremely condensed and simplified form, this can be seen as the general evolution of fashion until the beginning of the twentieth century. Did World War I signal the end of an era, the end of a way of life that had, until then, determined the premises on which fashion was based, despite all the variables? Yes, to a certain degree. But it is important to note that a half century later, World War II upset not just old habits and traditions but the very foundations of civilization; the evolution that took place after the first war was transformed after the second into a kind of revolution.

It is a given that those living during times of economic and social transformations—the fruits of more obvious political upheavals—are for the most part unaware that they are witnessing a "revolution" in the historical sense of the word. More often than not, they simply perceive that their material conditions are different from those of their ancestors. Very rarely can anyone date such changes.

Like so many facets of culture, fashion today has a split purpose: first, to accommodate human character, taking into account the traditions, sensibilities, desires, dreams—even the irrationality—of the people; and second, to adapt to modern society's impersonal utilitarianism and the cold, uniform nature of technology. Will fashion's artist-creators of the past give way to a new breed of garment engineers? Most likely, the former will have to abandon some of their dreams. But while the creative power of the designer may diminish, it is still individuals, with their innate need for balance, who will determine their own fashion choices.

Fashion has been a fact of daily life for centuries. People have seen clothes as a reflection of their existence and their personality for so long that fashion will never completely lose its natural elements, dependent on human sensibility, in favor of the soulless materialism of technology. Clothes will always be a refuge—perhaps the last—of personal taste and vanity. It is a mistake to think that human nature changes. Rather, it renews itself with each generation.

Fifty years ago, vague visions of the future foretold new conditions and unimaginable destinies, many of which have become aspects of our present reality: ways of thinking that are ambitious but often unfeasible; increasingly abstract and intellectual conceptions of art and architecture; a constantly growing dominance of science and technology; a staggering materialism in ways of life; an inordinately reduced sense of space; and a more and more frantic pace to daily existence.

It has become impossible to make a distinction between styles that will last, trends that will grow, and the passing fancies of a season. Yet fashion, in some ways a mere footnote to culture, nonetheless follows the vagaries of modern civilization and will always remain both a changing and an eternal form of human expression.

General Bibliography

BIBLIOGRAPHIES

COLAS, RENÉ: *Bibliographie générale du costume et de la mode*, 1933.
GIBBS-SMITH, C. H.: *Costume (Victoria and Albert Museum)*, London, 1931.
HILER, HILAIRE and MEYER: *Bibliography of Costume*, New York, 1939.
LAVER, JAMES: *Catalogue of the exhibition: The Literature of Fashion*, London, 1947.
LIPPERHEIDE, F. J. FREIHEER VON: *Katalog der Freiherrlich von Lipperheide'schen Kostümbibliothek*, Berlin, 1896–1905.
MARQUET DE VASSELOT, J. J. and WEIGERT, R. A.: *Bibliographie de la tapisserie et de la broderie en France*, 1935.
MONRO, ISABEL STEVENSON, and COOK, DOROTHY E.: *Costume Index*, New York, 1937.

GENERAL STUDIES

COSTUME

BEAULIEU, MICHÈLE: *Le Costume antique et médiévale*, 1951.
BEAULIEU, MICHÈLE: *Le Costume moderne et contemporain*, 1951.
BOEHN, MAX VON: *Die Mode: Menschen und Moden*, Munich, 1932.
DAVENPORT, MILLIA: *The Book of Costume*, New York, 1948.
KELLY, F. M. and SCHWABE, R.: *Historic Costume (1450–1790)*, London and New York, 1931.
LAVER, JAMES: *Taste and Fashion*, London, 1945.
LELOIR, MAURICE: *Histoire du costume*, 1935–1949.
MORRIS, HERBERT: *Costume and Fashion*, London, 1927–1933.
QUICHERAT, JULES: *Histoire du costume en France*, 1875.
SICHART, EMMA VON: *Praktische Kostümkunde*, Munich, 1926.
TILKE, MAX: *Studien zu der Entwicklungsgeschichte des Orientalischen Kostüms*, 1923.

ACCESSORIES

D'ALLEMAGNE, HENRI-RENÉ: *Les Accessoires du costume et du mobilier*, 1928.
CUNNINGTON, C. W. and PHYLLIS: *The History of Underclothes*, London, 1951.
FORRER, ROBERT: *Archäologisches zur Geschichte des Schuhes aller Zeiten*, Schoenenwerd, 1942.

JAFERT, ERNFRID: *Skomod och Skotillverkning*, Stockholm, 1938.
LIBRON, F. and CLOUZOT, H.: *Le Corset dans l'art et les moeurs du XIIe au XXe s.*, 1933.
WAUGH, NORA: *Corsets and Crinolines*, London, 1954.

TRADE AND INDUSTRY

BOURQUELOT, FÉLIX: *Etudes sur les Foires de la Champagne aux XIIe, XIIIe et XIVe siècles*, 1865–1866.
LACOUR-GAYET, JACQUES: *Histoire du Commerce*, 1950–1955.
PIRENNE, HENRI: *Histoire économique de l'Occident médiéval*, 1951.
STEIN, SIR AUREL: *On Ancient Central Asian Tracks*, London, 1910.

TEXTILES

ALGOUD, H.: *La Soie: Art et histoire*, 1928.
ALGOUD, H.: *Le Décor des soieries françaises des origines à 1815*, 1931.
BIZON: *Dictionnaire des tissus anciens et modernes*, 1857.
CLOUZOT, H.: *Les Toiles imprimées et les indiennes de traite*, 1942.
COX, R.: *Les Soieries d'art, des origines à nos jours*, 1914.
ERRERA, I.: *Catalogue des étoffes anciennes et modernes... (Musées Royaux des Arts Décoratifs de Bruxelles)*, Brussels, 1908.
FALKE, O. VON: *Kunstgeschichte der Seidenweberei*, Berlin, 1936.
HENNEZEL, H. D': *Pour comprendre les tissus d'art*, 1930.
MIGEON, G.: *Les Arts du tissu*, 1909.
PFISTER, R.: *Les Toiles imprimées de Fostat et l'Hindoustan*, 1938.
PODREIBER, F.: *Storia dei tessuti d'arte in Italia*, Bergamo, 1928.
VIDAL DE LA BLACHE, P.: *Note sur l'origine du commerce de la soie, par voie de mer*, 1897.
WEIBEL, A. C.: *Two Thousand Years of Textiles*, Detroit, 1952.
WESCHER, F.: 'Cotton and Cotton Trade in the Middle Ages' in *Ciba Review*, no. 64 (February 1948).

TRADES AND TECHNIQUES

ARNOLD WACE, JANET: *Patterns of Fashion, 1660–1860*, London, 1964.
SINGER, C, HOLMYARD, E. J., and HALL, A. R.: *A History of Technology*, Oxford, 1954.
WAUGH, NORAH: *The Cut of Men's Clothes, 1600–1900*, London, 1964.

DICTIONARIES AND MANUALS

CABROL, DON: *Dictionnaire d'archéologie chrétienne*, 1912.
DIDEROT, D.: *Encyclopédie*, 1751–1772.
FRANKLIN, A.: *Dictionnaire des arts, métiers et professions*, 1906.
GAY, VICTOR: *Glossaire archéologique*, 1887–1928.
JAUBERT, P.: *Dictionnaire raisonné universel des Arts et Métiers*, 1773.
RICH, A.: *Dictionnaire des antiquités romaines et grecques*, 1861.
SAXARY DES BRULONS, J.: *Dictionnaire universel du Commerce*, 1759–1775.

PERIODICALS

Bulletin de la Société de l'Histoire du Costume, 1908–1911.
Cahiers Ciba, Ciba Review, Ciba Rundschau, 1946 on.
Chronicle of the Museum for the Arts of Decoration of the Cooper Union, New York, 1934–1959.
Costumes et uniformes, 1912–1914.
Mitteilungen der Gesellschaft für Historische Kostüm und Waffenkunde, Berlin, 1955–1959.
Waffen und Kostüm Kunde, 1959 on, Munich.

Glossary

ABA Probably derived from the name of a coarse fabric, used in the East for short, open-fronted coats which took the same name.

ACUCHILLADOS Spanish name for *slashings*.

ADRIENNE see SACK GOWN

AGAL Modern Arab head-dress similar to certain ancient Sumerian styles. It consists of a scarf wound round the head and held in place by its own fringes tucked into the roll. The *kaffiyeh* is similar.

AIGUILLETTES see POINTS

ALB Long white linen tunic (tunica alba) formerly worn by lay citizens as well as priests. Abandoned as a secular costume towards the 6th century, it became an exclusively liturgical garment. Until the end of the 15th century it was decorated with two orfrays, one on the front and another on the back, and a similar orfray along the sleeved hems, called *parure* or *parement*.

ALBANIAN HAT Hat popularized by portraits of Henri IV. It had a high crown and raised front, trimmed with a feather.

AMADIS SLEEVE Tight-fitting sleeve continuing on the back of the hand, invented in 1684 by Mlle Le Rochois, an actress at the Opera who had unsightly arms. The name stuck to this type of sleeve, which is frequently found in the 19th century.

AMICE see AUMUSSE

AMICTUS In ancient Rome, the generic term applied to all draped outer garments or *indumenta*.

AMIGAUT Slit at the neck of both male and female garments to make them easier to put on. Also a decorative panel in front of the armhole.

ANAXYRIDES Greek name for Persian long trousers.

ANDRIENNE see SACK GOWN

APRON Originally a piece of cloth which women tied round their waists before sitting down to table 'to preserve their gowns'. This purely utilitarian model occasionally reached elegance, which turned it into a luxury garment. In the 17th century it was called a *laisse-tout-faire*; in the 18th century it was made in silver or gold lace and ladies wore it out of coquetry, but without bibs which were reserved for servant's aprons. By analogy, the name apron was given to the front of the skirt or dress when it carried special decoration or trimming or, on the contrary, was plain in a patterned skirt.

ATTIFFET 16th century women's head-dress, forming an arc on either side of the forehead, covered by a veil falling in a point over the brow. Widows wore it in black.

AUMUSSE A simple head-dress in the form of a flat hood falling on to the shoulders, worn by both sexes. The clerical hood often included bands falling forward to the chest (13th and 14th centuries). From then on it was only worn by canons and as they developed the habit of lifting a fold over the arm it finally became reduced to a simple band of fur, the emblem of the wearers.

BAGNOLETTE Little hooded cape fastened under the chin and at the foot with gathers: sometimes it was also gathered at the neck in a little cape covering the shoulders (1st third of 18th century).

BAGWIG see COIFFURE EN BOURSE

BAIGNEUSE Large, finely-tucked bonnet accompanying the négligée: it was worn originally in the bath, but later spread to daytime town wear (*c.* 1775–90).

BALANDRAN Name given in the South of France to the medieval rain cape whose form remained in use for a long time. It was worn under this name in various countries in the 16th to 17th centuries.

BALLANTINE see RETICULE

BAMBERGES Shinguards of the Carolingian period.

BANYAN Name given in England to men's jackets in Indian linen cloth. They were half-length and used for town and indoor wear.

BARBET(TE) Veil fixed above the ears either to the hair or to the head-dress, hiding women's chins and necks. The *barbet*, with the *coverchief*, formed the *wimple* worn from the 12th to 15th centuries by old women and widows. It was compulsory for nuns, who have retained it.

BARDOCUCULLUS see CUCULLUS

BARRETTE see BIRETTA

BAS DE COTTE / DE JUPE / DE ROBE In the Louis XIV period this term was used for the lower part of the petticoat or skirt, which went with the petticoat or skirt body, covered by the gown body. In the 18th century the *bas the robe* was a detachable train which formed part of ladies' court dress, known as *grand habit*, and which could be removed after the presentation or ceremony that called for formal dress.

BASQUINE or **VASQUINE** Contrary to the opinion of certain 19th-century authors, this was not a corsage or bodice but 'a very wide skirt held well out on circles'. It was confused with the farthingale and was also known as an *hochoplis*. Sometimes only the front was in rich material, the rest being hidden by the gown. In Spain it was called the *basquina*.

BATTANT L'ŒIL 'Head-dress whose sides project well in front of the face, over the temples and eyes; cut in curves and projecting so far forwards that it strikes the cheek and eye when the wind catches it'.

BELUQUE Probably a type of women's mantle in the 15th century.

BERET A sort of round woollen cap, flat or full-volumed, held on the head by a simple hemmed edge or a straight, semi-stiff band. It can be related to the medieval biretta, but when this head-dress was adopted in the Romantic period it was allegedly inspired by the coiffure of Béarnais women, though the resemblance is actually very tenuous. Since then it has been worn in a great variety of forms, the best-known of which are the Basque beret and the Tam O'Shanter.

BERNE see SBERNIA

BIBIS In 1883–4 a type of bonnet but much less voluminous than the hats of the preceding years. At first they fitted tightly to the sides of the head; later they flared out all round the face, tied on with lace-decorated ribbons, beside which the long ringlets of the time dangled down. Though scorned as unfashionable, they were still worn around 1840. About 1879 women wore minute, highly-fanciful hats perched on top of their chignons, and revived the name *bibi*. The name persisted, colloquially, for any small, elegant hat.

BIRETTA Originally a head-dress, difficult to distinguish from the *aumusse* (late 13th, early 14th centuries). In the 16th century the name was transferred to round caps, which became square on top once a hatter had the idea of fitting them on a rigid frame, giving the shape still worn by the clergy.

BIRRUS Garment forming a hooded cloak, made of rough cloth, worn by Romans of all classes under the last Emperors.

BLANCHET Variety of doublet: long cotton camisole, generally white, which originally earned it its name. With sleeves and a collar, it was often fur-lined and worn over the shirt. The name remained even when the blanchet was made in all colours.

BLIAUD Long overgown worn by both sexes from the 11th to the late 13th centuries. The women's version fitted closely at the bust and had long loose sleeves. It was worn with a belt. The male model, with narrower sleeves, was slit at the foot and covered by the coat of chain mail: it too was belted. The bliaud was often richly ornamented. A looser version, the SHORT BLIAUD, was worn by workers and soldiers.

BLOOMERS Women's trousers, invented in America by Mrs Bloomer in the mid-19th century and unsuccessfully launched by her in France and England. The name was forgotten until about 1895, then applied to short puffed knickers made in material matching little girls' frocks.

BOATER A round, flat-topped, flat-brimmed had hat that appeared about 1865, worn first by children, then by women, and later (about 1880) by men. Brought into fashion by boating enthusiasts, it became summer wear for men until 1930/35. For women the fashion is revived periodically, usually as a simple hat to wear with a summer dress, trimmed with a ribbon and a flat bow. Except in English school uniform it has largely disappeared since the 1939–45 war.

BODICE/CORPS/CORSAGE (1) CORPS: 17th century, synonym of bodice: the part of women's garments from the shoulders to the waist.
(2) CORSAGE: 18th century: sometimes synonym of corps (which was stiff whereas the corsage was supple). From the 19th century, a garment clothing the upper body: the upper part of a gown or an independent garment.

BOEMIO Three-quarter-length cape worn in Spain by men in the 16th century.

BOLERO Short jacket of Spanish inspiration. Also a woman's or child's hat, round and with a rolled brim as in Spanish hats.

BOMBAZEEN see FUSTIAN

BONNET Originally the stuff used for making all the types of headwear called bonnet. The term has survived applied to any head-dress other than a hat.

BONNET À BEC or **BONNET EN PAPILLON** Bonnet from the first half of the 18th century, covering the top of the head and forming a point over the forehead. The *papillon* itself was the lower edge of the bonnet, resting on the hair.

BOOT In the Middle Ages, it seems the term referred to a type of slipper, generally fur-lined – the *night-watch boot* – used also by religious orders. The 14th-century 'armed boots', strengthened with steel rods and mail, were probably the prototypes for the doeskin leather boots worn by men and women in the 14th and 15th centuries. The height of elegance was to wear only one. In the 17th century, when Henri IV had sent men to study leather-work in Hungary, boots became so fashionable that they were accepted in salons and on the dance-floor. The forms boots took varied according to their function: the *Cavalier boot*, with a very wide top, could be turned down for town wear, showing a silk or coloured leather lining. From the mid-17th century the boot became limited to riding, hunting and walking.

BOOT HOSE Very long stockings, flaring widely at the top, worn over silk stockings, with boots, in the 17th century. They were often made with only a strap under the instep.

BOUKINKAN see BUCKINGHAM

BOULEVART Second half of the 15th century. Short upper hose attached to the belt and covering only the groin and the upper thighs. They are seldom mentioned and examples are rare.

BOURDALOU Hat-ribbon, finer than grosgrain, round the foot of the crown of hats. This trimming is sometimes finished off with a buckle: it has been in use since the 17th century.

BOURRELET This is essentially a sausage of cloth stuffed with cotton or cloth waste. In all periods it has been used as a component for various purposes, in head-dresses, to support dresses, or for various trimmings; also as a CHILD'S PUDDING.

BOWLER HAT Man's hat with a rounded, medium height crown; it became fashionable towards 1863 as a very small hat, the shape being adopted for women's and children's hats. From 1868 it was more generally worn by men, but only informally with lounge suits. It was only accepted as town wear towards 1898 and until 1914 remained semi-informal – grey being a more formal shade. After the 1914–18 war, the top hat disappeared from everyday wear and the bowler became the formal hat, except for ceremonial occasions. It almost disappeared with the 1939–45 war.

BRACES In the mid-18th century, when *waistcoats* replaced vests and covered less of the breeches, men were obliged to wear braces of ribbon or cord. Towards 1803 stretch braces appeared, woven as a tube containing tiny springs; the rubber-elastic variety appeared only about 1840.

BRACTIATES Fastening pins used by the Merovingians.

BRAGUETTE see CODPIECE

BRANC Women's smock, worn especially in the 15th century.

BRASSARD In the gowns *à l'italienne* of the Charles VIII period the brassard was the part of the sleeve from the wrist to the elbow, joined to the *mancheron* of the upper sleeve by ribbons. In the Romantic period it was a fur-lined half-sleeve worn to protect the arms when outside at night. From the mid-19th century on it was a band of black cloth worn by men on the left arm as a sign of mourning; also a broad ribbon of white silk with a bow with long decorated ends worn by first communicants until the mid-20th century.

BREECHES / BRAIES / CHAUSSES / GRÈGUES / CULOTTES (1) BREECHES. Term first used in Britain in the 16th century; formerly known as HOSE, UPPER-STOCK, SLOPS.
(2) BRAIES or PETITS DRAPS. Sort of short drawers, probably Eastern in origin, held at the waist by a belt (*braiel* or *brayette*); adopted by the Germans, the Gallo-Romans and the Romans, in different materials and lengths. The lower edges were at first tucked into hose bound with thongs; as these grew longer the breeches became shorter, until they became the equivalent of the very short 15th-century trunks.
(3) CHAUSSES. Garment for the lower part of the body, covering the foot and leg. Short in the 7th century, held by thongs criss-crossed to the knee, they grew in length as garments became shorter, and finally rose to the groin; then in the 14th century they reached the waist and, with the new fashion for 'short robes' were joined to become true tights. Their name changed with the changing form: round hose and 'pointed' (on one side) hose were separate stockings, called 'empty between the legs'; stirrup hose (with a strap under the instep) or with full feet called 'full between the legs' were usually

joined. Full foot hose were sometimes soled; high hose were attached to the gippon by metal-tipped laces passed through eyes, usually seven in number; however, those worn by Joan of Arc had twenty points and laces. In the 16th century they were divided into upper and lower hose, but thereafter the term chausses always refers to upper hose.
(4) GRÈGUES. Type of chausses first seen about 1572, generally in cut bands revealing the lining which covered the inner padding. They had no codpieces and were most often richly decorated (with braid) and embroidered with gold and silver. Some are mentioned as 'made in the Spanish style'; however it seems that in Spain they were believed to be of Gascon origin. They were part of pages' uniform under Louis XIII, and survived under Louis XIV as *trousses*, whose form was very similar.
(5) CULOTTE. The word appeared in the last years of the 16th century, applied to nether chausses. But in the second half of the 17th century the culotte/breeches finally replaced chausses. Varying in length and tightness, they remained part of the dress of elegant men until, in the early 19th century, they were replaced by trousers. (Trousers had appeared during the French Revolution, and were considered revolutionary symbols, the Sansculottes having been the wildest element in the bloody days of the Revolutionary Tribunals.)

BRIGANDINE Doublet of cloth or leather covered by leaves or scales of metal, covered in turn with leather or cloth so as to show only the rivets holding this triple sheath together. It was excellent armour for a foot soldier because of its lightness. Its name comes from the brigands (foot soldiers) who first wore it and whose excesses gave the word its present pejorative meaning.

BROADCLOTH 19th century: any unpatterned one-coloured cloth.

BROCATELLE Originally a small-patterned brocade, it seems from the late 16th century on to have become a damasked cloth, a mixture of silk, cotton, lisle or wool, without silver or gold. It was also called 'Gates of Paris cloth' and *mézeline*. It seems to have been in the 18th century a cloth of little value.

BRODEQUIN A light boot whose form derives from the *cothurna* and the *caliga*: until the 16th century the brodequin was a light shoe worn inside boots and houseaux: it was also an instep-strap stocking which young men wore inside boots for weapon practice. Only in the 18th century is the brodequin found as a sort of boot. In the 19th century it was the footwear of elegant ladies, with a fine linen or silk leg, and was worn even for dancing. It was then by (ironic) analogy that the name was given to the short-legged army boots then in use. Liturgical brodequins, which were used for the consecration of bishops or the coronation of monarchs, were more like richly ornamented silk or velvet stockings.

BROIGNE War garment of the Carolingian and Roman periods, made of leather or strong linen reinforced with metal or horn.

BUCKSAIN Man's padded greatcoat with fairly wide sleeves, in fashion in 1850.

BUCKINGHAM Man's hat: a sort of cap with two visors, one flat and the other raised, worn in imitation of Buckingham's troops. This type of headgear was called *montera* in Spain.

BUFF JERKIN Late 16th and early 17th centuries: in military costume a sort of jacket, with or without sleeves, in cloth or, more generally, leather or hide.

BUSTLE or 'DRESS-IMPROVER' Whalebone half-cage whose shape changed with current fashion. Worn under the skirt, after the decline of the crinoline, on the hips, supporting the fullness of the back of the skirt and holding the more or less full *pouf*. Towards the end of the 19th century, the bustle was reduced to a small pad attached to the waist; it disappeared for good

towards 1899 with the vogue for flat-hipped skirts.

CABAN This was probably the first fitted coat with sleeves, introduced to Europe from the East through Venice in the mid-14th century. It was a coat with wide sleeves, not sewn up under the armpit, of Arab origin (*gaba*), closed in front and sometimes worn with a belt. Since then it has remained in current use in its original form.

CACHE-FOLIES Small wigs worn in the early 19th century to camouflage the cropped heads of women who had adopted the 'Titus' hairstyle after the Revolution.

CADOGANS see CLUBWIG

CAFTAN Originally the cremonial wrap presented by Turkish sovereigns to distinguish people whom they wanted to honour, and especially to foreign ambassadors. It is the prototype of all the garments with fitted backs and open fronts which were current in the Orient long before their introduction into the West.

CAGE see CRINOLINE

CAISSIA Lacedaemonian head-dress whose shape can still be traced in Greece.

CALASIRIS Egyptian tunic-shaped robe in semi-transparent white linen, sewn down the sides and sometimes pleated; also worn in Ionia. It was held in by a belt knotted at the waist.

CALCEUS Roman shoe or half-boot covering the foot and sometimes the leg up to calf level. It was also a low shoe whose straps reached quite high up the leg, reserved for Roman senators (*calceus patricius*). Another form whose point was bent upward was widespread in the Mediterranean countries, particularly Etruria, from where it passed to Rome. It was worn in the East during the greater part of the Middle Ages. The CALCEOLUS was a lighter, more elegant calceus worn by women.

CALE According to authorities, this was either a flat-topped cap covering only the top of the head, or a sort of beguin hood with two ribbons knotted under the chin.

CALECHE or CABRIOLET During the period of high, built-up hairstyles – 1775–83 – a sort of high hood on a hooped frame which folded back like a carriage roof. It reappeared in the Romantic period until 1840 as an adaption of the then fashionable overcoats with drawstrings into wide capes protecting the head.

CALIGA An enclosed shoe with a thick, nailed, sole, covering the foot and lower leg, worn by Roman soldiers and centurions but not by higher officers.

CALYPTRA Head-dress of the Byzantine Emperor, in the form of an arched polygon.

CAMELEURION Hemispherical crown worn by the Caesars, then by the Byzantine emperors.

CAMISIA see CHEMISE

CAMLET Camel-hair fabric made originally in Asia Minor, introduced to the West in the 12th century by returning Venetian and French travellers. It was made in Rheims, then in Amiens, where a silk mixture was used; and in the Low Countries, where wool was added. Probably in the 18th century Bourges began to make poor quality imitations which produced the word *camelote* (cf. tawdry). Until then it had been a beautiful rich cloth sometimes woven with silk and gold thread.

CAMOCAS A very beautiful silk cloth, often striped with gold and silver, made in a castle in Palestine; rich even when unpatterned, it had a satin base, diapered like fine linen, which a document dated 1401 calls *enamelled*. Used mostly in the 14th and 15th centuries.

CAMPAGUS Shoe of the Byzantine period, worn throughout the Middle Ages until the Carolingian period. It had a very high quarter fitted on the corners above the ankles, with laces which tied over the instep.

CANDYS see KANDYS

CANEZOU Small guimp with or without sleeves; its main feature was that it was tucked into the belt, where it stopped. Its greatest vogue was during the Romantic period, but it was worn from 1799 until about 1870.

CAN(N)ONS At the end of the 16th century and during a great part of the 17th, the canon was a sort of half-stocking, at first long and narrow, then wider and decorated with flounces and lace, worn between the nether hose and the boot; the thickly ruffled flounces fell over the boot turn-over, giving the impression that they were the turnovers of *boot hose*, but contemporary texts are very clear about the distinction. The canons attached to *petticoat breeches*, worn with low shoes, show that they were separate.

CAP Man's head-dress, flat and round, and always with a peak; originally popular and informal in character, it was accepted for travel and sport at the end of the 19th century.

CAPA Wide circular hooded cloak worn by men in Spain in the late 16th to 17th centuries. It was also worn in France (*cape à l'espagnole*) at the same time. The name was revived in the Romantic period for flowing evening cloaks.

CAPOTE (1) From the very late 18th century on, a woman's head-dress fitted closely round the chignon, with a wide flaring brim framing the face. The capote was worn until the end of the 19th century, with changes in detail, but the basic shape remained unaltered.
(2) see GREATCOAT

CAPPA FLOCCATA Round cap in hairy material, still worn by Greek shepherds.

CAPPUCCIO Italian name for the hood (*chaperon*).

CARACALLA A narrow, tight-fitting garment, sometimes hooded, with long sleeves; it was split in front and behind to the groin; worn by the Gauls. The Emperor Aurelius Bassanus introduced it to Rome, and thus was nick-named Caracalla. The Roman version was longer than the Gaullish original.

CARACO or PET-EN-L'AIR The caraco, borrowed from a French provincial costume, appeared towards 1768. It was essentially a gown *à la française*, cut off at hip level and forming a sort of short, peasant-style jacket. A similar model preceded it: the *casaquin*, a loose gown cut off at hip level; later the same was to happen to the English-style gown.

CARBATINA The commonest type of ancient footwear: a piece of oxhide forming a sole, turned up round the edges and over the toes and held over the instep by laces passed through holes pierced in the leather.

CARCAILLE Early 15th century: a flaring collar of *houppelandes* or pourpoints: rising to the ears.

CARMAGNOLE Jacket worn by French Revolutionaries in 1792–3.

CARRICK Originally a coachman's heavy coat: a box-coat.

CASAQUE see CASSOCK

CASAQUIN see CARACO

CASSOCK / CASAQUE A sort of unbelted overcoat, three-quarter length, with long or short slit sleeves, open-sided and almost invariably covered with braid and woven ornament. It was worn from the middle of the 16th century, mainly for hunting and riding. The origin of the name has been traced variously to Cossack dress, to the Hebrew casack and even the Gaulish *caracalla*.
The casaque was above all an outer garment; in the 19th century the name was applied to women's garments (or parts of garments) worn as overgowns or as coats; and, in the 20th century it refers to any form of blouse worn outside the skirt.

CASULA see CHASUBLE

CENDAL Silk material resembling taffeta. It was made in various qualities, so that it is sometimes

mentioned as a luxury fabric, sometimes as cheap lining material. Widely used during the Middle Ages, by the 17th century it was found only as lining.

CHACONNE Type of cravat made of a ribbon dangling from the shirt collar to the chest. It takes its name from the dancer Pécourt who danced a chaconne in 1692 with his cravat tied in this way.

CHADDAR or UTTARIYA Indo-Iranian shawl or mantle.

CHAINSE or CAINSIL A long tunic of fine linen cloth with long sleeves tightly-fitted at the wrists: always white, and usually finely-pleated. The sleeves could be seen under the *bliaud* sleeves. Authors do not agree as to whether the chainse was the same as the shirt or if it was worn over it. However, some ancient texts mention the wearing of a chainse and a shirt.

CHAMARRE A long, wide coat, open in front, with full-topped sleeves, generally fur-lined and heavily decorated with braid and *passementerie*, which explains the origin of the French word 'chamarrer'. It first appeared about 1490, the transformation into a rich garment of a sheepskin coat – the samarra – worn by Spanish shepherds.

CHAPEAU-BRAS In the 18th century, to avoid disarranging their wigs, elegants developed the habit of carrying their hats in their hands, then under the left arm (hence 'arm hats'). Towards 1778–80 we find false hats, imitating *tricornes*, but completely flat, in cardboard covered with taffeta, called 'broken hats'.

CHAPERON Hood with a short cape known as a COLLET or GULERON: it appeared at the end of the 12th century and stayed in use until the mid-15th century, with some variations.

CHARLOTTE Large woman's hat, named after Queen Charlotte of England (1784); a wide tightly-gathered crown, the brim covered with a generous flounce. Modified and lightened, this hat returned to fashion in the late 19th and early 20th centuries, for women and children.

CHASUBLE Originally an outer garment, circular in shape with an opening for the head, generally without a hood. It was the CASULA, so-called because it enclosed the wearer like a little house. Abandoned as secular costume about the 6th century, it remained a liturgical garment; the neck was edged with a small piece of fabric which developed into a T-shape and suggested the cruciform arrangement adopted about the 14th century. The shape of chasubles was reduced over the centuries to free the arms, and finally kept nothing of its original form until the 19th century brought a renewal of the traditional form.

CHAUSSE Alternative name for the epitoga.

CHAUSSES see BREECHES

CHAUSSES EN BOURSES Early 17th-century breeches made in bands and padded so they swelled out at the bottom, ending in a flattened balloon shape.

CHAUSSES EN TONNELET see VENETIANS

CHEMISE Descended from the antique CAMISIA; a light undergarment for both sexes.

CHEMISE GOWN Amply cut muslin gown 'as worn by our French ladies in America', with sleeves fitting tightly at the wrists; the dress fitted closely at the waist but loosely at the throat 'after the fashion of a chemise'. It opened down the front and was fastened by a pin at the top and a ribbon sash at the waist as in the *robe à la lévite*.

CHERUSQUE or CHERUSSE Corruption of the term *collarette à la Lyons* which at the time of the Revolution was a lace border which stood up at the neck of women's deeply-cut dresses. Dressmakers wrote it 'cherusse'; men 'chérusque'; under the First Empire, the name was given to the starched lace collarettes of court costume.

CHILD'S PUDDING Small round hats for children made of cloth or straw, forming a shock-absorber to protect them if they fell.

CHINTZ Linen, originally Persian, printed and wax-glazed, often wrongly called glazed percale.

CHITE Painted linen, originally from Chitta (India) which started the fashion for painted linens in the 17th and 18th centuries.

CHITON Ancient Greek garment. Originally a type of linen, then a tunic of that cloth, then the tunic in any sort of cloth. Essentially an undergarment, worn at first like the *exomis*, leaving the right-shoulder bare, then held over both shoulders by a fibula.

CHLAINE Woollen cloak of Homeric period, worn by shepherds and warriors; discarded by the latter for the shorter *chlamys*.

CHLAMYS Short, light Greek garment, trapeze-shaped. Originally from Thessaly, but adopted throughout Greece. It could be draped in various ways. Seldom worn by the Romans. The name survived for royal and military cloaks and mantles of the Merovingian and Carolingian periods, whose shape was analogous if not wholly similar.

CHOPINES Spanish name for the raised PATTENS worn by women to increase their height.

CINGULUM Band or belt worn by women beneath the breasts, to gird in the tunic. Man's belt worn on the hips over the tunic so that it would be tucked up for active exercise.

CIRCASSIENNE A variant of the gown *à la polonaise*; it had three back panels, differing from the polonaise by its very short sleeves which exposed the long or half-length sleeves of the under-bodice.

CLAVI Purple bands vertically decorating the tunics of Roman dignitaries. Senators were entitled to a broad band (*laticlaves*) and knights to two narrow bands (*angusti claves*) which ran from each shoulder to the foot of the tunic.

CLUBWIG (CADOGANS) About 1785 a man's wig with one pigtail tied with a narrow ribbon and with a bulge at the end; women took up this hairstyle and wore either single or double cadogans. The style returned to fashion, particularly for young girls who had not yet put up their hair, in the late 19th and early 20th centuries.

COAT OF ARMS Sort of long tunic strengthened with metal rings, worn from the 11th century on. After the adoption of the coat of mail and the hauberk, the armed coat of arms became a sort of parade tunic worn over the armour, and kept in France until the 17th century for heralds of arms and certain grades of palace guards. It still survives in Britain in connection with the College of Heralds.

CODPIECE At the end of the 15th century, a piece of cloth designed to cover the opening of the hose, attached by two buckles to the front of the hose. In the 16th century this piece became protuberant and so voluminous that it could serve as a pocket.

COIF Piece of linen or cloth following the shape of the head and worn under the helmet or hood; it differs from the CALE in that it has no chinstrap (13th–15th centuries). By extension, the word was applied to hat- and wig-linings, and also the nightcap. Today the term is used only for traditional regional head-dresses and the light lining used in hats.

COIFFURE EN BOUFFONS Women's hairstyle from the end of the reign of Louis XIII: tufts of crimped hair over the temples, while the forehead was covered by a fringe known as a *garcette*.

COIFFURE EN BOURSE About 1730 'it was a fashion taken from horses': men's hair was held in a little black ribbon bag tied with a rosette. For many years this style was not admitted to balls or in court, but its popularity spread gradually, so that it was universally adopted. Also called a BAGWIG.

COIFFURE EN CADENETTES 17th century: hairstyle invented by the sire de Cadenet which entailed letting a lock of hair (a 'moustache') fall on either side of the face; these were wound with ribbons and tied with a bow. Worn by men and women in the early years of Louis XIII.

The name was revived in the 18th century for a male hairstyle with two long locks held back by a ribbon on the back of the head, but which could be untied and left to dangle.

COIFFURE EN RAQUETTE Women's hairstyle, last quarter of the 16th century, with hair swept up all round the face, puffed out over the temples and supported by a hoop.

COLLET MONTE or ROTONDE After the ruff men wore a linen collar with a card or tin base. Women also wore a standing, fan-shaped, lace-trimmed collar.

COLOBIUM Sort of blouse or sleeveless coat worn in ancient Gaul and in popular costume throughout the Middle Ages. The liturgical colobium, derived from a Roman secular garment, worn by freemen and, in particular, senators, was a long linen tunic, sleeveless or short-sleeved; it was soon abandoned for the dalmatic.

COMBINATIONS Several articles of underwear joined into one; chemise-drawers-pantaloon (1892); pantaloon-petticoat (1897); bodice-pantaloon-petticoat (1898).

COMPERES Small false front in two pieces fixed to the edge of the bodice and simulating a waistcoat.

CONCH Sort of large shell-shaped hat in gauze or light crepe, mounted on a tin framework, which seems to have been worn mainly in France by widows in the late 16th and early 17th centuries. At the same time a similar veil, but generally much bigger and made of pale gauze, seems to have had a great vogue in England.

CONQUE see CONCH

CONSIDÉRATIONS see PANIERS

COPE Originally a hooded cloak designed for protection against rain. In civilian costume, where it survived until about the 15th century, it sometimes had sleeves and a hood; it also served as a ceremonial garment for men and women. It was fastened in the centre front with a large hook, not on the shoulder as in other mantles. Once it was adopted by the clergy as ceremonial wear, it was always sleeveless and decorated whith rich orfrays. The original hood was replaced by a decorative imitation which gradually lost its meaning and was moved below the shoulder line. As with the chasuble, the original line was restored in the 19th and 20th centuries.
The UNIVERSITY GOWN, reathr different from the civilian cloak, was closed, and had two slits on the front or sides for the arms to pass through.

CORDOBAN LEATHER Goat skin, simply-tanned 'but not with gall like the leather they call Morocco'. The art of preparing this leather came from Cordoba and the craftsmen allowed to use it for making shoes in the Middle Ages were cordwainers.

CORNET The more or less long point of the hood. At the end of the 15th century it became separate as a women's cap, covering the skull and temples with the point standing up for greater comfort. The term remained in use in the 17th and 18th centuries for the linen head-dresses worn by women of the people, while burgher's wives could be in broadcloth and 'damoiselles' in velvet. This is how the term still refers to the head-dresses of French peasants and nuns. As the point of the hood was sometimes rolled round the head in the Middle Ages, the name was also used for the ornaments, hoops and bands round the crown of the hat.

CORNET HAT Women's hat with gathered crown and narrow brim, fashionable in the Directoire period.

CORPS see BODICE

CORPS PIQUÉ or CORPS À BALEINE In the 16th century, under the influence of Spanish fashions, women wore a sort of quilted camisole fitted with a bust or busk of varnished wood to stiffen it. In the 17th and 18th centuries the garment took the form of an underbodice fitted with whalebones, tightly laced and held on by shoulder straps. It gradually disappeared in the last years of the 18th century when a corset (lightly boned bodice) replaced it under more flowing gowns; then at the end of the century the Classical revival in dress did away with it altogether.

CORSAGE see BODICE.

CORSET (1) Middle Ages: sort of long or short surcoat with or without sleeves, worn by men from the mid-12th to mid-15th centuries. From the 14th to 16th centuries a woman's gown, laced in front and fur-lined for winter.
(2) 17th century: 'Garment for upper part of woman's body, with or without sleeves' (Monet, Dict). Sort of bodice which often replaced the bodice in the 18th century, but more supple and supported by only two busks.
(3) 19th century: under forms which vary from a lightly-boned bodice in the early years of the century, to a rigid cuirass from the mid-century on; a support whose form varied according to considerations of fashion and contours.

COTEHARDIE Though the term occurs frequently, few details are known about this garment which was worn from the late 13th to the 15th centuries. For men it seems to have been a surcoat open in front, split and buttoned at the sides. The sleeves were wide at first, then false. It is also mentioned as a sort of dressing gown, and it seems the name was also given to the first short gowns for men.

COTERON Little coat, worn by the people; a sort of fatigue coat.

COTHURNES High boot, Greek in origin, worn by huntsmen; it covered the whole foot and leg up to calf level; laced in front and fitting either foot. It was also, for tragedians, a shoe made of a very thick cork sole designed to increase the actor's height (the buskin) – it was ungraceful and always hidden by the long robe. This last form, with adaptions, provided the inspiration for the early 19th-century fashions, giving its name to a light sandal-type shoe, tied with laces criss-crossed up the leg.

COUREUR Very tight-fitting caraco with very short basques, worn by women during the Revolutionary period.

CRACKOW SHOES see POULAINES

CRAMIGNOLE Man's cap with turned-up brim cut away all round, worn in the late 15th and early 16th centuries. Made originally of velvet trimmed with pompoms, feathers etc., then, until the early 17th century, with hosiery work. The original style was much older, but had no particular name.

CRAVAT Ornamental neckwear thought to have been inspired in 1668 by a Croatian regiment who wore it and whose name became corrupted. Except for the greater part of the 18th century, it has stayed in current use though undergoing numberless transformations until the present.

CREMONA CRAVAT Cravat worn in 1702 (after the capture of Cremona) which was a plain ribbon decorated with gathers along each edge.

CREPIDA A Greek shoe similar to the Roman carbatina, formed by a thick sole with a narrow piece of leather covering the side of the boot, pierced along the top with several holes through which a thong passed attaching it to the instep. Sometimes the edges had leather buckles through which the strips passed.

CRIARDES Early 18th century: underskirts of gummed linen prefiguring paniers.

CRINOLINE Originally a cloth of horsehair and woven for officer's collars, and then used for civilian collars in the Romantic period, then for women's underskirts designed to support the skirts which from 1842 became gradually wider. These underskirts in crinoline or crinoline were replaced about 1850 by numerous petticoats, first starched, then boned. These were supplanted about 1856 by lighter metallic cages which became gradually more flexible until 1867 when they disappeared, giving way to a few boned hoopes round the foot of the skirt. The term crinoline remained attached to the swollen shape of the skirt, even when the fabric which originally bore the name was no longer used.

CRISPIN 'Coat without collar or arm-holes' designed in 1826 to protect actresses waiting in the wings from draughts; it was adopted by men, women and children.

CROTALIA Fanciful name given by Roman ladies to earrings made of several pear-shaped beads, large enough to make sounds like castanets.

CUCULLUS Name given in Rome to the hoods of working clothes, by analogy with the cornet used by grocers; from the hood, the name extended its meaning to include the garment of which it was part, like the bardocucullus or cucullus of the bards.

CUERPO BAXO Spanish name for the quilted, boned, sleeveless bodice worn in the 16th century with the basquine.

CULOT Very short tight breeches worn during the reign of Henri III.

CULOTTE see BREECHES

CHAUSSURES À CRIC / À PONT-LEVIS Early 17th-century shoes with heels, so-called because they resembled a bridge raised by a jack (cric). Others claim the name à cric was invented because the shoes creaked.

DABIKI In the 15th century, Dabiki, a suburb of Damietta, produced robes woven with gold, and linen turbans embroidered with gold, in stuff so light that fifty yards of dabiki could go into one turban.

DAGGINGS 15th-century German fashion; adopted mainly at the court of Burgundy; the hems of garments and sleeves, the ends of bands etc. were cut in various patterns – toothed, with long cut-out leaves and even, inside the leaves, bands of pertuisé work – cut open-work in small patterns.

DALMATIC Long, wide-sleeved blouse falling to the feet in white Dalmation wool, decorated with vertical purple bands. Considered effeminate during the Roman Empire, it was later adopted as part of Christian liturgical dress.

DAMASK Originally a silk fabric made in Damascus, with self-coloured patterns of flowers, branches and animals in satin finish contrasting with the slightly textured taffeta background. Multi-coloured damasks are lampas.

DAMASKIN A sort of brocatelle or multi-coloured damask with flower motifs in gold or silver.

DEVANTIÈRE 17th century: woman's riding costume split at the back.

DEVICE In the Middle Ages, a figured object or emblem adopted as a distinguishing sign: the broom (planta genista) for Charles VI, the plane for Jean sans Peur, etc. Several objects might be taken by one person, who often wore them embroidered on his clothes. What is today called the motto ('legend') was then called the mot (word).

DHOTI Into-Iranian loin-cloth/kilt/pagne, also called paridhana.

DIPHTERA Cretan cloak formed of an animal skin or thick woollen cloth covering the shoulders.

DOGALINE Venetian fashion of the Middle Ages and 16th century, a straight loose gown worn by men and women; it featured a very wide sleeve whose lower edge was fastened up to the shoulder, completely revealing the undergown sleeve. There was an ephemeral revival of this fashion in France during the Romantic period.

DORMEUSE Cap with a ruched border fitting tightly to the head, held by a ribbon tied on the top of the head. It was worn at night, hence the name. For daytime wear, the dormeuse had a brim turned up on the nape, and pinners. Though abandoned by fashionable women about 1770 it remained current among the people until the French Revolution.

DOUBLET/POURPOINT Originally a quilted garment, i.e. padded with cotton or waste, held in place by stitching; worn under the hauberk. It was a variety of gippon or gambeson in rich cloth, which passed from military to civil costume and became an outer garment from the early 14th century. In the 16th century and up to the middle of the 17th century it was a garment worn by all men; the shape and trimmings changed, but its basis character remained unaltered.

DRAWERS Nether undergarments worn from the 16th century onwards by ladies; men's drawers in the 17th century were of linen or hide. It seems that at that time they were already worn by Europeans in India.

DUCKBILL SHOES Exaggeratedly wide shoes which succeeded the *poulaine* in the late 15th and early 16th centuries.

ENGAGÉANTES Lace cuffs with two or three tiered ruffles, finishing women's gown sleeves under Louis XIV: still worn in the 18th century with gowns *à la française*.

EPHOD A sort of corselet supported by shoulder straps and worn by the Jewish high priest; then used in Christian priestly costume during the first years of Christianity.

EPITOGA Originally a cloak, worn over the toga; a wide, ungathered unbelted robe, sometimes with bell sleeves. It appeared as academic dress in the 13th century. It was also a sort of hood worn by the Presidents and *greffiers* of the French parliament, for ceremonies, covering only the shoulders. It was the medieval hood reduced to symbolic form as part of academic and magisterial robes. Also known as the *chausse* or *épomine*.

EPOMINE Hood: alternative name for EPITOGA.

ESCAFFIGNONS or ESCHAPINS 16th century: very light flat shoes, generally slashed on top. The term already existed in the 12th century for a light shoe in rich material.

ESCOFFION Wrongly given by some authors as the name for tall hairstyles covered by a net snood worn in the early 15th century. The term, which appeared only in the 16th century, refers to women's coifs of silk or gold thread net. From the Italian *scuffia*. Later the word lost its original meaning and referred to a popular head-dress.

ESPRITS Aigrettes stuck upright in the hair or hat, first quarter of the 19th century.

ESTACHES see POINTS

ESTIVAUX see STIVALI

ESTRAIN Straw used for hat-making in the Middle Ages.

EXOMIDE Very short sleeveless Greek tunic completely open down the right side, later adopted by the Romans. It was the tunic of the working classes. The term EXOMIS was sometimes used for the pallium when it was draped so as to leave the right shoulder bare.

FACES Flat locks of hair framing the face of Dandies in the Directoire period.

FACINGS Edging of fine fur or rich cloth, used from the 12th century to face fine garments, as revers or *passepoils*, while the garment was lined with more ordinary cloth or fur. These trimmings were purely for decoration. The term was then extended to cover all the revers of the body or sleeves of a garment: this meaning still survives today. In the 18th century the *parement* was the long band, generally decorated, which edged the fronts of the gown *à la française*: narrow on the bodice, but broadening on the lower part of the gown. In England this ornament often stopped at the waist, leaving the skirt plain. *Parements d'aube* were bands either embroidered or appliquéd on to the hem and round the cuffs of *albs*. Originally continuous, in the 19th century they were imitated with *parements interrompus* in rectangles.

FALLING RUFF (FRAISE À LA CONFUSION) Last form of the ruff in France during the reign of Henri IV: unstarched and falling in tiers on the shoulders.

FALSE GOWN Fashion from England which, in the 18th century, borrowed it from French little girl's styles and converted it into a women's dress. It consisted of a tight bodice with skirt gathered all round. A broad ribbon tied at the back formed a belt. It was called a false gown because it did not have an overgown open over a petticoat but was in one piece.

FALSE SLEEVES In the 14th century, the habit of letting the unbuttoned lower part of sleeves hang down gave rise to this fashion; long panels fell from the elbow, sometimes to ankle-length. Originally an integral part of the sleeve, they were later sewn to the sleeve, and were sometimes in contrasting fabrics.

FARDEGALIJN Dutch name for the FARTHINGALE.

FAROUS Modern Iraqui loincloth.

FARTHINGALE / VERTUGADIN Spanish fashion of the late 15th century introduced into France in the 16th century. A coarse linen underskirt was stretched over thick iron wire which supported the skirts. Under Charles IX it was replaced by a thick roll worn round the waist, which held the gathers of the top of the skirt which then fell in ample folds to the ground. This was called the *vertugadin français*. At the end of the 16th century the addition of a stiff circular *plateau* (plate) forms the farthingale known as a *tambour* or *drum farthingale*.

FEMINALIA / FEMORALIA Sort of short drawers attached at the waist and reaching to the knees. They were worn only by Roman troops serving in cold Northern climates, and were probably imported to Rome from Gaul by Augustus.

FERRERUOLO Long cape with velvet collar and no hood, worn by Spanish men in the 16th century.

FERRONIÈRE Small jewel attached to a fine chain holding it on the forehead. Romantic head-dress using the jewel on *Madonna bandeaux* inspired by the Leonardo da Vinci Virgin known as *La Belle Ferronière*.

FIBULA Pin or brooch, used in ancient times to attach or fasten male and female garments like the chlamys or palla, but not the toga, which was held in place by the manner in which it was draped.

FICHU Small black lace scarf which women knotted around their necks so that the points fell on the chest. Mentioned from 1779 on, but its greatest vogue coincided with the beginning of the French Restoration. The term came from the long leather loop which hung from horses' croups in the Middle Ages to aid mounting.

FICHU MENTEUR Fichu worn by women in the late 18th century in the neck of coats and open dresses; it was draped so that it exaggerated the figure and increased the size of the bust.

FIELTRO Man's three-quarter length cape with high collar and hood, worn in 16th-century Spain.

FLAMMEUM Marriage veil worn by Roman brides on their wedding day. It was dark flame colour and covered the wearer from head to foot throughout the ceremony. The bridegroom removed it only on reaching their new home.

FLOUNCE From the end of the 18th century on, a band of cloth or lace fluting round a garment to which it is attached only by its upper edge. In the 17th and 18th centuries it was called a *furbelow*.

FONTANGES HEAD-DRESS About 1678, women's hairstyle, with the hair swept up and held by a ribbon; with important modifications it lasted until the end of Louis XIV's reign, complicated by a cap and various accessories.

FRAC Man's garment wider than the coat, without outer pockets and with a turned down collar. It appeared about 1767 and remained

an informal garment, worn through part of the 19th century. Its cut then changed, the tails growing narrower and shorter. By the mid-19th century it was a formal jacket with basques, cut away at the waist in front.

FROCK COAT (1) English garment similar to the FRAC, but the name also applied to more formal embroidered coats known as *French frocks*. Knights' models often had several collars.
(2) REDINGOTE (masculine). French, from the English *riding-coat* (a term never used in England): a heavy, wide-cut, collared coat for men, worn for riding and travelling. It appeared about 1725. In the 19th century it was worn over or instead of the coat. Then it replaced the coat for town wear; the front panels were in one piece instead of being cut like those of the *habit*. Gradually it became the ceremonial garment when the frock coat was no longer daytime wear. It disappeared after the 1914–18 war.
(3) REDINGOTE (feminine). Garment adapted for women about 1785; a lighter version of the male redingote, whose cut and sometimes collars it borrowed. But it remained a gown, open a waistcoat and skirt, and not a surtout. However, under the Empire it appeared as an overcoat, then reappeared as a gown during the Restoration and Romantic period. Until the Second Empire it was essentially a gown buttoning all the way down the front. Its fashion ended under the Second Empire; from 1874 it reappeared as a coat, fairly severe in cut.

FULLBOTTOMED WIG (BINETTE) Light wig, with three locks of hair, invented for Louis XIV at the end of the 17th century by sieur Binet, wigmaker.

FUSTIAN Cloth of cotton or cotton crosswoven with flax or linen. Originally made in Fustat, near Cairo, hence its name. It was for undergarments and linings. Fustian with two 'right' sides was bombazeen. The name is sometimes applied to an undergarment made of fustian.

GABARDINE see CABAN

GALABIJEH Modern gown worn by Egyptian fellahin.

GALERUS In Rome, a rounded cap of animal skin worn by peasants and huntsmen. A cape of the same shape but made of the skin of sacrificed animals with an olive wood point was reserved for pontiffs. Similar to the *tutulus* in shape.

GALLANTS Mid-17th century: small ribbon bows worn in the hair and scattered about the clothes.

GALLICAE Low Gaulish shoe with one or more thick soles, the upper exposing the instep, sometimes laced on top.

GAMBESON Quilted, padded garment worn under armour; it passed into civilian costume in the 14th century under the name of *juppe*, gippon, pourpoint or doublet.

GAMURRA 16th-century Italian women's garment, often mentioned but never clearly described; it seems to have been midway between the *simarre* and a late form of *houppelande*.

GARCETTE see COIFFURE EN BOUFFONS

GARDE-CORPS Garment for both sexes which, in the early 14th century, replaced the surcoat or was worn over it. It is confused with the *corset*; normally loose and flowing, with sleeveless or with short, wide sleeves, it disappeared at the end of the 14th century.

GARNACHE Surcoat or robe worn for extra warmth; similar in shape to the HOUSSE.

GARNEMENT Each of the individual pieces composing a *robe* in the Middle Ages (cf. ROBE); the word is retained in English: garment.

GARTERS (1) Ribbon tied round the leg to hold up the stocking.
(2) Band, usually fastened with a buckle, holding the edge of knee-breeches to the leg.

GAULLE see CHEMISE GOWN

GIBUS see OPERA HAT

GIGOT SLEEVES see LEG-OF-MUTTON SLEEVES.

GIPON / GIPPON also called jupe, jupel, jupon in the Middle Ages. A sort of doublet made of padded, quilted material. It was an undergarment and the breeches were attached to it; in the mid-14th century it became indistinguishable from the doublet and the jacket made in rich materials which replaced it.

GIRDLE À LA VICTIME 1796: a vividly coloured sash passing over the shoulders, crossed at the back and tied round the waist.

GONELLE / GONNE Long tunic, worn by both sexes in the Merovingian and Roman periods; it was adopted as monastic costume. It also became the long coat of knights. The male style generally reached only half-way down the legs. The word is related to the English *gown* and the Italian *gonnellone*, soutane.

GORGET / GORGERETTE 14th and 15th century: any costume accessory covering the neck and throat, decorated in silk, wool, linen or fur. 17th century: more generally a neckerchief in Holland cloth or silk called a *gorge de Paris*. 18th century tulle or ribbon ruche edging a square décolleté.

GORGIAS Gauze used in the late 15th century to mask the pronounced décolleté of women's dresses; by extension, the plunging neckline itself and any other provocative elegance. Related to the English word gorgeous.

GOWN À LA FRANÇAISE In the mid-18th century, the sack GOWN gave way to a dress consisting of a close-fitting bodice, opening in front on a triangular *stomacher*, which was generally richly decorated; at the back, two large double pleats fell freely from the middle of the collar, spreading to the ground. Universally worn at first, it remained current as a ceremonial gown until the French Revolution, even when other lighter fashions became widespread.

GOWN À LA LEVANTINE 1778: '...a gown so comfortable, and so simple to put on and take off that it has earned the name of *négligée de la volupté*'. Fastened on the chest with a pin; only the foot of the back was pleated; skirt opening down the front; worn over an undergarment whose Amadis sleeves passed through the Levantine's half-sleeves.

GOWN À LA LÉVITE Inspired by the costumes worn by the choirs in *Athalie*; a straight dress held at the waist by a long scarf whose ends fell over the underskirt (1799).

GOWN À L'ANGLAISE About 1778–85: a gown without boned bodice or paniers, characterized by a long boned point reaching down the middle of the back to below the waist. The front closed over a waistcoat; the sides of the skirt opened on a petticoat usually of the same material.

GOWN À LA POLONAISE One of the first soft dresses of the last third of the 18th century. Characteristic features: fastened at the top of the boned bodice, then cut away to show a tight-fitting waistcoat; sabot sleeves trimmed with *petits bonshommes*; over the underskirt it formed three draped panels held up by drawstrings. Its variants did not alter these basic features. After 1866, the polonaise, inspired by the 18th-century gown, remained in fashion for over twenty years. Open-fronted, it was draped in a pouf behind.

GOWN À LA SULTANE 1781: dress opening in front over an underskirt of a different colour.

GOWN À LA TURQUE 1799: gown which, by its elegance, caused crowds to gather at the Palais Royal when it first appeared. It had a tight bodice, with a turn-down collar, flaring sleeves, pleated corset and a draped belt knotted over one hip.

GOWN À L'INSURGENTE One of the fashions inspired by the American War of Independence; however, it was only a 'gown *à l'anglaise* with pagoda sleeves which was widely worn by Anglo-American women'. It was tucked like 17th-century dresses.

GRANATZA Long sleeved gown, originally Assyrian: the exact cut is unknown. The Persians transmitted it to the Byzantines.

GREATCOAT / OVERCOAT (1) Early 18th-century English surtout/overcoat with a flat collar topped with a smaller collar that could be raised to protect the face; in France it became the redingote.
(2) CAPOTE In 1775, a woman's mantle enveloping the wearer from head to toe. In 1804 'man's mantle with a collar and a wide shoulder-cape'. A wide cloak, generally in heavy cloth, with or without a hood, appearing as part of military and college uniforms and some civilian uniforms.
(3) PALETOT. Originally called a *paltok*. 15th century: a short outer garment, unfitted, with full sleeves; generally decorated with gold and stones. 16th and 17th centuries: assimilated to the *hoqueton*, whereas it had previously been confused with the short manteline. Late 17th century: a sleeveless surtout worn by peasants. It reappears in the mid-19th century, first as a woollen riding garment for men which attracted bitter criticism. Next the name is extended to very varied and fanciful women's garments before being applied (about 1843) to a coat, of varying length, but considered inelegant for at least twenty years. Ultimately it was accepted for women, girls and children with streamlined forms which have survived to the present.
(4) PARDESSUS. Only towards the second third of the 19th century was the term used to describe the coat – a type of heavy-sleeved paletot – worn by men. In women's costume, the term was used during the 19th century for all top garments, classic or fanciful in conception: visites, paletots, mantelets, scarves etc., in light or heavy materials. *Pardessus de chambre* even appeared alongside morning peignoirs.

GREAVES Under names that vary according to the period, a costume accessory covering the leg from ankle to knee.

GRÈGUES see BREECHES

GUARD-INFANTA Large farthingale still worn in Spain in the 17th century.

GUÉRIDONS Paniers made of very large hoops fastened together with tape.

GUIMP Originally a piece of light material with which women surrounded their face, letting it fall over their neck and chest, in the 14th and 15th centuries. The style spread, particularly for widows and nuns. Only in the late 19th century did the term guimp begin to be used for a little short chemise generally in tulle or other very light stuff, designed to cover the neck of very open dresses. It is possible the term may at first have referred to light silk cloth and become attached to the articles made of the stuff.

GULERON / COLLET / PATTE Part of the chaperon covering the shoulders.

HABIT In the Middle Ages, garments in general, whether men's or women's; in the 17th century, for men, the two-piece suit of clothes (doublet and breeches) or three-piece, with the mantle, or four-piece, with the stockings, all in the same cloth or colour. COURT HABIT in the 17th and 18th centuries meant men's clothes, and the GRAND HABIT women's, worn only at court and at festivities where the court was present. In the second half of the 18th century the male JUSTAUCORPS became lighter and took the name of HABIT À LA FRANÇAISE, which survives to the present day in certain liveries. The habit *à la française*, plain or embroidered, remained the elegant men's costume during part of the 19th century. Gradually the lapels took shape, the top became open and became evening dress, while the town 'habit' coat gave way to the REDINGOTE, which in turn was supplanted by the morning coat, which kept its form. The word habit also referred to clothes with a particular purpose, for example riding-habit and religious habit.

HAÏK ROYAL Light pleated, carefully draped garment worn in Egypt by Pharaohs and queens, which covered the body though revealing it by transparency. Its real name is still unknown; it is called *haïk* because of its similarity to the Arab garment, which was also made from a large scarf which lends itself to the same draped effects.

HAINCELIN Short houppelande which took its name from Charles VI's fool, Haincelin Coq. It differed from the normal houppelande in that both its sleeves were embroidered, whereas the houppelande had embroidery on only one sleeve.

HALF-BEAVER In the 17th and 18th centuries beaver hats were the most prized and the dearest; hats were made of a mixture – half beaver hair and half other hair – known as half-beaver.

HAT BAND see BOURDALOU

HAT PIN When the hat was no longer tied with ribbons under the chin, hat pins appeared. They were long, so as to go through the crowns of all shapes of hats, and were more or less richly decorated at one end. Between 1910 and 1914 they were so long that it was compulsory to fit the points with *point guards*. The hat pin disappeared in about 1925, when short hair became fashionable.

HAUBERK Shirt of mail.

HELM / HELMET / CASQUE Military headgear made of metal or leather. The name was used by analogy in the 19th century, when women's hats with hemispherical crowns and visor-like brims were named helmets or half-helmets.

HENNIN Insulting term used for tall, horned head-dresses, considered wrongly to have been the name of the hairstyle and the tall conical hat.

HÉRIGAUTE Type of *housse* or *garde-corps* worn in the late 13th and early 14th centuries. It was open at the sides and similar in shape to the *dalmatic*.

HEUZE / HOUSEAUX Middle Ages, from the 9th century on. Tall leather thick-soled boots sometimes leaving the end of the foot uncovered, which sometimes led to their being confused with gaiters or leggings. Some covered half the leg, others rose to mid-thigh. They disappeared towards the end of the 15th century.

HIMATION Greek mantle, made from a large rectangle of cloth which could be draped in various ways. Worn by both sexes.

HOOP-PETTICOAT English name for paniers in the 18th century.

HOQUETON / AVQUETON Tight-fitting padded tunic, a type of *gambeson*. Derived from the Arabic *alcoton* (cotton), which was used to make it. In the 16th century it was part of parade uniforms for certain companies, and was often decorated with gold and precious stones.

HORNED HEAD-DRESS Women's tall head-dresses from the late 14th and the first third of the 15th centuries; sometimes incorrectly referred to as *hennin*.

HOSE Liturgical hose covering the foot and part of the leg, knitted or cut from cloth, were already worn in the early Middle Ages. They served as a model for the short cloth hose which grew longer in the 14th and 15th centuries, finally becoming to all intents and purposes full-length tights. In the early 16th century they were divided into *upper hose*, now underpants (shorts) and lower hose or stockings. The first knitting machines, invented in England, appeared about 1527 and silk stockings then became current; but the industry only developed under Henri IV; ordinary stockings were made of coarse worsted, and only luxury stockings of silk. Cotton stockings were very fashionable in the last third of the 18th century, and lisle thread under Louis-Philippe. There were successive fashions for stockings with embroidery, openwork or lace insets from the 18th century to the early 20th.

HOUPPELANDE Full overdress, with wide flaring sleeves and a funnel-shaped collar called CARCAILLE, worn by men, women and children from about 1375 to 1425. Generally made of rich, ornate stuff. In the 17th century the term was applied to 'a full riding coat cut like a BALANDRAN', split and buttoned down the front and at the sides. It was thought to have come, probably, from Upland in Sweden. Since then, the word has appeared only occasionally, meaning a man's or woman's full overcoat.

Housse Outer garment with wide, short sleeves forming a cape or PÈLERINE, buttoned in front, with two little tabs below the neck. Its length varied. Often confused with the *gamache*, similar in shape but without tabs.

Huik 17th century: heavy Flemish mantle covering the head and body. Later it was combined with a flat felt hat which, after 1630, was crowned with a little tuft on a stalk rising from a skullcap on the head.

Huque Outer garment, a short flowing robe, open at the sides, worn in both military and civilian costume; the knight's style was slit in front. Often edged with fur and decorated with embroidery or precious stones. Worn during all the 15th century; under Louis XI its length increased to cover the feet.

Hurluberlu (Hurlupe) About 1671, a woman's hairstyle in which short curls covered the entire head.

Huve Women's head-dress, late 14th and early 15th centuries. Sort of tapered cornet projecting, held to each side of the head by long pins. The folds fell over the neck. Possibly the name may have designated the cloth before it was applied to the way it was folded.

Indiennes 17th and 18th centuries: name given to all Eastern painted and printed stuffs, whatever their country of origin.

Indigo In ancient times and the Middle Ages, the most precious dye, popular and admired in spite of its high price. Its use spread after the discovery of the sea-route to the Indies by Vasco da Gama (1498). Extracted from the indigo and isotis (pastel) plants.

Indumentum In Rome, general term for any garment or accessory that covered part of the body.

Instita see Stola.

Ipsiboe (Modes à l') *Ipsiboe,* a satirical novel by the Vicomte d'Arlincourt published in 1823, was so successful that for several years an Ipsiboe style prevailed in everything; in particular there was a colour 'Ipsiboe', a yellowish beige which enjoyed a great vogue.

Ispahanis Name given to precious cloths made in Almeria (Spain) by the Moravids from the 8th to 11th centuries, noted particularly in Antioch in the 12th century.

Jabot Originally the neck opening of the chemise, and its lace trimmings, showing through the opening at the doublet. Appeared mid-17th century, stayed in fashion through the 18th and the early part of the 19th centuries, when men's shirt fronts were trimmed with pleated jabots. These disappeared as men's clothing became more plain and restrained. It appeared in women's clothing in the late 19th and early 20th centuries, as lace or embroidered trimmings.

Jack Sort of padded military doublet worn from the late 13th to late 15th centuries. Made of up to 30 superimposed layers of cloth, fitted closely to the torso. Worn over the hauberk, – or haubergeon – and could be in very rich cloth when not worn by soldiers: it then became confused with the doublet.

Jacket 14th to 16th centuries: man's garment deriving from the *jaque* but more closely-fitted, worn mainly by the poor. Considered a peasant garment, hence its name (*jaquette*), Jacques being a name widely used in the country. This sort of blouse remained, in the 17th and even the 18th centuries, a garment for little boys not yet in breeches.

Jansenists see Paniers

Jaquette Woman's jacket of the late 19th century, inspired by the 17th-century hongreline, hunting jackets, etc.

Jerkin (1) Kind of outer doublet worn in England in the late 16th and early 17th centuries: sleeveless, with loose sleeves or, when in hide, with sleeves in a rich cloth.
(2) The Justaucorps was, as the name indicates, a tight-fitting garment already worn for some time in military costume when (about 1670) it was adopted by civilians. With some changes in detail, it remained in use until the mid-19th century, when its cut and ornament were simplified and it became the habit *à la française.*

Jockey / Jokey Flounce forming an epaulette, placed at the top of the sleeve from about 1825; still mentioned in 1870.

Journade Inspired by the Italian *giornea,* a sort of flowing *cassock* with wide slit sleeves; its form underwent changes, for in texts it is confused often with the paletot, manteline, hoqueton. It seems to have been a parade or display garment. (About the mid-15th to mid-16th century.)

Jubon Long sleeved camisole buttoned all the way down (16th to 17th centuries) often in panels, worn in Spain by men under the doublet and by women under certain gowns, like the *galerilla.*

Jupe From the Arabic *djuba,* jacket. In the Middle Ages confused with Gippon but also meant women's jacket; the two senses survived to the 17th-century, when men still wore '*juppes de chasse*' and women wore under the gown, the *corps* and *bas de iupe.* Only in 1672 did the Dict. de l'Acad. define jupe: 'Part of women's costume, from the waist to the feet'. The term then disappeared from men's costume, except for the panels of certain garments. From then on *jupe/skirt* corresponds to the modern definition. 17th-century women wore 3 jupes one on top of the other; the *modeste,* a top skirt, often trailing; the *friponne* in the middle, which covered the *secrète* underskirt, the last two being ground length.

Justaucorps see Jerkin

Kaffiyeh see Agal

Kakofnitch Russian women's head-dress in the form of a tiara or diadem.

Kandys Tight-sleeved caftan, Persian in origin, worn by the Byzantine emperor.

Kaunakès Long haired fur pelt worn in Sumer in the pre-Agadean period, *c.* 3000 BC. At the end of this period the name passed to a hairy cloth similar in appearance.

Kepresh War head-dress of the Pharaoh; a tall tiara covered with projecting circles, perhaps metal rings.

Kilt see Plaid

Klaft Pharaonic head-dress in striped cloth on which a sparrowhawk was woven. It fitted over the temples, the broken folds falling over the ears; the head-dress shown on the sphinx.

Kontush / Contouche Generously cut caftan-shaped mantle worn in Poland. The term passed to Germany and the Nordic countries where it referred to women's gowns, *robes volantes* or *gowns à la française* worn in the 18th century.

Kyne Greek soldier's helmet, made of leather.

Lacerna Flowing hooded cloak, open fronted and fastened with a buckle or brooch at the throat, taken by the Romans from the Gauls: wide enough to be worn over the toga.

Laisse-tout-faire see Tablier

Landrines / Lazarines Under Louis XIII, boots with widely flared tops, reaching half-way up the leg; soft enough to be turned up for riding.

Languti Indian loincloth.

Leading strings / Tatas Long narrow strips of cloth attached to the shoulders of small children's dresses to hold them by when they began to walk (17th and 18th centuries). In England in the 18th century, young girls wore these bands of cloth, reminiscent of the hanging sleeves of the 16th and 17th centuries, until marriage.

Leg-of-mutton sleeves Sleeves worn from 1828 to 1837, with a huge puff at the top of the sleeve. The fashion was revived from 1893 to 1899.

Licinium Linen loincloth.

Lodier Thick padded and quilted wrap used in the early 17th century to make a sort of roll over the hips to increase their bulk. This mode was short lived.

Loincloth Band of material wound round the hips like a short shirt and worn in the past and now by primitive peoples.

Loros Scarf worn by Byzantine emperors.

Love locks see Coiffure en cadenettes

Lower stocks Silk or woollen cloth stockings showing beneath upper stock.

Madder Plant yielding a bright red dye. Jean Athen, a Persian settled in France in the early 18th century, acclimatized it in the Comtat Venaissin.

Mafors Long narrow veil, generally covering the head and falling over the shoulders, worn by women (6th to 11th centuries).

Maheutres Cylindrical pads used to trim the shoulders of tight gippon sleeves, *c.* 1450, to broaden the shoulders. Not to be confused with the padded, gathered sleeves of preceding years.

Mamillare see Strophium

Mancheron Though there is confusion in the texts over this term, it seems the mancheron was, in the 16th century and perhaps before, a half-sleeve of silk or velvet which showed under the wide sleeves of gowns and houppelandes. The mancheron of a gown or houppelande could also be the slashed half-sleeves from the elbow up, through which the mancheron of the doublet could be seen. These explanations taken from Nicol's *Dictionnaire* seem to indicate that the term was applied to any half-sleeve whether it covered the upper or lower arm.

Maniakes Collar worn by Byzantine emperors.

Manteau / Mantua In the 17th century, the overdress, that is, the gown worn over the bodice and petticoat.

Manteline Short parade garment worn over the armour; usually richly decorated, sometimes hooded; in some texts it is confused with the journade or paletot. Late 15th to early 16th centuries.

Mantilla In Spain, late 16th century, a reduced version of the old *manto;* a large shawl worn by women and widows, and also by young girls, who had to cover their head so as to show only one eye. The mantilla covered only the head and shoulders, as it does now.

Mantle It seems the term appeared at the beginning of the 15th century in the sense of a cloak, which it has kept ever since. It was the most simple and widespread outer garment; a large rectangle of thick stuff gathered at the neck, without sleeves, often with a hood whose shape, round or pointed, has changed little since the Middle Ages.

Mappa Large piece of cloth used to give signals at games, or as a table napkin.

Marlotte 16th century women's garment. Sort of half-length mantle, completely open in front, the back falling in symmetrical folds. The very short sleeves were puffed and the standing collar could take a ruff. This garment can be compared with the Spanish *ropa,* but it has no connection with the *marlota,* a man's coat on the lines of a caftan, with hanging sleeves, worn only for tourneys and bullfights.

Marramas Cloth of gold, oriental in origin,

449

also made in Lucca, the principal source, in the 14th century. It was used mainly for ecclesiastical ornament.

MARTINGALE BREECHES 16th-century breeches with a movable panel between the legs, held to the belt by buttons and points.

MASK Theatrical accessory in ancient times, adopted in the late Middle Ages and especially, in the 16th and 17th centuries, by women, for whom it replaced the *touret de nez*, to protect the wearer's complexion and preserve her incognito. It took various names according to its shape and the period.

MATHILDE Broad, vertical band of embroidery decorating women's dress-fronts about 1804–5 after the exhibition of 'Queen Matilda's Tapestry' (the Bayeux Tapestry). This decoration was later modified by the extension of the embroidery along the foot of the dress, and was called 'inverted T' or 'inverted Y'.

MEDICI COLLAR Name given in the 14th century to women's standing collars, recalling those worn in the 16th century, popularized by protraits of Marie de Médicis, but already current by 1580.

MENAT Egyptian necklace, particular emblem of the goddess Hathor.

MILITARY TUNIC Appears in military uniform in the 17th century.

MITRA In its original meaning, a scarf with tie-tapes at the ends, so that it could be worn in various ways according to the wearer's needs. It formed a swathed, draped head-dress worn by the inhabitants of Persia, Arabia and Asia Minor and by Grecian women. It covered the head and framed the chin and neck. The Asiatic mitra worn by the Phrygians was a woollen cap with a turned-down point, with cords fastening under the chin. This was the *Phrygian cap*. In Greek art the mitra is used to characterize the Trojans; the Greeks considered it effeminate.

MITRE Derived from the ancient Eastern mitra. Appears in the Christian liturgy in the 7th century. It seems that at first bishops wore a gold circlet, more or less ornate, which was later lined with a crown. In the 12th century, the crown split into two lobes, one on either side; the central split, from the brow to the nape of the neck, became more accentuated in the course of the century, and by the end of the 12th century the points had moved round 90 degrees and were now back to front; their decoration varies in degree but the basic form, slightly heightened, has not changed since then.

MOB CAP Linen nightcap worn by women in the mid-18th century. Towards 1780 it was a cap with a pleated border worn under large bonnet hats.

MOGHUL BREECHES see PYJAMA

MOTTO see DEVICE

MOUFLES or MITONS Fingerless gloves worn in the Merovingian period; the name was applied to various gloves used for hunting or rough work. By analogy the name was applied, in the late 14th and early 15th centuries, to an extension of the sleeve covering the hand.

MOUSTACHE see COIFFURE EN CADENETTES

MUFF 18th century on, a band of fur or fur-lined fabric protecting the hands from the cold.

MULEUS Red or violet boot worn by Roman patricians who had served as magistrates. Some authors think it was confused with the *calceus patricius* of Roman senators.

MUSLIN The first fabrics from Mosul were silk with gold. It seems it was only in the 18th century that the name was given to a wide variety of light fabrics also from the East. This cotton stuff owed its name to its texture, covered with tiny bumps which reminded one of foam (French: *mousse*), so that its present name has no connection with Mosul. It enjoyed a great vogue in the 19th century when it was worn plain or printed during all the first half of the century.

NAGES Black frieze skirts worn in full mourning.

NORFOLK JACKET Jacket in English cloth, adopted by men for sport and travel, and by boys for hiking dress; main feature a half-belt catching in the full back. The fashion was set by the Prince of Wales (later Edward VII) at the end of the 19th century, when he wore it with baggy knickerbockers.

OLICULA Hooded cape worn by Roman women.

OPERA HAT Collapsible top hat flattened by an internal spring so that it could be carried under the arm. First, about 1825–30, there was the *elastic hat*, which unfortunately tended to lose its shape. It was dethroned by the *gibus*, whose easily operated spring held the shape stiffly when expanded; from its appearance in 1823, the Opera hat remained part of evening and theatre wear until the early 20th century.

PAENULA In Rome a kind of round hooded blouse with an opening for the head. Sometimes the front was split to the groin to facilitate walking. It was made in heavy material or leather and was worn for travel or in bad weather.

PAGNE see LOINCLOTH

PAGODA SLEEVES Men's coat sleeves about 1729 were called pagoda sleeves when the deep cuff reaching to the elbow narrowed in, instead of flaring out like the wide cuffs *en bottes* of the preceding years. The sleeves of women's dresses in the 18th century were pagoda sleeves when they flared out conically, with cuffs. The term reappears in the 19th century, during the Second Empire, with the flaring sleeves on women's gowns.

PAISON Greek name for the trousers worn by the Persians.

PALATINE Little fur stole which takes its name from the Princess Palatine who, during the hard winter of 1676, wore an old fur as a cravat.

PALETOT see GREATCOAT

PALLA Latin name for the Greek women's *peplos*. It was the ceremonial garb of rich Roman ladies; it was draped like the peplos and generally open down one side. But sometimes the side was sewn up and the palla was then put on like any other closed garment.

PALLIUM Main piece of the *amictus* or outer garment of the Greeks, as the toga was in the Roman amictus. A long square or rectangle of wool, draped and fastened at the neck or on the shoulder by a brooch (*fibula*). The Greeks had various ways of draping it and gave each a different name. Women also wore it, again in varying ways. Among Greek bishops who were already wearing it in the 3rd century, it was considered a symbol of pastoral dignity. In the 6th century, when it was worn by the Pope, it was transformed, passing over the shoulders to fall down the left side; in the 8th century it was no more than a V-shaped band over the chest, falling over the other garments. In the 10th century, the V became a circle finishing in two vertical bands back and front. Under this form it became a particular piece of insignia granted to bishops by the Pope. However, it is possible that the intermediate V-form of pallium shown at Ravenna may be descended from the *loros*, the Byzantine scarf, while the circular form returned to ancient tradition remaining the emblem of the Roman church.

PANAMA Panama hats for men were very fashionable at the end of the 19th century and the beginning of the 20th century. Made at first of exotic leaves, they were later imitated in *latanier* or finely-worked poplar wood. They were soft straw hats with rounded crowns.

PANIERS Following after CRIARDES, paniers were underskirts stretched over metal hoops: round at first, then *en coupole* (dome) or *en guéridon* (round table), they appeared about

1718–20 and remained in fashion under various forms until the French Revolution. Oval paniers were called *paniers à coudes*. The top hoop was called the *traquenard*. *Paniers à bourelets* (roll paniers) had a thick roll at the foot to make the skirt flare out. *Paniers anglais* had eight hoops. Toward the middle of the century the one-piece panier was replaced by two pieces, one on each hip. By 1750 only half-paniers were worn; known as *jansenistes*, they were kept for Court ceremonies after the invention of *considérations*, light paniers supporting skirts without numerous underskirts.

PANTALETTES From the end of the First Empire to about 1865 little girls' pantaloons showed below the dress hem.

PANTALOONS Women's undergarment; originally, in the 19th century, linen or silk pants. Then, after a tentative mode for pantaloons showing below the dress hem (1809) they became more sophisticated and acquired flounces of lace or embroidery at the foot. They remained long until about 1870, then became progressively shorter until 1914, when they were simply short, straight knickers.

PAPILLON see BONNET

PARAGAUDION Originally a gold-embroidered band which gave its name to the Persian tunic, decorated with embroidery in gold, which the emperor of Byzantium presented to vassal sovereigns.

PARDESSUS see GREATCOAT

PAREMENT(S) see FACINGS

PARIDHANA see DHOTI

PARTI-COLOURED DRESS Garment divided vertically in half in two colours of cloth; in vogue at the beginning of the 12th century and the end of the 14th century. Livery garments were often *partis*, quartered in the colours of the lord of the town.

PASSACAILLE Fashionable dance (*passacaglia*), whose name was given to the cord attaching the muff to the waist, under Louis XIV.

PASSEMENT Original name given to all forms of lace, in the 16th–17th centuries, whether in thread, silk or metal; gradually the name *dentelle* was given to lighter work made with shuttles or needle, while passement developed into PASSEMENTERIE describing all kinds of woven ornament.

PATAGIUM Long band of purple or gold decorating the fronts of women's tunics, similar to the *clavus* worn by men.

PATNA Printed cloth imported from Patna on the Ganges, one of the first fabrics imported in 1640, probably by Portuguese traders, as with SURATES/SURAHS, from Surah, north of Bombay.

PATTENS In the Middle Ages and the 16th century, shoe, thick soled or raised on high heels, worn mainly in Spain (*chopine*) and Venice, and by imitation, in France. It was worn over the slipper and generally made of worked or decorated leather or velvet. In the Middle Ages it was also a shoe fitted with an iron blade, for skating.

PEASCOD BELLY False hump of stuffing and cotton lengthened into a horn-shape which filled out men's doublets, in the Henri III period; it recalled doublets *à la poulaine* (or Polish) because it was supposed to have been brought back from Poland by Henri III. However, they already existed in Spain in 1587 and the shape was then explained as an imitation of cuirasses, made in this form to deflect bullets.

PEEL Man's light jacket, in vogue in 1850.

PÈLERINE Name given in the 18th century to a short cape covering the shoulders, similar to those worn by Watteau's 'Pilgrims' (*Pèlerins* and *Pèlerines*). The word has kept the original meaning, though it is sometimes applied to longer garments.

PELICON Fur-lined garment worn between chemise and cote, 12th to 15th centuries.

PELISSE Though the *pelisson* was known in the

Middle Ages, only in the 18th century do we find a women's mantle, related to the cape and the tippet, wide and padded, fur-edged, with two arm slits, sometimes with a hood. Worn in the early 19th century and Romantic period for evening outings. In the late 19th and early 20th centuries the term applied only to a heavy fur coat worn by men, especially with evening dress. Also, 19th century to 1930, a long, hooded, padded coat for small children.

PEPLOS Greek women's garment; large rectangle of cloth, the top folded down, round the torso and pinned on each shoulder; the right side was open and the edges of the material fell in loose drapery. Like all Greek garments its form depended on the way it was draped. Lacedaemonian women had originaly worn a simpler model, without the draped fold. The frequently-used word *peplum* is only the Latin transposition of *peplos*, describing the same garment worn in Rome under the name *palla*.

PERIZOMA Short, close fitting trunks worn by the Etruscans, Iberians and Sardinians.

PERO Boot made of hairy undressed hide, worn by agricultural workers under the Romans.

PERSE Painted cloth from the Coromandel Coast, thought to be Persian. It was enormously fashionable in the 18th century, and again in the mid-19th century.

PETASUS Flat-crowned, broad-brimmed hat taken from Greece by the Romans; it was held on by strings tied under the chin or behind the head. It is to be seen with two wings in most representations of Mercury.

PETIT BORD Small, elaborately fashioned hat worn about 1830–50, said to have been inspired by toques of the Renaissance period, but which differed from them by the variety of its shapes and trimmings.

PETITE OIE Set of ribbons which, in the mid-17th century, was used to trim men's suits, and which became very large when petticoat breeches were worn.

PETITS BONSHOMMES Sort of fine linen bracelet made of several frills, used to edge the sleeves of gowns *à la française* (after 1722).

PETTICOAT BREECHES Upper stocks with wide, loose, flowing legs, richly decorated; fashionable in the mid-17th century until about 1675.

PHAROS One of the forms of the peplos worn by Greek women; mentioned by Homer; belted at the waist.

PIANELLE 16th-century Italian shoe, often defined as a *pantoufle* or carpet slipper; though pantoufle-shaped in France, it was nonetheless adapted for outdoor wear, protected by pattens.

PICCADILS Notches made in the sleeve openings and necks of garments. This fashion gave its name to Piccadilly, which was being built on the outskirts of London while this fashion was current.

PIERROT It is difficult to define, from the texts, the exact function of the *pierrot* worn in France from about 1784 until the Revolution; it seems to have been a *caraco*, or at any rate a small garment worn like a caraco, but much more fanciful in cut and trimming.

PIGACHE Shoe with long, upturned, pointed toe, recalling the Classical *calceus repandus*; in fashion during the 12th century. Probably the term referred to the upturned point rather than to the shoe itself.

PILEUS Felt cap worn under very varied forms in Rome by men. The Phrygian cap had a point, folded over; the Grecian model was ovoidal in shape; Roman freedmen wore a tubular cap.

PLAID Scottish national costume, made in heavy woollen material, checked in the colours of the clan. It was originally draped over the shoulders and worn round the waist, but was later simplified when it was divided into two parts; one was wound round the waist to form the KILT; the other was worn over one shoulder like a blanket (PLAID). In the 19th century the fashion for Scottish styles introduced by the

Romantic movement led to the widespread export of Scottish tartans, which were used, in various periods, to make cloaks known as plaids.

PLEUREUSES / AMAZONES / WEEPERS From 1900 on, ostrich feathers, with each strand lengthened with another strand, first gummed but later tied.

POCKETS In the Middle Ages clothes did not have pockets; objects were held in the split (AMICAUT) of the neck opening, in the corner of the hood and later in the codpiece which opened like a box, or, lastly, in bags of various forms. Wide sleeves were adopted, as purses could be hidden in them, particularly in the armpit opening, known as the *gusset*. With the fashion for breeches tailors began to incorporate pockets in them, but these were so large they could conceal weapons, so that they were forbidden, at least temporarily, in France, in 1573.

In the 17th century the pocket was still a small independent bag attached to the gusset. It is only with the appearance of the justaucorps that we find pockets, vertical at first, then horizontal (about 1684). In the 18th century women's pockets were hung outside the paniers and were reached by a slit on either side of the dress. Coats, jackets, and men's waistcoats were fitted with pockets from the late 17th century on; this was not possible with the very tight breeches worn in the 18th century; at first small watch-pockets were placed in front, and at last, in the last quarter of the century, at the sides.

POINTS Metal-tagged laces that replaced the sewn *estaches*, to attach the upper hose to the gippon or the doublet.

POLONAISE see GOWN À LA POLONAISE

POLOS Greek women's hat, 5th century BC, already worn in Daedalic Crete.

PONCHO Large rectangle of unsewn cloth, with an opening in the centre for the head; a prototype of the simplest form of primitive garment, it was worn in the earliest periods, and is still worn by many South American peoples.

PORCUPINE HEAD-DRESS / PORC-EPIC Style with the hair cut short and standing up like bristles (1798).

POSTILLON Gathered or ruffled basque at the foot of the bodice back; very fashionable in 1860–61, still mentioned in 1888.

POUFS AU SENTIMENT About 1780, women's voluminous hairstyles on which the most varied trimmings might find a place.

POULAINES Shoes said to be in the Polish style, which appeared at the end of the 14th century and were worn until the reign of Louis XI, in spite of numerous edicts attempting to forbid them. Perhaps inspired by Oriental modes known since ancient times (see CALCEUS) they consisted of an exaggerated lengthening of the shoe point, far more accentuated than the 11th-century *pigaches*, called CRACKOW SHOES in England.

POURPOINT see DOUBLET

POWDERING The fashion of powdering wigs began under Louis XIV, but it was in the 18th century that the vogue for powder spread and became universal. Hairdressers and barbers called the operation *poudrage* or *accommodage*, powdering or arranging; they emerged from the process white with powder, which earned them the nickname of *merlans* (whitings).

PRÉTINTAILLES Decoration for women's gowns: coloured materials cut out and appliqued to the gowns (late 17th century).

PRINCESS DRESS Appeared about 1865: one piece in front, all the fullness taken to the back over the cage which had lengthened backwards. The fashion for these dresses increased continually once, after the decline of the crinoline, dresses became absolutely flat in front; the general volume decreased according to fashion.

PSHENT Cap in the form of a truncated cone worn by the Pharaohs.

PUDDING-BASIN CUT 15th-century hairstyle: the hair was shaved on the neck and temples, leaving a skullcap of hair on the top of the head.

Widespread in England, France, Italy but never worn in Germany.

PURPLE Dye extracted from the *murex brandis*, reserved for important people in ancient times. It was yellow when collected; exposure to sunlight turned it red, then deep violet.

PYJAMA The name comes from the Hindustani *epai-jama*. Though still worn in the 20th century under this name, pyjamas were already worn in England in the 17th century and were then known as Moghul breeches.

RABAT 17th century: collar of linen and lace worn over the doublet. Ecclesiastics wore a narrower model. The narrow rabat remained an accessory for ecclesiastical town dress for a long time. In the 19th century it was a lingerie ornament worn on women's bodices.

REBATO Brass wire support worn in Spain by men and women to support the ruff, which was thus held at an unusual angle.

REBRAS 13th and 17th centuries: the equivalent of revers, whether the upturned brim of a hat or the revers of a coat, the cuff of a glove, or a lingerie ornament.

REDINGOTE see FROCK COAT

RETICULE The transparent gowns of the Directoire period and the following years made no provision for pockets, so women took to carrying handbags known as *ballantines* and *reticules*, known colloquially as *ridicules*, terms which stayed in use until the early years of the 19th century to refer to women's handbags.

REVERS The turned-back edge of a coat, waistcoat, or bodice. See also FACINGS.

RHENO Very short coat in reindeer skin, typically Germanic, worn in Gaul during the Merovingian period.

RHINEGRAVES see PETTICOAT BREECHES.

RICINIUM Square veil worn by Roman women on their heads, then in Gaul until the Carolingian period, for offering sacrifices and other occasions. The IRICINIUM was a smaller veil folded in half, worn on the head, particularly as a sign of mourning.

ROBE Originally, all the furniture and effects belonging to a person; then his collection of clothes.

ROBE À LA CRÉOLE see CHEMISE GOWN

ROBE ANGLAISE About 1880 to 1900, a child's dress.

ROBE DE CHAMBRE / ROBE VOLANTE In the 17th century the word had nothing of the modern sense of *déshabillé*: it was simply a gown differing from the court gown, and was admitted to the *chambres* of the royal apartments outside receptions and ceremonies. The robe de chambre was only a *déshabillé* for men; it took on the same function for women only in the 19th century.

ROBE DÉGUISÉE 15th century: the term used for garments in new and daring fashions reserved for the most elegant wear. The term contrasts with *robe de commune et ancienne guise* (ordinary clothes).

ROBE GIRONNÉE / À PLIS GIRONNÉS 15th century: loose dress with pleats, fixed at the waist, which fell like organ pipes.

ROBE LONGUE / ACADEMIC DRESS 13th century on: long costume worn by academics and religious orders.

ROCHET / ROQUET Small collarless coat worn in the Louis XIII period. The sleeves reached no further than the elbow and split along their full length so that it could be turned inside-out. Worn by some gentlemen at first, it was handed on to lackeys and ended up on the backs of buffoons in the Italian comedy.

ROLL see BOURRELET

ROND Louis XIII period: a sausage-shaped pad over which women built their hair.

ROPA Spanish women's outer garment, opening all the way down the front, with a straight collar and sleeves bouffant at the top (16th and early 17th centuries).

ROPILLA Doublet adopted in Spain about 1550: very close-fitting, half-length basques and hanging sleeves.

ROQUELAURE Large, full overcoat with cape, called after the Duke of Roquelaure.

ROTONNE Lower collar of a man's redingote in the 18th century.

ROWEL Round of yellow cloth or felt which was compulsory wear for Jews in the 13th century, imposed by the Lateran Council and again by the Narbonne Council. Sometimes it was green; in the 14th century it was sometimes red and white.

RUFF Costume accessory for both sexes in the late 16th and 17th centuries: a pleated, starched collarette worn throughout western Europe, whose form and size varied considerably with the country and the time. In Spain it was known as the *gran gola*: it was worn throughout the greater part of the 17th century, much later than in France, and survived even later in the form of the *golilla* until the early years of the 18th century.

SABLE The finest, rarest and most celebrated type of marten fur. Already known in ancient times, it was keenly sought after in the Middle Ages when the fashion for fur-lined clothes was very widespread. After the 15th century the fashion for skins died out completely, and furs were hardly used except as trimming until the 19th century. Sable continued to be the luxury fur *par excellence* until the 20th century, when it was dethroned by mink.

SABLÉ A sort of cloth woven from very fine beads, used in the 18th century for shoes and small objects – purses, ornaments etc.

SABOT PANTALOONS 1891: pantaloons, wide at the bottom; the close-fitting leg was turned up outside.

SABOT SLEEVE Sleeve of the gown *à la polonaise*, fitting tightly over the elbow; the foot might be decorated with *petits bonshommes*.

SACCOZ Byzantine Imperial robe.

SACK GOWN / ROBE VOLANTE / ANDRIENNE / ADRIENNE A loose dress flaring out at the bottom, the back attached to the neckband with gathers at first, then with pleats. It was worn from about 1704 to about 1730–35.

SACRISTAN Light brass wire farthingale with five or six hoops, still worn in Spain towards 1675–80.

SAGUM / SAIE Originally a cloak worn by the ancient Celts. It was made from hairy cloth recalling goatskin, square or rectangular, draped over the left shoulder and pinned on the right. The word *saie* used by most costume historians is probably the result of confusion with *saye* and the 16th-century *sayon*.

SAIE / SAYE 16th century: coat with cape- or ordinary sleeves, front-buttoned, worn with or without a belt: particularly a garment worn by pages. Its basques were sometimes long; designed for show, generally in rich material, and very similar to the hoqueton.

SAILOR SUIT Costume inspired by the uniforms of French and English sailors, adopted for boys from about 1862 until the mid-20th century. A constant feature is the square collar, trimmed with narrow white braid. A variant was developed for girls, with a pleated skirt replacing the trousers.

SAMITE Silk cloth which must have been related to CENDAL, but richer and stronger, probably because the silk warp and weft were supported by finely-interwoven wire which hardly showed on the right side. Philip the Long and his wife wore robes of samite lined with cendal on their

coronation day. Manufacture of plain samite stopped at the end of the Middle Ages, and that of figured samites survived only a short time in Italy.

SAMPOT Piece of cloth which the Cambodians wind around the waist and take up between their legs, draping it to form something like trousers.

SANDAL Footwear derived from the Roman *solea* adopted by certain religious orders: a leather sole strapped on to the foot. The Greek SANDALIUM, worn only by women, resembled the *calceolus*, with an upper protecting the toes. The modern sandal usually has an upper, and a quarter fitting the heel. When it resembles the solea it is called a *spartiate* or barefoot sandal.

SARONG Long cloth wound round the body, for example in Malaya.

SAYON Some authors have defined the sayon as a Gaulish cassock, though this is not confirmed by documents. The term appears in the 16th century, denoting a sleeved cassock, belted at the waist; sometimes it was of medium length, like a doublet, and sometimes it fell to the feet. During much of the 16th century the sayon was worn in the form of the shorter *saye*.

SBERNIA Outer garment worn by women in the 16th century, especially in Spain and Italy. It was a sort of long scarf draped from a pin on the left shoulder; it is found in England in the 17th century. Originally the term referred to coarse woollen material from Ireland (Hibernia), used for soldiers' blankets. This gives the French word *berner*, the practical joke of tossing a man in a blanket held by four others.

SCARF Originally a satchel worn over one shoulder. In the early 14th century the name passed from the object to the way it was worn, and the strip of cloth worn first obliquely from shoulder to hip, then tied at the waist. Later the name was extended to the piece of cloth women wore on their heads and shoulders when they went out without their overgowns (17th century); it was called a 'cape' when it was decorated. It was only in the 19th century that scarves of fine material acquired the place they now occupy in women's wardrobes.

SEGMENTUM Band of cloth of gold or precious stuff used to decorate the garments of Roman women.

SERAPIS Long tunic of fine pleated stuff worn by Persian women, and borrowed from the Lydians by the Greeks of Asia Minor.

SERPENTAUX Women's hairstyle, with barely-curled hair hanging down; it followed the coiffure *en bouffons* under Louis XIII.

SHAWL Large rectangle of woollen or any other material. In modern times, the fashion was exported from England to France (1790), and remained well established throughout the 19th century. The finest were from Kashmir: they were imitated, but never equalled, in England, France and Scotland. Shawls were also made in silk, percale, muslin, net etc., which were often given names inspired by the theatre, for example the Esmeralda shawl and the Maranâ shawl (1836).

SHENTI Sort of loincloth worn in Egypt, made of a long narrow piece of linen cloth passed between the legs. The end, folded over, forms a projecting tab above the waist, enabling the wearer to tighten the garment. Pharaohs are often portrayed wearing only the shenti.

SIGLATON Gold brocade originating from the East; made in Lucca from the 14th century. It was used for very luxurious garments.

SIMARRA In Italy, an outer gown whose form varies from province to province, but which was always opened over an undergown. It was sometimes made in one piece and sometimes cut at the waist: the equivalent of the Spanish *ropa* and French *marlotte*. For men it was a long, long-sleeved gown worn in Venice by senators in the 14th and 15th centuries. The name continued to be used, by analogy, to

describe the gowns of magistrates, chancellors, cardinals, etc.

SINDON Egyptian cloak made of a large draped piece of linen.

SKARAMANGION Long Persian gown, fur-lined and buttoned at the side. In Constantinople it was a fur-lined tunic belted at the waist.

SCARABICON Outer garment of high Byzantine dignitaries.

SKIRADION Head-dress worn by Byzantine dignitaries.

SKULL CAP Small hemispherical cap covering the top of the head; sometimes flat, sometimes with a rounded point or even a short tail; 12th and 15th centuries. Later its form varied; in the 17th century it was adopted by the clergy.

SLASHINGS Small openings made in a garment, showing the lining. Slashings (*crevés*, *chiquetades*) were made in garments, shoes and gloves. The smallest slashings were called *mouchetures*. In the 17th century slashing was less used; it was replaced by long-edged cuts serving the same purpose. During the French Restoration and the Romantic period the historical allusions prevalent in fashion resurrected slashing, particularly in the sleeves of women's dresses.

SLIPPERS Originally called *solers*. From the 12th century this term described footwear covering the foot as far as the instep. The name derives from the ancient *solea*, but the shape was different: solers cover the foot and vary in form – unlined, strapped, and so on. They were made of leather (Cordoban) or of cloth. They have undergone all manner of changes dictated by fashion.

SLOPS Large unpadded breeches which extended to the knees.

SNOOD Already worn in ancient times, it was a net, used in the 13th century to cover headgear. In the 15th and 16th centuries nets decorated with pearls and jewels were worn directly over the hair. They disappeared at the end of the 16th century, and reappeared under the Second Empire, when for a short time low chignons were held in a snood of fine silk cord sometimes decorated with steel beads.

SOCCUS / SOCQ (1) Wide ceremonial cloak (Middle Ages); open, fastened on the right shoulder, worn by the king for his coronation and other major ceremonies.
(2) A sort of slipper or shoe without fastening, completely covering the foot; worn in Greece by both sexes. In Rome it was reserved for women and comic actors as opposed to the *cothurne* of tragedians. Also known as SOCQ.

SOLEA The simplest form of Roman sandal: a wooden sole with a cord passing over the foot.

SOLERS see SLIPPERS

SOLITAIRE About 1725 on: with hairstyles *en bourse* men generally wore a ribbon bow round the bourse behind the neck; its long ends were knotted in front of the shirt collar. The term formerly described women's neck-bows.

SOLLERET Piece of armour protecting the foot.

SOMBRERO Man's hat adopted in Spain at the beginning of the 17th century: the shape, however, had been used for a long time in the Iberian peninsula. It was worn throughout Europe in the 17th century. It was a soft hat with or without an ostrich feather; the Spaniards turned up the brim on the right side. A 16th-century French text mentions 'a sombrero flat as a pancake'.

SORQUENIE / SOUCANIE Tunic fitting tightly over the bust; worn by women from the 13th to the 19th century. The word was then applied to the smocks (*souquenilles*) of coachmen and ostlers.

SOTTANA 12th and 13th centuries: in Italy, a tunic undergown; sometimes in plain material, sometimes in alternate, differently coloured bands of linen cloth. Young girls wore the sottana as an outer gown.

SOULETTE / SOLETTE In the Louis XIII period, a leather band that passed over the instep and under the patten, to hold it to the boot. It fitted over the *surpied*, a large piece of leather cut in a quatrefoil trimming the boot instep.

SPENCER Short jacket reaching to the waist with long sleeves that covered the hand, worn mainly by women in the Directoire period and, with various changes, during a large part of the 19th century. It was always in a colour which contrasted with the dress. Men wore it for a short time under the Consulate, but it does not seem to have become part of male costume until very recently, under the modified form of an evening dress jacket without tails, generally in linen, for summer evening functions. By analogy, the name was extended to women's undergarments (the short bodice).

STEINKIRK CRAVAT After the battle of Steinkirk (1692) Mlle Le Rochois, a singer at the Opera, appeared in the role of Thetis with a lace cravat thrown negligently over her neck, like the officers surprised by the battle; the fashion immediately spread through Paris. Men wore the ends of their cravats tucked into a coat buttonhole, while women tucked theirs into their corset laces.

STEMMA Circlet set with gems and decorated with hanging ornaments, sometimes topped with a cross, worn by the Byzantine emperors.

STEPHANOS Crown sent by Byzantine emperors to vassal monarchs and high dignitaries.

STIVALI 12th to late 14th century: light boots fitted close to the leg in France, wider in England; high and soft, usually black but sometimes red. They were summer footwear. The name survives in the German *stiefel* and the Italian *stivale*.

STOLA Typical garment of the Roman woman, and the toga of the Roman citizen. Long and loose, it was worn over the chemise and fastened to the body by two belts, one under the breasts and one on the hips. Its distinctive ornament was the INSITA, a panel sewn below the belt and trailing on the ground, covering the feet at the back.

STOLE Liturgical ornament probably derived from the *orarium* or *lorum*, a kind of scarf worn by certain Roman dignitaires as a sign of office: a long band which the priest wears over the amict and under the chasuble. Some authors see in it the descendant of the Roman *stola* which, cut off, would probably have formed a long scarf, but there is no proof of this. By analogy the name given to fur scarves in the 19th century.

STROPHIUM Scarf wound into a long even cord and tied round the body to support the breasts. It was worn over a short tunic, unlike the *mamillare*, worn next to the skin.

SUBLIGACULUM Piece of cloth passed round the waist and between the thighs, fastened under the fork: it made sort of short trousers like those worn by boatmen. For decency's sake actors wore it on stage.

SUBUCULA Under-tunic of wool, worn under the true tunic.

SUCCINTA Wide belt worn by both sexes in Rome, to gird in garments at the waist so that they could be tucked up for walking.

SUFFIBULUM Large rectangle of white cloth worn on the head hanging down behind, fastened with a brooch under the chin. Worn by Vestals and priests during sacrifices.

SUIT From the late 19th century, an ensemble for men, comprizing jacket, waistcoat and trousers in the same material, and matching frockcoat and waistcoat with striped trousers.

SUPPARIUM Short linen garment which Roman women wore over the subucula.

SURATE / SURAH see PATNA

SURCOAT A long garment worn over the cote, replacing the BLIAUD in the 12th century. It could be sleeveless, or have halfsleeves or very tight long sleeves. Men wore it in varying lengths, often split for riding; women wore a style – particularly in the 14th century – with a very long wide skirt.

SURPIED see SOULETTE

SURTOUT Term used for a very long time for men's cloaks and coats, whatever their form.

SWEDISH HAT Large felt hat popularized by musketeers' dress; taken from the Swedish troops who wore it during the Thirty Years' War.

SYNTHESIS A sort of tunic, though the exact form is unknown, worn by the Romans for meals; but never, except during the Saturnalia, in public.

TABARD A kind of military and a ceremonial coat from the 13th–16th centuries, recalling the dalmatic, with its free hanging back and front and its short wing sleeves. It was worn mainly in tourneys, 'the long parts back and front for the Herald if he was King at Arms, and the long parts along the arms if he was only Poursuivant'. However, the same texts also relate the tabard to the wide-draped 'Reiter coats', though their exact shape is unknown.

TABLION Oblong embroidered with the image of the monarch, decorating the chlamys worn by the Byzantine empress and vassal sovereigns.

TAILORED COAT Introduced in 1910, a woman's coat with severe English cut, always worn buttoned.

TAILORED SUIT Woman's costume composed of a jacket and skirt, mannish in cut; English, late 19th century.

TALARIS TUNIC A long-sleeved, long-girded tunic worn by women and elderly men.

TASSEAU / TASSEL Late 15th century: a triangle of cloth, usually black, filling in the bodice neckline.

TASSETTES 17th century: basques of the doublet.

TEBENNA An Etruscan cloak, sometimes completed with a hooded cape.

TEMPLET Metal ornament round which women's hair was rolled above the ears in the 15th century.

THÉRÈSE A loose head-dress in the form of a hood which could be worn over the tall bonnets of the 1775–90 period. It remained in use and is still mentioned in 1835–40, but with a cape protecting the shoulders.

THOLIA A hat with a pointed crown and flat brim, worn by Greek women.

THORAKION A coat-of-arms (crest) of the empresses of Byzantium.

TIARA National head-dress of all south-west Asiatic peoples: a soft crown held in place by a narrow ribbon round the head; the style worn by kings was stiff. That worn by the Hebrew high priest was higher and recalled the present tiara of the popes, on which the crowns symbolizing sovereign power were added successively from the 12th to the 14th century.

TIBIALES High leggings worn by Roman huntsmen or soldiers, sometimes adopted by delicate men like Augustus.

TIPPET (1) Medieval: streamer hanging from the sleeve of a cothardie.
(2) From the 16th century, a kind of short shoulder cape.

TOGA The main outer garment worn by the Romans; it was their national costume, as the pallium was for the Greeks. It was usually made of white wool; its dimensions and the way it was worn changed in the course of time. It is thought that it was originally fairly short and slightly taken in at the waist, but its dimensions increased under the Republic, which led to changes in the manner of draping it. In the Augustan period it became still larger, and was cut in a complete circle; its drapery became so complicated that it finally went out of fashion because of its inconvenience. The *toga praetexta*, with a purple band woven in, was taken from the Etruscans and worn with the *bulla* by freeborn children of both sexes; it was worn like the toga. The ordinary toga, in plain white wool, was called *toga virilis*.

TOGA GABIANA Roman toga, tight-fitting, with one fold thrown over the head and the other taken behind over the hips to form a belt.

TOGA TRABEA Short Etruscan toga decorated with purple bands; the royal robe adopted by Romulus and his successors. It was worn later by consuls and knights in solemn public ceremonies; though smaller than the toga, it was draped in the same way.

TONTILLO Farthingale with steel hoops still worn in Spain at the end of the 17th century.

TORQUE Roman and Gallo-Roman necklace in the form of a variously ornamented circle.

TOUR / TOUR DE CHEVEUX False hair worn on the front of the head.

TOURET Woman's head-dress: originally (13th–15th centuries) a veil covering the forehead, as in certain coifs worn by nuns. This arrangement must have changed, for in the 16th century it was only the edge of the head-dress, and in particular the decorated part of women's coiffures. It was also a mourning head-dress at the courts of France and Burgundy; a veil in two pieces, one of which covered the top of the face, while the other hid the chin, becoming the BARBETTE in the 14th century. The *touret de nez*, worn in winter, was a band of cloth attached to the ear-flaps of the hood, and covering the nose and even the eyes, for it was fitted with a 'pane of crystalline'. It was the original of the *cachenez* and the *loup*.

TOURET DE COL see GORGET

TRABEA (1) Toga, see TOGA TRABEA
(2) Brocaded scarf worn by consuls of the late Roman Empire, and of the Basilean period in Byzantium.

TRAQUENARD see PANIERS

TRESSOIR Golden plait of silk worked with metal and gems, worn by women in the 13th century.

TROUSERS Worn since the earliest times by horse-riding steppe peoples. In their present form, introduced to western Europe by the Venetians, particularly in the 16th century by the Italian Comedy. They were adopted in France by advanced factions during the Revolution; they were only accepted as informal wear at the beginning of the 19th century. They were worn as part of semi-formal dress during the French Restoration, and became generally worn after 1930.

TROUSSES 17th century: upper hose which did not hang down, but fitted the thighs tightly 'like those worn in the last century'. They are a survival of the 16th century *grègues*, preserved in the ceremonial costume of Knights of the King's Orders and in pages' costumes.

TROUSSOIR Hook designed to lift the long gowns worn by women at the end of the 14th century; in the 16th century, also a flowing scarf hanging down one side, on which women hung various small objects.

TRUFFEAU / TRUFFE Some authors interpret these as false hair worn on the temples, or the pads used in the tall nairstyles of the late 14th and 15th centuries. 15th-century texts mention 'fine stuffs to make *truffes* for the head of the queen' (which might mean coiffure pads), and also truffes of leaves and flowers in gold thread to hang from a necklace.

TRUNK HOSE Upper hose or leg garment which extended from waist to knee.

TUNIC À LA MAMELUCK Reminiscent of Napoleon's Egyptian campaign: a woman's tunic, half-length, with long or short sleeves, in vogue about 1801–2 and worn later as *Juive* or *tunique à la Juive*.

TUNIC À LA ROMAINE Long gauze or lawn tunic, with a very high waist and long sleeves;

one form of the classically-inspired Directoire styles ('modes à l'antique').

TURBAN Eastern head-dress formed of a cap round which a long piece of cloth (wool, cotton or silk) is rolled, starting in the middle of the tall woollen or felt crown and criss-crossing until the ends are tucked into the folds. Fine red cotton stuff was used to make turbans; the name derives from the stuff. By analogy the name is used of women's hats inspired by this Eastern head-dress. The fashion recurred each time literary events brought a return to fashion of things Eastern.

TUTULUS Roman women's hairstyle, with all the hair piled up in a cone on the top of the head; also a conical woollen cap, worn in particular in some seminaries.

TZITSAKION Eastern garment adopted by the court of Byzantium.

UPPER STOCKS Breeches or hose which covered the lower part of the trunk as well as the upper part of the leg.

UTTARIYA see CHADDAR

VAIR Fur of the northern grey squirrel; it was blue-grey on top and white underneath. When it was arranged in alternate squares of back and belly fur, it was *menu vair*; when the squares were larger, it was *grand vair* or *gros vair*. This fur was reserved exclusively for the robes of kings or high magistrates.

VENETIANS Late 16th- and early 17th-century breeches whose bouffant shape took the form of a long oval tied at the knee by garter-ribbons.

VERDINGALE see FARTHINGALE

VERDUGO Literally, a rod or wand: a supple branch used in Spain in 1468 for the first rigid frames designed to support the fullness of gowns. This developed into the FARTHINGALE.

VEST (1) In the 17th and 18th centuries, a man's garment worn under the JUSTAUCORPS, generally in rich material for the two fronts and the sleeve cuffs, the rest being made of lining material. Originally very long, the vest was

gradually shortened and simplified until, in the middle of the reign of Louis XV, it became the waistcoat.
(2) In the 19th century the word is applied to either a man's garment (informal or formal, uniform jacket, hunting jacket, etc.) or women's small jackets completing or accompanying certain dresses. Such were the zouave jacket, the Garibaldi jacket, the Figaro jacket, the bolero jacket. They were very short, often sleeveless or short-sleeved, and could, depending on their elegance, be worn in town, in villeggiatura, or informally (Second Empire).

VESTES Term used in Rome for the pieces of woven cloth draped by the wearer.

VISAGIÈRE Open part of the hood around the face.

VISITE Cloak in the form of a large printed shawl, buttoning in front and with two front slits edged with embryonic sleeves. The visite, which appeared in 1845, could be long or short, in cashmere or any other cloth, and was still worn in 1885.

VITTA Bandeau worn round the head by all freeborn Roman women, to hold their hair back and to distinguish then.

VLIEGER Woman's garment corresponding to the Spanish *ropa*, worn in the Low Countries until about 1640; it disappeared at the same time as the large ruff.

VOLANT Light unlined jerkin worn in the second third of the 18th century as a surtout. It had no pockets, buttons or buttonholes on the sleeves, or tabs; the neck was fastened with a button.

WAISTCOAT From the Louis XVI period waistcoats were worn under all men's outer garments: coat, riding-coat, frock coat, jacket, etc. It has shrunk in size, as have the outer garments; its main feature has always been to have only the front in fine materials and the back in lining material. Between 1800 and 1830 the fashion was to wear several waistcoats, one on top of the other.

Similarly in women's costume, it is a 'front' buttoned down the middle, trimming the opening of a very *enchancrée* gown. It appeared under the name of *compères* with the gown *à l'anglaise* about 1778, of *soubreveste* with the Circassian style; then from 1850 on it reappeared periodically.

WALKING SUIT 1901: suit with a skirt barely touching the ground; in the following year it was three to four inches off the ground.

WATTEAU PLEAT Box pleat sweeping down from the shoulders to the hem in the loose back of a gown – which, however, was fitted at the front and sides. It was popular about 1745. Many of the paintings of Watteau (1684–1721) show a similar type of gown.

WEEPERS (1) White bands worn on the sleeve facings of coats and jerkins for deep mourning; 17th and 18th centuries.
(2) Ostrich feathers: see PLEUREUSES.

WIMPLE see GUIMP

WITCHOURA Hooded, fur-trimmed overcoat of Polish origin; the sleeves could be left hanging. Wider than the redingote, less stiff than the pelisse, the witchoura appeared in 1808 and was very fashionable under the Empire; it was even worn by young men. It reappeared during the Romantic period.

WOAD Alternative name for pastel or *isatis tinctoria*.

ZANCHA / ZANGA / TZANGA Boot fitting the leg tightly and rising very high; in soft black leather. During the Roman period it was worn by Eastern peoples under their trousers.

ZÔNA In Greece from the 9th century BC, a broad flat belt which girls wore on the hips. It was discarded only when they were married, the husband unfastening it after the ceremony. The ordinary belt (*cingulum*) was below the breasts.

ZOUAVE PANTALOONS 1890: a wide pantaloon with the legs gathered below the knee into a tight band trimmed with a frill.

Index

458